FINANCIAL AND MANAGEMENT ACCOUNTING

DIAMOND HANSEN MURPHY

Donna K. Ulmer
Southern Illinois University at Edwardsville

COLLEGE DIVISION South-Western Publishing Co.

Cincinnati Ohio

Sponsoring Editor: David L. Shaut
Developmental Editor: Linda A. Spang
Production Editor II: Sharon L. Smith
Production House: Litten Editing and Production
Designer: Joseph M. Devine
Marketing Manager: Michael J. O'Brien

CONTENTS

TO THE STUDENT

This study guide, a supplement to *Introductory Accounting: Concepts and Applications* by Michael Diamond, Don Hansen, and David Murphy, is designed to assist you in reviewing important concepts and testing your understanding of the material. The study guide contains the following:

- **CHAPTER REVIEW.** A summary of the important points in each chapter.

- **KEY TERMS TEST.** A test of your understanding of the key terms in each chapter.

- **CHAPTER QUIZ.** Multiple choice, true-false, and completion questions to test your comprehension of the chapter material.

- **EXERCISES.** A test of your ability to apply the concepts.

- **ANSWERS.** Suggested solutions appear at the end of each chapter.

- **GUIDELINES FOR MEMORANDUM PREPARATION.** A sample memorandum and general suggestions for writing memoranda are contained in Appendix A.

- **FACTOR TABLES.** Present value and future value factor tables are included in Appendix B of the study guide for your convenience.

The following sequence is recommended to make the most effective use of your study time.
- Read the assigned chapter in the text.
- Read the Chapter Review in the study guide. Add your notes or questions to the Chapter Review.
- Complete the Key Terms Test, Chapter Quiz, and Exercises in the study guide.
- Review any difficult topics if necessary.
- Prepare text exercises and problems assigned by your instructor.

Additional suggestions to assist you in your course preparation are:
- Try to understand the important concepts and how they are applied. Do not try to memorize formulas and plug in numbers without first understanding *why* the formulas work.
- Ask questions when you do not understand. If you do not understand something, write your questions down so that you can ask at a later time. Simply formulating the questions may help you clarify your thinking.
- Always attempt to answer questions and problems before looking at the solution. This tests your understanding of the material and indicates the areas that need further study.

CHAPTER 1

ACCOUNTING: ITS NATURE AND FUNCTIONS

CHAPTER REVIEW

- Accounting is the language of business.

- Understanding financial accounting concepts can enable:
  - Stockbrokers to spot a company's strengths and weaknesses.
  - Loan officers to determine quickly a client's financial strength.
  - Company treasurers to make good decisions and recommendations.
  - Regulators and elected officials to make crucial decisions regarding the economic climate in their states.

ACCOUNTING AND ITS FUNCTIONS

- **Accounting** is a system of providing quantitative information that is useful in making economic decisions.

- Accounting information is used by:
  1. internal users, such as managers.
  2. external users, such as stockholders and creditors.

- The **accounting system** is the set of methods and procedures used to record, classify, and summarize the financial information to be distributed to users. The accounting system is part of the overall information system in an organization.

The Record-Keeping Function

- The record-keeping function involves keeping track of an organization's transactions.

- **Transactions** are business events that are measured in monetary terms and recorded in the financial records.

Classifying and Summarizing Transactions

- First, transactions must be classified into similar categories. For example, all transactions affecting cash are aggregated to determine the amount of cash at a point in time.

  Then this data is summarized into accounting reports.

1

- **Financial statements** are concise accounting reports that communicate financial information about a particular enterprise to users.

A Broader View of Accounting

- A broader view of accounting involves:
  1. <u>observation</u> and <u>selection</u> of significant variables about the activities of an organization.
  2. the <u>measurement</u> of these selected variables.
  3. the <u>analysis</u> of data to identify relevant information for long-term and operating decision making.
  4. the <u>disclosure</u> of the information to the various decision makers.

Observation and Selection of Events

- The selection of events to measure is particularly important because it determines what information will be communicated to financial statement users.

- Accounting usually has focused only on economic events involving monetary transactions. However, data important in determining the future prospects of an enterprise, such as market share, are often included in internal management reports even though such data traditionally have not been reported in a firm's published financial statements.

- Accountants need to understand what information various decision makers need and how they make decisions so that the accounting system can provide relevant and reliable information.

Measurement

- Accounting measurement includes two activities:
  1. Identifying what the accountant should measure. Should the accountant measure current value, historical cost, or liquidation value of a particular item? For financial statement purposes, accountants focus primarily upon measuring the historical cost of an item.
  2. Selecting the most appropriate measurement technique. For example, in the U.S., accountants usually use dollars to measure financial statement items.

Analysis and Disclosure

- Financial analysis is the process of examining and understanding the significance of important relationships among elements of financial data.

- Information that is likely to affect an individual's decisions should be disclosed even if the information is usually not included on a financial statement.

Accounting and Decision Making

- The expanded view of accounting emphasizes providing information that is useful in decision making.

- The primary users of corporate financial information are:
  - the firm's management
  - present and potential investors
  - present and potential creditors
  - government agencies, such as the Internal Revenue Service
  - the general public

ACCOUNTING AND FORMS OF BUSINESS ENTERPRISES

- The three major types of business organizations are:
  1. sole proprietorship
  2. partnership
  3. corporation

Sole Proprietorships

- A **sole proprietorship** is a business entity owned by one individual.

- Advantages of a sole proprietorship include:
  1. ease of establishment
  2. low organization cost
  3. limited legal requirements

- A **business entity** is a distinct economic unit whose transactions are kept separate from those of its owners.

- For accounting purposes, a sole proprietorship and its owner are considered separate entities. Accounting for the sole proprietorship is limited to the transactions of the business and excludes the owner's personal transactions.

- A sole proprietorship and its owner are <u>not</u> separate <u>legal</u> entities. Legally, the sole proprietor is personally responsible for the debts of the business.

Partnerships

- A **partnership** is a business entity that is owned by two or more individuals. Examples of partnerships include CPA firms and law firms.

- A partnership is considered a separate accounting entity from its owners; however, the partners and partnership are <u>not</u> separate legal entities.

3

Corporations

- A **corporation** is a business entity that is viewed as legally separate and distinct from its owners. Owners of a corporation are called stockholders. Ownership in a corporation is designated by stock certificates.

- Because a corporation is a separate legal entity, stockholders have **limited liability**--their liability is limited to the amount they have invested in the corporation.

- The stockholders elect a board of directors. The board of directors appoints the officers of the corporation (president, vice-president, treasurer, and secretary) to manage the business.

- Two different types of corporations are:
  1. publicly owned corporations
  2. closely held corporations

- **Publicly owned corporations** are corporations whose stock is traded (bought and sold) by the public on stock exchanges, such as the New York Stock Exchange or the American Stock Exchange (AMEX). Publicly traded corporations are required to follow Securities and Exchange Commission (SEC) requirements.

- Stock in a closely held corporation is not traded publicly and may be owned by a family, a few shareholders, or a single individual.

- During the late 1980's many publicly held corporations went private using a leveraged buyout where management and others borrowed large amounts to repurchase all the corporation's stock.

- Owners need financial reports to:
  - evaluate the corporation's performance.
  - evaluate management's performance.
  - decide whether to retain, sell, or add to their investment in the corporation.

PRIMARY USERS OF ACCOUNTING INFORMATION

- Primary users of accounting information can be divided into two major categories:
  1. external users
  2. internal users

- External users are decision makers outside the corporation. External users include:
  - present and potential investors
  - present and potential creditors
  - government agencies
  - the general public

- Internal users are decision makers within the organization. The primary internal user of accounting information is the firm's management.

4

External Users of Accounting Information

- **Financial accounting** is the study of the concepts, standards, and procedures used to prepare financial information distributed to external users.

Present and Potential Investors and Creditors

- Investors use financial statements and other information to make decisions about increasing, decreasing, or maintaining their investment in an organization.

- Creditors, when deciding whether to extend a loan to a company, use financial statements to evaluate whether the corporation can repay its debts.

Governmental Agencies

- Governmental agencies that use financial information about a firm include:
  - the Internal Revenue Service (IRS) to determine the amount of taxes due the government
  - the Securities and Exchange Commission
  - the Interstate Commerce Commission
  - the Resolution Trust Agency (an agency established by Congress to oversee the bailout of troubled savings and loans)
  - state public utility commissions when setting and/or approving utility rates
  - state insurance commissions when setting and/or approving insurance rates

- **Governmental accounting** is the practice of accounting as it relates to governmental organizations.

The General Public

- The public often relies on financial information summarized in financial statements to evaluate the actions of large corporations, such as General Motors and IBM.

Other External Users

- Other external users of accounting information include:
  - labor unions to help them assess a company's ability to increase employee wages
  - potential employees when evaluating the long-range prospects of a firm before deciding to accept an employment offer

External Users' Need for Generally Accepted Accounting Principles

- External users must rely on others to prepare reliable financial information for their use.

5

- **Generally accepted accounting principles (GAAP)** are the concepts and standards for external financial reporting. GAAP represents a consensus at a particular time on how accounting information should be recorded, what information should be disclosed, how it should be disclosed, and which financial statements should be prepared.

- GAAP provides a common financial language to enable informed users to read and interpret financial statements.

- Two groups involved in determining GAAP are:
  1. the American Institute of Certified Public Accountants (AICPA), the professional organization of CPAs.
  2. the Financial Accounting Standards Board (FASB), an independent organization from the AICPA charged with setting accounting standards for financial reporting.

Internal Users of Accounting Information--Company Management

- Managers are the primary internal users of accounting information.

- Managers use accounting information to:
  1. pinpoint problems.
  2. help select appropriate solutions.
  3. assist when making business decisions.
  4. assess organizational performance.

- **Management accounting** is the system and the procedures for providing information for managerial activities.

- Management accountants are not constrained by GAAP in developing accounting information to meet their particular needs.

ACCOUNTANTS--THE PROVIDERS OF ACCOUNTING INFORMATION

- Professional accountants may work in:
  - public accounting
  - private accounting
  - government accounting

Public Accountants

- **Public accounting** is the field of accounting that provides a variety of accounting services to clients for a fee.

- A professional accountant who works in a public accounting firm is usually a **certified public accountant (CPA)**. CPAs are licensed by individual states to practice accounting after:
  1. passing the Uniform CPA exam administered by the AICPA, and
  2. satisfying the education and experience requirements of the particular state.

- The Big Six public accounting firms are:
  - Arthur Andersen
  - Coopers & Lybrand
  - Deloitte & Touche
  - Ernst & Young
  - KPMG Peat Marwick
  - Price Waterhouse

- Services that public accounting firms provide include:
  - auditing and accounting services
  - tax preparation and tax planning
  - management advisory services

Auditing and Accounting Services

- An **audit** is an objective and independent third-party examination of an organization's financial statements. Publicly held corporations are required by federal securities law to have their financial statements audited.

- An auditor:
  - evaluates the firm's accounting system.
  - performs tests to determine whether economic transactions have been properly recorded.
  - gathers other evidence to ensure that all relevant economic events have been appropriately reported or disclosed.
  - issues an auditor's report.

- The **audit report**:
  - identifies the financial statements audited.
  - describes the nature and scope of the audit.
  - contains the auditor's opinion.

- The **auditor's opinion** states whether the financial statements present fairly the firm's financial position, results of operations, and cash flows.

- In an unqualified or "clean" audit report, the auditor does not express any qualifications about the fairness of the presentation of the financial statements.

- CPA firms also provide an accounting service called reviews and compilations where the accounting firm reviews a company's records or helps in preparing the financial statements.

Tax Preparation and Planning

- CPAs often:
  1. prepare income tax returns for clients.
  2. assist clients in tax planning by providing advice about the possible tax consequences of a particular decision.

Management Advisory Services

- In addition to audit and tax departments, CPA firms have management advisory services departments to provide clients with business advice and consulting services.

Management Accountants

- A **management accountant** works for a single firm and is responsible for collecting, processing, and reporting information.

- Tasks performed by management accountants include:
  - determining the cost of items produced
  - budgeting
  - internal auditing
  - taxation
  - financial reporting

- The chief accounting officer for a private enterprise typically is known as the controller.

- The head financial officer is often called the treasurer.

- A **Certified Management Accountant (CMA)** is an accountant who has passed the CMA exam which is administered by the **Institute of Management Accountants (IMA).**

- A **Certified Internal Auditor (CIA)** is an accountant who has passed the CIA exam which is administered by the Institute of Internal Auditors.

- An **internal auditor** is a specialized management accountant who performs an audit function within an organization.

- An internal auditor performs:
  - **compliance audits** to determine whether employees are following management's policies and procedures.
  - **operational audits** to assess the efficiency and effectiveness of operations within an organizational unit.

Governmental Accountants

- Governmental accountants are employed by governmental agencies and bodies, such as:
  - the Internal Revenue Service (IRS)
  - the Federal Bureau of Investigation (FBI)
  - the General Accounting Office (GAO)
  - state departments of revenue
  - counties
  - cities
  - school districts

ACCOUNTANTS AND ETHICAL BEHAVIOR

- Ethical behavior involves choosing actions that are "right," "proper," and "just."

- A common principle underlying ethics is the belief that each member of a group bears some responsibility for the well-being of other members of the group. For example, a corporation that produces toxic waste may have to decide between making more profit or reducing pollution to satisfy a community's desire for a clean environment.

- Ethical norms are effected by cultural factors. For example, in the U.S. bribery is considered illegal and unethical, whereas in certain foreign countries bribes are considered an accepted business practice.

Accountants' Ethical Responsibilities

- Accountants have a significant ethical responsibility because they supply accounting information to users who make important economic decisions based on the information.

Implications for Public Accounting

- In order for financial statement users to rely on the auditor's opinion, they must have confidence in the auditor's integrity.

Implications for Management Accounting

- A corporation's objective of profit maximization should be constrained by the requirement that profits be achieved through legal and ethical means.

Ethical Standards for Accountants

- Organizations commonly establish standards of conduct for their managers and employees.

- The AICPA and the IMA have established ethical standards for accountants.

FINANCIAL STATEMENTS AND THEIR ELEMENTS

- Financial statements are concise reports that summarize transactions for a particular period of time.

- The four main financial statements are:
  - balance sheet
  - income statement
  - statement of cash flows
  - retained earnings statement

- The heading for financial statements consists of three items:
  1. the name of the enterprise
  2. the title of the statement
  3. the date of the statement

Balance Sheet

- The **balance sheet** presents the financial position of a firm at a particular date.

- The body of the balance sheet contains three major categories:
  1. assets
  2. liabilities
  3. stockholders' equity

- **Assets** are the economic resources of the firm that are expected to have future benefit.

- **Liabilities** are the firm's financial obligations to its creditors.

- **Owners' equity** is the owners' residual interest in the assets of a firm. The residual interest usually is viewed as the assets that remain after all the liabilities have been paid.

- For a corporation, owners' equity is called **stockholders' equity**.

- The **account form of balance sheet** is the format in which assets are listed on the left and liabilities and stockholders' equity are listed on the right.

- The **report form of balance sheet** is a vertical balance sheet format with liabilities and stockholders' equity listed below assets.

The Accounting Equation

- The **accounting equation** is:

$$\text{Assets} = \text{Liabilities} + \text{Owners' Equity}$$

- For a corporation, the accounting equation is:

$$\text{Assets} = \text{Liabilities} + \text{Stockholders' Equity}$$

- The two sides of the accounting equation must always be equal. The left-hand side of the equation shows the economic resources controlled by a firm and the right-hand side shows the claims against those resources.

- The accounting equation can be restated as follows:

$$\text{Assets} - \text{Liabilities} = \text{Stockholders' Equity}$$

Assets

- Assets are a firm's economic resources.

- An item can be classified as an asset when it:
  1. results from a past transaction.
  2. has a historical cost.
  3. is expected to provide <u>future economic benefits</u>.
  4. is owned or controlled by the enterprise.

- Examples of assets include:
  - Cash: coins, currency, checks.
  - Marketable securities: investments in stocks and bonds of other companies.
  - Notes receivable: written promises from others to pay a specific amount at a specific time in the future.
  - Accounts receivable: Accounts receivable arise from sales on credit and represent future cash collections.
  - Inventory: Inventories represent items held for resale.
  - Prepaid expenses: payments for goods or services that will be used in the future, such as prepaid insurance and prepaid rent.
  - Property, plant, and equipment: assets such as land, buildings, equipment, furniture and fixtures that provide long-term benefits but that, except for land, usually wear out over time.
  - Patents: exclusive right granted by the federal government to make a product or use a process.

- Assets generally are listed on the balance sheet in order of their **liquidity** (the ease with which the item can be converted to cash).

Liabilities

- Liabilities are a firm's economic obligations.

- Liabilities consist of money or services that the firm owes its creditors.

- Examples of liabilities include:
  - Accounts payable: Accounts payable arise from the purchase of goods and services from suppliers on credit.
  - Notes payable: formal written promises to repay the lender at a certain time in the future usually resulting from borrowing from banks or other creditors. Unlike accounts payable, notes payable require the payment of interest to the lender.
  - Wages payable: wages owed employees for work performed.
  - Interest payable: interest owed to creditors.

- Liabilities are usually listed on the balance sheet according to their due dates with short-term liabilities listed first.

- If a business is dissolved, creditors have a primary claim and must be paid first while the owners have a secondary claim and receive anything left after the creditors are paid.

Owners' Equity

- Owners' equity is the owners' residual interest in the assets of the firm. Sometimes owners' equity is referred to as net assets.

- **Net assets** is calculated as follows:

Net Assets = Assets - Liabilities

- Owners' equity increases when:
  - the owners invest assets in the firm
  - the firm makes a profit

- Owners' equity decreases when:
  - the firm issues a dividend (distributes cash or other assets to its owners), or
  - the firm has unprofitable operations (net loss)

Stockholders' Equity

- The owners' equity section of a balance sheet for a corporation is called stockholders' equity.

- Two components of stockholders' equity are:
  - capital stock
  - retained earnings

- **Capital stock** represents the amount invested by owners of a corporation.

  Shares of stock in a publicly held corporation are easily transferable.

  Once a corporation issues shares of stock, the corporation is not affected by subsequent sales of these shares in the market.

- **Retained earnings** represents the portion of stockholders' equity (resulting from the cumulative profitable operations of the corporation) that has not been distributed as dividends to shareholders.

- Retained earnings is:
  1. increased by profitable operations.
  2. reduced by net losses.
  3. reduced by distribution of dividends.

Concepts Related to the Balance Sheet

- Accounting concepts related to the balance sheet are:
  - the historical cost convention
  - the going-concern assumption

- The **historical cost convention** requires that assets and liabilities be recorded in the accounting system at their original or acquisition cost and not be adjusted for subsequent changes in value.

For example, if a corporation purchased land for $100,000 in 1994 and in 1996 the land is worth $120,000, on the 1996 balance sheet for the corporation the land would still be shown at its historical cost of $100,000.

A major advantage of historical cost is its **objectivity**. Information is objective if it is reliable, verifiable, and not subject to different interpretations. Historical cost is verifiable because different people could agree on the same acquisition cost. Appraisals often are not objective because different people might assign different market values to the same asset.

- The **going concern assumption** is the assumption that a firm will continue to operate indefinitely unless there is evidence to the contrary.

Income Statement

- The **income statement** is the financial statement that reports the results (profit or loss) of a firm's operations over a period of time.

- Major components of an income statement include:
  - revenues
  - expenses
  - income before taxes
  - net income

Revenues

- **Revenues** are the price of goods or services provided to customers.

- Sales of goods and services can be for:
  - cash, or
  - on credit (resulting in an account receivable)

- An account receivable is a promise of cash to be received in the future.

- In general, both cash sales and credit sales are revenues to the firm at the point of sale, regardless of when the cash is received.

Expenses

- **Expenses** are the resources used up by a firm during a particular period of time in the process of earning revenue.

- An expense is recorded on the income statement in the period in which it was incurred, even though it may be paid in cash during a subsequent period. An expense is incurred when the firm receives the service or other benefit.

- Examples of expenses include:
  - cost of items sold to customers
  - salaries
  - utilities
  - rent
  - interest
  - taxes

Net Income

- **Net income** is calculated as follows:

$$\text{Net Income} = \text{Revenue} - \text{Expenses}$$

- Net income results when revenues exceed expenses. A **net loss** results when expenses exceed revenues.

- Net income increases a corporation's net assets and retained earnings.

Retained Earnings Statement

- The **retained earnings statement** is a financial statement that explains the change in retained earnings from the beginning of an accounting period to the end of the period.

- Items that affect retained earnings include:
  - net income (increases retained earnings)
  - net loss (reduces retained earnings)
  - dividends (reduce retained earnings)

- Dividends are not expenses. Instead, dividends reduce retained earnings.

Statement of Cash Flows

- The **statement of cash flows** is a financial statement that discloses the effects of a firm's operating, financing, and investing activities.

- A firm can obtain cash from three primary sources:
  - operating activities
  - investing activities
  - financing activities

- Cash flows from operating activities include only revenues and expenses received or paid in cash during the period. *Cash flow from operating activities is not the same as net income.*

- Investing activities relate to the receipt and payment of cash from the sale or purchase of:
  - property, plant, and equipment
  - long-term investments

- Financing activities include:
  - issuing stock
  - paying dividends
  - borrowing from creditors for long-term debt
  - repaying creditors for long-term debt

Relationships Among the Financial Statements

- The balance sheet, income statement, retained earnings statement, and the statement of cash flows all are interrelated. **Articulation** refers to the relationships among these basic financial statements that tie the financial statements together.

KEY TERMS TEST

There are many new key terms introduced in this chapter. The following is provided to assist you in reviewing the new terminology. Indicate which of the following terms best matches the statements listed below by placing the appropriate letter(s) in the blank preceding the statement.

KEY TERMS

A. account form of balance sheet
B. articulation
C. assets
D. balance sheet
E. compliance audits
F. financial accounting
G. financial statements
H. generally accepted accounting principles
I. going-concern assumption
J. governmental accounting
K. historical cost convention
L. income statement

M. liabilities
N. objectivity
O. operational audits
P. partnership
Q. public accounting
R. report form of balance sheet
S. retained earnings
T. retained earnings statement
U. sole proprietorship
V. statement of cash flows
W. stockholders' equity
X. transactions

DEFINITIONS

___ 1. Concise reports that summarize specific transactions for a particular period of time.

___ 2. The field of accounting that provides a variety of accounting services to clients for a fee.

___ 3. A business entity, owned by two or more individuals, that is not legally independent of the owners.

___ 4. Economic resources that a firm owns or controls.

___ 5. The financial statement that reports the results (profit or loss) of a firm's operations over a period of time.

___ 6. The format in which assets are listed on the left and liabilities and stockholders' equity on the right of the balance sheet.

_____ 7. The portion of stockholders' equity (resulting from the cumulative profitable operations) that has not been distributed to owners.

_____ 8. Audits that determine whether employees are following management's policies and procedures.

_____ 9. The concepts and standards underlying accounting for financial reporting purposes.

_____ 10. The practice of accounting within a governmental entity.

_____ 11. The assumption that a firm will continue to operate indefinitely.

_____ 12. The practice of recording assets and liabilities in the accounting system at their acquisition cost and not adjusting the amounts for subsequent changes in value.

_____ 13. The financial obligations of a firm to its creditors.

_____ 14. A characteristic of information which is reliable, verifiable, and not subject to different interpretations.

_____ 15. A business entity, owned by one individual, that is not legally independent of the owner.

_____ 16. The vertical balance sheet format with liabilities and stockholders' equity listed below assets.

_____ 17. Business events of a particular enterprise which are measured in monetary terms and recorded in its financial records.

_____ 18. The financial statement that discloses the effects of a firm's operating, financing, and investing activities.

_____ 19. Assesses the efficiency and effectiveness of operations within an organizational unit.

_____ 20. The owners' residual interest in the assets of a corporation.

_____ 21. The financial statement that presents the financial position of a firm at a particular point in time.

_____ 22. A financial statement that explains the change in retained earnings from the beginning of an accounting period to the end of the period.

_____ 23. The relationships among the basic financial statements which tie the financial statements together.

_____ 24. The study of concepts and procedures used to prepare financial information for external users.

Test your recall of the remaining key terms as follows: Read the following definitions of key terms and try to recall as many key terms as you can without assistance. Write your answers in the spaces provided. If you need assistance, refer to the list of key terms at the end of this section.

25. _____ _____ consists of the system and procedures for providing information for managerial activities.

26. The _____ _____ is the part of an organization's overall information system which includes the principles, methods, and procedures used to record, classify, and summarize financial information to be distributed to decision makers.

27. The _____ _____ ____ _____ _____ _____ or _____ is the professional organization of CPAs.

28. _____ _____ is the stockholder's equity account where owners' investment in the stock of a corporation is reported.

29. The _____ _____ is: Assets = _____ + Owners' Equity.

16

30. _____ is the price of goods sold or services rendered by a firm to others in exchange for cash or other assets or to satisfy liabilities.

31. A(n) _____ is the objective and independent third-party examination of an organization's financial statements.

32. _____ _____ is the owners' residual interest in the assets of a firm.

33. A(n) _____ is viewed legally as being separate and distinct from its owners, who are called stockholders.

34. _____ _____ _____ or _____ are accountants who are licensed by individual states to practice accounting after having met a number of education and experience requirements, and who have passed the Uniform CPA exam.

35. The _____ _____ _____ _____ or _____ is an independent organization which is responsible for the establishment of generally accepted accounting principles.

36. A(n) _____ _____ performs an audit function within an organization and is not independent of the organization.

37. _____ _____ is an attribute of corporations where stockholders' liability is limited to the extent of their investment in the corporation.

38. The _____ ___ _____ _____ or _____ is the professional organization for management accountants.

39. A(n) _____ _____ _____'s stock is bought and sold by the public often on exchanges such as the New York or American Stock Exchange.

40. _____ _____ is calculated as assets minus liabilities and is the same amount as stockholders' equity.

41. A(n) _____ _____ expresses the auditor's professional opinion about the fairness of the financial statements being audited.

42. A _____ _____ is an economic unit whose transactions are kept separate from those of its owners.

43. _____ are the resources used up by the firm during a particular period of time in the process of earning revenues.

44. The difference between revenues and expenses in an accounting period is called either _____ _____ or _____ _____.

45. _____ is the ease with which an item can be converted to cash.

46. A(n) _____ _____ is an accountant who works for a single firm and is responsible for collecting, processing, and reporting financial information.

KEY TERMS:

accounting equation
accounting system
American Institute of
  Certified Public Accountants, AICPA
audit
audit report
business entity
capital stock
certified public accountants, CPAs
corporation
expenses
Financial Accounting Standards Board, FASB
Institute of Management Accountants, IMA

internal auditor
liabilities
limited liability
liquidity
management accountant
management accounting
net assets
net income
net loss
owners' equity
publicly owned corporation
revenue

Compare your answers to those at the end of the chapter and review any key terms missed before proceeding.

CHAPTER QUIZ

Circle the single best answer.

1. All businesses are required to follow Securities and Exchange Commission regulations: (a) true; (b) false

2. Big 6 accounting firms usually provide three services: audit, tax, and consulting: (a) true; (b) false

3. A sole proprietorship is considered a separate legal entity from the owner: (a) true; (b) false

4. A sole proprietorship is considered a separate accounting entity from the owner: (a) true; (b) false

5. A partnership is considered a separate legal entity from the owners: (a) true; (b) false

6. A partnership is considered a separate accounting entity from the owners: (a) true; (b) false

7. A corporation is considered a separate legal entity from the owners: (a) true; (b) false

8. A corporation is considered a separate accounting entity from the owners: (a) true; (b) false

9. Accounting changes over time according to economic needs: (a) true;
   (b) false

10. Stockholders in a corporation have unlimited liability: (a) true;
    (b) false

11. Publicly owned corporations are owned by the government and operated to
    benefit the public: (a) true; (b) false

12. Both the AICPA and the IMA have established ethical standards for
    accountants: (a) true; (b) false

13. Assets have future economic benefit: (a) true; (b) false

14. Cash inflow from operating activities is equal to net income for the
    year: (a) true; (b) false

Write your answers in the spaces provided.

15. List the three major types of business organizations.
    1. _____
    2. _____
    3. _____

16. List the four primary financial statements.
    1. _____
    2. _____
    3. _____
    4. _____

17. The primary external users of accounting information are:
    1. _____
    2. _____

18. The primary internal user of accounting information is _____.

19. The three primary sources from which a firm can obtain cash are:
    1. _____ activities
    2. _____ activities
    3. _____ activities

20. If a company's assets equal $100,000 and stockholders' equity equals
    $30,000, then liabilities must equal $_____.

21. If a company's liabilities equal $60,000 and stockholders' equity is
    $50,000, then assets must equal $_____.

22. On January 1 a company's assets totaled $200,000 and liabilities equaled
    $120,000. During the year, stockholders' equity increased by $25,000 and
    liabilities decreased by $40,000. At December 31, total assets would be
    $_____.

**Compare your answers to those at the end of the chapter and review any
questions missed before proceeding.**

EXERCISE 1

Richard Barker opened a landscaping business on January 1, 1995. Listed below are the transactions that occurred in January. For each transaction, indicate if it would be recognized in preparing Richard's personal records and/or recognized in accounting for his business, Barker's Landscaping Services. Some transactions may be recorded in both entities' records, while some transactions may not be recorded in either set of records. The first one has been done for you.

| | RECOGNIZE IN: | |
TRANSACTION	PERSONAL RECORDS	BUSINESS RECORDS
Example: Richard invests $10,000 of his personal funds in the landscaping business.	YES	YES
1. Richard personally borrowed $25,000 from a local bank using his home as security for the loan. Richard intends to use the money to buy equipment for the landscaping business.	_____	_____
2. Richard invests the $25,000 in the business in exchange for capital stock.	_____	_____
3. The business pays $20,000 in cash to buy landscaping equipment and a used truck.	_____	_____
4. The business rents a building, paying $1,000 in cash.	_____	_____
5. Richard hired a college student to work part time in the business beginning in March.	_____	_____

EXERCISE 2

On January 1, 1995, Claire Koch opened a dry-cleaning business called Koch Cleaners Inc. The following transactions occurred during the first year of the firm's existence.

1. Claire invested $40,000 of her personal funds in the business, in exchange for 4,000 shares of capital stock.

2. The firm purchased a small building for $35,000, of which $15,000 was paid in cash and the remainder was borrowed from a local bank.

3. The firm purchased equipment for $15,000 cash.

4. Various supplies were purchased. The supplies cost $3,000 and were purchased on account, and no payments were made on this account during the current year.

5. Services provided during the year amount to $150,000. By year-end, $120,000 of this amount had been collected in cash.

6. Various operating expenses of $100,000 were incurred during the year. As of year-end, $85,000 of these expenses had been paid in cash.

7. Interest expense on the bank loan amounted to $2,000 and was unpaid at year-end.

8. Taxes of $6,000 were incurred and paid during the year.

Required:

Using the information provided, prepare the following financial statements:

1. An income statement for the year ended December 31, 1995. Use the following expense categories: operating expenses, interest expense, and income tax expense.

2. A statement of cash flows for the year ended December 31, 1995.

3. A balance sheet as of December 31, 1995.

NOTE: If you have difficulty in determining the amounts for the financial statements, use the format on the following page to organize the information and keep track of how the transactions affect the different accounts. The first transaction has been done for you.

EXERCISE 2 (continued)

	CASH	ACCOUNTS RECEIVABLE	SUPPLIES	EQUIPMENT	BUILDING	ACCOUNTS PAYABLE	INTEREST PAYABLE	BANK LOAN PAYABLE	CAPITAL STOCK	RETAINED EARNINGS	REVENUE	OPERATING EXPENSES	INTEREST EXPENSE	TAX EXPENSE
1.	+40,000								+40,000					

```
╔══════════════════════════════════════╗
║  ANSWERS                               ║
╚══════════════════════════════════════╝
```

KEY TERMS
 1. (G) financial statements
 2. (Q) public accounting
 3. (P) partnership
 4. (C) assets
 5. (L) income statement
 6. (A) account form of balance sheet
 7. (S) retained earnings
 8. (E) compliance audits
 9. (H) generally accepted accounting principles
10. (J) governmental accounting
11. (I) going-concern assumption
12. (K) historical cost convention
13. (M) liabilities
14. (N) objectivity
15. (U) sole proprietorship
16. (R) report form of balance sheet
17. (X) transactions
18. (V) statement of cash flows
19. (O) operational audits
20. (W) stockholders' equity
21. (D) balance sheet
22. (T) retained earnings statement
23. (B) articulation
24. (F) financial accounting
25. Management accounting
26. accounting system
27. American Institute of Certified Public Accountants, (AICPA)
28. Capital stock
29. accounting equation, Liabilities
30. Revenue
31. Audit
32. Owners' Equity
33. corporation
34. Certified public accountants, CPAs
35. Financial Accounting Standards Board, FASB
36. Internal auditor
37. Limited liability
38. Institute of Management Accountants, IMA
39. publicly owned corporation
40. Net assets
41. audit report
42. business entity
43. Expenses
44. net income, net loss
45. Liquidity
46. management accountant

CHAPTER QUIZ

1. b False. Only publicly traded corporations are required to follow SEC regulations.
2. a True
3. b False. A sole proprietorship is not considered a separate legal entity from its owner.
4. a True
5. b False. A partnership is not considered a separate legal entity from its owners.
6. a True
7. a True
8. a True
9. a True
10. b False. Stockholders' liability is usually limited to the amount they have invested in the corporation.
11. b False. A publicly owned corporation's stock is bought and sold by the public.
12. a True
13. a True
14. b False. Cash inflow from operating activities is not the same as net income. Cash inflows from operating activities include only revenues and expenses received or paid in cash during the period.
15. 1. sole proprietorship
    2. partnership
    3. corporation
16. 1. income statement
    2. balance sheet
    3. statement of cash flows
    4. statement of retained earnings
17. 1. stockholders
    2. creditors
18. management
19. 1. operating
    2. investing
    3. financing
20. $70,000
21. $110,000
22. $185,000

Supporting Calculations:

	Assets	=	Liabilities	+	Stockholders' Equity
Beginning Balance	$200,000	=	$120,000	+	$80,000
Change			(40,000)		25,000
			--------		-------
Ending Balance	$185,000	=	$ 80,000	+	$105,000

EXERCISE 1

TRANSACTION	RECOGNIZE IN: PERSONAL RECORDS	BUSINESS RECORDS
1. Richard personally borrowed $25,000 from a local bank using his home as security for the loan. Richard intends to use the money to buy equipment for the landscaping business.	YES	NO
2. Richard invests the $25,000 in the business in exchange for capital stock.	YES	YES
3. The business pays $20,000 in cash to buy landscaping equipment and a used truck.	NO	YES
4. The business rents a building, paying $1,000 in cash.	NO	YES
5. Richard hired a college student to work part time in the business beginning in March.	NO	NO

EXERCISE 2
1.

Koch Cleaners Inc.
Income Statement
For the Year Ended December 31, 1995

Revenue		$150,000
Expenses:		
Various operating expenses	$100,000	
Interest expense	2,000	
Total expenses before income taxes		102,000
Income before taxes		$ 48,000
Income tax expense		6,000
Net income		$ 42,000

EXERCISE 2 (continued)

2.
_____

Koch Cleaners Inc.
Statement of Cash flows
For the Year Ended December 31, 1995

_____

Cash flows from operating activities:		
Cash received from customers	$120,000	
Various expenses and taxes paid ($85,000 + $6,000)	(91,000)	
Net cash provided by operating activities		$29,000
Cash flows from investing activities:		
Purchase of building	($35,000)	
Purchase of equipment	(15,000)	
Net cash used by investing activities		(50,000)
Cash flows from financing activities:		
Issuance of bank loan payable	$20,000	
Issuance of capital stock	40,000	
Net cash provided by financing activities		60,000
Net increase in cash		$39,000
Cash balance, January 1, 1995		0
Cash balance, December 31, 1995		$39,000

EXERCISE 2 (continued)

3.

Koch Cleaners Inc.
Balance Sheet
December 31, 1995

Assets		Liabilities and Stockholders' Equity	
Cash	$ 39,000	Liabilities:	
Accounts receivable	30,000	Accounts payable	$ 18,000
Office supplies	3,000	Interest payable	2,000
Equipment	15,000	Bank loan payable	20,000
Building	35,000		
	———	Total liabilities	$ 40,000
		Stockholders' equity:	
		Capital stock	$ 40,000
		Retained earnings*	42,000
		Total stockholders' equity	$ 82,000
		Total liabilities and stockholders' equity	
Total assets	$122,000		$122,000

*The balance in retained earnings is calculated as follows:

Beginning Retained Earnings + Income - Dividends = Ending Retained Earnings
$-0-   + $42,000 - $-0-   = $42,000

Because this is the firm's first year of operation, there is no beginning balance in retained earnings. In addition, no dividends were declared. As a result, the ending balance of retained earnings equals net income for the year of $42,000.

EXERCISE 2 (continued)

Note: The following worksheet can be used to organize information about transactions and determine the ending account balances.

	CASH	ASSETS ACCOUNTS RECEIVABLE	SUPPLIES	EQUIPMENT	BUILDING	LIABILITIES ACCOUNTS PAYABLE	INTEREST PAYABLE	BANK LOAN PAYABLE	ST. EQUITY CAPITAL STOCK	RETAINED EARNINGS	REVENUE REVENUE	EXPENSES OPERATING EXPENSES	INTEREST EXPENSE	TAX EXPENSE
1.	+40,000								+40,000					
2.	-15,000				+35,000			+20,000						
3.	-15,000			+15,000										
4.			+3,000			+3,000								
5.	+120,000	+30,000									+150,000			
6.	-85,000					+15,000						+100,000		
7.							+2,000						+2,000	
8.	-6,000													+6,000
	$39,000	$30,000	$3,000	$15,000	$35,000	$18,000	$2,000	$20,000	$40,000	-0-*	$150,000	$100,000	$2,000	$6,000

*This is the retained earnings balance before net income is closed to retained earnings.

28

CHAPTER 2

ACCOUNTING AS AN INFORMATION SYSTEM-- RECORDING BALANCE SHEET TRANSACTIONS

```
╔══════════════════════════════════╗
║  CHAPTER REVIEW                   ║
╚══════════════════════════════════╝
```

THE ACCOUNTING INFORMATION SYSTEM

- An **accounting information system** is a system designed to provide financial information about economic entities.

- The objective of an accounting system is to process accounting transactions and provide useful information to decision makers.

- Three components of the accounting information system are:
  - inputs: new data about economic events.
  - transaction process: the set of rules and conventions that accountants use to record, classify, and summarize the inputs.
  - outputs: the accounting reports provided to users.

- Outputs for external users are produced by the **financial accounting information system**, a subsystem of the overall accounting system.

- The main objective of the financial accounting information system is to prepare the following financial statements in accordance with GAAP for external users:
  - income statement
  - retained earnings statement
  - balance sheet
  - statement of cash flows

- Outputs for internal users are produced by the **management accounting information system**, another subsystem of the overall accounting system.

  The main objective of the management accounting information system is to produce accounting information (reports) for managerial use, such as:
  - performance reports
  - budgets
  - other reports needed by managers to make decisions

The Information Systems Role of the Accountant

- Three important system roles that accountants play are:
  - users
  - designers
  - auditors

- As users, accountants enter transactions into the accounting system, then use the system to process the transactions and to generate reports and financial statements for decision makers.

- As designers, accountants and other information specialists work together to design and implement manual and computer-based information systems.

- As auditors, accountants review and test information systems to ensure the systems are correctly processing transactions.

Data Input Criteria for the Financial Accounting System

- To be recorded in the financial accounting system, economic events must be:
  - transactions for the business entity
  - quantifiable or measurable in monetary terms
  - verifiable

Business Entity Assumption

- The **business entity assumption** is the concept that a business is independent and distinct from its owners.

- Only business transactions and events related to an entity's economic activities should be included in the accounting system. Owners' personal transactions should not be recorded in the accounting system of the business.

Quantifiability

- **Quantifiability** is the concept that economic events must be measured and expressed in numerical (primarily monetary) terms.

Verifiability

- **Verifiability** is the concept that data related to a transaction or event must be available and that if two or more qualified persons examined the same data, they would reach essentially the same conclusions about the proper accounting treatment for the transaction.

Recognizing Transactions

- In addition to deciding if an event meets the criteria as an input to the accounting system, accountants must also decide *when* to recognize (record) the event in the accounting records.

- Business transactions are entered in the accounting system at their historical cost and are not changed with subsequent increases in value until another transaction takes place.

- Generally, accountants do not recognize mutual promises to perform until one or both parties actually perform.

EFFECTS OF TRANSACTIONS ON THE FINANCIAL ACCOUNTING SYSTEM

- The following accounting equation summarizes the contents of the balance sheet.

$$\text{Assets = Liabilities + Owners' Equity}$$

- The accounting equation is part of the transformation process that converts data into useful information.
  1. All transactions are recorded in accounts. An **account** is a record that summarizes all transactions that affect a particular category of asset, liability, or stockholders' equity.
  2. For the accounting equation to remain in balance, each transaction must involve a change in at least two accounts.

COMPONENTS OF THE ACCOUNTING SYSTEM

- The major components of the financial accounting system consist of the following:

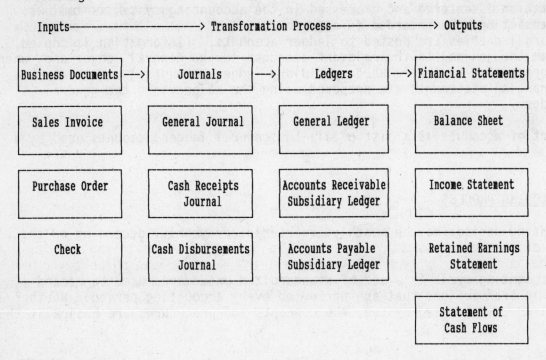

Inputs —————————> Transformation Process —————————> Outputs

Business Documents	--->	Journals	--->	Ledgers	--->	Financial Statements
Sales Invoice		General Journal		General Ledger		Balance Sheet
Purchase Order		Cash Receipts Journal		Accounts Receivable Subsidiary Ledger		Income Statement
Check		Cash Disbursements Journal		Accounts Payable Subsidiary Ledger		Retained Earnings Statement
						Statement of Cash Flows

- The components of the system are similar whether the system is manual or computerized.

31

The Journal

- The **journal** is the record where transactions are initially recorded in chronological order.

- The general journal can be used to record all types of transactions.

- Special journals are used to record a specific type of transaction. For example, the cash receipts journal is used to record cash receipts and the cash disbursements journal is used to record cash payments.

The Ledger

- A **ledger** is a book or computerized record of specific accounts where the effects of all transactions that affect a specific account are summarized.

- A **general ledger** contains a specific account for each item listed on the financial statements.

- A **subsidiary ledger** is a back-up or more detailed record for an account in the general ledger. For example, Accounts Receivable is an account in the general ledger and the Accounts Receivable subsidiary ledger contains individual accounts receivable for each customer.

- Information is entered and processed in the accounting system as follows:
  1. Transactions are recorded in a journal.
  2. Journal entries are posted to ledger accounts. (Information is copied from the journal to the relevant accounts in the general ledger and, when appropriate, to the related subsidiary ledger accounts.)
  3. Financial statements are prepared using the balances in the general ledger.

- A **chart of accounts** is a list of all the general ledger accounts used by a firm.

THE RECORDING PROCESS

- Accounting periods may be monthly, quarterly, or yearly, depending on the needs of the business.

- The **accounting cycle** is a set of standardized procedures used to record economic transactions that are performed every accounting period. Whether a manual or computerized system, the concepts and procedures are basically the same.

- The accounting cycle consists of the following procedures:

  During the accounting period:
  - Record transactions in the journal.
  - Periodically post journal entries to ledger accounts.

  At the end of the accounting period:
  - Prepare the unadjusted trial balance.
  - Prepare the worksheet (optional).
  - Prepare adjusting entries.
  - Post adjusting entries to the ledger accounts and prepare the adjusted trial balance.
  - Prepare the financial statements.
  - Prepare closing entries, post to the ledger accounts, and prepare a post-closing trial balance.

Recording Transactions in the Ledger

- In a manual accounting system a ledger contains a separate page for each account.

- **T accounts** are used to represent individual ledger accounts for analysis purposes. A T account for cash might appear as follows:

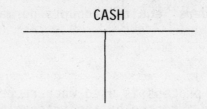

CASH

- For every increase in an asset account, there is a corresponding:
  - decrease in another asset account, or
  - increase in a liability account, or
  - increase in a stockholders' equity account.

Understanding Debits and Credits

- In accounting, the terms debit and credit are used as shorthand ways of indicating if an entry is made on the left or the right side of an account.

- A **debit** is an entry on the *left* side of an account.

  Debits:
  - increase asset accounts.
  - decrease liability accounts.
  - decrease stockholders' equity accounts.

- A **credit** is an entry on the *right* side of an account.

Credits:
- decrease asset accounts.
- increase liability accounts.
- increase stockholders' equity accounts.

- The debit and credit rules are summarized below.

Assets		=	Liabilities		+	Stockholders' Equity	
Debit	Credit		Debit	Credit		Debit	Credit
Increases	Decreases		Decreases	Increases		Decreases	Increases
+	-		-	+		-	+

- When **double-entry accounting** is used, debits must equal credits for each transaction recorded.

  For example, if an asset account is increased (debited), there must be a corresponding:
  - decrease in another asset account (credit), or
  - an increase in a liability or stockholders' equity account (credit)

- Asset accounts normally have debit balances.

- Liabilities and stockholders' equity accounts normally have credit balances.

Analyzing Transactions

- The following three-step process is used when recording transactions:
  1. Determine the accounts affected by the transaction and whether they are asset, liability, or stockholders' equity accounts.
  2. Decide whether each of these accounts is increased or decreased.
  3. Make the appropriate debit and credit entries in the specific accounts.

Recording Transactions in the Journal

- Conventions used when recording entries in the journal include:
  - Debits are always listed first, with the account title beginning at the left margin of the account titles column.
  - The credit portion of the entry is then recorded, indented slightly from the left margin.
  - If the entry is a compound entry that involves more than two accounts, all the debits are recorded before the credits.
  - The dollar amounts are entered in the respective Debit and Credit columns on the same line as the account titles. No dollar signs are used.
  - A short explanation is usually included under the entry.
  - When the journal entry is posted to the ledger account, the number of the ledger account to which the entry is placed in the Ref. (references) column of the journal in order to cross-reference the journal to the ledger.

• A sample entry is shown below.

Date	Account Title	Ref.	Debit	Credit
1995				
Jan. 30	Land	150	20,000	
	Building	165	100,000	
	Cash	101		40,000
	Notes Payable	205		80,000

Posting to the Ledger

• **Posting** is the process of transferring recorded transaction data from a journal to a ledger.

• Posting can take place daily, semimonthly, monthly, or yearly.

• If a computer is used to record transactions, posting can be performed instantaneously as the transactions are recorded.

THE TRIAL BALANCE

• The **trial balance** is a list of all general ledger accounts and their corresponding account balances. The trial balance is a check to see whether equal amounts of debits and credits have been posted to the ledger.

• If the trial balance is in balance (debits equal credits), this indicates that:
1. the same dollar amounts of debits and credits have been posted, and
2. the accounts have been correctly balanced.

• If the trial balance is in balance, this does not necessarily indicate that no errors have been made. For example, an entire entry may have been omitted from the journal, yet the trial balance would still be in balance.

Errors in the Trial Balance

• Some of the more common errors that may occur in the trial balance include:
1. An addition error was made in totaling the trial balance.
2. A debit may have been posted as a credit or vice versa.
3. Part of an entry may not have been posted.
4. A dollar amount may have been misposted due to a transposition or misplaced decimal point.
5. The ledger accounts are incorrectly balanced.
6. An incorrect balance is transferred to the trial balance from a ledger account.
7. A journal entry does not balance.

KEY TERMS TEST

Test your recall of the key terms as follows: Read the following definitions of key terms and try to recall as many key terms as you can *without assistance*. Write your answers in the spaces provided. If you need assistance, refer to the list of key terms at the end of this section.

1. A(n) _____ is an entry on the left side of an account.

2. The _____ is a book or computerized record of specific accounts where the effects of all transactions on those accounts are recorded.

3. The _____ _____ _____ consists of the interrelated parts and procedures used to process accounting transactions and provide useful information to decision makers.

4. The main objective of the _____ _____ _____ _____ is to produce accounting information (reports) for managerial use.

5. The _____ _____ is the standard set of accounting procedures performed in sequence every accounting period.

6. The _____ _____ is the record that contains a specific account for each item listed on the financial statements.

7. The process of transferring recorded transaction data from a journal to a ledger is called _____.

8. The _____ _____ is a list of all general ledger accounts and their corresponding account balances at a point in time.

9. The _____ _____ _____ is a list of all of the general ledger accounts used by a firm.

10. The _____ is the record where transactions are initially recorded in chronological order.

11. _____ is the concept that economic events must be measured and expressed in numerical terms.

12. _____ is the concept that data related to a transaction or event must be available, and that two or more qualified persons would reach the same conclusions about the proper accounting treatment of the transaction or event if they examined the data.

13. A(n) _____ _____ is a shorthand representation of an individual ledger account.

14. A(n) _____ is an entry on the right side of an account.

15. The _____ _____ is a detailed record of the effects of all transactions on a specific entity within a general ledger account.

16. The concept that a business is independent and distinct from its owners is known as the _____ _____ _____.

17. The system of accounting where every transaction is represented by equal debits and credits is called _____ _____.

18. The main objective of the _____ _____ _____ _____ is to prepare financial statements for external users.

KEY TERMS:

accounting cycle s)
accounting information system 3)
business entity assumption 16)
chart of accounts 9)
credit 14)
debit 1)
3) double-entry accounting
financial accounting 18)
   information system
general ledger 6)

journal 10)
ledger 11)
management accounting
   information system 4)
posting 7)
quantifiability 11)
2) subsidiary ledger
1) T account
trial balance 8)
verifiability 12)

Compare your answers to those at the end of the chapter and review any key terms missed.

CHAPTER QUIZ

Circle the best answer.

1. The accounting equation is: assets plus liabilities equals stockholders' equity: (a) true; (b) false

2. Asset accounts are increased by credits: (a) true; (b) false

3. Posting is the process of transferring account balances from the ledger accounts to the post-closing trial balance: (a) true; (b) false

4. If the trial balance is in balance (debits equal credits), this proves that the accounting system is free of errors: (a) true; (b) false

5. All of the following are considered source documents except: (a) sales invoices; (b) purchase orders; (c) cash register tapes; (d) ledgers; (e) checks

6. Retained earnings is a(n): (a) asset account; (b) liability account; (c) stockholders' equity account; (d) revenue account; (e) none of the above

7. If the beginning balance for the Cash account was $13,000, and during the year $30,000 was collected from customers, $20,000 was paid for rent, insurance and wages, and $5,000 was paid in taxes, the ending balance in the Cash account would be: (a) $5,000; (b) $8,000; (c) $18,000; (d) $23,000

8. If assets increase by $10,000, for the accounting equation to remain in balance: (a) liabilities must increase by $10,000; (b) liabilities must decrease by $10,000; (c) stockholders' equity must decrease by $10,000; (d) assets must decrease by $10,000; (e) a or c; (f) a or d

Write your answers in the spaces provided.

9. List three roles that accountants play in the information system.
   1. _____
   2. _____
   3. _____

10. List in order eight steps in the accounting cycle.
   1. _____
   2. _____
   3. _____
   4. _____
   5. _____
   6. _____
   7. _____
   8. _____

Circle the correct answer.

11. Asset accounts are increased by (circle one: debits, credits).

12. Liability accounts are increased by (circle one: debits, credits).

13. Stockholders' equity accounts are decreased by (circle one: debits, credits).

14. Accounts Receivable is a(n) (circle one: asset, liability, stockholders' equity) account and is increased by (circle one: debits, credits).

15. Accounts Payable is a(n) (circle one: asset, liability, stockholders' equity) account and is increased by (circle one: debits, credits).

16. Capital Stock is a(n) (circle one: asset, liability, stockholders' equity) account and is decreased by (circle one: debits, credits).

17. Supplies is a(n) (circle one: asset, liability, stockholders' equity) account and is decreased by (circle one: debits, credits).

18. Notes Payable is a(n) (circle one: asset, liability, stockholders' equity) account and is increased by (circle one: debits, credits).

19. Office Equipment is a(n) (circle one: asset, liability, stockholders' equity) account and is decreased by (circle one: debits, credits).

20. Retained Earnings is a(n) (circle one: asset, liability, stockholders' equity) account and is increased by (circle one: debits, credits).

21. Cash is a(n) (circle one: asset, liability, stockholders' equity) account and is increased by (circle one: debits, credits).

22. Wages Payable is a(n) (circle one: asset, liability, stockholders' equity) account and is decreased by (circle one: debits, credits).

23. Inventory is a(n) (circle one: asset, liability, stockholders' equity) account and is decreased by (circle one: debits, credits).

24. Interest Payable is a(n) (circle one: asset, liability, stockholders' equity) account and is increased by (circle one: debits, credits).

25. Prepaid Rent is a(n) (circle one: asset, liability, stockholders' equity) account and is increased by (circle one: debits, credits).

Compare your answers to those at the end of the chapter and review any questions missed.

EXERCISES

TIP: When working homework, study guide, or examination problems, read the requirements *before* reading the problem. This saves time because then as you read the problem, you can begin thinking of how to use the problem information to answer the requirements. In addition, as you read the problem, underline or circle any important numbers or information. Use the margins to jot down ideas and make notes as you read through the problem.

EXERCISE 1

On December 31, 1994 the Grant Company had the following account balances:

Cash	$15,000
Accounts Receivable	25,000
Supplies	8,000
Equipment	30,000
Accounts Payable	12,000
Notes Payable	40,000
Capital Stock	22,000
Retained Earnings	4,000

EXERCISE 1 (continued)

During January 1995, the following events occurred:

a. On January 1, a new office building was leased for $1,000 per month. Six months of rent were paid in advance on January 1.
b. One of the owners contributed $5,000 to the firm in exchange for 1,000 shares of capital stock.
c. The business purchased a new computer costing $3,500. At the time of purchase, $1,000 was paid in cash with the remainder due in March.
d. The old computer, which cost $500 when purchased, was sold for $500, of which $200 was received in cash and the remainder was on account.
e. An installment of $2,000 was paid on the bank loan.
f. Supplies costing $500 were purchased on account.
g. Accounts receivable of $7,000 were collected.
h. The remainder due from the sale of the old computer was collected.
i. Accounts payable of $1,200 were paid.

Required:

Complete the following chart as follows:
1. Enter the beginning balances for each account at January 1, 1995.
2. Show the effect of each transaction on the accounting equation. (Do not give totals after each transaction.)
3. Determine the ending balance in each account at January 31, 1995.

CASH	ACCOUNTS RECEIVABLE	PREPAID RENT	SUPPLIES	EQUIPMENT	ACCOUNTS PAYABLE	NOTES PAYABLE	CAPITAL STOCK	RETAINED EARNINGS

EXERCISE 2

For each of the following accounts indicate:
1. whether the account is an asset, liability, or stockholders' equity
   account, and
2. whether the normal balance is a debit or credit

ACCOUNT	TYPE OF ACCOUNT	NORMAL ACCOUNT BALANCE
Retained earnings		
Notes payable		
Supplies		
Prepaid rent		
Fees collected in advance from customers		
Accounts payable		
Accounts receivable		
Patent		
Equipment		
Land		
Capital stock		
Wages payable		
Inventory		
Cash		

EXERCISE 3

The following transactions occurred during the month of June, 1995.

June 1: Noah Anthony started Josh's Dog Grooming and Boarding Service by
         contributing $40,000 to the business in exchange for 1,000 shares of
         capital stock.

June 2: The business purchased a building, including land, for $30,000, in
         cash. The land has a value of $5,000 and the building a value of
         $25,000.

June 3: Supplies costing $2,000 were purchased on account.

June 4: The business purchased equipment costing $12,000, paying $3,000 in
         cash and borrowing the remainder from a local bank.

June 20: The firm paid the account payable that resulted from the purchase of
         supplies.

Required:

1. Label the following blank T accounts with an account title, then enter the
   above transactions in the appropriate T accounts, labeling each transaction
   with the date it occurred.

2. Balance the T accounts.

41

EXERCISE 4

On June 1, 1995 Marsha M. Moore opens an ice cream parlor, MMM's Ice Cream. The following events occur during the month of June.

June 1: Marsha invests $50,000 cash in the business in exchange for 500 shares of capital stock.

June 10: The corporation purchases a small building, including land, for $40,000 cash. The land has a value of $4,000 and the building a value of $36,000.

June 12: The company purchases furniture and freezers for $8,000, financing the purchase with a one-year bank loan.

June 15: Ice cream totaling $1,000 is purchased on account and recorded in an account called Ice Cream Inventory. The ice cream is purchased from Quinn's Ice Creamery.

June 16: Supplies costing $900 are purchased on account and recorded in an account called Supplies Inventory. The supplies are purchased from Steve's Supplies Inc.

June 20: The corporation pays $800 on the account payable incurred on June 15.

Required:

1. Record the transactions in the general journal on the following page.

TIP: When making journal entries, use the following approach:
1. Determine which accounts are affected by the transaction.
2. For each account, determine whether it is an asset, liability, or stockholders' equity account.
3. Decide whether each account is increased or decreased by the transaction.
4. Make the appropriate debit or credit to each account.
   Although debits and credits may seem confusing at first, simply remember the following:

   Asset accounts are increased by **debits**.

   Liability accounts are increased by **credits**.

   Stockholders' Equity accounts are increased by **credits**.

MMM'S ICE CREAM

GENERAL JOURNAL

DATE	ACCOUNT TITLES	REF.	DEBIT	CREDIT

2. Post the transactions to the appropriate T accounts.

EXERCISE 4 (continued)

EXERCISE 4 (continued)

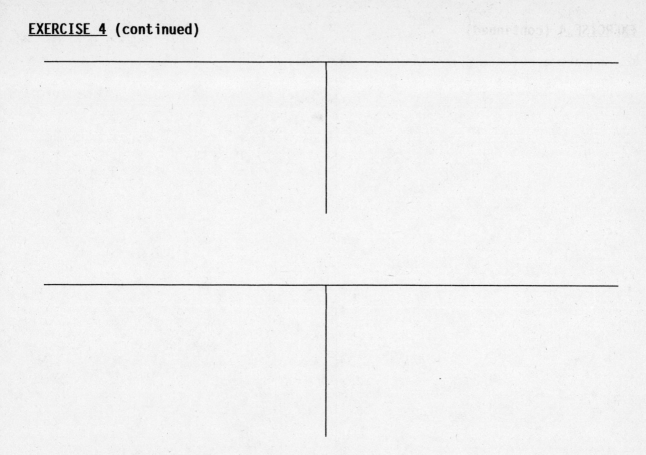

3. Prepare a trial balance at June 30, 1995.

4. Prepare a balance sheet at June 30, 1995.

```
┌────────────────────────────────────────────────────────┐
║  ANSWERS                                                 ║
└────────────────────────────────────────────────────────┘
```

KEY TERMS
1. debit
2. ledger
3. accounting information system
4. management accounting information system
5. accounting cycle
6. general ledger
7. posting
8. trial balance
9. chart of accounts
10. journal
11. Quantifiability
12. Verifiability
13. T account
14. credit
15. subsidiary ledger
16. business entity assumption
17. double-entry accounting
18. financial accounting information system

CHAPTER QUIZ
1. b False. The accounting equation is: Assets = Liabilities + Stockholders'
   Equity.
2. b False. Asset accounts are increased by debits and decreased by credits.
3. b False. Posting is the process of transferring information from the
   journal to ledger.
4. b False. There can be errors even if the trial balance is in balance, as
   for example, when an entire entry is omitted from the general
   journal or a debit or credit is posted to the wrong account.
5. d
6. c
7. c $18,000   ($13,000 + $30,000 - $20,000 - $5,000 = $18,000)
8. f
9. 1. users
   2. designers
   3. auditors
10. 1. Record transactions in the journal.
    2. Post journal entries to ledger accounts.
    3. Prepare the unadjusted trial balance.
    4. Prepare the worksheet (optional).
    5. Prepare adjusting entries.
    6. Post adjusting entries and prepare the adjusted trial balance.
    7. Prepare the financial statements.
    8. Prepare closing entries, post to ledger accounts, and prepare a post-
       closing trial balance.
11. debits
12. credits
13. debits
14. asset, debits
15. liability, credits

50

16. stockholders' equity, debits
17. asset, credits
18. liability, credits
19. asset, credits
20. stockholders' equity, credits
21. asset, debits
22. liability, debits
23. asset, credits
24. liability, credits
25. asset, debits

EXERCISE 1

		ASSETS			=	LIABILITIES	+	ST. EQUITY	
	CASH	ACCOUNTS RECEIVABLE	PREPAID RENT	SUPPLIES	EQUIPMENT	ACCOUNTS PAYABLE	NOTES PAYABLE	CAPITAL STOCK	RETAINED EARNINGS
Beg. Bal.	$15,000	$25,000	$ -0-	$8,000	$30,000	$12,000	$40,000	$22,000	$4,000
a.	-6,000		+6,000						
b.	+5,000							+5,000	
c.	-1,000				+3,500	+2,500			
d.	+200	+300			-500				
e.	-2,000						-2,000		
f.				+500		+500			
g.	+7,000	-7,000							
h.	+300	-300							
i.	-1,200					-1,200			
	$17,300	$18,000	$6,000	$8,500	$33,000	$13,800	$38,000	$27,000	$4,000

Assets = Liabilities + Stockholders' Equity
$17,300+$18,000+$6,000+$8,500+$33,000 = ($13,800+$38,000) + ($27,000+$4,000)
$82,800 = $51,800 + $31,000
$82,800 = $82,800

51

EXERCISE 2

ACCOUNT	TYPE OF ACCOUNT	NORMAL ACCOUNT BALANCE
Retained earnings	St. Equity	CR
Notes payable	Liability	CR
Supplies	Asset	DR
Prepaid rent	Asset	DR
Fees collected in advance from customers	Liability	CR
Accounts payable	Liability	CR
Accounts receivable	Asset	DR
Patent	Asset	DR
Equipment	Asset	DR
Land	Asset	DR
Capital stock	St. Equity	CR
Wages payable	Liability	CR
Inventory	Asset	DR
Cash	Asset	DR

<u>EXERCISE 3</u>

CASH

	DR			CR	
6/1		40,000			
			6/2		30,000
			6/4		3,000
			6/20		2,000
6/30		5,000			

SUPPLIES

	DR			CR	
6/3		2,000			
6/30		2,000			

LAND

	DR			CR	
6/2		5,000			
6/30		5,000			

BUILDING

	DR			CR	
6/2		25,000			
6/30		25,000			

EXERCISE 3 (continued)

EQUIPMENT

DR		CR
6/4	12,000	
6/30	12,000	

ACCOUNTS PAYABLE

DR		CR	
		6/3	2,000
6/20	2,000		
		6/30	-0-

NOTE PAYABLE

DR		CR	
		6/4	9,000
		6/30	9,000

CAPITAL STOCK

DR		CR	
		6/1	40,000
		6/30	40,000

EXERCISE 4

MMM'S ICE CREAM

GENERAL JOURNAL

DATE	ACCOUNT TITLES	REF.	DEBIT	CREDIT
1995				
June 1	Cash		50,000	
	Capital Stock			50,000
	To record sale of capital stock.			
June 10	Land		4,000	
	Building		36,000	
	Cash			40,000
	To record the purchase of land and building.			
June 12	Equipment		8,000	
	Notes Payable			8,000
	To record the purchase of furniture and freezers.			
June 15	Ice Cream Inventory		1,000	
	Accounts Payable: Quinn's Ice Creamery			1,000
	To record the purchase of ice cream inventory on account.			
June 16	Supplies Inventory		900	
	Accounts Payable: Steve's Supplies			900
	To record the purchase of supplies on account.			
June 20	Accounts Payable: Quinn's Ice Creamery		800	
	Cash			800
	To record payment on account.			

CASH

	DR		CR	
6/1	50,000			
			6/10	40,000
			6/20	800
6/30	9,200			

SUPPLIES INVENTORY

	DR		CR
6/16	900		
6/30	900		

ICE CREAM INVENTORY

	DR		CR
6/15	1,000		
6/30	1,000		

LAND

	DR		CR
6/10	4,000		
6/30	4,000		

BUILDING

DR		CR
6/10	36,000	
6/30	36,000	

EQUIPMENT

DR		CR
6/12	8,000	
6/30	8,000	

ACCOUNTS PAYABLE: QUINN'S ICE CREAMERY

DR		CR	
		6/15	1,000
6/20	800		
		6/30	200

ACCOUNTS PAYABLE: STEVE'S SUPPLIES

DR		CR	
		6/16	900
		6/30	900

NOTES PAYABLE

DR	CR
	6/12 8,000
	6/30 8,000

CAPITAL STOCK

DR	CR
	6/1 50,000
	6/30 50,000

3.

MMM's Ice Cream
Trial Balance
June 30, 1995

ACCOUNT	DEBIT	CREDIT
Cash	$ 9,200	
Supplies Inventory	900	
Ice Cream Inventory	1,000	
Land	4,000	
Building	36,000	
Equipment	8,000	
Accounts Payable (200 + 900)		$ 1,100
Notes Payable		8,000
Capital Stock		50,000
Totals	$59,100	$59,100

4.

MMM's Ice Cream
Balance Sheet
June 30, 1995

Assets:
 Cash $ 9,200
 Supplies Inventory   900
 Ice Cream Inventory   1,000
 Land   4,000
 Building   36,000
 Equipment   8,000
                ———
  Total Assets $59,100
                     =====

Liabilities:
 Accounts Payable $ 1,100
 Notes Payable   8,000
               ———
  Total Liabilities $ 9,100

Stockholders' Equity:
 Capital Stock $50,000
               ———
  Total Stockholders' Equity   50,000
                 ———
  Total Liabilities and Stockholders' Equity $59,100
                    =====

CHAPTER 3

MEASURING AND RECORDING
INCOME STATEMENT TRANSACTIONS

```
CHAPTER REVIEW
```

- The profit earned by an enterprise is a yardstick that managers, investors, and creditors use to evaluate the future prospects of a business. Thus one of the most important parts of the accounting process is the recognition, measurement, and recording of those economic transactions that affect the firm's income.

TRANSACTION PROCESSING CYCLES

- A **transaction cycle** is a sequence of related steps used to process a series of repetitive transactions.

- Two transaction processing cycles in most merchandising firms (firms that sell goods to the public) are:
  1. the revenue cycle
  2. the expenditure cycle

Revenue Cycle

- The **revenue cycle** processes transactions related to the sale of goods and services.

- The revenue cycle, which processes sales and cash receipts transactions, has three major subsystems:
  1. **Order entry system**. The order entry system validates the order, checks the customer's credit status, and checks inventory quantities to make sure sufficient inventory exists to fill the customer's order. Once the order had been approved, the ordered goods are withdrawn from inventory and taken to shipping where they are packaged for shipment. A **shipping notice** informs the customer that the goods have been shipped.
  2. **Billing system**. Using the shipping invoice as input, the billing system records the sales transaction and prepares and mails an **invoice** indicating how much the customer owes.
  3. **Cash receipts system**. The cash receipts system processes the cash received from cash and credit sales. The cash receipts system records the receipt of customers' checks and reduces the customers' outstanding accounts receivable balance by the amount received.

Expenditure Cycle

- The **expenditure cycle** processes transactions related to the acquisition and use of goods and services.

- The expenditure cycle, which processes expenditure and cash disbursement transactions, has three major subsystems:
  1. **Purchasing system.** The purchasing system generates a **purchase order** (a formal, external request for the purchase of goods or services from a vendor). After the purchase order is reviewed and approved, it is mailed to the vendor.
  2. **Receiving system.** In the receiving system, goods received are counted and compared with the goods ordered (as shown on the purchase order). A **receiving report** shows the quantity of goods received and acts as input to the accounts payable and inventory systems.
  3. **Cash disbursements system.** Copies of the original purchase order, the receiving report, and the vendor's invoice are compared and differences reconciled, then the obligation to pay for goods and services received is recorded as an account payable. At the appropriate time, the liability is paid, and the cash disbursement is recorded.

- Revenue and expense transactions are recorded throughout the accounting period, and they are summarized periodically on an income statement, which measures the net income or loss of the organization.

MEASURING INCOME

- The income statement is the financial statement that lists the following components of income:
  - revenues
  - expenses
  - gains
  - losses
  - net income

Revenues and Expenses

- Revenues and expenses result from the firm's major operating activities, such as the sale of its goods or services during the period.

- Revenues are the prices of goods and services provided to customers in exchange for cash or other assets.

- Expenses are the dollar amounts of the resources used up by the firm during a particular period of time in the process of earning revenues.

- **Receipts** are the inflows of cash or other assets. Receipts are not the same as revenues. For example, cash received from a bank loan is not revenue, but a liability.

  Only receipts of cash that come from products sold or services performed for customers are considered revenue.

- **Expenditures** are outflows of cash or other assets or increases in liabilities. All expenditures are not necessarily expenses. For example, if a firm purchases an office building for cash, the building would be recorded as an asset, not an expense.

  Only expenditures that produce revenues in the current period and do not provide for future economic benefits are considered expenses.

Gains and Losses

- **Gains** are increases in equity (net assets) from activities other than revenues and investments by owners during the period.

- **Losses** are decreases in equity (net assets) from activities other than expenses or distributions to owners during the period.

- Revenues and expenses directly relate to producing and selling goods and services; gain and losses do not. For example, the sale of the firm's office building would result in a gain or loss.

Net Income

- **Net income** or **net loss** is the difference between the total of revenues and gains and the total of expenses and losses of the period.

- Net income results when revenues and gains exceed expenses and losses. A net loss results when expenses and losses exceed revenues and gains.

- Net income causes an increase in a firm's net assets (owners' equity), whereas a net loss causes a decrease in the firm's net assets.

Dividends

- **Dividends** are a return to the stockholders of some of the assets that have increased because of profits earned. Cash dividends are the most common types of dividend.

- If a dividend is issued when there is a negative balance (a deficit) in Retained Earnings, it is called a liquidating dividend.

- Dividends are <u>not</u> expenses. Dividends are a distribution of assets resulting from the corporation's accumulated profits; therefore, dividends do not appear on the income statement. Instead, dividends are deducted from retained earnings.

MAJOR CONCEPTS RELATED TO DETERMINING INCOME

- Concepts and conventions used when determining net income include:
  - the time period assumption
  - the matching convention
  - the accrual basis of accounting
  - the revenue realization principle

Time Period Assumption

- The **time period assumption** is the assumption that a firm's life can be divided into time periods, which can be a month, a quarter, or a year.

- At a minimum, firms prepare annual financial statements.

- Publicly held corporations also are required to issue quarterly financial statements, call **interim statements**.

- Most firms prepare monthly financial statements for internal purposes.

The Matching Convention

- The **matching convention** requires that the expenses incurred in a particular period be matched against the revenues that they helped generate during the period.

- The accrual basis of accounting provides the best matching of expenses with revenues.

Accrual Basis Versus Cash Basis of Accounting

Accrual Basis

- When the **accrual basis of accounting** is used, revenues, expenses, and other changes in assets, liabilities, and owners' equity are accounted for in the period in which the economic event occurs rather than when the actual cash is received or paid.

  Under the accrual basis, revenue is recognized when earned, and expenses are recognized when incurred. For example, revenue is recognized when goods or services are provided, regardless of when the cash is actually collected.

- Recall the following debit and credit rules that are used when making journal entries:

    Asset accounts are increased by **debits**.
    Liability accounts are increased by **credits**.
    Stockholders' equity accounts are increased by **credits**.
    Revenue accounts are increased by **credits**.
    Expense accounts are increased by **debits**.

- A cash sale is recorded by debiting (increasing) Cash and crediting (increasing) Sales Revenue as shown in the following entry:

  Debit: Cash
    Credit: Sales Revenue

- A credit sale is recorded by debiting (increasing) Accounts Receivable and crediting (increasing) Sales Revenue as follows:

  Debit: Accounts Receivable
    Credit: Sales Revenue

- When a credit sale occurs, revenue is recorded when the goods or services are provided. When the cash from the credit sale is collected, no revenue is recognized. The collection of accounts receivable would be recorded with the following entry to increase Cash and decrease Accounts Receivable:

  Debit: Cash
    Credit: Accounts Receivable

- Under the accrual basis, when cash is received before the good or service is provided, no revenue is recognized. Instead, a liability to perform the service or provide the good in the future is recorded when the cash is received. The liability is usually referred to as *unearned revenue*. The entry debits (increases) Cash and credits (increases) Unearned Revenue (a liability):

  Debit: Cash
    Credit: Unearned Revenue

- When the good or service is provided, the revenue earned is recorded by debiting (decreasing) Unearned Revenue and crediting (increasing) Revenue:

  Debit: Unearned Revenue
    Credit: Revenue

- Expenses are considered incurred when the goods or services are consumed by the enterprise, not necessarily when the cash outflow occurs.

  For example, salaries earned by employees in December are recorded as Salaries Expense in December even though the salaries may not be paid until January.

  The entry to record salaries expense incurred in December but not paid until January would be:

  Debit: Salaries Expense
    Credit: Salaries Payable

  The entry to record the payment of salaries in January would be:

  Debit: Salaries Payable
    Credit: Cash

65

- If a firm pays cash before an expense is incurred, the expense is recognized when the goods or services are consumed.

  For example, if a firm prepays rent, the entry to record the prepayment would record an asset, Prepaid Rent, and reduce cash.

  Debit: Prepaid Rent
    Credit: Cash

  When the service has been received, the expense is recorded and the asset reduced using the following entry:

  Debit: Rent Expense
    Credit: Prepaid Rent

Cash Basis

- When the **cash basis of accounting** is used, revenue is recognized when cash is received, and an expense is recognized when cash is paid.

- The cash basis of accounting is not a generally accepted accounting principle for external financial reporting purposes.

- The cash basis may be used by:
  - individuals to determine their taxable income.
  - doctors and lawyers who prepare financial statements solely for their own use.

REVENUE AND EXPENSE RECOGNITION

- The **realization principle** states revenue is earned and, therefore, should be recognized when:
  1. the earnings process is essentially complete, and
  2. there is objective evidence as to the exchange or sales price.

Sale as the Point of Revenue Recognition

- Normally revenues are considered earned when goods or services are provided.

Alternative Revenue Recognition Methods

- Alternative revenue recognition methods are used when industry characteristics make it reasonable to recognize revenue at a time other than the sale.

- Alternative revenue recognition methods include the following:
  1. The **percentage-of-completion method** recognizes revenue during construction in proportion to the amount of work completed on the project. This method is widely used by construction companies.
  2. Revenue may be recognized at the completion of production when indistinguishable goods, such as some agricultural products and precious metals, are sold in large, well-developed markets. Because the sale is ensured, the earnings process is considered complete at the end of production rather than at the point of sale.
  3. Under the installment method, revenues are recognized in proportion to the cash collected. This method is used infrequently and only when there is a great deal of uncertainty about the collectibility of the receivable.

Expense Recognition

- Under the accrual basis of accounting, expenses are recognized when they are incurred and matched against the corresponding revenues. This matching is accomplished by relating the expense to either:
  1. a particular product sold or service rendered, such as cost of goods sold, or
  2. a particular time period in which the revenue is recognized, such as insurance or rent. These expenses, called **period expenses**, are matched against revenues in the period during which the expenses are incurred.

RECORDING INCOME STATEMENT TRANSACTIONS

Understanding Debit and Credit Rules for Revenue and Expense Accounts

- The debit and credit rules for revenue and expense accounts follow the same rules as those for the retained earnings account, which is part of stockholders' equity.

Retained Earnings	
Debit	Credit
Decreases	Increases
-	+

Expense Accounts		Revenue Accounts	
Normal Balance: Debit		Normal Balance: Credit	

- The debit and credit rules for revenue and expense accounts are explained as follows:
  1. Revenues represent increases in retained earnings. Increases in retained earnings are recorded as credits on the right side of the account ledger. Therefore, increases in revenues are recorded as credits on the right side of the revenue account.
  2. Expenses represent decreases in retained earnings. Decreases in retained earnings are recorded as debits on the left side of the account. Therefore, because an increase in an expense represents a decrease in retained earnings, these increases are recorded as debits on the left side of expense accounts.

- At the end of the period, the net effect of the transactions recorded in the revenue and expense accounts is transferred to the retained earnings account.

- **Nominal** or **temporary accounts** are used only during the period and are zeroed at the end of each period. Income statement accounts (revenues and expense accounts) are temporary accounts.

- **Real** or **permanent accounts** are not zeroed at the end of each period. Instead, they maintain a running balance. Balance sheet accounts, including Retained Earnings, are permanent accounts.

Dividends

- The declaration and payment of a cash dividend is recorded directly as a reduction in retained earnings and does not represent an expense to the firm. The entry to record the declaration and payment of a cash dividend would be:

  Debit: Retained Earnings
    Credit: Cash

- Dividends often are declared several weeks prior to their payment. The following entry is made at the time the dividends are declared:

  Debit: Retained Earnings
    Credit: Dividends Payable

  When the dividend is paid, the following entry is made:

  Debit: Dividends Payable
    Credit: Cash

RELATIONSHIPS AMONG THE FINANCIAL STATEMENTS

- The balance sheet, income statement, and retained earnings statement are related to one another.

- A **comparative balance sheet** is a balance sheet in which data for two or more years is presented in adjacent columns.

- Two consecutive balance sheets are linked by the retained earnings statement.

- The retained earnings statement summarizes the factors (net income or net loss and dividends) that have caused retained earnings to change.

Beginning Retained Earnings + Net Income - Dividends = Ending Retained Earnings

- The income statement summarizes the changes in retained earnings due to profitable or unprofitable operations.

- The statement of cash flows explains changes in the cash account.

- The linkage among the financial statements is referred to as articulation.

KEY TERMS TEST

Test your recall of the key terms as follows: Read the following definitions of key terms and try to recall as many key terms as you can *without assistance*. Write your answers in the spaces provided. If you need assistance, refer to the list of key terms at the end of this section.

1. The method of accounting where revenues and expenses are recorded when cash is received or paid is known as the _____ _____ _____ _____.

2. The method of accounting where revenues, expenses, and other changes in assets, liabilities, and owners' equity are accounted for in the period in which the economic event takes place and not in the period in which cash is received or paid is known as the _____ _____ _____ _____.

3. _____ _____ are financial statements prepared at times other than at the end of a firm's fiscal year.

4. The _____ _____ states that revenue is earned and, therefore, should be recognized when (1) the earnings process is essentially complete, and (2) there is objective evidence as to the exchange or sales price.

5. The _____ _____ is the concept that expenses incurred in one time period to earn the revenues of that period should be offset against those revenues.

6. Expenses which cannot be directly related to a product or service and consequently are expensed in the period in which they are incurred are called _____ _____.

7. The _____ _____ consists of the sequence of related steps used to process a transaction.

8. The _____ _____ consists of the set of systems and procedures that process transactions related to the sale of goods and services.

9. The _____ _____ consists of the systems and procedures used to process transactions related to the acquisition and use of goods and services.

10. _____ are inflows of cash or other assets, which may not always represent revenues.

11. Outflows of cash or other assets or increases in liabilities which may not represent expenses are _____.

12. _____ are a return to the stockholders of some of the assets that have increased because of the profits earned.

13. The difference between the total of revenues and gains and the total of expenses and losses of a period is _____ _____ or _____ _____.

14. _____ are decreases in equity (net assets) from activities affecting the firm during the period other than expenses and distributions to its owners.

15. _____ are increases in equity (net assets) from activities other than revenues and investments by owners of the firm during a period.

16. The _____ _____ _____ is the division of a firm's life into time periods.

17. A(n) _____ _____ is a business document that informs the customer that the goods have been shipped.

18. A(n) _____ _____ is a report that shows the quantity of goods received from a vendor.

19. A(n) _____ _____ is a formal, external request for the purchase of goods or services.

20. A(n) _____ is a business document that bills a customer for a purchase transaction.

21. A(n) _____ _____ _____ is a balance sheet that shows account balances at two or more different points in time.

22. A revenue recognition method that recognizes revenue during construction in proportion to the amount of work completed on the project is the _____ _____.

23. A revenue recognition method where all of the revenue earned from the contract is recognized in the year that the project is 100% complete is called the _____ _____.

24. _____ _____ or _____ _____ are accounts that are zeroed at the end of an accounting period.

25. _____ _____ or _____ _____ are accounts that maintain a running balance that extends beyond an accounting period.

KEY TERMS:

accrual basis of accounting
cash basis of accounting
comparative balance sheet
completed-contract method
dividends
expenditure cycle
expenditures
gains
interim statements
invoice
losses
matching convention
net income
net loss

nominal accounts
permanent accounts
percentage-of-completion method
period expenses
purchase order
real accounts
realization principle
receipts
receiving report
revenue cycle
shipping notice
temporary accounts
time period assumption
transaction cycle

Compare your answers to those at the end of the chapter and review any key terms missed.

CHAPTER QUIZ

Write your answers in the spaces provided.

1. List the three major subsystems of the expenditure cycle.
   1. _____
   2. _____
   3. _____

2. List the three major subsystems of the revenue cycle.
   1. _____
   2. _____
   3. _____

3. The realization principle states that revenue should be recognized when:
   1. _____, and
   2. _____

4. Complete the following equation:

   Beginning   Ending
   Retained Earnings + _____ - _____ = Retained Earnings

5. Complete the following equation:

Beginning   Ending

Net Assets + _____ + _____ - _____= Net Assets

6. The two major components of stockholders' equity are:
   1. _____
   2. _____

Circle the best answer.

7. Receipts are the same as revenues: (a) true; (b) false

8. Expenditures are the same as expenses: (a) true; (b) false

9. Dividends are expenses that are listed on the income statement: (a) true; (b) false

10. The cash basis of accounting provides the best matching of expenses and revenues: (a) true; (b) false

11. Income statement accounts are temporary accounts that are zeroed at the end of each period: (a) true; (b) false

12. Revenue accounts are increased by: (a) debits; (b) credits

13. Expense accounts are increased by: (a) debits; (b) credits

14. The Retained Earnings account is increased by: (a) debits; (b) credits

15. Stockholders' equity accounts are increased by: (a) debits; (b) credits

16. Asset accounts are increased by: (a) debits; (b) credits

17. Liability accounts are increased by: (a) debits; (b) credits

18. Prepaid Insurance is which one of the following types of accounts: (a) asset; (b) liability; (c) stockholders' equity; (d) revenue; (e) expense

19. Sales is which one of the following types of accounts: (a) asset; (b) liability; (c) stockholders' equity; (d) revenue; (e) expense

20. Cost of Goods Sold is which one of the following types of accounts: (a) asset; (b) liability; (c) stockholders' equity; (d) revenue; (e) expense

21. Unearned Revenue is which one of the following types of accounts: (a) asset; (b) liability; (c) stockholders' equity; (d) revenue; (e) expense

22. Salaries Payable is which one of the following types of accounts: (a) asset; (b) liability; (c) stockholders' equity; (d) revenue; (e) expense

23. Retained Earnings is which one of the following types of accounts:
(a) asset; (b) liability; (c) stockholders' equity; (d) revenue;
(e) expense

24. If a company sells land with a cost of $10,000 for $12,500 cash, the
company should make which of the following entries to record the sale:

(a) Land	10,000	
Gain on sale		10,000
(b) Cash	12,500	
Land	10,000	
Gain on sale		22,500
(c) Cash	12,500	
Loss on sale	2,500	
Land		15,000
(d) Cash	12,500	
Land		10,000
Gain on sale		2,500

25. If the beginning balance of Retained Earnings was $100,000, net income
for the year was $20,000, and the ending balance of Retained Earnings was
$115,000, dividends for the year must have been: (a) $35,000; (b) $5,000;
(c) $15,000; (d) $10,000

EXERCISES

EXERCISE 1

Identify the transaction processing cycle and the accounting system that
would be used to process each of the following transactions.

Transaction Processing Cycles	Accounting Systems
Revenue cycle	Order entry system
Expenditure cycle	Billing system
	Cash receipts system
	Purchasing system
	Receiving system
	Cash disbursements system

Transaction	Transaction Processing Cycle	Accounting System
a. Ordered inventory		
b. Received a customer's order		
c. Prepared a customer's invoice		
d. Shipped goods to a customer		
e. Paid for inventory received		
f. Received a customer's payment		

73

EXERCISE 2

For each of the following transactions, indicate:
1. the accounts that would be affected
2. the type of account using the following symbols:
   A = Asset
   L = Liability
   S = Stockholders' equity
   R = Revenue or gain
   E = Expense or loss

3. whether the account would be increased or decreased.
4. whether the account would be debited or credited to record the transaction.

Transaction	Account	Type of Account	Increase/ Decrease	Debit/ Credit
Example: The firm records cash sales of $10,000.	*Cash* *Sales*	*A* *R*	*Increase* *Increase*	*Debit* *Credit*
a. The firm records credit sales of $80,000.				
b. A customer makes a payment on account.				
c. A customer makes a $500 deposit on an order to be delivered next year.				
d. The firm borrows $25,000 from a local bank.				
e. The firm buys $5,000 of supplies on account.				
f. The firm pays $3,000 on account.				
g. The firm sold marketable securities for $2,000 cash that it had purchased for $2,400 one year ago.				
h. The firm declares and pays a $3,000 dividend.				

74

EXERCISE 3

For each of the following transactions indicate:
1. whether the transaction resulted in a revenue, an expense, or neither in the month of June.
2. the amount of the revenue or expense.

Transaction	Revenue/Expense/Neither	Amount
a. The firm borrowed $20,000 from a local bank on June 2.		$_____
b. Credit sales for June totaled $35,000.		$_____
c. The firm collected $40,000 on account for credit sales made in May.		$_____
d. A customer placed a special order to be delivered in September and made a $200 deposit.		$_____
e. The firm paid $600 for insurance that becomes effective July 1.		$_____
f. The firm paid $400 for employee wages for work performed in May.		$_____
g. The firm paid $4,000 for employee wages for work performed in June.		$_____
h. The firm purchased $3,000 of inventory, of which $2,000 was sold in June.		$_____
i. The firm repaid $1,000 in principal on the bank loan and $200 in interest.		$_____

EXERCISE 4

The balance sheet for Ravenwood, Inc. is as follows:

RAVENWOOD, INC.
BALANCE SHEET
DECEMBER 31, 1994

Assets:	
Cash	$ 10,000
Marketable securities	6,000
Accounts receivable	30,000
Inventory	50,000
Furniture and fixtures	40,000
Total assets	$136,000
Liabilities:	
Accounts payable	$ 15,000
Salaries payable	8,000
Bank loan payable	45,000
Total liabilities	$ 68,000
Stockholders' equity:	
Capital stock	$ 32,000
Retained earnings	36,000
Total stockholders' equity	$ 68,000
Total liabilities and stockholders' equity	$136,000

The following events occurred during 1995:
a. Inventory totaling $90,000 was purchased on account during the year.
b. Sales for the year amounted to $270,000, of which $25,000 was for cash and $245,000 was on account.
c. The cost of the inventory sold amounted to $100,000.
d. Salaries payable of $8,000 were paid on January 5, 1995; the salaries were earned by employees in 1994.
e. Salaries earned in 1995 totaling $60,000 were paid during the year.
f. Advertising of $900 and utilities of $600 were paid in cash.
g. Cash collections on account totaled $250,000.
h. Cash payments on account were $85,000.
i. The firm sold marketable securities for $4,000 cash that it had purchased for $3,500 one year ago.
j. The firm declared and paid a $7,000 dividend.
k. The firm paid $12,000 rent for the year.

76

EXERCISE 4 (continued)

Required:

1. Record the transactions in the general journal on the following page. Journal entry explanations are not necessary.

TIP: When making journal entries, use the following approach:

1. Determine which accounts are affected by the transaction.

2. For each account, determine whether the account is a(n):
   - Asset account
   - Liability account
   - Stockholders' equity account
   - Revenue account (or gain)
   - Expense account (or loss)

3. Determine whether each account is increased or decreased by the transaction.

4. Make the appropriate debit or credit to each account using the following debit and credit rules:

   Asset accounts are increased by **debits**.
   Liability accounts are increased by **credits**.
   Stockholders' equity accounts are increased by **credits**.
   Revenue (and gain) accounts are increased by **credits**.
   Expense (and loss) accounts are increased by **debits**.

   Revenue accounts are increased by credits because they increase retained earnings (a stockholders' equity account).

   Expense accounts are increased by debits because they decrease retained earnings.

RAVENWOOD, INC.

GENERAL JOURNAL

DATE	ACCOUNT TITLES	REF.	DEBIT	CREDIT
(a)				
(b)				
(c)				
(d)				
(e)				
(f)				
(g)				
(h)				
(i)				
(j)				
(k)				

EXERCISE 4 (continued)

2. Post the entries to the appropriate T accounts.

CASH		MARKETABLE SECURITIES	

ACCOUNTS RECEIVABLE		INVENTORY	

FURNITURE AND FIXTURES	

ACCOUNTS PAYABLE		SALARIES PAYABLE	

BANK LOAN PAYABLE		CAPITAL STOCK	

EXERCISE 4 (continued)

RETAINED EARNINGS	SALES

COST OF GOODS SOLD	SALARIES EXPENSE

ADVERTISING EXPENSE	UTILITIES EXPENSE

RENT EXPENSE	GAIN ON SALE OF MARKETABLE SECURITIES

EXERCISE 4 (continued)

3. Prepare a trial balance.

EXERCISE 4 (continued)

4. Prepare the following financial statements:
- income statement
- retained earnings statement
- comparative balance sheets for December 31, 1994 and December 31, 1995

EXERCISE 5

For each of the following transactions, indicate the amount of revenue or expense that would be recognized in June using:
(1) the cash basis
(2) the accrual basis

Transactions		Cash Basis	Accrual Basis
1. Cash sales during June	$14,000	_____	_____
2. Credit sales during June not yet collected	15,000	_____	_____
3. Cash collected from June credit sales	5,000	_____	_____
4. Cash collected from May's credit sales	7,000	_____	_____
5. Cash deposit received in June for an order to be delivered in July	2,000	_____	_____
6. Payment of May's telephone bill	500	_____	_____
7. June's salaries paid in July	4,000	_____	_____
8. Received a repair bill for services performed in June, to be paid in July	2,500	_____	_____
9. Payment of June rent	2,000	_____	_____
10. Payment of insurance for six months, June through December	3,000	_____	_____

EXERCISE 6

The following income statement was prepared using the cash basis of accounting.

MARTIN INCORPORATED
INCOME STATEMENT--CASH BASIS
FOR THE YEAR ENDED DECEMBER 31, 1995

Revenues:		
Sales		$320,000
Expenses:		
Wages	$60,000	
Insurance	9,000	
Rent	25,000	
Utilities	8,000	
Supplies	2,400	
Interest	1,000	105,400
Net income		$214,600

Additional information:

1. At year-end, 20% of sales had not yet been collected.
2. Interest of $200 was incurred but not paid at December 31, 1995.
3. One month's wages totaling $5,000 have not yet been paid.
4. Three years of insurance were paid on January 1, 1995.
5. $800 of office supplies was still on hand at December 31, 1995.

Required:

Prepare an income statement using the accrual basis.

ANSWERS

KEY TERMS TEST
1. cash basis of accounting
2. accrual basis of accounting
3. Interim statements
4. realization principle
5. matching convention
6. period expenses
7. transaction cycle
8. revenue cycle
9. expenditure cycle
10. Receipts
11. expenditures
12. Dividends
13. net income, net loss
14. Losses
15. Gains
16. time period assumption
17. shipping notice
18. receiving report
19. purchase order
20. invoice
21. comparative balance sheet
22. percentage-of-completion method
23. completed-contract method
24. Nominal, temporary accounts
25. Real, permanent accounts

CHAPTER QUIZ
1. 1. purchasing system
   2. receiving system
   3. cash disbursements system
2. 1. order entry system
   2. billing system
   3. cash receipts system
3. 1. the earnings process is essentially complete
   2. there is objective evidence as to the exchange or sales price

4.   Beginning   Ending
   Retained Earnings + Net Income - Dividends = Retained Earnings

5. Beginning   Ending
   Net Assets + Net Income + Capital Contributions - Dividends = Net Assets

6. 1. capital stock or common stock
   2. retained earnings
7. b False
8. b False
9. b False Dividends are not expenses, and they do not appear on the income
            statement. Dividends are considered a distribution of assets
            and are deducted from retained earnings.

85

10. b   False   The accrual basis of accounting provides the best matching of expenses with revenues.
11. a   True
12. b
13. a
14. b
15. b
16. a
17. b
18. a
19. d
20. e
21. b
22. b
23. c
24. d
25. b $100,000 + $20,000 - Dividends = $115,000
              Dividends = $5,000

EXERCISE 1

Transaction	Transaction Processing Cycle	Accounting System
a. Ordered inventory	Expenditure cycle	Purchasing system
b. Received a customer's order	Revenue cycle	Order entry system
c. Prepared a customer's invoice	Revenue cycle	Billing system
d. Shipped goods to a customer	Revenue cycle	Order entry system
e. Paid for inventory received	Expenditure cycle	Cash disbursements system
f. Received a customer's payment	Revenue cycle	Cash receipts system

EXERCISE 2

Transaction	Account	Type of Account	Increase/ Decrease	Debit/ Credit
a. The firm records credit sales of $80,000.	Accounts Receivable Sales	A R	Increase Increase	Debit Credit
b. A customer makes a payment on account.	Cash Accounts Receivable	A A	Increase Decrease	Debit Credit
c. A customer makes a $500 deposit on an order to be delivered next year.	Cash Unearned Revenue	A L	Increase Increase	Debit Credit
d. The firm borrows $25,000 from a local bank.	Cash Notes Payable	A L	Increase Increase	Debit Credit
e. The firm buys $5,000 of supplies on account.	Supplies Accounts Payable	A L	Increase Increase	Debit Credit
f. The firm pays $3,000 on account.	Accounts Payable Cash	L A	Decrease Decrease	Debit Credit
g. The firm sold marketable securities for $2,000 cash that it had purchased for $2,400 one year ago.	Cash Loss on Sale of Marketable Securities Marketable Securities	A E A	Increase Increase Decrease	Debit Debit Credit
h. The firm declares and pays a $3,000 dividend.	Retained Earnings Cash	S A	Decrease Decrease	Debit Credit

EXERCISE 3

Transaction	Revenue/Expense/Neither	Amount
a. The firm borrowed $20,000 from a local bank on June 2.	Neither	$ -0-
b. Credit sales for June totaled $35,000.	Revenue	$35,000
c. The firm collected $40,000 on account for credit sales made in May.	Neither	$ -0-
d. A customer placed a special order to be delivered in September and made a $200 deposit.	Neither	$ -0-
e. The firm paid $600 for insurance that becomes effective July 1.	Neither	$ -0-
f. The firm paid $400 for employee wages for work performed in May.	Neither	$ -0-
g. The firm paid $4,000 for employee wages for work performed in June.	Expense	$4,000
h. The firm purchased $3,000 of inventory, of which $2,000 was sold in June.	Expense	$2,000
i. The firm repaid $1,000 in principal on the bank loan and $200 in interest.	Expense	$200

EXERCISE 4

1.

RAVENWOOD, INC.

GENERAL JOURNAL

DATE	ACCOUNT TITLES	REF.	DEBIT	CREDIT
(a)	Inventory		90,000	
	Accounts Payable			90,000
(b)	Cash		25,000	
	Accounts Receivable		245,000	
	Sales			270,000
(c)	Cost of Goods Sold		100,000	
	Inventory			100,000
(d)	Salaries Payable		8,000	
	Cash			8,000
(e)	Salaries Expense		60,000	
	Cash			60,000
(f)	Advertising Expense		900	
	Utilities Expense		600	
	Cash			1,500
(g)	Cash		250,000	
	Accounts Receivable			250,000
(h)	Accounts Payable		85,000	
	Cash			85,000
(i)	Cash		4,000	
	Gain on Sale of Marketable Securities			500
	Marketable Securities			3,500
(j)	Retained Earnings		7,000	
	Cash			7,000
(k)	Rent Expense		12,000	
	Cash			12,000

EXERCISE 4 (continued)

2.

CASH			
1/1 Bal.	10,000	(d)	8,000
(b)	25,000	(e)	60,000
(g)	250,000	(f)	1,500
(i)	4,000	(h)	85,000
		(j)	7,000
		(k)	12,000
12/31 Bal.	115,500		

MARKETABLE SECURITIES			
1/1 Bal.	6,000	(i)	3,500
12/31 Bal.	2,500		

ACCOUNTS RECEIVABLE			
1/1 Bal.	30,000	(g)	250,000
(b)	245,000		
12/31 Bal.	25,000		

INVENTORY			
1/1 Bal.	50,000	(c)	100,000
(a)	90,000		
12/31 Bal.	40,000		

FURNITURE AND FIXTURES		
1/1 Bal.	40,000	
12/31 Bal.	40,000	

ACCOUNTS PAYABLE			
(h)	85,000	1/1 Bal.	15,000
		(a)	90,000
		12/31 Bal.	20,000

SALARIES PAYABLE			
(d)	8,000	1/1 Bal.	8,000
		12/31 Bal.	-0-

BANK LOAN PAYABLE		
	1/1 Bal.	45,000
	12/31 Bal.	45,000

CAPITAL STOCK		
	1/1 Bal.	32,000
	12/31 Bal.	32,000

EXERCISE 4 (continued)

RETAINED EARNINGS

(j)	7,000	1/1 Bal.	36,000
		12/31 Bal.	29,000

SALES

	(b)	270,000
	12/31 Bal.	270,000

COST OF GOODS SOLD

(c)	100,000	
12/31 Bal.	100,000	

SALARIES EXPENSE

(e)	60,000	
12/31 Bal.	60,000	

ADVERTISING EXPENSE

(f)	900	
12/31 Bal.	900	

UTILITIES EXPENSE

(f)	600	
12/31 Bal.	600	

RENT EXPENSE

(k)	12,000	
12/31 Bal.	12,000	

GAIN ON SALE OF MARKETABLE SECURITIES

	(i)	500
	12/31 Bal.	500

91

EXERCISE 4 (continued)

3.

RAVENWOOD, INC.
TRIAL BALANCE
DECEMBER 31, 1995

ACCOUNT	DEBIT	CREDIT
Cash	$115,500	
Marketable securities	2,500	
Accounts receivable	25,000	
Inventory	40,000	
Furniture and fixtures	40,000	
Accounts payable		$ 20,000
Salaries payable		-0-
Bank loan payable		45,000
Capital stock		32,000
Retained earnings		29,000
Sales		270,000
Cost of goods sold	100,000	
Salaries expense	60,000	
Advertising expense	900	
Utilities Expense	600	
Rent expense	12,000	
Gain on sale of marketable securities		500
Totals	$396,500	$396,500

4.

RAVENWOOD, INC.
INCOME STATEMENT
FOR THE YEAR ENDED DECEMBER 31, 1995

Revenues:		
Sales	$270,000	
Gain on sale of marketable securities	500	$270,500
Expenses:		
Cost of goods sold	$100,000	
Salaries expense	60,000	
Advertising expense	900	
Utilities expense	600	
Rent expense	12,000	173,500
Net income		$ 97,000

EXERCISE 4 (continued)

RAVENWOOD, INC.
RETAINED EARNINGS STATEMENT
FOR THE YEAR ENDED DECEMBER 31, 1995

Retained earnings, January 1, 1995	$ 36,000
Add: Net income for 1995	97,000
Less: Dividends declared in 1995	(7,000)
Retained earnings, December 31, 1995	$126,000

RAVENWOOD, INC.
COMPARATIVE BALANCE SHEETS

Assets	December 31, 1995	December 31, 1994
Cash	$115,500	$ 10,000
Marketable securities	2,500	6,000
Accounts receivable	25,000	30,000
Inventory	40,000	50,000
Furniture and fixtures	40,000	40,000
Total assets	$223,000	$136,000

Liabilities and Stockholders' Equity		
Liabilities:		
Accounts payable	$ 20,000	$ 15,000
Salaries payable	-0-	8,000
Bank loan payable	45,000	45,000
Total liabilities	$ 65,000	$ 68,000
Stockholders' equity:		
Capital stock	$ 32,000	$ 32,000
Retained earnings	126,000	36,000
Total stockholders' equity	$158,000	$ 68,000
Total liabilities and stockholders' equity	$223,000	$136,000

EXERCISE 5

Transactions		Cash Basis	Accrual Basis
1. Cash sales during June	$14,000	$14,000	$14,000
2. Credit sales during June not yet collected	15,000		15,000
3. Cash collected from June credit sales	5,000	5,000	
4. Cash collected from May's credit sales	7,000	7,000	
5. Cash deposit received in June for an order to be delivered in July	2,000	2,000	
6. Payment of May's telephone bill	500	500	
7. June's salaries paid in July	4,000		4,000
8. Received a repair bill for services performed in June, to be paid in July	2,500		2,500
9. Payment of June rent	2,000	2,000	2,000
10. Payment of insurance for six months, June through December	3,000	3,000	500

EXERCISE 6

MARTIN INCORPORATED
INCOME STATEMENT--ACCRUAL BASIS
FOR THE YEAR ENDED DECEMBER 31, 1995

Revenues:		
Sales		$400,000*
Expenses:		
Wages ($60,000 + $5,000)	$65,000	
Insurance ($9,000 x 12/36)	3,000	
Rent	25,000	
Utilities	8,000	
Supplies ($2,400 - $800)	1,600	
Interest ($1,000 + $200)	1,200	103,800
Net income		$296,200

*.80X = $320,000
 X = $400,000

CHAPTER 4

COMPLETING THE ACCOUNTING CYCLE

CHAPTER REVIEW

OVERVIEW

- The accounting cycle includes the following steps:

  During the period:
  - Record business transactions in the journal.
  - Post the journal entries to the ledger.

  At the end of the period:
  - Prepare the unadjusted trial balance.
  - Prepare adjusting entries.
  - Post adjusting entries to the ledger.
  - Prepare an adjusted trial balance.
  - Prepare a worksheet (optional).
  - Prepare financial statements.
  - Make closing entries and post to the ledger accounts.
  - Prepare a post-closing trial balance.

- The final steps in the accounting cycle (preparing adjusting entries, financial statements, and closing entries) are discussed in this chapter. This part of the accounting cycle often involves analysis and judgment and separates the work of the accountant from that of the bookkeeper.

ADJUSTING ENTRIES

- **Adjusting entries** are made at the end of each accounting period to ensure:
  1. the proper matching of revenues and expenses, and
  2. that the financial statements reflect all relevant economic events that occurred during the period.

- Different types of adjusting entries are as follows:
  1. nonmonetary assets acquired in one period and used up in subsequent periods, such as supplies, prepaid insurance, and depreciation.
  2. nonmonetary liabilities recorded in one period with associated revenues earned in subsequent period(s), such as unearned revenue.
  3. accrued revenues where cash is received after earnings are recognized, such as interest receivable.
  4. accrued expenses where cash is paid in a period after benefits are received, such as interest payable and salaries payable.
  5. estimates of expenses are matched with current period revenues, such as uncollectible accounts.
  6. correction of current and past period errors.

Nonmonetary Assets Acquired in One Period and Used Up in Subsequent Periods

- **Nonmonetary assets** are assets that do not represent future claims to fixed amounts of cash, such as prepaid items, office supplies, inventories, buildings, and equipment.

- **Monetary assets** are cash and the right to receive a specific amount of cash, such as receivables.

- Adjusting entries are used to match the cost of nonmonetary assets against the revenues for the period as the services or benefits are consumed.

Supplies

- The entry to record the purchase of supplies throughout the year would be:

    Debit: Offices Supplies (Asset Account)
     Credit: Cash (or Accounts Payable)

- At the end of the accounting period, the cost of the supplies remaining on hand is determined, and the following adjusting entry is made to record the amount of supplies used:

    Debit: Supplies Expense
     Credit: Supplies

- The adjusting entry transfers the cost of the supplies used from the supplies account (an asset account) to the supplies expense account.

- The cost of the supplies used during a period is calculated as follows:

      Beginning balance of supplies
    + Purchases of supplies during the period
    = Supplies available for use
    - Ending balance of supplies
    = Supplies used during the period (supplies expense)

- The balance in the supplies account after the adjusting entry is posted represents the cost of the supplies on hand that are available for future use.

- The balance in the supplies expense account after the adjusting entry is posted represents the cost of the supplies used during the period.

Prepaid Assets

- **Prepaid assets** represent payments made in advance for the right to receive future services or benefits. Examples include:
  - prepaid insurance
  - prepaid rent
  - prepaid subscriptions

- The matching convention requires that the costs of these assets be allocated between the current and future periods.

- When prepaid insurance is purchased, the following entry is made:

  Debit: Prepaid Insurance (Asset Account)
   Credit: Cash (or Accounts Payable)

- The following adjusting entry is necessary to reduce the asset account by the amount that has expired:

  Debit: Insurance Expense
   Credit: Prepaid Insurance

- After the adjusting entry is posted:
  - the remaining balance in the asset account, Prepaid Insurance, represents the future benefits of the insurance policy.
  - the balance in the Insurance Expense account represents the amount of expired benefits.

- When making adjusting entries for prepaid rent and other prepaid assets, follow these steps:
  1. Estimate the monthly cost of benefits to be received from the asset, using the following general formula:

     Cost of the Asset/Total Number of Months Benefits Are to Be Received

  2. Expense the amount of the asset used or consumed. The adjusting entry decreases the asset account and records an expense for the amount of benefits used or expired.

Depreciation

- The matching convention requires that a portion of nonmonetary assets, such as plant and equipment, be systematically allocated against the revenues generated by the use of these assets.

- Depreciation is the allocation of the <u>cost</u> of an asset to the periods benefited.

- Examples of depreciable assets include:
  - equipment
  - buildings
  - furniture and fixtures
  - automobiles
  - machines

- Land is not depreciated because it does not lose its future benefits.

- Notice that depreciation is an allocation of the asset's <u>cost</u> and does not attempt to determine the current market value of the asset.

- The asset's **useful life** or **economic life** is management's estimate of how long the asset will provide economic benefits to the firm. An asset's physical life and economic life can differ. For example, a computer's physical life may be 10 years, but its economic life may be only three years.

  When estimating the useful life of an asset, management makes a best estimate of the useful life of long-lived assets using broad guidelines established by the accounting profession and past experience.

- **Residual value** or **salvage value** is an estimate of what an asset will be worth at the end of its useful life.

- An asset's **depreciable base** is calculated as follows:

$$\text{Depreciable Base} = \text{Acquisition Cost} - \text{Residual Value}$$

- **Straight-line depreciation** allocates an equal amount of the asset's cost to each accounting period during its useful life.

- Straight-line depreciation is calculated as follows:

  Annual Depreciation Expense = Depreciable Base/Estimated Useful Life

  Annual Depreciation Expense = (Acquisition Cost - Residual Value)/Estimated Useful Life

- The entry to record the acquisition of equipment for cash would be:

  Debit: Equipment
   Credit: Cash

- The adjusting entry to record depreciation expense would be:

  Debit: Depreciation Expense
   Credit: Accumulated Depreciation: Equipment

- Note that the credit is made to the Accumulated Depreciation account rather than directly to the Equipment account. Accumulated Depreciation is a **contra-asset account** (an account that offsets the balance in another account).

  Using the contra-asset account to record accumulated depreciation permits the accounting system to maintain both the original historical cost of the asset in one account (Equipment) and the amount of depreciation recorded to date in another account (Accumulated Depreciation: Equipment).

- **Net book value** is the historical cost less accumulated depreciation. For example, net book value for equipment would be calculated as follows:

$$\begin{aligned}
&\text{Equipment (cost)} \\
&- \text{Accumulated depreciation} \\
&= \text{Net book value}
\end{aligned}$$

Nonmonetary Liabilities Recorded in One Period With Associated Revenues Earned in Subsequent Period

- Unearned revenues arise whenever an enterprise receives cash or other assets prior to a sale or the performance of a service.

- Unearned revenues are considered **nonmonetary liabilities** because the liability is reduced by the performance of a service or the delivery of goods, not by a cash payment.

- An example of unearned revenue is subscription money collected by a publisher of a magazine before the magazine is delivered.

- The entry to record the receipt of cash before a good or service is provided is as follows:

   Debit: Cash
      Credit: Unearned Revenue

- At the end of the accounting period, the following adjusting entry is needed to record the portion that has been earned as revenue:

   Debit: Unearned Revenue
      Credit: Revenue

- The balance of the unearned revenue account is reported on the balance sheet as a liability.

- The portion that has been earned is recorded as revenue and reported on the income statement.

Accruals

- **Accruals** are adjusting entries made to record revenues or expenses that are continuously earned or incurred but which have not been recorded because cash has not yet been received or paid.

- Examples of accruals include:
  - interest revenue
  - interest expense
  - salaries expense

99

- Accruals should be made for:
  1. revenues or expenses that are earned in one period and for which cash will be received in a subsequent period, and
  2. expenses that are incurred in one period and for which cash will be paid in a subsequent period.

Accrued Revenues

- Examples of accrued revenue include:
  - interest revenue
  - rental revenue

- The adjusting entry to record accrued revenue recognizes revenue in the accounting period in which it is earned, even though the cash will be received in following periods.

- The entry to record a note receivable would be:

      Debit: Note Receivable
         Credit: Cash

- At the end of the accounting period, any interest earned but not yet received in cash should be recorded as revenue using the following adjusting entry:

      Debit: Interest Receivable
         Credit: Interest Revenue

- At the maturity date of the note, the following entry is made:

      Debit: Cash
         Credit: Note Receivable
         Credit: Interest Receivable
         Credit: Interest Revenue (interest earned in the current period)

- Interest is payment for the use of money.

- Most loans are interest bearing and have the following characteristics:
  1. **Principal (or face amount):** the amount lent or borrowed.
  2. **Maturity date:** the date the loan must be repaid.
  3. **Maturity value:** the total of the principal plus interest at the maturity date.
  4. **Interest rate:** the percentage rate, which is usually stated in annual terms and must be prorated for periods shorter than a year.

- In general, interest can be calculated as follows:

$$i = p \times r \times t$$

where:
i = interest
p = principal of the loan
r = annual interest rate
t = applicable time period in fractions of a year

Accrued Expenses

- **Accrued expenses** are expenses incurred in one accounting period that will be paid in a subsequent accounting period.

- Examples of accrued expenses include:
  - interest expense
  - salaries expense
  - tax expense
  - rental expense

- Adjusting entries are used to record the expense in the period in which it is incurred, even though the cash will not be paid until the following period.

Accrued Interest Expense

- The entry to record the issuance of a note payable would be:

  Debit: Cash
    Credit: Notes Payable

- The following adjusting entry would be used to record the accrual of interest incurred but not yet paid:

  Debit: Interest Expense
    Credit: Interest Payable

- The entry to record the payment of principal and interest in the next accounting period would be:

  Debit: Notes Payable
  Debit: Interest Payable
  Debit: Interest Expense (interest incurred in the current period)
    Credit: Cash

Accrued Salaries Expense

- An adjustment is necessary when the date that salaries are paid does not correspond to the last date of the accounting period. Accrued salaries expense must be recorded for salaries earned by employees but unpaid at the end of the accounting period.

- The adjusting entry to record accrued salaries would be:

  Debit: Salaries Expense
    Credit: Salaries Payable

- The entry to record the payment of salaries in the next accounting period would be:

  Debit: Salaries Payable (salaries owed at the end of the prior period)
  Debit: Salaries Expense (current period salaries)
    Credit: Cash

COMPLETING THE ACCOUNTING CYCLE

- The five steps in the accounting cycle after the adjusting entries have been recorded in the general journal are:

  1. Post the adjusting entries to the ledger accounts.
  2. Prepare an adjusted trial balance.
  3. Prepare financial statements:
     a. Income statement.
     b. Retained earnings statement.
     c. Balance sheet.
     d. Statement of cash flows.
  4. Make closing entries and post to the ledger accounts.
  5. Prepare a post-closing trial balance.

Posting Adjusting Entries to the General Ledger

- After the adjusting entries are recorded in the general journal, they are posted to the appropriate ledger accounts.

Adjusted Trial Balance

- An **adjusted trial balance** is a list of all the accounts and the account balances after the adjusting entries have been posted.

Financial Statements

- Three financial statements prepared from the adjusted trial balance are:
  1. Income statement
  2. Retained earnings statement
  3. Balance sheet

- The statement of cash flows cannot be prepared directly from the adjusted trial balance. Cash receipts and cash disbursements must be analyzed to prepare this statement. Essentially, there must be a conversion from the accrual basis to the cash basis of accounting.

Closing Entries

- **Closing entries** are made at the end of the period and are used to accomplish two objectives:
  1. Eliminate the balances in the revenue and expense accounts so that the income statement accounts begin the subsequent period with zero balances.
  2. Update the retained earnings balance to reflect the results of operations for the current period.

The Closing Process--A Summary

- The closing process contains the following four steps:
  1. Bring revenue accounts to zero by closing them to the Income Summary account. Because revenue accounts have credit balances, revenues accounts are closed by debiting the revenue account(s) and crediting the Income Summary account.
  2. Bring expense accounts to zero by closing them to the Income Summary account. Because expense accounts have debit balances, expense accounts (and loss accounts) are closed by crediting the expense accounts and debiting the Income Summary account.
  3. Bring the Income Summary account to zero by closing it to the Retained Earnings account.
  4. If a Dividends Declared account is used, also close it to the Retained Earnings account.

Post-Closing Trial Balance

- The **post-closing trial balance** is a trial balance prepared from the ledger accounts after the closing entries have been posted. The post-closing trial balance helps ensure that these entries have been posted correctly.

- Only balance sheet accounts appear on the post-closing trial balance because all the income statement accounts have been closed to zero balances.

- The retained earnings balance that appears on the post-closing trial balance is the ending balance for retained earnings because the closing entries closed all the income statement statement accounts to the retained earnings account.

GENERAL LEDGER SYSTEMS

- Two sources of inputs to a computer-based general ledger system are:
  1. Automated journal entries that are generated by transaction processing systems, such as revenue and expenditure journal entries to record sales, cost of goods sold, collections and payments on account, expenses and related transactions.
  2. Manual journal entries that include all journal entries not generated by a transaction processing system, such as adjusting entries.

- A **system flowchart** is a diagram that summarizes:
  - the inputs to a system, and
  - the outputs generated by a system.

KEY TERMS TEST

Test your recall of the key terms as follows: Read the following definitions of key terms and try to recall as many key terms as you can *without assistance*. Write your answers in the spaces provided. If you need assistance, refer to the list of key terms at the end of this section.

1. _____ _____ are journal entries prepared at the end of an accounting period to recognize transactions in the proper accounting period.

2. _____ _____ are assets that do not represent future claims to fixed amounts of cash.

3. _____ _____ are nonmonetary assets whose benefits affect more than one accounting period.

4. _____ is the systematic allocation of the cost of an asset to the time periods benefited.

5. _____ _____ is a depreciation method that results in an equal allocation of the asset's cost to each accounting period during its estimated service life.

6. _____ _____ or _____ _____ is a measure of the service potential that the current user may expect from the asset.

7. _____ _____ or _____ _____ is an estimate of what the asset will be worth at the end of its life.

8. A(n) _____ _____ is an account that partially or wholly offsets the balance in another account.

9. _____ _____ _____ is the difference between the historical cost of an asset and its accumulated depreciation.

10. _____ _____ are liabilities that are not fixed in amount.

11. A(n) _____ is an adjusting entry that records revenue or expense before cash is received or paid.

12. _____ _____ is revenue that is earned over time but for which the corresponding cash is received periodically.

13. _____ _____ are expenses that are incurred in one accounting period and will be paid in a subsequent accounting period.

14. The trial balance prepared before adjusting journal entries have been recorded and posted is the _____ _____ _____.

15. The trial balance prepared after adjusting entries have been posted is the _____ _____ _____.

16. _____ _____ are journal entries made at the end of an accounting period to (1) update the Retained Earnings balance to reflect the results of operations, and (2) eliminate the balances in the revenue and expense accounts so that the income statement accounts begin the subsequent period with zero balances.

17. The trial balance prepared after the closing entries have been posted is the _____ _____ _____.

18. A(n) _____ _____ is a diagram that depicts the flows into and out of an information system.

19. _____ is the amount of money borrowed on a loan.

20. The _____ _____ is the date when a loan becomes due and payable.

21. The _____ _____ is the total amount to be paid on a loan at its maturity date. This amount is normally the sum of the principal amount of a loan plus interest on a loan.

22. _____ _____ are cash or the right to receive a specific amount of cash, such as a receivable.

23. The annual percentage rate charged for use of borrowed money is the _____ _____.

24. The _____ _____ is the acquisition cost of an asset less its estimated residual value.

25. The _____ _____ _____ is a manual or computer-based accounting system that accepts journal entry input and posts those entries to a general ledger.

26. The _____ _____ _____ is a temporary holding account used in the closing process.

KEY TERMS:

accrual
accrued expenses
accrued revenue
adjusted trial balance
adjusting entries
closing entries
contra account
depreciable base
depreciation
economic life
general ledger system
income summary account
interest rate
maturity date

maturity value
monetary assets
net book value
nonmonetary assets
nonmonetary liabilities
post-closing trial balance
prepaid assets
principal
residual value
salvage value
straight-line depreciation
system flowchart
unadjusted trial balance
useful life

Compare your answers to those at the end of the chapter and review any key terms missed.

CHAPTER QUIZ

1. Below are listed the steps in the accounting cycle. Arrange the steps in the order in which they occur by numbering the steps 1 though 8.

   _____ Prepare closing entries.

   _____ Prepare an unadjusted trial balance.

   _____ Prepare financial statements.

   _____ Prepare adjusting entries.

   _____ Post journal entries to the ledger.

   _____ Post adjusting entries and prepare an adjusted trial balance.

   _____ Prepare a post-closing trial balance.

   _____ Record transactions in the journal.

Use the following information to answer the next two questions.

On January 1, 1995, supplies on hand totaled $1,500. During the year, $3,000 of supplies were purchased. At December 31, 1995, a count of supplies revealed $800 of supplies on hand.

2. Supplies expense for 1995 would be: (a) $700; (b) $2,200; (c) $2,300; (d) $4,500; (e) $3,700

3. After the adjusting entry at December 31, 1995, is made, the balance in the Supplies account would be: (a) $3,000; (b) $800; (c) $5,300; (d) $4,500; (e) $3,700

Use the following information to answer the next five questions.

On April 1, 1995, Dunker, Inc. purchased new equipment costing $90,000. The equipment is expected to have a useful life of ten years and a $10,000 residual value. The company uses straight-line depreciation and is on a calendar year.

4. The depreciable base for the equipment would be: (a) $90,000; (b) $80,000; (c) $9,000; (d) $100,000

5. Depreciation expense for 1995 would be: (a) $6,000; (b) $8,000; (c) $9,000; (d) $10,000

6. Depreciation expense for 1996 would be: (a) $6,000; (b) $8,000; (c) $9,000; (d) $10,000

7. Accumulated depreciation at December 31, 1996, would be: (a) $9,000; (b) $10,000; (c) $14,000; (d) $18,000

8. Net book value of the equipment at December 31, 1996, would be: (a) $90,000; (b) $80,000; (c) $70,000; (d) $76,000

Use the following information to answer the next two questions.

On May 1, 1995, the Campbell Company borrowed $20,000 from a local bank and issued a one-year note payable. The annual interest rate on the note was 12%, and the interest was due when the note matured.

9. At December 31, 1995, Campbell should record interest expense of: (a) $-0-; (b) $800; (c) $1,600; (d) $2,400

10. When the note matures on May 1, 1996, Campbell should record interest expense of: (a) $-0-; (b) $800; (c) $1,600; (d) $2,400

Use the following information to answer the next four questions.

On June 1, 1995, the Campbell Company purchased a two-year insurance policy for $4,800.

11. In 1995, the Campbell Company should record insurance expense of: (a) $-0-; (b) $1,400; (c) $2,400; (d) $2,800; (e) $4,800

12. The balance in the Prepaid Insurance account on the December 31, 1995 balance sheet would be: (a) $-0-; (b) $2,400; (c) $2,800; (d) $3,400; (e) $4,800

13. In 1996 the Campbell Company should record insurance expense of: (a) $-0-; (b) $1,400; (c) $2,400; (d) $2,800; (e) $4,800

14. The balance in the Prepaid Insurance account on the December 31, 1996 balance sheet would be: (a) $-0-; (b) $3,600; (c) $2,400; (d) $1,200; (e) $1,000

Use the following information to answer the next two questions.

The Campbell Company pays salaries on Friday for the workweek ending on that day. Weekly salaries total $10,000. December 31 falls on a Tuesday.

15. The adjusting journal entry to accrue salaries expense at December 31 should record salaries expense in the amount of: (a) $-0-; (b) $4,000; (c) $6,000; (d) $10,000

16. The entry Campbell would make on January 3 to record the payment of salaries would include a debit to the Salaries Expense account in the amount of: (a) $-0-; (b) $4,000; (c) $6,000; (d) $10,000

Use the following information to answer the next three questions.

For special orders the Campbell Company requires payment in full at the time the special order is placed. On August 1, 1995, Campbell received a special order from a customer and received a $2,000 payment for the order. Campbell recorded the $2,000 as unearned revenue. At December 31, 1995, 75% of the special order had been filled.

17. The adjusting entry at December 31, 1995, should record revenue in the amount of: (a) $-0-; (b) $500; (c) $1,500; (d) $2,000

18. The Unearned Revenue account appearing on the December 31, 1995, balance sheet should have a balance of: (a) $-0-; (b) $500; (c) $1,500; (d) $2,000

19. The Unearned Revenue account is a(n): (a) asset account; (b) liability account; (c) stockholders' equity account; (d) revenue account; (e) expense account

20. The following information is provided about the Campbell Company for 1995:

    Net assets at the beginning of the year $220,000
    Net assets at the end of the year   290,000
    Dividends declared   30,000
    Capital stock issued   40,000

    Net income for the year must have been: (a) $30,000; (b) $40,000; (c) $60,000; (d) $70,000

Use the following information to answer the next two questions.

    The following information has been provided about Granite, Inc.:

    Total liabilities, ending balance $340,000
    Capital stock, ending balance   650,000
    Net income   120,000
    Dividends declared   80,000
    Retained earnings, ending balance   290,000

21. Total assets at the end of the year must have been: (a) $1,140,000; (b) $1,060,000; (c) $1,020,000; (d) $990,000

22. The beginning balance in the Retained Earnings account must have been: (a) $210,000; (b) $250,000; (c) $330,000; (d) $370,000

23. Prepaid insurance amounted to $2,500 at the beginning of the year and $900 at the end of the year. The income statement for the year showed insurance expense of $4,000. Insurance purchased during the year must have been: (a) $1,500; (b) $2,400; (c) $3,600; (d) $4,000

24. At the beginning of the year, the balance in a firm's Unearned Subscription Revenue account was $3,000, and at the end of the year, it was $1,200. During the year, the firm received an additional $3,500 in subscription receipts. Revenue earned during the year must have been: (a) $1,800; (b) $2,300; (c) $5,300; (d) $6,500

25. Jones owns a 9% note receivable that was acquired on March 1, 1995. On July 1, 1995, the interest receivable account showed a balance of $6,000 and there have been no receipts of interest or principal. The principal of the note must be: (a) $120,000; (b) $145,000; (c) $160,000; (d) $200,000

26. The Seahorse Company purchased a building on January 2, 1995. It is being depreciated at a straight-line rate of $4,500 per year. At the end of its useful life of 40 years, it will have a salvage value of $20,000. The building's purchase price must have been: (a) $150,000; (b) $160,000; (c) $180,000; (d) $200,000

EXERCISES

EXERCISE 1

The Smith Company began operations on January 1, 1995. The company's year-end is December 31, and it makes adjusting entries once a year at that time. During 1995, the following transactions occurred:

a. On January 5, the company purchased $600 of office supplies for cash. On September 4, the company purchased another $800 of office supplies on account. A year-end count of office supplies revealed that $300 of supplies were still on hand.
b. On April 1, the firm purchased a two-year insurance policy for $2,400.
c. On August 1, the company received $12,000 cash from a tenant for one year's rent for office space.
d. On March 1, 1995, the company borrowed $10,000 from a local bank at 9% interest. The interest and principal are due in one year.
e. Wages accrued but unpaid at December 31 totaled $3,000.

Required:

For each of the above transactions prepare:
1. The initial journal entry to record the transaction.
2. If necessary, the adjusting entry at December 31. Include supporting calculations in the journal entry explanation.

SMITH COMPANY
GENERAL JOURNAL

DATE	ACCOUNT TITLES	REF.	DEBIT	CREDIT
(a)	Initial Entries:			
	Adjusting Entry:			
(b)	Initial Entry:			
	Adjusting Entry:			
(c)	Initial Entry:			
	Adjusting Entry:			
(d)	Initial Entry:			
	Adjusting Entry:			
(e)	Initial Entry:			
	Adjusting Entry:			

EXERCISE 2

The unadjusted trial balance for Oak Haven, Inc. is shown below.

OAK HAVEN, INC.
UNADJUSTED TRIAL BALANCE
DECEMBER 31, 1995

ACCOUNT	DEBIT	CREDIT
Cash	$ 15,000	
Marketable securities	2,500	
Accounts receivable	25,000	
Inventory	40,000	
Office supplies	1,000	
Prepaid insurance	2,000	
Land	10,000	
Building	50,000	
Furniture and fixtures	8,000	
Accounts payable		$ 20,000
Bank loan payable		45,000
Capital stock		32,000
Retained earnings		18,500
Sales		120,000
Cost of goods sold	64,000	
Salaries expense	12,000	
Advertising expense	2,500	
Utilities expense	1,500	
Repairs and maintenance expense	3,000	
Gain on sale of land		1,000
Totals	$236,500	$236,500

Additional information:

a. At the end of the year, office supplies on hand totaled $200.
b. The prepaid insurance policy was purchased during the year for $2,000. It became effective on October 1, 1995, and has a two-year term.
c. The building and furniture and fixtures were purchased at the beginning of the year. The building has a useful life of 40 years and no salvage value. The furniture and fixtures have a five-year useful life and a residual value of $2,000.
d. Salaries earned but unpaid at year-end were $700.
e. The bank loan has been outstanding since May 1. The interest (10%) and principal are due next year.
f. On January 5, 1996, December's utility bill of $90 arrived.

EXERCISE 2 (continued)

Required:

1. Prepare the necessary adjusting entries. Include supporting calculations in the journal entry explanations.

OAK HAVEN, INC.

GENERAL JOURNAL

DATE	ACCOUNT TITLES	REF.	DEBIT	CREDIT
	ADJUSTING ENTRIES			
(a)				
(b)				
(c)				
(d)				
(e)				
(f)				

2. After transferring the balances of the accounts from the trial balance to the T accounts, post the entries to the appropriate T accounts.

CASH

MARKETABLE SECURITIES

ACCOUNTS RECEIVABLE

INVENTORY

OFFICE SUPPLIES

PREPAID INSURANCE

LAND

BUILDING

ACCUMULATED DEPRECIATION: BUILDING

FURNITURE AND FIXTURES

EXERCISE 2 (continued)

ACCUMULATED DEPRECIATION:
FURNITURE AND FIXTURES

ACCOUNTS PAYABLE

INTEREST PAYABLE

SALARIES PAYABLE

BANK LOAN PAYABLE

CAPITAL STOCK

RETAINED EARNINGS

SALES

COST OF GOODS SOLD

SALARIES EXPENSE

ADVERTISING EXPENSE

UTILITIES EXPENSE

REPAIRS AND MAINTENANCE EXPENSE

GAIN ON SALE OF LAND

OFFICE SUPPLIES EXPENSE

INSURANCE EXPENSE

DEPRECIATION EXPENSE

INTEREST EXPENSE

EXERCISE 2 (continued)

3. Prepare an adjusted trial balance.

EXERCISE 2 (continued)

4. Prepare the following financial statements:
   - an income statement
   - a statement of retained earnings
   - a balance sheet

5. Prepare closing entries.

OAK HAVEN, INC.

GENERAL JOURNAL

DATE	ACCOUNT TITLES	REF.	DEBIT	CREDIT
	CLOSING ENTRIES			

EXERCISE 2 (continued)

6. Prepare a post-closing trial balance.

ANSWERS

KEY TERMS TEST
1. Adjusting entries
2. Nonmonetary assets
3. Prepaid assets
4. Depreciation
5. Straight-line depreciation
6. Useful life, economic life
7. Residual value, salvage value
8. contra account
9. Net book value
10. Nonmonetary liabilities
11. accrual
12. Accrued revenue
13. Accrued expenses
14. unadjusted trial balance
15. adjusted trial balance
16. Closing entries
17. post-closing trial balance
18. system flowchart
19. Principal
20. maturity date
21. maturity value
22. Monetary assets
23. interest rate
24. depreciable base
25. general ledger system
26. income summary account

CHAPTER QUIZ
1.   7   Prepare closing entries.
      3   Prepare an unadjusted trial balance.
      6   Prepare financial statements.
      4   Prepare adjusting entries.
      2   Post journal entries to the ledger.
      5   Post adjusting entries and prepare an adjusted trial balance.
      8   Prepare a post-closing trial balance.
      1   Record transactions in the journal.
2. e $1,500 + $3,000 - $800 = $3,700
3. b Supplies on hand of $800
4. b $90,000 - $10,000 = $80,000
5. a ($90,000 - $10,000)/10 years = $8,000/year
     $8,000 x 9/12 = $6,000
6. b ($90,000 - $10,000)/10 years = $8,000/year
7. c $6,000 + $8,000 = $14,000
8. d $90,000 - $14,000 = $76,000
9. c $20,000 x 12% x 8/12 = $1,600
10. b $20,000 x 12% x 4/12 = $800
11. b $4,800 x 7/24 = $1,400
12. d $4,800 x 17/24 = $3,400
13. c $4,800 x 12/24 = $2,400

14. e $4,800 - $1,400 - $2,400 = $1,000$, or $4,800 \times 5/24 = $1,000$
15. b $10,000 \times 2/5 = $4,000$
16. c $10,000 \times 3/5 = $6,000$
17. c $2,000 \times 75\% = $1,500$
18. b $2,000 - $1,500 = 500, or $2,000 \times 25\% = 500
19. b liability account
20. c $220,000 + $40,000 + \text{Net Income} - $30,000 = $290,000$
$$\text{Net Income} = $60,000$$
21. d $340,000 + $650,000 = $990,000$
22. b Beginning Retained Earnings $+ $120,000 - $80,000 = $290,000$
$$\text{Beginning Retained Earnings} = $250,000$$
23. b $2,500 + X - $4,000 = 900
$$X = $2,400$$
24. c $3,000 + $3,500 - X = $1,200$
$$X = $5,300$$
25. c $\text{Principal} \times 9\% \times 5/12 = $6,000$
$$\text{Principal} = $6,000/0.0375$$
$$\text{Principal} = $160,000$$
26. d $4,500 \times 40 = $180,000 + $20,000 = $200,000$

EXERCISE 1

SMITH COMPANY

GENERAL JOURNAL

DATE	ACCOUNT TITLES	REF.	DEBIT	CREDIT
(a)				
1/5	Supplies		600	
	Cash			600
	To record the purchase of supplies for cash.			
9/4	Supplies		800	
	Accounts Payable			800
	To record the purchase of supplies on account.			
12/31	Supplies Expense		1,100	
	Supplies			1,100
	To record supplies used. $600 + $800 - $300 = $1,100$			
(b)				
4/1	Prepaid Insurance		2,400	
	Cash			2,400
	To record the purchase of a two-year insurance policy.			

EXERCISE 1 (continued)

| 12/31 | Insurance Expense | 900 | |
| | Prepaid Insurance | | 900 |

To record expired insurance.
$2,400 x 9/24 = $900

(c)
| 8/1 | Cash | 12,000 | |
| | Unearned Rent Revenue | | 12,000 |

To record one year of rent received in advance.

| 12/31 | Unearned Rent Revenue | 5,000 | |
| | Rent Revenue | | 5,000 |

To record rent revenue earned.
$12,000 x 5/12 = $5,000

(d)
| 3/1 | Cash | 10,000 | |
| | Bank Loan Payable | | 10,000 |

To record the issuance of a note payable.

| 12/31 | Interest Expense | 750 | |
| | Interest Payable | | 750 |

To record accrued interest.
$10,000 x 9% x 10/12 = $750

(e)
| 12/31 | Wage Expense | 3,000 | |
| | Wages Payable | | 3,000 |

To record accrued wages.

1.   OAK HAVEN, INC.

                                  GENERAL JOURNAL

DATE	ACCOUNT TITLES	REF.	DEBIT	CREDIT

                                  ADJUSTING ENTRIES

(a)   Office Supplies Expense   800
         Office Supplies   800

      To record office supplies used during the period.
      $1,000 - $200 = $800

(b)   Insurance Expense   250
         Prepaid Insurance   250

      To record insurance used during the period.
      $2,000 x 3/24 = $250

(c)   Depreciation Expense   2,450
         Accumulated Depreciation: Building   1,250
         Accumulated Depreciation: Furniture and Fixtures   1,200

      To record depreciation expense for the period.
      Building: $50,000/40 years = $1,250
      Furniture and Fixtures: ($8,000 - $2,000)/5 years = $1,200

(d)   Salaries Expense   700
         Salaries Payable   700

      To record accrued salaries.

(e)   Interest Expense   3,000
         Interest Payable   3,000

      To record interest payable.
      $45,000 x 10% x 8/12 = $3,000

(f)   Utilities Expense   90
         Accounts Payable   90

      To record December utility bill received
      in January.

2.

CASH			MARKETABLE SECURITIES		
Bal.	15,000		Bal.	2,500	
12/31 Bal.	15,000		12/31 Bal.	2,500	

ACCOUNTS RECEIVABLE			INVENTORY		
Bal.	25,000		Bal.	40,000	
12/31 Bal.	25,000		12/31 Bal.	40,000	

OFFICE SUPPLIES			PREPAID INSURANCE		
Bal.	1,000	(a) 800	Bal.	2,000	(b) 250
12/31 Bal.	200		12/31 Bal.	1,750	

LAND			BUILDING		
Bal.	10,000		Bal.	50,000	
12/31 Bal.	10,000		12/31 Bal.	50,000	

ACCUMULATED DEPRECIATION: BUILDING			FURNITURE AND FIXTURES		
		(c) 1,250	Bal.	8,000	
		12/31 Bal. 1,250	12/31 Bal.	8,000	

EXERCISE 2 (continued)

ACCUMULATED DEPRECIATION: FURNITURE AND FIXTURES

	(c)	1,200
	12/31 Bal.	1,200

ACCOUNTS PAYABLE

	Bal.	20,000
	(f)	90
	12/31 Bal.	20,090

INTEREST PAYABLE

	(e)	3,000
	12/31 Bal.	3,000

SALARIES PAYABLE

	(d)	700
	12/31 Bal.	700

BANK LOAN PAYABLE

	Bal.	45,000
	12/31 Bal.	45,000

CAPITAL STOCK

	Bal.	32,000
	12/31 Bal.	32,000

RETAINED EARNINGS

	Bal.	18,500
	12/31 Bal.	18,500

SALES

	Bal.	120,000
	12/31 Bal.	120,000

COST OF GOODS SOLD

Bal.	64,000	
12/31 Bal.	64,000	

SALARIES EXPENSE

Bal.	12,000	
(d)	700	
12/31 Bal.	12,700	

EXERCISE 2 (continued)

ADVERTISING EXPENSE

Bal.	2,500		
12/31 Bal.	2,500		

UTILITIES EXPENSE

Bal.	1,500		
(f)	90		
12/31 Bal.	1,590		

REPAIRS AND MAINTENANCE EXPENSE

Bal.	3,000		
12/31 Bal.	3,000		

GAIN ON SALE OF LAND

		Bal.	1,000
		12/31 Bal.	1,000

OFFICE SUPPLIES EXPENSE

(a)	800		
12/31 Bal.	800		

INSURANCE EXPENSE

(b)	250		
12/31 Bal.	250		

DEPRECIATION EXPENSE

(c)	2,450		
12/31 Bal.	2,450		

INTEREST EXPENSE

(e)	3,000		
12/31 Bal.	3,000		

3.

OAK HAVEN, INC.
ADJUSTED TRIAL BALANCE
DECEMBER 31, 1995

ACCOUNT	DEBIT	CREDIT
Cash	$ 15,000	
Marketable securities	2,500	
Accounts receivable	25,000	
Inventory	40,000	
Office supplies	200	
Prepaid insurance	1,750	
Land	10,000	
Building	50,000	
Accumulated depreciation: Building		$ 1,250
Furniture and fixtures	8,000	
Accumulated depreciation: Furn. and Fixtures		1,200
Accounts payable		20,090
Interest payable		3,000
Salaries payable		700
Bank loan payable		45,000
Capital stock		32,000
Retained earnings		18,500
Sales		120,000
Cost of goods sold	64,000	
Salaries expense	12,700	
Advertising expense	2,500	
Utilities Expense	1,590	
Repairs and maintenance expense	3,000	
Gain on sale of land		1,000
Office supplies expense	800	
Insurance expense	250	
Depreciation expense	2,450	
Interest expense	3,000	
Totals	$242,740	$242,740

4.

OAK HAVEN, INC.
INCOME STATEMENT
FOR THE YEAR ENDED DECEMBER 31, 1995

Revenues:
Sales	$120,000	
Gain on sale of land	1,000	$121,000

Expenses:
Cost of goods sold	$ 64,000	
Salaries expense	12,700	
Advertising expense	2,500	
Utilities expense	1,590	
Repairs and maintenance expense	3,000	
Office supplies expense	800	
Insurance expense	250	
Depreciation expense	2,450	
Interest expense	3,000	90,290

Net income	$ 30,710

OAK HAVEN, INC.
RETAINED EARNINGS STATEMENT
FOR THE YEAR ENDED DECEMBER 31, 1995

Retained earnings, January 1, 1995	$ 18,500
Add: Net income for 1995	30,710
Less: Dividends declared in 1995	0
Retained earnings, December 31, 1995	$ 49,210

EXERCISE 2 (continued)

OAK HAVEN, INC.
BALANCE SHEET
DECEMBER 31, 1995

Assets

Cash		$ 15,000
Marketable securities		2,500
Accounts receivable		25,000
Inventory		40,000
Office supplies		200
Prepaid insurance		1,750
Land		10,000
Building	$50,000	
Less: Accumulated depreciation	(1,250)	48,750
Furniture and fixtures	$ 8,000	
Less: Accumulated depreciation	(1,200)	6,800
Total assets		$150,000

Liabilities and Stockholders' Equity

Liabilities:	
Accounts payable	$ 20,090
Interest payable	3,000
Salaries payable	700
Bank loan payable	45,000
Total liabilities	$ 68,790
Stockholders' equity:	
Capital stock	$ 32,000
Retained earnings	49,210
Total stockholders' equity	$ 81,210
Total liabilities and stockholders' equity	$150,000

5.   OAK HAVEN, INC.

                           GENERAL JOURNAL

DATE	ACCOUNT TITLES	REF.	DEBIT	CREDIT
	CLOSING ENTRIES			
12/31	Sales		120,000	
	Gain on Sale of Land		1,000	
	Income Summary			121,000
	To close revenue accounts.			
12/31	Income Summary		90,290	
	Cost of Goods Sold			64,000
	Salaries Expense			12,700
	Advertising Expense			2,500
	Utilities Expense			1,590
	Repairs and Maintenance Expense			3,000
	Office Supplies Expense			800
	Insurance Expense			250
	Depreciation Expense			2,450
	Interest Expense			3,000
	To close expense accounts.			
12/31	Income Summary		30,710	
	Retained Earnings			30,710
	To close the Income Summary account to Retained Earnings.			

6.

OAK HAVEN, INC.
POST-CLOSING TRIAL BALANCE
DECEMBER 31, 1995

ACCOUNT	DEBIT	CREDIT
Cash	$ 15,000	
Marketable securities	2,500	
Accounts receivable	25,000	
Inventory	40,000	
Office supplies	200	
Prepaid insurance	1,750	
Land	10,000	
Building	50,000	
Accumulated depreciation: Building		$ 1,250
Furniture and fixtures	8,000	
Accumulated depreciation: Furn. and Fixtures		1,200
Accounts payable		20,090
Interest payable		3,000
Salaries payable		700
Bank loan payable		45,000
Capital stock		32,000
Retained earnings		49,210
Sales		0
Cost of goods sold	0	
Salaries expense	0	
Advertising expense	0	
Utilities Expense	0	
Repairs and maintenance expense	0	
Gain on sale of land		0
Office supplies expense		0
Insurance expense		0
Depreciation expense		0
Interest expense		0
Totals	$152,450	$152,450

Notice that all the temporary accounts have $-0- balances after closing.
Another option is to list only the permanent accounts and not list the
temporary accounts that have $-0- balances on the post-closing trial balance.

CHAPTER 5

FINANCIAL STATEMENTS:
THE OUTPUT OF THE SYSTEM

```
╔══════════════════════════════════════════════════════════╗
║  CHAPTER REVIEW                                           ║
╚══════════════════════════════════════════════════════════╝
```

ACCOUNTING STANDARD SETTING

- The development of generally accepted accounting principles (GAAP) is a complex process involving a mixture of theory, governmental regulation, and conventions derived from actual practice.

- Generally accepted accounting principles are not collected in a single book or codified in state or federal law. (Although generally accepted accounting principles in the United States are not state or federal law, in many European countries the government is the primary standard setter.)

- Generally accepted accounting principles include concepts, opinions, standards, and regulations from various sources. The major groups involved in the standard-setting process include:
  1. the American Institute of Certified Public Accountants (AICPA)
  2. the Financial Accounting Standards Board (FASB)
  3. the Securities and Exchange Commission (SEC)
  4. the American Accounting Association (AAA)
  5. the Governmental Accounting Standards Board (GASB)

The American Institute of Certified Public Accountants

- The AICPA is the major professional organization of CPAs. In the past the AICPA has formed several committees to develop accounting standards, including:
  1. the Committee on Accounting Procedures (CAP), and
  2. the Accounting Principles Board (APB) that went out of existence in 1973.

- Auditing guidelines and standards continue to be set by the AICPA.

Financial Accounting Standards Board

- The Financial Accounting Standards Board (FASB) was created in 1973 as an organization independent of the AICPA.

- The primary purpose of the FASB is to develop accounting standards.

- The Statements and Concept Statements issued by the FASB and the earlier opinions issued by the APB form a major portion of generally accepted accounting principles.

Securities and Exchange Commission

• The Securities and Exchange Commission (SEC) has the legal authority from Congress to determine accounting standards, but until recently has basically accepted the standards determined by the accounting profession, sometimes modifying them.

• The Securities and Exchange Commission was established by Congress during the Great Depression that followed the stock market crash of 1929. The securities laws of 1933 and 1934 that founded the SEC gave it the power to establish accounting principles governing the form and content of financial statements of companies issuing securities for sale to the public.

• For many years, the SEC set principles for publicly-held companies that reflected the existing standards developed by the private sector of the accounting profession, the APB and the FASB. More recently, however, the SEC has issued several technical pronouncements that were at variance with those of the public accounting profession. In these cases, the accounting profession has usually had to conform its rules to those of the SEC.

American Accounting Association

• The **American Accounting Association (AAA)** is a professional association of accountants, principally academics and practicing accountants, who are concerned with accounting education and research.

Governmental Accounting Standards Board

• The purpose of the Governmental Accounting Standards Board (GASB) is to establish and improve financial accounting standards for state and local governments.

ACCOUNTING CONCEPTS AND CONVENTIONS

Objectives of Financial Reporting

• The FASB considers present and potential investors and creditors to be the primary users of financial statements.

• Financial reporting should provide information that is useful to users making investment and credit decisions.

• The users need information concerning the possibility of receiving cash flows from investments or loans. This data can best be provided by giving investors and creditors information about the enterprise's:
  • resources
  • claims to those resources
  • changes in resources

Important Concepts, Conventions, and Principles

- Financial statements in the United States rest on a set of agreed upon accounting concepts and conventions that can be grouped into three categories:
  1. basic assumptions about the accounting environment
  2. qualitative characteristics of accounting information
  3. the generally accepted accounting conventions

Basic Assumptions About the Accounting Environment

- The basic assumptions about the accounting environment are:
  - **Business entity**: Business entities are separate economic units that control resources and obligations and must have separate and distinct records.
  - **Going concern**: There is an assumption that a particular business enterprise will continue in existence long enough to carry out its objectives and commitments.

Qualitative Characteristics of Accounting Information

- Qualitative characteristics of accounting information are:
  - **Quantifiability**: Money is the basic measuring unit, which means that in the United States, items included in the accounting system must be quantifiable in dollars.
  - **Relevance**: Accounting information is relevant if it is capable of making a difference in a decision.
  - **Reliability**: Accounting information is reliable if it measures without bias what it is supposed to measure. **Verifiability** is a prime ingredient of reliability.
  - **Comparability**: Accounting information is comparable if it enables users to identify similarities and differences between two sets of economic events.
  - **Consistency**: Consistency refers to using the same accounting principles in different periods.
  - **Conservatism**: Uncertainties in accounting are resolved by choosing from the alternatives the one that produces the lowest asset valuation or the least amount of income.
  - **Materiality**: Accounting information is material if the judgment of a reasonable user would have been changed or influenced by the omission or misstatement of the information.
  - **Full Disclosure**: All information useful to an informed decision maker should be disclosed.

Generally Accepted Accounting Conventions

- Generally accepted accounting conventions are:
  - **Historical cost**: Historical cost is the primary valuation method used in financial statements. Assets are recorded at their acquisition cost and are usually not adjusted for increases in value until a sale has occurred.
  - **Time period**: Although a business enterprise is assumed to have an indefinite life, measurement of financial condition and operations must be made at relatively short intervals, such as quarterly or yearly.
  - **Matching**: Under the matching concept, expenses must be offset against the revenues earned in the period. Thus expenses of the period are matched against the revenues of the same period, and the result is net income or loss for the period.
  - **Revenue recognition**: Revenue is usually recognized for accounting purposes when goods are delivered or services performed. In some cases, revenue is recognized before or after the delivery of goods or the performance of services.

Accounting Concepts and General Purpose Financial Statements: A Summary

- The assumptions, qualitative characteristics, and accounting conventions ensure that financial information is useful to the variety of groups who are likely to use it for decision-making purposes.

CLASSIFIED BALANCE SHEETS

- The purpose of the balance sheet is to present the financial position of a company at a specific date.

- The balance sheet helps financial statement users answer the following types of questions:
  - What is the company's overall financial strength?
  - How liquid is the company?
  - Will the company be able to meet its short-term obligations?
  - What proportion of the company's assets has been contributed by creditors and investors, respectively?
  - How does the company's financial position compare with that of others in the same industry?

- **Consolidated financial statements** are the combined financial statements, with certain eliminations, of a parent company and its subsidiaries.

Assets

- Most balance sheets contain up to five categories in the assets section:
  1. current assets
  2. long-term investments
  3. property, plant, and equipment
  4. intangible assets
  5. other assets

Current Assets

- **Current assets** are cash or other assets reasonably expected to be realized in cash or sold within one year or the normal operating cycle of a business, whichever is longer.

- The **operating cycle** of a business is the time it takes a firm to go from cash back to cash. An enterprise uses its cash or incurs payables to purchase or manufacture merchandise for resale. The inventory is then sold, and the enterprise receives cash or a receivable. The operating cycle is completed when the receivables from credit sales are collected and the payables are paid.

CASH-->INVENTORY-->ACCOUNTS RECEIVABLE-->CASH

- Most firms have an operating cycle of less than one year.

- Examples of companies with operating cycles longer than one year are construction companies, tobacco growers, distillers, and cattle breeders.

- Current assets include:
  - cash
  - short-term investments or marketable securities (securities that are readily marketable and that management intends to sell within one year or the operating cycle, whichever is longer)
  - accounts receivable
  - notes receivable (due within one year or the operating cycle, whichever is longer)
  - inventory
  - supplies
  - prepaid items (In some situations, prepaid expenses may benefit several years or operating cycles. Because these amounts are usually not material, however, common practice is to show the entire amount as a current asset. If the long-term prepaid items are material, the noncurrent portion is listed under Other Assets.

Long-Term Investments

- **Long-term investments** include:
  - cash not available for current use.
  - securities (stocks and bonds) not classified as current.
  - property, plant, and equipment not used in production but held for resale or future use.
  - special cash accounts called sinking funds, which are established to purchase property, plant, and equipment or to repay bonds and other long-term debts.

Property, Plant, and Equipment

- Property, plant, and equipment are assets purchased by the firm to generate future revenues.

- Excluding land, which does not lose its future benefits, the matching convention requires that a portion of these assets be systematically allocated against the revenues generated by the use of these assets.

- **Depreciation** is the allocation of a portion of the cost of the assets to the periods benefited.

- The original historical cost of the asset is recorded in an asset account, such as Equipment.

  When recording depreciation, instead of reducing the asset account directly, depreciation is accumulated in a separate account, Accumulated Depreciation.

- The **net book value** or book value of the asset is calculated as follows:

Book Value = Cost of Asset - Accumulated Depreciation

- Property, plant, and equipment may include:
  - land (which is not depreciated).
  - buildings.
  - plants.
  - factories.
  - equipment.
  - leasehold improvements, such as air conditioning and construction made by the individual or firm that is leasing (the lessee) a particular property. At the end of the lease these improvements revert to the owner of the property; they are not the property of the lessee.
  - assets under capital lease, which are assets leased under long-term agreements.

Intangible Assets

- **Intangible assets** are assets that have no physical or tangible characteristics but are agreements, contracts, or rights that provide economic benefits to the firm, the use of a certain production process, trade name, or similar item.

- Examples of intangible assets include:
  - patents
  - trademarks
  - copyrights
  - franchises
  - goodwill

- **Goodwill** is the difference between the cost of the net assets acquired in a purchase and the fair market value of those assets.

  Goodwill cannot be recorded unless a firm is purchased by another and the purchaser pays more than the fair market value for the net assets acquired.

- Intangible assets are amortized. The cost of the intangible assets is written off over the shorter of the:
  - useful life or
  - economic life

Other Assets

- Other Assets is a catchall category that many firms use for assets that do not fit into any other category.

Liabilities

- Liabilities represent the economic obligations of the firm.

- For balance sheet purposes, liabilities are usually divided into two categories:
  1. current liabilities
  2. long-term liabilities or noncurrent liabilities

Current Liabilities

- **Current liabilities** are liabilities that will either be paid or will require the use of current assets within one year or one operating cycle, if the operating cycle exceeds one year.

  Examples of current liabilities include:
  - short-term notes payable
  - accounts payable
  - taxes payable
  - interest payable
  - taxes payable
  - unearned income (advances from customers)
  - current portion of long-term debt (the portion of long-term debt payable within 12 months from the balance sheet date)

Long-Term Liabilities

- Liabilities that do not meet the criteria to be considered current are classified as noncurrent or long-term.

- Examples of long-term liabilities include:
  - bonds payable
  - mortgages payable
  - leases
  - long-term bank loans payable
  - **deferred income taxes** (taxes incurred based on the current year's accounting income that may not be payable to the government until a future period)

- The portion of long-term liabilities that is due within the next 12 months or the operating cycle (if longer than one year) is classified as a current liability.

Stockholders' Equity

- Stockholders' equity includes:
  - common stock (or capital stock)
  - capital in excess of par value
  - retained earnings

- The total of the common stock and the capital in excess of par value represents the stockholders' investment in the corporation.

- Retained earnings represents the accumulated earnings of the business less any distributions to stockholders.

- The Retained Earnings account balance is calculated as:

Beginning Retained Earnings + Net Income - Dividends = Ending Retained Earnings

THE USES AND LIMITATIONS OF CLASSIFIED BALANCE SHEETS

Measuring Liquidity

- Financial statement users are interested in a firm's liquidity (whether the firm has enough current assets to pay its current liabilities and to respond to changes in the business environment).

- Two measures of liquidity are:
  1. working capital
  2. the current ratio

Working Capital

- **Working capital** is calculated as follows:

Working Capital = Current Assets - Current Liabilities

- Working capital represents the amount of current assets that the firm has available to respond to its business needs after repaying all of its current liabilities.

- Creditors often require a firm to maintain a certain minimum level of working capital.

Current Ratio

- The **current ratio** is calculated as follows:

Current Ratio = Current Assets/Current Liabilities

- A firm's current ratio should be compared with the industry average.

- Most financial analysts would probably agree that for many industries a ratio of 2.0 is sufficiently high for most firms.

Long-Term Measures of Financial Strength

- Two measures of a firm's long-term financial strength are:
  1. debt-to-equity ratio
  2. debt-to-total-assets ratio

Debt-to-Equity Ratio

- The **debt-to-equity ratio** is calculated by the following formula:

Debt-to-Equity Ratio = Total Liabilities/Total Stockholders' Equity

- The debt-to-equity ratio measures the relative risk assumed by creditors and owners. The higher the ratio, the more difficult it will be for a firm to raise additional capital by increasing long-term debt.

Debt-to-Total-Assets Ratio

- The **debt-to-total-assets ratio** is calculated as follows:

Debt-to-Total-Assets Ratio = Total Liabilities/Total Assets

- The debt-to-total-assets ratio measures the amount of assets provided by the creditors versus the amount provided by the stockholders. (Assets must be provided by creditors, stockholders, or profitable operations.)

- A ratio higher than the industry average indicates that the creditors have provided a larger share of the firm's assets than is common in the industry. When this is the case, a banker or other creditor may be unwilling to extend additional credit.

Limitations of the Balance Sheet

- The following problems limit the usefulness of balance sheets:
  1. Limited definition of assets. Assets are defined as economic resources, controlled by an enterprise, that have future benefits and are quantifiable in monetary terms with benefits that are measurable and verifiable. A number of items that one might consider assets, such as good management and research and development efforts, do not meet these criteria and are not considered assets. Therefore, not all of the real economic assets that a firm owns or controls are listed on the balance sheet.
  2. Use of historical cost. Net assets on a firm's balance sheet are recorded at historical cost or net book value. Therefore, investors or creditors cannot use the balance sheet to determine the current value of the company's net assets.
  3. Arbitrary cost allocation. The matching convention ensures that the costs of assets that benefit several periods are allocated to those periods. This requires the use of allocations, such as depreciation, that are based on estimates.
  4. Use of different accounting methods. Another limitation of the balance sheet is that alternative generally accepted accounting principles are available under current standards. Management can choose among alternatives, and this makes it difficult to compare and contrast the financial positions of various firms.

CLASSIFIED INCOME STATEMENTS

- The purpose of the income statement is to provide financial statement users with information concerning the profitability of an enterprise for a particular period of time.

- The income statement lists:
  - revenues
  - expenses
  - gains and losses (Gains and losses result from the sale of assets other than the sale of goods and services.)

- By analyzing the income statement, the investor or creditor can answer such questions as:
  1. Did the company earn a profit this year, and if so, how does it compare with its profits from other years?
  2. What is the company's gross profit on sales, and is it large enough to cover other operating expenses?
  3. What are the various components of revenues and expenses, and how do they compare with those of prior years?
  4. Did the firm generate enough revenues from operations to pay the current interest charges?
  5. How profitable is the firm compared with others in the industry?

Income Statement Format and Categories

- Published income statements are rather condensed, whereas the income statements prepared for management use are quite detailed.

Gross Profit on Sales

- **Gross profit on sales** (sometimes referred to as gross profit or gross margin) is calculated as follows:

> Sales
> − Cost of goods sold
> = Gross profit

Operating and Administrative Expenses

- **Operating expenses** are the costs incurred to conduct normal business operations.

- Operating expenses generally include:
  - selling expenses, such as sales commissions and advertising.
  - general and administrative expenses, such as office salaries, rent, utilities, and insurance.

Operating Profit

- **Operating profit** (or income from operations) is calculated as follows:

> Sales
> − Cost of goods sold
> = Gross profit
> − Operating expenses
> = Operating profit

Other Income and Expenses

- **Other revenues (income) and expenses** include:
  - rent revenue
  - investment revenue from dividends
  - interest revenue
  - gains from sales of property, plant, and equipment
  - losses from sales of plant and equipment
  - interest expense

Earnings Before Income Taxes and Net Earnings

- Earnings (income) before taxes and net income are calculated as follows:

> **Sales**
> **- Cost of goods sold**
> **= Gross profit**
> **- Operating expenses**
> **= Operating profit**
> **+/- Other revenues and expenses**
> **= Earnings before taxes**
> **- Income tax expense**
> **= Net income**

Other Data

- Income statements of publicly-held corporations may include such categories as:
  - discontinued operations
  - extraordinary items
  - the effects of changes in accounting methods

- **Earnings per share (EPS)** data are required to be disclosed on the income statement.

USES AND LIMITATIONS OF CLASSIFIED INCOME STATEMENTS

- Investors and creditors can use the income statement to answer questions about a firm's profitability.

Measuring Profitability

- Two measures of profitability are:
  1. gross profit percentage
  2. profit margin percentage

Gross Profit Percentage

- The **gross profit percentage** is calculated as follows:

> **Gross Profit Percentage = Gross Profit/Sales**

- The gross profit percentage reveals what percentage of each sales dollar is gross profit.

Profit Margin Percentage

- The **profit margin percentage** is calculated as follows:

Profit Margin Percentage = Net Income/Sales

- The profit margin percentage reveals what percentage of each sales dollar is profit. For example, a profit margin of 10% indicates that 10 cents of every dollar of sales is profit.

Return on Investment

- Two ratios used by investors and creditors to determine how effectively management is operating a business and the return that is accruing to the various equity holders on their investment are:
  1. return on assets
  2. return on stockholders' equity

Return on Assets

- **Return on assets** is calculated as follows:

Return on Assets = Net Income/Average Total Assets

- Return on assets measures how efficiently a firm is using its assets or resources to produce profits.

Return on Stockholders' Equity

- **Return on stockholders' equity** measures the return that stockholders are receiving on their investment, and it is calculated as follows:

Return on Stockholders' Equity = Net Income/Average Stockholders' Equity

Limitations of the Income Statement

- Limitations of the income statement include:
  - the use of historical costs
  - the problems associated with cost allocation
  - the use of different accounting methods

RETAINED EARNINGS STATEMENTS AND STATEMENT OF STOCKHOLDERS' EQUITY

- The retained earnings statement discloses the items that have caused a change in retained earnings.

- Retained earnings is:
  - increased by net income
  - decreased by a net loss
  - decreased by dividends

- The **statement of stockholders' equity** details the changes in all the stockholders' equity accounts.

STATEMENT OF CASH FLOWS

- The purpose of the statement of cash flows is to provide information about the cash receipts and cash disbursements during a period.

- The statement of cash flows is useful in answering the following questions:
  1. What are the sources of the firm's cash?
  2. What proportion of the firm's cash is generated internally (from operations)?
  3. What other financing and/or investing activities took place during the year?
  4. Why was the firm profitable, although there was only a slight increase in cash?

- The statement of cash flows has three major categories:
  1. cash flows from operating activities
  2. cash flows from investing activities
  3. cash flows from financing activities

- Operating activities are primarily those related to sales of the firm's goods and services.

  The income statement measures income as defined by generally accepted accounting principles, whereas the statement of cash flows measures only cash inflows and outflows. Net income and cash provided from operations are different concepts.

- Cash flows from investing activities result primarily from:
  - lending cash to others and collecting cash from repayment of loans.
  - purchasing and selling securities.
  - purchasing and selling property, plant, and equipment.

- Cash flows from financing activities result from:
  - cash obtained from the issuance of debt.
  - cash in repayment of debt.
  - cash received when issuing stock.
  - payment of cash dividends.

OTHER ELEMENTS OF ANNUAL REPORTS OF PUBLICLY-HELD COMPANIES

- Publicly-held companies are required to provide stockholders with an annual report of their activities.

- The annual report includes:
  - the firm's financial statements.
  - explanatory notes to the financial statements.
  - the auditor's report.
  - management's statement of responsibility for financial reporting.
  - management's discussion and analysis of results of operations and financial condition.

Notes to the Financial Statements

- The full-disclosure principle requires that a firm's financial statements provide users with all relevant information about the various transactions of the firm.

- Financial statements are accompanied by notes, which are narrative explanations of the important aspects of various items.

Auditor's Report

- Public companies are required by U.S. securities laws to engage CPAs to conduct an annual audit.

- The general purpose of the audit is to assure users that the financial statements are prepared in accordance with generally accepted accounting principles (GAAP).

- The **auditor's report** expresses an opinion on whether or not the financial statements are presented fairly in conformity with generally accepted accounting principles.

- An unqualified or clean opinion states that the financial statements are fairly presented in accordance with GAAP.

- The auditors do not examine every transaction but examine on a test basis evidence supporting the amounts and disclosures in the financial statements.

THE FINANCIAL REPORTING SYSTEM

- Accounting exists to provide useful financial information to decision makers.

- A **financial reporting system** is a manual or computer-based system that uses accounting data that has been collected and summarized in ledgers to produce financial reports and financial statements.

- The financial reporting system receives inputs from two different files:
  1. the general ledger file
  2. the chart of accounts file

- The financial reporting system uses the data contained in the general ledger to produce the financial statements.

- The chart of accounts file contains information about where the various general ledger accounts are placed on the different financial statements.

- Computer-based accounting systems are used extensively because they provide two significant advantages over manual systems:
  1. Computers can process information much more rapidly than individuals can.
  2. A computer system that has been correctly programmed will consistently process data correctly.

APPENDIX: CORPORATE INCOME STATEMENTS

- One of the primary purposes of the income statement is to help users predict future income patterns. To separate recurring from nonrecurring transactions, generally accepted accounting principles require that the following four major components of income be shown separately on the income statement:
  1. Income from continuing operations
  2. Discontinued operations
  3. Extraordinary items
  4. Cumulative effect of changes in accounting methods or principles

Income from Continuing Operations

- **Income from continuing operations** includes all of the recurring and usual transactions that the firm enters into as it produces its goods and services, such as:
  - sales
  - cost of goods sold
  - operating expenses
  - other income and expenses

- Income from continuing operations indicates how profitable the corporation has been and how profitable it might be on a recurring and continuing basis.

- **Intraperiod income tax allocation** refers to the allocation of total income tax expense among the four components of income:
  1. Income from continuing operations (shown both before and after taxes)
  2. Discontinued operations (shown net of tax)
  3. Extraordinary items (shown net of tax)
  4. Cumulative effects of accounting changes (shown net of tax)

- **Interperiod income tax allocation** refers to the allocation of income taxes among different accounting periods.

Discontinued Operations

- Results from discontinued operations and the gain or loss from the disposal of the discontinued operations should be shown separately from continuing operations.

- A **segment** is a separate major line of business or class of customer. A segment may be a subsidiary, a division, or a department, as long as its activities can be clearly distinguished from other assets.

Extraordinary Items

- **Extraordinary items** are gains and losses that result from transactions which are both:
  1. unusual in nature, and
  2. infrequent in occurrence

- An unusual event or transaction is one that is highly abnormal or is clearly only incidentally related to the enterprise's ordinary and typical activities, taking into account the environment in which the entity operates.

- For an event to be infrequent in occurrence, it should be of a type that would not reasonably be expected to recur in the foreseeable future, again taking into account the environment in which the entity operates.

- The entity's environment includes such factors as the characteristics of the industry in which the entity operates, its geographical location, and the extent of governmental regulations.

- Example of extraordinary items include:
  - destruction by an earthquake and other natural disasters.
  - expropriation of assets by a foreign government.
  - gains and losses due to prohibition under a new law.
  - gains and losses on early extinguishment of debt.

- Examples of items that are not considered extraordinary include:
  - effects of strikes against the firm and/or competitors and major suppliers.
  - changes in accounting estimates and methods.

Types of Accounting Changes

- Over a period of time, a firm is likely to make two different types of accounting changes:
  1. a change in accounting method.
  2. a change in accounting estimate.

- A **change in accounting method** results when a firm changes from one generally accepted accounting principle or method to another generally accepted one.

- A **change in accounting estimate** occurs when a firm changes a particular estimate, such as an asset's depreciable life, as a result of new information that was not available when the original estimate was made.

Change in Method or Principle

- There are different methods of determining bad debts, cost of goods sold, and depreciation expense. Once a particular method is chosen, accountants feel that it should be consistently used unless a change to a different method is preferable, or unless revision of a particular accounting standard mandates the change.

- When there is a change in accounting method, current accounting rules generally require that the cumulative effect of the change be included in income of the current period.

Change in Estimate

- In order to make the allocations required under the matching convention, accountants must make estimates.

- Examples of estimates that must be made include:
  - service lives for depreciable assets
  - uncollectible accounts
  - residual values
  - warranty costs

- A change in estimate affects only the current period in which the change is made and future periods.

KEY TERMS TEST

Test your recall of the key terms as follows: Read the following definitions of key terms and try to recall as many key terms as you can *without assistance*. Write your answers in the spaces provided. If you need assistance, refer to the list of key terms at the end of this section.

1. Financial statements with subcategories for each of the major reporting categories are known as _____ _____ _____.

2. The _____ _____ _____ is an information system that uses the accounting data which has been collected and summarized in ledgers to produce financial reports and financial statements.

3. _____ _____ are gains and losses that result from transactions which are both: (1) unusual in nature, and (2) infrequent in occurrence.

4. A(n) _____ _____ _____ _____ results when a firm changes from one generally accepted accounting principle or method to another generally accepted one.

150

5. A(n) _____ _____ _____ _____ occurs when a firm changes a particular estimate, such as an asset's depreciable life, as a result of new information that was not available when the original estimate was made.

6. A(n) _____ is a separate major line of business or class of customer.

7. _____ _____ _____ _____ refers to the allocation of income taxes among different accounting periods.

8. _____ _____ _____ _____ refers to total income tax expense being divided among the four components of income.

9. _____ _____ are financial statements prepared for a single accounting entity consisting of a parent company and its subsidiaries.

10. _____ _____ are cash and other assets that are expected to be converted into cash or sold or consumed during the normal operating cycle of a business or within one year, whichever is longer.

11. The time it takes a firm to go from cash back to cash is known as the _____ _____.

12. An account whose balance is used to offset the balance in another account is known as a(n) _____ _____.

13. _____ _____ are assets not available for current use.

14. _____ is the systematic allocation of the cost of a long-lived asset to the accounting periods that benefit from the use of the asset.

15. _____ _____ _____ is the difference between the balance in an account and a corresponding contra account.

16. _____ is the difference between the cost of the net assets acquired in a purchase and the fair market value of those assets.

17. _____ _____ are assets that have no physical or tangible characteristics.

18. _____ _____ are liabilities that will be paid in cash or liquidated through the use of another current asset within one year or the normal operating cycle, whichever is longer.

19. The _____ _____ _____ _____ _____ is that portion of long-term debt which is scheduled to be paid within one year or the normal operating cycle, whichever is longer.

20. _____ _____ _____ are income taxes whose payment has been postponed to a future period.

21. _____ _____ is a measure of short-term liquidity computed as the difference between current assets and current liabilities.

151

22. A measure of liquidity computed by dividing current assets by current liabilities is the _____ _____.

23. The _____ _____ is a measure of the use of financial leverage computed by dividing total liabilities by total stockholders' equity.

24. The _____ _____ is a measure of long-term financial strength computed by dividing total liabilities by total assets.

25. _____ _____ _____ _____ is the difference between net sales and cost of goods sold.

26. _____ _____ are the costs incurred to conduct normal business operations.

27. _____ _____ is the difference between gross profit on sales and operating expenses.

28. _____ _____ _____ _____ are revenue and expenses earned and incurred other than from operations.

29. _____ _____ _____ or _____ is a measure of profitability, computed by dividing net income by the number of shares of stock that are outstanding.

30. The _____ _____ _____ is a measure of profitability, computed by dividing gross profit on sales by sales.

31. The _____ _____ _____ is a profitability measure computed by dividing net income by sales.

32. _____ _____ _____ is a measure of management effectiveness computed by dividing net income by average total assets.

33. _____ _____ _____ _____ is a measure of management effectiveness computed by dividing net income by average stockholders' equity.

34. The financial statement that explains the change in total stockholders' equity from the beginning to the end of a reporting period is called the _____ _____ _____ _____.

35. An external opinion on the fairness of financial statements is called a(n) _____ _____.

36. _____ _____ _____ _____ includes all of the recurring and usual transactions that the firm enters into as it produces its goods and services.

37. _____ is a characteristic of information that is present when several individuals or measures would reach similar conclusions.

KEY TERMS:

auditors' report	gross profit percentage
change in accounting estimate	income from continuing operations
change in accounting method	intangible assets
classified financial statements	interperiod income tax allocation
consolidated statements	intraperiod income tax allocation
contra account	long-term investments
current assets	net book value
current liabilities	operating cycle
current portion of long-term debt	operating expenses
current ratio	operating profit
debt-to-equity ratio	other revenues and expenses
debt-to-total-assets ratio	profit margin percentage
deferred income taxes	return on assets
depreciation	return on stockholders' equity
earnings per share, EPS	segment
extraordinary items	statement of stockholders' equity
financial reporting system	verifiability
goodwill	working capital
gross profit on sales	

Compare your answers to those at the end of the chapter and review any key terms missed.

CHAPTER QUIZ

Write your answers in the spaces provided.

1. The operating cycle is the time it takes a firm to go from cash back to cash. Complete the following:

   Cash---> _____ ---> _____ ---> Cash

2. List the five categories of assets on a classified balance sheet.
   1. _____
   2. _____
   3. _____
   4. _____
   5. _____

3. List two categories of liabilities on a classified balance sheet.
   1. _____
   2. _____

4. List three parts of stockholders' equity.
   1. _____
   2. _____
   3. _____

5. The cost of intangible assets is amortized over the shorter of the:
   1. _____ or
   2. _____

6. Working capital is calculated as:

   Working Capital = _____ - _____

7. The current ratio is calculated as:

   Current Ratio = _____ / _____

8. The debt-to-equity ratio is calculated as:

   Debt-to-Equity Ratio = _____ / _____

9. The debt-to-total-assets ratio is calculated as:

   Debt-to-Total-Assets Ratio = _____ / _____

10. The gross profit percentage is calculated as:

    Gross Profit Percentage = _____ / _____

11. The profit margin percentage is calculated as:

    Profit Margin Percentage = _____ / _____

12. Return on assets is calculated as:

    Return on Assets = _____ / _____

13. Return on stockholders' equity is calculated as:

    Return on Stockholders' Equity = _____ / _____

14. Complete the following:

                    Sales

                  - _____

                  = _____

                  - Operating expenses

                  = _____

              +/- _____

                  = Earnings before taxes

                  - _____

                  = _____

15. The three major categories on the statement of cash flows are:
    1. _____
    2. _____
    3. _____

16. The four major components of income that must be shown separately on the income statement are:
    1. _____
    2. _____
    3. _____
    4. _____

17. Extraordinary items are gains and losses that result from transactions that are both:
    1. _____, and
    2. _____

Circle the single best answer.

18. Which of the following is a governmental agency: (a) American Institute of Certified Public Accountants; (b) Securities and Exchange Commission; (c) American Accounting Association; (d) Financial Accounting Standards Board

19. The primary objective of financial reporting is to provide information that is useful to: (a) creditors; (b) management; (c) investors; (d) a & b; (e) b & c; (f) a & c

Use the following information to answer the next five questions.

Godfrey, Inc.
List of Accounts
December 31, 1995

Accounts receivable	$ 3,500
Accounts payable	2,500
Bonds payable	12,000
Bond sinking fund	3,800
Cash	2,000
Common stock	8,000
Copyright, net of amortization	4,500
Current maturity of long-term debt	3,000
Interest payable	400
Inventory	4,000
Note receivable, due 1-1-98	1,000
Land	9,000
Marketable securities	1,200
Mortgage payable less current portion	5,000
Prepaid insurance	800
Plant and equipment	20,000
Supplies	600
Retained earnings	?
Salaries payable	500
Taxes payable	750

20. Total current assets would be: (a) $10,500; (b) $10,700; (c) $11,500; (d) $12,100

21. Total long-term investments would be: (a) $3,800; (b) $4,800; (c) $9,800; (d) $14,000

22. Total property, plant, and equipment would be: (a) $20,000; (b) $23,800; (c) $29,000; (d) $34,000

23. Total intangible assets would be: (a) $4,500; (b) $3,800; (c) $3,000; (d) $1,200

24. Retained earnings at December 31, 1995 would be: (a) $16,750; (b) $17,250; (c) $18,250; (d) $18,650

Use the following information to answer the next six questions.

The following information has been provided for Godfrey, Inc. for the year ended December 31, 1995.

Sales commissions	$ 20,000
Gain on sale of land	2,000
Sales	140,000
Interest expense	1,500
Insurance expense	1,000
Advertising expense	6,000
Cost of goods sold	80,000
Dividends declared and paid	10,000
Depreciation on the office building	5,000
Income tax rate	40%

25. Gross profit would be: (a) $23,500; (b) $33,500; (c) $40,000; (d) $60,000

26. Other revenues and expenses would be: (a) ($500); (b) ($3,500); (c) $500; (d) $3,500

27. Total selling expenses would be: (a) $28,500; (b) $26,000; (c) $20,000; (d) $6,000

28. Total general and administrative expenses would be: (a) $6,000; (b) $7,000; (c) $7,500; (d) $8,500

29. Earnings before income taxes would be: (a) $16,500; (b) $26,500; (c) $28,500; (d) $31,500

30. Net income would be: (a) $16,500; (b) $17,100; (c) $28,500; (d) $36,000

31. If a company borrows $10,000 on a six-month note, the effect of this transaction on the current ratio would be to: (a) decrease the current ratio; (b) increase the current ratio; (c) have no effect on the current ratio

32. If a company borrows $20,000 on a two-year note, the effect of this transaction on the debt-to-total-assets ratio would be to: (a) decrease the debt-to-total-assets ratio; (b) increase the debt-to-total-assets ratio; (c) have no effect on the debt-to-total-assets ratio

33. (Appendix) A $100,000 loss resulting from the worst flood in over 100 years that destroyed the company's warehouse and inventory would be classified as an extraordinary item: (a) true; (b) false

34. (Appendix) A $5,000 loss resulting from the disposal of an obsolete computer would be classified as an extraordinary item: (a) true; (b) false

35. (Appendix) A $25,000 write-off of a bankrupt customer's account would be classified as an extraordinary item: (a) true; (b) false

36. (Appendix) A $50,000 loss due to a strike by employees would be classified as an extraordinary item: (a) true; (b) false

37. (Appendix) A $30,000 loss resulting because one of the pesticides the company produces was banned by the EPA would be classified as an extraordinary item: (a) true; (b) false

EXERCISE 1

Financial accounting uses a set of agreed upon accounting concepts and conventions that are listed below:

A. Business entity
B. Comparability
C. Conservatism
D. Consistency
E. Full disclosure
F. Going concern
G. Historical cost

H. Matching
I. Materiality
J. Quantifiability
K. Relevance
L. Reliability
M. Revenue recognition
N. Time period

Required:

1. In column (1) below, match each of the concepts and conventions with its definition.
2. In column (2) below, identify whether it is:
   (A) an assumption
   (Q) a qualitative characteristic
   (C) a generally accepted accounting convention

---

(1)   (2)

_F_ _____ 1. A business enterprise will continue in existence long enough to carry out its objectives and commitments.

_E_ _____ 2. All information useful to an informed decision maker should be disclosed.

_H_ _____ 3. Expenses must be offset against the revenues earned in the period.

_B_ _____ 4. A characteristic of information that exists when the similarities and differences between two sets of economic events can be understood.

_D_ _____ 5. A characteristic of information that is present when the same accounting procedures and policies are used from one period to another.

_A_ _____ 6. Separate economic units that control resources and obligations must have separate and distinct records.

_M_ _____ 7. Revenue is usually recorded when goods are delivered and services are performed.

_J_ ____ 8. Financial statements only represent the effects of economic events which can be represented in numerical terms.

_C_ ____ 9. Uncertainties in accounting are resolved by choosing the alternative that produces the lowest asset valuation or the least amount of income.

____ ____ 10. Relative importance or significance of an item to an informed decision maker.

_N_ ____ 11. Although a business enterprise is assumed to have an indefinite life, measurement of financial condition and operations must be made at relatively short intervals, such as quarterly or yearly.

_G_ ____ 12. A characteristic of information that actually represents what it purports to represent.

____ ____ 13. A characteristic of accounting information that is capable of making a difference in a decision because it has predictive and/or feedback value.

_G_ ____ 14. Assets are recorded at their acquisition cost and are usually not adjusted for increases in value until a sale has occurred.

EXERCISE 2

The following list of accounts (in alphabetical order) was prepared by the Lewis Company at December 31, 1995:

Accounts payable	$ 8,000
Account receivable	24,000
Accumulated depreciation: building	10,000
Accumulated depreciation: equipment	4,000
Advertising expense	2,400
Bonds payable	12,000
Bond sinking fund	9,000
Building	120,000
Cash	2,000
Common stock	40,000
Copyright, net of amortization	11,000
Cost of goods sold	70,000
Current maturity of long-term debt	2,500
Depreciation expense: building	3,000
Depreciation expense: equipment	5,000
Dividends declared and paid	?
Equipment	80,000
Income tax rate	40%
Insurance expense	1,500
Interest expense	3,200
Interest payable	400
Interest revenue	500
Inventory	6,000
Land	4,500
Loss on sale of marketable securities	300
Marketable securities	1,500
Mortgage payable less current portion	100,000
Note receivable, due 12-31-97	5,500
Patents, net of amortization	7,500
Prepaid insurance	840
Retained earnings, January 1, 1995	78,180
Retained earnings, December 31, 1995	93,240
Sales	150,000
Salaries payable	1,200
Sales commissions	10,000
Taxes payable	500

Required:

1. On the following page, prepare in good form a classified balance sheet at December 31, 1995.

EXERCISE 2 (continued)

Use this page for your answer to Requirement 1.

<u>EXERCISE 2</u> (continued)

2. Prepare in good form an income statement for the year ended December 31, 1995. Separate operating expenses into selling expenses and general and administrative expenses.

3. Prepare in good form a statement of retained earnings for the year ended December 31, 1995.

EXERCISE 2 (continued)

4. Calculate the following ratios:

a. Working capital

b. Current ratio

c. Debt-to-equity ratio

d. Debt-to-total-assets ratio

e. Gross profit percentage

f. Profit margin percentage

g. Return on assets

h. Return on stockholders' equity

EXERCISE 3

For each of the following activities, indicate:
(1) whether the activity should be classified as:
   (O) an operating activity
   (I) an investing activity
   (F) a financing activity
(2) whether the activity results in:
   (+) an increase in cash
   (-) a decrease in cash

---

(1)   (2)

_____ _____ 1. The firm collected $20,000 in cash sales.

_____ _____ 2. Cash dividends of $5,000 were paid.

_____ _____ 3. Land was sold for $8,000.

_____ _____ 4. Common stock was issued for $15,000.

_____ _____ 5. Equipment costing $9,000 was purchased.

_____ _____ 6. The firm paid $200 in interest.

_____ _____ 7. The firm repaid a $2,000 note payable.

KEY TERMS TEST
1. classified financial statements
2. financial reporting system
3. Extraordinary items
4. Change in accounting method
5. Change in accounting estimate
6. Segment
7. Interperiod income tax allocation
8. Intraperiod income tax allocation
9. Consolidated statements
10. Current assets
11. operating cycle
12. contra asset
13. Long-term investments
14. Depreciation
15. Net book value
16. Goodwill
17. Intangible assets
18. Current liabilities
19. Current portion of long-term debt
20. Deferred income taxes
21. Working capital
22. current ratio
23. debt-to-equity ratio
24. debt-to-total-assets ratio
25. Gross profit on sales
26. Operating expenses
27. Operating profit
28. Other revenues and expenses
29. Earnings per share, EPS
30. Gross profit percentage
31. profit margin percentage
32. Return on assets
33. Return on stockholders' equity
34. statement of stockholders' equity
35. auditors' report
36. Income from continuing operations
37. Verifiability

CHAPTER QUIZ
1. Cash--->Inventory--->Accounts Receivable--->Cash
2. 1. Current assets
   2. Long-term investments
   3. Property, plant, and equipment
   4. Intangible assets
   5. Other assets
3. 1. Current liabilities
   2. Noncurrent liabilities (or long-term liabilities)

4. 1. Capital stock (or common stock)
   2. Capital in excess of par value
   3. Retained earnings
5. 1. Useful life or 2. Economic life
6. Working Capital = Current Assets - Current Liabilities
7. Current Ratio = Current Assets/Current Liabilities
8. Debt-to-Equity Ratio = Total Liabilities/Total Stockholders' Equity
9. Debt-to-Total-Assets Ratio = Total Liabilities/Total Assets
10. Gross Profit Percentage = Gross Profit/Sales
11. Profit Margin Percentage = Net Income/Sales
12. Return on Assets = Net Income/Average Total Assets
13. Return on Stockholders' Equity = Net Income/Average Stockholders' Equity
14.

> Sales
> - Cost of goods sold
> = Gross profit
> - Operating expenses
> = Operating profit
> +/- Other revenues and expenses
> = Earnings before taxes
> - Income tax expense
> = Net income

15. 1. Cash flows from operating activities
   2. Cash flows from investing activities
   3. Cash flows from financing activities
16. 1. Income from continuing operations
   2. Discontinued operations
   3. Extraordinary items
   4. Cumulative effect of changes in accounting methods or principles
17. 1. Unusual in nature, and
   2. Infrequent in occurrence
18. b
19. f
20. d $3,500 + $2,000 + $4,000 + $1,200 + $800 + $600 = $12,100
21. b $3,800 + $1,000 = $4,800
22. c $9,000 + $20,000 = $29,000
23. a $4,500
24. c ($3,500 + $3,800 + $2,000 + $4,500 + $4,000 + $1,000 + $9,000 + $1,200 + $800 + $20,000 + $600) - ($2,500 + $12,000 + $8,000 + $3,000 + $400 + $5,000 + $500 + $750) = $18,250
25. d $140,000 - $80,000 = $60,000
26. c $2,000 - $1,500 = $500
27. b $20,000 + $6,000 = $26,000
28. a $5,000 + $1,000 = $6,000
29. c ($140,000 + $2,000) - ($80,000 + $20,000 + $6,000 + $5,000 + $1,000 + $1,500) = $28,500
30. b $28,500 - ($28,500 x 40%) = $17,100
31. a
32. b
33. a
34. b
35. b
36. b
37. a

167

EXERCISE 1

(1)   **(2)**

F   A   **1.** A business enterprise will continue in existence for a period of time long enough to carry out its objectives and commitments.

E   Q   **2.** All information useful to an informed decision maker should be disclosed.

H   C   **3.** Expenses must be offset against the revenues earned in the period.

B   Q   **4.** A characteristic of information that exists when the similarities and differences between two sets of economic events can be understood.

D   Q   **5.** A characteristic of information that is present when the same accounting procedures and policies are used from one period to another.

A   A   **6.** Separate economic units that control resources and obligations must have separate and distinct records.

M   C   **7.** Revenue is usually recorded when goods are delivered and services are performed.

J   Q   **8.** Financial statements only represent the effects of economic events which can be represented in numerical terms.

C   Q   **9.** Uncertainties in accounting are resolved by choosing the alternative that produces the lowest asset valuation or the least amount of income.

I   Q   **10.** Relative importance or significance of an item to an informed decision maker.

N   C   **11.** Although a business enterprise is assumed to have an indefinite life, measurement of financial condition and operations must be made at relatively short intervals, such as quarterly or yearly.

L   Q   **12.** A characteristic of information that actually represents what it purports to represent.

K   Q   **13.** A characteristic of accounting information that is capable of making a difference in a decision because it has predictive and/or feedback value.

G   C   **14.** Assets are recorded at their acquisition cost and are usually not adjusted for increases in value until a sale has occurred.

EXERCISE 2

1.

Lewis Company
Balance Sheet
December 31, 1995

Assets

Current assets:
Cash	$ 2,000
Marketable securities	1,500
Accounts receivable	24,000
Inventory	6,000
Prepaid insurance	840

Total current assets $ 34,340

Investments:
Note receivable, due 12-31-97	$ 5,500
Bond sinking fund	9,000

Total long-term investments $ 14,500

Property, plant, and equipment:
Land		$ 4,500
Building	$120,000	
Less: Accumulated depreciation	10,000	110,000
Equipment	$ 80,000	
Less: Accumulated depreciation	4,000	76,000

Total property, plant, and equipment $190,500

Intangible assets:
Copyright, net	$ 11,000
Patents, net	7,500

Total intangible assets $ 18,500

Total assets $257,840

EXERCISE 2 (continued)

Liabilities and Stockholders' Equity

Current liabilities:
Accounts payable	$ 8,000
Current maturities of long-term debt	2,500
Interest payable	400
Salaries payable	1,200
Taxes payable	500
Total current liabilities	$ 12,600

Noncurrent liabilities:
Bonds payable	$ 12,000
Mortgage payable	100,000
Total noncurrent liabilities	$112,000
Total liabilities	$124,600

Stockholders' equity:
Common stock	$ 40,000
Retained earnings	93,240
Total stockholders' equity	$133,240
Total liabilities and stockholders' equity	$257,840

EXERCISE 2 (continued)

2.

Lewis Company
Income Statement
For the Year Ended December 31, 1995

Sales		$150,000
Cost of goods sold		(70,000)
Gross profit		$ 80,000

Operating expenses:

Selling expenses:			
Advertising expense	$ 2,400		
Sales commissions	10,000		
Total selling expenses		$12,400	
General and administrative expenses:			
Depreciation expense: building	$ 3,000		
Depreciation expense: equipment	5,000		
Insurance expense	1,500		
Total general and administrative expenses		9,500	
Total operating expenses			(21,900)
Income from operations			$ 58,100
Other revenues and expenses:			
Interest revenue	$ 500		
Interest expense	(3,200)		
Loss on sale of marketable securities	(300)		
Total nonoperating income			(3,000)
Income before taxes			$ 55,100
Income tax expense (40%)			(22,040)
Net income			$ 33,060

171

EXERCISE 2 (continued)

3.

Lewis Company
Statement of Retained Earnings
For the Year Ended December 31, 1995

Retained earnings, January 1, 1995	$ 78,180
Add: Net income	33,060
	$111,240
Less: Dividends*	(18,000)
Retained earnings, December 31, 1995	$ 93,240

* $78,180 + $33,060 - Dividends = $93,240
            Dividends = $18,000

4.a. Working Capital = Current Assets - Current Liabilities
           = $34,340 - $12,600 = $21,740

  b. Current Ratio = Current Assets/Current Liabilities
           = $34,340/$12,600 = 2.73

  c. Debt-to-Equity Ratio = Total Liabilities/Total Stockholders' Equity
           = $124,600/$133,240 = 93.52%

  d. Debt-to-Total-Assets Ratio = Total Liabilities/Total Assets
           = $124,600/$257,840 = 48.32%

  e. Gross Profit Percentage = Gross Profit/Sales
           = $80,000/$150,000 = 53.33%

  f. Profit Margin Percentage = Net Income/Sales
           = $33,060/$150,000 = 22.04%

  g. Return on Assets = Net Income/Total Assets[a]
           = $33,060/$257,840 = 12.82%

  h. Return on Stockholders' Equity = Net Income/Stockholders' Equity[b]
           = $33,060/$133,240 = 24.81%

[a]If available, average total assets is used. In this exercise, only the year end balance of total assets is available.

[b]If available, average stockholders' equity is used. In this exercise, only the ending balance of stockholders' equity is available.

EXERCISE 3

(1)	(2)	
O	+	**1.** The firm collected $20,000 in cash sales.
F	-	**2.** Cash dividends of $5,000 were paid.
I	+	**3.** Land was sold for $8,000.
F	+	**4.** Common stock was issued for $15,000.
I	-	**5.** Equipment costing $9,000 was purchased.
O	-	**6.** The firm paid $200 in interest.
F	-	**7.** The firm repaid a $2,000 note payable.

CHAPTER 6

MANAGEMENT CONTROLS, FRAUDULENT FINANCIAL REPORTING, AND ACCOUNTING INFORMATION SYSTEMS

```
┌─────────────────────────────────────────┐
│  CHAPTER REVIEW                           │
└─────────────────────────────────────────┘
```

- **Expectation gap** is the difference between what the public perceives auditors should do and what they in fact do.

INSTANCES OF FRAUDULENT FINANCIAL REPORTING

- **Fraudulent financial reporting** is the intentional misstatement of financial reports.

- Fraudulent financial reporting may result in:
  - overstatement of assets
  - understatement of liabilities
  - overstatement of income

Fraudulent and Questionable Financial Reporting Practices

- Examples of fraudulent financial reporting practices include:
  - falsifying or altering records or documents.
  - omitting transactions from records and documents.
  - misapplying accounting policies.
  - failing to disclose significant information.
  - creating and recording fictitious transactions.

Questionable Financial Reporting

- **Questionable reporting practices** involve legal but deceptive methods to improve financial statements or other financial data.

- Although questionable reporting practices are not fraudulent in a legal sense, many might consider them deceptive, unethical, or immoral.

- Examples of questionable financial reporting practices include:
  - using the most "liberal" accounting policy permitted under GAAP.
  - opinion shopping (shopping around for an auditor who will find questionable accounting practices acceptable).
  - modifying estimates to boost income in less profitable years, as for example, reducing estimates for uncollectible accounts expense in order to increase income.
  - failing to write off obsolete inventory that has no value.

- Often there is disagreement over what behaviors are considered unethical or inappropriate, especially with respect to managing short-term earnings.

Fraudulent Financial Reporting and the Accounting Profession

- The accounting profession is responding to the need for greater confidence and ensurance of integrity.

- The AICPA has revised some of its auditing standards and issued new ones, referred to as expectation gap standards, which have expanded the role of the auditor in evaluating internal control and detection fraud.

- Congress also has addressed some of these concerns in various hearings investigating the role of the auditor in fraud detection, oversight procedures by the SEC, and other matters related to the audit process and fraudulent financial reporting.

- There has been a call for increased teaching of ethics in business schools.

THE FINANCIAL REPORTING SYSTEM FOR PUBLIC COMPANIES

- The three major components of the financial reporting system for public companies are:
  1. public companies
  2. independent public accountants
  3. oversight bodies such as the SEC

- Management bears the primary responsibility for the preparation and content of the financial statements.

- The CPA, through the audit opinion, reports on the fairness of the financial statements, and the several oversight bodies affect financial reporting through standard setting and monitoring of compliance.

- A key area is the accounting department, which is responsible for the actual preparation of the firm's financial statements. The controller and the chief financial officer, who report to the chief executive officer, oversee the accounting department.

- The legal department reviews financial statements and annual report disclosures for compliance with various state and federal securities laws.

- The internal audit department oversees the firm's compliance with its own internal controls.

- The board of directors, through its audit committee, is ultimately responsible to shareholders for the content of the financial reports.

THE IMPORTANCE OF INTERNAL CONTROL AND THE INTERNAL CONTROL FRAMEWORK

- A strong internal control system can:
  1. reduce the incidence of fraudulent financial reporting.
  2. reduce errors in the published financial statements.

Definition of Internal Control

- **Internal control** consists of the practices and procedures used by an enterprise to
  - safeguard assets
  - prevent and detect errors, and
  - reduce the risk of irregularities in the accounting system.

Elements of an Internal Control Structure

- An entity's control structure consists of three elements:
  1. the control environment
  2. the accounting system
  3. control procedures

The Control Environment

- The **control environment** is the organizational climate and structure within which the accounting and control systems operate.

- The internal control environment or "corporate culture" is a major factor in contributing to the overall integrity of the financial reporting process. Management is responsible for establishing the appropriate control environment in which financial reporting occurs.

- A company's management is responsible for the preparation and integrity of the firm's financial statements.

- The board of directors is ultimately responsible to shareholders for management's performance and actions. Both the Treadway Commission and the Framework Study recommend that the board of directors establish an audit committee to provide oversight in regard to the preparation and integrity of the firm's financial statements.

  The audit committee consists of directors who are not part of the company's management and has responsibility for selecting the firm's auditors.

The Accounting System

- The **accounting system** consists of the methods and records established by management to identify, assemble, analyze, classify, record, and report an entity's transactions and to maintain accountability for the firm's assets and liabilities.

Control Procedures

- **Control procedures** are the transaction processing steps established by management to provide reasonable assurance that the firm's objective will be met.

- Three categories of control procedures are:
  1. **operations controls** that provide reasonable assurance that business activities such as purchases, sales, and production are performed in accordance with management's authorizations.
  2. **financial reporting controls** that provide reasonable assurance that financial records and reports are reliable.
  3. **compliance controls** that provide reasonable assurance that an enterprise complies with local, state, and federal regulations.

- Features common to all effective systems include:
  - separation of duties
  - clear lines of authority
  - maintenance of formal policies and procedures
  - physical control over assets and records
  - adequate documents and checks
  - hiring and development of competent, trustworthy personnel

- Separation of duties refers to each of the following duties being handled by a different individual or group within the organization:
  - authorizing economic activities
  - custody of assets
  - accountability for assets

- For example, the cashier (the person who receives cash collections from customers who are paying their accounts) should not have access to the accounts receivable records because a dishonest person could steal the funds and conceal the theft by authorizing a bad debt write-off to that account.

Legislative Influences on Internal Control

Foreign Corrupt Practices Act

- The **Foreign Corrupt Practices Act** prohibits the payment of bribes to foreign officials and requires publicly traded companies to:
  1. keep reasonably detailed records which accurately reflect company financial activities.
  2. establish and maintain a system of internal control to provide reasonable assurance that transactions are properly authorized, recorded, and accounted for.

INTERNAL CONTROL AND COMPUTER-BASED ACCOUNTING SYSTEMS

- In a manual accounting system, the segregation of duties is one of the most common control procedures.

- In a computer-based accounting system, most of the accounting functions are concentrated within the computer, thus making it impossible to increase control over the system by segregating accounting functions. The development of other control procedures becomes necessary.

Control Categories

- Two broad categories of controls in a computer environment are:
  1. **general controls**, such as hardware and system security controls, that are pervasive global controls affecting all system users.
  2. **application controls** that have been tailored to reduce specific risks in a given system.

- An **error** is an <u>unintentional</u> misstatement of financial information.

- An **irregularity** is the <u>intentional</u> misstatement of financial information. For example, authorizing a bad debt write-off to conceal the theft of funds is an irregularity.

- **Preventive controls** are controls designed to <u>prevent</u> the occurrence of errors or irregularities.

- **Detective controls** are controls designed to <u>detect</u> errors and irregularities after they have occurred.

- **Corrective controls** are controls designed to facilitate the correction of an error or an irregularity after it has been detected. Journal entry descriptions is an example of a corrective control.

- Application controls can be classified into:
  1. **input controls** that prevent or detect and facilitate the correction of erroneous input.
  2. **process controls** that either prevent or detect and facilitate the correction of errors during processing.
  3. **output controls** that either prevent or detect and facilitate the correction of erroneous output.

General Controls

- General controls are pervasive global controls that affect all system users and all application systems.

- The different types of general controls and their objectives are:

Control Type	Control Objective
Hardware controls	Detection
System security controls	Prevention
Systems development procedures	Prevention
Integrity controls	Correction
Segregation of MIS function	Prevention

Hardware Controls

- **Hardware controls** are general controls that operate whenever the computer hardware is used.

- Hardware controls are designed to prevent and detect errors caused by hardware malfunctions, power fluctuations, and interference by other electronic devices.

- **Surge protectors** are preventive controls installed on computer systems to guard against hardware failures caused by sudden fluctuations in electrical power.

- Hardware controls that are detective controls include the following:
  - **Parity checks** are hardware controls that detect data errors when characters are transferred from any device to the computer system.
  - A **dual-read control** reads each character twice when transferring data from a magnetic disk into the central processing unit.
  - A **read-after-write control** ensures that data is correctly transferred from the computer to a magnetic disk. A read-after-write control reads data after it is written to a disk and compares the data that was written with the data that should have been written to detect write errors.

System Security Controls

- **System security controls** are controls that prevent unauthorized access to or destruction of system resources.

- Examples of system security controls include the following:
  - **Password protection** restricts access to computer systems to authorized system users. Individuals must have a valid password to gain access to many computer systems.
  - **Physical security controls** prevent unauthorized access to or destruction of a computer facility.

Systems Development Procedures

- **Systems development procedures** are general controls that ensure that application systems are properly designed and installed.

- Examples of systems development procedures include:
  - documentation standards
  - testing standards
  - review and approval procedures

Integrity Controls

- **Integrity controls** are corrective controls that minimize losses due to data and system destruction.

- The two most common integrity controls are:
  1. back-up procedures
  2. disaster plans

Segregation of MIS Functions

- Effective segregation of MIS functions is a preventive control.

- Critical functions that should be segregated include:
  - data origination
  - data entry
  - computer operations
  - computer file library maintenance
  - output distribution
  - systems design
  - programming

- An individual who is able to perform two or more of these functions is able to misuse system resources.

  For example, a data entry operator who is able to originate transaction data could create a fictitious company and then prepare fraudulent accounts payable input that resulted in the payment of nonexistent liability to the fictitious company.

Application Controls

- Application controls are designed to minimize specific risks in application systems, such as:
  - the preparation and submission of invalid or unauthorized input
  - data entry errors
  - file processing errors
  - loss or misplacement of output

• As part of their role as system designers, accountants identify the risks that an accounting system may be subject to and then design appropriate controls to reduce those risks.

Auditors assess the adequacy of controls in accounting systems as part of every audit.

Internal controls can only provide reasonable assurance, not guarantees, regarding:
• the effectiveness and efficiency of operations.
• the reliability of financial reporting.
• the compliance with applicable laws and regulations.

• Three different categories of application controls that are designed to prevent and detect errors are:
1. input controls
2. process controls
3. output controls

• The different types of application controls and their objectives include:

Control Type	Control Objective
Input	
Review and approval	Preventive
Edits	Detective
Direct data entry	Preventive
Processing	
Edits	Detective
File labels	Preventive
Recovery and restart procedures	Corrective
Output	
Control log	Detective
Distribution list	Preventive

Input Controls

• **Input controls** are controls designed to prevent or detect and correct erroneous input.

• The objective of input controls is to provide reasonable assurance that all valid, and only valid, data are input for processing.

- Common input controls include the following:
  - **Transaction review and authorization controls** are preventive controls to prevent the submission of data that contains errors or that is unauthorized. For example, in some systems, accountants transfer information contained on business documents such as invoices and time cards onto journal entry forms that are reviewed and approved by an accounting supervisor before the forms are submitted to data processing for input into an accounting system.
  - **Edits** are detective controls that identify and reject input that appears to be erroneous and include:
    - **journal entry balance edits** that compare the sum of the debits in a journal entry with the sum of the credits to ensure that every journal entry balances.
    - **limit tests** that reject transactions which include amounts that are either less than or greater than a predetermined limit.
    - **range test** that rejects transactions which include an amount that does not fall within an allowable range.
    - **direct data entry procedures** that allow input to be entered directly from source documents, with minimal human intervention, such as grocery store checkouts that use bar code scanners.

Process Controls

- Process controls are controls designed to prevent or detect and correct processing errors.

- Process controls are controls that provide reasonable assurance that the results of computer processing are valid.

- Process controls include the following:
  - **Edits.** The same types of edits that were used to validate input can also be used to validate the results of computer processing.
  - **File labels** are preventive controls that physically and logically identify computer files. An external label provides human-readable file identification on a specific diskette or magnetic tape. An internal label provides computer program-readable file identification.
  - **Recovery and restart procedures** are corrective controls that facilitate the resumption of processing after abnormal program termination.

Output Controls

- Output controls are controls that provide reasonable assurance that output is complete and properly distributed.

- Most transaction processing systems print output control logs so that computer operators can check off each report as it is printed and thus verify that all reports and documents which should be printed are actually printed.

- Systems should also print distribution lists that:
  - identify each printed report.
  - identify the individual(s) who is supposed to receive the output.

KEY TERMS TEST

Test your recall of the key terms as follows: Read the following definitions of key terms and try to recall as many key terms as you can *without assistance*. Write your answers in the spaces provided. If you need assistance, refer to the list of key terms at the end of this section.

1. _____ _____ is the difference in perceived responsibilities between accountants and auditors and the general public.

2. _____ _____ _____ is the intentional misstatement of financial reports.

3. _____ _____ _____ involve legal but deceptive methods to improve financial statements or other financial data.

4. _____ _____ consists of the practices and procedures used by an enterprise to reduce the risk of errors and irregularities in an accounting system.

5. _____ _____ _____ is the environment, accounting system, and control procedures used to provide a reasonable assurance that management's objectives are met.

6. The organizational climate and structure within which the accounting and control systems operate is known as the _____ _____.

7. The _____ _____ consists of the procedures and technology used to identify, assemble, analyze, classify, record, and report an entity's transactions and to maintain accountability for the firm's assets and liabilities.

8. _____ _____ are the transaction processing steps established by management to provide reasonable assurance that the firm's objectives will be met.

9. _____ _____ are controls that provide a reasonable assurance that business activities are performed in accordance with management's authorizations.

10. _____ _____ _____ are controls that provide a reasonable assurance that financial records and reports are reliable.

11. _____ _____ are controls that provide a reasonable assurance that an enterprise complies with local, state, and federal regulations.

12. The _____ _____ _____ _____ requires that publicly traded companies establish an adequate accounting system and internal controls.

13. _____ _____ are pervasive global controls that affect all system users.

14. _____ _____ are controls that have been tailored to reduce specific risks in a given information system.

15. The unintentional misstatement of financial information is a(n) _____.

16. A(n) _____ is the intentional misstatement of financial information.

17. _____ _____ are controls designed to prevent the occurrence of errors or irregularities.

18. _____ _____ are controls designed to detect errors and irregularities after they have occurred.

19. _____ _____ are controls designed to facilitate the correction of an error or irregularity after it has been detected.

20. _____ _____ are controls designed to prevent or detect and correct erroneous input.

21. _____ _____ are controls designed to prevent or detect and correct processing errors.

22. _____ _____ are controls designed to prevent or detect and correct output errors and irregularities.

23. _____ _____ are general controls that operate whenever the computer hardware is used.

24. A(n) _____ _____ is a hardware control that is installed on many computer systems to prevent hardware failures caused by sudden fluctuations in electrical power.

25. _____ _____ are hardware controls that detect data errors when information is transferred into a computer.

26. A hardware control that detects errors when a computer reads data from a disk is a(n) _____ _____.

27. A(n) _____ _____ is a hardware control that detects errors when data are recorded on a magnetic disk.

28. _____ _____ _____ are general controls that ensure that application systems are properly designed and installed.

29. _____ _____ is a general control that restricts access to computer systems to authorized system users.

30. _____ _____ _____ are general controls that prevent unauthorized access to or destruction of a computer facility.

31. _____ _____ _____ are general controls that ensure that application systems are properly designed and installed.

32. _____ _____ are corrective controls that minimize losses due to data and system destruction.

33. _____ _____ _____ _____ _____ are controls that prevent the submission of data that contains errors or that is unauthorized.

34. _____ _____ _____ _____ is an edit that ensures that debits equal credits in every journal entry.

35. A(n) _____ _____ is a control that rejects transactions which include amounts that are either less than or greater than a predetermined limit.

36. A(n) _____ _____ is a control that rejects transactions which include an amount that does not fall within an allowable range.

37. _____ _____ _____ _____ are procedures and devices that allow input to be entered directly from source documents, with minimal human intervention.

38. _____ _____ are controls that physically and logically identify computer files.

39. _____ _____ _____ _____ are corrective controls that facilitate the resumption of processing after abnormal program termination.

40. _____ are detective controls that identify and reject input which appears to be erroneous.

KEY TERMS:

accounting system
application controls
compliance controls
control environment
control procedures
corrective controls
detective controls
direct data entry procedures
dual-read control
edits
error
expectation gap
file labels
financial reporting controls
Foreign Corrupt Practices Act
fraudulent financial reporting
general controls
hardware controls
input controls
integrity controls

internal control
internal control structure
irregularity
journal entry balance edit
limit test
operations controls
output controls
parity checks
password protection
physical security controls
preventive controls
process controls
questionable reporting practices
range test
read-after-write control
recovery and restart procedures
surge protector
systems development procedures
system security controls
transaction review and
    authorization controls

Compare your answers to those at the end of the chapter and review any key terms missed.

CHAPTER QUIZ

Write your answers in the spaces provided.

1. List the three major components of the financial reporting system for public companies.
   1. _____
   2. _____
   3. _____

2. _____ bears the primary responsibility for the preparation and content of the financial statements.

3. List the three elements of an entity's control structure.
   1. _____
   2. _____
   3. _____

4. Two main objectives of internal control are:
   1. _____
   2. _____

5. Three categories of control procedures are:
   1. _____
   2. _____
   3. _____

6. List five different types of general controls in a computer environment.
   1. _____
   2. _____
   3. _____
   4. _____
   5. _____

7. Three different categories of application controls used in a computer environment to prevent and detect errors are:
   1. _____
   2. _____
   3. _____

8. Separation of duties is an internal control measure. List the three duties that always should be performed by different individuals.
   1. _____
   2. _____
   3. _____

EXERCISES

EXERCISE 1

For each of the following situations, indicate if the action described would be considered a(n):
(A) acceptable practice (legal and ethical)
(Q) questionable practice (a practice that is legal but might be considered deceptive, unethical, or immoral)
(F) fraudulent practice (a practice that involves the intentional misstatement of financial information)

_____

_____ 1. Sales were far below budget for the year, and in order to spur sales, the firm offered a 10% discount on sales placed before the company's December 31 year end.

_____ 2. A manager made arrangements with a customer to accept delivery of $20,000 worth of merchandise in December with the understanding that the customer would return the merchandise in January for a full refund.

_____ 3. Employees were asked to change the date on all travel vouchers for December 1995 to January 1996.

_____ 4. Management decided to switch from the LIFO inventory method to the FIFO method in order to boost income in the current year.

_____ 5. To increase income, management revised the estimated life of production equipment from 8 years to 15 years.

EXERCISE 2

For each of the following controls, indicate:

1. whether the control is a:

   (G) General control
   (A) Application control

2. whether the control is a:

   (P) Preventive control
   (D) Detective control
   (C) Corrective control

_____

(1)   (2)

_____ _____ 1. A surge protector was installed on the computer system to guard against hardware failures caused by sudden fluctuations in electrical power.

_____ _____ 2. Journal entry balance edits compare the sum of the debits in the journal entry with the sum of the credits to ensure that every journal entry balances.

_____ _____ 3. File labels are placed on magnetic disk containers.

_____ _____ 4. Distribution lists are used to identify individuals who are supposed to receive printouts.

_____ _____ 5. Individuals must have a valid password to gain access to the computer system.

_____ _____ 6. The disaster plan was implemented when the computer facilities were flooded.

ANSWERS

KEY TERMS TEST
1. Expectation gap
2. Fraudulent financial reporting
3. Questionable reporting practices
4. Internal control
5. Internal control structure
6. control environment
7. accounting system
8. Control procedures
9. Operations controls
10. Financial reporting controls
11. Compliance controls
12. Foreign Corrupt Practices Act
13. General controls
14. Application controls
15. error
16. irregularity
17. Preventive controls
18. Detective controls
19. Corrective controls
20. Input controls
21. Process controls
22. Output controls
23. Hardware controls
24. surge protector
25. Parity checks
26. dual-read control
27. Read-after-write control
28. System security controls
29. Password protection
30. Physical security controls
31. Systems development procedures
32. Integrity controls
33. Transaction review and authorization controls
34. Journal entry balance edit
35. limit test
36. range test
37. Direct data entry procedures
38. File labels
39. Recovery and restart procedures
40. Edits

CHAPTER QUIZ

1. 1. public companies
   2. independent public accountants
   3. oversight bodies such as the SEC
2. Management
3. 1. the control environment
   2. the accounting system
   3. control procedures
4. 1. safeguard assets
   2. prevent and detect errors
5. 1. operations controls
   2. financial reporting controls
   3. compliance controls
6. 1. hardware controls
   2. system security controls
   3. systems development procedures
   4. integrity controls
   5. segregation of MIS function
7. 1. input controls
   2. process controls
   3. output controls
8. 1. authorization
   2. custody of assets
   3. accountability for assets (recording)

EXERCISE 1

A   1. Sales were far below budget for the year, and in order to spur sales, the firm offers a 10% discount on sales placed before the company's December 31 year end.

F   2. A manager made arrangements with a customer to accept delivery of $20,000 worth of merchandise in December with the understanding that the customer would return the merchandise in January for a full refund.

F   3. Employees were asked to change the date on all travel vouchers for December 1995 to January 1996.

Q   4. Management decided to switch from the LIFO inventory method to the FIFO method in order to boost income in the current year.

Q   5. To increase income, management revised the estimated life of equipment from 8 years to 15 years.

EXERCISE 2

(1)	(2)	
G	D	1. A surge protector was installed on the computer system to guard against hardware failures caused by sudden fluctuations in electrical power.
A	D	2. Journal entry balance edits compare the sum of the debits in the journal entry with the sum of the credits to ensure that every journal entry balances.
A	P	3. File labels are placed on magnetic disk containers.
A	P	4. Distribution lists are used to identify individuals who are supposed to receive printouts.
G	P	5. Individuals must have a valid password to gain access to the computer system.
G	C	6. The disaster plan was implemented when the computer facilities were flooded.

CHAPTER 7

THE REVENUE CYCLE:
SALES, RECEIVABLES, AND CASH

CHAPTER REVIEW

THE REVENUE CYCLE

- Different types of firms are:
  1. merchandising firms, such as Wal-Mart, which purchase finished goods for resale to the public.
  2. manufacturing firms, such as IBM, which produce goods for sale primarily to merchandisers or dealerships.
  3. service firms, such as law firms and accounting firms, which provide services to clients.

- One of the transaction cycles is the revenue cycle that processes operating activities which generate revenue.

- The application systems in the revenue cycle for merchandising firms are:
  1. the order entry system, which processes customer orders.
  2. the shipping system, which insures that goods are withdrawn from the firm's inventory and shipped to customers.
  3. the accounts receivable system, which insures that the correct customer is billed on a timely basis.
  4. the cash receipts system, which processes customer payments.

RECOGNITION AND MEASUREMENT OF SALES TRANSACTIONS

- Merchandising firms may have:
  1. cash sales
  2. credit sales

- Manufacturing firms are more likely to make only credit sales.

- When the sale is for cash, the amount of revenue recognized is the amount of cash received (the agreed-upon sales price less any trade or quantity discounts) not including any sales taxes collected.

- If the sale is made on credit, the amount of revenue recognized is based on the net realizable value of the receivable.

- The **net realizable value** of the receivable is the agreed-upon sales price prior to sales taxes less any trade or quantity discounts and sales discounts.

Trade and Quantity Discounts and Sales Taxes

- **Trade discounts** are price reductions offered to a certain class of buyers.

- **Quantity discounts** are reductions from the list price based on quantity purchases.

- Both trade and quantity discounts are adjustments to the sales price. Generally accepted accounting principles require that transactions be recorded at the agreed-upon price, net of these discounts.

- Most states and many counties and cities impose sales or excise taxes. These taxes usually are imposed on the consumer, with the retailer collecting and remitting them to the taxing authority. The retailer recognizes a liability for the amount of the tax and does not include it in sales revenue.

- The entry to record a cash sale is:

      Debit: Cash
         Credit: Sales
         Credit: Sales Taxes Payable

- The entry that is made when sales taxes are remitted to the taxing authority is:

      Debit: Sales Taxes Payable
         Credit: Cash

- Sales taxes apply only to retail sales; they do not apply to goods sold by a manufacturer to a merchandiser for resale.

- Although financial reporting rules do not require explicit recognition of trade or quantity discounts, management may want to keep records of these discounts to monitor them.

Sales Discounts

- **Sales discounts** are cash reductions offered to customers who purchase merchandise on account and pay for the goods within a specified time period as a means of encouraging prompt payment.

- A sales discount of 2/10, n/30 indicates that a 2% discount is allowed if payment is made within ten days of the invoice date. The full price is due within 30 days of the invoice date.

- A sales discount of n/30 indicates the entire invoice price is due within 30 days of the invoice date.

- A service charge or finance charge is often charged on accounts that are outstanding over 30 days.

- There are two methods used to record sales discounts:
  1. the gross method
  2. the net method

Gross Method

- The **gross method of accounting for sales discounts** records the sale and receivable at the gross amount before any discount.

- Entries for the gross method are:
  1. Entry to record the sale of merchandise on account:

     Debit: Accounts Receivable (gross amount)
       Credit: Sales (gross amount)

  2. Entry to record the customer's payment within the discount period:

     Debit: Cash
     Debit: Sales Discounts
       Credit: Accounts Receivable

  3. Entry to record the customer's payment after the discount period:

     Debit: Cash
       Credit: Accounts Receivable

- Sales Discounts is a contra-sales account that is deducted from gross sales to arrive at net sales shown on the income statement.

Net Method

- The **net method of accounting for sales discounts** records the receivable and sale after deducting the allowable discount. The net method is based on the assumption that the customer will take the discount.

- Entries for the net method are:
  1. Entry to record the sale of merchandise on account:

     Debit: Accounts Receivable (net amount)
       Credit: Sales (net amount)

  2. Entry to record the customer's payment within the discount period:

     Debit: Cash
       Credit: Accounts Receivable

  3. Entry to record the customer's payment after the discount period:

     Debit: Cash
       Credit: Sales Discounts Not Taken
       Credit: Accounts Receivable

- Sales Discounts Not Taken is a revenue account listed under Other Revenues and Expenses on the income statement.

Credit Card Sales

- Credit cards are accepted by retailers because:
  1. they stimulate business.
  2. cash is often received sooner than are payments on accounts carried by the business.
  3. it can be cheaper to accept a credit card than to carry individual accounts because the risk of bad debts is shifted to the credit card company.

- Credit card companies charge for their services and for the risk of bad debts. Most credit cards charge between 2% and 5% of the sales price to process a credit card sale. This charge is deducted from the total cash receipts credited to the retailer's account when the sale is processed. The sale is shown at the agreed-upon sales price before the credit card service charge. The credit card service charge is considered an expense.

Sales Returns and Allowances

- **Sales returns** occur when a customer returns an item for a cash refund or a credit on account. It is called a credit because, from the retailer's point of view, it reduces (credits) accounts receivable or cash.

- **Sales allowances** are a reduction in the actual sales price, and the customer keeps the merchandise.

- A **credit memorandum** is prepared to document the sales return or allowance transaction.

- The entry used to record sales returns and allowances would be:

  Debit: Sales Returns and Allowances
     Credit: Accounts Receivable (or Cash)

- If a firm has material sales returns and allowances, the matching principle requires that sales returns and allowances be recorded in the period of sale, making it necessary to estimate sales returns and allowances.

- For most companies, sales returns and allowances are not material, so such an estimate is rarely made.

MEASUREMENT AND VALUATION OF ACCOUNTS RECEIVABLE

Uncollectible Accounts

- **Uncollectible accounts** are receivables that the firm is unable to collect in full from the customer.

- The ability of a firm to collect its credit sales depends on:
  1. how strict the firm is in granting credit.
  2. the particular credit policies of the firm, such as the use of sales discounts or interest charges on uncollected accounts.
  3. general economic conditions.

- In large firms, the credit department is responsible for granting credit as well as for subsequently collecting accounts. In deciding initially whether to grant credit or extend credit limits, the firm must obtain information about customers, such as their financial condition and past credit history. The information can be obtained through credit applications and credit-rating bureaus.

- In theory, a firm should extend credit to all customers from whom the cash ultimately collected will (through either partial or full payment on account) exceed the total of the cost of the goods sold plus other incremental selling and general and administrative expenses. As long as the uncollectible accounts do not exceed the incremental profits from sales to customers in this credit class, the firm will be better off.

Accounting for Uncollectible Accounts

- Bad debt expense should be recognized in the period in which the sale took place and the receivable was generated, not in the period in which management determined that the customer was unable or unwilling to pay.

- Under the **allowance method** the uncollectible accounts expense for the period is matched against the sales for that period.

- The **uncollectible accounts expense** is the amount of current period sales that are not expected to be collected. Uncollectible accounts expense must be estimated in the period of sale. An estimate is required because it is impossible to know with certainty which outstanding accounts will be uncollectible.

Recording Uncollectible Accounts Expense

Recording Original Estimate

- The journal entry to record sales during the year would be:

  Debit: Accounts Receivable
      Credit: Sales

- The entry to record cash collected on account during the year would be:

  Debit: Cash
      Credit: Accounts Receivable

- The adjusting entry to record estimated uncollectible accounts would be:

    Debit: Uncollectible Accounts Expense (or Bad Debt Expense)
    Credit: Allowance for Uncollectible Accounts

- Uncollectible accounts expense is a selling expense on the income statement. (Some firms show it as a deduction from gross sales in arriving at net sales.)

- The Allowance for Uncollectible Accounts is a contra-asset account with a credit balance. The allowance account is a permanent account that is not closed each year and thus may have a beginning balance.

- Instead of reducing accounts receivable directly, an allowance account is used because a firm does not know which particular accounts will ultimately be uncollectible.

- The balance sheet presentation is as follows:

Accounts receivable	**$100,000**
Less: Allowance for uncollectible accounts	**8,000**
Accounts receivable, net	**$ 92,000**

Recording Actual Write-Off

- Once a specific account is determined to be uncollectible, the following entry is made to write off the account:

    Debit: Allowance for Uncollectible Accounts
    Credit: Accounts Receivable: Customer Account Name

- The entry must be posted to both the general ledger accounts receivable and to the accounts receivable subsidiary ledger.

- The entry to write off an account decreases the allowance account and the accounts receivable account by the same amount but has no effect on the net realizable value of the receivable, as the following example illustrates:

	Before Write-Off	After Write-Off of a $1,000 Account
Accounts receivable	$100,000	$99,000
Less: Allowance for uncollectible accounts	8,000	7,000
Net realizable value of accounts receivable	$ 92,000	$92,000

Recording Subsequent Collection of Accounts Previously Written Off

- In some cases a customer whose account has been written off will pay part or all of the account later.

- Two entries are needed to record the collection of an account that has been previously written off.

  The first entry reverses the entry to write off the account and reinstates the customer's account receivable:

  Debit: Accounts Receivable: Customer's Name
     Credit: Allowance for Uncollectible Accounts

  The second entry is the normal cash receipts entry to record a collection from a customer:

  Debit: Cash
     Credit: Accounts Receivable

Estimating Uncollectible Accounts Expense

- Two approaches to estimating the allowance for uncollectible accounts are:
  1. the percentage-of-net-sales method
  2. the aging method

Percentage-of-Net-Sales Method

- The **percentage-of-net-sales method** is a method of determining the amount of uncollectible accounts expense by analyzing the relationship between net credit sales and uncollectible accounts expense of prior years.

- The percentage-of-net-sales method is often called the income statement approach because it attempts to estimate the amount of uncollectible accounts expense.

Aging Method

- The **aging method** is a method of estimating the balance in the Allowance for Uncollectible Accounts by analyzing the age of each accounts receivable account. The accountant attempts to estimate what percentage of outstanding receivables at year-end will ultimately not be collected; this amount becomes the desired ending balance in the Allowance for Uncollectible Accounts.

- The percentages are based on past experience adjusted for current economic and credit conditions.

- The aging method is based on the assumption that the longer an account is outstanding, the less likely it is to be collected, and a higher percentage is applied to the older accounts.

- The aging method is often called the balance sheet approach because it attempts to estimate the net realizable value of the accounts receivable.

Comparison of the Percentage-of-Net-Sales Method and the Aging Method

- Both the percentage-of-net-sales method and the aging method are generally accepted accounting principles because both attempt to match revenues and expenses in the proper accounting period.

- The percentage-of-net-sales method determines the amount of uncollectible accounts expense for a period, and the aging method determines the net realizable balance of accounts receivable for the balance sheet.

- In applying generally accepted accounting principles, management has a choice of methods, and these choices affect the firm's financial statements. Once a method of estimating bad debts is chosen, it should be consistently followed to enhance the comparability of the firm's financial statements.

Difference Between Estimates and Actual Experience

- Regardless of which method is used, the actual accounts written off seldom equal the estimates made in the prior year. Estimates are necessary because the accountant attempts to match revenues and expenses. Most individuals feel that the benefits of this proper matching outweigh the disadvantages of using estimates.

MANAGEMENT CONTROL AND ANALYSIS OF RECEIVABLES

- Control procedures over receivables include:
1. Proper authorization of receivables to be written off as uncollectible. Only the controller or an individual who does not have day-to-day operational control over receivables or cash should authorize a write-off or a sales return. Written authorization should be attached to the customer's subsidiary ledger or file. These controls will ensure that an employee is not able to steal a cash payment on account and conceal the theft by recording the transaction in a customer's account as a bad debt or a sales return.
2. Monitoring the age and size of the accounts receivable balance.
3. Use of a cash budget to forecast collections of receivables. The ability to convert receivables into cash quickly is important in maintaining the firm's liquidity.

Receivable Analysis: Turnover and Collection Period

- Two statistics to monitor receivables are:
1. the receivable turnover
2. the average collection period

- The **receivable turnover** is computed as follows:

Receivable Turnover = Credit Sales/Average Accounts Receivable

- The **average collection period** shows, on average, how long an account is outstanding.

- The average collection period is calculated as:

Average Collection Period = 365 Days/Receivable Turnover

- Management is interested in reducing the turnover period and thus quickly turning receivables into cash. If sales are made on a 2/10, n/30 basis, the turnover should be close to 12 times in a year, and the average age of receivables should be less than 30 days.

- A firm can generate cash by selling accounts receivable to a bank or other lender or borrowing against the accounts to obtain immediate cash.

Budgeting Cash Collections

- By knowing when cash deficiencies and surpluses are likely to occur, a firm's management can plan to:
  - borrow cash when needed.
  - repay loans when there is excess cash.

- The principal sources of cash inflow are from:
  1. cash sales
  2. collection of cash from sales on credit

- Management would compare estimated cash inflows to estimated cash expenditures to determine whether the firm is in need of short-term cash financing.

CLASSIFICATION OF CASH AND RECEIVABLES

- Cash is included in the current assets section of the balance sheet.

- Cash may be excluded from the current assets section when:
  - Restrictions on the cash make it unavailable for current use, such as a sinking fund where cash is put in a special fund to repay bonds or for the future purchase of a building. Sinking funds are shown in the long-term investments section of the balance sheet.
  - Cash on deposit in foreign countries where regulations prohibit its being returned to the United States or used in current operations.
  - When a company overdraws its bank account and has a cash overdraft. Cash overdrafts are shown as a liability in the current liabilities section of the balance sheet.

- Accounts receivable that arise from ordinary sales are classified as current assets.

- Other receivables that might arise from loans to outsiders, employees, or stockholders should be listed separately from accounts receivable.

- If the receivable is due within a year or the operating cycle, it should be classified as current.

- If the receivable arises from a loan to a stockholder or employee and there is no definite due date, it should be considered noncurrent and included in either the long-term investments or other assets section of the balance sheet.

OTHER OPERATING REVENUES

- Other types of revenues include:
  - interest
  - dividends
  - gain on the sale of fixed assets

REVENUE CYCLE APPLICATION SYSTEMS

- Two systems flowchart symbols are:
  1. the manual input symbol
  2. the on-page connector symbol

- The **manual input symbol** shows where data is input into a computer system from a standard keyboard.

- The **on-page connector symbol** is used to connect two flowchart symbols when a connector line can not be easily used.

- Application systems used to process revenue-cycle transactions include:
  1. the order entry system (transaction processing system)
  2. the cash receipts system (accounting system)
  3. the accounts receivable system (accounting system)
  4. the shipping system (transaction processing system)

Order Entry System

- Customer purchase orders are entered into the computerized order entry system as they are received.

- The order entry system reads data contained on two master files:
  1. the customer master file
  2. the inventory master file

- Information on the customer master file is used to perform a credit check.

- Data on the inventory master file is checked to verify that sufficient quantities of the ordered goods are on hand to fill the order.

- The order entry system prints an order acknowledgment, which is mailed to the customer confirming that an order has been received and informing the customer that the ordered goods will be shipped.

- The order entry system prints an order register (a detailed list of every order that was processed by the order entry system).

Shipping System

- The unfilled order file is input into the shipping system. The system reads the customer's name and address from the customer master file to be printed on the shipping notice.

- The shipping system updates the inventory master file.

- An **update** changes the contents of a master file. The shipping system updates or changes the quantity on hand for various items in inventory as goods are withdrawn from inventory and shipped to customers.

- The shipping system also updates the unfilled order file by moving filled orders from the unfilled order file to the filled order file.

Accounts Receivable System

- Inputs into the accounts receivable system include:
  1. filled order file
  2. credit memoranda
  3. write-off of bad debts

- The accounts receivable system reads the customer's name and address from the customer master file so that the invoice can be printed. The accounts receivable system also updates the customer master file by adding the current transaction amount to the customer's account balance.

- The customer master file is the computer-based accounts receivable subsidiary ledger.

- The invoice file contains invoice detail rather than account detail, thus providing more detail than the customer master file.

- The accounts receivable system also generates journal entries to record all of the accounts receivable transactions that have been processed.

Cash Receipts System

- The objective of the cash receipts system is to properly record all cash receipt transactions.

- Remittance advices are entered into the system.

- A **remittance advice** is a business document returned by a customer that identifies their account number and the amount being paid on their account.

- The remittance advice is printed with the invoice and is detached by the customer when they pay the invoice.

- The cash receipts system prints a cash receipts register every day, after the day's cash transactions have been processed.

- The register lists every cash receipts transaction processed by the system.

- The remittance advices and the register together provide a detective control over the payments received. Detective controls are controls that help protect against errors.

- The accounts receivable system generates general ledger journal entries and also updates the customer master file (subsidiary ledger) and the invoice file to record the amounts paid on accounts and invoices.

- The balance in the accounts receivable account in the general ledger should always be the same as the totals in the customer master file and the invoice register.

Types of Computer Files

- The accounts receivable system makes use of two different types of files:
  1. master files
  2. transaction files

- A **master file** is a file that contains relatively permanent information about an entity.
  - The customer master file contains permanent information about:
    - customers
    - customer names and addresses
    - account balances
  - The inventory master file contains permanent information about inventory items such as:
    - item numbers
    - descriptions
    - selling price
    - quantity on hand

- A **transaction file** contains information that is used to update a master file.

- The unfilled order file is used to update the inventory master file.

- The filled order file is used to update the customer master file.

- Journal entries in the general ledger entries file are used to update the general ledger master file.

Indicate which of the following items best matches the statements listed below by placing the appropriate letter in the blank preceding the statement.

     A. order entry system
     B. accounts receivable system
     C. cash receipts system
     D. shipping system

_____ 19. The application system that prints an order acknowledgment that is mailed to the customer.

_____ 20. The application system that prints invoices.

_____ 21. The application system that uses information in the customer master file to perform a credit check.

_____ 22. The application system that updates the quantity of inventory on hand as goods are withdrawn from inventory.

_____ 23. The application system that uses data on the inventory master file to verify that sufficient quantities of the ordered goods are on hand to fill the order.

EXERCISES

EXERCISE 1

The following data relates to the receivables of Naper Company as of December 31, 1995 (prior to any adjusting entries):

Net credit sales	$2,500,000
Accounts receivable balance	300,000
Allowance for uncollectible accounts (debit balance)	2,000

Based on past experience, the firm estimates that 2.5% of all credit sales will be uncollectible.

Required:

1. Prepare the adjusting entry at December 31, 1995, to record bad debt expense using the percentage-of-net-sales method.

2. Determine the balance in Uncollectible Accounts Expense after the adjusting entry.

3. Determine the balance in the Allowance for Uncollectible Accounts after the adjusting entry.

4. Prepare the balance sheet presentation of accounts receivable at December 31, 1995.

EXERCISE 2

The following data relates to the receivables of Barber Company as of December 31, 1995 (prior to any adjusting entries):

Net credit sales	$2,500,000
Accounts receivable balance	300,000
Allowance for uncollectible accounts (debit balance)	2,000

An aging of accounts receivable at December 31, 1995, revealed the following:

Age	Total	Estimated Percentage Uncollectible
Current	$180,000	4%
31-60 days	40,000	12%
61-90 days	20,000	18%
91-120 days	50,000	24%
Over 120 days	10,000	40%
	$300,000	

Required:

1. Make the adjusting entry at December 31, 1995, to record bad debt expense.

2. Determine the balance in Uncollectible Accounts Expense after the adjusting entry.

3. Determine the balance in the Allowance for Uncollectible Accounts after the adjusting entry.

4. Prepare the balance sheet presentation of accounts receivable at December 31, 1995.

5. Prepare the entry to record the write-off of a $2,000 uncollectible account on January 10, 1996.

EXERCISE 3

The following transactions were selected from the records of Jerry Retailers:

January 2:   Sold merchandise to the George Corporation for $12,000 cash.
January 12: Sold merchandise on account to the Kramer Company for $8,000.
             Terms 2/10, n/30.
January 15: Sold merchandise on account to the Louise Company for $6,000.
             Terms 2/10, n/30.
January 21: Received payment from Kramer Company net of the discount.
January 30: Received payment from the Louise Company.

Required:

1. Prepare the necessary entries to record these sales, assuming that Jerry
   Retailers uses the gross method to record sales discounts.

2. Prepare the necessary entries to record the sales, assuming that Jerry
   Retailers uses the net method to record sales discounts.

EXERCISE 4

Hillary's Department Store has found from past experience that 30% of its sales are for cash. The remaining 70% use credit. An aging schedule for accounts receivable reveals the following pattern.

20% of credit sales are paid in the month of sale.
60% of credit sales are paid in the month following sale.
15% of credit sales are paid in the second month following sale.
5% of credit sales are never collected.

The department store has developed the following sales forecast:

March	$50,000
April	64,000
May	48,000
June	70,000
July	80,000

Required:

Prepare a schedule of cash receipts for June and July.

	June	July

KEY TERMS TEST
1. Trade discounts
2. Quantity discounts
3. Net realizable value
4. sales discount
5. gross method of accounting for sales discounts
6. net method of accounting for sales discounts
7. Sales returns
8. Sales allowances
9. credit memorandum
10. Uncollectible accounts
11. allowance method
12. Uncollectible accounts expense
13. percentage-of-net-sales method
14. aging method
15. Receivable turnover
16. manual input symbol
17. on-page connector symbol
18. register
19. update
20. remittance advice
21. master file
22. transaction file
23. average collection period

CHAPTER QUIZ
1. 1. merchandising
   2. manufacturing
   3. service
2. 1. order entry system
   2. shipping system
   3. accounts receivable system
   4. cash receipts system
3. 1. gross method
   2. net method
4. Receivable Turnover = Credit Sales/Average Accounts Receivable
5. Average Collection Period = 365 Days/Receivable Turnover
6. 1. cash sales
   2. collections of cash from sales on account
7. a True
8. b False A credit memorandum is used to document a <u>sales</u> return or allowance.
9. b False Bad debt expense should be recognized in the period in which the sale occurred.
10. b False Debit the Allowance for Uncollectible Accounts and credit Accounts Receivable.
11. b False Income and assets are not affected.
12. a True
13. a 2% x $260,000 = $5,200
14. c $500 + $3,200 = $3,700

15. b
16. c   5% x $400,000 = $20,000
17. b $800,000/[($220,000 + $280,000)/2] = 3.2
18. c   365/3.2 = 114 days
19. A. order entry system
20. B. accounts receivable system
21. A. order entry system
22. D. shipping system
23. A. order entry system

EXERCISE 1

1.

DATE	ACCOUNT TITLES	REF.	DEBIT	CREDIT
12/31/95	Uncollectible Accounts Expense		62,500	
	Allowance for Uncollectible Accounts			62,500

2.

Uncollectible Accounts Expense

Adj.	62,500	
12/31 Bal.	62,500	

3.

Allowance for Uncollectible Accounts

12/31	2,000		
		Adj.	62,500
		12/31 Bal.	60,500

4.

Accounts receivable	$300,000
Less: Allowance for uncollectible accounts	60,500
Net accounts receivable	$239,500

EXERCISE 2

1.

Age	Total	Estimated Percentage Uncollectible	Total
Current	$180,000	4%	$ 7,200
31-60 days	40,000	12%	4,800
61-90 days	20,000	18%	3,600
91-120 days	50,000	24%	12,000
Over 120 days	10,000	40%	4,000
	$300,000		

Required balance	$31,600
Unadjusted balance (debit)	2,000
Amount of adjusting entry	$33,600

2.

Uncollectible Accounts Expense

Adj.	33,600	
12/31 Bal.	33,600	

3.

Allowance for Uncollectible Accounts

12/31	2,000		
		Adj.	33,600
		12/31 Bal.	31,600

4.

Accounts receivable	$300,000
Less: Allowance for uncollectible accounts	31,600
Net accounts receivable	$268,400

5.

DATE	ACCOUNT TITLES	REF.	DEBIT	CREDIT
1/10/96	Allowance for Uncollectible Accounts		2,000	
	Accounts Receivable			2,000

EXERCISE 3

1.

DATE	ACCOUNT TITLES	REF	DEBIT	CREDIT
1/02/95	Cash		12,000	
	Sales			12,000
1/12/95	Accounts Receivable: Kramer Company		8,000	
	Sales			8,000
1/15/95	Accounts Receivable: Louise Company		6,000	
	Sales			6,000
1/21/95	Cash ($8,000 x 98%)		7,840	
	Sales Discounts ($8,000 x 2%)		160	
	Accounts Receivable: Kramer Company			8,000
1/30/95	Cash		6,000	
	Accounts Receivable: Louise Company			6,000

2.

DATE	ACCOUNT TITLES	REF.	DEBIT	CREDIT
1/02/95	Cash		12,000	
	Sales			12,000
1/12/95	Accounts Receivable: Kramer Company ($8,000 x 98%)		7,840	
	Sales			7,840
1/15/95	Accounts Receivable: Louise Company ($6,000 x 98%)		5,880	
	Sales			5,880
1/21/95	Cash		7,840	
	Accounts Receivable: Kramer Company			7,840
1/30/95	Cash		6,000	
	Sales Discounts Not Taken			120
	Accounts Receivable: Louise Company			5,880

EXERCISE 4

	June	July
Cash sales		
(30% x $70,000)	$21,000	
(30% x $80,000)		$24,000
Credit sales:		
Current month:		
(20% x 70% x $70,000)	9,800	
(20% x 70% x $80,000)		11,200
First month following sale:		
(60% x 70% x $48,000)	20,160	
(60% x 70% x $70,000)		29,400
Second month following sale:		
(15% x 70% x $64,000)	6,720	
(15% x 70% x $48,000)		5,040
Total cash collections	$57,680	$69,640

CHAPTER 8

THE EXPENDITURE CYCLE: PURCHASES AND PAYABLES

```
╔═══════════════════════════════════════════════════════════════╗
║  CHAPTER REVIEW                                                 ║
╚═══════════════════════════════════════════════════════════════╝
```

- The expenditure cycle processes:
  - purchases of goods and services
  - payments to suppliers for goods and services
  - payments for other operating activities such as employee wages
  - incurrences and payments of taxes
  - incurrences and payments of interest

LIABILITY RECOGNITION, MEASUREMENT, AND VALUATION

- Liabilities represent the economic obligations of the enterprise.

- Liabilities can be either:
  - **monetary liabilities**: obligations that are payable in a fixed sum of money, such as accounts payable, notes payable, and wages payable, or
  - **nonmonetary liabilities**: obligations to provide fixed amounts of goods and services, such as revenues received in advance of a sale.

Classification of Liabilities on the Balance Sheet

- Liabilities are classified as either:
  - current liabilities, or
  - noncurrent liabilities

- Current liabilities are obligations that use current assets or create new current liabilities.

- Current liabilities include:
  - accounts payable
  - short-term notes payable
  - current maturities of long-term debt (the principal portion of a long-term liability due within the next 12 months)
  - interest payable
  - taxes payable
  - other accrued payables

- Noncurrent liabilities are liabilities that will not be satisfied within one year or within the operating cycle (if longer than one year).

- Examples of long-term liabilities include:
  - mortgages payable
  - bonds payable
  - lease obligations

- The portion of noncurrent liabilities that is currently due is classified as a current liability.

Measurement and Valuation of Current Liabilities

- Like assets, liabilities originally are measured and recorded according to the historical cost principle. When incurred, the liability is measured and recorded at the current market value of the asset or service received.

- Current liabilities are generally valued on the balance sheet at their face value, while long-term liabilities are shown at their present value.

- **Present value** is the concept that the value of money is affected by time.

  One dollar today (a present value) is worth more than one dollar received one year from now (a future value) because cash on hand today can be invested and earn a return.

- With current liabilities, the difference between value today and future cash outlay is not material because of the short time span between the time the liability is incurred and the time it is paid. Current liabilities are shown at the amount of the future principal payment.

TYPES OF CURRENT LIABILITIES

- Liabilities often are divided into two major types:
  1. those whose amounts usually are known.
  2. contingent liabilities which depend on some future event.

Existing Liabilities with Known Amounts

- Examples of existing current liabilities with known amounts include:
  - accounts payable
  - wages payable
  - interest payable
  - current maturities of long-term debt
  - dividends payable

- The accounting issues related to these liabilities are:
  - determining their existence and amount.
  - ensuring that they are recorded in the proper accounting period.

Contingent Liabilities

- **Contingent liabilities** are potential future liabilities whose existence is contingent upon some future event.

- Generally, the amount of these liabilities must be estimated; the actual amount cannot be determined until the event that confirms the liability occurs.

- Examples of contingent liabilities include:
  - product warranties and guarantees
  - pending or threatened litigation
  - guarantee of others' indebtedness

- Two types of contingent liabilities are:
  1. contingent liabilities that are accrued.
  2. contingent liabilities that are not accrued.

Contingent Liabilities That Are Accrued

- Under generally accepted accounting principles, contingent liabilities are accrued only if:
  1. the potential liability is probable, and
  2. the amount can be reasonably estimated.

- Examples include product warranties and premiums.

- Because the matching convention requires warranty expense to be recorded in the period of the sale, not when the repair is made, estimates must be used.

- The entry to record the sale would be:

    Debit: Cash (or Accounts Receivable)
      Credit: Sales

- The entry to record the estimated liability for product guarantees would be:

    Debit: Product Guarantee Expense
      Credit: Estimated Liability for Product Guarantees

- The entry to record actual expenditures incurred for product guarantees during the year would be:

    Debit: Estimated Liability for Product Guarantees
      Credit: Cash, Supplies, Accrued Wages, etc.

Contingent Liabilities That Are Not Accrued

- Contingent liabilities that are not probable and/or whose amounts cannot be reasonably estimated are not accrued on the company's books. Instead, they are usually disclosed in the notes to the financial statements.

- Examples of contingent liabilities that are not accrued include:
  - pending litigation
  - certain guarantees of indebtedness

- Pending litigation is usually reported through footnote disclosure. However, if it is probable that the litigation is going to result in a liability and the amount of the liability can be estimated, it should be accrued.

ACCOUNTING ISSUES RELATED TO PAYABLES ARISING FROM OPERATIONS

- Operating activities which give rise to expenses and corresponding liabilities include:
  1. the purchase of inventories for resale.
  2. purchase of employee services (including fringe benefits and retirement benefits).
  3. other accrued liabilities related to operations.
  4. the incurrence of income taxes.

Purchase of Inventories for Resale

- **Inventories** are:
  - items held for resale to customers in the normal course of business, or
  - items that are to be consumed in producing or manufacturing goods or rendering services.

- For merchandising and manufacturing companies, inventories often are the single largest current asset.

- Inventory purchases should be recorded at the time title passes from the seller to the buyer.

- The historical cost of inventory includes the cash equivalent price of the item plus all costs incurred by the purchasing company for freight and handling to deliver the merchandise to a location for its use or sale.

- The historical cost of inventory purchases is calculated as follows:

> **Purchase Cost**
> **- Purchase Discounts**
> **- Purchase Returns and Allowances**
> **+ Freight Charges**
> **= Cost of Inventory**

Recording Purchase Discounts

- Two methods of accounting for **purchase discounts** are:
  1. the gross method
  2. the net method

- The **gross method of recording purchase discounts** records the purchase of merchandise inventory and the payable at the gross amount before any discount.

- The payroll system:
  - accesses the employee master file to retrieve pay rate and deduction information for each employee.
  - calculates each employee's pay.
  - generates the following outputs:
    - payroll checks
    - a payroll register
    - payroll tax and deduction reports
    - payroll general journal entries

Payroll Tax Liabilities

- Payroll tax liabilities include:
  - federal withholding
  - state withholding
  - social security taxes
  - unemployment taxes

Withheld From Employee Paycheck	Payroll Tax Paid by Employer
Federal income tax	
State income tax	
Union dues	
Social security taxes--employee share	Social security taxes--employer share
	Unemployment taxes

- The federal government and many state governments require the employer to withhold income taxes from employee's paychecks and to remit these taxes to the appropriate federal and state governments.

- **FICA (Federal Insurance Contribution Act) taxes** usually are referred to as social security taxes. FICA taxes are levied on both the employer and the employee.

- In addition to their share of social security taxes, employers must pay federal and state unemployment taxes.

- The entry made by the employer to record payroll would be:

  Debit: Wages Expense
    Credit: Federal Withholding Income Taxes Payable
    Credit: State Withholding Income Taxes Payable
    Credit: Union Dues Withheld
    Credit: FICA Taxes Payable (Employee's share)
    Credit: Cash

- The entry to record the employer's payroll taxes would be:

  Debit: Payroll Taxes Expense
    Credit: FICA Taxes Payable (Employer's share)
    Credit: State Unemployment Taxes Payable
    Credit: Federal Unemployment Taxes Payable

- The entry to record the payment of the liabilities is as follows:

  Debit: FICA Taxes Payable
  Debit: Federal Withholding Income Taxes Payable
  Debit: State Withholding Income Taxes Payable
  Debit: Union Dues Withheld
  Debit: State Unemployment Taxes Payable
  Debit: Federal Unemployment Taxes Payable
    Credit: Cash

Compensated Absences

- **Compensated absences** are absences for which the employee will continue to be paid, such as vacation and sick pay.

- Under current accounting practices, a firm should accrue the liability for these benefits as they are earned.

- The entry to record the estimated liability for vacation pay would be:

  Debit: Vacation Pay Expense
    Credit: Accrued Vacation Pay (liability account)

- When the employees take their vacation and are paid, the employer makes the following entry to remove the liability and record the payment of cash:

  Debit: Accrued Vacation Pay
    Credit: Cash

- The economic environment of the 1990s has seen many companies "downsizing" and offering inducements to current employees to leave or accept early retirement in an effort to combat rising costs. Inducements often include a full year's pay. Current accounting pronouncements require that the costs associated with these special termination programs be recognized when they are offered.

Pension and Post-Retirement Health Care Costs

- A **pension** is an agreement in which an employer promises to make certain payments to employees after they retire.

- **Post-retirement health care costs** are the insurance costs that the employer agrees to pay for health and similar insurance on behalf of the employee.

- The employee earns these benefits today, even though the actual benefit may not be realized until some future date. Thus, the expense of these programs must be recognized in the current period when the related employee's salary is recognized, not deferred until the employee actually takes advantage of them.

- When current pension funding is less than the current pension expense, the firm must recognize an additional pension liability. Conversely, a prepaid asset is recognized when current pension funding exceeds the current pension expense.

Post-Retirement Benefits

- Post-retirement benefits can include the employer's contributions to health care plans, life insurance premiums, and other assistance plans.

- Recently the FASB changed the accounting standards for post-retirement benefits by requiring that firms currently recognize the expense and liability associated with the post-retirement benefits that are earned in the current period and will be paid when the employee retires.

Other Liabilities Related to Operations

Interest Expense and Interest Payable

- The FASB considers interest expense to be an operating item. However, for the most part, the notes and loans that give rise to the interest expense are considered a financing activity or transaction.

Local, State, and Federal Taxes

- Many local and state jurisdictions impose sales taxes on retail sales. The federal government also imposes excise taxes and luxury taxes on the sale of certain items.

- The selling firm usually collects the sales and excise taxes and remits them to the taxing authority.

Advances from Customers

- **Unearned revenue** results when a firm receives cash in advance of performing some service or providing some goods. Because the firm has an <u>obligation</u> to provide the goods or services in the future, unearned revenues is considered a liability.

- Examples of unearned revenues include:
  - subscriptions
  - dues received in advance
  - prepaid rent

- Unearned revenues are generally classified as current liabilities.

- The entry to record the receipt of an advance payment or deposit from a customer and the corresponding liability would be:

    Debit: Cash
      Credit: Advances from Customers (or Unearned Revenues)

- The entry to remove the liability and record the revenue when the goods or services are provided would be:

    Debit: Advances from Customers (or Unearned Revenues)
    Credit: Sales

Accounting for Corporate Income Taxes

- There often are differences between generally accepted accounting principles (GAAP) and the Internal Revenue Code (IRC) because the objectives of GAAP and the IRC are different.

- The objectives of GAAP are aimed at providing investors and users of financial statements with reliable and relevant financial information.

- The objectives of the tax law include social equity, ease of administration, political considerations, and ensuring that individuals and corporations are taxed when they have the ability to pay.

- Management of a firm may use one accounting method for financial statement purposes and another method for tax purposes. For example, straight-line depreciation might be used for financial reporting purposes and accelerated depreciation used for tax purposes.

- **Accelerated depreciation methods** allow a greater amount of depreciation in the earlier years of an asset's life.

- Prudent management will select those accounting methods permitted by the IRC that minimize the firm's taxable income, thus reducing its cash outflow for taxes.

Sources of Differences Between Accounting Income and Taxable Income

- Differences between accounting income and taxable income can be classified as:
1. permanent differences
2. temporary differences

- **Permanent differences** enter into the determination of accounting income but never into the determination of taxable income.

An example of a permanent difference is interest on state and local bonds. Interest on state and local bonds is included when calculating accounting income for financial reporting purposes, but it is not included in taxable income because it is nontaxable under the IRC.

- **Temporary differences** result when a transaction affects taxable income in a different period from when it affects pretax accounting income.

- **Pretax accounting income** is income based on generally accepted accounting principles before income tax expense is deducted.

- Two points with regard to temporary differences are:
  1. temporary differences affect two or more periods: the period in which the difference originates and the later period when it turns around or reverses.
  2. over the life of a single transaction, the amount of accounting and taxable income or expense related to that transaction will be the same. It is just a question of when temporary differences affect accounting and taxable income.

- Temporary differences include the following examples:

Transaction	Accounting Method	Tax Method
Rent received in advance	Recognized when earned	Recognized when cash is received
Installment sales	Recognized at point of sale	Installment basis; income recognized as cash collected
Construction contracts	Percentage-of-completion	Completed contract
Inventories	FIFO	Average cost
Depreciation	Straight-line	Accelerated depreciation

The Need for Interperiod Income Tax Allocation

- **Interperiod income tax allocation** is reporting the tax effects of temporary differences in the balance sheet as assets and liabilities.

- The journal entry to record tax expense including deferred taxes would be:

  Debit: Income Tax Expense
     Credit: Income Taxes Payable
     Credit: Deferred Income Taxes

- Income tax expense relates to accounting income for financial reporting purposes.

- Income taxes payable is the amount of tax actually owed.

- Deferred income taxes equals the difference between the income tax expense and income taxes payable.

SPECIAL ISSUES INVOLVED IN RECORDING INVENTORY TRANSACTIONS

Inventory Systems

- Two different accounting information systems used to account for inventories are:
  1. perpetual inventory system
  2. periodic inventory system

Perpetual Inventory System

- The **perpetual inventory system** keeps a continuous record of inventory on hand and cost of goods sold.

- An example of a perpetual inventory system is the optical scanner in grocery stores that keeps track of inventory quantities.

- The entry to record the purchase of inventory using a perpetual inventory system would be:

  Debit: Merchandise Inventory
     Credit: Accounts Payable

- The entries to record a sale using a perpetual inventory system would be:

  Debit: Cash
     Credit: Sales

  Debit: Cost of Goods Sold
     Credit: Merchandise Inventory

- Under the perpetual system when inventory is purchased, the merchandise inventory account is debited (increased).

  As inventory is sold, the merchandise inventory account is credited (decreased).

- Although the ending balance in the merchandise inventory account should equal the actual cost of inventory on hand, it rarely does because of clerical errors, spoilage, and theft.

  A physical count of inventory to determine the actual quantity of inventory on hand should be made at least once a year at the end of the accounting period. The balance in the merchandise inventory account is then adjusted to agree with the actual ending inventory on hand as determined by a physical count.

Periodic Inventory System

- A **periodic inventory system** does not keep a continuous record of inventories and cost of goods sold. Instead, these items are determined only periodically, usually at the end of each accounting period.

- Although the periodic system may be easier to use for record-keeping purposes, it does not have the ability to provide information about inventory shrinkage.

- When the periodic system is used, inventory purchases are not debited to the merchandise inventory account. Instead, they are recorded in a separate account called Purchases. In addition, no entry is made to reduce inventory and record the cost of inventory sold for a particular sale.

- Before adjusting entries are made at the end of the accounting period, the inventory account will reflect the amount of inventory at the beginning of the year.

- The entry to record the purchase of inventory using the periodic system would be:

    Debit: Purchases
      Credit: Accounts Payable

- The entry to record a sale would be:

    Debit: Cash
      Credit: Sales

- Notice there is no entry to update inventory when a sale is made.

Determining Cost of Goods Sold and Ending Inventory

- Under the periodic system, ending inventory is determined by a physical count and cost of goods sold is calculated as follows:

Beginning inventory
+ Inventory purchases
= Goods available for sale
- Ending inventory
= Cost of goods sold

Adjusting and Closing Entries Under the Periodic System

- The adjusting entry to adjust inventory to the ending balance and create the
* Cost of Goods Sold account would be:

    Debit: Merchandise Inventory (ending)
    Debit: Cost of Goods Sold
      Credit: Purchases
      Credit: Merchandise Inventory (beginning)

- For convenience, merchandise inventory is labeled beginning and ending; however, there is only one ledger account, Merchandise Inventory.

- The closing entry to close the Cost of Goods Sold account would be:

    Debit: Income Summary
      Credit: Cost of Goods Sold

Taking a Physical Inventory

- When a perpetual inventory system is used, the physical inventory verifies that the firm has the inventory that its records show it has.

- When a periodic inventory system is used, a physical inventory is needed to determine cost of goods sold.

- The two steps in taking a physical inventory are:
  1. the item count
  2. the determination of inventory's cost

- In taking a physical inventory, special care must be taken to ensure that:
  1. all items of inventory to which the firm has legal title are counted.
  2. items that have been sold but are still physically present are not counted in the seller's year-end inventory.
  3. all items that required special analysis, such as goods in transit, goods on consignment, and goods in public warehouses, are not overlooked.

Goods in Transit

- **Goods in transit** are goods that have been purchased but have not yet been received by the purchaser.

  If title has passed to the buyer:
  1. the seller records a sale and a receivable or cash and does not include the item in ending inventory.
  2. the buyer records the payable or the payment of cash and the purchase and includes the item in ending inventory.

  If title has not passed to the buyer, no sale or purchase has occurred, so the inventory is included in the seller's ending inventory.

Goods on Consignment

- **Goods on consignment** are goods held by a firm for resale, but title remains with the manufacturer of the product.

- When the retail firm sells the consigned goods, it receives a commission.

Goods in Public Warehouses

- **Goods in public warehouses** are goods that a firm may own but which are stored in a public warehouse, rather than a warehouse that the firm owns.

- If a firm has title to the goods in the warehouses, they must be included in the ending inventory. Failure to count these items will understate the ending inventory, net assets, and profits for the period.

Sales, Purchases, and Cost of Goods Sold Summarized

- The following partial income statement summarizes sales and cost of goods sold:

PARTIAL INCOME STATEMENT

Gross sales
   Less: Sales returns and allowances
         Sales discounts
Net sales

Cost of goods sold:
  Beginning inventory
  Purchases
  Less: Purchase returns and allowances
       Purchase discounts
Net purchases
Add: Freight-in

Cost of goods available for sale
  Less: Ending inventory
Cost of goods sold

Gross profit on sales

- Most published financial statements are not detailed and usually only contain amounts for net sales and cost of goods sold.

BALANCE SHEET PRESENTATION OF LIABILITIES

- The liability section of the balance sheet is divided into two sections:
  1. current liabilities
  2. noncurrent liabilities (or long-term liabilities)

EXPENDITURE CYCLE APPLICATION SYSTEMS

- Four application systems found in the expenditure cycle are:
  1. purchasing system
  2. receiving system
  3. accounts payable system
  4. cash disbursements system

- The purchasing and receiving systems are transaction processing systems that do not generate journal entries.

- The accounts payable and cash disbursements systems are accounting systems that use information from the transaction processing systems to generate journal entries.

The Purchasing System

- The purpose of the **purchasing system** is to maintain adequate inventory stock levels by generating purchase orders when the quantity-on-hand plus the quantity-on-order is less than the reorder point.

- The **reorder point** is the stock level at which additional units of an inventory item should be purchased to meet expected demand.

- The purchasing system:
  1. updates the quantity-on-order in the inventory master file when an order is placed.
  2. prints purchase orders and an order register that lists every purchase order printed.
  3. sends data to an open purchase order file used by the receiving system to ensure that received goods were actually ordered.

The Receiving System

- The purpose of the **receiving system** is to control and record information about goods as they are received from vendors and to compare the items received with those ordered.

- This control prevents the acceptance of goods which were not ordered.

- The receiving system:
  1. transfers data from the open purchase order file to the closed purchase order file.
  2. prints a receipt register that lists the purchase orders that have been closed and the items that have been received.

- Receiving clerks enter quantity received data into the receiving system; however, they typically do not have access to cost data. The cost data is processed by the accounts payable system.

The Accounts Payable System

- The **accounts payable system** records a liability for the purchase of inventory after an invoice has been received and input into the system and after the system has compared the invoice with the information in the closed purchase order file. This comparison is made to provide reasonable assurance that only valid liabilities, those incurred for goods that have actually been received, are processed.

- The accounts payable system:
  1. records the purchase liability.
  2. updates the inventory master file.

```
┌─────────────────────────────────────────────────────────────────┐
║  EXERCISES                                                        ║
└─────────────────────────────────────────────────────────────────┘
```

EXERCISE 1

During the month of September, STAC Enterprises (the seller) entered into the following transactions with BRG, Inc. (the buyer).

September 4:   STAC Enterprises sold merchandise to BRG, Inc. on account. The sale totaled $20,000, and the terms were 2/10, n/30.

September 10: BRG, Inc. returned $4,000 of merchandise because it was defective.

September 11: STAC Enterprises made an additional sale of $8,000 on account to BRG, terms 2/10, n/30.

September 12: STAC received the required payment for the September 4 sale.

September 27: STAC received full payment on the September 11 purchase from BRG, Inc.

BRG uses the periodic inventory system.

Required:

1. Make all the required entries on the books of STAC Enterprises assuming that the firm uses the gross method of recording sales.

DATE	ACCOUNT TITLES	REF.	DEBIT	CREDIT

EXERCISE 1 (continued)

2. Make all the required entries on the books of BRG, Inc. assuming that the firm uses the gross method of recording purchases.

DATE	ACCOUNT TITLES	REF.	DEBIT	CREDIT

EXERCISE 1 (continued)

3. Make all the required entries on the books of STAC Enterprises assuming that the firm uses the net method of recording sales.

DATE	ACCOUNT TITLES	REF.	DEBIT	CREDIT

EXERCISE 1 (continued)

4. Make all the required entries on the books of BRG, Inc. assuming that the firm uses the net method of recording purchases.

DATE	ACCOUNT TITLES	REF.	DEBIT	CREDIT

EXERCISE 2

Weller Electronics manufactures and sells cellular phones. The retail price of each unit is $300, and Weller warrants each phone for 24 months. During 1995 the firm sold 1,000 units and incurred actual warranty costs of $18,000. Past experience indicates that Weller will incur warranty costs of $20 per unit.

Required:

Make the summary journal entries during 1995 to record the above events. Assume that all sales are for cash.

DATE	ACCOUNT TITLES	REF.	DEBIT	CREDIT

EXERCISE 3

The payroll expense for the Ziegfield Corporation for the week ending
September 4, 1995 is $25,000. The entire payroll is subject to FICA taxes of
8%, but only 90% is subject to state unemployment taxes of 5.4% and federal
unemployment taxes of 0.8%. Federal income taxes of $4,000, state income
taxes of $1,500, and union dues of $500 were withheld.

Required:

1. Prepare the journal entry to record payroll.

DATE	ACCOUNT TITLES	REF.	DEBIT	CREDIT

2. Prepare the journal entry to record payroll taxes.

DATE	ACCOUNT TITLES	REF.	DEBIT	CREDIT

3. Prepare the journal entry to record the payment of payroll liabilities.

DATE	ACCOUNT TITLES	REF.	DEBIT	CREDIT

ANSWERS

KEY TERMS TEST
1. Monetary liabilities
2. nonmonetary liabilities
3. Present value
4. Inventories
5. gross method of recording purchase discounts
6. net method of recording purchase discounts
7. Purchase returns and allowances
8. freight-in
9. Transportation-in
10. FICA taxes, social security taxes
11. Compensated absences
12. pension
13. Post-retirement health care costs
14. Unearned revenue
15. Permanent differences
16. Temporary differences
17. pretax accounting income
18. Accelerated depreciation methods
19. Interperiod income tax allocation
20. perpetual inventory system
21. periodic inventory system
22. Physical inventory
23. Goods in transit
24. Goods on consignment
25. Goods in public warehouses
26. purchasing system
27. receiving system
28. reorder point
29. accounts payable system
30. check register
31. contingent liabilities
32. Purchase discounts
33. freight-out

CHAPTER QUIZ
1. 1. current
   2. noncurrent
2. 1. the potential liability is probable
   2. the amount can be reasonably estimated
3. 1. purchasing system
   2. receiving system
   3. accounts payable system
   4. cash disbursements system
4. 1. permanent
   2. temporary

5. Beginning inventory
    + Purchases
    = Goods available for sale
    - Ending inventory
    = Cost of goods sold

6. b False GAAP requires that warranty expense be recorded in the period
             of sale.
7. a True
8. b False Freight-out is not added to the cost of merchandise purchased.
             Instead, freight-out is classified as a selling expense.
             Freight-in is added to the cost of merchandise purchased.

9. a True
10. a
11. a
12. c
13. b
14. b
15. c, d
16.

Inventory count	$215,000
Adjustment:	
a.	- 50,000
b.	-0-
c.	+ 25,000
d.	+ 1,000
e.	+ 15,000
Ending inventory	$206,000

17. E. Payroll system
18. B. Receiving system
19. D. Cash disbursements system
20. C. Accounts payable system
21. A. Purchasing system

EXERCISE 1

1.

DATE	ACCOUNT TITLES	REF.	DEBIT	CREDIT
Sep. 4	Accounts Receivable		20,000	
	Sales			20,000
	To record sale on account, terms 2/10, n/30.			
10	Sales Returns and Allowances		4,000	
	Accounts Receivable			4,000
	To record the return of $4,000 of defective merchandise.			
11	Accounts Receivable		8,000	
	Sales			8,000
	To record $8,000 ﹍ e on account, terms 2/10, n/30.			
12	Cash		15,680	
	Sales Discounts		320	
	Accounts Rece able			16,000
	To record the ﹍ollection of September 4 sale. ($20,000 - $4,000) x 98% = $15,680			
27	Cash		8,000	
	Accounts Receivable			8,000
	To record the collection of September 11 sale.			

EXERCISE 1 (continued)

2.

DATE	ACCOUNT TITLES	REF.	DEBIT	CREDIT
Sep. 4	Purchases		20,000	
	Accounts Payable			20,000
	To record purchase on account, terms 2/10, n/30.			
10	Accounts Payable		4,000	
	Purchase Returns and Allowances			4,000
	To record the return of $4,000 of defective merchandise.			
11	Purchases		8,000	
	Accounts Payable			8,000
	To record $8,000 purchase on account, terms 2/10, n/30.			
12	Accounts Payable		16,000	
	Purchase Discounts			320
	Cash			15,680
	To record the payment for September 4 purchase. ($20,000 - $4,000) x 98% = $15,680			
27	Accounts Payable		8,000	
	Cash			8,000
	To record the payment of September 11 purchase.			

3.

DATE	ACCOUNT TITLES	REF.	DEBIT	CREDIT
Sep. 4	Accounts Receivable		19,600[a]	
	Sales			19,600
	To record sale on account, terms 2/10, n/30.			
10	Sales Returns and Allowances		3,920[b]	
	Accounts Receivable			3,920
	To record the return of $4,000 of defective merchandise.			
11	Accounts Receivable		7,840[c]	
	Sales			7,840
	To record $8,000 sale on account, terms 2/10, n/30.			
12	Cash		15,680	
	Accounts Receivable			15,680
	To record the collection of September 4 sale.			
27	Cash		8,000	
	Accounts Receivable			7,840
	Sales Discounts Not Taken			160
	To record the collection of September 11 sale.			

[a] $20,000 x 98% = $19,600
[b] $ 4,000 x 98% = $ 3,920
[c] $ 8,000 x 98% = $ 7,840

EXERCISE 1 (continued)

4.

DATE	ACCOUNT TITLES	REF.	DEBIT	CREDIT
Sep. 4	Purchases		19,600[a]	
	Accounts Payable			19,600
	To record purchase on account, terms 2/10, n/30.			
10	Accounts Payable		3,920[b]	
	Purchase Returns and Allowances			3,920
	To record the return of $4,000 of defective merchandise.			
11	Purchases		7,840[c]	
	Accounts Payable			7,840
	To record $8,000 purchase on account, terms 2/10, n/30.			
12	Accounts Payable		15,680	
	Cash			15,680
	To record the payment for September 4 purchase.			
27	Accounts Payable		7,840	
	Purchase Discounts Lost		160	
	Cash			8,000
	To record the payment of September 11 purchase.			

[a] $20,000 x 98% = $19,600
[b] $ 4,000 x 98% = $ 3,920
[c] $ 8,000 x 98% = $ 7,840

EXERCISE 4 (continued)

2.

DATE	ACCOUNT TITLES	REF.	DEBIT	CREDIT

ADJUSTING ENTRY

1995
Dec. 31 Merchandise Inventory (ending)   43,000

         Cost of Goods Sold   415,500

         Purchase Returns and Allowances   3,000

         Purchase Discounts   8,000

            Purchases   410,000

            Freight-In   4,500

            Merchandise Inventory (beginning)   55,000

         To adjust inventory to ending balance and create
Cost of Goods Sold account.

CLOSING ENTRIES

1995
Dec. 31 Sales   650,000

            Sales Returns and Allowances   12,000

            Sales discounts   2,500

            Income Summary   635,500

         To close revenue accounts.

     31 Income Summary   415,500

            Cost of Goods Sold   415,500

         To close Cost of Goods Sold account.

CHAPTER 9

INVENTORY VALUATION

CHAPTER REVIEW

INTRODUCTION

- Inventories held by merchandising firms are goods purchased for resale.

- Manufacturing firms can have three types of inventories:
  1. **Raw materials inventory**: stores of materials, usually purchased from outside suppliers, that are eventually converted into finished goods.
  2. **Work-in-process inventory**: stores of partially completed goods.
  3. **Finished goods inventory**: stores of fully completed goods ready for sale to customers.

- Both merchandising and manufacturing firms must determine:
  1. the cost of ending inventory
  2. the cost of goods sold

INVENTORIES AND INCOME DETERMINATION

- The cost of goods available for sale must be allocated between:
  - the items sold (cost of goods sold)
  - the items remaining (ending inventory)

- Cost of goods sold is calculated as follows:

    Beginning inventory
    + Purchases
    = Goods available for sale
    - Ending inventory
    = Cost of goods sold

Measuring Ending Inventories and Income

- Cost of goods sold appears on the income statement, and ending inventory appears as an asset on the balance sheet.

- The allocation of the cost of goods available for sale between ending inventories and cost of goods sold affects both the balance sheet and the income statement.

- A measurement error in cost of goods sold affects:
  - gross profit
  - gross profit percentage
  - net income

- A measurement error in ending inventory causes an error in:
  - current assets
  - total assets
  - working capital
  - current ratio

- In addition, a measurement error in determining ending inventory affects two periods, because the ending inventory for one period becomes the beginning inventory for the next period.

Effect of an Ending Inventory Measurement Error

- The effects of inventory measurement errors are summarized below:
  1. Overstating ending inventory:
     - understates cost of goods sold
     - overstates gross profit
     - understates net income
  2. Understating ending inventory:
     - overstates cost of goods sold
     - understates gross profit
     - understates net income
  3. Overstating beginning inventory:
     - overstates cost of goods sold
     - understates gross profit
     - understates net income
  4. Understating beginning inventory:
     - understates cost of goods sold
     - overstates gross profit
     - overstates net income

- Because ending inventory for Year 1 becomes beginning inventory for Year 2, if ending inventory in Year 1 is overstated, beginning inventory for Year 2 is overstated. The error is self-canceling over the two-year period; however, inventories, cost of goods sold, gross profit, and net income will be misstated each year.

DETERMINING THE COST OF ENDING INVENTORIES

- Determining the cost of ending inventories involves two steps:
  1. The actual quantity of items on hand at the end of the period is determined by taking a physical count of inventory. A physical inventory is required at least once a year, regardless of whether a firm uses the perpetual or the periodic inventory system.
  2. Costs are attached to each item in inventory using a cost flow pattern.

METHODS OF ATTACHING COSTS TO ENDING INVENTORY

- The four cost flow assumptions that are acceptable under GAAP are:
  1. first-in, first-out (FIFO)
  2. last-in, first-out (LIFO)
  3. average cost
  4. specific identification

- **First-in, first out (FIFO)** assumes that the first costs in are the first costs out to cost of goods sold.

- **Last-in, first-out (LIFO)** assumes that the last costs in are the first costs out to cost of goods sold.

  When the LIFO method is used, it is important to maintain separate layers of costs of ending inventory.

- The **average cost** method attaches an average cost to both the cost of goods sold and the ending inventory.

  A weighted average cost per unit is calculated by dividing the total cost of goods available for sale by the total number of units available for sale.

  Average Cost Per Unit = Cost of Goods Available for Sale/Units Available for Sale

- The **specific identification method** determines the actual acquisition cost of each individual item in the ending inventory.

  The specific identification method is used most often in firms whose products have high unit costs, are easily differentiated, and are sold in relatively low volumes. For example, an automobile dealer uses auto serial numbers to record the exact cost of every car sold and every car remaining in inventory.

  When the specific identification method is used, there is more potential to manipulate the firm's income by selecting the particular unit cost to recognize as cost of goods sold.

- The cost flow assumptions assume that costs flow in one of the four different patterns (FIFO, LIFO, average cost, or specific identification) regardless of how the goods physically flow into and out of the firm.

Comparing the Methods

Rising Prices and FIFO

- In a period of rising prices, of the three inventory costing methods, FIFO produces the lowest cost of goods sold because the earliest and the lowest costs are allocated to cost of goods sold. This means that FIFO produces the highest gross profit, net income, and ending inventory amounts.

- Many accountants approve of using FIFO because ending inventories are recorded at costs that approximate their current acquisition or replacement cost. Thus, inventories are realistically valued on the firm's balance sheet.

- Accountants criticize FIFO because it matches the earliest costs against current sales and results in the highest gross profit. Some accountants argue that these profits are overstated.

- **Inventory profits** are profits that are realized when current revenue is matched with low historical inventory costs that do not approximate the current replacement cost of inventory.

- A **holding gain** is profit that is caused by the increase in the acquisition price of the inventory between the time that the firm purchased the item and when it was sold.

Rising Prices and LIFO

- In a period of rising prices, LIFO results in the highest cost of goods sold because the latest and highest costs are allocated to cost of goods sold. This results in the lowest gross profit, net income, and ending inventory amounts.

- Under LIFO, the ending inventory is recorded at the lowest cost because the earliest and lowest prices are allocated to inventory. If a company switched to LIFO 20 years ago, the original LIFO layers, if unsold, would be cost at 20-year-old prices.

- LIFO is criticized because the inventory cost on the balance sheet often is unrealistically low. Therefore, working capital, the current ratio, and current assets tend to be understated.

  However, many argue that LIFO provides a more realistic income figure because it eliminates a substantial portion of inventory profit.

- In summary, in periods of rising prices, LIFO usually provides a realistic income statement at the expense of the balance sheet.

  Conversely, FIFO provides a realistic balance sheet at the expense of the income statement.

  In a period of falling prices, the reverse is true. In either case, average cost will fall between FIFO and LIFO.

How Current Cost Can Alleviate the Problem

- **Current cost** is an item's current acquisition cost.

- When current costs are used, cost of goods sold is recorded at the current cost of the item at the time of its resale.

- Thus, the gross profit figure (the difference between sales and the current cost of goods sold) represents income available to the firm to cover operating expenses after maintaining its ability to purchase new inventory.

- On the balance sheet, ending inventory is recorded at the current cost at the statement date. The difference between the current cost of the ending inventory and its historical cost is considered a holding gain.

- Current cost accounting is not a generally accepted accounting principle for primary financial statements. FASB Statement No. 33, as amended by Statement No. 89, suggests that firms disclose income from continuing operations on a current-cost basis and the current-cost amounts of inventory and property, plant, and equipment at the end of the year. Not many firms choose to make these disclosures.

CHOOSING AMONG GENERALLY ACCEPTED ACCOUNTING PRINCIPLES

- In many instances, management can choose one accounting method for tax purposes and another method for financial reporting purposes. For example, management can use accelerated depreciation for tax purposes and straight-line depreciation for financial reporting purposes.

Motivation for Selecting Certain Accounting Methods

- The motivation of management when selecting accounting methods for tax purposes is often to postpone or reduce current tax payments.

- The selection of accounting principles for external financial reporting may be motivated by:
  - increasing the "bottom line" (net income)
  - enhancing management's own compensation
  - providing reliable financial reports

- The motivations in selecting accounting principles for tax purposes may conflict with those in selecting accounting principles for financial reporting purposes, because often management wishes to reduce taxable income while at the same time increasing reported accounting income.

In many cases, this is not a problem because management can select one principle for tax purposes and another for financial reporting purposes. When deciding whether to use FIFO or LIFO, however, this is not the case.

Selecting FIFO or LIFO

• The Internal Revenue Code contains a provision called the *LIFO conformity rule*, which requires a company to use LIFO for financial reporting purposes if LIFO is used for tax purposes.

This is one of the few situations in which the choice of accounting principles for tax and financial reporting purposes cannot be made independently.

The LIFO conformity rule is intended to keep business from reporting low earnings (using LIFO) to the government while reporting high earnings (using FIFO) to stockholders and other financial statement users.

• In periods of rising prices, LIFO will reduce the current period's taxable income and taxes, thus increasing cash flows. It is argued that increased cash flows enhance stockholders' wealth, even though reported earnings are lower. Further, many financial analysts have begun to evaluate a firm's quality of earnings.

• **Quality of earnings** is a qualitative measure of the extent to which reported earnings are the result of economic events rather than the result of accounting principles.

• Accounting research has generally indicated that the stock market is not fooled by reported earnings and recognizes the value of the increased cash flows available to LIFO firms versus those available to FIFO firms.

Issues Related to LIFO

• Some of the issues and problems related to LIFO that can decrease its advantages are:
1. Falling prices. LIFO-based earnings and income taxes are higher when prices decrease because the latest and lowest prices are allocated to cost of goods sold.
2. LIFO liquidation. **LIFO liquidation** is the sale of prior year inventory layers and occurs when a firm sells more units than it purchases in any one year. LIFO layers that have built up in the past are liquidated and included in the current period's cost of goods sold. The result is a lower cost of goods sold, higher gross profit, higher taxable income, and higher taxes.
3. Purchasing behavior. The use of LIFO, especially in connection with the periodic inventory method, offers management a certain degree of flexibility to manipulate profits. By timing purchases at year-end, management is able to determine what costs will be allocated to cost of goods sold.
4. Inventory turnover. **Inventory turnover** is the rate at which a company sells its inventory. The advantage of LIFO over FIFO is not as great when a company has a high turnover rate.

INVENTORY VALUATION--LOWER OF COST OR MARKET

- **Lower of cost or market (LCM)** is a conservative approach to inventory valuation that reports inventory at the lower of historical acquisition cost or the current market value.

  The concept of conservatism takes precedence over the historical cost convention. There is an assumption that a decrease in the replacement cost of an item will result in a corresponding decrease in its sales price and the loss should be recognized in the period when the price decline occurs, not in a later period when the item is sold.

- When applying the lower-of-cost-or-market rule:
  1. Determine the cost of ending inventory using one of the following cost flow assumptions:
     - LIFO
     - FIFO
     - average cost
     - specific identification
  2. Determine market (replacement cost to purchase a similar item)
  3. Determine the lower of cost or market

- Under generally accepted accounting principles, the comparison can be made on:
  1. an item-by-item basis
  2. a group-of-items basis, or
  3. the inventory as a whole

- The item-by-item method is the most conservative and results in the lowest inventory value because increase in the value of one item cannot offset decreases in other items, as is the case under the group and total inventory methods.

Lower of Cost or Market and Income Taxes

- For tax purposes, only FIFO (not LIFO) can be used in conjunction with lower of cost or market.

- For generally accepted accounting purposes, LIFO combined with lower of cost or market is a valid method.

- For tax purposes, lower of cost or market can be applied only on an item-by-item basis. The group and total inventory methods cannot be used.

USING INVENTORY DATA FOR DECISION MAKING

- Because inventories have a substantial effect on both the balance sheet and the income statement, they offer important data to investors and managers in evaluating a firm's financial performance and position.

- Two ratios often used are:
  1. **Gross profit percentage** calculated as follows:

     Gross Profit Percentage = Gross Profit/Sales

  2. **Inventory turnover** calculated as follows:

     Inventory Turnover = Cost of Goods Sold/Average Inventory

     Inventory Turnover in Days = 365 Days/Inventory Turnover

- Inventory turnover indicates how quickly a firm is able to sell its inventory. The more quickly the inventory turns over:
  1. the less cash the firm has tied up in inventory.
  2. the less need there is for inventory financing.
  3. the less chance there is for obsolescence or spoilage.

- Too quick a turnover may result in stockouts and lost sales.

- *Just-in-Time (JIT) manufacturing and purchasing* has materials delivered just in time for production needs and goods produced just in time for customers to buy them.

- A firm using JIT would want very low inventories and a very high inventory turnover.

- Inventory turnover is sensitive to the cost flow assumption used. When prices are rising, inventory turnover under LIFO is apt to be higher than under FIFO because under LIFO, cost of goods sold (the numerator) is higher, and average inventories (the denominator) is lower.

THE DESIGN OF ACCOUNTING SYSTEMS FOR INVENTORIES

- Often management may choose among several different generally accepted accounting principles, and the choice may affect the reported financial position and net income of the firm.

  The selection of an accounting principle or method may also have a significant effect on the design of the accounting information system.

EXERCISE 1 (continued)

2. LIFO

3. Average cost

EXERCISE 2

The Mollett Company uses the lower-of-cost-or-market convention in valuing its inventory. The company has divided its product into two groups, with two types within each group. The following schedule presents the relevant data as of December 31.

	Group 1		Group 2	
	Type A	Type B	Type C	Type D
Number of units	60	150	150	220
Selling price per unit	$25	$30	$40	$15
Replacement cost per unit—12/31	10	15	18	14
Cost per unit	8	16	20	12

Required:

Determine at what amount the ending inventory should be shown, assuming that the firm applies the lower-of-cost-or-market rule using:

1. An item-by-item basis.

2. A group basis.

3. A total inventory basis.

EXERCISE 2

			LCM Item-by-Item	LCM Group	LCM Total
Group 1					

Type A Cost = 60 x $ 8 = $ 480   Market = 60 x $10 = $ 600 $ 480
Type B Cost = 150 x $16 = 2,400   Market = 150 x $15 = 2,250   2,250

Total Group 1 $2,880 $2,850 $2,850

Group 2

Type C Cost = 150 x $20 = $3,000   Market = 150 x $18 = $2,700   2,700
Type D Cost = 220 X $12   2,640   Market = 220 x $14 = 3,080   2,640

Total Group 2 $5,640 $5,780   5,640

Total inventory $8,520 $8,630 $8,520

                                                                       $8,070 $8,490 $8,520

1. Item-by-item: $8,070
2. Group: $8,490
3. Total inventory: $8,520

EXERCISE 3

Cost of goods sold--Year 1	$380,000
Corrections:	
Beginning inventory overstated	(10,000)
Ending inventory understated	(5,500)
Corrected cost of goods sold	$364,500

Cost of goods sold--Year 2	$400,000
Corrections:	
Beginning inventory understated	5,500
Corrected cost of goods sold	$405,500

1.

	Year 1	Year 2
Sales	$600,000	$540,000
Cost of goods sold	364,500	405,500
Gross profit	$235,500	$134,500
Operating expenses	140,000	115,000
Net income	$ 95,500	$ 19,500

2.

Retained earnings--end of Year 2	$450,000
Add: increase in net income--Year 1	15,500
Less: decrease in net income--Year 2	(5,500)
Adjusted retained earnings	$460,000

PRESENT VALUE MODULE

CHAPTER REVIEW

INTRODUCTION

- The time value of money is the concept that a dollar received today is worth more than a dollar to be received one year from today.

- The dollar received today can be invested to earn a return.

SIMPLE VERSUS COMPOUND INTEREST

- Interest is payment for the use of money.

- There are two types of interest:
  1. **Simple interest**: the interest is paid each interest period.
  2. **Compound interest**: instead of being paid each period, the interest is added to the previous balance. In following periods, interest is earned on the interest added to the balance.

- Interest can be compounded annually, quarterly, monthly, daily, or continuously.

- If interest is compounded quarterly, there are four interest periods in each year. If the annual interest rate is 12%, the quarterly rate would be 3%.

        Annual Interest Rate/Interest Period Per Year
        = 12%/4 periods = 3% per interest period

FUTURE VALUE OF A SINGLE AMOUNT

- **Future value of a single amount** is the amount to which the investment will grow by a future date if interest is compounded.

- If interest is compounded, the future value can be calculated as follows:

$$\text{Future Value} = p(1 + i)^n$$

where: p = principal amount or present value
        i = interest rate
        n = number of compounding periods

- The future value can also be calculated using future value factors (FVF) contained in Table 1 of Appendix B of this study guide. The following formula is used to calculate future values:

Future Value = Future Value Factor x Principal (Present Value)

- For example, the future value in two years of $1,000 invested today, earning 10% interest compounded annually, would be calculated as follows:

Future Value = Future Value Factor (10%, n=2) x Present Value
             = 1.21000 x $1,000
             = $1,210

If interest was compounded quarterly, the interest rate would be 2.5% per quarter (10% annual rate/4 periods per year). There would be a total of 8 interest periods (2 years x 4 interest periods per year). The future value would be calculated as follows:

Future Value = Future Value Factor (2.5%, n=8) x Present Value
             = 1.21840 x $1,000
             = $1,218.40

- This formula can also be used to determine the required interest rate. For example, assume you invest $1,000 for five years. The rate of return necessary to accumulate $1,469.33 at the end of five years is determined as follows:

Future Value = Future Value Factor x Present Value
Future Value Factor = Future Value/Present Value
Future Value Factor = $1,469.33/$1,000.00
Future Value Factor = 1.46933

In Table 1, locate the future value factor of 1.46933, n=5. This factor is found under 8%, the required rate of return.

PRESENT VALUE OF A SINGLE AMOUNT

- The **present value of a single amount** is the amount that must be invested now in order to produce a given future amount assuming compounding at a given interest rate.

- The present value of a future amount can be calculated using the following formula:

Present Value = Present Value Factor x Future Value

- The present value factors for a single amount are found in Table 3 of Appendix B.

- The present value of $2,000 to be received in 3 years, earning 9% interest would be calculated as follows:

$$\text{Present Value} = \text{Present Value Factor (9\%, n=3)} \times \text{Future Value}$$
$$= .77218 \times \$2,000$$
$$= \$1,544,36$$

FUTURE VALUE OF AN ANNUITY

- An **annuity** is a series of equal cash flows.

- A payment made at the beginning of the period is called an *annuity due*.

- A payment made at the end of the period is called an *ordinary annuity*.

- The **future value of an annuity** is the sum of all the periodic payments plus the interest that has accumulated.

- The future value of an annuity is calculated using the following formula:

$$\text{Future Value of an Annuity} = \text{FVAF} \times \text{Present Value Annuity}$$

where FVAF = Future Value Annuity Factor. Future value annuity factors are contained in Table 2 of Appendix B of this study guide.

- The future value of $1,000 to be received each year for 5 years, earning 10% interest, would be:

$$\text{Future Value of an Annuity} = \text{FVAF (10\%, n=5)} \times \text{Present Value Annuity}$$
$$= 6.10510 \times \$1,000$$
$$= \$6,105.10$$

- The amount of interest earned can be determined as follows:

Future value	$6,105.10
Annuity payments ($1,000 x 5 years)	(5,000.00)
Interest earned	$1,105.10

PRESENT VALUE OF AN ANNUITY

• The **present value of an annuity** is the value today of a series of equal payments that occur in the future.

• The present value of an annuity is calculated using the following formula:

Present Value of an Annuity = PVAF x Future Value Annuity

where PVAF = Present Value Annuity Factor.

• Present value annuity factors are contained in Table 4 of Appendix B.

• The present value of a 3-year, $2,000 annuity earning 10% interest would be:

Present Value of an Annuity = PVAF (10%, n=3) x Future Value Annuity
= 2.48685 x $2,000
= $4,973.70

ACCOUNTING APPLICATIONS OF THE TIME VALUE OF MONEY

• Present values are used to value long-term liabilities.

KEY TERMS TEST

Test your recall of the key terms as follows: Read the following definitions of key terms and try to recall as many key terms as you can *without assistance*. Write your answers in the spaces provided. If you need assistance, refer to the list of key terms at the end of this section.

1. _____ _____ is the interest amount for one or more periods, assuming that the amount on which interest is computed stays the same.

2. _____ _____ is interest computed on the principal plus any previously accrued interest.

3. The _____ _____ _____ _____ _____ _____ is the amount of a current single amount taken to a future date at a specified interest rate.

4. The _____ _____ _____ _____ _____ _____ is the value of a future promise to pay or receive a single amount at a specified interest rate.

5. A(n) _____ is a series of equal payments or receipts at regular intervals.

6. The _____ _____ _____ _____ _____ is the amount of a series of payments or receipts taken to a future date at a specified interest rate.

7. The _____ _____ _____ _____ _____ is the present value of a series of future promises to pay or receive an annuity at a specified interest rate.

KEY TERMS:

annuity
compound interest
future value of an annuity
future value of a single amount

present value of an annuity
present value of a single amount
simple interest

Compare your answers to those at the end of the chapter and review any key terms missed.

CHAPTER QUIZ

Write your answers in the spaces provided.

1. Two types of interest are:
    1. _____
    2. _____

2. The present value of a single amount can be calculated using factors and the following formula:

    Present Value of a Single Amount = _____ X _____

3. The present value of an annuity can be calculated using factors and the following formula:

    Present Value of an Annuity = _____ X _____

4. The future value of a single amount can be calculated using factors and the following formula:

    Future Value of a Single Amount = _____ X _____

5. The future value of an annuity can be calculated using factors and the following formula:

Future Value of an Annuity = _____ x _____

Circle the best answer.

6. The present value of $10,000 to be received 5 years from now and earning an annual return of 8% is: (a) $6,210; (b) $6,805.80; (c) $4,000; (d) $4,693.30

7. The present value of a 5-year annuity of $10,000, earning an annual return of 8% is: (a) $31,700.50; (b) $34,029; (c) $37,910; (d) $39,927.10

8. $10,000 invested today and earning an annual return of 8% would have a future value at the end of 6 years of: (a) $12,226.53; (b) $15,233.40; (c) $15,868.70; (d) $16,301.70

9. The future value of a $10,000 annuity for 6 years, earning 8% would be: (a) $98,974.70; (b) $73,359.30; (c) $69,753.20; (d) $58,666.67

EXERCISES

EXERCISE 1

A generous grandfather has offered to deposit enough money in an account to pay your college tuition for four years, starting one year from today. The account would earn 9% interest, and college tuition would be $12,000 per year. How much should your grandfather deposit in the account today?

EXERCISE 2

In five years you plan to buy a house, and you want to save $20,000 for the down payment. If you earn 7% annually, how much would you have to invest at the end of each of the next five years in order to accumulate $20,000?

EXERCISE 3

If you invest $15,000 today and earn 12% compounded quarterly, how much would you have at the end of six years?

EXERCISE 4

If you have a $5,000 investment that will accumulate to $7,518.12 at the end of seven years, what rate of interest would you earn, compounded annually?

ANSWERS

<u>KEY TERMS TEST</u>
1. Simple interest
2. Compound interest
3. future value of a single amount
4. present value of a single amount
5. annuity
6. future value of an annuity
7. present value of an annuity

<u>CHAPTER QUIZ</u>
1. 1. simple interest
   2. compound interest
2. Present Value of a Single Amount = Present Value Factor x Future Value
3. Present Value of an Annuity = PVAF x Future Value Annuity
4. Future Value of a Single Amount = Future Value Factor x Present Value
5. Future Value of an Annuity = FVAF x Present Value Annuity
6. b ($10,000 x .68058) = $6,805.80
7. d ($10,000 x 3.99271) = $39,927.10
8. c ($10,000 x 1.58687) = $15,868.70
9. b ($10,000 x 7.33593) = $73,359.30

<u>EXERCISE 1</u>

Present Value of an Annuity = PVAF (9%, n=4) x FV Annuity
                           = 3.23972 x $12,000
                           = $38,876.64

<u>EXERCISE 2</u>

Future Value of an Annuity = FVAF x PV Annuity
                  $20,000 = 5.75074 x PV Annuity
               PV Annuity = $20,000/5.75074
               PV Annuity = $3,477.81

<u>EXERCISE 3</u>

12%/4 interest periods = 3% per quarter

6 years x 4 periods = 24 interest periods

FV of a Single Amount = FV Factor (3%, n=24) x PV
                      = 2.03279 x $15,000
                      = $30,491.85

EXERCISE 4

PV of a Single Amount = PV Factor (n=7) x FV
                $5,000 = PV Factor (n=7) x $7,518.12
            PV Factor = $5,000/$7,518.12
            PV Factor = 0.66506

A PV Factor of 0.66506, n=7, corresponds to 6% interest.

CHAPTER 10

INVESTMENTS IN
OPERATING AND INTANGIBLE ASSETS

CHAPTER REVIEW

INTRODUCTION

- **Operating assets** are the assets used to conduct business operations and include:
  1. property, plant, and equipment
  2. intangible assets

CAPITAL BUDGETING

- **Capital budgeting** is the process of planning, setting goals and priorities, arranging financing, and identifying criteria for making long-term investments.

- Capital budgeting decisions involve choosing among competing investment alternatives.

- Capital budgeting decisions such as the purchase of operating assets are basically cash flow decisions. The firm gives up cash flows today (the purchase price) and in the future (operating outlays) in the expectation of receiving a greater amount of cash flows in the future as the asset generates revenues and/or produces cost savings.

NONCURRENT, NONMONETARY ASSETS

- Noncurrent, nonmonetary assets often are categorized as either:
  1. tangible assets, or
  2. intangible assets.

- **Tangible assets** are assets that have physical substance and include:
  - property, plant, and equipment.
  - **natural resources** (physical substances that, when taken from the ground, produce revenues for the firm). Examples of natural resources include oil, natural gas, coal, iron ore, uranium, and timber.

- **Intangible assets** are assets that have no physical substance. Instead, they provide future benefit to the firm by providing the right of ownership or legal benefits. Examples of intangibles assets include:
  - patents
  - copyrights
  - leaseholds
  - trademarks
  - franchises
  - goodwill

- All noncurrent, nonmonetary assets have the following common characteristics:
  1. They represent future economic services.
  2. They benefit several accounting periods.
  3. They are systematically allocated to the periods in which the benefits are received (except for land).

Future Services Not Held for Resale

- Property, plant, and equipment are acquired by an enterprise because of their ability to generate future revenues and ultimately cash flows.

- Assets not currently being used in the merchandising or production process are not included in the property, plant, and equipment category. For example, a warehouse that is no longer being used or land held for speculation are included in the long-term investment category on the balance sheet.

  Land that a real estate firm holds for resale is shown in the inventory section of the balance sheet.

Long-Term Nature of the Assets

- The economic or service life of a noncurrent, nonmonetary asset is the period of time that a firm expects to receive benefits from the asset.

Allocation of Benefits to Accounting Periods

- The matching convention requires that the cost of expired benefits be matched with the revenues they produce.

- The major categories of noncurrent, nonmonetary assets and the expenses associated with the cost allocation process are listed below:

Asset Category	Expense
Tangible assets	
Land	None
Plant, buildings, equipment	Depreciation
Natural resources	Depletion
Intangible assets	Amortization

CAPITAL VERSUS REVENUE EXPENDITURES

- An **expenditure** is the payment of an asset or incurrence of a liability in exchange for another asset or for a service rendered.

- A **capital expenditure** is an expenditure that results in the acquisition of an operating asset.

- A **revenue expenditure** is the purchase of goods or services whose benefits are consumed in the current period.

- Capital expenditures affect several future accounting periods, whereas revenue expenditures affect only the current period.

- If an error is made and a capital expenditure is recorded as a revenue expenditure:
  1. The current period's income will be understated because the entire expenditure was expensed when only a portion of it, the current year's depreciation, should have been expensed.
  2. Future periods' income will be overstated because no depreciation expense is recorded in those years.

  Over the useful life of the asset the error is self-correcting, but the interim incomes are misstated.

MEASURING AND RECORDING THE ACQUISITION COST OF PROPERTY, PLANT, AND EQUIPMENT

- The acquisition cost of property, plant, and equipment includes all reasonable and necessary costs required to get the asset in place and ready for use.

- The acquisition cost of equipment includes:
  - transportation costs
  - insurance in transit
  - installation
  - testing costs
  - normal repairs needed before putting the asset into service

- The acquisition cost of land includes:
  - purchase price of the land
  - real estate commissions
  - title fees
  - legal fees
  - delinquent property taxes
  - the cost to drain, grade, and clear

Cash Acquisitions

- The acquisition price of property, plant, and equipment is the cash price paid plus all other costs necessary to get the asset ready to use.

Other Methods of Acquiring Property, Plant, and Equipment

- A firm can acquire property, plant, and equipment in a variety of ways other than by direct cash purchase, such as:
  - basket purchases
  - noncash exchanges
  - donations
  - self-construction
  - leases

Basket Purchases

- Property, plant, and equipment often are purchased together in one lump sum. The agreed upon purchase price represents the total cost of both the building and the land.

- In a basket purchase, the total purchase price must be allocated between the individual assets.

Noncash Exchanges

- The acquisition price of the asset is equal to the cash given plus the fair market value of any noncash consideration.

- If it is difficult or impossible to determine with reasonable accuracy the fair market value of the noncash consideration, the market value of the particular asset that is purchased should be used.

- For example, if stock is issued in exchange for land, the land would be recorded at the fair market value of the stock.

      Debit: Land
        Credit: Capital Stock

Donations

- Donated assets are recorded at their fair market value at the time they are received.

- The entry to record a donated asset would be:

      Debit: Land
        Credit: Donated Capital

Self-Constructed Assets

- **Self-constructed assets** are assets such as a building or equipment that is constructed by the enterprise.

- The acquisition cost of self-constructed assets includes:
  - materials and labor used in the construction process.
  - overhead costs, such as supervisory labor, utilities, and depreciation on the factory building.
  - interest costs incurred during construction and related to the financing of the construction.

Leasing Operating Assets

- Leasing operating assets is in some cases similar to financing a purchase through a bank loan.

- If the lease is in substance a purchase, the asset acquired is recorded in the property, plant, and equipment section of the balance sheet.

- The leased asset is depreciated.

- The lease liability is shown as a liability (current for payments within the next twelve months and noncurrent for the remaining payments) on the balance sheet.

THE ACCOUNTING CONCEPT OF DEPRECIATION

- **Depreciation** is the process of allocating the cost of operating assets to the periods in which the enterprise receives benefits from these assets.

- **Depletion** is the allocation of the cost of natural resources to the periods in which the enterprise receives benefits from the assets.

- **Amortization** is the process of allocating the cost of intangible assets to the proper accounting periods.

Depreciation Is an Allocation Process

- The cost of the asset is allocated to the periods in which the enterprise receives benefits from the asset.

Depreciation Is Not a Valuation Concept

- A common misconception is that depreciation represents a decrease in the value of an asset.

- Depreciation is used to allocate the <u>cost</u> of an asset over its estimated useful life, regardless of current market value.

Depreciation Is Not a Direct Source of Cash

• Another common misconception regarding depreciation is that it is a source of cash.

• Depreciation is a noncash expense because it does not require a cash payment at the time the expense is recorded.

• The cash outlay occurs when the payment for the related asset is made.

What Causes Depreciation?

• Two factors that cause a tangible asset to give up its economic benefits are:
1. deterioration
2. obsolescence

Physical Deterioration

• Tangible assets deteriorate because of use, the passage of time, and exposure to the elements such as weather.

Obsolescence

• **Obsolescence** is the process of becoming outdated, outmoded, or inadequate.

• Certain high-tech equipment, such as computers, are subject to rapid obsolescence.

METHODS OF COMPUTING DEPRECIATION

• The four most common depreciation methods are:
1. straight-line
2. units-of-production
3. declining-balance
4. sum-of-the-years-digits

Factors in Computing Depreciation

• Factors in computing depreciation are:
1. Residual or salvage value (management's best estimate of what an asset will be worth at the time of its disposal)
2. **Depreciable cost.** Depreciable cost or depreciable base is calculated as follows:

Depreciable Cost = Acquisition Cost - Residual Value

3. **Estimated useful or economic life.** Estimated useful life is the service potential that the current user may expect from an asset.

Methods of Computing Depreciation

Straight-Line Depreciation Method

- **Straight-line depreciation** is calculated as follows:

   Straight-Line Depreciation = (Cost - Salvage Value)/Useful Life

- When the straight-line method is used, depreciation expense is the same amount each year.

- Straight-line depreciation is widely used because of its simplicity and the fact that it allocates an equal amount of expense to each period of the asset's life.

Units-of-Production Depreciation Method

- The **units-of-production depreciation** method assumes that the primary depreciation factor is use rather than the passage of time.

- When the units-of-production method is used, depreciation per unit is calculated as follows:

   Depreciation Per Unit = (Cost - Salvage Value)/Estimated Total Production in Units

- Depreciation expense is calculated as:

   Depreciation Expense = Depreciation Per Unit x Number of Units

Accelerated Depreciation Methods

- **Accelerated depreciation methods** allocate a greater portion of an asset's cost to the early years of its useful life and less to later years.

- Accelerated depreciation methods are based on the assumption that some assets produce greater benefits or revenues in their earlier years, and thus a greater portion of their cost should be allocated to those years.

- The two most common accelerated methods are:
   1. declining-balance depreciation
   2. sum-of-the-years-digits depreciation

Declining-Balance Depreciation

- **Declining-balance depreciation** calculates yearly depreciation by applying a fixed percentage rate to an asset's remaining book value at the beginning of each year.

- Declining-balance depreciation is calculated as follows:

Declining-Balance Depreciation = Declining-Balance Rate x Book Value at Beginning of Year

- Double-declining balance depreciation uses a rate that is double the straight-line rate.

- 150%-declining-balance depreciation uses a rate that is 150% of the straight-line rate.

Sum-of-the-Years-Digits Depreciation Method

- Under the **sum-of-the-years-digits** depreciation method, the asset's depreciable base (cost less salvage value) is multiplied by a declining rate.

- Sum-of-the-years-digits depreciation is calculated as follows:

(Cost - Salvage Value) x SYD Rate

- The sum-of-the-years-digits (SYD) rate is a fraction where:
  - the numerator equals the number of years remaining in the asset's life at the beginning of the year, and
  - the denominator is the sum of the digits of the asset's useful life.

Comparison of Depreciation Methods

- Management can choose straight-line depreciation for financial reporting purposes and accelerated depreciation for tax purposes. This allows a firm to report higher income for financial statement purposes and lower income for tax return purposes.

- Theoretically, for financial reporting purposes, the best depreciation method is the one that allocates the cost of the individual asset to the years of its useful life in the same pattern as the benefits or revenues that the asset produces.

Selecting a Depreciation Method for Tax Purposes

- Under the Tax Reform Act of 1986, depreciable business property other than real estate is assigned to one of six classes or recovery periods.

- Recovery periods prescribe the length of time over which various assets can be written off or depreciated.

- Some of the recovery periods are:

3-Year Class	Small tools
5-Year Class	Light trucks, automobiles, computer equipment, typewriters, calculators, copiers, assets used in research and development, oil and gas drilling, construction, and the manufacture of products such as chemical and electronic components
7-Year Class	Office furniture and fixtures and most other machinery and equipment

- The Tax Reform Act of 1986 developed the Modified Accelerated Cost Recovery System (MACRS).

- Tax rules for depreciation require use of the half-year convention. This means that for tax purposes, property is depreciated for half the taxable year in which it is placed in service, regardless of when use actually begins.

- During the early years of an asset's life, depreciation expense for tax purposes exceeds depreciation expense for financial reporting purposes. Higher depreciation expense for tax purposes means lower taxable income and thus lower tax payments. In later years, these benefits reverse and depreciation for financial reporting purposes exceeds that for tax purposes.

  The fact that tax payments are deferred until later years benefits the firm, since it is able to invest and earn a return on the cash saved through lower taxes in the early years.

OTHER PROBLEMS RELATED TO DEPRECIATION

Depreciation for a Partial Year

- Two common conventions used to calculate partial-year depreciation are:
  1. Depreciation expense is calculated for the entire year if the asset is purchased in the first half of the year. If the asset is purchased in the last half of the year, no depreciation is taken.
  2. Six months of depreciation is taken in the year of purchase and six months in the year of retirement or disposal, regardless of the date of actual disposal. This is called the six-month convention and is built into the IRS tax depreciation tables for assets other than real estate.

Revision of Depreciation

- Useful economic life and residual value are estimates made at the time an asset is purchased. Later events may require that these original estimates be revised.

- Changes in depreciation estimates are handled by spreading the remaining undepreciated base (undepreciated cost or book value less estimated residual value) of the asset over the years of the new remaining useful life. Only <u>current</u> year's and <u>future</u> years' depreciation are affected.

- The remaining depreciable base is spread over the new remaining life.

  Revised Depreciation Expense = Remaining Depreciable Base/Remaining Useful Life

  Revised Depreciation Expense = (Book Value - Residual Value)/Remaining Useful Life

- A change in depreciation method, such as a change from sum-of-the-years-digits to straight-line depreciation, requires a separate item on the income statement labeled as a cumulative effect of an accounting change.

Arbitrary Allocation

- Depreciation expense is an example of an allocation that is based on estimates.

- In analyzing financial statements with ratios and other techniques, it is important to keep in mind that these estimates limit the usefulness of the financial information.

Inflation and Depreciation

- Historical cost is the primary basis for recording assets; periodic depreciation is based on the historical cost of assets. Many people feel that when price levels rise in the economy, historical-cost depreciation overstates profits and does not provide a reasonable picture of a firm's financial position.

- In the United States, the FASB urges public companies to make supplemental disclosure of certain current costs; however, not many companies provide these supplemental disclosures.

- In countries where inflation is a chronic economic problem, it is often required that companies disclose inflation-adjusted data.

ACCOUNTING FOR SUBSEQUENT EXPENDITURES

Revenue Expenditures

- Revenue expenditures are expenditures for the purchase of goods and services whose benefits are used up or consumed in the current period.

- Revenue expenditures are usually for repairs and maintenance.

- **Repairs or maintenance** is an expenditure that maintains the asset's expected level of service or output, neither extending its useful life nor increasing the quantity or quality of its output.

- The entry to record revenue expenditures would be:

  Debit: Repairs and Maintenance
    Credit: Cash (or Payables)

Capital Expenditures Subsequent to Purchase

- Capital expenditures benefit several accounting periods.

- Capital expenditures may be:
  1. the acquisition of an operating asset
  2. additions
  3. betterments
  4. extraordinary repairs

- **Additions** are enlargements, such as the addition of a new wing to an existing building.

- **Betterments** are improvements to existing assets, such as installing energy-efficient windows.

- **Extraordinary repairs** consist of major reconditioning or overhaul of existing assets, such as the overhaul of an engine.

- Capital expenditures either:
  1. extend the asset's useful life, or
  2. increase the quantity or quality of its output.

- In the case of an addition to a building, the entry to record the capital expenditure would be:

  Debit: Asset account
    Credit: Cash (or Liability)

- For other capital expenditures, the entry usually is:

  Debit: Accumulated Depreciation
    Credit: Cash (or Liability)

DISPOSAL OF OPERATING ASSETS

- Disposal of operating assets occurs through:
  - retirements
  - sales
  - trade-ins

- Two entries to record a disposal are:
  1. record depreciation up to the date of disposal
  2. record the gain or loss on disposal

Sale of Operating Assets

- The gain or loss on the sale of operating assets is calculated as:

  Cash (or other assets) received
  - Book value (cost - accumulated depreciation)
  = Gain or loss on sale

- A gain occurs if the cash or other assets received (referred to as consideration) are greater than the book value at the time of sale.

- A loss occurs if the consideration received is less than the book value at the time of sale.

- The entry to record a gain on the sale of equipment would be:

  Debit: Cash
  Debit: Accumulated Depreciation
    Credit: Equipment (cost)
    Credit: Gain on Disposal of Equipment

- The entry to record a loss on the sale of equipment would be:

  Debit: Cash
  Debit: Accumulated Depreciation
  Debit: Loss on Disposal of Equipment
    Credit: Equipment

Trade-in of Operating Assets

- When an operating asset is traded in for a similar one, a gain is not recognized, though a loss is always recognized.

Method of Disposal	Is Gain/Loss Recognized?
Sale of asset at realized gain	Yes
Sale of asset at realized loss	Yes
Trade-in of asset for similar asset at realized gain	No
Trade-in of asset for similar asset at realized loss	Yes

Gain Realized But Not Recognized

- <u>Realized</u> refers to an actual economic gain.

- <u>Recognized</u> means the gain is recorded in the accounting records.

- When an asset is traded in on a similar asset, the gain is realized but not recognized.

- The cost basis of the new asset is calculated as follows:

> **Book value of old asset**
> **+ Cash paid**
> **= Cost basis of new asset**

- The entry to record the trade-in of similar assets when the gain is unrecognized is:

  Debit: Asset (New)
  Debit: Accumulated Depreciation: Old Asset
   Credit: Asset (Old)
   Credit: Cash

Loss Realized and Recognized

- When an asset is traded in on a similar asset, the loss is both realized and recognized. Any realized losses must be recognized because of the concept of conservatism.

- The entry to record the trade-in for a similar asset when a loss is realized is:

  Debit: Asset (New)
  Debit: Accumulated Depreciation: Old Asset
  Debit: Loss on Disposal of Asset
   Credit: Asset (Old)
   Credit: Cash

ACCOUNTING INFORMATION SYSTEMS FOR OPERATING ASSETS

- The components of an operating-asset accounting system include:
  1. control policies and procedures.
  2. the procedures or computer programs designed to process transactions.

Operating Asset Controls

- Operating asset controls include:
  1. Only authorized employees are permitted access to assets.
  2. Complete inventory records provide detective and corrective controls. The inventory records should identify the location of each operating asset and, when appropriate, the individual responsible for the asset.
  3. Adequate insurance coverage.
  4. Authorization controls to control operating asset transactions. Authorization is often required before an operating asset is purchased.
  5. Assurance that once authorized, the transactions are properly recorded in the operating asset records.

Operating Asset Records and Systems

- The three major sources of input into this system are:
  1. disbursement vouchers for the initial acquisition of an asset.
  2. disposal authorizations to provide evidence of managements' approval for the disposal of an asset.
  3. asset adjustment forms used to document changes in depreciation estimates and to document additional capital expenditures associated with an asset.

- The operating-asset accounting system:
  1. updates the operating-asset master file.
  2. prints reports.
  3. generates the necessary journal entries.
  4. periodically computes depreciation for all operating assets and generates the depreciation journal entries.

- The most common reports printed by an operating-asset accounting system are:
  1. the **operating-asset ledger**: a report that lists each operating asset and its corresponding acquisition date, cost, book value, salvage value, depreciation method, and life.
  2. the **location list**: a report that identifies each asset and its corresponding custodian and location.
  3. the **depreciation register**: a report that lists the current depreciation expense as computed for each operating asset.

- A **data base management system** is a program that accesses data for other application programs and users and manages the physical storage of data.

- The **relational data base** organizes data into tables and provides users and application programs with access to the necessary rows and columns of data.

  Columns in an operating-asset relational data base would include the asset identification number, asset description, and asset cost.

INTANGIBLE ASSETS

- Intangible assets are noncurrent, nonmonetary assets that have no physical properties.

- Two categories of intangible assets are:
  1. **specifically identifiable intangible assets**: intangibles whose costs can be easily identified as part of the cost of the asset and whose benefits generally have a determinable life. Examples include:
     - patents
     - copyrights
     - trademarks
     - franchises
     - leaseholds
  2. intangibles that are not specifically identifiable: intangibles that represent some right or benefit that has an indeterminate life and whose cost is inherent in a continuing business. An example is goodwill.

Accounting Problems Related to Intangible Assets

Determining Acquisition Cost

- Intangible assets originally are recorded at cost.

- The cost of an intangible asset includes all the expenditures necessary to get the intangible asset ready for its intended use. This would include the purchase price and any legal fees.

Research and Development Costs

- **Research and development costs** are expenditures incurred in discovering, planning, designing, and implementing a new product or process.

- Because it is difficult to measure the ultimate benefits that accrue from research and development expenditures, the FASB requires that all research and development costs be expensed in the period incurred.

Amortization of Intangible Assets

- The intangible asset should be amortized over its useful economic life or legal life, whichever is shorter, not to exceed 40 years.

Gains and Losses on Disposition

- When intangible assets are sold or disposed of, the gain or loss is calculated as:

> Cash received
> - Book value of intangible asset
> = Gain or loss

Accounting for Intangible Assets

Patents

- A **patent** is an exclusive right to use, manufacture, process, or sell a product.

- When a patent is purchased from the inventor, its cost includes its acquisition cost and other incidental costs, such as legal fees.

- The legal costs of successfully defending a patent also are capitalized as part of its cost.

- If a patent results from successful research and development efforts, its cost is only the legal or other fees necessary to patent the invention, product, or process. All research and development costs expended to develop the patent must be written off to expense in the period the expenditure occurs.

- A patent has a legal life of 17 years; however, its useful economic life may be less than 17 years, as in the case of computer chips.

- Patents should be amortized over their remaining legal life or economic life, whichever is shorter.

- The entry to record patent amortization would be:

    Debit: Amortization Expense
      Credit: Patent

Goodwill

- **Goodwill** is the present value of the excess earnings of a particular enterprise.

- Goodwill can only result when an entire business is purchased. The purchase price is first allocated to the identifiable net assets based on their fair market value. Any remaining portion is considered goodwill and is recorded by a debit to the Goodwill account. The entry to record a purchase is shown below.

    Debit: Inventory
    Debit: Property, Plant, and Equipment
    Debit: Other Assets
    Debit: Goodwill
      Credit: Liabilities
      Credit: Cash

- Goodwill is amortized over a period not exceeding 40 years.

OTHER DIMENSIONS OF ACCOUNTING FOR INVESTMENTS IN OPERATING ASSETS

International Dimensions of Accounting for Operating Assets

- Accounting for operating assets varies considerably in the international environment.

KEY TERMS TEST

Test your recall of the key terms as follows: Read the following definitions of key terms and try to recall as many key terms as you can *without assistance*. Write your answers in the spaces provided. If you need assistance, refer to the list of key terms at the end of this section.

1. _____ _____ are assets that are used to conduct business operations.

2. _____ _____ is the process of planning, setting goals and priorities, arranging financing, and identifying criteria for making long-term investments.

3. _____ _____ are assets that have physical substance and capabilities.

4. Physical substances that, when taken from the ground, produce revenues for a firm are _____ _____.

5. _____ _____ are assets that have no physical substance; rather, they give the enterprise the right of ownership or use.

6. A(n) _____ is the payment of an asset or the incurrence of a liability in exchange for another asset or for a service rendered.

7. An expenditure that results in the acquisition of an operating asset is a(n) _____ _____.

8. _____ _____ are the purchases of goods or services whose benefits are consumed in the current period.

9. A(n) _____ _____ is a building or piece of equipment constructed by the enterprise.

10. _____ is the process of allocating the cost of operational assets such as plant and equipment to the period in which the enterprise receives benefits from these assets.

11. _____ is the allocation of the cost of natural resources to the period in which the enterprise receives benefits from these assets.

12. _____ is the allocation of the cost of intangible assets to the period in which the enterprise receives benefits from these assets.

13. _____ is the process of becoming outdated, outmoded, or inadequate.

14. _____ _____ is the difference between an asset's acquisition cost and its estimated residual value.

15. _____ _____ _____ is the service potential that the current user may expect from the asset.

16. _____ _____ is a method where yearly depreciation is calculated by dividing an asset's depreciable cost by its estimated useful life.

17. _____ is a depreciation method that assumes that the primary depreciation factor is use rather than the passage of time.

18. Depreciation methods that allocate a greater portion of an asset's cost to the early years of its useful life and, consequently, less to later years are known as _____ _____ _____.

19. _____ _____ is a depreciation method in which yearly depreciation is calculated by applying an operating percentage rate to an asset's remaining book value at the beginning of each year.

20. _____ is an accelerated depreciation method in which the asset's depreciable base (cost less salvage value) is multiplied by a declining rate.

21. _____ _____ _____ is an expenditure that maintains the asset's expected level of service or output and neither extends its useful life nor increases the quantity or quality of its output.

22. _____ are asset enlargements, such as the addition of a new wing to an existing building.

23. _____ are improvements to existing assets.

24. _____ _____ is major reconditioning or overhaul of existing assets.

25. A(n) _____ _____ is a report that lists each operating asset and its corresponding acquisition date, cost, book value, salvage value, depreciation method, and life.

26. A(n) _____ _____ is a report that identifies each asset and its corresponding custodian and location.

27. A(n) _____ _____ is a report that lists the current depreciation expense as computed for each operating asset.

28. A(n) _____ _____ _____ _____ is a program that accesses data for other application programs and users and manages the physical storage of the data.

29. A(n) _____ _____ _____ is a data base in which data is stored in tabular form.

30. Those intangibles whose costs can be easily identified as part of the cost of the asset and whose asset's benefits generally have a determinable life are referred to as _____ _____ _____ _____.

31. _____ _____ _____ _____ are costs and expenditures incurred in discovering, planning, designing, and implementing a new product or process.

32. A(n) _____ is an exclusive right to use, manufacture, process, or sell a product.

33. _____ is the present value of the excess earnings of a particular enterprise.

KEY TERMS:

accelerated depreciation methods
additions
amortization
betterments
capital budgeting
capital expenditure
data base management system
declining-balance depreciation
depletion
depreciable cost
depreciation
depreciation register
estimated useful life
expenditure
extraordinary repairs
goodwill
intangible assets

location list
natural resources
operating assets
operating-asset ledger
obsolescence
patent
relational data base
repair or maintenance
research and development costs
revenue expenditures
self-constructed assets
specifically identifiable intangible assets
straight-line depreciation
sum-of-the-years-digits
tangible assets
units-of-production

Compare your answers to those at the end of the chapter and review any key terms missed.

CHAPTER QUIZ

Write your answers in the spaces provided.

Indicate the expense that is associated with the cost allocation process for each of the following assets:

Asset   Expense
_____   _____

1. Natural resources: _____

2. Buildings: _____

3. Intangible assets: _____

4. Land: _____

5. Equipment: _____

6. Two factors that cause a tangible asset to give up its economic benefits are:
   1. _____
   2. _____

7. List the four most common depreciation methods.
   1. _____
   2. _____
   3. _____
   4. _____

8. Depreciable cost is calculated as:

   Depreciable Cost = _____ - _____

9. Straight-line depreciation is calculated as:

   Straight-Line Depreciation = (_____ - _____) / _____

10. The gain or loss on the sale of operating assets is calculated as:

   _____

   - _____

   = _____

11. The three major sources of input into the accounting information system for operating assets are:
    1. _____
    2. _____
    3. _____

12. The most common reports printed by an operating-asset accounting system are:
    1. _____
    2. _____
    3. _____

13. Intangible assets are amortized over:
    1. _____, or
    2. _____
    whichever is shorter but not to exceed _____ years.

Circle the best answer.

14. Depreciation is the decrease in the value of an asset: (a) true; (b) false

15. Revenue expenditures increase the quantity or quality of output: (a) true; (b) false

16. A gain resulting from the trade-in of an asset for a similar asset is recognized: (a) true; (b) false

17. A realized loss resulting from the trade-in of an asset for a similar asset is recognized: (a) true; (b) false

18. Research and development costs are expensed in the period incurred: (a) true; (b) false

19. Painting a warehouse that has been used in operations for the past eight years would be a: (a) revenue expenditure; (b) capital expenditure

20. Installing a new energy-efficient heating system in the office building would be considered a: (a) revenue expenditure; (b) capital expenditure

21. Overhauling the engine of the company's delivery truck would be considered a: (a) revenue expenditure; (b) capital expenditure

22. Adding on a new wing to the existing office building would be considered a: (a) revenue expenditure; (b) capital expenditure

23. Repairing the roof of the warehouse would be considered a: (a) revenue expenditure; (b) capital expenditure

24. Replacing the entire roof of the warehouse would be considered a: (a) revenue expenditure; (b) capital expenditure

25. Production equipment is generally classified as five-year property for tax purposes: (a) true; (b) false

Use the following information to answer the next two questions.

Land and building were purchased for $500,000 cash. At the time of purchase, the land was appraised at $150,000 and the building was appraised at $450,000.

26. The land should be recorded on the purchaser's books at: (a) $100,000; (b) $125,000; (c) $150,000; (d) none of the above

27. The building should be recorded on the purchaser's books at: (a) $375,000; (b) $400,000; (c) 450,000; (d) none of the above

28. Equipment with a list price of $20,000 was purchased on account with terms of 2/10, n/30. Other costs incurred for cash were:

Shipping	$800
Installation	250
Testing on new equipment	100

The equipment should be recorded on the purchaser's books at: (a) $20,350; (b) $20,650; (c) $20,750; (d) $21,050

29. At the beginning of 1992, the Miller Corporation purchased equipment for $400,000. At the time of purchase, the equipment was estimated to have a $40,000 residual value at the end of its 12-year life. At the beginning of 1995, management revised its estimate of the remaining useful life to 5 years.

Depreciation expense for 1995 would be: (a) $80,000; (b) $68,500; (c) $62,000; (d) $54,000

30. The Wilson Company agreed to purchase the Jones Corporation for $300,000 cash. The Wilson Company will acquire the following Jones Corporation assets and liabilities:

	Book Value	Fair Market Value
Current assets	$ 45,000	$ 60,000
Property, plant, and equipment	320,000	400,000
Liabilities	210,000	210,000

As a result of the purchase, the Wilson Company should record goodwill in the amount of: (a) $50,000; (b) $110,000; (c) $145,000; (d) $160,000

Compare your answers to those at the end of the chapter and review any questions missed.

EXERCISES

EXERCISE 1

Lugge, Inc. purchased production equipment used to manufacture electronic components for $250,000. The asset is estimated to have a residual value of $50,000 and a useful life of five years or 10,000 hours. Hours used are as follows:

Year	Hours Used
1	1,000
2	2,400
3	3,000
4	2,000
5	1,600

Required:

Calculate annual depreciation for each of the next five years under each of the following methods, and complete the following depreciation schedules under each method.

1. Straight-line:

Year	Cost	Depreciation Expense[a]	Accumulated Depreciation	Book Value
1	$250,000			
2				
3				
4				
5				

[a] Supporting calculations for straight-line depreciation expense:

EXERCISE 1 (continued)

2. Units-of-production:

Year	Cost	Depreciation Expense[b]	Accumulated Depreciation	Book Value
1	$250,000			
2				
3				
4				
5				

[b] Supporting calculations for units-of-production depreciation expense:

3. Double-declining-balance:

Year	Cost	Depreciation Expense[c]	Accumulated Depreciation	Book Value
1	$250,000			
2				
3				
4				
5				

[c] Supporting calculations for double-declining-balance depreciation expense:

EXERCISE 1 (continued)

4. Sum-of-the-years-digits:

Year	Cost	Depreciation Expense[d]	Accumulated Depreciation	Book Value
1	$250,000			
2				
3				
4				
5				

[d] Supporting calculations for sum-of-the-years-digits depreciation expense:

5. For tax purposes, the production equipment is considered five-year property. Using the following MACRS percentages, calculate depreciation expense for tax purposes.

Year	MACRS Percentage	Depreciation Expense
1	20.00%	
2	32.00%	
3	19.20%	
4	11.52%	
5	11.52%	
6	5.76%	

EXERCISE 2

The following information about two operating assets of the Griffith Company at December 31, 1995 was provided:

Delivery truck, cost	$25,000
Less: Accumulated depreciation	15,000
Book value	$10,000
Production equipment, cost	$70,000
Less: Accumulated depreciation	49,000
Book value	$21,000

At the time of purchase, the delivery truck had no residual value and a five-year useful life and the production equipment had no residual value and a ten-year useful life. Straight-line depreciation is used for both assets.

On April 1, 1996 the production equipment was traded in for new equipment. The firm received a trade-in allowance of $15,000. The list price of the new equipment is $80,000. On October 1, 1996, the delivery truck was sold for $12,000.

Required:

1. Prepare the necessary journal entries to record the exchange of the production equipment on April 1, 1996.

2. Prepare the necessary journal entries to record the disposal of the delivery truck on October 1, 1996.

318

EXERCISE 3

The Green Machine, a manufacturer of lawn mowers and other equipment, had the following intangible assets on December 31, 1995 (the company's year-end):

a. On August 1, 1995 the company patented a new lawn mower developed by the firm. Expenses of $100,000 were incurred in the development of the mower. Legal fees and costs associated with obtaining the patent totaled $12,000. The company plans to amortize the patent over its legal life beginning on August 1, 1995.
b. On January 2, 1994 the company purchased a patent for a lawn trimmer for $16,000 cash. The patent was registered with the U.S. Patent Office on January 2, 1993. The firm estimates that the patent has a remaining economic life of twenty years.

Required:

Prepare all necessary journal entries to record the above events for 1995. (Round amounts to dollars.)

ANSWERS

KEY TERMS TEST
1. Operating assets
2. Capital budgeting
3. Tangible assets
4. natural resources
5. Intangible assets
6. expenditure
7. capital expenditure
8. Revenue expenditures
9. self-constructed asset
10. Depreciation
11. Depletion
12. Amortization
13. Obsolescence
14. Depreciable cost
15. Estimated useful (or economic) life
16. Straight-line depreciation
17. Units-of-production
18. accelerated depreciation methods
19. Declining-balance depreciation
20. Sum-of-the-years-digits
21. Repair or maintenance
22. Additions
23. Betterments
24. Extraordinary repairs
25. operating-asset ledger
26. location list
27. depreciation register
28. data base management system
29. relational data base
30. specifically identifiable intangible assets
31. Research and development costs
32. patent
33. Goodwill

CHAPTER QUIZ
1. depletion
2. depreciation
3. amortization
4. none
5. depreciation
6. 1. deterioration
   2. obsolescence
7. 1. straight-line
   2. units-of-production
   3. declining-balance
   4. sum-of-the-years-digits
8. Depreciable Cost = Cost - Residual Value
9. Straight-Line Depreciation = (Cost - Residual Value)/Useful Life

10. Cash received
    - Book value
    = Gain or loss

11. 1. disbursement vouchers
    2. disposal authorizations
    3. asset adjustment forms
12. 1. operating-asset ledger
    2. location list
    3. depreciation register
13. 1. the useful or economic life, or
    2. the legal life
    whichever is shorter but not to exceed **40** years
14. b False Depreciation is the allocation of an asset's cost to the
                periods benefited.
15. b False
16. b False A gain resulting from the trade-in of an asset for a similar
                asset is not recognized.
17. a True
18. a True
19. a
20. b
21. b
22. b
23. a
24. b
25. b False Production equipment is generally considered seven-year
                property for tax purposes except for equipment used for
                research and development and equipment used for production of
                chemical and electronic components.

26. b $500,000 x [$150,000/($150,000 + $450,000)] = $125,000
27. a $500,000 x [$450,000/($150,000 + $450,000)] = $375,000
28. c ($20,000 x 98%) + $800 + $250 + $100 = $20,750
29. d ($400,000 - $40,000)/12 years = $30,000 depreciation expense per year
       $30,000 x 3 years = $90,000 accumulated depreciation
       [($400,000 - $90,000) - $40,000]/5 years = $54,000 revised depreciation
30. a Fair market value of net assets = $60,000 + $400,000 - $210,000
                                       = $250,000
       Goodwill = $300,000 - $250,000 = $50,000

EXERCISE 1

1. Straight-line:

Year	Cost	Depreciation Expense[a]	Accumulated Depreciation	Book Value
1	$250,000	$40,000	$ 40,000	$210,000
2	250,000	40,000	80,000	170,000
3	250,000	40,000	120,000	130,000
4	250,000	40,000	160,000	90,000
5	250,000	40,000	200,000	50,000

[a] Straight-Line Depreciation = (Cost - Residual Value)/Useful Life
= ($250,000 - $50,000)/5 years
= $40,000 per year

2. Units-of-production:

Year	Cost	Depreciation Expense[b]	Accumulated Depreciation	Book Value
1	$250,000	$20,000	$ 20,000	$230,000
2	250,000	48,000	68,000	182,000
3	250,000	60,000	128,000	122,000
4	250,000	40,000	168,000	82,000
5	250,000	32,000	200,000	50,000

[b] Units-of-Production Depreciation = (Cost - Residual Value)/Total Hours
= ($250,000 - $50,000)/10,000 hours
= $20 per hour

Year	Hours Used Per Year	x	Depreciation Per Hour	=	Depreciation Expense
1	1,000	x	$20	=	$20,000
2	2,400	x	20	=	48,000
3	3,000	x	20	=	60,000
4	2,000	x	20	=	40,000
5	1,600	x	20	=	32,000

322

EXERCISE 1 (continued)

3. Double-declining-balance:

Year	Cost	Depreciation Expense[c]	Accumulated Depreciation	Book Value
1	$250,000	$100,000	$100,000	$150,000
2	250,000	60,000	160,000	90,000
3	250,000	36,000	196,000	54,000
4	250,000	4,000	200,000	50,000
5	250,000			

[c] Double-Declining-Balance Rate = 2 x Straight-Line Rate
= 2 x (1/5)
= 40%

Year	Book Value at Beg. of Year	x DDB Rate	=	Depreciation Expense
1	$250,000	x 40%	=	$100,000
2	150,000	x 40%	=	60,000
3	90,000	x 40%	=	36,000
4	54,000	x 40%	=	~~21,600~~* $4,000

*Year 4 depreciation would be $4,000 because the book value cannot be less than the residual value of $50,000.

4. Sum-of-the-years-digits:

Year	Cost	Depreciation Expense[d]	Accumulated Depreciation	Book Value
1	$250,000	$66,667	$ 66,667	$183,333
2	250,000	53,333	120,000	130,000
3	250,000	40,000	160,000	90,000
4	250,000	26,667	186,667	63,333
5	250,000	13,333	200,000	50,000

[d] Sum-of-the-Years-Digits Depreciation:

Year	(Cost - Residual Value)	x SYD Rate	=	Depreciation Expense
1	($250,000 - $50,000)	x 5/15	=	$66,667
2	($250,000 - $50,000)	x 4/15	=	53,333
3	($250,000 - $50,000)	x 3/15	=	40,000
4	($250,000 - $50,000)	x 2/15	=	26,667
5	($250,000 - $50,000)	x 1/15	=	13,333

EXERCISE 1 (continued)

5.

Year	Cost	x	MACRS Percentage	=	Depreciation Expense
1	$250,000	x	20.00%	=	$50,000
2	$250,000	x	32.00%	=	$80,000
3	$250,000	x	19.20%	=	$48,000
4	$250,000	x	11.52%	=	$28,800
5	$250,000	x	11.52%	=	$28,800
6	$250,000	x	5.76%	=	$14,400

EXERCISE 2

1.

DATE	ACCOUNT TITLES	REF.	DEBIT	CREDIT
Apr. 1	Depreciation Expense: Equipment		2,500	
	Accumulated Depreciation: Equipment			2,500

To record depreciation to date of sale.
$70,000/7 years x 3/12 = $2,500

DATE	ACCOUNT TITLES	REF.	DEBIT	CREDIT
Apr. 1	Equipment (New)		80,000	
	Accumulated Depreciation: Equipment			
	($49,000 + $2,500)		51,500	
	Loss on Trade-In of Equipment		3,500	
	Equipment (Old)			70,000
	Cash			65,000

To record trade-in of equipment. Loss on trade-in
is calculated as follows.

Book value ($70,000 - $51,500)	$18,500
Trade-in allowance	15,000
Loss on trade-in	($ 3,500)

(If the trade-in had resulted in a gain, the gain would not have been
recognized.)

EXERCISE 2 (continued)

2.

DATE	ACCOUNT TITLES	REF.	DEBIT	CREDIT
Oct. 1	Depreciation Expense: Delivery Truck		3,750	
	Accumulated Depreciation: Delivery Truck			3,750
	To record depreciation to date of sale.			
	$25,000/5 years x 9/12 = $3,750			
Oct. 1	Cash		12,000	
	Accumulated Depreciation: Delivery Truck			
	($15,000 + $3,750)		18,750	
	Delivery Truck			25,000
	Gain on Sale of Delivery Truck			5,750

To record sale of delivery truck. Gain on sale
is calculated as follows.

Cash received	$12,000
Less: Book value ($25,000 - $18,750)	6,250
	———
Gain on sale	$ 5,750

EXERCISE 3

DATE	ACCOUNT TITLES	REF.	DEBIT	CREDIT
1995				
Aug. 1	Research and Development Expense		100,000	
	Cash or Payables			100,000
Aug. 1	Patent		12,000	
	Cash or Payables			12,000
Dec. 31	Amortization Expense		294	
	Patent: Lawn Mower			294
	$12,000/17 years x 5/12 = $294			
Dec. 31	Amortization Expense		1,000	
	Patent: Lawn Trimmer			1,000
	$16,000/16 years = $1,000			

CHAPTER 11

INVESTMENTS IN DEBT
AND EQUITY SECURITIES

CHAPTER REVIEW

INVESTMENTS

- Different types of investors include:
  1. corporations
  2. mutual funds
  3. bank trust departments
  4. insurance companies
  5. individuals

- Two major types of securities are:
  1. Equity securities. **Equity securities** are any securities, such as common and preferred stock, that represent an ownership interest in an enterprise.
  2. Debt securities. **Debt securities** are any securities that represent a creditor relationship with a firm or government agency. Examples of debt securities include corporate bonds and U.S. Treasury securities.

- Stock is publicly traded if it is traded on:
  1. a national stock exchange such as the New York Stock Exchange or the American Stock Exchange.
  2. a regional stock exchange such as the Pacific Stock Exchange.
  3. the over-the-counter market (NASDAQ).

- A publicly-held corporation must comply with regulations of both:
  1. the Securities and Exchange Commission (SEC) and
  2. the exchange on which the stock is listed.

- The 10-K is a report that publicly traded corporations must file with the SEC. The 10-K contains the corporation's financial statements, which have been audited by a certified public accountant.

THE NATURE OF DEBT AND EQUITY SECURITIES

- Accounting for investments in debt and equity securities depends upon:
  1. the nature of the securities (debt versus equity).
  2. management's intention to sell the securities or hold them to maturity.
  3. the degree of influence or control that the investment gives the investor.

- The current accounting standards for different investments are summarized below:

Amount of Influence or Control	Percentage Owned	Accounting Treatment
1. No significant influence or control		
a. All debt securities		
• Held-to-maturity debt securities	Up to 100%	Amortized cost
• Trading securities debt securities	Up to 100%	Fair value--unrealized holding gains or losses in *current period's income*
• Available-for-sale debt securities	Up to 100%	Fair value--unrealized holding gains or losses in *stockholders' equity*
b. Equity securities (less than 20% ownership)		
• Trading equity securities	Less than 20%	Fair value--unrealized holding gains or losses in *current period's income*
• Available-for-sale equity securities	Less than 20%	Fair value--unrealized holding gains or losses in *stockholders' equity*
2. Significant influence or control	20% to 50%	Equity method
3. Controlling interest	More than 50%	Consolidated financial statements

- No significant influence or control exists when the investor is unable to have an important impact on either the financing or operating policies of the investee. Under current accounting standards, it is presumed that there is no significant influence or control for:
1. all debt securities.
2. all equity securities that are nonvoting stock.
3. equity securities that represent less than 20% of the voting stock.

- Significant influence exists when an investor can influence, but cannot control, the operating and financing policies of the investee. Significant influence can be evidenced by:
  • the investor's having a seat on the board of directors.
  • other intercompany transactions.
  • interchange of management personnel.
  • technological interdependencies.

Current accounting standards presume that significant influence, but not control, exists when the investor holds at least 20%, but not more than 50%, of the voting stock of another company.

- A controlling interest exists when an investor is able to determine both the financial and operating policies of another company. Control is presumed when the investor owns more than 50% of the voting stock of another company.

DEBT AND EQUITY SECURITIES: NO INFLUENCE OR CONTROL

Accounting for Certain Equity Securities and Debt Securities

- FASB Statement No. 115 applies to:
  1. all investments in debt securities.
  2. investments in equity securities that have a readily determinable fair market value and no significant influence or control exists.

- FASB Statement No. 115 does not apply to:
  1. equity securities accounted for by the equity method of accounting (20% to 50% ownership).
  2. investments in consolidated subsidiaries (over 50% ownership).

- According to FASB Statement No. 115, debt and equity securities with a readily determinable fair market value must be classified into one of the following three categories:.

  1. **Held-to maturity securities**: Debt securities that management intends to hold to maturity. In order to classify a debt security in this category, management must not only have the intent to hold them to maturity but must also have the ability to do so. Equity securities are not included in this category because they do not have a maturity date.

  2. **Trading securities**: Debt and equity securities that are purchased and held primarily for sale in the near term. Securities in this category are purchased and held principally for the purpose of selling them in the near future, and thus are held for a short period of time. Management purchases these securities with the intent of generating short-term trading profits.

  3. **Available-for-sale securities**: These are debt and equity securities that are not classified as either held-to-maturity or trading securities.

- Management must make the appropriate classification when the particular security is purchased; however, management should reassess this classification at the end of each accounting period.

Held-to-Maturity Securities

- This category includes debt securities that management intends to hold to maturity and also has the ability to do so.

- At the time of purchase, held-to-maturity securities are recorded at cost. The entry to record the purchase of held-to-maturity securities is:

  Debit: Investment in Held-to-Maturity Securities
    Credit: Cash

- Interest income, including the amortization of premiums and discounts (discussed in the next chapter), is included in the current period's earnings.

- The entry to record interest is:

  Debit: Cash
   Credit: Interest Revenue

- The entry to record interest receivable is:

  Debit: Interest Receivable
   Credit: Interest Revenue

- The entry to record receipt of interest receivable is:

  Debit: Cash
   Credit: Interest Receivable

- Held-to-maturity securities are reported on the balance sheet at amortized cost.

- Because these debt securities will be held to maturity, no recognition is given to increases or decreases in market values unless there is a permanent loss in value, such as might occur if the firm issuing the bonds entered bankruptcy proceedings.

Trading Securities

- Trading securities are either debt or equity securities whose market prices are readily determinable and are purchased and held for sale in the near term. In effect, management purchases these securities in the hope of realizing a short-term trading profit.

- Trading securities are first recorded at cost. The entry to record the purchase of trading securities is:

  Debit: Investment in Trading Securities
   Credit: Cash

- Dividends and interest are recorded in the current period's income as earned. The entry to record interest earned is:

  Debit: Cash
   Credit: Interest Revenue

  The entry to record dividends received is:

  Debit: Cash
   Credit: Dividend Revenue

- On the balance sheet date, the trading securities are adjusted to fair value and any unrealized holding gains and losses that result from the adjustment are reflected in the current period's earnings.

- The entry to record an unrealized holding gain on trading securities is:

  Debit: Investment in Trading Securities
    Credit: Unrealized Holding Gain or Loss on Trading Securities

- The entry to record an unrealized holding loss is:

  Debit: Unrealized Holding Gain or Loss on Trading Securities
    Credit: Investment in Trading Securities

- A credit to the Unrealized Holding Gain or Loss on Trading Securities account to record an unrealized holding gain increases earnings.

- A debit to the Unrealized Holding Gain or Loss on Trading Securities account to record an unrealized holding loss decreases earnings.

- Unrealized holding gains and losses appear on the income statement under Other Income and Expenses.

- A debit to the Investment in Trading Securities account increases the account balance, while a credit to the Investment in Trading Securities account decreases the account balance.

- After adjustment, the balance in the Investment in Trading Securities account should be the fair value of the securities on the balance sheet date.

- The Investment in Trading Securities is classified as a current asset on the balance sheet.

- When an investor sells a trading security, a gain or loss is realized. (The gain or loss is unrealized if the security has not been sold.)

  The gain or loss is calculated as follows:

  Selling price of the trading securities
  - Fair value of trading securities
  = Gain or loss on sale of trading securities

  The entry to record the sale of a trading security at a loss would be:

  Debit: Cash
  Debit: Loss on Sale of Trading Securities
    Credit: Investment in Trading Securities

  The entry to record the sale of a trading security at a gain would be:

  Debit: Cash
    Credit: Gain on Sale of Trading Securities
    Credit: Investment in Trading Securities

Available-For-Sale Securities

- Available-for-sale securities are either current or noncurrent debt or equity securities that are not classified as either trading or held-to-maturity securities. If management's intention is to hold these securities beyond one year or the firm's operating cycle, they would be classified as a noncurrent asset; otherwise they would be considered current.

- The primary difference between accounting for available-for-sale securities and trading securities is that any unrealized holding gains and losses are reported as a separate item in stockholders' equity until realized, instead of being included in the current period's income.

- The entry to record the purchase of available-for-sale securities is:

    Debit: Investment in Available-for-Sale Securities
       Credit: Cash

- Dividends and interest are recorded as income when they are earned.

- At each balance sheet date, the securities are valued at their fair value. Any unrealized holding gain or loss is considered a component of stockholders' equity and not included in the current period's income.

- The entry to record an unrealized holding loss on available-for-sale securities is:

    Debit: Unrealized Holding Gain or Loss on Available-for-Sale Securities
       Credit: Investment in Available-for-Sale Securities

- The entry reduces the available-for-sale securities to their fair value.

- The Unrealized Holding Gain or Loss on Available-for-Sale Securities account is a separate component in stockholders' equity.

- The entry to record an unrealized holding gain on available-for-sale securities is:

    Debit: Investment in Available-for-Sale Securities
       Credit: Unrealized Holding Gain or Loss on Available-for-Sale
                  Securities

- The Investment in Available-for-Sale Securities account would be shown at the fair value of the securities.

- The Unrealized Holding Gain or Loss on Available-for-Sale Securities account is a permanent account that is a component of stockholders' equity. If it has a debit balance, it reduces stockholders' equity. If it has a credit balance, it increases stockholders' equity.

Summary

- Accounting for debt securities and equity securities where no significant influence or control exists is summarized below:

Security	Accounting Treatment
Held-to-maturity securities: Debt securities that are expected to be held to maturity.	Reported at amortized cost. No recognition of unrealized gains or losses. Interest income recognized in current earnings.
Trading securities: Debt securities purchased and held for sale in the near term. Equity securities, less than 20% ownership, purchased and held for sale in the near term.	Fair value. Unrealized gains and losses recognized in current earnings. Interest and dividend income recognized in current earnings.
Available-for-sale securities: Debt securities purchased and not classified as held-to-maturity or trading securities. Equity securities, less than 20% ownership, purchased and not classified as trading securities.	Fair value. Unrealized gains and losses not included in current earnings, but shown as part of stockholders' equity. Interest and dividend income recognized in current earnings.

Evaluation of FASB Statement No. 115

- FASB Statement No. 115 represents a major shift away from the historical cost model. The economic environment of the late 1980s and early 1990s caused many financial statement users to question the relevance of historical costs when fair values were readily available. The Securities and Exchange Commission was particularly adamant in its push towards fair value accounting for financial instruments.

OWNERSHIP INTEREST BETWEEN 20% AND 50%

- The equity method is used to account for ownership interests between 20% and 50%.

- The **equity method** is a method of accounting for investments when the investment is first recorded at its acquisition cost and is subsequently adjusted to reflect changes in balance sheet value of the investee.

- When the equity method is used, the investment is recorded at acquisition cost. The entry to record the acquisition would be:

    Debit: Investment in XYZ Company
      Credit: Cash

- As the investee earns net income, its stockholders' equity increases; the investor then recognizes its proportionate share of the increase as investment revenue. The entry to record the investor's proportionate share of investee income would be:

    Debit: Investment in XYZ Company
      Credit: Investment Revenue

- Under the equity method, dividends declared are not considered income but rather a reduction in the investment account. A cash dividend reduces the net assets (stockholders' equity) of the investee, so the investor records a proportionate decrease in its investment account. Under the equity method, investors recognize income as the investee earns it rather than at the time dividends are declared and received.

    The entry to record the receipt of dividends would be:

    Debit: Cash
      Credit: Investment in XYZ Company

- The equity method ensures that the balance in the investment account equals the investor's proportionate share of the net assets purchased.

OWNERSHIP INTEREST ABOVE 50%--ACCOUNTING FOR MERGERS AND ACQUISITIONS

- Control exists when the investor owns more than 50% of the investee's stock.

- A **parent company** is a corporation that owns the majority of stock in another corporation.

- A **subsidiary** is a corporation that is wholly or partially owned by another corporation.

- The parent company and the subsidiary or subsidiaries are separate legal entities, so they each maintain separate records and prepare separate financial statements for internal purposes.

- On the parent's books, the investment in the subsidiary is accounted for by the equity method of accounting. Since the parent and subsidiary represent one economic unit, the parent company prepares consolidated financial statements to be distributed to external users.

Consolidated Financial Statements

- **Consolidated financial statements** are financial statements of a parent company and its subsidiaries presented as if the separate organizations were one economic entity.

- Although the assets, liabilities, revenues, and expenses of all the entities are combined to provide a single set of financial statements, certain eliminations and adjustments are necessary to ensure that only arm's-length transactions between independent parties are reflected in the consolidated statements.

- Intercompany transactions that must be eliminated include:
  1. intercompany sales between parent company and subsidiary.
  2. intercompany loans between parent company and subsidiary.
  3. intercompany stock investment accounts.

- FASB Statement No. 94, except for minor exceptions, requires the consolidation of all majority-owned subsidiaries in order to eliminate off-balance-sheet financing.

- Acquisitions must be accounted for using either:
  1. the **purchase method**, a consolidation method which assumes that the company's shareholders have sold out their interest to the parent company or
  2. the **pooling of interests method**, a consolidation method which assumes that the subsidiary's shareholders are now stockholders of the parent company.

- When the purchase method is used, all assets and liabilities are revalued to their fair market values, and any remaining excess cost is considered goodwill.

- When the pooling-of-interests method is used, all of the assets and liabilities of the subsidiary are combined with the parent's assets and liabilities at their net book value. Furthermore, under a pooling of interests, in the year of acquisition the subsidiary's earnings for the entire year are combined with the parent's earnings.

- The major differences between the purchase method and the pooling-of-interests method are summarized below:

	Method of Consolidation	Recording of Net Assets	Subsidiary's Earnings
Purchase method:	Acquisition of more than 50% of a subsidiary's voting stock for cash and/or other assets, debt, or securities.	Subsidiary's assets are valued to fair market value. Excess of cost over fair market value, if any, is considered goodwill. Goodwill is amortized over a maximum of 40 years.	In year of acquisition, earnings of subsidiary are combined with those of the parent from date of acquisition.
Pooling-of-interests method:	Acquisition of substantially all (90% or more) of the subsidiary's voting stock for voting stock of parent.	Subsidiary's net assets are shown on consolidated balance sheet at book value. As a result, no goodwill is recognized. Retained earnings of subsidiary are carried over.	In year of acquisition, earnings of subsidiary are combined with those of the parent for the entire year.

INTERNATIONAL ASPECTS OF ACCOUNTING FOR LONG-TERM INVESTMENTS

- Use of the equity method as well as the preparation and dissemination of consolidated financial statements has been a common practice in the United States for a long time. Only within the last two decades have these accounting treatments become common worldwide. However, not all countries consolidate both similar and dissimilar subsidiaries, as is now the practice in the United States. Also, the recognition and handling of goodwill varies greatly throughout the world.

SYSTEMS AND CONTROL ISSUES RELATED TO INVESTMENTS

- The system designed to account for investments, like all manual and computer-based accounting systems, should provide reasonable assurance that all authorized investment transactions are properly recorded.

- Accounting for three different events in the life of an investment are:
  1. investment acquisition
  2. recognition of investment revenue
  3. disposal of investment

- Management approval is the primary control over accounting for acquisitions and disposals.

- When preparing consolidated financial statements, general ledger account balances, after intercompany transactions have been eliminated, are used. The elimination entries do not affect the account balances in the general ledgers of the separate companies, only the amounts reported on the consolidated financial statements.

- Consolidated financial statements are accurate only if all intercompany transactions are correctly identified and eliminated. The use of consolidated software increases control over the consolidation process because the software is able to scan all transactions to identify intercompany transactions.

KEY TERMS TESTS

Test your recall of the key terms as follows: Read the following definitions of key terms and try to recall as many key terms as you can *without assistance*. Write your answers in the spaces provided. If you need assistance, refer to the list of key terms at the end of this section.

1. _____ _____ are preferred and common stock.

2. _____ _____ are bonds.

3. _____ _____ are debt securities that management intends to hold to maturity.

4. _____ _____ are debt and equity securities that are purchased and held primarily for sale in the near term.

5. _____ _____ are debt and equity securities that are not classified as either trading securities or held-to-maturity securities.

6. The _____ _____ is a method of accounting for investments when the investment is first recorded at its acquisition cost and is subsequently adjusted to reflect changes in balance sheet value of the investee.

7. A corporation that owns the majority of stock in another corporation is referred to as a(n) _____ _____.

8. A corporation that is wholly or partially owned by another corporation is referred to as a(n) _____.

9. _____ _____ _____ are financial statements of a parent company and its subsidiaries presented as if the separate organizations were one economic entity.

10. The _____ _____ is a consolidation method that assumes that the company's shareholders have sold out their interest to the parent company.

11. The _____ _____ is a consolidation method that
assumes that the subsidiary's stockholders are now stockholders of the
parent company.

KEY TERMS:

available-for-sale securities
consolidated financial statements
debt securities
equity method
equity securities
held-to-maturity securities

parent company
pooling-of-interests method
purchase method
subsidiary
trading securities

**Compare your answers to those at the end of the chapter and review any key
terms missed.**

CHAPTER QUIZ

Write your answers in the spaces provided.

1. List two methods used to account for acquisitions of 50% to 100% of
   another company.
   1. _____
   2. _____

**For each of the following investments, indicate the appropriate accounting
treatment.**

Investment	Accounting Treatment
2. Held-to-maturity securities	_____
3. Trading securities	_____
4. Available-for-sale securities	_____
5. Investment in stock, between 20% and 50% ownership interest	_____
6. Investment in stock, more than 50% ownership interest	_____

Circle the best answer.

7. The Unrealized Holding Gain or Loss on Available-for-Sale Securities account appears on the income statement: (a) true; (b) false

8. When the equity method is used, the receipt of dividends by the investor is recorded by debiting Cash and crediting Dividend Income: (a) true; (b) false

9. A gain or loss that results when an investor sells stock is a realized loss: (a) true; (b) false

Compare your answers to those at the end of the chapter and review any questions missed.

EXERCISES

EXERCISE 1

At the beginning of 1995, Sun Inc. held the following portfolio of trading equity securities:

Security	Number of Shares	Total Cost	Market Value
Alistair	80	$ 6,000	$ 6,300
Baker	120	4,000	3,500
Compton	180	9,000	8,500
		$19,000	$18,300

During 1995, Sun Inc. entered into the following transactions:
a. Sold 90 shares of Compton for $4,000 net of commissions.
b. Purchased 110 shares of Deker for $50 per share, including commissions.
c. Fair values at December 31, 1995 were:

Stock	Fair Value
Alistair	$ 6,100
Baker	3,400
Compton	4,500
Deker	5,400
	$19,400

EXERCISE 1 (continued)

Required:

1. Prepare all the necessary journal entries for 1995.

GENERAL JOURNAL

DATE	ACCOUNT TITLES	REF.	DEBIT	CREDIT

EXERCISE 1 (continued)

2. How would the trading securities be shown on the balance sheet at December 31, 1995?

3. Assume that all securities were held throughout 1996 and that at the end of 1996 their fair values were as follows:

Stock	Fair Value
Alistair	$ 6,200
Baker	4,100
Compton	4,600
Deker	5,600
	$20,500

(All securities remain classified as trading securities.)

Make the required entry at December 31, 1996.

DATE	ACCOUNT TITLES	REF.	DEBIT	CREDIT

EXERCISE 2

At the beginning of 1995 the Ringo Company purchased a 40% interest in the Starr Corp. The purchase price was $40,000, which represented a 40% interest in the book value of Starr's net assets at that time. At the beginning of 1995, the book value of Starr's net assets were $100,000. During 1995, Starr reported the following:

Net income	$60,000
Dividends paid	35,000

Required:

1. Make the appropriate entries on Ringo's books to reflect these events during the current year.

DATE	ACCOUNT TITLES	REF.	DEBIT	CREDIT

2. What is the balance in the investment account at the end of the year?

EXERCISE 3

On January 2, 1995 Columbus Company purchased 20, $1,000 9% bonds of Cummins Corporation at par. The bonds pay interest every January 2 and July 1. The bonds are considered held-to-maturity securities.

Required:

1. Make the required journal entry on January 2, 1995 to record the purchase.

DATE	ACCOUNT TITLES	REF.	DEBIT	CREDIT

2. Make the required journal entry on July 1, 1995.

DATE	ACCOUNT TITLES	REF.	DEBIT	CREDIT

EXERCISE 3 (continued)

3. Make the required journal entry at December 31, 1995.

DATE	ACCOUNT TITLES	REF.	DEBIT	CREDIT

4. Make the required journal entry at January 2, 1996.

DATE	ACCOUNT TITLES	REF.	DEBIT	CREDIT

EXERCISE 4

At the beginning of 1995 the Bryant Corp. purchased two long-term investments. The first purchase was a 35% interest in the common stock of Jane Company for $1.75 million. The second purchase was a 12% interest (12,000 shares) in the common stock of Quinn, Inc., for $480,000. These shares are available for sale but will not be sold within the next 12 months. The following data are available regarding these companies:

Company	Reported Income	Dividends Declared and Paid	Fair Value Per Share, 12/31/95
Jane Corp.	$600,000	$180,000	$51
Quinn, Inc.	800,000	200,000	36

Required:

1. Which accounting method should be used to account for the:

   a. Jane Corp. investment: _____

   b. Quinn, Inc. investment: _____

2. How much income should be reported by Bryant Corp. for the year ended December 31, 1995 as a result of the investment in:

   a. Jane Corp.: $_____

   b. Quinn, Inc.: $_____

3. On Bryant's 1995 balance sheet, at what amount should the investment be valued for the:

   a. Jane Corp.: $_____

   b. Quinn, Inc.: $_____

ANSWERS

KEY TERMS TEST
1. Equity securities
2. Debt securities
3. Held-to-maturity securities
4. Trading securities
5. Available-for-sale securities
6. equity method
7. parent company
8. subsidiary
9. Consolidated financial statements
10. purchase method
11. pooling-of-interests method

CHAPTER QUIZ
1. 1. purchase method
   2. pooling-of-interests method

Investment	Accounting Treatment
2. Held-to-maturity securities	Amortized cost
3. Trading securities	Fair value Unrealized holding gains or losses in current period's income
4. Available-for-sale securities	Fair value Unrealized holding gains or losses in stockholders' equity
5. Investment in stock, between 20% and 50% ownership interest	Equity method
6. Investment in stock, more than 50% ownership interest	Consolidated financial statements

7. b False The Unrealized Holding Gain or Loss on Available-for-Sale Securities account is included in stockholders' equity.
8. b False The receipt of dividends is recorded by debiting Cash and crediting the Investment account.
9. a True

EXERCISE 1

1.

GENERAL JOURNAL

DATE	ACCOUNT TITLES	REF.	DEBIT	CREDIT
a.	Cash		4,000	
	Loss on Sale of Trading Securities		250	
	Investment in Trading Securities			4,250

To record sale of 90 shares of Compton for $4,000.

Sales price	$4,000
Fair value at beginning of year	
($8,500 x 1/2)	4,250
Loss on sale	($ 250)

b.	Investment in Trading Securities (110 x $50)		5,500	
	Cash			5,500

To record purchase of 110 shares of Deker at $50 per share.

c.	Unrealized Holding Gain or Loss on Trading Securities		150	
	Investment in Trading Securities			150

To record decrease in fair value of securities at December 31, 1995.

Supporting calculations:

Fair value of securities at beginning of 1995	$18,300
Fair value of Compton shares sold	(4,250)
	$14,050
Cost of Deker shares purchased	5,500
Balance in Investment in Trading Securities account	$19,550
Fair value at end of 1995	19,400
Unrealized holding loss at December 31, 1995	$ 150

2.   Investment in trading securities $19,400

EXERCISE 1 (continued)

3.   GENERAL JOURNAL

DATE	ACCOUNT TITLES	REF.	DEBIT	CREDIT
	Investment in Trading Securities		1,100	
	Unrealized Holding Gain or Loss on			
	Trading Securities			1,100
	To record unrealized holding gain on trading securities.			

Fair value at December 31, 1996	$20,500	
Fair value at December 31, 1995	19,400	
Unrealized holding gain	$ 1,100	

EXERCISE 2

1.   GENERAL JOURNAL

DATE	ACCOUNT TITLES	REF.	DEBIT	CREDIT
	Investment in Starr Corp.		40,000	
	Cash			40,000
	To record investment in Starr Corp.			
	Investment in Starr Corp.		24,000	
	Investment Revenue			24,000
	To record investment revenue.			
	($60,000 x 40% = $24,000)			
	Cash		14,000	
	Investment in Starr Corp.			14,000
	To record receipt of dividend.			
	($35,000 x 40% = $14,000)			

2. Balance in investment account:

Investment in Starr Corp.

Beg. bal.	40,000		
	24,000	14,000	
End. bal.	50,000		

EXERCISE 3

GENERAL JOURNAL

DATE	ACCOUNT TITLES	REF.	DEBIT	CREDIT
1.				
1995				
Jan. 2	Investment in Held-to-Maturity Securities			
	(20 x $1,000)		20,000	
	Cash			20,000
2.				
1995				
July 1	Cash		900	
	Interest Revenue			900
	($20,000 x 9% x 6/12)			
3.				
1995				
Dec. 31	Interest Receivable		900	
	Interest Revenue			900
4.				
1996				
Jan. 2	Cash		900	
	Interest Receivable			900

EXERCISE 4

1. a. Jane Corp. investment: equity method

  b. Quinn, Inc. investment: Available-for-sale security: Fair value--
unrealized holding gains or losses in stockholders' equity

2. a. Jane Corp.: $600,000 x 35% = $210,000

  b. Quinn, Inc.: $200,000 x 12% = $24,000
The unrealized holding loss of $48,000 would not be included in the
current year's income. Instead, it would be shown as a component of
stockholders' equity.

3. a. Jane Corp.: $1,750,000 + ($600,000 x 35%) - ($180,000 x 35%) =
$1,750,000 + $210,000 - $63,000 = $1,897,000

  b. Quinn, Inc.: Fair value = 12,000 x $36 = $432,000

CHAPTER 12

LONG-TERM DEBT FINANCING

CHAPTER REVIEW

NATURE AND FEATURES OF BONDS

- A **bond** is a written agreement between a borrower and a lender in which the borrower agrees to:
  1. repay a stated sum on a future date.
  2. make periodic interest payments at specified dates.

- Bonds can be issued by:
  - local governments
  - state governments
  - federal governments
  - not-for-profit institutions, such as universities
  - corporations

Features of Bonds

- A bond certificate specifies the terms of the bond agreement between the issuer and the investor, including:
  - the denomination of the bond
  - the maturity date
  - the stated rate of interest
  - the interest payment terms

Denomination of the Bond

- Individual bonds usually have a **denomination** of $1,000. The denomination, or principal, of a bond is often referred to as:
  - face value
  - maturity value
  - par value

- In the United States, after bonds are issued by large publicly held companies, they are traded on the New York Bond Exchange.

Maturity Date

- The **maturity date** is the date that the principal of the bond is to be repaid.

Stated Interest Rate and Interest Payment Dates

- The **stated interest rate** is the interest rate stated on the face of the bond at the time of sale. The stated interest rate is also called the nominal interest rate. The stated rate does *not* change over the life of the bond.

- The **market interest rate** is the interest rate being paid in the marketplace. The market rate may differ from the stated rate. The market rate depends on such factors as prevailing interest rates in the economy and the perceived risk of the company.

- Management attempts to set the stated rate as close as possible to the market interest rate that exists at the time bonds are issued.

- Most bonds pay interest semiannually (every six months). A 10% bond that pays interest semiannually would pay 5% interest every six months (10%/2 periods = 5% per period).

- **Zero-coupon bonds** do not pay interest periodically. Zero-coupon bonds are issued at a discount (below par value). At maturity, the bondholder receives the maturity value. The difference between the issue price and the maturity value is the amount of interest earned over the life of the bond.

Other Agreements

- **Bond indentures** are written convenants that are part of the bond agreement. Bond indentures usually include restrictions as to dividends, working capital, and the issuance of additional long-term debt. The purpose of the agreement is to ensure that the borrower will maintain a strong enough financial position to meet the interest and principal payments.

Types of Bonds

- Different types of bonds include:
  - term bonds
  - serial bonds
  - unsecured bonds
  - convertible bonds
  - callable bonds

Term Versus Serial Bonds

- **Term bonds** are bonds whose entire principal matures on the same date.

- **Serial bonds** are bonds that mature at specific intervals, such as every five years.

- Most corporate bonds are term bonds, while serial bonds are often issued by state or local municipalities.

Secured Versus Unsecured Bonds

- **Unsecured bonds**, or debentures, are bonds that are issued without any security to back them.

- **Mortgage bonds** are bonds secured by the borrower's collateral or specified assets. Should the borrower default, the borrower's collateral is used to repay the bondholders.

Convertible Bonds

- **Convertible bonds** may at some future specified date be exchanged for (converted into) the firm's common stock. This conversion feature allows the firm to issue the bond at a lower interest rate.

- Convertible bonds are usually callable (the issuer is able to call or redeem the bonds prior to maturity).

Bond Prices

- Bond prices are quoted in terms of 100. For example, a bond price of 100 means that the bond is selling at 100% of its face value. This is referred to as *selling at par*.

- A $1,000 bond that is selling at 105 would sell for $1,050 ($1,000 x 105%). A bond that sells for more than par value is selling at a *premium*.

- A $1,000 bond that is selling at 96 would sell for $960 ($1,000 x 96%). A bond that sells for less than par value is selling at a *discount*.

Determination of Bond Prices

- The two types of cash flows associated with bonds are:
  1. Face value at maturity.
  2. Interest payments. The interest payments are usually made semiannually and are calculated as follows:

Interest Payment = Face Value x Stated Rate x Time

- The selling price of the bond is the present value of two cash flows (maturity value and interest payments) discounted at the market rate of interest.

- The selling price of a bond is calculated as follows:

  Present value of interest payments
  + Present value of maturity value
  = Selling price of bonds

- The market rate is the rate that investors are demanding for investments of similar risk.

- The **yield rate**, or effective interest rate, is the prevailing market rate when a bond is issued.

- If the stated rate = market rate at issuance, then the selling price = par. The investor is receiving the return demanded.

- If the stated rate < market rate at issuance, then the selling price < par. The investor is receiving less than the return demanded and pays less than par for the bond (the bond sells at a discount). The price of the bond is bid down until it yields a rate of return equal to the prevailing market rate for investments of similar risk.

- If the stated rate > market rate at issuance, then the selling price > par. The investor is receiving more than the return demanded, so the investor pays more than par for the bond (the bond sells at a premium). If the stated rate is higher than the market rate, the demand for these bonds will cause their price to be bid up, and they will be issued at a premium.

- Remember that the stated rate is specified on the bond and does not change over its life. Market rates of interest constantly change as economic conditions change. When there is a general rise in interest rates, the bond market declines. When interest rates decline, bond prices tend to rise. (There is an inverse relationship between the market rate and bond prices.) Subsequent price changes in the bonds are not reflected in the accounting records of the issuer or the investor.

Determination of Interest Rates on Individual Bond Issues

- Underwriters often agree to purchase the entire bond issue at a certain price and then assume the risks involved in selling the bonds to institutions and/or private investors.

- Management and the underwriters attempt to set the stated rate as close as possible to the prevailing market rate, but there is a lag time between the time the decision must be made about the stated rate and the time the bonds are actually issued. Economic and financial events during the interim may often cause changes in the rates, so bonds are usually issued at a discount or premium.

Determination of Bond Risk and Future Price Changes

- Not only is the entire bond market affected by changes in interest rates, but individual bonds are also subject to price changes due to perceived changes in their individual risk.

- *Junk bonds* are bonds that carry a high rate of interest due to their high risk.

- Financial advisory services, such as Standard and Poor's and Moody's, rate the bonds of major corporations, states, and cities. The higher the rating, the less risky the bond will be in the opinion of the rating service. Firms with high ratings can issue bonds with a lower stated interest rate than firms with lower ratings.

ACCOUNTING FOR BONDS BY ISSUERS

Bonds Issued at Par or Face Value

- If the stated interest rate equals the market rate for similar investments at the issue date, the bonds will be issued at par.

Bonds Issued at Par on an Interest Date

- The entry to record the issuance of bonds at par on an interest payment date would be:

      Debit: Cash
        Credit: Bonds Payable

- The entry to record the payment of semiannual interest would be:

      Debit: Interest Expense
        Credit: Cash

    The interest payment is calculated as follows:

    Interest Payment = Face Value x Stated Rate x Time

- The adjusting entry to record accrued interest between interest payment dates would be:

      Debit: Interest Expense
        Credit: Interest Payable

- The entry to record payment of accrued interest would be:

      Debit: Interest Payable
        Credit: Cash

Bonds Issued at Par Between Interest Dates

- When bonds are issued between interest dates, the investor pays the issuing corporation for the interest that has accrued since the last interest date. The investor will receive the entire six months' interest on the next interest payment date, regardless of how long the bonds have been held.

  For example, if an investor buys bonds two months after the last interest payment date, when purchasing the bonds the investor must pay the issuing corporation the two months of accrued interest. On the next interest payment date, the investor will receive an interest payment for six months of interest. Thus, the investor will net four months of interest (the period of time the investor has held the bonds).

- The entry to record the issuance of bonds and accrued interest would be:

  ```
  Debit:    Cash
   Credit:    Interest Payable
   Credit:    Bonds Payable
  ```

- The entry to record the next interest payment would be:

  ```
  Debit:    Interest Expense
  Debit:    Interest Payable
   Credit:  Cash
  ```

Bonds Issued at Other Than Face Value

- If the stated rate is less than the market interest rate at the issue date, the bonds will be issued at a discount.

- If the stated rate is greater than the market interest rate, the bonds will be issued at a premium.

Recording Bonds Issued at a Discount

- The **effective interest rate** is the prevailing market rate at issuance.

- The entry to record the issuance of bonds at a discount would be:

  ```
  Debit:    Cash                        [proceeds received]
  Debit:    Discount on Bonds Payable   [cash minus face value]
   Credit:  Bonds Payable               [face value]
  ```

- The discount account is a contra-liability account that is deducted from the bonds payable account on the balance sheet in order to arrive at the bonds' net carrying value.

- In effect, the discount should be thought of as additional interest expense that is recognized over the life of the bonds. Remember that bonds are issued at a discount because the stated interest rate is below the market rate.

- The discount must be amortized (written off) over the life of the bond.

- Two methods used to amortize a discount (or premium) are:
  1. the straight-line method.
  2. the effective-interest method. The effective-interest method must be used unless the straight-line method is not materially different.

- The straight-line method allocates the discount evenly over the remaining life of the bond.

  Straight-Line Amortization = Total Discount/Number of Interest Periods

- The entry to record the cash interest payment and the amortization of the discount would be:

  Debit: Interest Expense
    Credit: Discount on Bonds Payable
    Credit: Cash

Notice that the amortization of the discount increases interest expense.

- At maturity, the discount should be fully amortized and the following entry made to record the repayment of principal at maturity:

  Debit: Bonds Payable
    Credit: Cash

Recording Bonds Issued at a Premium

- The entry to record the issuance of bonds at a premium would be:

  Debit: Cash
    Credit: Premium on Bonds Payable
    Credit: Bonds Payable

- The premium account is an **adjunct account**; it is added to the Bonds Payable account to determine the bonds' carrying value.

- The premium should be thought of as a reduction in interest expense. The bonds were issued at a premium because the stated rate was higher than the prevailing market rate. The premium represents the present value of the extra interest that the bondholders will receive.

- The entry to record the cash interest payment and amortization of the premium would be:

  Debit: Interest Expense
    Debit: Premium on Bonds Payable
    Credit: Cash

Notice that the amortization of the premium decreases interest expense.

- The effect of the entry is to decrease the carrying value of the bonds as the premium account is reduced each period. By the time the bonds reach maturity, their carrying value is reduced to the face value amount.

Applying the Effective-Interest Method

- Under the **effective-interest method** the effective rate of interest at the time of issue is used to calculate interest expense.

- Effective interest expense is calculated as follows:

Interest Expense = Bond Carrying Value x Effective Interest Rate x Time

- Recall that the cash interest payment is calculated as follows:

Interest Payment = Face Value x Stated Rate x Time

- Amortization under the effective-interest method is calculated as:

Amortization = Interest Payment - Interest Expense

Accounting for the Retirement of Bonds

- Different ways that bonds can be retired include:
  1. repayment at maturity
  2. early extinguishment of debt before maturity
  3. conversion into capital stock

Retirement of Bonds at Maturity

- When bonds are repaid at maturity, the journal entry is:

  Debit: Bonds Payable
      Credit: Cash

Notice that any discount or premium is amortized to zero at the time of the last interest payment.

Bond Sinking Fund

- A **sinking fund** is a collection of cash or other assets set apart to be used for a specific purpose, such as bond repayment.

- A bond sinking fund is used to pay the interest and repay the principal of the bonds.

- The sinking fund is an asset account shown under the investment section of the balance sheet.

Early Extinguishment of Debt

- **Early extinguishment of debt** occurs whenever a firm's long-term debt is retired before maturity.

- Bonds can be retired early in the following ways:
  1. The issuing corporation repurchases the bonds on the market.
  2. If the bonds are callable, the issuing corporation has the right to buy back the bonds before maturity at a specified price.

- When a firm extinguishes debt prior to maturity, there will be a gain or a loss calculated as follows:

      Reacquisition price
    - **Carrying value of bonds**
    = **Gain or loss on early extinguishment of debt**

- If the reacquisition price exceeds the carrying value of the bonds, there is a loss.

- If the reacquisition price is less than the carrying value of the bonds, there is a gain.

- The gain or loss is considered extraordinary and must be shown as a separate item on the income statement.

- The entry to record the early extinguishment of debt is:

  Debit: Bonds Payable
  Debit: Extraordinary Loss on Early Extinguishment of Debt
      Credit: Discount on Bonds Payable
      Credit: Cash

ACCOUNTING FOR BONDS BY INVESTORS

- Accounting for the purchase of bonds is similar to accounting for the issuance of bonds except that the investor records an asset, Investment in Bonds, rather than a liability, Bonds Payable.

- The accounting standards for bonds depends upon whether the bonds are considered to be:
  1. held-to-maturity securities
  2. trading securities
  3. available-for-sale securities

- Held-to-maturity securities are classified as long-term until the year prior to their maturity.

- Trading debt securities are classified as current assets.

- Available-for-sale debt securities can be classified as either long-term or current depending upon whether or not management's intention is to sell these securities within the operating cycle or twelve months.

Accounting for Held-to-Maturity Bonds

• The acquisition cost of bonds includes:
  1. the purchase price
  2. brokerage commissions
  3. any other costs related to the purchase

Accounting at Acquisition

• If bonds are purchased between interest dates, the investor must pay the issuer or previous bondholder for any accrued interest since the last interest payment date.

• The entry to record the purchase of held-to-maturity bonds plus accrued interest would be:

   Debit: Investment in Held-to-Maturity Bonds
   Debit: Interest Receivable
     Credit: Cash

• The discount or premium is not recorded in a separate account. Instead, the Investment in Held-to-Maturity Bonds account is shown at the carrying value of the bonds.

Amortizing the Discount or Premium

• The effective-interest method should be used to amortize a discount or premium unless there is no material difference between the effective-interest method and the straight-line method.

• The entry to record the first semiannual interest payment after purchase and the discount amortization is:

   Debit: Cash   [face value x stated rate x 6/12]
   Debit: Investment in
              Held-to-Maturity Bonds   [discount amortization]
     Credit: Interest Receivable   [interest accrued at purchase]
     Credit: Interest Revenue   [6 months' interest - accrued interest]

• The entry to record subsequent semiannual interest payments and discount amortization is:

   Debit: Cash
   Debit: Investment in Held-to-Maturity Bonds
     Credit: Interest Revenue

• Held-to-maturity bonds are reported on the balance sheet at amortized cost (cost plus unamortized premium or cost minus unamortized discount). No adjustment is made for unrealized gains or losses due to changes in fair value.

Accounting at Maturity

- When the bonds mature, the investor receives the face value of the bonds regardless of whether they were originally purchased at a discount or premium. The entry to record the receipt of the face value by the investor would be:

    Debit: Cash
      Credit: Investment in Held-to-Maturity Bonds

Accounting for Available-for-Sale Securities

- Available-for-sale securities are reported at *fair value* rather than amortized cost.

Adjustment to Fair Value

- The entry to record the purchase of available-for-sale bonds plus accrued interest would be:

    Debit: Investment in Available-for-Sale Bonds
    Debit: Interest Receivable
      Credit: Cash

- The entry to record the first semiannual interest payment after purchase and the discount amortization is:

    Debit: Cash   [face value x stated rate x 6/12]
    Debit: Investment in Available-
            for-Sale Bonds   [discount amortization]
      Credit: Interest Receivable   [interest accrued at purchase]
      Credit: Interest Revenue   [6 months' interest - accrued interest]

- The entry to record subsequent semiannual interest payments and discount amortization is:

    Debit: Cash
    Debit: Investment in Available-for-Sale Bonds
      Credit: Interest Revenue

- On the balance sheet date, the bonds are adjusted to fair value. Any unrealized holding gain or loss is calculated as follows:

    Fair value of bonds at balance sheet date
    - Current balance in the Investment in Available-for-Sale Bonds account
    = Unrealized holding gain or loss on available-for-sale bonds

- The entry to record an unrealized holding gain would be:

    Debit: Investment in Available-for-Sale Bonds
     Credit: Unrealized Holding Gain or Loss on Available-for-Sale Bonds

Notice that the unrealized holding gain is recorded with a credit.

- The entry to record an unrealized holding loss would be:

    Debit: Unrealized Holding Gain or Loss on Available-for-Sale Bonds
     Credit: Investment in Available-for-Sale Bonds

- The Unrealized Holding Gain or Loss on Available-for-Sale Bonds is a stockholders' equity account. If the bonds were classified as trading securities, the unrealized holding gain or loss would be reported on the income statement.

Sale of Bonds Prior to Maturity

- If an investor sells available-for-sale bonds prior to maturity, the gain or loss is calculated as follows:

      Cash proceeds received for bonds (sales price less commissions)
    - Carrying value of bonds
    = Gain or loss on sale of available-for-sale bonds

- If the bonds are sold between interest payment dates, two entries are necessary at the time of sale.

1. The entry to record the discount amortization up to the date of sale would be:

    Debit: Investment in Available-for-Sale Bonds
     Credit: Interest Revenue

2. The entry to record the sale of bonds at a loss and the receipt of accrued interest since the last interest payment date would be:

    Debit: Cash
    Debit: Loss on Sale of Available-for-Sale Bonds
     Credit: Investment in Available-for-Sale Bonds
     Credit: Interest Revenue

The cash received consists of two parts:
1. the sales price of the bonds
2. accrued interest since the last interest payment date

OTHER FORMS OF LONG-TERM DEBT

- Other types of long-term debt, besides bonds, include:
  - mortgages payable
  - leases

Mortgages Payable

- A **mortgage** is a promissory note secured by an asset whose title is pledged to the lender.

- Mortgages are generally payable in equal installments.

- Each mortgage payment consists of:
  1. interest
  2. repayment of principal

- The entry to record the purchase of a building and the issuance of a mortgage is:

     Debit: Building
       Credit: Mortgage Payable
       Credit: Cash

- The entry to record the mortgage payment is:

     Debit: Interest Expense   [principal x rate x time]
     Debit: Mortgage Payable   [payment minus interest expense]
       Credit: Cash   [mortgage payment]

Leases

- A **lease** is a contractual agreement between the **lessor** (owner of the property) and the **lessee** (the user of the property), giving the lessee the right to use the lessor's property for a specific period of time in exchange for cash payments.

- Leasing is used in the airline, retail, hotel, and computer industries.

Types of Leases

- There are two types of leases:
  1. **Capital lease.** A lease that is essentially a financing agreement to purchase an asset and meets one or more of the FASB Statement No. 13's criteria for a capital lease.
  2. **Operating lease.** A lease that does not meet the FASB's criteria to be considered a financing lease. An operating lease is viewed as a rental agreement.

  The entry to record the annual lease payment for an operating lease records the entire lease payment as an expense:

     Debit: Lease Expense
       Credit: Cash

- Capital leases are accounted for essentially as a purchase of an asset. A lease rather than a bank loan is used to finance the purchase.

- Under a capital lease, an asset and a liability are recorded on the lessee's books as if a purchase had taken place. The liability is recorded at the present value of the required lease payments using an appropriate interest rate.

- At inception, the entry to record the present value of the lease payments as an asset and a liability would be:

  Debit: Lease Equipment under Capital Lease (asset account)
     Credit: Obligation under Capital Lease (liability account)

- The Leased Equipment under Capital Lease account is shown under the property, plant, and equipment section of the balance sheet.

- The Obligation under Capital Lease account is a liability which is classified as part current and part long-term.

- Each lease payment consists of 2 parts:
  1. interest, and
  2. repayment of principal

- The entry to record the lease payment is:

  Debit: Interest Expense
  Debit: Obligation under Capital Lease
     Credit: Cash

  The debit to Obligation under Capital Lease account reduces the liability for the amount of the repayment of principal.

- The leased equipment is depreciated over its useful life. The adjusting entry to record depreciation related to the lease is:

  Debit: Depreciation Expense
     Credit: Accumulated Depreciation: Leased Equipment

Operating Versus Capital Leases

- Prior to the issuance of FASB Statement No. 13, some managers had a definite bias to classify leases as operating leases.

- If a lease is considered an operating lease, no liability is recorded on the balance sheet for the required lease payments. **Off-balance-sheet financing** occurs when the lessee in substance makes an installment purchase but records it as an operating lease, thereby not having to record the liability on the balance sheet.

- FASB Statement No. 13 corrected a number of obvious situations in which agreements that were in substance capital leases were being accounted for as operating leases.

USING LONG-TERM DEBT INFORMATION IN DECISION MAKING

- **Leverage** is the use of debt to finance asset purchases.

- Highly leveraged companies have a greater proportion of their assets financed through debt than do companies that are less leveraged.

- Leverage can provide a positive return to stockholders as long as the after-tax cost of borrowing is less than the returns the company can earn on the assets it owns.

- Leverage magnifies income; however, leverage also magnifies losses.

Ratio Analysis

- Ratios used to measure leverage and the debt-paying ability of a company include:
  1. the equity ratio
  2. the debt ratio

Equity and Debt Ratios

- The **equity ratio** measures the proportion of assets supplied by the stockholders versus the proportion supplied by creditors.

- The equity ratio, a measure of leverage, is calculated as:

$$\textbf{Equity Ratio = Total Stockholders' Equity/Total Assets}$$

- The **debt ratio** measures the amount of assets supplied by creditors. The debt ratio is calculated as:

$$\textbf{Debt Ratio = Total Liabilities/Total Assets}$$

- The debt ratio can also be calculated as:

$$\textbf{Debt Ratio = 100\% - Equity Ratio}$$

Debt-to-Equity Ratio

- The debt-to-equity ratio is calculated as follows:

$$\textbf{Debt-to-Equity Ratio = Total Liabilities/Total Stockholders' Equity}$$

Times Interest Earned Ratio

• The times interest earned ratio provides an indication of the ability of a company to meet the required interest payments.

• Times interest earned is calculated as:

Times Interest Earned = Income Before Interest and Taxes/Interest Expense

DECISION SUPPORT SYSTEMS

• The decision to issue bonds can have a significant effect on a firm's financial position and operating results.
  1. The issuance of bonds increases total liabilities, which in turn, affects the firm's debt-to-equity ratio.
  2. Required bond interest payments result in an increase in interest expense on the income statement and a corresponding decrease in net income.
  3. Cash is needed to make periodic interest payments and redeem the bonds at maturity.

• A variety of tools have evolved to help accountants and other financial managers assess the potential effects of debt and investment transactions.

• A **decision support system (DSS)** is a flexible computer-based system that helps individuals analyze quantitative data in complex decision situations.

• A typical DSS includes two types of analysis:
  1. What-if analysis. What-if analysis tries to determine the most likely effect of changes in one or more decision parameters on the decision outcome. Data is manipulated by the decision maker, and the model computes the expected outcome.
  2. Goal-seeking analysis. Goal-seeking analysis attempts to make changes in decision parameters so that a desired outcome will be achieved. The data is manipulated by the model after the user specifies the desired outcome.

• A DDS can help an accountant or a manager make more informed decisions.

KEY TERMS TEST

Test your recall of the key terms as follows: Read the following definitions of key terms and try to recall as many key terms as you can *without assistance*. Write your answers in the spaces provided. If you need assistance, refer to the list of key terms at the end of this section.

1. A(n) _____ is a written agreement between a borrower and a lender in which the borrower agrees to repay a stated sum on a future date and in most cases to make periodic interest payments at specified dates.

2. _____ is the face value of a bond.

3. The date that the principal on the bond is to be repaid is the _____ _____.

4. _____ _____ are bonds whose entire principal is due in one payment.

5. _____ _____ are bonds that are payable on various dates.

6. The _____ _____ _____, or _____ _____ _____, is the interest rate stated on the face of the bond at the time of sale.

7. The _____ _____ _____ is the interest rate being paid in the marketplace.

8. _____ _____ _____ are bonds that do not pay interest periodically.

9. Written covenants that are part of the bond agreement are called _____ _____.

10. _____ _____ are bonds that are issued without any security to back them.

11. Bonds which can be exchanged, at some future specified date, into a firm's common stock are _____ _____.

12. The _____ _____, or _____ _____ _____, is the actual interest rate at which a bond is used.

13. A(n) _____ _____ is an account that increases the balance in another related account.

14. The _____ _____ is a method of determining periodic interest, in which the effective interest rate is applied to the carrying value of the bond at the beginning of the period.

15. A(n) _____ _____ is a collection of cash or other assets set apart to be used for a specific purpose, such as bond repayment.

16. _____ _____ _____ _____ is the redemption of a bond prior to its maturity date.

17. A(n) _____ is a promissory note secured by an asset whose title is pledged to the lender.

18. A(n) _____ is a contractual agreement between the lessor and the lessee, giving the lessee the right to use the lessor's property for a specified period of time in exchange for stipulated cash payments.

19. The owner of the property that is leased to the lessee is known as the _____.

20. The person who leases and uses the leased property is the _____.

21. _____ _____ are leases that do not meet the FASB's criteria to be considered a financing lease.

22. A type of lease that is essentially a financing agreement to purchase an asset is called a(n) _____ _____.

23. _____ _____ is the use of financing instruments that are not recorded as liabilities on the balance sheet.

24. _____ _____ are bonds that are secured by the borrower's collateral or specified assets.

25. _____ is the use of debt to finance asset purchases.

26. The _____ _____ measures the proportion of total assets supplied by shareholders and is calculated by dividing total stockholders' equity by total assets.

27. The _____ _____ measures the proportion of assets provided by debt holders and is calculated by dividing total liabilities by total assets.

28. _____ _____ _____ is the ratio of the income that is available for interest payments to the annual interest expense and is calculated by dividing income before interest and taxes by the annual interest expense.

29. _____ _____ _____, or _____, are flexible computer-based systems that help individuals analyze quantitative data in complex decision situations.

KEY TERMS:

adjunct account
bond
bond indentures
capital lease
convertible bonds
decision support systems, DSS
debt ratio
denomination
early extinguishment of debt
effective-interest method
effective interest rate
equity ratio
lease
lessee
lessor
leverage

market interest rate
maturity date
mortgage
mortgage bonds
nominal interest rate
off-balance-sheet financing
operating leases
serial bonds
sinking fund
stated interest rate
term bonds
times interest earned
unsecured bonds
yield rate
zero coupon bonds

Compare your answers to those at the end of the chapter and review any key terms missed.

CHAPTER QUIZ

Write your answers in the spaces provided.

1. When issuing bonds, the two types of payments that a borrower agrees to make are:
   1. _____
   2. _____

2. If bond interest is paid semiannually, bond interest payments are calculated as follows:

   Bond Interest Payment = _____ X _____ X _____

3. If bond interest is paid semiannually, effective interest expense is calculated as:

   Interest Expense = _____ X _____ X _____

4. _____ often agree to purchase an entire bond issue and then assume the risks involved in selling the bonds to investors.

5. List two financial advisory services that evaluate a bond's risk and publish bond ratings for major corporations:
   1. _____
   2. _____

6. The Investment in Available-for-Sale Bonds account is classified as a current asset if _____.

7. The gain or loss on the sale of available-for-sale bonds is calculated as follows:

   _____

   _____

   = Gain or loss on sale of bonds

8. Each mortgage payment consists of:
   1. _____
   2. _____

9. List the two different types of analyses that a decision support system (DSS) usually provides:
   1. _____
   2. _____

10. The equity ratio is calculated as:

    Equity Ratio = _____ / _____

11. The debt ratio is calculated as:

Debt Ratio = _____ / _____

12. The debt-to-equity ratio is calculated as:

Debt-to-Equity Ratio = _____ / _____

13. Times interest earned is calculated as:

Times Interest Earned = _____ / _____

Circle the best answer.

14. At the time of issuance, a bond's stated rate was 10% and the market rate was 12%. The bond will sell at a premium: (a) true; (b) false

15. If the stated rate equals the market rate at issuance, the bond will sell at par: (a) true; (b) false

16. Debentures are secured bonds: (a) true; (b) false

17. Convertible bonds may at some future date be converted into a firm's common stock: (a) true; (b) false

18. Junk bonds carry a high rate of interest due to their high risk: (a) true; (b) false

19. Companies may use either the straight-line method or the effective-interest method of amortizing a bond premium or discount: (a) true; (b) false

20. Total interest expense over the life of a bond is the same under the straight-line and the effective-interest methods: (a) true; (b) false

21. Leverage magnifies income and reduces losses: (a) true; (b) false

22. Which one of the following rates does not change over the life of a bond? (a) market rate; (b) stated rate

23. Which of the following methods of amortizing bond discounts and premiums allocates the discount or premium evenly over the life of the bond? (a) straight-line; (b) effective-interest

24. A lease that results in the recording of an asset and a liability is a(n): (a) operating lease; (b) capital lease

Use the following information to answer the next four questions.

On January 2, 1995 the Hirsch Company issued $200,000 of 5-year, 8% bonds at 85.27936 to yield 12%. The bonds pay interest semiannually on January 2 and July 1. The company uses the effective-interest method to amortize bond premiums and discounts.

25. The amount of cash the firm would receive from the issuance of the bonds would be: (a) $85,279.36; (b) $170,558.72; (c) $177,381.06; (d) $200,000.00

26. From January 2, 1995 until January 2, 1996, the firm would pay interest in the amount of: (a) $11,269; (b) $13,644; (c) $14,190; (d) $16,000

27. From January 2, 1995 until January 2, 1996, the firm would incur interest expense of: (a) $12,800.60; (b) $14,240.48; (c) $20,601.05; (d) $20,647.05

28. Over the ten-year life of the bond, the firm would incur interest expense of: (a) $189,441.28; (b) $160,000.00; (c) $142,615.86; (d) $130,558.72

Use the following information to answer the next four questions.

The following information was provided for the Ortegren Company:

Total assets	$1,000,000
Total stockholders' equity	400,000
Pretax income from operations	120,000
Interest expense	20,000

29. The equity ratio would be: (a) 52%; (b) 50%; (c) 40%; (d) 38%

30. The debt ratio would be: (a) 40%; (b) 50%; (c) 52%; (d) 60%

31. The debt-to-equity ratio would be: (a) 150%; (b) 67%; (c) 60%; (d) 40%

32. The times interest earned ratio would be: (a) 6; (b) 7; (c) 9.4; (d) 10

Compare your answers to those at the end of the chapter and review any questions missed.

EXERCISES

EXERCISE 1

On January 2, 1995, the Compton Corporation issued $100,000, ten-year 12% bonds. The bonds were issued to yield 10% and pay interest every January 2 and July 1. The company uses the effective-interest method to amortize the bond discount or premium.

Required:

1. Calculate the issue price of the bonds.

2. Make the entry to record the issue of the bonds on January 2, 1995.

DATE	ACCOUNT TITLES	REF.	DEBIT	CREDIT

3. Make the entry to record the first interest payment on July 1, 1995.

DATE	ACCOUNT TITLES	REF.	DEBIT	CREDIT

4. If the company has a December 31 year-end, make the appropriate entry at December 31, 1995.

DATE	ACCOUNT TITLES	REF.	DEBIT	CREDIT

5. Make the entry to record the interest payment on January 2, 1996.

DATE	ACCOUNT TITLES	REF.	DEBIT	CREDIT

EXERCISE 2

Using the information from the previous exercise, answer the following requirements assuming the company uses the straight-line method to amortize the discount or premium.

Required:

1. Make the entry to record the issue of the bonds on January 2, 1995.

DATE	ACCOUNT TITLES	REF.	DEBIT	CREDIT

2. Make the entry to record the first interest payment on July 1, 1995.

DATE	ACCOUNT TITLES	REF.	DEBIT	CREDIT

3. If the company has a December 31 year-end, make the appropriate entries at December 31, 1995.

DATE	ACCOUNT TITLES	REF.	DEBIT	CREDIT

4. Make the entry to record the interest payment on January 2, 1996.

DATE	ACCOUNT TITLES	REF.	DEBIT	CREDIT

EXERCISE 3

On January 2, 1995 the O'Boyle Corporation issued $100,000 of five-year bonds. The bonds have a stated rate of 8% and were issued at 108.42488 to yield 6%. Interest is payable annually on January 2 of each year.

Required:

1. Compute the following amortization table for the bonds using the straight-line amortization method.

Date	Cash Interest	Interest Expense	Amortization	Carrying Value
01-02-95				$
01-02-96	$	$	$	
01-02-97				
01-02-98				
01-02-99				
01-02-00				

2. Compute the following amortization table for the bonds using the effective-interest amortization method.

Date	Cash Interest	Interest Expense	Amortization	Carrying Value
01-02-95				$
01-02-96	$	$	$	
01-02-97				
01-02-98				
01-02-99				
01-02-00				

EXERCISE 4

The Hampton Corporation issued $400,000 of 20-year, 12% term bonds on March 1, 1995. The bonds were issued at par and pay interest semiannually every January 2 and July 1.

Required:

1. Prepare the journal entry to record the issuance of the bonds on March 1, 1995.

DATE	ACCOUNT TITLES	REF.	DEBIT	CREDIT

2. Prepare the journal entry to record the interest payment on July 1, 1995.

DATE	ACCOUNT TITLES	REF.	DEBIT	CREDIT

3. Prepare the adjusting journal entry on December 31, 1995, the firm's year-end.

DATE	ACCOUNT TITLES	REF.	DEBIT	CREDIT

EXERCISE 5

On March 1, 1995, the Houlihan Manufacturing Company purchased $10,000 of six-year 9% bonds at a price of 93. The bonds were dated January 2, 1995 and pay interest semiannually on January 2 and July 1. Houlihan uses the straight-line method of interest amortization and uses a December 31 year-end. The bonds have a fair value of 102 at December 31, 1995 and a fair value of 97 at December 31, 1996. Houlihan sold the bonds at 99 on July 1, 1997.

Required:

1. Assuming that Houlihan classifies the bonds as trading securities, prepare the entries that Houlihan would make to account for the bonds.

DATE	ACCOUNT TITLES	REF.	DEBIT	CREDIT

EXERCISE 5 (continued)

2. How would your answer to requirement 1 change if Houlihan classified the bonds as available-for-sale securities?

EXERCISE 6

On January 2, 1995, the Potter Corporation purchased a building for $100,000. The firm made a 20% down payment and took out a mortgage payable over 2 years, at a rate of $3,766 monthly. The first payment is due February 2, 1995, and the interest rate is 12%.

Required:

1. Make the entry to record the purchase of the building.

DATE	ACCOUNT TITLES	REF.	DEBIT	CREDIT

2. Complete the following mortgage amortization table for the first six mortgage payments. (Round amounts to dollars.)

Date	Payment	Monthly Interest	Principal	Carrying Value of Mortgage
01-02-95				$
02-02-95	$	$	$	
03-02-95				
04-02-95				
05-02-95				
06-02-95				
07-02-95				

3. Make the entries to record the first two mortgage payments.

DATE	ACCOUNT TITLES	REF.	DEBIT	CREDIT

379

EXERCISE 7

On January 2, 1995, the Powers Corporation leased an office building from
Control Systems, Inc. The Powers Corporation agreed to make 10 annual lease
payments of $15,930 each beginning on December 31, 1995. Assume the capital
lease has a present value of $90,000 based on a 12% interest rate. The
Powers Corporation uses straight-line depreciation and estimates that the
building will have a ten-year life with no salvage value.

Required:

1. Prepare the necessary journal entry to record the lease for the Powers
   Corporation on January 2, 1995.

DATE	ACCOUNT TITLES	REF.	DEBIT	CREDIT

2. Prepare the journal entry to record the first lease payment on December
   31, 1995.

DATE	ACCOUNT TITLES	REF.	DEBIT	CREDIT

3. Prepare the journal entry to record depreciation related to the lease.

DATE	ACCOUNT TITLES	REF.	DEBIT	CREDIT

4. How would the building and the related lease liability be shown on the
   December 31, 1995 balance sheet of the Powers Corporation?

```
╔═══════════════════════════════════╗
║  ANSWERS                          ║
╚═══════════════════════════════════╝
```

KEY TERMS TEST

1. bond
2. Denomination
3. maturity date
4. Term bonds
5. Serial bonds
6. stated interest rate, nominal interest rate
7. market interest rate
8. Zero coupon bonds
9. bond indentures
10. Unsecured bonds
11. convertible bonds
12. yield rate, effective interest rate
13. adjunct account
14. effective-interest method
15. sinking fund
16. Early extinguishment of debt
17. mortgage
18. lease
19. lessor
20. lessee
21. Operating leases
22. capital lease
23. Off-balance-sheet financing
24. Mortgage bonds
25. Leverage
26. equity ratio
27. debt ratio
28. Times interest earned
29. Decision support systems, DSS

CHAPTER QUIZ

1. 1. interest payments
   2. maturity value
2. Bond Interest Payment = Face Value x Stated Rate x 6/12
3. Interest Expense = Carrying Value x Effective Rate
4. Underwriters
5. 1. Standard and Poor's
   2. Moody's
6. management intends to sell the bonds within the operating cycle or twelve months

7.   Cash proceeds received for bonds
     - Carrying value of bonds
     = Gain or loss on sale of bonds

8. 1. interest
   2. repayment of principal

9. 1. what-if analysis
   2. goal-seeking analysis
10. Equity Ratio = Total Stockholders' Equity/Total Assets
11. Debt Ratio = Total Liabilities/Total Assets
12. Debt-to-Equity Ratio = Total Liabilities/Total Stockholders' Equity
13. Times Interest Earned = Income Before Interest and Taxes/Interest Expense
14. b False The bond will sell at a discount.
15. a True
16. b False Debentures are unsecured bonds.
17. a True
18. a True
19. b False Companies must use the effective-interest method to amortize a
               bond premium or discount unless the straight-line method is not
               materially different.
20. a True
21. b False Leverage magnifies income and magnifies losses.
22. b
23. a
24. b
25. b $200,000 x 85.27936% = $170,558.72
26. d $200,000 x 8% = $16,000

27. c Interest Expense = Carrying Value x Effective Rate
       July 1 1995: $170,558.72 x 12% x 6/12 $10,233.52
       January 2, 1996: [$170,558.72 + ($10,233.52 - $8,000)] x 6%   10,367.53
                                                                       _____
                                                                       $20,601.05
                                                                       ===========

28. a $200,000 x 8% = $16,000/year x 10 years = $160,000.00
       Discount ($200,000 - $170,558.72)   =   29,441.28
                                                   _____
       Interest expense $189,441.28
                                                   ============

29. c $400,000/$1,000,000 = 40%
30. d ($1,000,000 - $400,000)/$1,000,000 = 60%
31. a $600,000/$400,000 = 150%
32. b ($120,000 + $20,000)/$20,000 = 7 times

EXERCISE 1

1. Present value of interest payments:
    Face value x stated rate x time x PVAF (n = 20, 5%)
    $100,000 x 12% x 6/12 x 12.46221 $ 74,773.26

    Present value of maturity value:
    $100,000 x PVIF (n = 20, 5%)
    $100,000 x .37689   37,689.00
                                                                 _____
    Issue price $112,462.26
                                                                 ============

382

EXERCISE 1 (continued)

2.

DATE	ACCOUNT TITLES	REF.	DEBIT	CREDIT
1995				
Jan. 2	Cash		112,462.26	
	Bonds Payable			100,000.00
	Premium on Bonds Payable			12,462.26

3.

DATE	ACCOUNT TITLES	REF.	DEBIT	CREDIT
1995				
July 1	Interest Expense		5,623.11	
	Premium on Bonds Payable		376.89	
	Cash			6,000.00

Interest expense = $112,462.26 x 10% x 6/12 = $5,623.11
Cash = $100,000 x 12% x 6/12 = $6,000.00
Premium amortization = $6,000.00 - $5,623.11 = $376.89

4.

DATE	ACCOUNT TITLES	REF.	DEBIT	CREDIT
1995				
Dec. 31	Interest Expense		5,604.27	
	Premium on Bonds Payable		395.73	
	Interest Payable			6,000.00

Interest expense = ($112,462.26 - $376.89) x 10% x 6/12 = $5,604.27
Interest payable = $100,000 x 12% x 6/12 = $6,000.00
Premium amortization = $6,000.00 - $5,604.27 = $395.73

5.

DATE	ACCOUNT TITLES	REF.	DEBIT	CREDIT
1996				
Jan. 2	Interest Payable		6,000.00	
	Cash			6,000.00

EXERCISE 2

1.

DATE	ACCOUNT TITLES	REF.	DEBIT	CREDIT
1995				
Jan. 2	Cash		112,462.26	
	Bonds Payable			100,000.00
	Premium on Bonds Payable			12,462.26

2.

DATE	ACCOUNT TITLES	REF.	DEBIT	CREDIT
1995				
July 1	Interest Expense		5,376.89	
	Premium on Bonds Payable		623.11	
	Cash			6,000.00

Cash = $100,000 x 12% x 6/12 = $6,000.00
Premium amortization = $12,462.26/20 periods = $623.11
Interest expense = $6,000.00 - $623.11 = $5,376.89

3.

DATE	ACCOUNT TITLES	REF.	DEBIT	CREDIT
1995				
Dec. 31	Interest Expense		5,376.89	
	Premium on Bonds Payable		623.11	
	Interest Payable			6,000.00

4.

DATE	ACCOUNT TITLES	REF.	DEBIT	CREDIT
1996				
Jan. 2	Interest Payable		6,000.00	
	Cash			6,000.00

EXERCISE 3

1.

Date	Cash Interest	Interest Expense	Amortization	Carrying Value
01-02-95				$108,424.88
01-02-96	$8,000.00[a]	$6,315.02[c]	$1,684.98[b]	106,739.90[d]
01-02-97	8,000.00	6,315.02	1,684.98	105,054.92
01-02-98	8,000.00	6,315.02	1,684.98	103,369.94
01-02-99	8,000.00	6,315.02	1,684.98	101,684.96
01-02-00	8,000.00	6,315.04	1,684.96[e]	100,000.00

[a]Face value x stated rate = $100,000.00 x 8% = $8,000.00
[b]$108,424.88 - $100,000.00 = $8,424.88/5 interest periods = $1,684.98
[c]$8,000.00 - $1,684.98 = $6,315.02
[d]Carrying value - amortization = $108,424.88 - $1,684.98 = $106,739.90
[e]rounded

2.

Date	Cash Interest	Interest Expense	Amortization	Carrying Value
01-02-95				$108,424.88
01-02-96	$8,000.00[a]	$6,505.49[b]	$1,494.51[c]	106,930.37[d]
01-02-97	8,000.00	6,415.82	1,584.18	105,346.19
01-02-98	8,000.00	6,320.77	1,679.23	103,666.96
01-02-99	8,000.00	6,220.02	1,779.98	101,886.98
01-02-00	8,000.00	6,113.02	1,886.98[e]	100,000.00

[a]Face value x stated rate = $100,000.00 x 8% = $8,000.00
[b]Carrying value x effective rate = $108,424.88 x 6% = $6,505.49
[c]Interest payment - interest expense = $8,000.00 - $6,505.49 = $1,494.51
[d]Carrying value - amortization = $108,424.88 - $1,494.51 = $106,930.37
[e]rounded

EXERCISE 4

1. Entry to record issuance of bonds:

DATE	ACCOUNT TITLES	REF.	DEBIT	CREDIT
1995				
Mar. 2	Cash		408,000	
	Interest Payable			8,000
	Bonds Payable			400,000

Interest payable = $400,000 \times 12\% \times 2/12 = \$8,000$

2. Entry to record interest payment:

DATE	ACCOUNT TITLES	REF.	DEBIT	CREDIT
1995				
July 1	Interest Expense		16,000	
	Interest Payable		8,000	
	Cash			24,000

Interest expense = $400,000 \times 12\% \times 4/12 = \$16,000$
Cash = $400,000 \times 12\% \times 6/12 = \$24,000$

3. Adjusting entry at December 31, 1995:

DATE	ACCOUNT TITLES	REF.	DEBIT	CREDIT
1995				
Dec. 31	Interest Expense		24,000	
	Interest Payable			24,000

Interest expense = $400,000 \times 12\% \times 6/12 = \$24,000$

EXERCISE 5

1.

DATE	ACCOUNT TITLES	REF.	DEBIT	CREDIT
1995				
Mar. 1	Investment in Trading Bonds		9,300	
	Interest Receivable		150	
	Cash			9,450
	To record investment in six-year, 9% bonds.			
	Investment in bonds = $10,000 x .93 = $9,300			
	Interest receivable = $10,000 x 9% x 2/12 = $150			
July 1	Cash		450	
	Investment in Trading Bonds		40	
	Interest Receivable			150
	Interest Revenue			340
	To record the receipt of interest and amortization.			
	Cash = $10,000 x 9% x 6/12 = $450			
	Discount amortization = $700/70 months = $10/month			
	$10 x 4 months = $40			
Dec. 31	Interest Receivable		450	
	Investment in Trading Bonds		60	
	Interest Revenue			510
	To record the accrual of interest and amortization.			
Dec. 31	Investment in Trading Bonds		800	
	Unrealized Holding Gain or Loss on			
	Investment in Trading Bonds			800
	To record increase in fair value of trading bonds.			
	Fair value at 12/31/95 ($10,000 x 1.02)			$10,200
	Current balance ($9,300 + $40 + $60)			9,400
	Unrealized holding gain			$ 800
1996				
Jan. 2	Cash		450	
	Interest Receivable			450
	To record the receipt of interest.			
July 1	Cash		450	
	Investment in Trading Bonds		60	
	Interest Revenue			510
	To record the receipt of interest and amortization.			

EXERCISE 5 (continued)

DATE	ACCOUNT TITLES	REF.	DEBIT	CREDIT
Dec. 31	Interest Receivable		450	
	Investment in Trading Bonds		60	
	Interest Revenue			510
	To record the accrual of interest and amortization.			
Dec. 31	Unrealized Holding Gain or Loss on Investment in			
	Trading Bonds		620	
	Investment in Trading Bonds			620
	To record decrease in fair value of trading bonds.			

Fair value at 12/31/96 ($10,000 x .97) $ 9,700
Current balance ($10,200 + $60 + $60)   10,320

Unrealized holding loss $ 620

DATE	ACCOUNT TITLES	REF.	DEBIT	CREDIT
1997				
Jan. 2	Cash		450	
	Interest Receivable			450
	To record the receipt of interest.			
July 1	Cash		450	
	Investment in Trading Bonds		60	
	Interest Revenue			510
	To record the receipt of interest and amortization.			
July 1	Cash		9,900	
	Gain on Sale of Bonds			140
	Investment in Trading Bonds			9,760
	To record sale of bonds and realized holding gain.			

Sales price ($10,000 x .99) $9,900
Current balance ($9,700 + $60)   9,760

Gain on sale $ 140

EXERCISE 5 (continued)

2. The following account titles would change:
   a. Investment in Available-for-Sale Bonds would replace Investment in Trading Bonds.
   b. Unrealized Holding Gain or Loss on Available-for-Sale Bonds would replace Unrealized Holding Gain or Loss on Trading Bonds.

   In addition, the unrealized holding gain or loss on available-for-sale bonds is a stockholders' equity account and would not affect current earnings.

EXERCISE 6

1. Entry to record the purchase of the building:

DATE	ACCOUNT TITLES	REF.	DEBIT	CREDIT
1995				
Jan. 2	Building		100,000	
	Cash			20,000
	Mortgage Payable			80,000

2. Mortgage amortization table:

Date	Payment	Monthly Interest	Principal	Carrying Value of Mortgage
01-02-95				$80,000
02-02-95	$3,766	$800[a]	$2,966[b]	77,034[c]
03-02-95	3,766	770	2,996	74,038
04-02-95	3,766	740	3,026	71,012
05-02-95	3,766	710	3,056	67,956
06-02-95	3,766	680	3,086	64,870
07-02-95	3,766	649	3,117	61,753

[a]Carrying Value x Rate x Time = $80,000 x 12% x 1/12 = $800
[b]Payment - Interest = $3,766 - $800 = $2,966
[c]Carrying Value - Principal = $80,000 - $2,966 = $77,034

3. Entries to record first two mortgage payments:

DATE	ACCOUNT TITLES	REF.	DEBIT	CREDIT
1995				
Feb. 2	Interest Expense		800	
	Mortgage Payable		2,966	
	Cash			3,766
Mar. 2	Interest Expense		770	
	Mortgage Payable		2,996	
	Cash			3,766

EXERCISE 7

1. Entry to record the lease:

DATE	ACCOUNT TITLES	REF.	DEBIT	CREDIT
1995				
Jan. 2	Leased Property under Capital Lease		90,000	
	Obligation under Capital Lease			90,000

2. Entry to record the first lease payment:

DATE	ACCOUNT TITLES	REF.	DEBIT	CREDIT
1995				
Dec. 31	Interest Expense		10,800	
	Obligation under Capital Lease		5,130	
	Cash			15,930

Interest expense = $90,000 \times 12\% = \$10,800$
Reduction of liability = $\$15,930 - \$10,800 = \$5,130$

3. Entry to record depreciation of leased asset:

DATE	ACCOUNT TITLES	REF.	DEBIT	CREDIT
1995				
Dec. 31	Depreciation Expense		9,000	
	Accumulated Depreciation: Leased Property			9,000

Depreciation expense = $\$90,000/10$ years = $\$9,000$

4. Assets:
Leased property	$90,000	
Less: Accumulated depreciation	9,000	
	$81,000	
	=======	

Liabilities:
Obligation under Capital Lease $84,870[a]
                                  =======

[a]$90,000 - $5,130 = $84,870 (of which $5,746 is current).

390

CHAPTER 13

EQUITY FINANCING--CORPORATIONS

CHAPTER REVIEW

CHARACTERISTICS OF A CORPORATION

- A corporation is a separate legal entity from its owners.

- A corporation may sue or be sued and may be taxed.

Advantages of the Corporate Form of Organization

- Advantages of the corporate form of organization include:
  1. Limited liability for stockholders. The owners' liability is limited to the amount they have invested in the corporation. Creditors can look only to the assets of the corporation to satisfy their claims.
  2. Transferability of ownership. Ownership in a corporation is evidenced by possession of a share of stock, which usually can be transferred to another without any restrictions.
  3. Ease of capital formation. Limited liability and transferability of ownership make it easier for a corporation to raise capital than for a sole proprietorship or a partnership.

Disadvantages of the Corporate Form of Organization

- Disadvantages of the corporate form of organization include:
  1. Double taxation. The earnings of a corporation are subject to taxes up to 34%. When corporate earnings are distributed to stockholders in the form of dividends, the dividends are not deductible by the corporation but are taxable to the recipient. In effect, corporate earnings are taxed twice, once at the corporate level and again at the individual shareholder level.
  2. Government regulation. Corporations are chartered by a state and thus must comply with various state and federal regulations. For smaller companies, the cost of complying with these regulations may outweigh the other benefits of the corporate form of business organization.
  3. For smaller companies, the limited liability feature of a corporation may be a disadvantage in raising capital. Because of this feature, creditors have claims against only the assets of a corporation; if a corporation defaults, the creditors have no recourse against the owners. As a result, smaller, closely held corporations often find that loans from bankers and other creditors are limited to the amount of security offered by the corporation. In other cases, the shareholders may have to sign an agreement pledging their personal assets as security.

FORMATION AND ORGANIZATION OF A CORPORATION

Forming a Corporation

- The first step in forming a corporation is for at least three individuals, generally the corporate president, vice-president, and secretary-treasurer, to file an application with the appropriate state official, often the secretary of state.

- Once the articles of incorporation have been approved by the appropriate state official, they are referred to as the *corporate charter*.

- **Organization costs** are the costs incurred to start a business, including:
  - legal costs
  - filing and incorporation fees
  - promotion costs
  - printing and engraving costs

- Organization costs are usually listed in the Other Assets section of the balance sheet.

Stockholders

- The stockholders are the owners of the corporation.

- Ownership in a corporation is evidenced by stock certificates. A stock certificate is a legal document that shows the number, type, and par value (if any) of the shares issued by the corporation.

- In large corporations, the shareholders do not participate in the day-to-day operation of the business.

- Stockholders elect a **board of directors** to establish broad corporate policies and appoint senior management.

- Rights of stockholders include:
  1. The right to attend all stockholders meetings.
  2. The right to vote for the board of directors. Stockholders who do not attend the meetings are able to vote through a proxy. A **proxy** is a legal document, signed by a stockholder, giving another person the right to vote the shares in the manner he or she deems best.
  3. The right to vote on major corporate policies and decisions such as proposed mergers and consolidations.
  4. The right to receive a proportionate share of all dividends declared by the board of directors.
  5. Upon liquidation of the corporation, the right to a proportionate share of remaining corporate assets after all the claims of the creditors have been satisfied.
  6. The preemptive right gives existing stockholders the right to purchase shares of a new stock issue in proportion to the shares already owned. This right ensures that the ownership of the current stockholders is not diluted by the issuance of additional shares.

Board of Directors and Senior Management

- The board of directors and the chairperson of the board are elected by the stockholders.

- The board's primary functions are to:
  1. determine general corporate policies.
  2. appoint senior management.
  3. protect the interests of stockholders and creditors.

EQUITY SECURITIES

- Two major types of capital stock are:
  1. common stock
  2. preferred stock

Common Stock

- **Common stock** is a capital stock that must be issued by all corporations.

- Common stock is the only type of stock with voting rights.

- In the event of corporate liquidation, common shareholders will not receive any assets until the claims of creditors and preferred stockholders are satisfied.

Preferred Stock

- **Preferred stock** generally has the following preferences and characteristics:
  1. Preference as to dividends.
  2. Cumulative dividends.
  3. Preference over common stockholders upon liquidation.
  4. Callable shares.
  5. No voting rights.

Preferred Dividends

- Preferred stockholders must receive all of the dividends to which they are entitled before any dividends can be declared and paid to the common stockholders.

- Preferred stock usually has the amount of its dividends stated on the stock certificate in one of two ways:
  1. the actual dollar amount of the dividend may be stated on the stock certificate or
  2. the dividend is stated as a percentage of par value.

- **Par value** is a stated amount printed on the stock certificate. For example, if dividends are declared, 8% preferred stock with a $100 par value would have dividends of $8 per share (8% x $100 par).

- Many consider preferred stock more stable and less risky than common stock.

Cumulative Versus Noncumulative Preferred Stock

- Many issues of preferred stock are cumulative (preferred stockholders do not lose their claim to undeclared dividends). The right to receive these undeclared dividends accumulates over time and must be paid in full before common stockholders can receive any dividends.

- If the preferred stock is noncumulative, any dividends not declared in the current year will lapse, and preferred stockholders will lose their claim to such dividends.

- **Dividends in arrears** are accumulated unpaid dividends on cumulative preferred stock. Dividends in arrears plus current year preferred dividends must be paid before common stockholders receive any dividends.

- Dividends in arrears are not liabilities of the corporation; however, full disclosure requires that any dividends in arrears be disclosed in the notes to the financial statements.

Participating Versus Nonparticipating Preferred Stock

- When preferred stock has a participating feature, in addition to the stated dividend, preferred stockholders can participate with common shareholders in additional dividends.

- When full participation exists, the common shareholders receive dividends at the same rate as preferred, and any excess dividends are split on a proportionate basis between common and preferred shareholders.

- Most preferred stock is *not* participating; the preferred stockholders receive only the stated dividend rate, regardless of how profitable the company is.

- The preferred stockholder who purchases cumulative nonparticipating preferred stock trades off a possible higher return for less risk.

- Normally, preferred stock has preference in the event of corporate liquidation. After the creditors are satisfied, preferred shareholders must be fully satisfied before common stockholders can receive any assets. Most preferred stock has an actual stated liquidation value per share that the shareholder will receive if liquidation occurs.

Other Features of Preferred Stock

- **Convertible preferred stock** is a preferred stock that can be converted into common stock at a stated rate and time.

- **Redeemable preferred stock** is preferred stock that can be returned for a stated price by the stockholder to the issuing corporation.

- **Callable preferred stock** gives the issuing corporation, at its option, the right to repurchase the stock at a specified price. The **call premium** is the difference between the call price and the par value of preferred stock. The call provision gives the corporation the flexibility to retire preferred stock with a high dividend rate and replace it with new stock at a lower rate.

COMPONENTS OF STOCKHOLDERS' EQUITY

- Stockholders' equity consists of the following components:
  1. contributed capital, including
     - preferred stock, par value
     - common stock, par value
     - additional paid-in capital on preferred stock
     - additional paid-in capital on common stock
     - donated capital
     - resale of treasury stock above its cost
  2. retained earnings
  3. treasury stock

Contributed Capital

- **Contributed capital** is the total capital contributed by stockholders and others.

- Contributed capital has two components:
  1. **Legal (stated) capital.** Legal capital is usually equal to the par or stated value of all of the capital stock that has been issued.
  2. **Additional paid-in capital.** Additional paid-in capital is the amount invested by owners in excess of the par value of the stock purchased.

- **Par value** of common or preferred stock is an amount designated in the articles of incorporation or by the board of directors and is printed on the stock certificate.

- The board of directors has the right to set the par value of stock at any amount it desires. Because it is unlawful in most states to issue stock below its par value, the board usually sets a relatively low par value, such as $1, $5, or $10.

- **No par stock** has no stated or par value.

- Number of shares authorized is the number of shares that the corporation is allowed to issue.

- Shares issued represent the number of shares the corporation has actually issued to date.

- Outstanding shares are the difference between the shares issued and the shares held as treasury stock.

Additional Paid-in Capital

- Sources of additional paid-in capital are:
  1. Issue of stock in excess of the par or stated value.
  2. Resale of treasury stock (stock repurchased by the corporation) above its cost.
  3. Donated capital, such as when a city or municipality offers a corporation land on which to locate its plant. Donated assets are recorded at their fair market value using the following entry:

Debit:	Asset Account
Credit:	Donated Capital

Retained Earnings

- Retained earnings result from a business's profitable operations.

- Dividends reduce retained earnings.

- The balance in the Retained Earnings account is calculated as follows:

  Beginning Retained Earnings + Income - Dividends = Ending Retained Earnings

Treasury Stock

- Treasury stock is a corporation's own stock that the corporation has repurchased.

Debit Items in Stockholders' Equity

- Direct deductions to stockholders' equity include:
  - unrealized losses on long-term investments
  - cumulative foreign currency translation adjustments

ACCOUNTING FOR THE ISSUANCE OF STOCK

- Large public corporations often issue stock through **underwriters** (brokerage firms), such as Merrill Lynch, that purchase the entire stock issue for a stated price.

- The underwriters assume the risks in marketing the stock.

Stock Issued for Cash

- Stock may have:
  - a par value
  - no par with a stated value
  - no par with no stated value

- The entry to record the issuance of par value stock is:

Debit:	Cash	[issue price]
Credit:	Common Stock	[par value]
Credit:	Paid-in Capital in Excess of Par	[issue price - par value]

- The entry to record the issuance of no par stock is:

Debit:	Cash	[issue price]
Credit:	Common Stock	[issue price]

- The entry to record the issuance of no par, stated value stock is:

Debit:	Cash	[issue price]
Credit:	Common Stock	[stated value]
Credit:	Paid-in Capital in Excess of Stated Value	[issue price - stated value]

Stock Issued for Noncash Assets

- A corporation may receive land, buildings, or other assets in exchange for its stock.

- The assets or services received should be recorded at:
  1. the fair market value of the stock issued at the date of the transaction or
  2. the fair market value of the assets or services received if it is not feasible to determine the fair market value of the stock issued.

- The entry to record the issuance of common stock in exchange for land would be:

Debit:	Land	
Credit:	Common Stock	
Credit:	Paid-in Capital in Excess of Par	

DIVIDENDS

Cash Dividends

- The amount and regularity of cash dividends are two of the factors that affect the market price of a firm's stock. Many corporations, therefore, attempt to establish a regular quarterly dividend pattern that is maintained or slowly increased over a number of years.

- There must be a positive balance in retained earnings in order to issue a dividend. If there is a deficit (debit or negative balance) in retained earnings, any dividend would represent a return of invested capital and is therefore called a *liquidating dividend*.

- In addition to having a positive balance in retained earnings, a firm must also have the necessary cash available to pay a cash dividend.

Declaration of Dividends

- Three dates are significant to the declaration and payment of dividends:
  1. **Declaration date**. The declaration date is the date on which the board of directors declares the dividend. At that time, the dividend becomes a liability of the corporation and is recorded with the following entry on the declaration date:

     Debit: Retained Earnings (or Dividends Declared)
       Credit: Dividends Payable

     A Dividends Declared account can be debited instead of Retained Earnings. At year-end the Dividends Declared account is closed to Retained Earnings.

  2. **Date of record**. Only stockholders on the date of record will receive the dividend. No entry is made on the date of record.

  3. **Payment date**. The payment date is the date that the dividend is actually paid. The entry made on the payment date is:

     Debit: Dividends Payable
       Credit: Cash

Noncash Dividends

- When a noncash dividend or (*property dividend*) is issued, the property is revalued to its current market value as of the date of declaration, and a gain or loss is recognized on the revaluation of the assets.

- The entry to record the declaration of a property dividend is:

  Debit: Retained Earnings
    Credit: Property Dividends Payable

- The entry to record the distribution of a property dividend in the form of marketable securities is:

  Debit: Property Dividend Payable
    Credit: Investment in Marketable Securities

STOCK DIVIDENDS AND STOCK SPLITS

Stock Dividends

- A **stock dividend** is a distribution of the corporation's own stock to current shareholders on a proportional basis.

- Most stock dividends are given only to common stockholders.

- When investors receive a stock dividend, the original cost of their shares is divided by the total number of shares (including the shares of the stock dividend) to arrive at a new cost per share.

- After the stock dividend, each individual shareholder owns the same proportionate share of the corporation as he or she did before.

- No income is recognized on the stock dividends by the stockholder when the stock dividend is received.

- A corporation may issue a stock dividend rather than a cash dividend for a number of reasons:
  1. A stock dividend conserves cash, thus allowing the firm to use its cash for growth and expansion.
  2. Stock dividends transfer a part of retained earnings to permanent capital (referred to as **capitalizing retained earnings**) making that part of retained earnings unavailable for future cash dividends.

Small Stock Dividends

- A small stock dividend is less than 20% to 25%.

- The entry to record the declaration and issuance of a small stock dividend is:

Debit:	Retained Earnings	[fair market value of stock dividend]
Credit:	Common Stock	[par value]
Credit:	Paid-in Capital in Excess of Par	[fair market value - par value]

- After the stock dividend is recorded, total stockholders' equity remains the same. The only difference is in the components of stockholders' equity:
  1. Retained earnings is decreased.
  2. Contributed capital is increased.

Large Stock Dividends

- A large stock dividend is greater than 20% to 25%.

- Because large stock dividends can affect the market price of the stock, par value (instead of market value) is used to record the stock dividend.

- The entry to record the declaration and issuance of a large stock dividend is:

  Debit: Retained Earnings   [par value]
    Credit: Common Stock   [par value]

Stock Splits

- A **stock split** occurs when a corporation increases the number of its common shares and proportionately decreases their par value or stated value. The number of outstanding shares increases, and the market price per share decreases.

- The main reason that a corporation decides to split its stock is to decrease the stock price per share. When the market price per share is too high, the stock loses its attractiveness to many investors.

- Although no journal entry is required to record a stock split, some firms make a memorandum entry noting the stock split.

- As a result of a stock split, there is no change in either total stockholders' equity or in the individual components. Only the par value and the number of issued and outstanding shares are different.

- When a stock split occurs, the corporation reduces the par value of its stock and increases the number of shares issued and outstanding. The old shares are canceled, and shares with the new par value are issued.

- The total market value of each stockholders' investment immediately after the split will be about the same as before the split.

- With stockholders' equity remaining the same, both stock splits and large stock dividends serve to:
  - reduce the market price per share.
  - increase the number of shares issued and outstanding.

TREASURY STOCK AND RETIREMENT OF CAPITAL STOCK

- **Treasury stock** is the corporation's own capital stock, either common or preferred, that has been issued and subsequently reacquired by the firm but not canceled.

- Treasury stock does not:
  1. have the right to vote.
  2. receive dividends.
  3. receive assets upon liquidation.

- Reasons why a firm may reacquire its own capital stock include:
  1. to acquire additional shares for employee stock option or bonus plans.
  2. to acquire shares for mergers and acquisitions.
  3. in order to support the price of its stock.
  4. because the firm may believe the stock is a good investment.
  5. to stop a hostile takeover.

Accounting for Treasury Stock

- Treasury stock is a reduction in stockholders' equity. Treasury stock is not an asset.

Recording the Purchase of Treasury Stock

- The entry to record the purchase of treasury stock is:

  Debit: Treasury Stock
    Credit: Cash

- The treasury stock is recorded at cost and is shown as a negative item in stockholders' equity.

- The purchase of treasury stock reduces both assets and stockholders' equity.

Recording Subsequent Sales of Treasury Stock

- A firm cannot record a profit or loss on the resale of treasury stock because tax and accounting rules do not allow a corporation to increase retained earnings by dealing in its own stock.

- If the resale price of the treasury stock is greater than the original cost, the entry to record the sale of treasury stock is:

  Debit: Cash   [resale price of treasury stock]
    Credit: Treasury Stock   [cost of treasury stock]
    Credit: Paid-in Capital from Sale of
                      Treasury Stock Above Cost   [resale price - cost]

- If treasury stock is resold at a price that is less than its original cost, the difference between the cost and the resale price is debited to the following accounts in the following order:
  1. Paid-in Capital from Sale of Treasury Stock account until there is a $-0- balance in the account.
  2. Paid-in Capital in Excess of Par account (if necessary) until there is a $-0- balance.
  3. Retained Earnings account (if necessary).

401

Retirement of Capital Stock

- A corporation may repurchase its stock with the intent to retire it rather than to hold it in the treasury.

OTHER ITEMS AFFECTING RETAINED EARNINGS

- Other transactions that affect retained earnings include:
  - prior period adjustments
  - appropriations of retained earnings
  - foreign currency adjustments

Prior Period Adjustments

- **Prior period adjustments** are transactions that relate to an earlier accounting period but which were not determinable in the earlier period, such as the correction of an error in the financial statements of a prior period.

- When single-year statements are published, the error is corrected by adjusting the beginning balance of Retained Earnings on the retained earnings statement.

- A journal entry is made to record the correction. For example, the entry to correct the understatement of depreciation would be:

```
Debit:        Retained Earnings
   Credit:        Accumulated Depreciation: Building
```

- In addition, the prior period adjustment would be explained in the notes to the financial statements.

- When comparative financial statements are presented and the error is in an earlier financial statement that is being presented for comparative purposes, that statement should be revised to correct the error. If the error is in a year for which the financial statements are not being presented, the correction is made through a prior period adjustment to the earliest retained earnings balance presented.

Appropriation of Retained Earnings

- An **appropriation of retained earnings** is a transfer of a portion of the retained earnings account to a separate retained earnings account. The sole purpose of such a transfer is to indicate to stockholders and others that the balance in Appropriated Retained Earnings is not available for dividends.

- The board may appropriate retained earnings in order to limit dividends voluntarily, in the hope of conserving cash for projects such as the purchase of new buildings, or because creditors may have forced the board to limit dividends.

- The entry to appropriate retained earnings is:

    Debit: Retained Earnings
     Credit: Appropriated Retained Earnings: Plant Expansion

- After retained earnings is appropriated, total retained earnings remains the same, but it is divided into two parts:
1. appropriated retained earnings
2. unappropriated retained earnings

- Although retained earnings may be appropriated, there is no guarantee that the cash will be there for its intended use.

- Corporations seldom appropriate retained earnings. Instead, voluntary or required dividend restrictions are disclosed in the notes to the financial statements.

USE OF STOCK INFORMATION

- After the stock of a major corporation is issued, it trades on a national exchange, such as the New York Stock Exchange or the American Stock Exchange.

- To evaluate a corporation, present and potential investors and creditors look at the market price of the stock and other indicators.

Market Value

- The market value per share refers to the price at which a particular stock is currently trading.

- The stock's market price is affected by such factors as:
  - general economic conditions
  - interest rates
  - the perceived risk of the company
  - expectations concerning future profits
  - present and expected dividends

- The yield (the rate of return that a stockholder would receive if the stock were purchased at its latest price) is calculated as follows:

Yield = Annual Dividend/Current Market Price

- The **price-earnings (P-E) ratio** is a ratio used by many investors and analysts to compare stocks and is calculated as follows:

Price-Earnings Ratio = Current Market Price/Earnings Per Share

- If a stock is selling at a P-E ratio of 12, the stock is selling at 12 times its earnings per share.

- **Earnings per share (EPS)** shows the amount of current earnings available to common stockholders on a per share basis.

   EPS = Net Income/Average Number of Common Shares Outstanding

Book Value per Share

- **Book value per share** of common stock indicates the equity that one share of stock has in the net assets (assets minus liabilities) of a corporation.

- Because the firm's net assets are recorded at historical cost less the write-offs to date, book value is in terms of these historical costs, not in terms of market value or liquidation value.

- The market price of a corporation's stock may be above or below the book value per share.

- When a firm has only common stock outstanding, the book value per share is calculated as follows:

   Book Value Per Share = Total Stockholders' Equity/Number of Common Shares Outstanding

FINANCIAL CYCLE CONTROLS

- The revenue transaction cycle records transactions related to selling goods and services to customers.

- The expenditure transaction cycle records transactions related to acquiring goods and services to sell to customers.

- The financial cycle is a collection of systems that process transactions and events involving the acquisition and use of capital resources.

- The **financial cycle** records two types of business transactions:
  1. capital acquisition transactions
  2. capital investment transactions

- The systems found within the financial cycle are:
  - the general ledger system
  - the financial reporting system
  - the operating asset or property accounting system

- Capital is acquired through:
  1. the issuance of long-term debt instruments, such as bonds
  2. medium- to long-term bank loans, such as mortgages
  3. the issuance of stock

Controls

- The most common and most effective controls over debt and equity transactions are:

1. Authorization controls. Organizations should have formal procedures for the authorization of bank loans, bond issues, and stock transactions. Most frequently, approval by the board of directors is required before an organization can enter into a long-term bank loan or issue bonds or stock. Approval of the chief financial officer or treasurer is usually required for less material short-term bank loans.

2. Segregation of functions. Transactions are authorized by the board of directors or the treasurer. Transactions are recorded by the controller's staff, thus segregating transaction authorization and transaction recording functions.

   The independent trustee, independent registrar, and transfer agent provide an external review over transaction authorization and execution.

   An **independent trustee** is an individual or organization, usually a bank, who performs transaction processing functions for a bond issue. The trustee maintains a record of all bondholders and updates the list when they sell their bonds to others. The trustee also maintains physical control over the bond certificates and cancels old certificates and issues new ones when bonds are traded.

   The **independent registrar** represents the stockholders and reviews all stock transactions to ensure that they have been approved by a company's board of directors.

   The **transfer agent** maintains a record of all of the stockholders, updates the record when stock is traded, issues new shares of stock to new owners, cancels certificates when they are sold, and pays dividends to the stockholders.

3. Document controls. Document controls used to prevent the loss or theft of stock and bond certificates include:
   - Documents should always be stored in a secure, locked location.
   - Access to the unissued documents should be restricted and controlled.
   - Documents should be prenumbered and accounted for.

KEY TERMS TEST

Test your recall of the key terms as follows: Read the following definitions of key terms and try to recall as many key terms as you can *without assistance*. Write your answers in the spaces provided. If you need assistance, refer to the list of key terms at the end of this section.

1. _____ _____ are the costs incurred to start a business, including legal costs, filing and incorporation fees, promotion costs, and printing and engraving costs.

2. The _____ _____ _____ is a group of individuals, elected by stockholders, who establish broad corporate policy and hire top management.

3. A(n) _____ is a legal document, signed by a stockholder, giving another person the right to vote the shares in the manner they deem best.

4. _____ _____ is stock that has preferential rights over and above those of common stock.

5. _____ _____ is an amount designated by the articles of incorporation or board of directors and printed on the stock certificates.

6. _____ _____ _____ are accumulated unpaid dividends on cumulative preferred stock.

7. _____ _____ _____ is preferred stock that can be converted into common stock at a stated rate and time.

8. _____ _____ _____ is preferred stock that can be callable and that can be returned by the stockholder to the corporation under certain circumstances.

9. _____ _____ _____ is preferred stock that may be repurchased at the option of the corporation.

10. The difference between the call price and the par value of preferred stock is the _____ _____.

11. _____ _____ is legal capital plus any additional capital contributed by the owners.

12. _____ _____ is the minimum amount that can be reported as contributed capital, usually equal to the par or stated value of all of the capital stock that has been issued.

13. _____ _____ _____ is the amount invested by owners in excess of the par value of the stock that they have purchased.

14. _____ _____ _____ is stock that does not have a stated or par value.

15. _____ are brokerage firms that, for a stated price, purchase an entire stock issue and assume the risks involved in marketing the stock to their clients.

16. The _____ _____ is the date that dividends are declared by the board of directors.

17. The _____ _____ _____ is the date that stockholders are entitled to receive their dividends.

18. The date that a dividend is actually paid is the _____ _____.

19. A(n) _____ _____ is a proportional distribution of a corporation's own stock to its shareholders.

20. _____ _____ _____ is converting retained earnings into permanent capital, usually through the issuance of stock dividends.

21. _____ _____ is a corporation's own stock that it has repurchased.

22. _____ _____ _____ are transactions that relate to an earlier accounting period but which were not determinable in the earlier period.

23. _____ _____ _____ _____ is the transfer of a portion of the retained earnings account to a separate retained earnings account.

24. _____ _____ is a class of capital stock issued by all corporations and has voting rights.

25. A(n) _____ _____ is an increase in the number of shares of stock outstanding with a proportional decrease in the par or stated value of the stock.

26. The _____ _____ is the current market price of a stock divided by its earnings per share.

27. _____ _____ _____, or _____, is net income divided by the average number of common shares outstanding during a year.

28. The equity that one share of stock has in the net assets of a corporation is _____ _____ _____ _____.

29. The _____ _____ is a collection of systems that process transactions and events involving the acquisition and use of capital resources.

30. An individual or organization, usually a bank, who performs transaction processing functions for a bond issue is a(n) _____ _____.

31. An individual or firm that represents the stockholders in stock transactions is the _____ _____.

32. A(n) _____ _____ maintains a record of all of the stockholders, updates the record when stock is traded, issues new shares of stock to new owners, cancels certificates when they are sold, and pays dividends to the stockholders.

KEY TERMS:

additional paid-in capital	independent trustee
appropriation of retained earnings	legal capital
board of directors	no par stock
book value per share	organization costs
call premium	par value
callable preferred stock	payment date
capitalizing retained earnings	preferred stock
common stock	price-earnings ratio
contributed capital	prior period adjustments
convertible preferred stock	proxy
date of record	redeemable preferred stock
declaration date	stock dividend
dividends in arrears	stock split
earnings per share, EPS	transfer agent
financial cycle	treasury stock
independent registrar	underwriters

Compare your answers to those at the end of the chapter and review any key terms missed.

CHAPTER QUIZ

Write your answers in the spaces provided.

1. List three advantages of the corporate form of organization.
   1. _____
   2. _____
   3. _____

2. List two disadvantages of the corporate form of organization.
   1. _____
   2. _____

3. Organization costs are usually listed in the _____ _____ section of the balance sheet.

4. List the two major types of capital stock.
   1. _____
   2. _____

5. The dividend yield is calculated as:

   Yield = _____ / _____

6. The price-earnings ratio is calculated as:

   Price-Earnings Ratio = _____ / _____

7. Book value per share is calculated as:

   Book Value Per Share = _____ / _____

8. The three systems found within the financial cycle are:
   1. _____
   2. _____
   3. _____

9. List three general types of controls over debt and equity transactions.
   1. _____
   2. _____
   3. _____

Circle the single best answer.

10. A firm cannot record a gain or loss on the resale of treasury stock:
    (a) true; (b) false

11. Appropriating retained earnings ensures that cash will be available for a specific purpose: (a) true; (b) false

12. Components of contributed capital include all of the following except:
    (a) common stock; (b) retained earnings; (c) paid-in capital in excess of par; (d) all of the above are components of contributed capital

Use the following information to answer the next seven questions.

The stockholders' equity section of the December 31, 1995 balance sheet of Katrina Technologies appeared as follows:

Preferred stock, 8%, $100 par value, cumulative, 60,000 shares authorized, ? shares issued	$5,000,000
Common stock, $10 par value, 100,000 shares authorized, 25,000 shares issued	?
Paid-in capital in excess of par: common stock	1,000,000
Retained earnings	1,200,000

13. The number of preferred shares issued is: (a) 60,000; (b) 40,000; (c) 50,000; (d) 30,000

14. What amount should be recorded in the common stock account? (a) $250,000; (b) $750,000; (c) $500,000; (d) $1,000,000

15. What was the total issue price of the common stock? (a) $250,000; (b) $2,000,000; (c) $1,750,000; (d) $1,250,000

16. What is the total legal capital of the corporation? (a) $6,000,000; (b) $6,250,000; (c) $5,250,000; (d) $6,450,000

17. What is the total contributed capital of the corporation? (a) $6,000,000; (b) $6,250,000; (c) $5,250,000; (d) $6,450,000

18. What is the amount of the total required preferred dividends? (a) $400,000; (b) $480,000; (c) $200,000; (d) $240,000

19. What is the amount of total stockholders' equity? (a) $6,250,000; (b) $6,000,000; (c) $5,250,000; (d) $7,450,000

Use the following information to answer the next three questions.

Data from the 1995 annual report of the DK Corporation is as follows:

Total common stockholders' equity	$2,000,000
Net income from 1995	$500,000
Number of common shares outstanding	400,000
Dividends declared during 1995	$ 0.50 per share
Market price at end of 1995	$10.00 per share
EPS for 1995	$1.25

20. The dividend yield for 1995 is: (a) 4%; (b) 5%; (c) 40%; (d) 20%

21. The price-earnings ratio is: (a) 4; (b) 5; (c) 8; (d) 20

22. The book value per share is: (a) $5.00; (b) $6.25; (c) $10.00; (d) $8.25

23. The Toto Corporation has the following shares of stock outstanding:

Common stock, $10 par	40,000 shares
Preferred stock, cumulative, 5%, $100 par	10,000 shares

The board of directors made the following funds available for dividends during 1993, 1994, and 1995:

1993	$40,000
1994	65,000
1995	70,000

Determine the amount of dividends that the preferred and common stockholders will receive each year.

	1993	1994	1995
Preferred stock	_____	_____	_____
Common stock	_____	_____	_____
Total	_____	_____	_____

EXERCISES

EXERCISE 1

The Derek Corporation was organized in 1995 and was authorized to issue 100,000 shares of $2 par value common stock and 20,000 shares of 7%, $100 par value preferred stock. The following stock transactions took place during 1995:

January 30: Issued 40,000 shares of common stock at $10 per share.

February 2: The city of Hometown donated land to the corporation for a building site. The land had a fair market value of $20,000.

April 14: Issued 500 shares of common stock to the firm's accountant in connection with the organization of the corporation. The fair market value of the accountant's fees was $10,000.

December 5: Issued 5,000 shares of preferred stock at $110 per share.

Required:

1. Prepare the journal entries to record these events.

DATE	ACCOUNT TITLES	REF.	DEBIT	CREDIT

2. Assuming that net income for the year amounted to $100,000 and no dividends were declared, prepare the stockholders' equity section of the balance sheet at December 31, 1995.

EXERCISE 2

Willman Corporation has 20,000 shares of $10 par value common stock outstanding. All stock was originally issued at $16 per share. During the current year, the company entered into the following transactions related to its common stock:

January 9: The company repurchased 5,000 shares of its common stock at a price of $25 per share.

April 14: The company resold 2,000 of these shares at $28 per share.

June   10: The company resold the remaining 3,000 shares held in treasury at $20 per share.

Required: Prepare the journal entries to record these events.

DATE	ACCOUNT TITLES	REF.	DEBIT	CREDIT

EXERCISE 3

Synnet has 200,000 shares of $5 par value common stock outstanding and 50,000 shares of 6%, $100 par value preferred stock outstanding. During October, the board of directors made the following dividend declaration.

On October 1, the board of directors declared that the preferred dividend would be paid on December 1 to preferred stockholders of record on November 20.

On October 15, the board of directors declared a $2 per share dividend payable on December 1 to common stockholders of record on November 20.

Required:

1. Make all the necessary entries related to the declaration and payment of the preferred dividends.

DATE	ACCOUNT TITLES	REF.	DEBIT	CREDIT

2. Make all the necessary entries related to the declaration and payment of the common dividends.

DATE	ACCOUNT TITLES	REF.	DEBIT	CREDIT

EXERCISE 4

On December 31, 1995, the stockholders' equity section of the Gates Corporation appeared as follows:

Gates Corporation
Partial Balance Sheet
December 31, 1995

Stockholders' equity:

Common stock, $5 par value, 400,000 shares authorized, 100,000 shares issued and outstanding	$ 500,000
Paid-in capital in excess of par	800,000
Retained earnings	2,000,000
Total stockholders' equity	$3,300,000

Required:

1. Assume that on January 2, 1996, the board of directors declared and issued a 10% stock dividend. At that time, the stock was selling at $20 per share. Prepare the stockholders' equity section of the balance sheet after the declaration.

2. Assume that instead of issuing a stock dividend, the board of directors declared a 2-for-1 stock split on January 2. Prepare the stockholders' equity section of the balance sheet after the stock split.

EXERCISE 5

At the beginning of 1995, Schuster Incorporated's retained earnings balance
was $600,000. During the year, the firm's net income amounted to $250,000,
and dividends of $80,000 were paid. During the preparation of the 1995
financial statements, it was discovered that annual depreciation expense on
equipment of $20,000 had not been recorded in either 1994 and 1995.

Required:

1. Assuming that the current year's books have not been closed and that the
   reported income of $250,000 does not reflect the depreciation on the
   equipment, make the necessary entries to correct the error. Ignore taxes.

DATE	ACCOUNT TITLES	REF.	DEBIT	CREDIT

2. If single-year statements are published, prepare the retained earnings
   statement for 1995, based on the correction made in requirement 1.

ANSWERS

KEY TERMS TEST
1. Organization costs
2. board of directors
3. proxy
4. Preferred stock
5. Par value
6. Dividends in arrears
7. Convertible preferred stock
8. Redeemable preferred stock
9. Callable preferred stock
10. call premium
11. Contributed capital
12. Legal capital
13. Additional paid-in capital
14. No par stock
15. Underwriters
16. declaration date
17. date of record
18. payment date
19. stock dividend
20. Capitalizing retained earnings
21. Treasury stock
22. Prior period adjustments
23. Appropriation of retained earnings
24. Common stock
25. stock split
26. price-earnings ratio
27. Earnings per share, EPS
28. book value per share
29. financial cycle
30. independent trustee
31. independent registrar
32. transfer agent

CHAPTER QUIZ
1. 1. Limited liability
   2. Transferability of ownership
   3. Ease of capital formation
2. 1. Double taxation
   2. Government regulation
3. Other Assets
4. 1. Common stock
   2. Preferred stock
5. Yield = Annual Dividend/Current Market Price
6. Price-Earnings Ratio = Current Market Price/Earnings Per Share
7. Book Value Per Share = Total Stockholders' Equity/Number of Common Shares Outstanding
8. 1. General ledger system
   2. Financial reporting system
   3. Operating asset system

9. 1. Authorization controls
    2. Segregation of functions
    3. Document controls

10. a True

11. b False Retained earnings can be appropriated, but that does not guarantee that the cash will be available for its intended use. The entry to appropriate retained earnings does not involve cash.

12. b

13. c $5,000,000/$100 par = 50,000 shares issued

14. a $10 par x 25,000 shares issued = $250,000

15. d Par ($10 par x 25,000 shares)   = $ 250,000
    Paid-in capital in excess of par = 1,000,000

    Total issue price of common stock = $1,250,000

16. c Common stock, par value   = $ 250,000
    Preferred stock, par value   = 5,000,000

    Total legal capital   = $5,250,000

17. b Preferred stock, par value   = $5,000,000
    Common stock, par value   =   250,000
    Paid-in capital in excess of par = 1,000,000

    Total contributed capital   = $6,250,000

18. a 8% x $5,000,000 = $400,000, or 8% x $100 par x 50,000 shares = $400,000

19. d Preferred stock, par value   = $5,000,000
    Common stock, par value   =   250,000
    Paid-in capital in excess of par = 1,000,000
    Retained earnings   = 1,200,000

    Total stockholders' equity   = $7,450,000

20. b $0.50/$10.00 = 5%

21. c $10.00/$1.25 = 8

22. a $2,000,000/400,000 = $5.00

23.

	1993	1994	1995
Preferred stock	$40,000[a]	$60,000[b]	$50,000
Common stock	-0-	5,000	20,000
Total	$40,000	$65,000	$70,000

418

a	Required dividends (5% x $100 par x 10,000 shares)	$50,000
	Dividends declared	40,000
	Dividends in arrears	$10,000

b	Dividends in arrears	$10,000
	1994 current year dividends	50,000
	Total preferred dividends	$60,000

	Total dividends	$65,000
	Total preferred dividends	60,000
	Total common dividends	$ 5,000

EXERCISE 1

1.

GENERAL JOURNAL

DATE	ACCOUNT TITLES	REF.	DEBIT	CREDIT
1995				
Jan. 30	Cash		400,000	
	Common Stock (40,000 x $2)			80,000
	Paid-in Capital in Excess of Par: Common Stock			320,000
	To record issue of 40,000 shares of $2 par value common stock at $10 per share.			
Feb. 2	Land		20,000	
	Donated Capital			20,000
	To record donation of land.			
Apr. 14	Organization Costs		10,000	
	Common Stock (500 x $2)			1,000
	Paid-in Capital in Excess of Par: Common Stock			9,000
	To record issue of 500 shares of common stock in connection with organization costs.			
Dec. 5	Cash		550,000	
	Preferred Stock (5,000 x $100)			500,000
	Paid-in Capital in Excess of Par: Preferred Stock			50,000
	To record the issue of 5,000 shares of preferred stock at $110 per share.			

EXERCISE 1 (continued)

2.

Derek Corporation
Partial Balance Sheet
December 31, 1995

Preferred stock, 7%, $100 par value, 20,000 shares authorized, 5,000 issued and outstanding	$ 500,000
Common stock, $2 par value, 100,000 shares authorized and 40,500 shares issued and outstanding	81,000
Paid-in capital in excess of par: preferred stock	50,000
Paid-in capital in excess of par: common stock	329,000
Donated capital	20,000
Retained earnings	100,000
Total stockholders' equity	$1,080,000

EXERCISE 2

GENERAL JOURNAL

DATE	ACCOUNT TITLES	REF.	DEBIT	CREDIT
Jan. 9	Treasury Stock		125,000	
	Cash (5,000 x $25)			125,000
	To record purchase of 5,000 shares of stock at $25 per share.			
Apr. 14	Cash (2,000 x $28)		56,000	
	Paid-in Capital from Sale of Treasury Stock Above Cost (2,000 x $3)			6,000
	Treasury Stock (2,000 x $25)			50,000
	To record sale of 2,000 shares of treasury stock at $28 per share.			
June 10	Cash (3,000 x $20)		60,000	
	Paid-in Capital from Sale of Treasury Stock Above Cost		6,000	
	Paid-in Capital in Excess of Par: Common Stock		9,000	
	Treasury Stock (3,000 x $25)			75,000
	To record sale of 3,000 shares of treasury stock at $20 per share.			

EXERCISE 3

1.   GENERAL JOURNAL

DATE	ACCOUNT TITLES	REF.	DEBIT	CREDIT

Declaration date:

Oct. 1   Retained Earnings — 300,000
             Dividends Payable: Preferred — 300,000

50,000 x $100 par x 6% = $300,000

Date of record: No entry

Payment date:

Dec. 1   Dividends Payable: Preferred — 300,000
             Cash — 300,000

2.   GENERAL JOURNAL

DATE	ACCOUNT TITLES	REF.	DEBIT	CREDIT

Declaration date:

Oct. 15   Retained Earnings — 400,000
              Dividends Payable: Common — 400,000

$2 x 200,000 shares = $400,000

Date of record: No entry

Payment date:

Dec. 1   Dividends Payable: Common — 400,000
             Cash — 400,000

EXERCISE 4

1.

Gates Corporation
Partial Balance Sheet
January 2, 1996

Stockholders' equity:

Common stock, $5 par value, 400,000 shares authorized, 110,000[a] shares issued and outstanding	$ 550,000
Paid-in capital in excess of par[b]	950,000
Retained earnings[c]	1,800,000
Total stockholders' equity	$3,300,000

[a] $10\% \times 100,000$ shares = 10,000 shares + 100,000 shares = 110,000 shares
[b] $800,000 + (10,000 \times \$15) = \$950,000$
[c] $\$2,000,000 - \$200,000 = \$1,800,000$

2.

Gates Corporation
Partial Balance Sheet
January 2, 1996

Stockholders' equity:

Common stock, $2.50 par value, 800,000 shares authorized, 200,000 shares issued and outstanding	$ 500,000
Paid-in capital in excess of par	800,000
Retained earnings	2,000,000
Total stockholders' equity	$3,300,000

EXERCISE 5

1.

GENERAL JOURNAL

DATE	ACCOUNT TITLES	REF.	DEBIT	CREDIT
1995				
Dec. 31	Retained Earnings		20,000	
	Accumulated Depreciation: Equipment			20,000
	To correct error in 1994 through a prior period adjustment.			
Dec. 31	Depreciation Expense: Equipment		20,000	
	Accumulated Depreciation: Equipment			20,000
	To record depreciation expense on equipment for 1995.			

2.

Schuster Incorporated
Statement of Retained Earnings
For the Year Ended December 31, 1995

Retained earnings, January 1, 1995	$600,000
Less: Prior period adjustment for error correction	(20,000)
Retained earnings, January 1, 1995 restated	$580,000
Net income for 1995[a]	230,000
Less: Dividends	(80,000)
Retained earnings, December 31, 1995	$730,000

[a] $250,000 - $20,000 = $230,000

CHAPTER 14

THE STATEMENT OF CASH FLOWS
AND FINANCIAL STATEMENT ANALYSIS

CHAPTER REVIEW

INTRODUCTION

- One of the primary objectives of financial reporting is to provide information that is useful to present and potential investors and creditors in making investment and credit decisions.

- Investors and creditors analyze the past performance of companies and assess their future prospects.

- This chapter discusses:
  - the statement of cash flows
  - other tools of financial analysis and interpretation

STATEMENT OF CASH FLOWS

- The primary financial statements are:
  1. balance sheet
  2. income statement
  3. statement of cash flows
  4. retained earnings statement or statement of changes in stockholders' equity

The Purposes of the Statement of Cash Flows

- The **statement of cash flows** discloses the effects of operating, financing and investing activities on a firm's cash flows.

- The two primary purposes of the cash flow statement are to provide:
  1. information about the firm's cash receipts and cash payments.
  2. information about the investing and financing activities of the firm.

- The statement of cash flows helps present and potential investors and creditors assess:
  1. The firm's ability to generate future cash flows.
  2. The firm's ability to meet its obligations and pay dividends and its need for outside financing.
  3. The reasons for the differences between income and cash receipts and payments.
  4. Both the cash and noncash aspects of the firm's investing and financing activities.

The Meaning of Cash Flows

- The cash flow statement should explain changes in both cash and cash equivalents.

- **Cash equivalents** are short-term, liquid investments, such as treasury bills, commercial paper, and money market funds, that are readily convertible into cash.

CAUSES OF CASH FLOWS

- Cash flows are classified into three categories:
  1. cash flows from operating activities
  2. cash flows from investing activities
  3. cash flows from financing activities

Investing Activities

- **Investing activities** are activities that involve the acquisition or sale of long-term assets.

- Cash inflows from investing activities include:
  - sale of plant and equipment
  - sale of long-term investments, such as stocks and bonds that are classified as held-to-maturity or available-for-sale securities

- Cash outflows from investing activities include:
  - purchase of plant and equipment
  - purchase of long-term investments, such as stocks and bonds that are classified as held-to-maturity or available-for-sale securities

Financing Activities

- **Financing activities** are activities that raise cash from outside sources by promising the providers of the cash a return on their investment and a return of their original investment.

- Cash inflows from financing activities include cash received from:
  - issuance of bonds
  - issuance of stocks
  - long-term borrowings, such as mortgages payable

- Cash outflows from financing activities include:
  - payment of cash dividends
  - repayment of bonds
  - repayment of long-term debt
  - retirement of stock

- Cash paid for accounts payable, wages payable, and income taxes payable are operating activities, not financing activities.

Operating Activities

- **Operating activities** are the major source of internally generated cash.

- Cash inflows from operating activities include:
  - cash sales
  - collection of accounts receivable
  - cash received for interest
  - cash received for dividends
  - proceeds from sales and maturities of trading securities

- Cash outflows for operating activities include:
  - payment for merchandise purchased
  - payment for salaries and wages
  - payment to suppliers for supplies, etc.
  - payment for insurance
  - payment for interest
  - payment for taxes
  - payment for trading securities purchased

- Cash flows from operating activities can be calculated using:
  1. the direct method or
  2. the indirect method.

Investing and Financing Activities Not Involving Cash Flows

- The FASB requires that information about noncash investing and financing activities be summarized in a separate schedule or disclosed in narrative form.

- An example of a noncash investing and financing activity would be acquiring land (an investing activity) by issuing common stock (a financing activity).

PREPARING A STATEMENT OF CASH FLOWS

- The five steps used when preparing a statement of cash flows are:
  1. Compute the change in cash for the period by finding the difference between the beginning and ending cash balance.

     Cash equivalents are highly liquid investments such as Treasury bills, money market funds, commercial paper, and marketable securities. Because of their liquidity, these short-term investments are treated as cash when preparing the statement of cash flows.

     (Long-term investments are placed in the investing section of the statement of cash flows.)
  2. Compute the cash flows from operating activities. Cash flows from operations can be calculated using the direct or the indirect method.
  3. Identify the cash flows from investing activities.
  4. Identify cash flows from financing activities.
  5. Prepare the statement of cash flows based on the information from the first four steps.

DETERMINING CASH FLOWS FROM OPERATING ACTIVITIES

- Two methods of presenting cash flows from operating activities are:
  1. The direct method. The **direct method** lists cash receipts from operations and cash payments related to operations.
  2. The indirect method. Instead of listing cash receipts and cash payments from operations, the **indirect method** starts with accrual net income and adjusts net income for the items that were included in net income that did not affect cash.

- Although the FASB prefers the direct method, it allows either the direct or indirect method of presenting cash flows from operating activities.

The Direct Method

- The income statement is prepared using the accrual basis. Adjustments must be made to sales, cost of goods sold, and the other operating expenses in order to determine cash flows from operating activities.

Cash Inflows from Operations

- Cash received from customers is the primary source of cash flows from operations and consists of:
  1. cash sales
  2. cash collected from customers on accounts receivable

- The relationship between accrual-basis and cash-basis income arising from receivables is as follows:

Accrual-Basis Revenue + Decrease in Receivables = Cash-Basis Revenue

or

Accrual-Basis Revenue - Increase in Receivables = Cash-Basis Revenue

- For example, assume the beginning balance in accounts receivable is $20,000 and the ending balance is $15,000. Assume sales are $200,000 and all are on credit. A T-account for accounts receivable would appear as follows:

ACCOUNTS RECEIVABLE

Beginning Balance	20,000		
Add: Credit sales	200,000	Deduct: Cash collections	X
Ending balance	15,000		

If accounts receivable decreased by $5,000 (from $20,000 to $15,000), this indicates that the company <u>collected</u> $5,000 <u>more</u> than the amount recorded as sales revenue. Therefore, cash collected must be $205,000.

When using the accrual basis to determine income, revenue is reported on the income statement when the goods or services are provided. The <u>collection of customers' accounts is a cash flow</u>.

Since the cash inflow is greater than accrual income reported, the decrease in accounts receivable needs to be added to accrual income to determine the cash basis.

- Cash received from customers is determined as follows:

> Accrual-basis sales
> - Increase in accounts receivable during the period
> + Decrease in accounts receivable during the period
> = Cash received from customers

Cash Outflows from Operations

- Cash outflows from operations include:
  - cash paid to suppliers for inventory
  - cash paid to employees for wages and salaries
  - cash paid for other operating expenses
  - cash paid for interest
  - cash paid for taxes

- The amount of cash paid for inventory is determined as follows:
  1. Analyze the inventory account. Determine the amount of inventory purchased as follows:

> Cost of goods sold
> + Ending inventory
> = Cost of goods available for sale
> - Beginning inventory
> = Inventory purchases

An increase in the inventory account indicates that the company purchased more goods during the year than it sold.

  2. Analyze the accounts payable account. The cash payments for inventory is determined as follows:

> Beginning balance in Accounts Payable
> + Inventory purchases
> = Maximum that could be paid
> - Ending balance in Accounts Payable
> = Cash payments for purchases of inventories

A decrease in accounts payable indicates that more goods were paid for during the year than were purchased.

- The relationships are summarized as follows:

   Accrual Cost of Goods Sold + Increase in Inventory = Net Purchases
   or
   Accrual Cost of Goods Sold - Decrease in Inventory = Net Purchases

   Net Purchases + Decrease in Accounts Payable = Cash Payments for Purchases
   or
   Net Purchases - Increase in Accounts Payable = Cash Payments for Purchases

- Cash outflows for various prepayments included in operating expenses are determined as follows:

   Prepaid expense
   - Decrease in prepaid account during period
   + Increase in prepaid account during period
   = Cash outflows for prepaids

- The relationship between accrual-basis and cash-basis expenses arising from the expiration of various prepayments is as follows:

   Accrual-Basis Expenses + Increase in Prepayments = Cash-Basis Expenses
   or
   Accrual-Basis Expenses - Decrease in Prepayments = Cash-Basis Expenses

- Cash outflows for all other operating expenses are calculated as follows:

   Other operating expenses
   - Increase in the accrued liabilities account
   + Decrease in the accrued liabilities account
   = Cash outflows for other operating expenses

- The amount of cash paid for taxes can be determined by analyzing the taxes payable account.

Accrual-Basis Tax Expense + Decrease in Taxes Payable = Cash Outflow for Taxes
or
Accrual-Basis Tax Expense - Increase in Taxes Payable = Cash Outflow for Taxes

- Cash paid for taxes is determined as follows:

   Taxes expense
   + Decrease in taxes payable
   - Increase in taxes payable
   = Cash paid for taxes

• Cash flows from operating activities can be summarized as follows:

        Cash received from customers
     - Cash paid to suppliers
     - Cash paid to employees
     - Cash paid for other operating expenses
     - Cash paid for interest
     - Cash paid for taxes

     = Net cash provided by operating activities

The Indirect Method

• The indirect method involves making adjustments to accrual-basis income in order to arrive at cash-basis income.

• When the balance in an asset account <u>decreases</u> during the year, cash-basis income is <u>higher</u> than accrual-basis income.

When the balance in an asset account <u>increases</u>, cash-basis income is <u>lower</u> than accrual-basis income.

When the balance in a liability account increases during the period, cash-basis income is <u>higher</u> than accrual-basis income.

When the balance in a liability account <u>decreases</u> during the year, cash-basis income is <u>lower</u> than accrual-basis income.

• AN EASY WAY TO REMEMBER THE NECESSARY ADJUSTMENT IS:
  • NONCASH ASSETS MOVE IN THE OPPOSITE DIRECTION OF CASH-BASIS INCOME.
  • LIABILITIES MOVE IN THE SAME DIRECTION AS CASH-BASIS INCOME.

• These relationships are summarized below:

Account	Change During Year	Cash-Basis Income in Relation to Accrual-Basis Income
Assets:		
Accounts receivable	Decrease	Higher
Accounts receivable	Increase	Lower
Other receivables (e.g., interest)	Decrease	Higher
Other receivables (e.g., interest)	Increase	Lower
Prepaid items (supplies, insurance)	Decrease	Higher
Prepaid items (supplies, insurance)	Increase	Lower
Liabilities:		
Payables (including interest)	Increase	Higher
Payables (including interest)	Decrease	Lower

431

- The four types of adjustments needed to convert accrual income to the cash basis are:

1. Add back to net income:
   - increases in current liabilities
   - decreases in noncash current assets

2. Deduct from net income:
   - decreases in current liabilities
   - increases in noncash current assets

   For example, if inventory remained the same and accounts payable decreased by $2,000, this indicates the company paid $2,000 more than it purchased on account.

   Therefore, the cash basis would be $2,000 less than accrual income, and the $2,000 decrease in accounts payable (a current liability) should be deducted from accrual income to determine the cash basis.

3. Add or deduct from net income the remaining items that are included in net income that do not affect cash flows, including:
   - depreciation expense
   - amortization expense of intangible assets
   - amortization of discounts on bonds payable
   - amortization of premiums on bonds payable

   Depreciation expense was deducted to arrive at net income but does not use cash; therefore, depreciation expense must be added back to net income to determine cash flow from operations.

   Amortization expense of intangible assets reduces income but does not reduce cash; therefore, amortization expense is added back to net income to calculate cash flow from operations.

   The amortization of the discount on bonds payable increased interest expense and thereby reduced net income but did not use cash. The amortization of the discount is added to net income to arrive at cash flows from operations.

   The amortization of premiums on bonds payable reduces interest expense, thereby increasing net income, but it is not a cash flow. Therefore, the amortization of a premium on bonds payable is deducted from net income to arrive at cash flow from operations.

4. Eliminate any items included in net income that belong in either the investing or financing sections.

   For example, the sale of long-term assets belongs in the investing section; however, the gain on the sale of the asset would be included in accrual net income.

   Also, the gain is not the amount of the cash flow. The gain is simply a calculation (the difference between the cash received and the book value of the asset).

The gain on sale should be _deducted_ from accrual income to find cash flow from operating activities. Then, the amount of _cash_ received from the sale should be shown as a cash inflow in the investing section.

A loss on the sale of a long-term asset should be _added_ to accrual income to find cash flow from operating activities. Then, the amount of _cash_ received from the sale should be shown as a cash inflow in the investing section.

FINANCIAL STATEMENT ANALYSIS

- **Financial statement analysis** is the set of techniques designed to provide relevant data to decision makers. It generally is based on a firm's published financial statements and other economic information about the firm and its industry.

- Three major techniques used in financial statement analysis are:
  1. horizontal analysis
  2. vertical analysis
  3. ratio analysis

Horizontal and Vertical Analysis

Horizontal Analysis

- **Horizontal analysis** focuses on the dollar and percentage changes in accounts from year to year.

- Use the following formula to calculate percentage changes:

Percentage Change = Amount of Dollar Change/Base-Year Amount

- Horizontal analysis can be used with the balance sheet and the income statement.

- For example, assume sales were $1,000,000 in 1994 and $1,400,000 in 1995. Horizontal analysis using a _base period_ follows.

	1994		1995	
	Dollars	%	Dollars	%
Net sales	$1,000,000	100%[a]	$1,400,000	140%[b]

[a] $1,000,000/$1,000,000
[b] $1,400,000/$1,000,000 (1995 sales/base year sales)

Trend Analysis

- **Trend analysis** is horizontal analysis that includes more than a single change from one year to the next.

433

- When more than two years are involved, index numbers are used instead of percentage changes.

- An index number can be calculated using the following formula:

Index Number = Index-Year Dollar Amount/Base-Year Dollar Amount

- Index numbers are particularly useful in measuring real growth, for example, by comparing the index number for sales growth to the rate of inflation for the same period as measured by an index such as the Consumer Price Index.

Vertical Analysis

- **Vertical analysis** is used to evaluate the relationships within a single financial statement in which all items on the statement are stated as a percentage of a selected item on the statement. These are called **common-dollar statements**.

- On the income statement, net sales is set equal to 100 percent and all other items appearing on the income statement are stated as a percentage of net sales.

- For example, assume the following results for 1995.

Net sales	$400,000
Cost of goods sold	240,000
Selling, general, and administrative expenses	60,000
Interest expense	10,000
Income tax expense	30,000

A common-dollar income statement appears below:

Common-Dollar Income Statement
For the Year Ended December 31, 1995

	Dollars	Percent
Net sales	$400,000	100.0%
Cost of goods sold	(240,000)	(60.0)[a]
Gross profit	$160,000	40.0
Selling, general, and administrative expenses	(60,000)	(15.0)
Operating income	$100,000	25.0
Interest expense	(10,000)	(2.5)
Income before taxes	$ 90,000	22.5
Income tax expense	(30,000)	(7.5)
Net income	$ 60,000	15.0%

[a]Cost of Goods Sold Percentage = Cost of Goods Sold/Net Sales
$$= \$240,000/\$400,000$$
$$= 60\%$$

- On a common-dollar balance sheet, total assets is set equal to 100 percent and each asset account is stated as a percentage of total assets. Each liability and stockholders' equity account is stated as a percentage of total equities.

- For example, assume the following information about assets for 1995.

Cash	$120,000
Accounts receivable	180,000
Inventory	300,000
Property, plant, and equipment	600,000

A common-dollar statement for assets only appears below:

Assets	Dollars	Percent
Cash	$ 120,000	10%[a]
Accounts receivable	180,000	15
Inventory	300,000	25
Property, plant, and equipment	600,000	50
Total assets	$1,200,000	100%

[a]Cash/Total Assets = $120,000/$1,200,000 = 10%

Ratio Analysis

- **Ratio analysis** is a method of expressing relationships among various items in a company's financial statements.

- The three most common financial statement user groups are:
  1. common and preferred stockholders
  2. short-term creditors
  3. long-term creditors

Common and Preferred Stockholder Ratios

- Earnings per share is a comparative figure of earnings on a per share basis and is calculated as:

  · Earnings per Share = (Net Income - Preferred Dividends)/Average Number of Common Shares Outstanding

- The price-earnings ratio is a comparative measure of how the market values the firm's earnings and is calculated as follows:

$$\text{Price-Earnings Ratio} = \text{Market Price per Common Share/Earnings per Share}$$

- The dividend yield is the dividend return to investors and is calculated as:

$$\text{Dividend Yield} = \text{Dividends per Share/Market Price per Share}$$

- Book value per share is the investors' share of assets at historical cost on a per share basis. It is calculated as follows:

$$\text{Book Value per Share} = \text{Common Stockholders' Equity/Number of Common Shares Outstanding}$$

- Return on total assets is a measure of how efficiently the firm's assets are employed. Return on total assets is calculated as:

$$\text{Return on Total Assets} = \text{(Net Income + Interest Expense)/Average Total Assets}$$

- Return on common stockholders' equity measures profitability of the investment to the owners and is calculated as:

$$\text{Return on Common Stockholders' Equity} = \text{(Net Income - Preferred Dividends)/Average Common Stockholders' Equity}$$

- The equity ratio measures the proportion of assets supplied by owners. The equity ratio is calculated as:

$$\text{Equity Ratio} = \text{Total Stockholders' Equity/Total Assets}$$

- The debt ratio measures the proportion of assets supplied by creditors. The debt ratio is calculated as:

$$\text{Debt Ratio} = \text{Total Liabilities/Total Assets}$$

- The gross profit percentage measures the percentage of gross profit per dollar of revenue and is calculated as:

$$\text{Gross Profit Percentage} = \text{Gross Profit/Sales}$$

- Profit margin is the percentage of net income per dollar of revenue and is calculated as:

$$\text{Profit Margin} = \text{Net Income/Sales}$$

Long-Term Creditor Ratios

- The debt-to-equity ratio is a measure of debt versus equity financing and is calculated as follows:

Debt-to-Equity Ratio = Total Liabilities/Total Stockholders' Equity

- Times interest earned is a measure of a firm's ability to meet interest payments. It is calculated as:

Times Interest Earned = Income before Interest and Taxes/Interest Expense

Short-Term Creditors

- The current ratio is a measure of the short-term liquidity of the firm. The current ratio is calculated as follows:

Current Ratio = Current Assets/Current Liabilities

- The quick ratio is a measure of the ability of a firm to meet immediate debt. The quick ratio is calculated as:

Quick Ratio = Monetary Current Assets/Current Liabilities

Monetary current assets include cash, marketable securities, and accounts receivable.

- Inventory turnover is a measure of how quickly inventory moves and is calculated as:

Inventory Turnover = Cost of Goods Sold/Average Inventory

- Accounts receivable turnover is a measure of how quickly receivables are collected and is calculated as:

Accounts Receivable Turnover = Net Credit Sales/Average Accounts Receivable

AUDIT OF COMPUTER-GENERATED FINANCIAL STATEMENTS

- Many organizations use computer-based accounting systems that rely on the financial reporting system to prepare the financial statements.

- Accountants:
  1. provide inputs to the financial reporting system.
  2. analyze and interpret the financial statements produced by the system (a user role).
  3. audit the financial statements and express an opinion on the fairness of the financial statements (the auditor role).

- The use of a computer-based accounting information system changes audit methods and techniques, but not the objective of the audit.

Nature of Internal Controls and Accounting Records

- Internal controls provide reasonable assurance that all and only valid transactions are processed and that the processing of transactions is complete and accurate.

- Internal controls, such as transaction authorization and the segregation of incompatible functions, and accounting records change when a computer-based system is used.

Auditing Computer-Based Accounting Systems

- The most common approach to auditing computer-based accounting systems is to **audit through the system** (audit computer-based accounting systems by testing control and processes within the system).

- To audit through the system, the following steps are used:
  1. An auditor prepares a set of test transactions or test data. **Test data** are transactions that have been specifically designed to test a specific control or system process.
  2. The auditor determines what the system response should be if the system is working correctly.
  3. The test data is input into the computer system, and the auditor compares the computer-generated results with his or her expectations.

KEY TERMS TEST

Test your recall of the key terms as follows: Read the following definitions of key terms and try to recall as many key terms as you can *without assistance*. Write your answers in the spaces provided. If you need assistance, refer to the list of key terms at the end of this section.

1. The _____ _____ _____ _____ is a required financial statement that discloses the effects of operating, investing, and financing activities on a firm's cash flows.

2. _____ _____ are short-term, liquid investments, such as commercial paper, money market accounts, and treasury bills, that can be converted into cash easily and without loss of principal.

3. Activities through which plant and equipment are acquired are _____ _____.

4. Nonoperating activities, such as selling stock or issuing bonds, that provide cash are _____ _____.

5. Transactions and events that provide cash but are not financing nor investing activities are _____ _____.

6. _____ _____ is a business activity that does not provide or use cash, such as depreciation.

7. The _____ _____ is a method used when preparing the statement of cash flows that lists cash receipts from operations and cash payments related to operations.

8. The _____ _____ is a method used when preparing the statement of cash flows that converts an accrual-basis income statement into a cash-basis income statement to determine cash flow from operations by adjusting items not affecting cash flows.

9. _____ _____ _____ is the set of techniques including horizontal, vertical, and ratio analysis designed to provide relevant data to decision makers.

10. _____ _____ focuses on the dollar and percentage changes in accounts from year to year.

11. _____ _____ is horizontal analysis that includes more than a single change from one year to the next.

12. _____ _____ evaluates the relationships within a single financial statement in which the appropriate total figure in the financial statement is set to 100%, and other items are expressed as a percentage of that figure.

13. _____ _____ are financial statements expressed in percentages where the appropriate figure is set to 100%, and other items are expressed as a percentage of that figure.

14. _____ _____ is a method of expressing relationships among various items in a company's financial statements.

15. _____ _____ _____ _____ is an approach to auditing computer-based accounting systems by testing controls and processes within the system.

16. _____ _____ are transactions that are prepared to test the adequacy of controls and processes in a system.

KEY TERMS:

audit through the system
cash equivalents
common-dollar statements
direct method
financial statement analysis
financing activities
horizontal analysis
indirect method

investing activities
noncash activity
operating activities
ratio analysis
statement of cash flows
test data
trend analysis
vertical analysis

Compare your answers to those at the end of the chapter and review any key terms missed.

CHAPTER QUIZ

Write your answers in the spaces provided.

1. The four main financial statements are:
   1. _____
   2. _____
   3. _____
   4. _____

2. On the statement of cash flows, the cash flows are classified as:
   1. _____ activities
   2. _____ activities
   3. _____ activities

3. _____ _____ are highly liquid investments, such as marketable securities, that are treated the same as cash when preparing the statement of cash flows.

4. The two methods that can be used to determine cash flow from operations are:
   1. _____
   2. _____

5. Cash inflows from operations include:
   1. _____
   2. _____
   3. _____
   4. _____

6. Cash outflows for operating activities include:
   1. _____
   2. _____
   3. _____
   4. _____

7. Cash inflows from investing activities include:
   1. _____
   2. _____

8. Cash outflows from investing activities include:
   1. _____
   2. _____

9. Cash inflows from financing activities include:
   1. _____
   2. _____

10. Cash outflows from financing activities include:
    1. _____
    2. _____
    3. _____

11. When auditing a computer-based accounting system, list the three steps used to audit through the system.
    1. _____
       _____
    2. _____
       _____
    3. _____
       _____

Circle the single best answer.

<u>Use the following information to answer the next four questions</u>.

The following balance sheets are for the Burns Company.

	1995	1994
Assets:		
Cash	$199,000	$160,000
Accounts receivable	25,000	30,000
Plant and equipment	90,000	70,000
Accumulated depreciation	(40,000)	(30,000)
Land	15,000	15,000
Total assets	$289,000	$245,000
Liabilities and stockholders' equity:		
Accounts payable	$ 15,000	$ 20,000
Bonds payable	35,000	10,000
Common stock	100,000	100,000
Retained earnings	139,000	115,000
Total liabilities and stockholders' equity	$289,000	$245,000

Additional information:

1. Equipment costing $20,000 was purchased at the end of the year. No equipment was sold during the year.
2. Net income for the year was $40,000.
3. Dividends of $16,000 were paid during the year.

12. The change in cash is: (a) $39,000 increase; (b) $44,000 increase; (c) $24,000 decrease; (d) $29,000 decrease

13. Cash flow from operating activities is: (a) $39,000 inflow; (b) $40,000 outflow; (c) $45,000 inflow; (d) $50,000 inflow

14. Cash flow from investing activities is: (a) $20,000 inflow; (b) $20,000 outflow; (c) $16,000 outflow; (d) $10,000 outflow

15. Cash flow from financing activities is: (a) $16,000 outflow; (b) $16,000 inflow; (c) $9,000 inflow; (d) $25,000 inflow

Compare your answers to those at the end of the chapter. Review any questions missed before proceeding.

Write your answers in the spaces provided.

16. Different financial statement users have different needs. A banker is concerned with _____.

17. A stockholder is interested in _____.

18. Management is interested in _____.

19. On a common-dollar balance sheet, _____ _____ is set equal to 100 percent.

20. On a common-dollar income statement, _____ _____ is set equal to 100 percent.

21. A ratio is more useful if compared to:
    1. _____
    2. _____
    3. _____

22. The _____ _____ is a stricter test than the current ratio of a company's ability to pay its debts when due.

23. Current Ratio = _____ /_____

24. Quick Ratio = _____ /_____

25. Accounts Receivable Turnover = _____ /_____

26. Inventory Turnover = _____ /_____

27. List 2 possible reasons for an unusually low inventory turnover:
    1. _____
    2. _____

28. Times Interest Earned = _____ /_____

29. Debt Ratio = _____ /_____

30. Profit Margin = _____ /_____

31. Earnings per Share = _____ /_____

32. Price-Earnings Ratio = _____ /_____

Compare your answers to those at the end of the chapter. Review any questions missed before proceeding.

Circle the single best answer.

Use the following information to answer the next eight questions.

The income statement for 1995 for the Dustin Company is presented below:

Sales revenue	$600,000
Cost of goods sold	(360,000)
Gross profit	$240,000
Operating expenses	(100,000)
Interest expense	(30,000)
Income before taxes	$110,000
Income taxes	(37,400)
Net income	$ 72,600

The balance sheet for 1995 is given below:

Cash	$ 10,000
Marketable securities	15,000
Accounts receivable	20,000
Inventory	30,000
Property, plant, and equipment	600,000
Total assets	$675,000
Current liabilities	$ 50,000
Long-term liabilities	225,000
Total liabilities	$275,000
Common stock	$150,000
Retained earnings	250,000
Total liabilities and equity	$675,000

The company had 100,000 shares of stock outstanding. At the end of 1995, the market value of the stock was $8.03 per share. Dividends of $50,000 were paid in 1995. Total assets have not changed during 1995.

33. The current ratio is: (a) 1.2; (b) 1.3; (c) 1.5; (d) 1.8

34. The quick ratio is: (a) 0.9; (b) 1.1; (c) 0.7; (d) 0.6

35. Accounts receivable turnover is: (a) 28.50; (b) 30.00; (c) 33.75; (d) 34.00

36. Inventory turnover is: (a) 8.3; (b) 9.0; (c) 10; (d) 12

444

37. The debt ratio is: (a) 24.5%; (b) 32.0%; (c) 41.0%; (d) 33.0%

38. Profit margin is: (a) 8.3%; (b) 9.5%; (c) 10%; (d) 12%

39. Earnings per share is: (a) $0.73; (b) $0.92; (c) $1.15; (d) $1.38

40. The price-earnings ratio is: (a) 5.9; (b) 7.2; (c) 9; (d) 11

Compare your answers to those at the end of the chapter. Review any questions missed before proceeding.

EXERCISES

EXERCISE 1

Listed below are transactions for Pierre & Company for the month of November. For each transaction, indicate how the item would appear on the statement of cash flows if the direct method is used.

1. Indicate whether the item is:
   (I) a cash inflow
   (O) a cash outflow
   (N) neither a cash inflow nor a cash outflow

2. Indicate how the item would be classified on the statement of cash flows using the following symbols:
   (O) operating activity
   (I) investing activity
   (F) financing activity
   (N) does not appear on the statement of cash flows

TRANSACTION	(1)	(2)
1. Credit sales for the month are $120,000.		
2. Cash sales for the month are $100,000.		
3. $20,000 of accounts receivable are collected.		
4. Five-year bonds are issued at the face value of $300,000.		
5. 2,000 shares of common stock are issued for $200,000.		
6. Paid $2,000 in interest on a note payable.		
7. The company borrows $40,000 from the bank and signs a 5-year note.		
8. New equipment is purchased for $50,000 cash.		
9. Repaid $10,000 in principal on a mortgage payable		
10. Paid $12,000 to employees for wages and salaries		
11. Cash dividends of $20,000 are declared; payment will be made in 30 days.		
12. Cash dividends of $20,000 are declared and paid immediately.		

EXERCISE 2

The following information pertains to the Casteel Company.

	12-31-95	12-31-94
Assets:		
Cash	$285,000	$240,000
Accounts receivable	30,000	50,000
Plant and equipment	115,000	80,000
Accumulated depreciation	(50,000)	(40,000)
Land	90,000	60,000
Total assets	$470,000	$390,000
Liabilities and stockholders' equity:		
Accounts payable	$ 30,000	$ 45,000
Bonds payable	50,000	95,000
Common stock	250,000	250,000
Retained earnings	60,000	80,000
Total liabilities and stockholders' equity	$390,000	$470,000

Additional information:

1. Equipment costing $35,000 was purchased at the end of the year. No equipment was sold during the year.

2. Net income for the year was $60,000.

3. Dividends of $40,000 were paid during the year.

Required:

1. Compute the change in the cash balance.

EXERCISE 2 (continued)

2. Compute cash flows from operating activities using the indirect method.

3. Compute cash flows from investing activities.

4. Compute cash flows from financing activities.

EXERCISE 3

The beginning and ending balances in each of the balance sheet accounts of the Sable Company are as follows:

Assets:	12-31-95	12-31-94
Cash	$ 100,000	$ 180,000
Accounts receivable	360,000	260,000
Inventory	460,000	400,000
Prepaid insurance	30,000	50,000
Total current assets	$ 950,000	$ 890,000
Land	$1,500,000	$1,200,000
Plant and equipment	1,400,000	1,000,000
Accumulated depreciation	(500,000)	(400,000)
Total noncurrent assets	$2,400,000	$1,800,000
Total assets	$3,350,000	$2,690,000
Liabilities and stockholders' equity:		
Accounts payable	$ 260,000	$ 300,000
Other accrued liabilities	132,000	122,000
Interest payable	30,000	20,000
Income taxes payable	150,000	200,000
Total current liabilities	$ 572,000	$ 642,000
Bonds payable	$ 700,000	$ 600,000
Common stock	1,100,000	800,000
Retained earnings	978,000	648,000
Total liabilities and stockholders' equity	$3,350,000	$2,690,000

EXERCISE 3 (continued)

The income statement for the Sable Company for 1995 is presented below:

THE SABLE COMPANY
INCOME STATEMENT
FOR THE YEAR ENDED DECEMBER 31, 1995

Sales revenue	$2,500,000
Cost of goods sold	(1,400,000)
Gross profit	$1,100,000
Operating expenses	(300,000)
Income before interest and taxes	$ 800,000
Interest expense	(50,000)
Income before taxes	$ 750,000
Income tax expense	(300,000)
Net income	$ 450,000

Additional information:

1. Dividends declared and paid during the year were $120,000.

2. Operating expenses included $100,000 of depreciation expense and $40,000 of insurance expense (prepaid insurance that expired during 1995).

3. Assume all accrued liabilities relate to operating expenses.

EXERCISE 3 (continued)

Required:

1. Prepare a statement of cash flows using the indirect method to determine
    cash flows from operating activities.

EXERCISE 3 (continued)

2.a. How much cash was collected from customers during the year?

b. How much cash was paid for interest expense during the year?

c. How much cash was paid for income taxes during the year?

3. Using the direct approach, prepare the operating activities section of the statement of cash flows.

EXERCISE 4

Comparative balance sheets for the Leigh Company for the past two years were as follows:

Assets:	12-31-95	12-31-94
Cash	$ 10,000	$ 8,000
Accounts receivable	24,000	30,000
Inventory	28,000	20,000
Prepaid rent	10,000	12,000
Total current assets	$ 72,000	$ 70,000
Land	$100,000	$100,000
Plant and equipment, net	550,000	500,000
Total noncurrent assets	$650,000	$600,000
Total assets	$722,000	$670,000
Liabilities and stockholders' equity:		
Accounts payable	$ 10,000	$ 8,000
Income taxes payable	6,000	5,000
Short-term notes payable	15,000	13,000
Total current liabilities	$ 31,000	$ 26,000
Bonds payable	$250,000	$230,000
Common stock, $10 par	$150,000	$150,000
Retained earnings	291,000	264,000
Total stockholders' equity	$441,000	$414,000
Total liabilities and stockholders' equity	$722,000	$670,000

A total of $18,000 in dividends were paid in 1995.
The market price of the common stock on December 31, 1995, was $30 per share.

EXERCISE 4 (continued)

Required:

1. Prepare a horizontal analysis using 1994 as the base year.
   (Round percentages to 1 decimal place.)

EXERCISE 4 (continued)

2. Prepare common-dollar comparative balance sheets for the two years for the Leigh Company. (Round percentages to 2 decimal places.)

EXERCISE 5

An income statement for the Leigh Company for 1995 is presented below:

THE LEIGH COMPANY
INCOME STATEMENT
FOR THE YEAR ENDED DECEMBER 31, 1995

Sales	$ 200,000
Cost of goods sold	(65,000)
Gross profit	$ 135,000
Selling, general, and administrative expenses ..	(40,000)
Operating income	$ 95,000
Interest expense	(20,000)
Income before taxes	$ 75,000
Income tax expense (40%)	(30,000)
Net income	$ 45,000

Required:

Prepare a common-dollar income statement for the Leigh Company. (Round percentages to 1 decimal place.)

EXERCISE 6

Required:

Using the information from Exercises 4 and 5, calculate the following ratios for 1995.

1. Short-term creditor ratios:

    a. Current ratio:

    b. Quick ratio:

    c. Accounts receivable turnover:

    d. Inventory turnover:

2. Long-term creditor ratios:

    a. Debt ratio:

    b. Times interest earned:

EXERCISE 6 (continued)

3. Common and preferred stockholder ratios:

   a. Profit margin:

   b. Return on common stockholders' equity:

   c. Earnings per share:

   d. Price-earnings ratio:

   e. Dividend yield:

   f. Book value per share:

ANSWERS

KEY TERMS TEST
1. statement of cash flows
2. Cash equivalents
3. investing activities
4. financing activities
5. operating activities
6. Noncash activity
7. direct method
8. indirect method
9. Financial statement analysis
10. Horizontal analysis
11. Trend analysis
12. Vertical analysis
13. Common-dollar statements
14. Ratio analysis
15. Audit through the system
16. Test data

CHAPTER QUIZ
1. 1. income statement
   2. balance sheet
   3. statement of cash flows
   4. retained earnings statement or statement of changes in stockholders' equity
2. 1. operating
   2. investing
   3. financing
3. Cash equivalents
4. 1. direct method
   2. indirect method
5. 1. cash sales
   2. collections of accounts receivable
   3. cash received for interest and dividends
   4. proceeds from sales and maturities of trading securities
6. Any four of the following:
   • payments to suppliers
   • payments for salaries and wages
   • payments for interest
   • payments for taxes
   • payments for merchandise purchased
   • payments for insurance
   • payments for trading securities purchased
7. 1. sale of property, plant, and equipment
   2. sale of long-term investments that are classified as held-to-maturity or available-for-sale securities
8. 1. purchase of property, plant, and equipment
   2. purchase of long-term investments that are classified as held-to-maturity or available-for-sale securities
9. 1. cash received from issuance of bonds
   2. cash received from issuance of stock

10. 1. payment of cash dividends
    2. repayment of long-term debt and bonds
    3. retirement of stock
11. 1. Prepare test data.
    2. Determine what the system response to test data should be.
    3. Input test data, and compare computer-generated results with expectations.
12. a $199,000 - $160,000 = $39,000 increase
13. d $40,000 + $5,000 + 10,000 - $5,000 = $50,000 inflow
14. b
15. c $25,000 - $16,000 = $9,000 inflow
16. the company's ability to repay loan principal and interest
17. earning a return on his or her investment
18. obtaining information that is useful in planning and controlling company operations
19. total assets
20. net sales
21. 1. past performance
    2. other companies in the same industry
    3. industry averages
22. quick ratio
23. Current Assets/Current Liabilities
24. (Cash + Marketable Securities + Receivables)/Current Liabilities
25. Net Credit Sales/Average Accounts Receivable
26. Cost of Goods Sold/Average Inventory
27. obsolete inventory, problems in the sales department, or the company is pricing its products too high
28. (Income before Taxes + Interest Expense)/Interest Expense
29. Total Liabilities/Total Assets
30. Net Income/Sales
31. (Net Income - Preferred Dividends)/Average Common Shares Outstanding
32. Market Price per Common Share/Earnings per Share
33. c ($10,000 + $15,000 + $20,000 + $30,000)/$50,000 = 1.5
34. a ($10,000 + $15,000 + $20,000)/$50,000 = 0.9
35. b $600,000/$20,000 = 30 times
36. d $360,000/$30,000 = 12 times
37. c $275,000/$675,000 = 41%
38. d $72,600/$600,000 = 12%
39. a $72,600/100,000 = $0.73
40. d $8.03/$0.73 = 11

EXERCISE 1

TRANSACTION	(1)	(2)
1. Credit sales for the month are $120,000.	N	N
2. Cash sales for the month are $100,000.	I	O
3. $20,000 of accounts receivable are collected.	I	O
4. Five-year bonds are issued at the face value of $300,000.	I	F
5. 2,000 shares of common stock are issued for $200,000.	I	F
6. Paid $2,000 in interest on a note payable.	O	O
7. The company borrows $40,000 from the bank and signs a 5-year note.	I	F
8. New equipment is purchased for $50,000 cash.	O	I
9. Repaid $10,000 in principal on a mortgage payable.	O	F
10. Paid $12,000 to employees for wages and salaries.	O	O
11. Cash dividends of $20,000 are declared; payment will be made in 30 days.	N	N
12. Cash dividends of $20,000 are declared and paid immediately.	O	F

EXERCISE 2

1. Change in the cash balance: $285,000 - $240,000 = $45,000

2. Cash flows from operating activities:

Net income	$ 60,000
Add (deduct) adjustments to convert to the cash basis:	
Decrease in accounts receivable	20,000
Depreciation expense	10,000
Increase in accounts payable	15,000
Net cash flow from operating activities	$105,000

3. Cash flows from investing activities:

Purchase of land	$(30,000)
Purchase of equipment	(35,000)
Net cash flow from investing activities	$(65,000)

4. Cash flows from financing activities:

Payment of dividends	$(40,000)
Issuance of bonds	45,000
Net cash flow from financing activities	$ 5,000

EXERCISE 3

1.

THE SABLE COMPANY
STATEMENT OF CASH FLOWS
FOR THE YEAR ENDED DECEMBER 31, 1995

Cash Flows From Operating Activities:		
Net income	$450,000	
Add (deduct) adjustments to convert		
net income to the cash basis:		
Depreciation expense	100,000	
Increase in accounts receivable	(100,000)	
Increase in inventory	(60,000)	
Decrease in prepaid insurance	20,000	
Decrease in accounts payable	(40,000)	
Increase in interest payable	10,000	
Decrease in income taxes payable	(50,000)	
Increase in accrued liabilities	10,000	
	—————	
Net cash flow from operating activities		$340,000
Cash Flows From Investing Activities:		
Acquisition of land	$(300,000)	
Acquisition of plant and equipment	(400,000)	
	—————	
Net cash flow from investing activities		(700,000)
Cash Flows From Financing Activities:		
Payment of cash dividends	$(120,000)	
Issuance of bonds	100,000	
Issuance of stock	300,000	
	—————	
Net cash flow from investing activities		280,000
Net decrease in cash		($ 80,000)

2.a. $2,400,000
 b. $40,000
 c. $350,000

EXERCISE 3 (continued)

3.

CASH FLOW FROM OPERATING ACTIVITIES
DIRECT APPROACH

	Income Statement	Adjustment	Cash Flow
Revenues	$2,500,000	$(100,000)[1]	$2,400,000
Cost of goods sold	(1,400,000)	(40,000)[2] (60,000)[3]	(1,500,000)
Depreciation expense	(100,000)	100,000	-
Insurance expense	(40,000)	20,000[4]	(20,000)
Other operating expenses	(160,000)[5]	10,000[6]	(150,000)
Interest expense	(50,000)	10,000[7]	(40,000)
Income tax expense	(300,000)	(50,000)[8]	(350,000)
Net income	$ 450,000		
Net cash flow from operating activities			$ 340,000

NOTE: Remember that when making adjustments to convert from the accrual to the cash basis, cash moves in the opposite direction of noncash current assets and cash moves in the same direction as current liabilities.

[1] Increase in accounts receivable
[2] Decrease in accounts payable
[3] Increase in inventory
[4] Decrease in prepaid insurance
[5] Calculated as follows:

Total operating expenses	$300,000
Less: depreciation expense	(100,000)
insurance expense	(40,000)
Other operating expenses	$160,000

[6] Increase in accrued liabilities
[7] Increase in interest payable
[8] Decrease in income taxes payable

462

EXERCISE 4

1.

THE LEIGH COMPANY
COMPARATIVE BALANCE SHEETS
DECEMBER 31, 1995 AND 1994

	12-31-95		12-31-94	
	Dollars	%	Dollars	%
Cash	$ 10,000	125.0	$ 8,000	100.0
Accounts receivable	24,000	80.0	30,000	100.0
Inventory	28,000	140.0	20,000	100.0
Prepaid rent	10,000	83.3	12,000	100.0
Total current assets	$ 72,000	102.9	$ 70,000	100.0
Land	$100,000	100.0	$100,000	100.0
Plant and equipment, net	550,000	110.0	500,000	100.0
Total noncurrent assets	$650,000	108.3	$600,000	100.0
Total assets	$722,000	107.8	$670,000	100.0
Accounts payable	$ 10,000	125.0	$ 8,000	100.0
Income taxes payable	6,000	120.0	5,000	100.0
Short-term notes payable	15,000	115.4	13,000	100.0
Total current liabilities	$ 31,000	119.2	$ 26,000	100.0
Bonds payable	$250,000	108.7	$230,000	100.0
Common stock, $10 par	$150,000	100.0	$150,000	100.0
Retained earnings	291,000	110.2	264,000	100.0
Total stockholders' equity	$441,000	106.5	$414,000	100.0
Total liabilities and stockholders' equity	$722,000	107.8	$670,000	100.0

EXERCISE 4 (continued)

2.

THE LEIGH COMPANY
COMMON-DOLLAR COMPARATIVE BALANCE SHEETS
DECEMBER 31, 1995 AND 1994

	12-31-95		12-31-94	
	Dollars	Percent	Dollars	Percent
Cash	$ 10,000	1.39%	$ 8,000	1.19%
Accounts receivable	24,000	3.32	30,000	4.47
Inventory	28,000	3.88	20,000	2.99
Prepaid rent	10,000	1.38	12,000	1.79
Total current assets	$ 72,000	9.97	$ 70,000	10.44
Land	$100,000	13.85	$100,000	14.93
Plant and equipment, net	550,000	76.18	500,000	74.63
Total noncurrent assets	$650,000	90.03	$600,000	89.56
Total assets	$722,000	100.00	$670,000	100.00
Accounts payable	$ 10,000	1.39	$ 8,000	1.19
Income taxes payable	6,000	0.83	5,000	.75
Short-term notes payable	15,000	2.07*	13,000	1.94
Total current liabilities	$ 31,000	4.29	$ 26,000	3.88
Bonds payable	$250,000	34.63	$230,000	34.33
Common stock, $10 par	$150,000	20.78	$150,000	22.39
Retained earnings	291,000	40.30	264,000	39.40
Total stockholders' equity	$441,000	61.08	$414,000	61.79
Total liabilities and stockholders' equity	$722,000	100.00	$670,000	100.00

*rounded

EXERCISE 5

THE LEIGH COMPANY
COMMON-DOLLAR INCOME STATEMENT
FOR THE YEAR ENDED DECEMBER 31, 1995

Sales	$200,000	100.0%
Cost of goods sold	(65,000)	(32.5)
Gross profit	$135,000	67.5
Selling, general, and administrative expenses	(40,000)	(20.0)
Operating income	$ 95,000	47.5
Interest expense	(20,000)	(10.0)
Income before taxes	$ 75,000	37.5
Income tax expense	(30,000)	(15.0)
Net income	$ 45,000	22.5

EXERCISE 6

1. Short-term creditor ratios:

a.

$$\text{Current Ratio} = \frac{\text{Current Assets}}{\text{Current Liabilities}}$$

$$= \frac{\$72,000}{\$31,000} = 2.32 \text{ to } 1$$

This indicates there are $2.32 in current assets for every $1.00 in current liabilities.

b.

$$\text{Quick Ratio} = \frac{\text{Quick Assets}}{\text{Current Liabilities}}$$

$$= \frac{\$10,000 + \$24,000}{\$31,000} = 1.10 \text{ to } 1$$

Leigh has $1.10 in quick assets for every $1.00 in current liabilities.

c.

$$\text{Accounts Receivable Turnover} = \frac{\text{Net Credit Sales}}{\text{Average Accounts Receivable}}$$

$$= \frac{\$200,000}{(\$24,000 + \$30,000)/2} = 7.41 \text{ times}$$

Accounts receivable turned over 7.41 times during the year.

d.

$$\text{Inventory Turnover} = \frac{\text{Cost of Goods Sold}}{\text{Average Inventory}}$$

$$= \frac{\$65,000}{(\$20,000 + \$28,000)/2} = 2.71 \text{ times}$$

Inventory turned over 2.71 times during the year.

2. Long-term creditor ratios:

a.

$$\text{Debt Ratio} = \frac{\text{Total Liabilities}}{\text{Total Assets}}$$

$$= \frac{\$281,000}{\$722,000} = .3892$$

About 39% of the company's assets are financed by creditors.

b.

$$\text{Times Interest Earned} = \frac{\text{Income Before Taxes + Interest Expense}}{\text{Interest Expense}}$$

$$= \frac{\$95,000}{\$20,000} = 4.75 \text{ times}$$

Operating income was 4.75 times the amount of interest expense.

EXERCISE 6 (continued)

3. Common and preferred stockholder ratios:

a.

$$\text{Profit Margin} = \frac{\text{Net Income}}{\text{Sales}}$$

$$= \frac{\$45,000}{\$200,000} = 22.5\%$$

The profit margin indicates that $0.225 of each $1 in sales is profit.

b.

$$\text{Return on Common Stockholders' Equity} = \frac{\text{Net Income - Preferred Dividends}}{\text{Average Common Stockholders' Equity}}$$

$$= \frac{\$45,000 - \$0}{(\$414,000 + \$441,000)/2} = .1053, \text{ or } 10.53\%$$

c.

$$\text{Earnings Per Share} = \frac{\text{Net Income - Preferred Dividends}}{\text{Average Common Shares Outstanding}}$$

$$= \frac{\$45,000 - \$0}{15,000 \text{ shares}} = \$3.00 \text{ per share}$$

d.

$$\text{Price-Earnings Ratio} = \frac{\text{Current Market Price}}{\text{Earnings Per Share}}$$

$$= \frac{\$30.00}{\$ 3.00} = 10$$

The price/earnings ratio indicates the stock is selling for 10 times its earnings.

e.

$$\text{Dividend Yield} = \frac{\text{Common Dividends Per Share}}{\text{Market Price Per Share}}$$

$$= \frac{\$ 1.20*}{\$30.00} = .04, \text{ or } 4\%$$

*$18,000 in dividends/15,000 shares = $1.20 per share

EXERCISE 6 (continued)

f.

$$\text{Book Value per Share} = \frac{\text{Common Stockholders' Equity}}{\text{Number of Common Shares Outstanding}}$$

$$= \frac{\$441,000}{15,000 \text{ shares}} = \$29.40$$

CHAPTER 15

COST CONCEPTS AND TERMINOLOGY

```
╔═══════════════════════════════════════════════════════════╗
║  CHAPTER REVIEW                                             ║
╚═══════════════════════════════════════════════════════════╝
```

ORGANIZATIONAL FRAMEWORK

- Organizations can be classified as:
  1. manufacturing
  2. merchandising
  3. service

- Manufacturing organizations convert raw materials into a finished product using labor and capital inputs (such as plant and equipment).

  General Motors is an example of a manufacturing firm that produces automobiles.

- Merchandising firms buy finished goods and resell the goods to consumers or other merchandising firms.

  Merchandising firms selling directly to consumers are sometimes referred to as *retailers*.

  Merchandising firms selling to other merchandising firms are often referred to as *wholesalers*.

  Examples of merchandisers include WalMart, K Mart, and Sears.

- Service organizations provide a service to customers.

  Examples of service firms include accounting firms, legal firms, medical practices, airlines, and insurance companies.

- Each type of organization needs cost information.

- Most cost concepts are applicable to all three types of organizations.

BASIC COST CONCEPTS

- A **cost** is the cash (or cash equivalent) exchanged for goods or services that are expected to produce current or future benefits.

- **Expenses** are <u>expired</u> costs (costs that are used up when generating revenue).

- A **loss** is a cost that expires without generating revenue.

- Expenses and losses appear on the income statement.

- **Assets** are <u>unexpired</u> costs. Assets are costs that still have future benefit, such as the cost of production equipment.

- Assets appear on the balance sheet.

- An **opportunity cost** is the benefit given up when one alternative is chosen over another. Opportunity costs are not usually recorded in the accounting system; however, opportunity costs should be considered when evaluating alternatives for decision making.

- A **differential cost**, or **incremental cost**, is the amount by which a cost differs between two alternatives.

- An **out-of-pocket cost** is a cost that involves a current cash outlay.

- A **sunk cost** is a cost for which an outlay has already been made and that cannot be changed by a present or future decision. Because sunk costs cannot be changed, they do not differ between alternatives and should have no bearing on the decision.

- **Controllable costs** can be influenced by a manager. Managers should be held accountable for only the costs they can control.

- **Noncontrollable costs** cannot be significantly influenced by a manager.

- **Direct costs** are traceable to a cost object.

- A **cost object** is any item or activity, such as products or departments, to which costs are assigned.

- **Indirect costs** are common to several cost objects. Indirect costs are not directly traceable to <u>one</u> particular cost object.

- Costs can be classified by
  1. function
  2. behavior

- The functional classification of costs is used for external reporting.

- The behavioral classification of costs is used for internal purposes, such as planning, control, and decision making.

FUNCTIONAL CLASSIFICATION OF COSTS

- The two major functional classifications of costs for a manufacturer are:
  1. **manufacturing costs**: costs associated with production
  2. **nonmanufacturing costs**: costs associated with selling and administration

Direct Manufacturing Costs

- **Direct manufacturing costs** are directly traceable to the product being manufactured. In a traditional multiple-product firm, two types of direct manufacturing costs are:
  1. **direct materials**: materials that become part of the product and are directly traceable to the product. Examples include wood in furniture.
  2. **direct labor**: labor used to convert direct materials into a finished product. Workers on an assembly line and production equipment operators are examples of direct labor.

Indirect Manufacturing Costs

- Indirect manufacturing costs cannot be traced to any one particular product.

- In a traditional, multiple-product manufacturing environment, indirect manufacturing costs consist of all manufacturing costs other than direct materials and direct labor.

- Indirect manufacturing costs are called **manufacturing overhead**.

- Examples of manufacturing overhead include:
  1. **indirect materials**, such as lubricating oil for production equipment. Indirect materials are necessary for production but do not become part of the finished product and are not directly traceable to any one product.

     Direct materials that are an insignificant part of the finished product, such as glue in furniture, are usually assigned to overhead.

  2. **indirect labor**, which consists of all factory labor other than those workers who are directly involved in transforming raw materials into a finished product. Examples include production-line supervisors, janitors, and maintenance workers.

     The premium paid for direct labor overtime is usually included in indirect labor. (Direct labor fringe benefits should be treated as a direct labor cost.)

Nonmanufacturing Costs

- Two categories of nonmanufacturing costs are:
  1. **selling costs**: costs necessary to market and distribute a product or service. Examples of selling costs include:
     - **order-getting costs**, such as salesperson's commissions and advertising.
     - **order-filling costs**, such as warehousing, customer service, and shipping.

471

2. **administrative costs**: all costs associated with the general administration of the organization that cannot be assigned to either marketing or manufacturing costs. Examples include top executive salaries, general accounting, and research and development.

Related Cost Concepts

Period Costs

- **Period costs** consist of nonmanufacturing (selling and administrative) costs.

- Period costs are expensed in the period incurred. Incurred means that the firm has become liable for payment. The payment of cash may or may not occur at the same time that the cost is incurred.

Product Costs

- **Product costs** are manufacturing costs that attach to the product and are first inventoried and later expensed as the product is sold.

- For <u>external financial reporting</u>, product costs consist of:
  - direct materials
  - direct labor
  - manufacturing overhead

- Product costs for financial reporting appear as an asset (Inventory) on the balance sheet until the goods are sold. When the goods are sold, product costs are recorded as an expense (Cost of Goods Sold).

- Managerial product costing is the product cost information used by managers for planning and decision making. For internal managerial use, different cost information might be needed for different purposes. For example, when pricing a product, a manager needs to consider <u>all</u> costs: direct materials, direct labor, overhead, and <u>selling and administrative</u> costs.

- One cost accounting system may be needed for inventory valuation (to satisfy external financial reporting requirements), another for managerial product costing, and a third for control.

Prime Costs and Conversion Costs

- **Prime costs** consist of direct material and direct labor costs.

- **Conversion costs** consist of direct labor and manufacturing overhead costs. Such costs are incurred to <u>convert</u> direct materials into a final product.

FINANCIAL STATEMENTS AND THE FUNCTIONAL CLASSIFICATION

• The functional classification of costs is required by the Securities and Exchange Commission (SEC) and the Financial Accounting Standards Board (FASB) for <u>external reporting</u>.

• Income computed using a functional classification frequently is referred to as **absorption-costing income** or **full-costing income** because <u>all manufacturing</u> costs are fully assigned or absorbed by the product.

• Under absorption costing, the two major functional categories of expenses are:
  1. cost of goods sold (manufacturing expenses)
  2. operating expenses (nonmanufacturing expenses)

• **Cost of goods sold** consists of the cost of direct materials, direct labor, and overhead attached to the units <u>sold</u> during a period.

• The **cost of goods manufactured** is the cost of direct materials, direct labor, and overhead attached to the units <u>produced</u> during a period.

Cost Flows: Manufacturing Firms

• **Work in process** consists of all partially completed units found in production at a given point in time.

• **Finished goods** are goods that are complete and ready for sale.

• Cost flows for a manufacturer are diagrammed below:

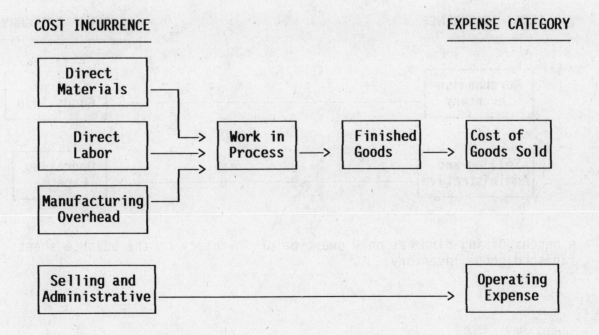

- As direct materials, direct labor, and manufacturing overhead are used in the production process, the associated costs are transferred to the Work-in-Process Inventory account.

- As the goods in process are completed, the associated costs are transferred to the Finished Goods Inventory account.

- As the goods are sold, the associated costs are transferred to the Cost of Goods Sold account. Thus, the product costs of direct materials, direct labor, and manufacturing overhead are not expensed until the goods are sold.

- A manufacturing firm will have three inventory accounts on the balance sheet:
  1. raw materials inventory
  2. work in process inventory
  3. finished goods inventory

Cost Flows: Merchandising Firms

- In a merchandising firm, cost of goods sold represents the acquisition cost of the goods rather than the manufacturing cost.

- When merchandise is purchased, it is recorded as inventory.

- When the merchandise is sold, the cost of the merchandise is transferred to an expense account, cost of goods sold.

- Cost flows for a merchandising firm are diagrammed below:

- A merchandising firm has only one type of inventory on the balance sheet: finished goods inventory.

Cost Flows: Service Organizations

- Cost flows for a service firm are diagrammed below:

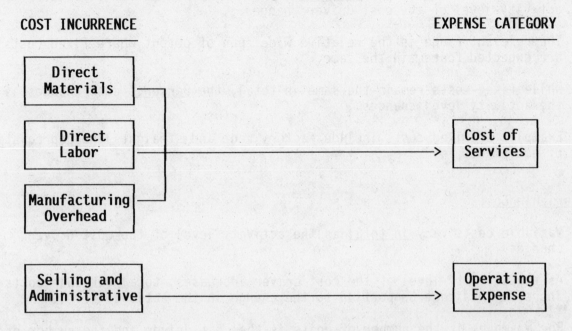

COST INCURRENCE   EXPENSE CATEGORY

- As materials (supplies), direct labor, and overhead (utilities, rent, etc.) are used to provide the service, these costs are expensed.

- Selling and administrative costs are expensed as incurred.

- Because service organizations cannot build inventories of services, there are no work in process or finished goods inventories.

- In regulated industries, service organizations are allowed to set a price that covers their costs and provides a specified rate of return.

- Deregulation has resulted in stiff competition. Managers need to know the cost of services so pricing decisions and profitability assessments can be made.

CLASSIFICATION BY COST BEHAVIOR

- **Cost behavior** is concerned with how costs change when activity changes.

- A **cost driver** is a factor (activity) that causes (drives) costs.

- Three types of cost behavior are:
  1. fixed costs
  2. variable costs
  3. mixed costs

Fixed Costs

- **Fixed costs** do <u>not</u> change <u>in total</u> within the relevant range as the activity level of the cost driver changes.

- The relevant range is the relative wide span of output where fixed costs are expected to remain the same.

- While fixed costs remain the same in total, the <u>per unit</u> cost changes as the activity level changes.

- Examples of fixed costs include factory rent and straight-line depreciation of equipment.

Variable Costs

- **Variable costs** vary <u>in total</u> as the activity level of the cost driver changes.

- As the activity level of the cost driver increases, total variable costs increase in direct proportion to the change in the activity level.

- For example, if the number of units is the cost driver and the number of units doubles, total variable costs would double.

- The variable cost <u>per unit of activity remains constant</u>.

- Total variable costs can be calculated as follows:

Total Variable Costs = Variable Cost Per Unit of Activity x Activity Level of Cost Driver

Fixed Versus Variable Costs

- The two graphs below illustrate how variable costs increase with activity while fixed costs remain the same.

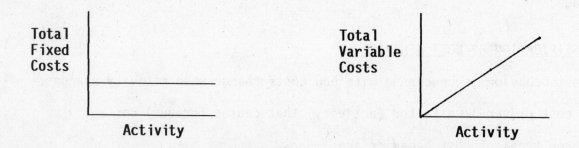

- Example: Assume NCP, Inc., manufactures racing bicycles. Each bicycle requires 1 handlebar costing $10 each. The handlebars are a direct material because they become part of the finished product, and they are a variable cost because the <u>total</u> handlebar cost <u>varies</u> with the number of bicycles produced.

If NCP produces 1 bicycle, the total cost for handlebars would be $10; if it manufactures 100 bicycles, the total cost for handlebars would be $1,000.

Bicycles	Handlebars	Cost Per Handlebar	Total Handlebar Cost
1	1	$10	$ 10
100	100	10	1,000
1,000	1,000	10	10,000
10,000	10,000	10	100,000

If NCP pays $5,000 per month to rent factory space large enough to produce up to 10,000 bicycles a month, the $5,000 rent would be classified as manufacturing overhead because it is a manufacturing cost other than direct materials or direct labor. In addition, the rent is a fixed cost because the cost is $5,000 a month whether NCP produces 1 bicycle or 10,000 bicycles.

Bicycles	Factory Rent
1	$5,000
10	5,000
1,000	5,000
10,000	5,000

Mixed Costs

- **Mixed costs** have both a fixed and a variable component.

- For example, if an equipment lease specified monthly payments of $1,000 plus $10 per hour the machine is used, the fixed portion is the $1,000 per month and the variable portion is the $10 per hour.

- The equation for a mixed cost is:

  Total Mixed Cost = Fixed Costs + Total Variable Costs

  Total Mixed Cost = Fixed Costs + (Variable Cost Per Unit of Activity x Activity Level)

Income Statement: Classification by Cost Behavior

Variable-Costing Income Statement

- A variable-costing income statement classifies costs by behavior as either fixed or variable using units sold as the cost driver.

- Variable-costing income is calculated as follows:

  Sales
  - **Variable expenses**
  = **Contribution margin**
  - **Fixed expenses**
  = **Variable-costing income**

- <u>Variable expenses</u> include:
  - **Variable cost of goods sold** consisting of variable manufacturing costs: direct materials, direct labor, and <u>variable</u> overhead. When calculating variable-costing income, only variable manufacturing costs are viewed as product costs.
  - **Variable selling and administrative expenses**

- <u>Fixed expenses</u> include:
  - fixed overhead
  - fixed selling and administrative expenses

- **Contribution margin** equals sales revenue less all variable expenses. Contribution margin represents the amount available to cover fixed expenses and provide profit.

- The variable-costing income statement provides information used for planning, control, and decision making.

Absorption-Costing Income Statement

- An absorption-costing income statement uses the functional approach and classifies costs as:
  1. Cost of Goods Sold consisting of:
     - direct materials
     - direct labor
     - variable <u>and</u> fixed overhead
  2. Selling and Administrative Expenses consisting of:
     - variable selling and administrative expenses
     - fixed selling and administrative expenses

- Note that all manufacturing costs including fixed overhead are viewed as product costs.

- Absorption-costing income is calculated as follows:

  Sales
  - **Cost of goods sold**
  = **Gross profit**
  - **Selling and administrative expenses**
  = **Absorption-costing income**

- A functional classification of costs is required for external financial reporting to stockholders.

Cost Behavior and Cost Systems

- Two cost systems can be found in practice:
  1. conventional or traditional cost systems
  2. activity-based cost systems (ABC systems)

- Currently, conventional cost systems are more widely used than ABC systems; however, use of ABC systems is increasing, especially among organizations using JIT manufacturing and advanced manufacturing technology.

- **Conventional cost systems** assume all costs can be classified as fixed or variable based on changes in the <u>volume</u> of production.

- **Activity-based cost systems** require additional cost drivers that are unrelated to the volume of the product produced. For example, setup costs are driven by the number of setups.

- ABC systems have the potential to:
  1. improve product costing accuracy by improving traceability of costs.
  2. improve the planning and control functions by improving the ability to forecast costs accurately.

KEY TERMS TEST

There are many new terms introduced in this chapter. The following is provided to assist you in reviewing the new terminology. Indicate which of the following terms best matches the statements listed on the following page by placing the appropriate letter(s) in the blank preceding the statement.

KEY TERMS

A. Asset	P. Indirect materials
B. Controllable cost	Q. Loss
C. Conversion cost	R. Manufacturing overhead
D. Cost of goods manufactured	S. Mixed costs
E. Cost of goods sold	T. Noncontrollable cost
F. Differential cost	U. Opportunity cost
G. Direct costs	V. Out-of-pocket cost
H. Direct labor	W. Period costs
I. Direct materials	X. Prime cost
J. Expense	Y. Product costs
K. Finished goods	Z. Relevant range
L. Fixed costs	AA. Selling costs
M. Incremental cost	BB. Sunk costs
N. Indirect costs	CC. Variable costs
O. Indirect labor	DD. Work in process

DEFINITIONS

___ 1. Costs that are the result of past decisions and cannot be changed by current or future actions.

___ 2. Materials that become part of the product and can be traced to the final product.

___ 3. All materials used in production that do not become part of the product.

___ 4. Labor used in manufacturing that is not part of transforming the raw materials into the product.

___ 5. Costs associated with inventory and expensed when the goods are sold.

___ 6. Partially completed units found in production at a given point in time.

___ 7. Goods that are complete and ready for sale.

___ 8. Costs that remain constant per unit of activity but vary in total.

___ 9. Costs that are expensed as incurred.

___10. Costs that are easily traceable to a cost object.

___11. Work involved in transforming direct materials into finished products.

___12. Direct labor cost plus manufacturing overhead cost.

___13. Costs that vary per unit of activity but remain constant in total within the relevant range.

___14. The range of activity over which cost behavior relationships are valid.

___15. Direct materials cost plus direct labor cost.

___16. All manufacturing costs other than direct materials and direct labor.

___17. An unexpired cost representing a current or future benefit to the firm.

___18. Costs incurred to market and distribute a firm's products or services.

___19. A cost that can be significantly influenced by a manager.

___20. A cost that expires without producing revenue.

___21. The cost of direct materials, direct labor, and overhead attached to the units sold.

___22. A cost that involves a current cash outlay.

___23. The cost of direct materials, direct labor, and overhead attached to the units produced in a period.

___24. The benefit sacrificed or foregone when one alternative is chosen instead of another.

___25. The amount by which a cost differs between two alternatives.

___26. A cost that cannot be significantly influenced by a manager.

___27. A cost that has expired to produce revenue.

___28. Costs that have both a fixed and a variable component.

___29. Costs that are common to several cost objects and cannot be traced to any single cost object.

Test your recall of the remaining key terms as follows. First, read the following definitions of key terms and try to recall as many key terms as you can <u>without assistance</u>. Write your answers in the spaces provided. If you need assistance, refer to the list of key terms at the end of this section.

30. _____ _____ _____ are manufacturing costs that can be easily traced to the product being manufactured.

31. Costs that cannot be reasonably assigned to marketing or manufacturing categories are _____ _____.

32. _____ _____ _____ is calculated by classifying costs according to cost behavior and then deducting these costs from revenue. Only variable manufacturing costs are viewed as product costs.

33. A(n) _____ is the cash or cash equivalent sacrificed for goods and services expected to product current or future benefits.

34. _____ _____ is the process of accounting for a cost from the point of incurrence to its expiration on the income statement.

35. _____ _____ are costs associated with selling and general administration.

36. _____ _____ are costs necessary to make a product and include the costs of direct materials, direct labor, and overhead.

37. _____ _____ _____ _____ is the total variable manufacturing costs attached to the units sold.

38. _____ _____ ____ ____ _____ is the cost of direct materials, direct labor, and variable overhead attached to the units produced in a period.

39. _____ _____ is calculated by deducting costs classified according to a functional classification under which all manufacturing costs are viewed as product costs.

40. A(n) _____ _____ _____, or _____ system, is a cost system that uses cost drivers in addition to units of product produced to describe cost behavior.

41. Sales revenue less all variable expenses equals _____ _____, the amount available to cover fixed expenses and provide for profit.

42. A(n) _____ _____ _____ is a cost system that uses only unit-based cost drivers to describe cost behavior and trace costs to products.

43. A factor that drives or causes activity costs is called a _____ _____.

481

44. Any objective or activity to which costs are assigned is a _____ _____.

KEY TERMS:

absorption-costing income
activity-based cost system, ABC
administrative costs
contribution margin
conventional cost system
cost
cost driver
cost flow

cost object
direct manufacturing costs
manufacturing costs
nonmanufacturing costs
variable-costing income
variable cost of goods manufactured
variable cost of goods sold

Compare your answers to those at the end of the chapter. Review any key terms missed.

CHAPTER QUIZ

1. Toys "R" Us is an example of: (a) a manufacturer; (b) a merchandiser; (c) a service company; (d) none of the above

2. Maytag is an example of: (a) a manufacturer; (b) a merchandiser; (c) a service company; (d) none of the above

3. Federal Express is an example of: (a) a manufacturer; (b) a merchandiser; (c) a service company; (d) none of the above

4. Contribution margin is: (a) revenue minus total costs; (b) revenue minus fixed costs; (c) revenue minus variable costs; (d) none of the above

5. Cost of goods sold consists of the following costs: (a) direct materials only; (b) direct materials and direct labor only; (c) direct materials, direct labor, and variable overhead; (d) direct materials, direct labor, variable overhead, and fixed overhead

6. Variable cost of goods sold consists of the following costs: (a) direct materials only; (b) direct materials and direct labor only; (c) direct materials, direct labor, and variable overhead; (d) direct materials, direct labor, variable overhead, and fixed overhead

7. When calculating variable-costing income: (a) all manufacturing costs are viewed as product costs; (b) only variable manufacturing costs are viewed as product costs; (c) manufacturing and nonmanufacturing costs are viewed as product costs; (d) only direct materials and direct labor are viewed as product costs

8. When absorption costing is used: (a) all manufacturing costs are viewed as product costs; (b) only variable manufacturing costs are viewed as product costs; (c) manufacturing and nonmanufacturing costs are viewed as product costs; (d) only direct materials and direct labor are viewed as product costs

9. Absorption costing and variable costing always result in the same amount of income: (a) true; (b) false

Use the following information to answer the next five questions

The Flowers Company estimated costs to be as follows at 50,000 units of production:

Direct materials	$ 75,000
Direct labor	150,000
Variable overhead	20,000
Fixed overhead	120,000
Variable selling and administration costs	10,000
Fixed selling and administration costs	80,000

10. The variable manufacturing cost per unit at a production level of 50,000 units would be: (a) $5.10; (b) $4.50; (c) $4.60; (d) $4.90

11. The variable manufacturing cost per unit at a production level of 60,000 units would be: (a) $3.75; (b) $4.08; (c) $4.25; (d) $4.90

12. The fixed manufacturing cost per unit at a production level of 50,000 units would be: (a) $1.60; (b) $2.40; (c) $4.00; (d) $4.20

13. The fixed manufacturing cost per unit at a production level of 60,000 units would be: (a) $2.00; (b) $2.40; (c) $3.34; (d) $3.50

14. The Flowers Company expects to produce 50,000 units. Another company asked Flowers to produce a special order of 8,000 units. No selling or administrative costs would be incurred as a result of the special order. Total incremental costs associated with the special order would be: (a) $28,800; (b) $36,800; (c) $39,200; (d) $40,800

Compare your answers to those at the end of the chapter and review any questions missed.

EXERCISES

EXERCISE 1

Classify each of the following costs using a functional classification and a behavioral classification (assuming a unit-based cost driver). Assume all depreciation is calculated using the straight-line method. Use the following abbreviations. The first one has been done for you.

Functional Classification:
  CGS: Cost of Goods Sold (Product Cost)
  S&A: Selling and Administrative Expenses (Period Cost)

Behavioral Classification:
  F: Fixed Cost
  V: Variable Cost

Cost Item	Functional Classification	Behavioral Classification
1. Direct materials	CGS	V
2. Depreciation of the office building		
3. Depreciation of the production equipment		
4. Depreciation of the factory building		
5. Sales commissions		
6. Base salaries paid to salespersons		
7. Direct labor		
8. Depreciation of the salespersons' cars		
9. Labor costs to inspect finished goods		
10. Property taxes on the factory building		
11. Property taxes on the office building		
12. Electricity to operate production equipment		
13. Production supervisor's salary		
14. Routine maintenance on production equipment performed daily		
15. Maintenance on production equipment based on equipment usage		

EXERCISE 2

ABE, Inc., expects to produce 20,000 toy tractors. Projected costs for 20,000 tractors are as follows:

Direct materials	$50,000
Direct labor	40,000
Manufacturing overhead:	
Supplies	4,000
Depreciation	20,000
Indirect labor	8,000
Power	6,000
Production supervisor's salary	24,000

Assume all cost items are either fixed or variable with respect to units produced.

Required:

1. Prepare a cost formula for each of the following costs:

   a. Direct materials _____

   b. Direct labor _____

   c. Variable overhead _____

   d. Fixed overhead _____

   e. Total manufacturing costs _____

2. Use the cost formulas developed in the previous requirement to compute the following costs if 25,000 toy tractors are produced:

   a. Total cost of direct materials $_____

   b. Total cost of direct labor $_____

   c. Total cost of variable overhead $_____

   d. Total cost of fixed overhead $_____

   e. Total manufacturing costs $_____

3. a. What is the total cost per unit if 20,000 units are manufactured?
      $_____

   b. What is the total cost per unit if 25,000 units are produced?
      $_____

   c. Why does the per unit cost change when production goes from 20,000 to 25,000 units?

EXERCISE 3

Angelina, Inc., manufactures sweatshirts. The company manufactured and sold 10,000 shirts in December 1995. Angelina has implemented JIT techniques, and as a result, there were no beginning or ending inventories in December.

The regular selling price is $15 per shirt. The following costs were incurred in December.

Direct materials	$15,000
Direct labor	30,000
Variable manufacturing overhead	10,500
Fixed manufacturing overhead	18,000[a]
Fixed selling and administrative costs	13,000
Variable selling and administrative costs:	
Sales commissions	12,000
Delivery costs	19,500

[a]Total fixed manufacturing overhead increases to $25,000 for production levels over 12,000 shirts.

Required:

1. Prepare an absorption-costing income statement for December 1995.

2. Prepare a variable-costing income statement for December 1995.

486

EXERCISE 3 (continued)

3. Angelina expected to produce and sell 10,000 shirts in January 1996. Costs for January 1996 were expected to be the same as costs in December 1995. In addition, Diane's Duds has indicated they would like to buy 2,000 shirts as a special order in January 1996. If Diane buys the shirts, no sales commissions would be paid on the order. In addition, Diane has agreed to pay all delivery costs. Determine the incremental costs that would be incurred by Angelina to produce the special order of 2,000 shirts.

4. What is the lowest price per shirt that Angelina would be willing to accept for the special order?

5. How would your answer in requirement (4) change if Angelina also had to pay delivery costs on the special order?

EXERCISE 3 (continued)

6. After Angelina agreed to make the special order for Diane, the Baumer Company wanted to place a special order for 3,000 shirts. What is the lowest acceptable price Angelina would be willing to accept for the Baumer Company special order? (Assume no sales commissions or delivery costs would be paid by Angelina.)

EXERCISE 4

Weiss & Company had the following beginning and ending inventories for the year 1995.

	Beginning	Ending
Raw materials	$80,000	$104,000
Work in process	40,000	57,200
Finished goods	30,000	54,000

During 1995, the following costs were incurred.

Purchase of raw materials	$520,000
Direct labor	400,000
Manufacturing overhead	840,000

Required:

Prepare a statement of cost of goods manufactured.

EXERCISE 5

The following information pertains to the York Company for the year ending December 31, 1995.

Sales	$840,000
Purchases of raw materials	220,000
Indirect labor	14,000
Indirect materials	9,000
Depreciation of factory equipment	50,000
Depreciation of factory buildings	29,000
Depreciation of administrative building	15,000
Marketing costs	130,000
Direct labor	110,000
Raw materials inventory, 12-31-95	22,000
Work in process, 1-1-95	54,000
Sales returns and allowances	17,000
Raw materials inventory, 1-1-95	33,000
Work in process, 12-31-95	45,000
Sales discounts	12,000
Finished goods inventory, 1-1-95	124,000
Finished goods inventory, 12-31-95	115,000

Required:

Prepare an absorption-costing income statement in good form for the York Company for the year ending December 31, 1995. Include a statement of cost of goods manufactured.

EXERCISE 6

The Jones Company currently produces one product, a cordless phone. The cost formula for the product is as follows.

$$\text{Total Manufacturing Cost} = \$400,000 + \$10X$$

where X is direct labor hours.

The Jones Company is considering production of another version of the cordless phone. The new version would be similar to the existing version except the new version would have a ten-number memory. The same cost formula would be used to estimate costs.

Estimates of activity for each product are as follows:

	Cordless Phone	Cordless Phone With Memory
Units of product	12,000	3,000
Direct labor hours	30,000	8,000

Required:

1. Estimate total manufacturing costs if only the original cordless phone is produced.

2. Estimate total manufacturing costs if both models of the cordless phone are produced.

KEY TERMS TEST

1. BB. Sunk costs
2. I. Direct materials
3. P. Indirect materials
4. O. Indirect labor
5. Y. Product costs
6. DD. Work in process
7. K. Finished goods
8. CC. Variable costs
9. W. Period costs
10. G. Direct costs
11. H. Direct labor
12. C. Conversion cost
13. L. Fixed costs
14. Z. Relevant range
15. X. Prime cost
16. R. Manufacturing overhead
17. A. Asset
18. AA. Selling costs
19. B. Controllable cost
20. Q. Loss
21. E. Cost of goods sold
22. V. Out-of-pocket cost
23. D. Cost of goods manufactured
24. U. Opportunity cost
25. F. Differential cost and M. Incremental cost
26. T. Noncontrollable cost
27. J. Expense
28. S. Mixed costs
29. N. Indirect costs
30. Direct manufacturing costs
31. administrative costs
32. Variable-costing income
33. cost
34. Cost flow
35. Nonmanufacturing costs
36. Manufacturing costs
37. Variable cost of goods sold
38. Variable cost of goods manufactured
39. Absorption-costing income
40. activity-based cost system, ABC
41. contribution margin
42. conventional cost system
43. cost driver
44. cost object

CHAPTER QUIZ

1. b
2. a
3. c
4. c
5. d
6. c
7. b
8. a
9. b
10. d   ($75,000 + $150,000 + $20,000)/50,000 units = $4.90 per unit
11. d
12. b   ($120,000/50,000 units) = $2.40 per unit
13. a   ($120,000/60,000 units) = $2.00 per unit
14. c   ($4.90 x 8,000 units) = $39,200

EXERCISE 1

Cost Item	Functional Classification	Behavioral Classification
1. Direct materials	CGS	V
2. Depreciation of the office building	S&A	F
3. Depreciation of the production equipment	CGS	F
4. Depreciation of the factory building	CGS	F
5. Sales commissions	S&A	V
6. Base salaries paid to salespersons	S&A	F
7. Direct labor	CGS	V
8. Depreciation of the salespersons' cars	S&A	F
9. Labor costs to inspect finished goods	CGS	V
10. Property taxes on the factory building	CGS	F
11. Property taxes on the office building	S&A	F
12. Electricity to operate production equipment	CGS	V
13. Production supervisor's salary	CGS	F
14. Routine maintenance on production equipment performed daily	CGS	F
15. Maintenance on production equipment based on equipment usage	CGS	V

EXERCISE 2

1. **a.** Direct materials cost = $2.50x
   ($50,000/20,000)

   b. Direct labor cost = $2.00x
   ($40,000/20,000)

   c. Variable overhead cost = $0.90x
   ($4,000 + $8,000 + $6,000)/20,000 units

   d. Fixed overhead cost = $44,000
   (Depreciation of $20,000 + Supervisor's salary of $24,000)

   e. Total manufacturing costs = $44,000 + $5.40x

2. **a.** ($2.50 x 25,000) = $62,500

   b. ($2.00 x 25,000) = $50,000

   c. ($0.90 x 25,000) = $22,500

   d. $44,000

   e. $44,000 + ($5.40 x 25,000) = $179,000

3. **a.** $7.60   [$5.40 + ($44,000/20,000)]

   b. $7.16   [$5.40 + ($44,000/25,000)]

   c. When volume increases, fixed cost <u>per unit</u> decreases because the same total cost is spread over more units. For example, the fixed manufacturing cost per unit at 20,000 units is $2.20 ($44,000/20,000 units). At 25,000 units, fixed manufacturing cost per unit is $1.76 ($44,000/25,000 units).

493

EXERCISE 3

1.
ANGELINA, INC.
ABSORPTION-COSTING INCOME STATEMENT
FOR THE MONTH ENDED DECEMBER 31, 1995

Sales ($15 x 10,000 units)		$150,000
Cost of goods sold:		
Direct materials	$15,000	
Direct labor	30,000	
Variable overhead	10,500	
Fixed overhead	18,000	73,500
Gross profit		$ 76,500
Less: operating expenses:		
Variable selling and administrative expenses	$31,500	
Fixed selling and administrative expenses	13,000	44,500
Income		$ 32,000

2.
ANGELINA, INC.
VARIABLE-COSTING INCOME STATEMENT
FOR THE MONTH ENDED DECEMBER 31, 1995

Sales ($15 x 10,000)			$150,000
Less: variable expenses:			
Variable cost of goods sold:			
Direct materials	$15,000		
Direct labor	30,000		
Variable manufacturing overhead	10,500		
Variable cost of goods sold		$55,500	
Variable selling and administrative costs		31,500	
Total variable costs			87,000
Contribution margin			$ 63,000
Less: fixed expenses:			
Fixed manufacturing overhead	$18,000		
Fixed selling and administrative costs	13,000		
Total fixed expenses			31,000
Income			$ 32,000

EXERCISE 3 (continued)

3. Manufacturing costs at 10,000 units of production:

	Total Cost	Per Unit Cost
Direct materials	$15,000	$1.50
Direct labor	30,000	3.00
Variable manufacturing overhead	10,500	1.05
Fixed manufacturing overhead	18,000	1.80
Total manufacturing costs	$73,500	$7.35

Manufacturing costs at 12,000 units of production:

		Total Cost
Direct materials	($1.50 x 12,000 units)	$18,000
Direct labor	($3.00 x 12,000 units)	36,000
Variable manufacturing overhead	($1.05 x 12,000 units)	12,600
Fixed manufacturing overhead		18,000
Total manufacturing costs		$84,600

Remember that <u>variable costs change in total</u> as production changes, while <u>fixed costs remain the same in total</u> within the relevant range.

The incremental costs associated with the special order of 2,000 shirts can be found by comparing total manufacturing costs at 10,000 units and at 12,000 units.

	10,000 Units	12,000 Units
Direct materials	$15,000	$18,000
Direct labor	30,000	36,000
Variable manufacturing overhead	10,500	12,600
Fixed manufacturing overhead	18,000	18,000
Total manufacturing costs	$73,500	$84,600

$11,100

The incremental costs incurred by Angelina to produce the special order of 2,000 shirts could also be calculated as follows:

		Incremental Costs
Direct materials	($1.50 x 2,000 units)	$ 3,000
Direct labor	($3.00 x 2,000 units)	6,000
Variable manufacturing overhead	($1.05 x 2,000 units)	2,100
Fixed manufacturing overhead		-
Total incremental costs		$11,100

EXERCISE 3 (continued)

4. The minimum price Angelina should accept for the special order would be
$5.55 per shirt calculated in one of two ways:

$$\frac{\text{Total Incremental Costs}}{\text{Number of Shirts}} = \frac{\$11,100}{2,000} = \$5.55 \text{ per shirt}$$

Because fixed costs remain the same, the incremental cost per unit could
also be calculated as follows:

Direct materials	$1.50
Direct labor	3.00
Variable manufacturing overhead	1.05
Total incremental cost per unit	$5.55

5. If Angelina also had to pay delivery charges on the special order,
the minimum price Angelina should accept for the special order would be
$7.50 calculated as follows:

Direct materials	$1.50
Direct labor	3.00
Variable manufacturing overhead	1.05
Delivery costs	1.95[a]
Total incremental cost per unit	$7.50

[a]Variable delivery cost per unit = $\dfrac{\$19,500}{10,000 \text{ shirts}} = \$1.95$ per shirt

6. If the Baumer Company also places a special order for 3,000 shirts, the
incremental costs associated with this special order would be:

		Incremental Costs
Direct materials	($1.50 x 3,000 units)	$ 4,500
Direct labor	($3.00 x 3,000 units)	9,000
Variable manufacturing overhead	($1.05 x 3,000 units)	3,150
Fixed manufacturing overhead	($25,000 - $18,000)	7,000
Total incremental cost of special order		$23,650

Notice that the special order of 3,000 shirts would result in a higher
level of fixed costs ($25,000 instead of $18,000). The increase in fixed
costs due to the special order would be $7,000.

The minimum Angelina could charge and break even on this special order
would be $7.89 per shirt ($23,650/3,000 shirts).

496

EXERCISE 4

WEISS & COMPANY
COST OF GOODS MANUFACTURED STATEMENT
FOR THE YEAR ENDING DECEMBER 31, 1995

Direct Materials:

Beginning inventory of raw materials	$ 80,000	
Add: Purchases of raw materials	520,000	
Cost of raw materials available for use	$600,000	
Less: Ending inventory of raw materials	104,000	
Direct materials used		$ 496,000
Direct labor		400,000
Manufacturing overhead		840,000
Total manufacturing costs		$1,736,000
Add: Beginning work in process inventory		40,000
		$1,776,000
Less: Ending work in process inventory		57,200
Cost of goods manufactured		$1,718,800

EXERCISE 5

YORK COMPANY
INCOME STATEMENT
FOR THE YEAR ENDING DECEMBER 31, 1995

Sales		$840,000
Less: Sales returns and allowances		17,000
Sales discounts		12,000
Net sales		$811,000
Cost of goods sold:		
Beginning finished goods inventory	$124,000	
Add: Cost of goods manufactured	452,000	
Cost of goods available for sale	$576,000	
Less: Ending finished goods inventory	115,000	461,000
Gross profit		$350,000
Less: Operating expenses:		
Selling expenses	$130,000	
General and administrative expenses	15,000	145,000
Income		$205,000

EXERCISE 5 (continued)

YORK COMPANY
COST OF GOODS MANUFACTURED
FOR THE YEAR ENDING DECEMBER 31, 1995

Direct Materials:

Beginning inventory of raw materials	$ 33,000	
Add: Purchases of raw materials	220,000	
Cost of raw materials available for use	$253,000	
Less: Ending inventory of raw materials	22,000	
Direct materials used		$231,000
Direct labor		110,000

Manufacturing overhead:

Indirect materials	$ 9,000	
Indirect labor	14,000	
Depreciation of factory equipment	50,000	
Depreciation of factory buildings	29,000	102,000
Total manufacturing costs		$443,000
Add: Beginning work in process inventory		54,000
		$497,000
Less: Ending work in process inventory		45,000
Cost of goods manufactured		$452,000

EXERCISE 6

1. Total Manufacturing Costs = $400,000 + ($10 × 30,000)
   = $700,000

2. Total Manufacturing Costs = $400,000 + $10(30,000 + 8,000)
   = $780,000

CHAPTER 16

JOB-ORDER COSTING

```
╔═══════════════════════════════════════════════════════════════╗
║  CHAPTER REVIEW                                                 ║
╚═══════════════════════════════════════════════════════════════╝
```

TWO ISSUES: COST MEASUREMENT AND COST ASSIGNMENT

• Total manufacturing costs must be measured, and then these costs must be associated with the units produced.

• **Cost measurement** consists of determining the cost of direct materials, direct labor, and manufacturing overhead used in production.

• **Cost assignment** is the process of associating costs with units produced.

Importance of Unit Costs

• Unit cost information is needed for:
  1. the financial reporting requirements of:
     • costing inventory
     • determining income
  2. decision making, such as product pricing

• Different cost information is needed for different purposes.

• **Full**, or **absorption**, **costing** is required for financial reporting. Full costing includes <u>all</u> manufacturing costs (direct materials, direct labor, variable overhead, and fixed overhead) in the unit cost.

• Full cost information may also be useful for some internal decisions, such as long-term pricing decisions or new product introduction decisions.

• Unit cost information used for external reporting may <u>not</u> supply the information needed for some internal decisions, especially short-run internal decisions. For example, incremental cost information is useful for special order decisions when there is excess capacity.

Production of Unit Cost Information

• In order to determine a cost per unit:
  1. costs are measured and
  2. the costs are assigned to units of product.

- Two **cost measurement systems** are:
  1. actual costing
  2. normal costing

- Two **cost assignment systems** are:
  1. job-order costing
  2. process costing

- Four possible cost accounting systems are:
  - actual job-order costing
  - actual process costing
  - normal job-order costing
  - normal process costing

- The two systems using actual costing are rarely used, because they do not provide product cost information on a timely basis.

Job-Order and Process Costing: Two Cost Assignment Systems

- Manufacturing firms can be divided into two major industrial types based on different manufacturing processes:
  1. job-order manufacturing
  2. process manufacturing

Job-Order Manufacturing and Costing

- A **job-order costing system** is a system where manufacturing costs are accumulated by job.

- Such a system is used when separate jobs are identifiable, such as a furniture manufacturer.

- Unit costs in a job-order system are calculated by dividing the total manufacturing cost of the job by the number of units produced in the job.

Process Manufacturing and Costing

- A **process costing system** is used where similar or homogeneous units are mass produced, such as the manufacture of paint or bricks.

- In a process costing system, production costs are accumulated by process or by department for a given period of time.

- Unit costs are calculated by dividing the process costs by the output for the period.

• A comparison of job-order and process costing follows:

Job-Order Costing	Process Costing
1. Wide variety of distinct products	1. Homogeneous products
2. Costs accumulated by job	2. Costs accumulated by process or department
3. Unit costs computed by dividing costs of the job by the number of units produced	3. Unit costs computed by dividing process costs of the period by the units produced in the period

Actual Costing and Normal Costing: Two Cost Measurement Approaches

Actual Costing

• An **actual cost system** uses actual costs for direct materials, direct labor, and overhead.

• The cost used for direct materials, direct labor, and overhead is the amount _actually_ incurred.

• Actual cost systems are rarely used, because they cannot provide accurate unit cost information on a timely basis.

• Another problem with using actual costs is that it can produce unit costs that fluctuate from period to period.

Per unit overhead costs must be achieved through an averaging process: manufacturing overhead costs are divided by the number of units produced during the period.

The averaging approach using actual overhead costs can yield per unit overhead costs that fluctuate dramatically from period to period because:
1. actual costs may vary from period to period and/or
2. the number of units may vary from period to period (nonuniform production levels).

• To avoid the fluctuations in per unit costs using actual overhead, the firm can wait until the end of the year and calculate a per unit cost based on total actual overhead costs for the year. This results in the same per unit overhead costs for all units produced that year.

However, if the per unit overhead cost cannot be calculated until the end of the year, then the unit cost information is received too late to be used when making marketing and operating decisions throughout the year.

Normal Costing

- A **normal costing system** uses:
  1. actual costs for direct materials
  2. actual costs for direct labor
  3. a predetermined rate for manufacturing overhead

- A normal costing system can supply unit cost information on a timely basis.

- The predetermined overhead rate is calculated by dividing <u>estimated</u> overhead costs by <u>estimated</u> production.

- Most manufacturers use a predetermined overhead rate, where the overhead rate is estimated before production begins.

- The predetermined overhead rate usually is based upon a time period of a year because this averages out the effects of month-to-month fluctuations in overhead costs and production volume.

- A job-order cost system that uses normal costing to measure costs is called a *normal job-order cost system.*

- A process cost system that uses normal costing is called a *normal process cost system.*

OVERHEAD APPLICATION: A NORMAL COSTING VIEW

- In normal cost systems, overhead is assigned to production using a predetermined overhead rate.

Predetermined Overhead Rates

- The **predetermined overhead rate** used in normal costing is calculated as:

$$\text{Predetermined Overhead Rate} = \frac{\textbf{Budgeted Manufacturing Overhead}}{\textbf{Budgeted Activity Level}}$$

- Budgeted overhead is the estimated overhead costs for the coming year.

- When determining budgeted activity for the year:
  1. identify a measure of production activity, such as direct labor hours or machine hours.
  2. estimate activity for the coming year.

- A predetermined overhead rate is calculated in advance, usually at the beginning of the year.

Measures of Production Activity

- **Cost drivers** or **causal factors** are factors that <u>cause</u> the consumption of overhead.

- Five common measures of activity (cost drivers) are:
  1. units produced
  2. direct labor hours
  3. direct labor dollars
  4. machine hours
  5. direct materials

- The cost driver that is most closely correlated to overhead consumption should be used.

Activity-Level Choices

- The estimate for activity level can be based on:
  1. **expected activity**, the <u>expected</u> production level of activity for the <u>next</u> year.
  2. **normal activity**, the <u>average</u> activity that the firm <u>expects</u> in the <u>long term</u>. For example, average activity for the next three to five years.
  3. **theoretical activity**, the <u>maximum output</u> possible under perfect operating conditions.
  4. **practical activity**, the <u>output</u> a firm can achieve if it operates <u>efficiently</u>. Efficient operations allow for equipment breakdowns, material shortages, etc.

- Normal activity and expected activity reflect consumer demand.

- Theoretical activity and practical activity reflect a firm's production capabilities.

- Because it uses the same activity level period after period, normal activity produces less fluctuation from period to period than expected activity.

The Basic Concept of Overhead Application

- **Applied overhead** is calculated as follows:

    Applied Overhead = Predetermined Overhead Rate x Actual Production Activity

- Since the predetermined overhead rate is based on estimates, applied overhead rarely is the same as actual overhead.

- Applied overhead will differ from actual overhead if either:
  1. <u>estimated overhead costs</u> used in calculating the predetermined overhead rate <u>differ</u> from the <u>actual costs</u> for the period or
  2. the <u>estimated activity level</u> used in calculating the predetermined overhead rate <u>differs</u> from the <u>actual activity level</u> for the period.

- The **overhead variance** is the difference between applied overhead and actual overhead.

- **Underapplied overhead** occurs when applied overhead is less than actual overhead for the period.

- **Overapplied overhead** occurs when applied overhead exceeds actual overhead for the period.

Disposition of Overhead Variances

- Underapplied or overapplied overhead may be accounted for in one of two ways:
  1. The entire overhead variance is allocated to cost of goods sold.
  2. The overhead variance is allocated among work-in-process inventory, finished goods inventory, and cost of goods sold.

- If the overhead variance is relatively small, underapplied or overapplied overhead may be treated as an adjustment to cost of goods sold.

- If the overhead variance is material, the variance must be allocated to the period's production.

- A period's overhead costs may appear in the following three accounts:
  1. work in process
  2. finished goods
  3. cost of goods sold

  Therefore, the overhead variance should be allocated to work in process, finished goods, and cost of goods sold based on the <u>applied overhead</u> in each account at the end of the period.

JOB-ORDER COSTING: GENERAL DESCRIPTION

- A **job-order cost sheet** is used to accumulate the manufacturing costs (direct materials, direct labor, and manufacturing overhead) associated with a job.

- See Exhibit 16-5 in the text for an example of a job-order cost sheet.

- The job-order cost sheets serve as a subsidiary work-in-process ledger.

- A **work-in-process file** is a collection of all job-order cost sheets. In a manual system, the work-in-process file is located in a filing cabinet, whereas in an automated system, the file is stored on magnetic tape or disk.

Materials Requisitions

- The **materials requisition form** is the source document used to record <u>direct materials</u> on the job-order cost sheet.

- <u>Indirect materials</u> are included in manufacturing overhead and assigned to jobs using the predetermined overhead rate.

Job Time Tickets

- **Time tickets** indicate the direct labor time worked on each job.

  See Exhibit 16-7 in the text for an example of a time ticket.

- Information on the time tickets is used to post direct labor costs to the job-order cost sheet for individual jobs.

- Indirect labor costs are included in manufacturing overhead and assigned to jobs using the predetermined overhead rate.

Overhead Application

- Overhead is assigned to jobs using a predetermined overhead rate.

Unit Cost Calculation

- When a job is completed, the unit cost is calculated as the total cost of the job divided by the number of units produced.

Unit Cost = Total Cost of Job/Number of Units Produced

- The job-order cost sheets for completed jobs serve as a subsidiary ledger for finished goods inventory.

JOB-ORDER COSTING: SPECIFIC COST FLOW DESCRIPTION

Accounting for Materials

- The materials account is used to account for:
  1. purchases of materials and supplies
  2. issuance of materials to production

- The entry to record the purchase of materials would be:

  Debit: Raw Materials
  Credit: Accounts Payable

- Materials requisition forms are used to make requests for materials from inventory.

- The entry to record the issuance of direct materials for use in production would be:

    Debit: Work in Process
      Credit: Raw Materials

- The materials requisition form is the source document used to record direct materials on the job-order cost sheet.

Accounting for Direct Labor Cost

- Time tickets indicate the direct labor time worked on each job.

- The entry to record direct labor costs would be:

    Debit: Work in Process
      Credit: Wages Payable

- The subsidiary ledgers for work in process (the job-order cost sheets) are updated to indicate the direct labor costs associated with each job.

Manufacturing Overhead

Overhead Application

- Manufacturing overhead is applied to work in process (and allocated to specific jobs) using a predetermined overhead rate established at the beginning of the period.

- The predetermined overhead rate is calculated as follows:

$$\text{Predetermined Overhead Rate} = \frac{\text{Budgeted Manufacturing Overhead Costs for the Year}}{\text{Budgeted Total Activity for the Year}}$$

- The activity used in calculating the predetermined rate could be units of product, direct labor hours, direct labor cost, machine hours, or units of material used.

- Overhead is allocated, or applied, to each job by multiplying the activity for that particular job by the predetermined rate. For example, if a firm selected direct labor hours as the activity, overhead would be applied by multiplying the number of hours worked on the particular job by the predetermined rate.

- The summary entry to record total overhead applied would be:

    Debit: Work in Process
      Credit: Manufacturing Overhead Control

- Overhead applied to a specific job would be recorded on the job-order cost sheet for that particular job.

Actual Overhead Costs

- Actual overhead costs are accumulated in the manufacturing overhead control account.

- Sources of actual manufacturing overhead costs are:
  1. indirect materials
  2. indirect labor, overtime premium, and idle time
  3. invoices received from outside suppliers for utilities, rent, repairs, property taxes, etc. The entry to record these costs would be:

     Debit: Manufacturing Overhead Control
        Credit: Accounts Payable

  4. internal transfers of costs, such as depreciation and the expiration of prepaid insurance. The entry to record such items would be:

     Debit: Manufacturing Overhead Control
        Credit: Accumulated Depreciation: Building
        Credit: Accumulated Depreciation: Equipment
        Credit: Prepaid Insurance

Overhead Variance

- Because estimates are used in determining the predetermined rate, actual overhead costs will probably differ from the amount of overhead applied.

- The balance in the Manufacturing Overhead Control account is the overhead variance.

- Underapplied overhead results when applied overhead is less than actual overhead for the period.

- Overapplied overhead results when applied overhead exceeds actual overhead for the period.

- Underapplied or overapplied overhead may be accounted for in one of two ways:
  1. closed to Cost of Goods Sold or
  2. allocated among:
     - Work-in-Process Inventory
     - Finished Goods Inventory
     - Cost of Goods Sold

Accounting for Finished Goods

- When a job is completed, the cost of the job is transferred from the Work-in-Process account to the Finished Goods account. The entry to record the transfer would be:

      Debit: Finished Goods
        Credit: Work in Process

- Thus, at the end of the period, the Work-in-Process account will have a balance only if there is uncompleted work in the factory.

- The costs of the particular jobs completed are summarized on job-order cost sheets. The job-order cost sheets for completed jobs are transferred from the work-in-process file to the finished goods file.

Accounting for Cost of Goods Sold

- As goods are sold, the associated costs are transferred from the Finished Goods account to the Cost of Goods Sold account. The entry to record the transfer would be:

      Debit: Cost of Goods Sold
        Credit: Finished Goods

- The entry to record the sale would be:

      Debit: Accounts Receivable
        Credit: Sales Revenue

- If the overhead variance is immaterial, it is treated as an adjustment to cost of goods sold at the end of the year.

  The entry to close overapplied overhead to cost of goods sold would be:

      Debit: Cost of Goods Sold
        Credit: Manufacturing Overhead Control

- **Normal cost of goods sold** is the cost of goods amount that is obtained when using per-unit normal cost. Normal cost of goods sold is the amount of cost of goods sold <u>before</u> adjustment for an overhead variance.

- **Adjusted cost of goods sold** is normal cost of goods sold <u>after</u> adjustment for an overhead variance.

Summary of Manufacturing Cost Flows

- The following diagram summarizes the flow of manufacturing costs.

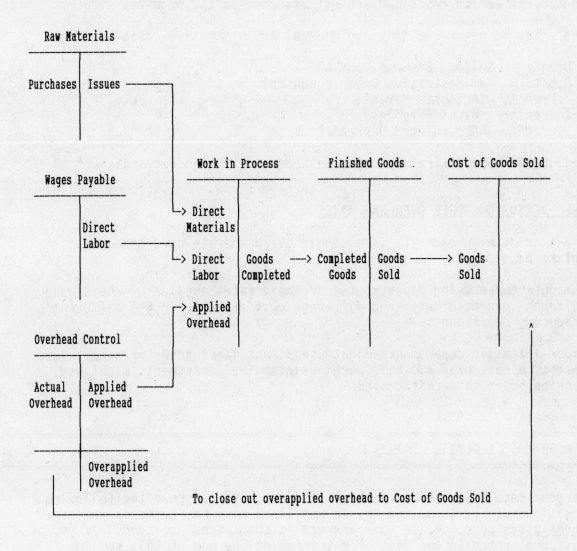

- Because cost of goods sold is an expense, it appears on the company's income statement.

- Raw materials inventory, work-in-process inventory, and finished goods inventory would appear in the current assets section of the company's balance sheet.

- Work-in-process inventory would also appear in the schedule of cost of goods manufactured, while finished goods inventory would also appear in the cost of goods sold section of the income statement.

Accounting for Nonmanufacturing Costs

- Selling and general administrative costs (nonmanufacturing costs) are considered period costs and are <u>not</u> assigned to the product.

- The entry to record selling and general administrative costs would be:

  Debit: Selling Expense Control
  Debit: Administrative Expense Control
     Credit: Accounts Payable
     Credit: Wages Payable
     Credit: Accumulated Depreciation

- Selling and administrative expenses appear on the income statement.

SINGLE VERSUS MULTIPLE OVERHEAD RATES

- A plantwide overhead rate is a single overhead rate used throughout the entire plant.

- A manufacturer using departmental overhead rates applies overhead using different overhead rates and different cost drivers for the different producing departments.

- Labor-intensive departments might use direct labor hours or direct labor cost as a cost driver, while machine-intensive departments might use machine hours as a cost driver.

KEY TERMS TEST

Test your recall of the key terms as follows. First, read the following definitions of key terms and try to recall as many key terms as you can <u>without assistance</u>. Write your answers in the spaces provided. If you need assistance, refer to the list of key terms at the end of this section.

1. The process of associating manufacturing costs with the units produced is called _____ _____.

2. The process of assigning dollar values to cost items is called _____ _____.

3. A document or record used to accumulate manufacturing costs for a job is a _____ _____ _____.

4. A document used to identify the cost of raw materials assigned to each job is a _____ _____ _____.

5. _____ _____ results when applied overhead is greater than the actual overhead cost incurred.

510

6. The _____ _____ is the difference between actual overhead and applied overhead.

7. A cost accumulation method that accumulates costs by process or department is a _____ _____ _____.

8. _____ _____ _____ is the maximum output possible for a firm under perfect operating conditions.

9. A(n) _____ _____ _____ is a cost measurement system in which actual manufacturing costs are assigned to products.

10. _____ _____ is the overhead assigned to production using a predetermined overhead rate.

11. _____ _____ _____ is the level of production activity expected for the coming period.

12. A(n) _____ _____ _____ accumulates manufacturing costs by job.

13. _____ _____ _____ is the average activity level that a firm experiences over more than one fiscal period.

14. A(n) _____ _____ _____ is a cost measurement system in which the actual costs of direct materials and direct labor are assigned to production and a predetermined rate is used to assign overhead costs to production.

15. _____ _____ _____ is the output a firm can achieve if it is operating efficiently.

16. The _____ _____ _____ is calculated as estimated overhead divided by the estimated level of production activity. It is used to assign overhead to production.

17. A document used to identify the cost of direct labor for a job is a _____ _____.

18. _____ _____ results when the actual overhead cost incurred is greater than applied overhead.

19. Normal cost of goods sold adjusted to include an overhead variance is called _____ _____ _____ _____ _____.

20. A(n) _____ _____ is a collection of open job-order cost sheets or job-order cost records.

21. The cost of goods sold amount calculated using per-unit normal cost is called _____ _____ _____ _____ _____.

KEY TERMS:

actual cost system
adjusted cost of goods sold
applied overhead
cost assignment
cost measurement
expected activity level
job-order costing system
job-order cost sheet
materials requisition form
normal activity level
normal costing system

normal cost of goods sold
overapplied overhead
overhead variance
practical activity level
predetermined overhead rate
process costing system
theoretical activity level
time ticket
underapplied overhead
work-in-process file

Compare your answers to those at the end of the chapter and review any key terms missed.

CHAPTER QUIZ

Circle the single best answer.

1. Material requisitions are used for recording: (a) materials purchased; (b) materials issued and used in production; (c) materials on hand in the storeroom; (d) none of the above

2. Which of the following is the average activity the firm expects in the long term? (a) practical activity; (b) theoretical activity; (c) normal activity; (d) expected activity

3. A department that is equipment-intensive would most likely use a predetermined departmental overhead rate based on which of the following cost drivers? (a) machine hours; (b) direct labor hours; (c) direct labor cost; (d) units of direct material used

4. Actual overhead rates are calculated as: (a) estimated total manufacturing overhead/estimated total activity; (b) estimated total manufacturing overhead/actual total activity; (c) actual total manufacturing overhead/actual total activity; (d) actual total manufacturing overhead/estimated total activity

5. The overhead costs of a given period might appear in all of the following except: (a) materials inventory; (b) work in process (c) finished goods; (d) cost of goods sold

6. In an absorption, or full, costing approach, all costs incurred become part of the cost of the finished product: (a) true; (b) false

7. For financial reporting, full, or absorption, costing must be used: (a) true; (b) false

8. A job-order cost system associates costs with particular jobs: (a) true; (b) false

9. A job-order cost system is especially appropriate for situations where basically homogeneous units flow through production on a fairly continuous basis: (a) true; (b) false

10. Time tickets indicate the direct labor time worked on each job: (a) true; (b) false

11. Underapplied or overapplied overhead must be allocated to materials inventory, work-in-process inventory, finished goods inventory, and cost of goods sold: (a) true; (b) false

12. The work-in-process account will have a balance only if there is uncompleted work in the factory: (a) true; (b) false

13. Finished goods is an expense account: (a) true; (b) false

14. Materials inventory, work in process, and cost of goods sold would appear in the assets section of the balance sheet: (a) true; (b) false

15. Most firms use actual costing because it provides product cost information on a timely basis: (a) true; (b) false

Use the following information to answer the next four questions.

Estimated manufacturing overhead	$320,000
Actual overhead costs incurred	$344,400
Estimated direct labor hours	40,000
Actual direct labor hours worked	42,000

16. The actual overhead rate for applying manufacturing overhead would be: (a) $7.62; (b) $8.00; (c) $8.20; (d) $8.61

17. The predetermined overhead rate for applying manufacturing overhead would be: (a) $7.62; (b) $8.00; (c) $8.20; (d) $8.61

18. If the predetermined overhead rate is used to apply overhead, applied manufacturing overhead would be: (a) $321,000; (b) $328,000; (c) $336,000; (d) $344,400

19. The amount of the overhead variance would be: (a) $24,400 overapplied; (b) $24,400 underapplied; (c) $8,400 overapplied; (d) $8,400 underapplied

Compare your answers to those at the end of the chapter. Review any questions missed.

EXERCISE 1

The Kircher Company allocates manufacturing overhead to units of product using an actual overhead rate.

The company incurred $520,000 of manufacturing overhead during the year, and the plant used 80,000 hours of direct labor costing $400,000.

Kircher uses direct labor hours for the cost driver.

Required:

1. What is Kircher's manufacturing overhead application rate?

2. When would the rate be calculated?

3. What are some of the problems associated with using an actual overhead application rate as opposed to using a predetermined overhead application rate?

EXERCISE 2

The Paine Company uses a predetermined overhead rate to apply manufacturing overhead to production. The rate is based on direct labor hours.

Estimates for the year 1995 are given below:

Estimated manufacturing overhead	$500,000
Estimated direct labor hours	50,000

During 1995 the Paine Company used 60,000 direct labor hours.

At the end of 1995, the Paine Company records revealed the following information:

Raw materials inventory	$ 40,000
Work-in-process inventory	100,000
Finished goods inventory	200,000
Cost of goods sold	700,000
Manufacturing overhead	510,000

Required:

1. Calculate the predetermined overhead rate for 1995.

2. Determine the amount of underapplied or overapplied manufacturing overhead for 1995.

3. If underapplied or overapplied manufacturing overhead is treated as an adjustment to cost of goods sold, determine the cost of goods sold amount that would appear on the company's income statement.

EXERCISE 3

Buss Inc. has two producing departments: assembly and finishing. The company has been using a plant wide predetermined overhead rate based on direct labor cost.

The following estimates were made for the current year:

	ASSEMBLY	FINISHING	TOTAL
Manufacturing overhead	$240,000	$160,000	$400,000
Direct labor cost	$300,000	$500,000	$800,000
Machine hours	15,000	10,000	25,000

Required:

1. Calculate a plant wide predetermined overhead rate for the current year based on direct labor cost.

2. Calculate separate departmental overhead rates based upon direct labor cost for assembly and machine hours for finishing.

EXERCISE 4

MLF Industries uses a job-order costing system and applies overhead on the basis of direct labor hours. At the beginning of 1995, management estimated that 200,000 direct labor hours would be worked and $600,000 of manufacturing overhead costs would be incurred.

During the year, the company actually worked 220,000 direct labor hours and incurred the following manufacturing costs:

Indirect labor	$140,000
Indirect materials	100,000
Insurance	50,000
Utilities	90,000
Repairs & maintenance	80,000
Depreciation	180,000
Direct materials used in production	540,000
Direct labor	700,000

Required:

1. Calculate the predetermined overhead application rate for 1995.

2. Determine the amount of manufacturing overhead applied to work in process during 1995.

3.   Determine the amount of underapplied or overapplied overhead for the
     year.

4.   If goods with a cost of $1,500,000 were completed and transferred to
     finished goods during 1995, determine the cost of goods in process at
     the end of the period.

5.   Prepare the journal entry to close underapplied or overapplied overhead
     to cost of goods sold.

EXERCISE 5

Cousins Incorporated uses a job-order costing system and a predetermined overhead rate based on machine hours.

At the beginning of the year, Cousins estimated manufacturing overhead for the year would be $50,000 and 8,000 machine hours would be used.

The following information pertains to December of the current year:

	Job No. 77	Job No. 79	Job No. 73	Totals
Work in process, December 1	$6,000	$2,500	$1,500	$10,000
December production activity:				
Materials requisitioned	$1,200	$800	$650	$2,650
Direct labor costs	$1,000	$400	$250	$1,650
Machine hours	300	200	100	600

Actual manufacturing overhead costs incurred in December were $5,000, of which $1,000 was depreciation on the factory building and $500 was depreciation on the production equipment.

Required:

1. Compute the predetermined overhead application rate.

2. Prepare the journal entries to record the activity for the month of December.

3. Determine the cost associated with each job.

4. If Job No. 77 was completed during December, what is the balance of Work in Process at December 31?

5. If there was no balance in the Manufacturing Overhead Control account on December 1, what is the balance at December 31?

6. Prepare the journal entry to close underapplied or overapplied overhead to cost of goods sold.

EXERCISE 6

DMF Industries uses a job-order costing system and a predetermined overhead rate based on direct labor cost.

Estimated manufacturing overhead for 1995 was $540,000, and estimated direct labor costs were $900,000.

On January 1, 1995, the company had the following inventories:

Raw materials	$ -0-
Work in process (Job No. 96)	$16,000
Finished goods	$ -0-

The following information pertains to the company's activities for the month of January 1995:

a. Purchased $150,000 of materials on account.

b. Job Nos. 97 and 98 were started during the month.

c. Materials requisitioned for production totaled $144,000, of which $6,000 was for indirect materials.

   The remainder was distributed as follows:

   Job No. 96...................$46,000
   Job No. 97.................. 70,000
   Job No. 98.................. 22,000

d. Factory payroll for the month totaled $100,000, of which $15,000 was for indirect labor. The direct labor was distributed as follows:

   Job No. 96...................$20,000
   Job No. 97.................. 35,000
   Job No. 98.................. 30,000

e. The company made adjusting entries at the end of January to record the following expenses:

   Depreciation................. $5,000
   Expired insurance........... 1,000

f. Other manufacturing costs not yet paid totaled $30,650.

g. Manufacturing overhead was applied using the predetermined overhead rate based upon direct labor cost.

h. Job Nos. 96 and 97 were completed during the month.

i. Job No. 96 was sold on account during the month at a selling price of 120% of manufacturing cost.

EXERCISE 6 (continued)

Required:

1. Prepare journal entries to record the manufacturing activities of the company for January, and post to the job-order cost sheets where appropriate.

EXERCISE 6 (continued)

2. Prepare T accounts for Raw Materials Inventory, Work-in-Process Inventory, Finished Goods Inventory, Cost of Goods Sold, and Manufacturing Overhead Control. Enter beginning balances (where appropriate), and post the transactions for January.

3. Prepare journal entries to dispose of the underapplied or overapplied overhead under the following two assumptions:

    a. Underapplied or overapplied overhead is treated as an adjustment to Cost of Goods Sold.

    b. Underapplied or overapplied overhead is allocated to Work-in-Process Inventory, Finished Goods Inventory, and Cost of Goods Sold. (Round your answers to dollars.)

EXERCISE 7

AEU Industries uses a job-order costing system. There are two production departments: machining and assembly. A predetermined overhead rate is used in each department.

The machining department bases its rate on machine hours, and the assembly department bases its rate on direct labor hours.

The company made the following estimates at the beginning of the current year:

	Machining	Assembly
Machine hours	20,000	15,000
Direct labor hours	7,000	40,000
Manufacturing overhead cost	$200,000	$800,000

The following information was available for Job No. 12-5, which was started and completed during December.

Job No. 12-5

	Machining	Assembly
Direct materials	$2,000	$ -0-
Direct labor cost	$1,200	$5,500
Direct labor hours	30	200
Machine hours	150	50

Required:

1. Calculate the predetermined manufacturing overhead rate used by each producing department.

2. Compute the total cost of Job No. 12-5.

KEY TERMS TEST
1. cost assignment
2. cost measurement
3. job-order cost sheet
4. materials requisition form
5. Overapplied overhead
6. overhead variance
7. process costing system
8. Theoretical activity level
9. actual cost system
10. Applied overhead
11. Expected activity level
12. job-order costing system
13. Normal activity level
14. normal costing system
15. Practical activity level
16. predetermined overhead rate
17. time ticket
18. Underapplied overhead
19. adjusted cost of goods sold
20. work-in-process file
21. normal cost of goods sold

CHAPTER QUIZ
1. b
2. c
3. a
4. c
5. a
6. b False   When using absorption costing, all <u>manufacturing</u> costs become part of the cost of the finished product.
7. a True
8. a True
9. b False   Process costing would be appropriate for situations where basically homogeneous units flow through production on a fairly continuous basis.
10. a True
11. b False   Underapplied or overapplied overhead would not be allocated to materials inventory. Also, if underapplied or overapplied overhead is immaterial, it could be treated as an adjustment to cost of goods sold.
12. a True
13. b False   Of the six control accounts, cost of goods sold is the only expense account. Finished goods is an inventory account that would appear in the current assets section of the balance sheet.
14. b False   The three inventory accounts are materials inventory, work-in-process inventory, and finished goods. Cost of goods sold appears on the income statement.
15. b False   Most firms do not use actual costing, because actual costs cannot be determined until the end of the period.

16. c ($344,400/42,000) = $8.20
17. b ($320,000/40,000) = $8.00
18. c ($8 x 42,000) = $336,000
19. d ($344,400 - $336,000) = $8,400 underapplied

EXERCISE 1

1. Actual overhead application rate:

   = Actual Total Manufacturing Overhead Costs/Actual Total Activity
   = $520,000/80,000 direct labor hours
   = $6.50 per direct labor hour

2. The actual overhead application rate would be calculated at the end of the period after actual overhead costs and actual activity have been determined.

3. When an actual overhead application rate is used, the unit cost information is received too late to be used when making marketing and operating decisions.

EXERCISE 2

1. Predetermined overhead rate:

$$= \frac{\text{Estimated Total Manufacturing Overhead}}{\text{Estimated Total Activity}}$$

$$= \frac{\$500,000}{50,000 \text{ DLH}} = \$10 \text{ per DLH}$$

2. Overapplied overhead for 1995:

Actual manufacturing overhead costs	$510,000
Manufacturing overhead applied during 1995 (60,000 DLH x $10 per DLH)	600,000
Overapplied overhead	$ 90,000

3. Adjusted cost of goods sold:

Cost of goods sold	$700,000
Overapplied overhead	90,000
Adjusted cost of goods sold	$610,000

Since overhead was overapplied, cost of goods sold is reduced.

EXERCISE 3

1.

$$\text{Plantwide Rate} = \frac{\text{Manufacturing Overhead}}{\text{Direct Labor Cost}}$$

$$= \frac{\$400,000}{\$800,000}$$

$$= 50\% \text{ of Direct Labor Cost}$$

2. Departmental rates:

$$\text{Assembly Application Rate} = \frac{\text{Manufacturing Overhead}}{\text{Direct Labor Cost}}$$

$$= \frac{\$240,000}{\$300,000}$$

$$= 80\% \text{ of Direct Labor Cost}$$

$$\text{Finishing Application Rate} = \frac{\text{Manufacturing Overhead}}{\text{Machine Hours}}$$

$$= \frac{\$160,000}{10,000 \text{ Hours}}$$

$$= \$16 \text{ Per Machine Hour}$$

EXERCISE 4

1.

$$\text{Predetermined Overhead Rate} = \frac{\text{Estimated Manufacturing Overhead}}{\text{Estimated Activity}}$$

$$= \frac{\$600,000}{200,000 \text{ DLH}}$$

$$= \$3.00 \text{ per DLH}$$

2. Manufacturing overhead applied to work in process during 1995:

$$= \text{Actual Activity} \times \text{Predetermined Rate}$$
$$= \quad 220,000 \text{ DLH} \quad \times \quad \$3.00 \text{ per DLH}$$
$$= \quad \$660,000$$

EXERCISE 4 (continued)

3.   Overapplied overhead for 1995:

MANUFACTURING OVERHEAD CONTROL

(Actual Costs)		(Applied)	
Indirect labor	140,000		
Indirect materials	100,000		
Insurance	50,000		
Utilities	90,000		
Repairs & maintenance	80,000		
Depreciation	180,000		
		Overhead applied	660,000
		Overapplied	20,000

4.
WORK IN PROCESS

Direct materials	540,000		
Direct labor	700,000		
Overhead applied	660,000		
		Goods Completed	1,500,000
Ending balance	400,000		

5.   Journal entry to close overapplied overhead to Cost of Goods Sold:

    Manufacturing Overhead Control.......... 20,000
            Cost of Goods Sold   20,000

Since overhead was overapplied, Cost of Goods Sold is reduced by $20,000.

EXERCISE 5

1.

$$\text{Predetermined Overhead Application Rate} = \frac{\$50,000}{8,000 \text{ Machine Hours}}$$

$$= \$6.25 \text{ Per Machine Hour}$$

EXERCISE 5 (continued)

2. Journal entries to record the activity for the month of December:

Entry to record issuance of direct materials for production:

```
Work in Process ......................... 2,650
      Raw Materials Inventory.............          2,650
```

Entry to record direct labor used in production:

```
Work in Process ......................... 1,650
      Wages Payable.......................          1,650
```

Entry to record actual overhead costs incurred during December:

```
Manufacturing Overhead Control ........... 5,000
      Accounts Payable ...................          3,500
      Accumulated Depreciation: Building...        1,000
      Accumulated Depreciation: Equipment..          500
```

Entry to record overhead applied during December:

```
Work in Process ......................... 3,750*
      Manufacturing Overhead Control ......          3,750
```

*($6.25 x 600)

3.

	Job No. 77	Job No. 79	Job No. 73
Work in Process, December 1	$ 6,000	$2,500	$1,500
December Production Activity:			
Materials	1,200	800	650
Direct labor	1,000	400	250
Manufacturing overhead			
$6.25 x 300 machine hours	1,875		
$6.25 x 200 machine hours		1,250	
$6.25 x 100 machine hours			625
Totals	$10,075	$4,950	$3,025

4. If Job No. 77 was completed during December, Work in Process at December 31 would have a balance of $7,975 (Job No. 79 at $4,950 and Job No. 73 at $3,025).

EXERCISE 5 (continued)

5. The balance in the Manufacturing Overhead Control account at December 31 could be calculated as follows:

MANUFACTURING OVERHEAD CONTROL

(Actual Costs)	(Applied)
5,000	3,750
Underapplied 1,250	

6. Journal entry to close underapplied overhead to cost of goods sold:

```
Cost of Goods Sold ................... 1,250
     Manufacturing Overhead Control....       1,250
```

Since overhead was underapplied, Cost of Goods Sold is increased by the entry.

EXERCISE 6

1. Journal entries to record manufacturing activities for January.

    a. Purchased materials on account:

```
Raw Materials Inventory............ 150,000
     Accounts Payable .............       150,000
```

    b. No entry required.

    c. Materials requisitioned for production:

```
Work in Process ................... 138,000
Manufacturing Overhead Control.....   6,000
     Raw Materials Inventory.......       144,000
```

    d. Factory payroll for January:

```
Work in Process ...................  85,000
Manufacturing Overhead Control.....  15,000
     Wages Payable.................       100,000
```

    e. Expenses recorded with adjusting entries:

```
Manufacturing Overhead Control......   6,000
     Accumulated Depreciation ......        5,000
     Prepaid Insurance .............        1,000
```

EXERCISE 6 (continued)

f. Other manufacturing costs not yet paid:

    Manufacturing Overhead Control...... 30,650
      Accounts Payable   30,650

g. Manufacturing overhead applied using a predetermined overhead rate:

$$\text{Predetermined Overhead Rate} = \frac{\text{Estimated Total Overhead}}{\text{Estimated Total Direct Labor Cost}}$$

$$= \frac{\$540,000}{\$900,000} = 60\% \text{ of Direct Labor Cost}$$

Entry to apply manufacturing overhead in January:

    Work in Process 51,000*
      Manufacturing Overhead Control..   51,000

*(60% x $85,000)

h. Job Nos. 96 and 97 were completed and transferred to finished goods.
(See the job-order cost sheets below for how the amounts were
determined).

    Finished Goods Inventory........... 220,000*
      Work in Process   220,000

*(Job No. 96 at $94,000 and Job No. 97 at $126,000)

i. Job No. 96 was sold during the month. (See the job-order cost sheets
below for how the amount was determined).

    Cost of Goods Sold 94,000
      Finished Goods Inventory.......   94,000

    Accounts Receivable 112,800*
      Sales Revenue   112,800

*($94,000 x 120%)

Job No. 96		Job No. 97		Job No. 98	
Balance	$16,000	Balance	$ -0-	Balance	$ -0-
DM	46,000	DM	70,000	DM	22,000
DL	20,000	DL	35,000	DL	30,000
OH	12,000[1]	OH	21,000[2]	OH	18,000[3]
Total	$94,000	Total	$126,000	Total	$70,000

[1]($20,000 x 60%)
[2]($35,000 x 60%)
[3]($30,000 x 60%)

2. T accounts for inventory accounts, Cost of Goods Sold, and Manufacturing Overhead Control:

RAW MATERIALS INVENTORY		WORK-IN-PROCESS INVENTORY			FINISHED GOODS INVENTORY		COST OF GOODS SOLD	
150,000		Bal. 16,000						
	144,000	DM 138,000						
		DL 85,000						
		OH 51,000						
			220,000		220,000			
						94,000	94,000	
6,000		70,000			126,000		94,000	

MANUFACTURING OVERHEAD CONTROL

(Actual Costs)		(Applied)
Indirect materials	6,000	
Indirect labor	15,000	
Depreciation		
and insurance	6,000	
Other costs	30,650	
		Overhead applied 51,000
Underapplied	6,650	

3 a. Underapplied overhead is closed to Cost of Goods Sold:

```
Cost of Goods Sold ..................... 6,650
     Manufacturing Overhead Control......        6,650
```

b. Applied overhead in Work in Process (Job No. 98) $18,000
Applied overhead in Finished Goods Inventory (Job No. 97)   21,000
Applied overhead in Cost of Goods Sold (Job No. 96)   12,000

Total applied overhead $51,000

EXERCISE 6 (continued)

Underapplied overhead is allocated to Work in Process, Finished Goods Inventory, and Cost of Goods Sold as follows:

$$\text{Work in Process:} \quad \frac{\$18,000}{\$51,000} \times \$6,650 = \$2,347$$

$$\text{Finished Goods:} \quad \frac{\$21,000}{\$51,000} \times \$6,650 = \$2,738$$

$$\text{Cost of Goods Sold:} \quad \frac{\$12,000}{\$51,000} \times \$6,650 = \$1,565$$

Entry to allocate underapplied overhead to Work in Process, Finished Goods Inventory, and Cost of Goods Sold:

```
Work in Process ........................ 2,347
Finished Goods Inventory................ 2,738
Cost of Goods Sold ..................... 1,565
     Manufacturing Overhead Control.....        6,650
```

EXERCISE 7

1. Machining Overhead Rate $= \dfrac{\text{Estimated Overhead}}{\text{Estimated Machine Hours}}$

$$= \frac{\$200,000}{20,000 \text{ Machine Hours}} = \$10 \text{ per Machine Hour}$$

Assembly Predetermined Overhead Rate $= \dfrac{\text{Estimated Overhead}}{\text{Estimated DLH}}$

$$= \frac{\$800,000}{40,000 \text{ DLH}} = \$20 \text{ per DLH}$$

2.

Job No. 12-5	
DM--Machining	$ 2,000
DL--Machining	1,200
DL--Assembly	5,500
OH--Machining	
($10 x 150 Machine Hours)	1,500
OH--Assembly	
($20 x 200 DLH)	4,000
Total	$14,200

CHAPTER 17

PROCESS COSTING

CHAPTER REVIEW

CHOICE OF A COST ACCUMULATION METHOD

- Cost accounting systems should be designed to fit the nature of the manufacturing operation.

- **Process costing** works well whenever relatively homogeneous products pass through a series of processes and receive <u>similar</u> amounts of manufacturing costs.

- A process is a series of operations performed on the product, such as mixing, molding, or packaging.

- **Job-order costing** works well whenever products pass through a series of processes that deal out <u>different</u> amounts of manufacturing costs.

- The manufacture of nearly any product requires three types of cost:
  1. direct materials
  2. direct labor
  3. manufacturing overhead

- The job cost system is designed to trace costs to a job.

- A process cost system traces the costs to the process instead of the job.

- Some manufacturing settings may need to use a blend of job-order and process costing.

- **Operation costing** is when job-order costing is used to assign material costs and process costing is used to assign conversion costs (direct labor and manufacturing overhead).

- The same accounts are used in the process costing system as in a job-order system with the exception of the number of work-in-process accounts. A different work-in-process account is required for each processing department.

- The major differences between process costing and job-order costing are summarized below:

Process Costing	Job-Order Costing
1. Homogeneous units pass through a series of similar processes.	1. Unique jobs are worked on during a time period.
2. Costs are accumulated by processing department.	2. Costs are accumulated by individual job.
3. Unit costs are computed by dividing the individual processing departments' costs by output. In addition, output is measured in equivalent units, not in units produced.	3. Unit costs are determined by dividing the total costs on the job-order cost sheet by the number of units in the job.
4. The cost of production report provides the detail for the Work-in-Process account for each processing department.	4. The job-order cost sheet provides the detail for the Work-in-Process account.

PROCESS MANUFACTURING AND PROCESS COSTING

Processing Patterns

- In a process manufacturing firm, units produced pass through a series of manufacturing steps or processes.

- The product may flow through the processing departments in different ways.

- The product may flow through the factory's processing departments using:
1. sequential processing or
2. parallel processing.

- **Sequential processing** is a method of process manufacturing in which units pass from one process to another in a sequential pattern and each unit is processed using the same series of steps.

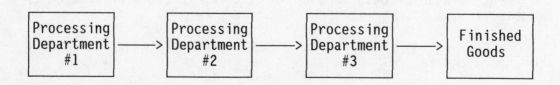

- Two examples of **parallel processing** are:
1. Two different products emerge from a common process and then each flows through its own separate series of processes for completion.

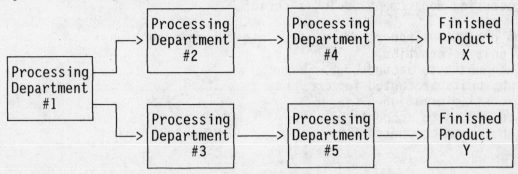

2. The products flow through their separate series of processes and then eventually flow through a common department.

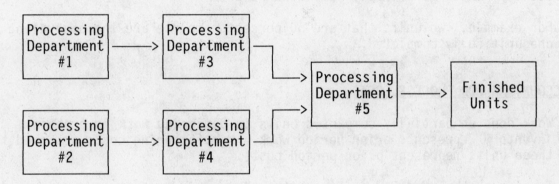

- No matter what the product flow, a unit cost is determined for each process and the cost of the finished product is the total of the unit costs accumulated as the product passes through the processing departments.

Process Costing: Cost Flows

- As raw materials are purchased, the cost of the materials are recorded in a Raw Materials Inventory account.

- As used, raw materials, direct labor, and manufacturing overhead are recorded in the Work-in-Process account.

- When goods are completed, their cost is transferred from the Work-in-Process account to the Finished Goods account.

- As goods are sold, their cost is transferred from the Finished Goods account to the Cost of Goods Sold account.

- In process costing, each processing department has its own Work-in-Process account.

- Costs transferred from a prior process to a subsequent process are called **transferred-in costs**.

Cost Accumulation: The Production Report

- The **production report** summarizes the manufacturing activity for a processing department during a period.

- The production report is divided into two main sections:
  1. unit information
     a. units to account for
     b. units accounted for
  2. cost information
     a. costs to account for
     b. costs accounted for

Output Measurement: The Concept of Equivalent Units

- **Equivalent units of output** is the expression of a processing department's activity in terms of fully completed units.

- For example, two units that are 50 percent complete are the equivalent of one unit fully completed.

ACCOUNTING FOR PROCESS COSTS

- Work done on partially completed units in beginning work in process inventory represents prior period work. Manufacturing costs assigned to these units represent prior period costs.

- Two approaches used for dealing with prior period output and prior period costs found in beginning work in process are:
  1. the weighted average method
  2. the first-in, first-out (FIFO) method

- The **weighted average costing method** combines the partially completed units in beginning work-in-process inventory with units produced in the current period to determine a weighted average equivalent units of production.

- The **FIFO costing method** excludes the equivalent units and costs in beginning work in process (prior period costs) from the current period unit cost calculations.

- Only current period work and current period costs are used to compute FIFO unit costs.

- If the cost of the manufacturing inputs remains fairly stable, the weighted average and FIFO method will produce very similar results.

- If costs of manufacturing inputs fluctuate from period to period, the FIFO method may be more useful for cost control, pricing decisions, and performance evaluation because the FIFO method concentrates on the current period's activity.

- Both the weighted average method and the FIFO method use the following general pattern to determine the cost of production:
  1. Analysis of the flow of physical units
  2. Calculation of equivalent units
  3. Computation of unit costs
  4. Valuation of inventories:
     a. cost of units transferred out
     b. cost of units in ending work in process
  5. Cost reconciliation

Weighted Average Costing

- The weighted average costing method combines the partially completed units in beginning work-in-process inventory with units produced in the current period to determine a weighted average equivalent units of production.

- Equivalent units of output using the weighted average method is calculated as:

  > **Units completed and transferred out***
  > **+ Equivalent units of production in ending work in process**
  > **= Equivalent production**

  *Notice that the weighted average method includes the partially completed units in beginning inventory with the units that were started and completed in the current period.

- The weighted average method also merges prior period costs with current period costs by adding manufacturing costs in beginning work in process to manufacturing costs incurred during the current period.

- The major advantage of the weighted average method is simplicity.

The Five Steps in the Production Report

Step One: Physical Flow Analysis

Units to account for:
    Units in beginning work in process
  + Units started during the period
  = Total units to account for

Units accounted for:
    Units completed
  + Units in ending work in process
  = Total units accounted for

```
┌─────────────────────────────────────────────────────────────────────────┐
│  Step Two:  Calculation of Equivalent Units--Weighted Average             │
│                                                                           │
│           Units completed and transferred out                            │
│         + Units in ending work in process x fraction complete             │
│         = Equivalent units of output                                      │
└─────────────────────────────────────────────────────────────────────────┘


┌─────────────────────────────────────────────────────────────────────────┐
│  Step Three:  Computation of Unit Cost                                    │
│                                                                           │
│  Costs to account for:                                                    │
│         Beginning work in process                                         │
│       + Costs added during the period                                     │
│       = Total costs to account for                                        │
│                                                                           │
│   Cost per equivalent unit = Total costs to account for/Equivalent units  │
└─────────────────────────────────────────────────────────────────────────┘


┌─────────────────────────────────────────────────────────────────────────┐
│  Step Four:  Valuation of Inventories                                     │
│                                                                           │
│   Costs accounted for:                                                    │
│                                                                           │
│         Units completed and transferred out                              │
│         (unit cost x equivalent units)                                    │
│                                                                           │
│       + Units in ending work in process                                   │
│         (unit cost x equivalent units)                                    │
│                                                                           │
│       = Total costs accounted for                                         │
└─────────────────────────────────────────────────────────────────────────┘


┌─────────────────────────────────────────────────────────────────────────┐
│  Step Five:  Cost Reconciliation                                          │
│                                                                           │
│  Compare total costs to account for with total costs accounted for        │
│  to determine that they are equal.                                        │
└─────────────────────────────────────────────────────────────────────────┘
```

SOME COMPLICATIONS OF PROCESS COSTING

Nonuniform Application of Manufacturing Inputs

- Equivalent units must be calculated for each category of manufacturing
  input.

- Equivalent units are calculated for:
  1. each type of material
  2. transferred-in costs (if any)
  3. conversion costs

- For example, if ending work in process contained 1,000 units and materials were 100% complete but conversion was only 40% complete, equivalent units would be calculated as follows:

$$\text{Equivalent units for materials } = 1{,}000 \times 100\% = 1{,}000$$
$$\text{Equivalent units for conversion} = 1{,}000 \times 40\% = 400$$

- A unit cost for materials and a unit cost for conversion would be calculated based upon the equivalent units for each.

KEY TERMS TEST

Test your recall of the key terms as follows. First, read the following definitions of key terms and try to recall as many key terms as you can <u>without assistance</u>. Write your answers in the spaces provided. If you need assistance, refer to the list of key terms at the end of this section.

1. _____ _____ involves determining whether the costs assigned to units transferred out and to units in ending work in process are equal to the costs in beginning work in process plus the manufacturing costs incurred in the current period.

2. The _____ _____ _____ is a unit-costing method that excludes prior-period work and costs in computing current-period unit work and costs.

3. A method of process manufacturing in which subunits pass through different sequential processes before being brought together in a final process is called _____ _____.

4. A method of process manufacturing in which units flow from one process to another in a sequential pattern is called _____ _____.

5. The _____ _____ _____ _____ merges prior-period work and costs with current-period work and costs.

6. The expression of a processing department's activity in terms of fully completed units is called _____ _____ _____ _____.

7. _____ _____ uses job-order costing to assign materials costs and process costing to assign conversion costs.

8. The _____ _____ summarizes the manufacturing activity for a department during a period and discloses physical flow, equivalent units, total costs to account for, unit cost computation, and costs assigned to goods transferred out and to units in ending work in process.

9. _____ _____ are the costs of a prior process.

10. A(n) _____ _____ _____ is a schedule that accounts for all units flowing through a department during a period.

KEY TERMS:

cost reconciliation   physical flow schedule
equivalent units of output   production report
FIFO costing method   sequential processing
operation costing   transferred-in costs
parallel processing   weighted average costing method

Compare your answers to those at the end of the chapter and review any key terms missed.

CHAPTER QUIZ

Write your answers in the spaces provided.

1. Cost accounting systems should be designed to fit the nature of the manufacturing operation. _____ costing works well whenever relatively homogeneous products pass through a series of processes and receive similar amounts of manufacturing costs. _____ costing works well whenever products pass through a series of processes that deal out different amounts of manufacturing costs.

2. The manufacture of nearly any product requires the following three types of costs:
   1. _____
   2. _____
   3. _____

3. In a process manufacturing firm, units pass through a series of processes. The product may flow through the processing departments using:
   1. _____ processing or
   2. _____ processing

4. Equivalent production is the expression of all activity of a processing department in terms of _____ _____ units.

5. Equivalent units using the weighted average costing method is calculated as:

   _____

   + _____

   = Equivalent units of output

6. Cost per equivalent unit using the weighted average costing method is calculated as:

   Cost per Equivalent Unit = _____ / _____

7. List the five sections of the cost of production report.
   1. _____
   2. _____
   3. _____
   4. _____
   5. _____

Circle the single best answer.

8. In a process costing system, costs are accumulated by jobs: (a) true; (b) false

9. In a process costing system, a cost of production report contains the detail for the work in process account: (a) true; (b) false

10. In a job-order costing system, unit costs are determined by dividing the total costs on the job-order cost sheet by the number of units in the job: (a) true; (b) false

11. The FIFO method is more useful for cost control purposes because it concentrates on the current period's activity: (a) true; (b) false

12. Job-order costing works well whenever relatively homogeneous products are produced on a continuous basis: (a) true; (b) false

13. Operation costing is when job-order costing is used to assign material costs and process costing is used to assign conversion costs: (a) true; (b) false

14. Costs transferred in from a prior process are handled in the same manner as materials: (a) true; (b) false

15. As raw materials are purchased, the cost of the materials is recorded in the Work-in-Process account: (a) true; (b) false

16. When using FIFO costing, work done on partially completed units in beginning work-in-process inventory is considered current period work: (a) true; (b) false

17. An advantage of the weighted average costing method is simplicity: (a) true; (b) false

Use the following information to answer the next six questions.

The Jones Company manufactures medicated shampoo. It passes through two processes: (1) mixing, where ingredients are added and blended together, and (2) packaging, where the shampoo is put into bottles and packed for shipment.

The following information pertains to the mixing department for September 1995.

	UNITS (POUNDS)
Work in process, September 1 (80% complete, materials; 70% complete, labor and overhead)	10,000

	UNITS (POUNDS)
Started during September	120,000
Work in process, September 30 (60% complete, materials; 40% complete, labor and overhead)	12,000

The costs of work in process at September 1 for the mixing department were as follows:

	MIXING DEPARTMENT
Work in process, September 1:	
Materials	$ 60,000
Direct labor	40,000
Overhead	25,000
Total	$125,000

Costs added by the mixing department during September were as follows:

	MIXING DEPARTMENT
Materials	$ 880,000
Direct labor	520,500
Overhead	208,600
Total costs added	$1,609,100

Using the weighted average costing method, calculate the following for the mixing department for September.

18. The equivalent units of production for materials is: (a) 118,000; (b) 125,200; (c) 130,000; (d) 142,000

19. The unit cost for materials is: (a) $5.69; (b) $7.07; (c) $7.23; (d) $7.51

20. The equivalent units of production for conversion is: (a) 112,000;
    (b) 118,000; (c) 122,800; (d) 130,000

21. The unit cost for conversion costs is: (a) $4.23; (b) $5.94; (c) $6.26;
    (d) $6.47

22. Cost of goods transferred out is: (a) $1,649,640; (b) $1,652,000;
    (c) $1,716,744; (d) $1,817,400

23. Cost of ending work in process is: (a) $77,640; (b) $82,632; (c) $85,128;
    (d) $90,120

Compare your answers to those at the end of the chapter and review any
questions missed.

EXERCISES

EXERCISE 1

Jax, Inc., manufactures a product that passes through two processes: assembly
and finishing. All manufacturing costs are added uniformly for both
processes.

Information for the assembly department for the month of November follows.

      Work in process, November 1:
        Direct materials $10,000
        Direct labor   15,000
        Overhead   8,000
        Number of units (20% complete)   6,000

During November, 20,000 units were completed and transferred to the finishing
department. The following costs were incurred by the assembly department
during November.

        Direct materials $35,000
        Direct labor   50,000
        Overhead   28,280

2,000 units that were 60% complete remained in assembly at November 30.

Required:

Complete the cost of production report on the following page for assembly for
November using the weighted average costing method.

EXERCISE 1 (continued)

JAX, INC.
COST OF PRODUCTION REPORT FOR NOVEMBER 1995
WEIGHTED AVERAGE COSTING METHOD

Unit Information

Units to account for:
Units in beginning work in process _____
Units started _____
Total units to account for _____

Equivalent Units

	Equivalent Units		
	Physical Flow	Materials	Conversion
Units completed	_____	_____	_____
Units in ending work in process	_____	_____	_____
Total units accounted for	_____	_____	_____

Cost Information: Calculation of Unit Costs

Costs to account for:

	Materials	Conversion	Total
Costs in beginning work in process	_____	_____	_____
Costs added	_____	_____	_____
Total costs to account for	_____	_____	_____
Cost per equivalent unit	_____	_____	_____

Cost Information: Costs Transferred Out and Cost of Ending Inventory

Costs accounted for:

	Transferred Out	Ending Work in Process	Total
Units transferred out (units x total unit cost)	_____		_____
Work in process--ending inventory:			
Materials (equivalent units x unit cost for materials)		_____	_____
Conversion (equivalent units x unit cost for conversion)		_____	_____
Total costs accounted for	_____	_____	_____

EXERCISE 2

Jim's Paint Products manufactures house paint. The ingredients are combined in the mixing department then put in gallon cans in the packaging department.

The following information pertains to the mixing department for May 1995.

	UNITS (GALLONS)
Work in process, May 1 (100% complete, materials; 60% complete, labor and overhead)	5,000
Started during May	80,000
Work in process, May 31 (100% complete, materials; 35% complete, labor and overhead)	9,000

Costs of work in process at May 1 in the mixing department were as follows:

	MIXING DEPARTMENT
Work in process, May 1:	
Materials	$34,000
Direct labor	23,000
Manufacturing overhead	15,000
Total	$72,000

The costs added by the mixing department during May were as follows:

	MIXING DEPARTMENT
Materials	$ 680,000
Direct labor	293,600
Manufacturing overhead	182,875
Total costs added	$1,156,475

Required:

Prepare a cost of production report using the weighted average costing method. The report should contain the following:
1. Physical flow of units
2. Equivalent units
3. Calculation of unit costs
4. Costs accounted for, showing costs transferred out and cost of ending work in process

EXERCISE 2 (continued)

Use this page for your answer.

EXERCISE 3

Information for the packaging department for Jim's Paint Products for May follows:

	UNITS (GALLONS)
Work in process, May 1 (20% converted)	2,000
Transferred in from the mixing department	76,000
Work in process, May 31 (70% converted)	8,000

The costs of the packaging department's work in process at May 1 were as follows:

	PACKAGING DEPARTMENT
Work in process, May 1:	
Costs transferred in from mixing department	$25,900
Direct labor	17,040
Manufacturing overhead	22,120
Total	$65,060

The costs added by the packaging department during May were as follows:

	PACKAGING DEPARTMENT
Direct labor	$240,000
Manufacturing overhead	560,000
Total costs added	$800,000

Required:

Using the information from Exercise 2 and the above information, prepare a cost of production report for the packaging department for May. The cost of production report should include the following:

1. Physical flow of units
2. Calculation of equivalent units
3. Calculation of unit costs
4. Costs accounted for, showing costs transferred out and the cost of ending work in process

EXERCISE 3 (continued)

Use this page for your answer.

EXERCISE 4

Required:

1. Using the information from the previous exercises, prepare the journal entries to summarize the activities in the mixing and packaging departments for May using the weighted average costing method.

2. Prepare T accounts for work in process for the mixing and packaging departments.

ANSWERS

KEY TERMS TEST
1. Cost reconciliation
2. FIFO costing method
3. parallel processing
4. sequential processing
5. weighted average costing method
6. equivalent units of output
7. Operation costing
8. production report
9. Transferred-in costs
10. physical flow schedule

CHAPTER QUIZ
1. process, job-order
2. 1. direct materials
   2. direct labor
   3. manufacturing overhead
3. 1. sequential
   2. parallel
4. fully completed
5. Units completed and transferred out
   Units in ending work in process x fraction complete
6. Total costs to account for/Equivalent units
7. 1. unit information: units to account for
   2. equivalent units
   3. computation of unit cost
   4. costs accounted for (calculation of costs transferred out
      plus cost of ending work in process inventory)
   5. cost reconciliation

8. b False A job-order costing system accumulates costs by jobs, while a
              process costing system accumulates costs by processing
              department.

9. a True
10. a True
11. a True
12. b False Process costing works well whenever relatively homogeneous
              products are produced on a continuous basis.

13. a True
14. a True
15. b False As raw materials are purchased, the cost is recorded as
              inventory. As raw materials are used in production, the cost
              is transferred to work in process.
16. b False The FIFO method does not include prior period costs in the
              current period unit cost.
17. a True
18. b (10,000 + 120,000 - 12,000) = 118,000 units completed
       [118,000 units completed + (12,000 units in ending inventory x 60%)] =
       125,200
19. d (60,000 + 880,000)/125,200 EUP = $7.51
20. c [118,000 units completed + (12,000 units in ending inventory x 40%)] =
       122,800
21. d ($40,000 + $25,000 + $520,500 + $208,600)/122,800 = $6.47
22. a [118,000 x ($7.51 + $6.47)] = $1,649,640
23. c [(7,200 x $7.51) + (4,800 x $6.47)] = $85,128

552

EXERCISE 1

JAX, INC.
COST OF PRODUCTION REPORT FOR NOVEMBER 1995
WEIGHTED AVERAGE COSTING METHOD

Unit Information

Units to account for:
Units in beginning work in process............................ 6,000
Units started..................................... 16,000

Total units to account for.. 22,000

Equivalent Units

	Equivalent Units		
	Physical Flow	Materials	Conversion
Units completed....................	20,000	20,000	20,000
Units in ending work in process...	2,000	1,200	1,200
Total units accounted for.........	22,000	21,200	21,200

Cost Information: Calculation of Unit Costs

Costs to account for:	Materials	Conversion	Total
Costs in beginning work in process	$10,000	$ 23,000	$ 33,000
Costs added......................	35,000	78,280	113,280
Total costs to account for........	$45,000	$101,280	$146,280
Cost per equivalent unit..........	$2.12	$4.78	$6.90

Cost Information: Costs Transferred Out and Cost of Ending Inventory

Costs accounted for:	Transferred Out	Ending Work in Process	Total
Units transferred out (20,000 x $6.90)................	$138,000		$138,000
Work in process--ending inventory:			
Materials (1,200 x $2.12)........		$2,544	2,544
Conversion (1,200 x $4.78).......		5,736	5,736
Total costs accounted for..........	$138,000	$8,280	$146,280

553

EXERCISE 2

JIM'S PAINT PRODUCTS
COST OF PRODUCTION--MIXING DEPARTMENT
FOR MAY 1995
WEIGHTED AVERAGE COSTING METHOD

Unit Information

Units to account for:
Units in beginning work in process............................. 5,000
Units started during May....................................... 80,000

Total units to account for..................................... 85,000

Equivalent Units

	Physical Flow	Materials	Conversion
Units completed	76,000	76,000	76,000
Units in ending work in process:			
Materials--9,000 x 100%........	9,000	9,000	
Conversion--9,000 x 35%........			3,150
Total units accounted for........	85,000	85,000	79,150

Cost Information: Calculation of Unit Costs

Costs to account for:

	Materials	Conversion	Total
Costs in beginning work in process..	$ 34,000	$ 38,000	$ 72,000
Costs added........................	680,000	476,475	1,156,475
Total costs to account for..........	$714,000	$514,475	$1,228,475
Cost per equivalent unit............	$8.40	$6.50	$14.90

Cost Information: Costs Transferred Out and Cost of Ending Inventory

Costs accounted for:

	Transferred Out	Ending Work in Process	Total
Units transferred out (76,000 x $14.90)...............	$1,132,400		$1,132,400
Work in process--ending inventory:			
Materials (9,000 x $8.40)........		$75,600	75,600
Conversion (3,150 x $6.50).......		20,475	20,475
Total costs accounted for..........	$1,132,400	$96,075	$1,228,475

554

EXERCISE 3

JIM'S PAINT PRODUCTS
COST OF PRODUCTION--PACKAGING DEPARTMENT FOR MAY 1995
WEIGHTED AVERAGE COSTING METHOD

Unit Information

Units to account for:
Units in beginning work in process.................................. 2,000
Units started in May (transferred in from Mixing)................ 76,000

Total units to account for..................................... 78,000

Equivalent Units

	Physical Flow	Transferred In	Conversion
Units completed	70,000	70,000	70,000
Units in ending work in process:			
Transferred-in--8,000 x 100%...	8,000	8,000	
Conversion--8,000 x 70%........			5,600
Total units accounted for....	78,000	78,000	75,600

Cost Information: Calculation of Unit Costs

Costs to account for:

	Transferred In	Conversion	Total
Costs in beginning work in process...	$ 25,900	$ 39,160	$ 65,060
Costs added.........................	1,132,400	800,000	1,932,400
Total costs to account for..........	$1,158,300	$839,160	$1,997,460
Cost per equivalent unit............	$14.85	$11.10	$25.95

Cost Information: Costs Transferred Out and Cost of Ending Inventory

Costs accounted for:

	Transferred Out	Ending Work in Process	Total
Units transferred out (70,000 x $25.95)...............	$1,816,500		$1,816,500
Work in process--ending inventory:			
Materials (8,000 x $14.85).......		$118,800	118,800
Conversion (5,600 x $11.10)......		62,160	62,160
Total costs accounted for.........	$1,816,500	$180,960	$1,997,460

EXERCISE 4

1. Journal entries for the mixing and packaging departments:

   Entry to record materials used in production:

   ```
   Work in Process: Mixing................ 680,000
        Raw Materials Inventory...........        680,000
   ```

   Entry to record direct labor:

   ```
   Work in Process: Mixing................ 293,600
        Wages Payable.....................        293,600
   ```

   Entry to record manufacturing overhead:

   ```
   Work in Process: Mixing................ 182,875
        Manufacturing Overhead Control.....        182,875
   ```

   Entry to record transfer of costs from the mixing department to the packaging department:

   ```
   Work in Process: Packaging............ 1,132,400
        Work in Process: Mixing..........          1,132,400
   ```

   Entry to record direct labor and manufacturing overhead costs in the packaging department in May:

   ```
   Work in Process: Packaging............. 800,000
        Wages Payable.....................        240,000
        Manufacturing Overhead Control.....        560,000
   ```

   Entry to record the transfer of costs from the packaging department to finished goods:

   ```
   Finished Goods Inventory.............. 1,816,500
        Work in Process: Packaging.......          1,816,500
   ```

EXERCISE 4 (continued)

2. T account for the mixing department:

Work in Process: Mixing Department

Beg. bal.	72,000			
Materials	680,000	Transferred		
DL	293,600	out to		
OH	182,875	packaging	1,132,400
End. bal.	96,075*			

*Agrees with costs assigned to ending work in process in Exercise 2.

T account for the packaging department:

Work in Process: Packaging Department

Beg. bal.	65,060			
Transferred		Transferred		
in costs	1,132,400	out to		
DL	240,000	finished		
OH	560,000	goods	1,816,500
End. bal.	180,960*			

*Agrees with costs assigned to ending work in process in Exercise 3.

CHAPTER 18

ALLOCATION:
SERVICE CENTER COSTS AND OTHER CONCEPTS

CHAPTER REVIEW

SERVICE DEPARTMENT COST ALLOCATION: FURTHER REFINEMENT OF OVERHEAD

- Two types of departments are:
  1. producing departments
  2. service departments

- **Producing departments** are responsible for manufacturing or creating the products or services sold to customers.

  Examples of producing departments include machining and assembly.

- **Service departments** provide support services for the producing departments.

  Examples of service departments include maintenance and security.

- Although service departments do not work directly on the products of an organization, the costs of providing these support services are part of the total product cost.

- The assignment of service department costs to units of product consists of a two-stage allocation:
  1. Service department costs are allocated to the producing departments.
  2. Allocated service department costs are included in the producing department's overhead rate. Then overhead is assigned to units of product.

- Thus, a producing department's overhead consists of two parts:
  1. overhead directly associated with the producing department.
  2. overhead allocated to the producing department from the service departments.

OBJECTIVES OF ALLOCATION

- The major objectives associated with the allocation of service department costs to producing departments and ultimately to specific products are:
  1. To obtain a mutually agreeable price
  2. To compute product-line profitability
  3. To predict economic effects for planning and control
  4. To value inventory
  5. To motivate managers

- Basic guidelines that should be followed when allocating service department costs are:
  1. Cost drivers (causal factors) should be used as the basis for cost allocation.
  2. Budgeted or expected costs, not actual costs, should be allocated.
  3. Costs should be allocated by behavior; fixed costs and variable costs should be allocated separately.

SELECTION OF COST-ALLOCATION BASES: CAUSAL FACTORS

- **Causal factors** are variables or activities that <u>cause</u> the incurrence of service costs.

- In general, causal factors should be used as the basis for allocating service costs.

- For example, if power costs were to be allocated, kilowatt hours would be the causal factor that could be used as the allocation base.

- Using causal factors results in more accurate product costs, and if causal factors are known, managers are better able to control the consumption of services.

Allocation: Budgeted Versus Actual Costs

- A general principle of performance evaluation is that managers should not be held responsible for costs or activities over which they have no control.

- Budgeted, not actual, costs should be allocated to producing departments so that the efficiencies or inefficiencies of the service departments are not passed on to the producing departments.

Cost Behavior: Separate Allocation of Fixed and Variable Costs

Allocation of Variable Costs

- Variable service costs increase, in total, as the quantity of service increases. As a producing department uses more of a service, the costs of the service department increase.

- Thus, variable costs should be allocated based on service usage.

- If the allocation is for product costing, the allocation is done at the beginning of the year on the basis of <u>budgeted</u> usage, so that a predetermined overhead rate can be computed. For <u>product costing</u>, the allocation of <u>variable</u> service department costs would be:

Budgeted Rate x <u>Budgeted</u> Usage

- If the allocation is for <u>performance evaluation</u>, the allocation of <u>variable</u> service department costs would be:

Budgeted Rate x <u>Actual</u> Usage

- Both budgeted and actual usage allocations are achieved by following four steps:
  1. Determine the budgeted rate. At the beginning of the year, the company determines what the variable cost per unit of service should be.
  2. Budget usage. Each producing department determines its expected or budgeted usage of the service for the year.
  3. Measure actual usage. The actual units of service used by each producing department are measured.
  4. Allocate variable service costs. Multiply the budgeted rate by the usage.
     a. For product costing, the formula is: budgeted rate x budgeted usage.
     b. For performance evaluation, the allocation is: budgeted rate x actual usage.

Allocation of Fixed Costs

- Fixed service costs are incurred to generate the capacity to provide the service.

- The service department's capacity is based on the long-term needs of the producing departments.

- Fixed service costs should be allocated based on the normal or practical activity of the producing departments.

- Three steps are involved in allocating fixed costs of a service department.
  1. Determine budgeted fixed costs of the service department.
  2. Calculate the allocation ratio.

Allocation Ratio = Producing Department Capacity/Total Capacity

  3. Allocate fixed costs.

Allocation = Allocation Ratio x Budgeted Fixed Service Costs

METHODS OF ALLOCATING SERVICE DEPARTMENT COSTS TO PRODUCING DEPARTMENTS

- Three methods used to allocate service department costs to producing departments are:
  1. direct method
  2. sequential, or step, method
  3. reciprocal method

The Direct Method of Allocation

• The direct method allocates service department costs directly to the producing departments based on relative use.

• This method ignores reciprocal services (services provided by one service department to another service department). For example, this method would ignore service provided by the data processing department to other service departments, such as personnel or maintenance.

• If a firm has two service departments--maintenance and data processing--and two producing departments--assembly and finishing--the allocation of service department costs using the direct method could be diagrammed as follows:

Maintenance   Data Processing   Assembly   Finishing

• <u>Variable service costs</u> can be allocated to producing departments in proportion to each producing department's <u>usage of the service</u>.

• <u>Fixed service costs</u> can be allocated to the producing departments in proportion to each producing department's normal or practical activity.

The Sequential Method of Allocation

• The **sequential (or step) method** allocates service department costs to the producing departments <u>and</u> to some service departments. Thus, the step method partially recognizes reciprocal services.

• The step method is applied in the following manner:
1. Select a service department and allocate its costs to the producing departments and service departments to which it provides services. (The service department with the greatest total costs is allocated first.)
2. Select another service department and allocate its cost to the producing departments and the remaining service departments.
3. Proceed in this manner until all of the service department costs have been allocated to the producing departments.

• Notice that once the costs of a service department are allocated, no further allocations are made to that service department.

- The allocation of service department costs under the step method can be diagrammed as follows:

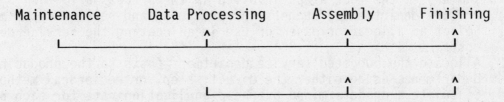

Maintenance   Data Processing   Assembly   Finishing

Reciprocal Method of Allocation

- The reciprocal method fully recognizes the reciprocal services provided by service departments to other service departments.

- The reciprocal method requires the use of simultaneous equations.

- The allocation of service department costs under the reciprocal method can be diagrammed as follows:

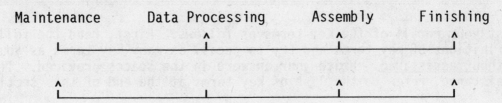

Maintenance   Data Processing   Assembly   Finishing

Departmental Overhead Rates and Product Costing

- Service department costs are allocated to the producing departments, and then the service department costs are included in the producing departments' overhead application rates.

- The flow of costs could be diagrammed as follows:

Service Department Costs	Producing Department Overhead Costs	Units of Product
	$400,000	
$200,000 ——————————>	$200,000	
	$600,000 ——————————>	

- The $600,000 of producing department overhead would be allocated to units of product using a cost driver such as direct labor hours or machine hours.

563

SUMMARY

- To summarize, the four steps involved in the process are:
  1. Prepare departmental budgets for producing and service departments.
  2. Select an allocation base for use in allocating the service department costs.
  3. Allocate the budgeted service department costs to the producing departments using either the direct, step, or reciprocal method.
  4. Calculate a predetermined overhead application rate for each producing department to apply total overhead costs to units of product produced.

- The accuracy of assigning overhead costs to units of product is dependent on:
  1. identifying and using a causal factor (allocation base) that is highly correlated with the incurrence of service department costs, and
  2. identifying a causal factor (cost driver) that is highly correlated to a product's consumption of a producing department's overhead costs.

KEY TERMS TEST

Test your recall of the key terms as follows. First, read the following definitions of key terms and try to recall as many key terms as you can without assistance. Write your answers in the spaces provided. If you need assistance, refer to the list of key terms at the end of this section.

1. A unit within an organization responsible for producing the products or services that are sold to customers is called a _____ _____.

2. A unit within an organization that provides essential support services for producing departments is called a(n) _____ _____.

3. The _____ _____ simultaneously allocates service costs to all user departments. It gives full consideration to interactions among service departments.

4. The _____ _____ is a method of allocating service costs that ignores any interactions that may exist among service departments.

5. _____ _____ are variables or activities that cause the incurrence of service costs.

6. The _____ _____ is a method of allocating service department costs that gives partial consideration to interactions among service departments.

KEY TERMS:

causal factors	producing department	sequential (or step) method
direct method	reciprocal method	service department

CHAPTER QUIZ

Circle the single best answer.

1. The direct method of allocating service department costs partially recognizes services that service departments provide to each other: (a) true; (b) false

2. The reciprocal method of allocating service department costs fully recognizes services that service departments provide to each other: (a) true; (b) false

3. Producing departments are responsible for producing the products sold to customers: (a) true; (b) false

4. Service departments are responsible for providing services directly to customers: (a) true; (b) false

5. Accounting is an example of a producing department: (a) true; (b) false

6. Maintenance is an example of a service department: (a) true; (b) false

7. The company cafeteria is an example of a producing department: (a) true; (b) false

8. Packaging is an example of a service department: (a) true; (b) false

9. One of the major objectives of allocation is to motivate managers: (a) true; (b) false

10. One of the major objectives of allocation is to value inventory: (a) true; (b) false

11. One of the major objectives of allocation is to compute product line profitability: (a) true; (b) false

12. Actual costs should always be used when allocating service department costs: (a) true; (b) false

13. Service department costs should be allocated directly to units of product: (a) true; (b) false

14. If the allocation is for performance evaluation, variable service department costs should be allocated based on the actual rate and actual usage: (a) true; (b) false

15. If the allocation is for product costing, variable service department costs should be allocated based on the budgeted rate and budgeted usage: (a) true; (b) false

16. Fixed service department costs should be allocated based on the practical capacity of the user departments: (a) true; (b) false

Use the following information to answer the next seven questions.

Mollet, Inc., often bids on jobs using a cost plus basis; therefore, in order to be competitive, it is important to determine costs as accurately as possible. The company operates two service departments (Department A and Department B) and two producing departments (Department C and Department D). Budgeted costs and normal activity levels are given below.

	Service Departments		Producing Departments	
	A	B	C	D
Overhead costs	$120,000	$160,000	$300,000	$240,000
Number of employees	8	12	40	60
Maintenance hours	3,000	400	8,000	2,000
Machine hours	--	--	12,000	1,500
Labor hours	--	--	1,800	15,000

The costs of Department A are allocated on the basis of number of employees, and the costs of Department B are allocated based on maintenance hours.

17. If the direct method is used, the Department A costs allocated to Department C would be: (a) $48,000; (b) $96,000; (c) $72,000; (d) $120,000

18. If the direct method is used, the Department B costs allocated to Department C would be: (a) $192,000; (b) $160,000; (c) $128,000; (d) $80,000

19. If Department C uses machine hours to allocate overhead to units of product, the overhead rate per machine hour for Department C would be: (a) $35.67; (b) $29.00; (c) $32.66; (d) $39.67

20. If Department D uses direct labor hours to allocate overhead to units of product, the overhead rate per direct labor hour for Department D would be: (a) $22.93; (b) $18.13; (c) $16.80; (d) $16.00

21. Estimates relating to a job that Mollet, Inc., plans to bid on are as follows:

Direct materials	$1,000
Direct labor	$600
Machine hours in Department C	20
Direct labor hours in Department D	30

    The estimate for the cost of the job would be: (a) $2,393; (b) $2,288; (c) $1,481; (d) $3,081

22. If the step method is used and the costs of the service department with the greatest total cost are allocated first, the Department B costs allocated to Department D would be: (a) $36,923; (b) $30,463; (c) $24,615; (d) $21,450

23. If the step method is used, the Department A costs allocated to Department C would be: (a) $60,649; (b) $62,769; (c) $62,980; (d) $69,280

EXERCISES

EXERCISE 1

Husmann Company has three service departments and two producing departments. Information for each department for 1995 is as follows:

	Service Departments			Producing Departments	
	Plant Administration	Plant Maintenance	Plant Cafeteria	Machining	Assembly
Budgeted overhead cost	$120,000	$100,000	$50,000	$200,000	$400,000
Direct labor hours	6,000	10,000	4,000	20,000	30,000
Square feet occupied	2,000	3,000	5,000	35,000	65,000
Number of employees	5	6	3	15	25

Plant administration costs are allocated based on direct labor hours; plant maintenance costs are allocated based on square footage occupied; and plant cafeteria costs are allocated based on the number of employees.

The company does not divide overhead into fixed and variable components. Predetermined overhead rates for the producing departments are based on direct labor hours.

Required:

Allocate the service department costs using the direct method. Then calculate the predetermined overhead rates the producing departments would use to apply overhead to units of product.

	Service Departments			Producing Departments	
	Plant Administration	Plant Maintenance	Plant Cafeteria	Machining	Assembly
Budgeted overhead cost	$120,000	$100,000	$50,000	$200,000	$400,000

567

EXERCISE 2

Required:

Using the information from the previous exercise, allocate the service department costs using the step method starting with the service department with the greatest total cost. Then calculate the predetermined overhead rates the producing departments would use to apply overhead to units of product.

	Service Departments			Producing Departments	
	Plant Administration	Plant Maintenance	Plant Cafeteria	Machining	Assembly
Budgeted overhead cost	$120,000	$100,000	$50,000	$200,000	$400,000

EXERCISE 3

There are three Sleepy Hollow Inns, one in each of the following cities:
Branson, Charleston, and Salem.

The central office provides computer services to each of the three motels.
Information pertaining to the computer center and the three motels follows.

	Computer Center	Branson	Charleston	Salem
Budgeted fixed costs	$150,000	--	--	--
Budgeted variable rate per hour	$25	--	--	--
Normal usage in hours	--	1,000	1,200	300
Actual fixed costs	$160,000	--	--	--
Actual variable costs	$70,000	--	--	--
Actual usage in hours	--	800	1,400	400

Required:

1. Using the direct method, allocate the computer costs to each motel
   location to provide information for setting room rates.

2. Using the direct method, allocate the computer center costs to each
   motel location assuming the purpose is to evaluate performance.

3. Did the total amount allocated in requirement 2 differ from the amount
   of costs incurred by the computer center?

EXERCISE 4

Taylor Bus Lines provides school bus service to two area school districts: Unit #1 and Unit #2.

Taylor has one service center that is responsible for service, maintenance, and cleanup of its buses. The costs of the service center are allocated to each operating unit on the basis of total miles driven.

During the first month of the year, the service center was expected to spend a total of $100,000. Of this total, $25,000 was viewed as being fixed. During the month, the service center incurred actual variable costs of $105,000 and actual fixed costs of $20,000.

The normal and actual miles logged by each unit are given below:

	Unit #1	Unit #2
Normal activity..........	170,000	80,000
Actual activity..........	175,000	90,000

Required:

1. Compute the predetermined service cost per mile driven.

2. Compute the costs that would be allocated at the end of the month to each unit for purposes of performance evaluation.

3. Determine the costs of the service center that were not allocated to the two units. Why were these costs not allocated to the operating units?

ANSWERS

KEY TERMS TEST
1. producing department
2. service department
3. reciprocal method
4. direct method
5. Causal factors
6. sequential (or step) method

CHAPTER QUIZ
1. b False The step method partially recognizes reciprocal services.
2. a True
3. a True
4. b False Service departments provide support services to the producing departments.
5. b False Accounting is an example of a service department.
6. a True
7. b False The company cafeteria would be an example of a service department.
8. b False Since packaging would work directly with the product, packaging would be considered a producing department.
9. a True
10. a True
11. a True
12. b False Budgeted costs, not actual costs, should be allocated.
13. b False First, service department costs are allocated to the producing departments. Then producing department overhead (including the allocated service department costs) is allocated to units of product.
14. b False If the allocation is for performance evaluation, variable service department costs should be allocated based on the <u>budgeted</u> rate and actual usage.
15. a True
16. a True
17. a $120,000 \times 40/100 = \$48,000$
18. c $160,000 \times 8,000/10,000 = \$128,000$
19. d $(\$300,000 + \$48,000 + \$128,000)/12,000 = \$39.67$
20. a $(\$240,000 + \$72,000 + \$32,000)/15,000 = \$22.93$
21. d $\$1,000 + \$600 + (\$39.67 \times 20) + (\$22.93 \times 30) = \$3,081$
22. c $160,000 \times (2,000/13,000) = \$24,615$
23. b $160,000 \times (3,000/13,000) = \$36,923$;
       $(\$120,000 + \$36,923) \times (40/100) = \$62,769$

EXERCISE 1

	Service Departments			Producing Departments	
	Plant Administration	Plant Maintenance	Plant Cafeteria	Machining	Assembly
Budgeted overhead cost	$120,000	$100,000	$50,000	$200,000	$400,000
Allocate plant administration (20,000/50,000, 30,000/50,000)	($120,000)			48,000	72,000
Allocate plant maintenance (35,000/100,000, 65,000/100,000)		($100,000)		35,000	65,000
Allocate plant cafeteria (15/40, 25/40)			($50,000)	18,750	31,250
Total producing department overhead to apply				$301,750	$568,250
Divided by DLH				20,000	30,000
Predetermined overhead rate				$15.0875	$18.9417

EXERCISE 2

	Service Departments			Producing Departments	
	Plant Administration	Plant Maintenance	Plant Cafeteria	Machining	Assembly
Budgeted overhead cost	$120,000	$100,000	$50,000	$200,000	$400,000
Allocate plant administration (10/64, 4/64, 20/64, 30/64)	($120,000)	18,750	7,500	37,500	56,250
Total cost in plant maintenance		$118,750			
Allocate plant maintenance (5/105, 35/105, 65/105)		($118,750)	5,655	39,583	73,512
Total cost in plant cafeteria			$63,155		
Allocate plant cafeteria (15/40, 25/40)			($63,155)	23,683	39,472
Total producing department overhead to apply				$300,766	$569,234
Divided by DLH				20,000	30,000
Predetermined overhead rate				$15.0383	$18.9745

EXERCISE 3

1.

	Branson	Charleston	Salem
Variable costs allocated:			
($25 x 1,000 hours)	$25,000		
($25 x 1,200 hours)		$ 30,000	
($25 x 300 hours)			$ 7,500
Fixed costs allocated:			
[(1,000 hours/2,500 hours) x $150,000]	60,000		
[(1,200 hours/2,500 hours) x $150,000]		72,000	
[(300 hours/2,500 hours) x $150,000]			18,000
Total costs allocated	$85,000	$102,000	$25,500

2.

	Branson	Charleston	Salem
Variable costs allocated:			
($25 x 800 hours)	$20,000		
($25 x 1,400 hours)		$ 35,000	
($25 x 400 hours)			$10,000
Fixed costs allocated:			
[(1,000 hours/2,500 hours) x $150,000]	60,000		
[(1,200 hours/2,500 hours) x $150,000]		72,000	
[(300 hours/2,500 hours) x $150,000]			18,000
Total costs allocated	$80,000	$107,000	$28,000

3. Actual costs incurred by the computer center equaled $230,000 ($70,000 + $160,000).

To prevent passing inefficiencies of service departments on to other departments, only budgeted service department costs are allocated.

Therefore, only the budgeted computer center costs of $215,000 were allocated to the three motels.

The $15,000 excess ($230,000 - $215,000) is charged to the computer center.

EXERCISE 4

1. $0.40 $100,000/250,000

2.

	Unit #1	Unit #2
Variable costs allocated:		
($0.30* x 175,000 miles)	$52,500	
($0.30 x 90,000 miles)		$27,000
Fixed costs allocated:		
[(170,000/250,000) x $25,000]	17,000	
[(80,000/250,000) x $25,000]		8,000
Total costs allocated	$69,500	$35,000

*Budgeted variable costs = $100,000 - $25,000 = $75,000
Variable rate per mile = $75,000/250,000 = $0.30

3.

Actual costs incurred	$125,000
- Total costs allocated ($69,500 + $35,000)	104,500
Unallocated	$ 20,500

These costs were not allocated to the operating units because the costs were associated with service department inefficiency.

CHAPTER 19

PRODUCT COSTING AND COST MANAGEMENT: THE ADVANCED MANUFACTURING ENVIRONMENT

CHAPTER REVIEW

LIMITATIONS OF CONVENTIONAL PRODUCT COSTING

- Over the past ten to twenty years, a revolution in manufacturing has occurred.

- Innovative practices developed by the Japanese, such as total quality control and just-in-time (JIT) manufacturing, have increased the competitive pressures felt by U.S. firms.

- In addition, the following changes have affected the competitive environment:
  1. computer-integrated manufacturing systems
  2. increased product complexity
  3. deregulation of service industries, such as airlines

- The **advanced manufacturing environment** is characterized by:
  1. firms engaged in intense competition
  2. a philosophy of continuous improvement, total quality control, and sophisticated technology

- As firms adopt new manufacturing strategies to remain competitive, the accounting system must change to produce more accurate product costs.

Overhead Assignment: The Source of the Problem

- Symptoms of an outdated cost system include:
  1. The outcome of bids is difficult to explain.
  2. Competitors' prices appear unrealistically low.
  3. Products that are difficult to produce show high profits.
  4. Operational managers want to drop products that appear profitable.
  5. Profit margins are hard to explain.
  6. The company has a highly profitable niche all to itself.
  7. Customers do not complain about price increases.
  8. The accounting department spends a lot of time on special projects.
  9. Some departments are using their own accounting system.
  10. Product costs change because of changes in financial reporting regulations.

- Traditional product costing methods may distort product costs.

- The problem usually is <u>not</u> related to assigning the costs of direct materials or direct labor, but arises when assigning overhead. (Direct materials and direct labor are directly traceable to units of product.)

- Using conventional unit-based, volume-related methods to assign overhead costs to products can result in distorted product costs.

- In a highly competitive environment, accurate cost information is critical for sound planning and decision making.

Overhead Costing: A Single-Product Setting

- If only a single product is manufactured in a facility, then all overhead costs are caused by and are traceable to that product.

Overhead Costing: Multiple-Product Setting with Unit-Based Cost Drivers

- When more than one product is produced in a manufacturing facility, the overhead costs are caused jointly by all the products.

- **Cost drivers** are factors that measure the demand placed on overhead activities by individual products.

- **Unit-based (volume-related) cost drivers** assign overhead to products using either plantwide or departmental rates.

Plantwide Overhead Rate

- A common method of assigning overhead to products is to compute a plantwide rate, using a unit-based (volume-related) cost driver, such as direct labor hours or machine hours.

Plantwide Rate = Total Overhead/Total Activity

This approach assumes that overhead cost variation can be explained by one cost driver.

Departmental Rates

- Another approach is to use departmental overhead rates. For example, a machine-intensive department might use machine hours as the cost driver. A labor-intensive department might use direct labor hours as the cost driver.

Problems with Costing Accuracy

- The main problem with the traditional approach to product costing is the assumption that a unit-based (volume-related) cost driver, such as machine hours or labor hours, causes all of the overhead cost.

- Overhead costs are not always driven or caused by the number of units produced. For example, <u>setup costs are related to the number of setups</u>.

Why Unit-Based Cost Drivers Fail

Nonunit-Related Overhead Costs

- **Nonunit**-based cost drivers are factors other than those related to the number of units produced that drive costs.

  For example, setup costs are not driven by the number of units, but by the number of setups, a nonunit-based cost driver.

- Using only unit-based cost drivers to assign nonunit-related overhead costs can create distorted product costs. The severity of distortion depends on the proportion of nonunit-related overhead costs. If nonunit-based overhead costs are only a small percentage of total overhead costs, the distortion of product costs would be small and the use of unit-based cost drivers might be acceptable.

Product Diversity

- **Product diversity** occurs when products consume overhead activities in different proportions.

- Reasons why products might consume overhead in different proportions include:
  - differences in product size
  - product complexity
  - setup time
  - size of batches

- **Consumption ratio** is the proportion of each activity consumed by a product.

- Product costs can be distorted if a unit-based cost driver is used and
  1. nonunit-based overhead costs are a significant proportion of total overhead
  2. the consumption ratios differ between unit-based and nonunit-based input categories.

ACTIVITY-BASED PRODUCT COSTING

- An **activity-based cost (ABC) system** uses a two-stage procedure:
  1. Overhead costs are traced to activities.
  2. Costs are traced to products.

- Conventional product costing also involves two stages; however, overhead costs are traced to departments (instead of activities) and then traced to products.

- Activity-based costing uses more cost drivers than the conventional system, which usually uses one or two unit-based cost drivers. Thus, activity-based costing improves product-costing accuracy and also provides information about the cost of activities.

- When using activity-based costing,
  - the first-stage procedure is activity grouping and cost assignment (tracing overhead costs to activities), and
  - the second-stage procedure is assigning costs to products.

First-Stage Procedure: Activity Grouping and Cost Assignment

- The first-stage procedure of activity-based costing consists of the following:
  1. Activities are identified.
  2. Costs are associated with the activities.
  3. Activities and their related costs are divided into homogeneous cost pools.
  4. Pool (overhead) rates are computed.

- The four steps of the first-stage procedure are explained below.

1. Activities are identified.

- An **activity** is work performed within an organization.

- Activity identification requires listing all the different kinds of work, such as materials handling and inspection.

- After activities are identified, they are classified into one of four general activity levels.
  - **Unit-level activities** are activities performed each time a unit is produced. For example, power is used each time a unit is produced.
  - **Batch-level activities** are activities performed each time a batch of products is produced. The costs of batch-level activities vary with the number of batches but are fixed with respect to the number of units in each batch. Examples include setups, inspections, production scheduling, and material handling.
  - **Product-level activities** are activities performed as needed to support the products. Examples include engineering changes and equipment maintenance.
  - **Facility-level activities** are activities that sustain a factory's general manufacturing process. Examples include plant management and security.

2. Costs are associated with the activities.

3. Activities and their related costs are divided into homogeneous cost pools.

- A **homogeneous cost pool** is a collection of overhead costs associated with activities that (1) have the same activity level and (2) use the same cost driver to assign costs to products.

  Thus, to be included in the same homogeneous cost pool, activities must satisfy two criteria:
  1. *activity-level criterion*: the activities are performed at the same general activity level (unit-level, batch-level, or product-level)
  2. *driver criterion*: the activities use the same cost driver.

- All unit-level activities that have the same cost driver would be grouped into homogeneous cost pools. For example, the unit-level category might have the following cost pools:
  - labor-related overhead cost pool
  - machine-related overhead cost pool
  - material-related overhead cost pool

  All batch-level activities that use the same cost driver would be grouped into homogeneous cost pools, and all product-level activities that use the same cost driver would be grouped into homogeneous cost pools.

- Unit-level costs vary as the number of units change; therefore, a unit-based cost driver can be used.

  Batch-level and product-level costs vary in proportion to factors other than changes in the number of units; therefore, they are assigned using nonunit-based cost drivers.

  Facility-level activities and costs are common to several products, and it is impossible to identify individual products that consume these activities. A pure ABC system would treat facility-level costs as period costs and would not assign them to products. In practice, facility-level costs might be allocated to individual products using unit-level, batch-level, or product-level cost drivers.

4. <u>**A pool rate for each cost pool is computed**</u>.

Pool Rate = Cost Pool/Activity Level of Cost Driver

<u>Second-Stage Procedure: Assigning Costs to Products</u>

- In the second stage, the costs of each overhead pool are traced to products. Costs associated with activities in the first three categories are assigned to products using cost drivers that reflect the cause-and-effect relationship between activity consumption and cost.

- The overhead assigned from each cost pool to each product is computed as follows.

$$\text{Applied Overhead} = \text{Pool Rate} \times \text{Cost Driver Units Used}$$

Comparison with Conventional Costing

- In a conventional system, the demand for overhead is assumed to be explained only by unit-based cost drivers. Thus, in a conventional system, the costs in the batch-level, product-level, and facility-level categories are treated as fixed costs--costs that do not vary as production volume changes.

  Allocation of fixed overhead using unit-based cost drivers may not reflect the activities actually being consumed by the products.

- ABC systems improve product-costing accuracy by recognizing that many of the so-called fixed overhead costs vary in proportion to changes other than production volume.

The Choice of Cost Drivers

- Two factors to consider when selecting cost drivers are:
  1. Minimize the cost of measuring the cost driver by selecting a cost driver that uses information already provided by the company's information system.
  2. Use cost drivers that directly measure overhead consumption. It is possible to replace a cost driver that directly measures consumption (inspection hours) with a cost driver that indirectly measures consumption (number of inspections) if there is a high correlation between the indirect cost driver and the actual consumption of overhead.

ABC and Service Organizations

- ABC can produce product-costing improvements in service organizations.

WHEN TO USE AN ABC SYSTEM

- Two fundamental requirements that must be met before an ABC system is considered are:
  1. Nonunit-based costs should be a significant percentage of total overhead costs. If they are immaterial, it does not matter how they are allocated to products.
  2. The consumption ratios of unit-based and nonunit-based activities must differ (there must be high product diversity). Otherwise, a conventional or an ABC system would produce the same cost assignment.

- When deciding whether to implement an ABC system, a manager must assess the tradeoff between:
  - **measurement costs**: costs associated with measurements required by the cost system.
  - **error costs**: costs associated with making poor decisions because of inaccurate product costs.

- An **optimal cost system** minimizes the sum of measurement costs and error costs.

- More complex systems have lower error costs and higher measurement costs.

- New information technology is decreasing measurement costs.

- Error costs increase as competition increases.

- As measurement costs decrease and error costs increase, a more accurate cost system is needed.

JIT MANUFACTURING AND PRODUCT COSTING

JIT Compared with Traditional Manufacturing

- JIT manufacturing is a demand-pull system.

- Products are produced only when necessary to satisfy customer demand.

- Each operation produces only what is necessary to satisfy the demand of the succeeding operation.

- Parts and materials arrive just in time to be used in production.

- Characteristics of JIT manufacturing that differ from traditional manufacturing include:
  1. Lower inventories. JIT manufacturing reduces inventory levels, since production is geared to demand.
  2. Manufacturing cells. Manufacturing cells consist of a set of machines needed to manufacture a particular product or product family.
  3. Interdisciplinary (multi-task) labor. Workers are trained to operate all machines within a cell resulting in interdisciplinary, not specialized, labor.
  4. A philosophy of total quality control. **Acceptable quality level** (AQL) is the traditional approach of permitting defects to occur as long as they do not exceed a certain level. **Total quality control** (TQC) strives for a defect-free manufacturing process. Poor quality cannot be tolerated in JIT manufacturing because, without inventories, a defective part stops production.
  5. Decentralization of services. JIT manufacturing decentralizes service functions to the cell level. For example, instead of one central location for raw materials, JIT uses multiple stock points, where each stock point is near where the material will be used.

JIT Compared with Traditional Manufacturing

JIT	Traditional
1. Pull-through system based on demand	1. Push-through system
2. Insignificant inventories	2. Significant inventories
3. Manufacturing cells	3. Departmental structure
4. Interdisciplinary labor	4. Specialized labor
5. Total quality control	5. Acceptable quality level
6. Decentralized services	6. Centralized services

Product-Costing Accuracy and JIT

- Under JIT's manufacturing cell structure, all the processes necessary for the production of a single product are collected in one area.

- The costs of operating the manufacturing cell are all directly traceable to the product produced.

- Under JIT, many costs formerly classified as indirect costs are now directly traceable to the product.

- One consequence of increasing the number of direct manufacturing costs is an increase in the accuracy of product costing.

- In a JIT system, the batch size is one unit of product. Thus, all batch-level activities become unit-level activities.

- In a JIT system, the levels of activities are:
  1. unit-level activities
  2. product-level activities
  3. cell-level activities (activities that sustain the cell process)
  4. facility-level activities

JIT and the Allocation of Service-Center Costs

- With JIT, many services are decentralized and the manufacturing of a product or component is all done within a manufacturing cell.

- Decentralization of services is accomplished through assigning people with specialized skills directly to product lines and by training direct laborers within cells to perform services formerly done by indirect laborers, such as maintenance service.

- Thus, many of the service costs can now be directly traced to a manufacturing cell and to the specific product.

- By making service costs directly traceable to products, managers have a better understanding of what it costs to produce a particular product.

JIT's Effect on Direct Labor Costs

- Two effects of implementing JIT and automating are:
  1. Direct labor decreases as a percentage of total manufacturing costs.
  2. Direct labor changes from a variable to a fixed cost. Under JIT, direct laborers perform multiple functions, such as doing maintenance work during slow production periods. Therefore, the level of direct labor costs tends to behave as a fixed cost and remains the same regardless of production level.

JIT's Effect on Inventory Valuation

- In a JIT environment, since inventory is kept at insignificant levels, GAAP guidelines for product costing of inventory are irrelevant.

- In a JIT environment, product-costing information is used for managerial decisions, such as pricing decisions, product profitability analysis, and make-or-buy decisions.

JIT's Effect on Job-Order and Process Costing

- Because costs are accumulated by manufacturing cells instead of jobs, JIT takes on the nature of a process-costing system.

- In a traditional process-costing system, it was necessary to calculate equivalent units of production because of partially completed units in beginning and ending work in process.

- With JIT manufacturing, there is no work-in-process inventory, so equivalent unit calculations are not necessary.

- Under JIT, unit costs are calculated as:

  Unit Cost = Cell's Costs for the Period/Units Produced During the Period

KEY TERMS TEST

Test your recall of the key terms as follows: Read the following definitions of key terms and try to recall as many key terms as you can <u>without assistance</u>. Write your answers in the spaces provided. If you need assistance, refer to the list of key terms at the end of this section.

1. Activities that are performed each time a batch is produced are _____ _____.

2. Activities that sustain the cell process but do not vary with cost drivers of other activity categories are _____ _____.

3. The proportion of an overhead activity consumed by a product is the _____ _____.

4. _____ _____ are factors that measure the demand placed on overhead activities by individual products.

5. A(n) _____ is a basic unit of work within an organization.

6. A(n) _____ _____ _____ is a collection of overhead costs associated with activities that have the same level and use the same cost driver to assign costs to products.

7. Costs incurred from measurements required by a cost system are _____ _____.

8. _____ _____ _____ are factors other than the number of units produced that explain the consumption of overhead.

9. Those activities performed to support the production of each different type of product are _____ _____.

10. _____ _____ _____, or _____, is a quality standard that demands perfection (zero defects).

11. _____ _____ _____, or _____, permits a predetermined number of defects.

12. A cost system that first traces costs to activities and then traces costs to products is a(n) _____ _____ _____.

13. A(n) _____ _____ _____ is characterized by intense competition, sophisticated technology, total quality control, and continuous improvement.

14. _____ _____ are performed each time a unit is produced.

15. Costs incurred from making bad decisions because of inaccurate product costs are _____ _____.

16. Those activities that sustain a facility's general manufacturing process are _____ _____.

17. A manufacturing approach that produces only what is necessary to satisfy the demand of the succeeding process (a demand-pull system) is _____ _____.

18. A(n) _____ _____ is a collection of machines dedicated to the production of a single product or subassembly.

19. A(n) _____ _____ _____ is a cost system that minimizes the sum of error costs and measurement costs.

20. _____ _____ occurs when products consume overhead in different proportions.

21. _____ _____ _____ are factors that increase in direct proportion to the number of units produced and which explain the consumption of unit-based overhead costs.

KEY TERMS:

acceptable quality level (AQL)
activity
activity-based cost system
advanced manufacturing environment
batch-level activities
cell-level activities
consumption ratio
cost drivers
error costs
facility-level activities
homogeneous cost pool

JIT manufacturing
manufacturing cell
measurement costs
nonunit-based cost drivers
optimal cost system
product diversity
product-level activities
total quality control (TQC)
unit-based cost drivers
unit-level activities

Compare your answers to those at the end of the chapter and review any key terms missed.

```
╔══════════════════════════════════════════════════════════╗
║  CHAPTER QUIZ                                              ║
╚══════════════════════════════════════════════════════════╝
```

Write your answers in the spaces provided.

1. List six ways JIT manufacturing differs from traditional manufacturing.
   1. _____
   2. _____
   3. _____
   4. _____
   5. _____
   6. _____

2. List three nonunit-based cost drivers.
   1. _____
   2. _____
   3. _____

3. In a highly competitive environment, accurate cost information is critical for the two management functions of _____ and _____ _____.

4. The two types of overhead rates used in the traditional approach to product costing are:
   1. _____
   2. _____

5. The overhead rates of the traditional approach to product costing use _____ cost drivers.

6. Activity-based cost systems use _____ cost drivers.

7. When activity-based costing is used, activities are classified into one of four categories:
   1. _____ activities
   2. _____ activities
   3. _____ activities
   4. _____ activities

8. When activity-based costing is used, the first-stage procedure involves identifying cost pools and calculating a pool rate for each cost pool. The pool rate is calculated as follows:

   Pool Rate = _____ / _____

9. The second stage of activity-based costing involves tracing the costs of each overhead cost pool to products. The overhead assigned to each product is calculated as follows:

   Applied Overhead = _____ x _____

10. In a JIT system, the four levels of activities are:
   1. _____ activities
   2. _____ activities
   3. _____ activities
   4. _____ activities

Circle the single best answer.

11. Unit-level costs are assigned using: (a) unit-based cost drivers;
    (b) nonunit-based cost drivers

12. Batch-level costs are assigned using: (a) unit-based cost drivers;
    (b) nonunit-based cost drivers

13. Product-level costs are assigned using: (a) unit-based cost drivers;
    (b) nonunit-based cost drivers

14. A conventional product costing system uses a two-stage procedure of (1)
    tracing overhead to activities, and (2) tracing the costs to products:
    (a) true; (b) false

15. With JIT manufacturing, labor costs are largely fixed in nature:
    (a) true; (b) false

16. The use of volume-based cost drivers, such as direct labor hours or
    machine hours, can produce distorted product costs: (a) true; (b) false

17. A product's consumption of overhead always increases in proportion to
    increases in production volume: (a) true; (b) false

18. With JIT manufacturing, direct labor costs decrease as a percentage of
    total manufacturing costs: (a) true; (b) false

19. In the new manufacturing environment, both manufacturing and
    nonmanufacturing costs are attributed to product lines in order to
    produce more accurate product-costing information for decision making:
    (a) true; (b) false

20. In a JIT environment, product-costing information is used primarily for
    inventory valuation for financial reporting: (a) true; (b) false

Use the following information to answer the next nine questions.

The following data is available for the two products, Model E and Model Z, that Pack Inc. manufactures.

Item	Quantity	Prime Costs	Machine Hours	Material Moves	Setups
Model E	350,000	$ 900,000	60,000	600,000	175
Model Z	100,000	250,000	15,000	400,000	75
Dollar value		$1,150,000	$400,000[a]	$500,000	$600,000

[a]The cost of maintenance

Currently, Pack uses a volume-based costing system that assigns the costs of maintenance, material handling, and setups to the models based on machine hours.

21. The volume-based plantwide overhead rate is: (a) $12.00; (b) $14.67; (c) $20,00; (d) $25.00

22. Overhead assigned to Model E is: (a) $1,500,000; (b) $1,200,000; (c) $880,200; (d) $720,000

23. Overhead assigned to Model Z is: (a) $300,000 (b) $375,000; (c) $220,050; (d) $320,000

24. The unit cost of Model E is: (a) $5.40; (b) $6.00; (c) $5.50; (d) $6.86

25. The unit cost of Model Z is: (a) $4.58; (b) $5.40; (c) $6.00; (d) $5.50

26. If activity-based costing is used, overhead assigned to Model E is: (a) $1,039,800; (b) $939,800; (c) $799,800; (d) $739,800

27. If activity-based costing is used, overhead assigned to Model Z is: (a) $359,950; (b) $279,950; (c) $380,000; (d) $459,950

28. If activity-based costing is used, the unit cost of Model E is: (a) $5.26; (b) $5.54; (c) $4.31; (d) $4.86

29. If activity-based costing is used, the unit cost of Model Z is: (a) $6.30; (b) $4.28; (c) $7.10; (d) $4.60

Write your answers in the spaces provided.

Use the following information to answer the next six questions.

Classify each of the following activities as a(n):
• unit-level activity
• batch-level activity
• product-level activity
• facility-level activity

30. Setups: _____

31. Electricity: _____

32. Plant management: _____

33. Engineering changes: _____

34. Inspections: _____

35. Plant security: _____

Use the following information to answer the next eleven questions.

Recently, Baker Inc. implemented a JIT manufacturing system. The system is designed so that each manufacturing cell produces a single product or component. Cell workers are responsible for the setup of machinery, maintenance of the machinery, and manufacturing the product.

Classify the following costs incurred by the company as:
• direct product costs or
• indirect product costs.

36. Parts for cell machinery: _____

37. Raw materials: _____

38. Depreciation on cell machinery: _____

39. Salaries of janitors: _____

40. Costs to set up machinery: _____

41. Maintenance of cell equipment: _____

42. Salary of cell supervisor: _____

43. Plant depreciation: _____

44. Salary of plant supervisor: _____

45. Oil for lubricating cell machinery: _____

46. Direct labor: _____

589

EXERCISES

EXERCISE 1

Paul's Plastics uses an activity-based cost system. The company produces Product X and Product Z. Information concerning the two products is given below.

	Product X	Product Z
Units produced	50,000	75,000
Machine hours	22,000	18,000
Direct labor hours	40,000	40,000
Material handling (number of moves)	10,000	15,000
Engineering labor (hours)	6,000	4,000
Setups	40	20
Maintenance (hours used)	1,500	1,000
Kilowatt hours	16,000	14,000
Inspections	18,000	12,000

The following overhead costs are reported:

Material handling	$ 70,000
Maintenance	50,000
Power	24,000
Engineering	60,000
Setups	75,000
Labor-related overhead	60,000
Machine-related overhead	120,000
Inspection	108,000

Required:

1. Using the format on the following page, classify the overhead activities as:
   - unit-level activities
   - batch-level activities
   - product-level activities

EXERCISE 1 (continued)

Unit-Level Activities:

_____

_____

_____

Batch-Level Activities:

_____

_____

_____

Product-Level Activities:

_____

_____

$3000 \times {}^{300}/_{100,000}$

9

$200 \times {}^{100,000}/_{100,000}$

$\$ 200$

$40 \times {}^{50,000}/_{200,000}$

20

$20 \times {}^{100,000}/_{100,000}$

20

$1 \times {}^{200000}/_{100,000}$

Overhead
Cost Per
    unit $\quad 251$

2. Group all overhead costs into homogeneous cost pools. Select a cost driver for each cost pool and compute a pool rate.

Homogeneous Cost Pool	Cost Driver	Pool Rate
_____ / _____		= _____
_____ / _____		= _____
_____ / _____		= _____
_____ / _____		= _____
_____ / _____		= _____
_____ / _____		= _____
_____ / _____		= _____

EXERCISE 1 (continued)

3. Using the pool rates, assign overhead costs to the two products and compute the overhead cost per unit for each. Round answers to two decimal places.

	Product X	Product Z
Unit-Level Activities:		
_____	_____	
_____		_____
_____	_____	
_____		_____
_____	_____	
_____		_____
Batch-Level Activities:		
_____	_____	
_____		_____
_____	_____	
_____		_____
_____	_____	
_____		_____
Product-Level Activities:		
_____	_____	
_____		_____
_____	_____	
_____		_____
Overhead cost per unit	$ _____	$ _____

EXERCISE 2

Peach, Inc., has identified the following overhead costs and cost drivers for next year.

Overhead Item	Expected Cost	Cost Driver	Expected Actual Transactions
Setup costs	$ 90,000	No. of setups	400
Ordering costs	50,000	No. of orders	4,000
Maintenance costs	150,000	Machine hours	25,000
Power	30,000	Kilowatt hours	75,000

The following are two of the jobs completed during the year:

	Job 700	Job 701
Direct materials	$1,200	$600
Direct labor	$900	$400
Units completed	250	100
Direct labor hours	40	20
Number of setups	2	1
Number of orders	10	4
Machine hours	50	40
Kilowatt hours	60	25

The company's normal activity is 5,000 direct labor hours.

Required:

1. Determine the unit cost for each job using direct labor hours to apply overhead.

2. Determine the unit cost for each job using the four cost drivers.

3. Which method produces the more accurate cost assignment? Why?

EXERCISE 3

Prior to installing a JIT system, Tori Inc. used machine hours to assign maintenance costs to its three products: 10-gauge, 20-gauge, and 30-gauge wire.

The maintenance costs totaled $200,000 per year. The machine hours used by each product and the quantity produced of each product are as follows:

	Machine Hours	Quantity Produced
10 gauge.......	10,000	5,000 rolls
20 gauge.......	15,000	6,000 rolls
30 gauge.......	25,000	8,000 rolls

After installing JIT, three manufacturing cells were created and the cell workers were trained to perform maintenance. Maintenance costs for the three cells still totaled $200,000; however, these costs are now traceable to each cell:

Cell, 10-gauge wire....................	$56,000
Cell, 20-gauge wire..................	70,000
Cell, 30-gauge wire.................	74,000

Required:

1. Compute the maintenance cost per roll for each type of wire before JIT is installed.

2. Compute the maintenance cost per roll for each type of wire after JIT is installed.

3. Explain why the maintenance cost per roll using JIT is more accurate than the cost per roll using the traditional approach.

EXERCISE 4

Hanover Manufacturing has four categories of overhead. The four categories and expected overhead costs for each category for next year are listed below.

Maintenance	$200,000
Materials handling	32,000
Setups	100,000
Inspection	120,000

Currently, overhead is applied using a predetermined overhead rate based upon budgeted direct labor hours. Fifty thousand direct labor hours are budgeted for next year.

The company has been asked to submit a bid for a proposed job. The plant manager feels getting this job would result in new business in future years. Usually bids are based upon full manufacturing cost plus 20 percent.

Estimates for the proposed job (Job No. P902) are as follows:

Direct materials	$6,000
Direct labor (1,000 hours)	$10,000
Number of material moves	12
Number of inspections	10
Number of setups	2
Number of machine hours	500

In the past, full manufacturing cost has been calculated by allocating overhead using a volume-based cost driver: direct labor hours. The plant manager has heard of a new way of applying overhead that uses cost pools and cost drivers.

Expected activity for the four activity-based cost drivers that would be used are:

Machine hours	20,000
Material moves	1,600
Setups	2,500
Quality inspections	4,000

Required:

1. a. Determine the amount of overhead that would be allocated to the proposed job if direct labor hours is used as the volume-based cost driver.

EXERCISE 4 (continued)

b. Determine the total cost of the proposed job.

c. Determine the company's bid if the bid is based upon full manufacturing cost plus 20 percent.

2. a. Determine the amount of overhead that would be applied to the proposed project if activity-based cost drivers are used.

b. Determine the total cost of the proposed job if activity-based costing is used.

c. Determine the company's bid if activity-based costing is used and the bid is based upon full manufacturing cost plus 20 percent.

EXERCISE 4 (continued)

3. Prepare a memorandum to the plant manager with your recommendation regarding the bid the company should submit. Include the reasons for your recommendation as well as any supporting calculations. (See Appendix A: Guidelines for Memorandum Preparation.)

```
+--------------------------------------------------------------+
|                          MEMORANDUM                          |
|                                                              |
|        DATE:                                                 |
|          TO:                                                 |
|        FROM:                                                 |
|     SUBJECT:                                                 |
+--------------------------------------------------------------+
|                                                              |
|                                                              |
|                                                              |
|                                                              |
|                                                              |
|                                                              |
|                                                              |
|                                                              |
|                                                              |
|                                                              |
|                                                              |
|                                                              |
|                                                              |
|                                                              |
|                                                              |
|                                                              |
|                                                              |
|                                                              |
|                                                              |
|                                                              |
+--------------------------------------------------------------+
```

EXERCISE 4

1. **a.** Total overhead = $200,000 + $32,000 + $100,000 + $120,000
   = $452,000

   Overhead rate = $452,000/50,000 direct labor hours
   = $9.04 per direct labor hour

   Overhead assigned to proposed job = $9.04 x 1,000 direct labor hours
   = $9,040

   b. Total cost of proposed job:

Direct materials	$ 6,000
Direct labor	10,000
Overhead applied	9,040
Total cost	$25,040

   c. Company's bid = Full manufacturing cost x 120%
   = $25,040 x 120%
   = $30,048

2. **a.** Maintenance: $200,000/20,000 = $10 per machine hour
   Materials handling: $32,000/1,600 = $20 per move
   Setups: $100,000/2,500 = $40 per setup
   Inspection: $120,000/4,000 = $30 per inspection

   Overhead assigned to proposed job:

Maintenance ($10 x 500)	$5,000
Materials handling ($20 x 12)	240
Setups ($40 x 2)	80
Inspection ($30 x 10)	300
Total overhead assigned to job	$5,620

   b. Total cost of proposed project:

Direct materials	$ 6,000
Direct labor	10,000
Overhead applied	5,620
Total cost	$21,620

   c. Company's bid = Full manufacturing cost x 120%
   = $21,620 x 120%
   = $25,944

EXERCISE 4 (continued)

3. Your memorandum should contain the following:

   1. A brief introductory sentence to inform the reader of the purpose of the memorandum.

       Example: This memorandum regards the recommended bid price for proposed Job No. P902.

   2. A concise and specific recommendation.

       Example: I recommend that Hanover Manufacturing submit a bid of $25,944 for Job No. P902.

   3. A discussion of the reasons why your recommendation should be followed.

       Example: This bid price was developed using activity-based costing (ABC) because ABC produces more accurate product costs and more competitive bids.

   4. Supporting calculations included in the body of the memorandum or attached on a separate page.

       Example: The bid price of $25,944 was determined as follows:

Direct materials		$ 6,000
Direct labor		10,000
Overhead assigned:		
Maintenance: ($10 x 500)	$ 5,000	
Materials handling ($20 x 12)	240	
Setups ($40 x 2)	80	
Inspections ($30 x 10)	300	
Total overhead assigned to job		5,620
Total cost		$21,620
Markup		x 120%
Bid price		$25,944

   5. A closing sentence.

       Example: If you have any questions, please contact me at Extension 76.

CHAPTER 20

COST BEHAVIOR AND CVP ANALYSIS

CHAPTER REVIEW

COST-VOLUME-PROFIT (CVP) ANALYSIS

- Cost-volume-profit analysis enables a firm to determine the sales (in units or dollars) necessary to attain a desired level of profit. CVP analysis is useful in assessing the effect of operating changes (such as changes in selling price or operating costs) upon profit.

- Two approaches to CVP analysis are:
  1. the **units-sold approach**, which measures sales in number of units.
  2. the **sales revenue approach**, which measures sales in terms of dollars of sales revenue.

- The variable costing income statement is the basis for CVP analysis.

- Variable costing income is calculated as:

  Profit Before Taxes = Sales Revenues - Variable Expenses - Fixed Expenses

  or

  Profit Before Taxes = (Selling Price per Unit)(X) + (Variable Cost per Unit)(X) - Fixed Expenses

  where X = units sold

CVP ANALYSIS: UNITS-SOLD APPROACH

Break-Even Point

- The **break-even point** is the point where total revenues equal total expenses and profit equals zero. This can be expressed as:

  Total Revenue - Total Variable Costs - Total Fixed Costs = $0

  or

  Total Revenue = Total Variable Costs + Total Fixed Costs

- To determine how many units must be sold in order to break even, solve for X (the number of units) in the following equation:

$$\text{Total Revenue} = \text{Variable Costs} + \text{Fixed Costs}$$

$$(\text{Selling Price per Unit})(X) = (\text{Variable Cost per Unit})(X) + \text{Fixed Costs}$$

$$X = \frac{\text{Fixed Costs}}{\text{Sales Price Per Unit} - \text{Variable Cost Per Unit}}$$

$$X = \frac{\text{Fixed Costs}}{\text{Contribution Margin Per Unit}}$$

- **Contribution margin per unit** is calculated as:

$$\text{Contribution Margin Per Unit} = \text{Selling Price Per Unit} - \text{Variable Cost Per Unit}$$

Profit Targets

- In order to earn a desired profit, total revenues must equal variable costs, fixed costs <u>and</u> desired profit.

$$\text{Total Revenue} = \text{Total Variable Costs} + \text{Total Fixed Costs} + \text{Desired Profit}$$

- To determine how many units must be sold in order to earn a desired profit, solve for X (the number of units) in the following equation:

$$\text{Total Revenue} = \text{Total Variable Costs} + \text{Total Fixed Costs} + \text{Desired Profit}$$

$$(\text{Selling Price Per unit})(X) = (\text{Variable Cost Per Unit})(X) + \text{Total Fixed Costs} + \text{Desired Profit}$$

$$X = \frac{\text{Fixed Costs} + \text{Desired Profit}}{\text{Selling Price Per Unit} - \text{Variable Costs Per Unit}}$$

$$X = \frac{\text{Fixed Costs} + \text{Desired Profit}}{\text{Contribution Margin Per Unit}}$$

- After fixed costs are covered, the contribution margin per unit above break-even volume is profit per unit.

- CVP analysis can also be done on an after-tax basis.

- If a firm knows desired after-tax profit, desired before-tax profit can be calculated as follows:

    Before-Tax Desired Profit x (1 - Tax Rate) = After-Tax Desired Profit

    Before-Tax Desired Profit = After-Tax Desired Profit/(1 - Tax Rate)

- By substituting [(after-tax profit)/(1 - tax rate)] for before-tax profit into the equation for CVP analysis, the equation becomes:

$$X = \frac{\text{Fixed Costs} + [(\text{After-tax Profit})/(1 - \text{Tax Rate})]}{\text{Contribution Margin Per Unit}}$$

Pricing Decisions

- Two approaches can be used to evaluate the effects of different pricing decisions on profit:
  1. total cost approach
  2. incremental approach

- The total cost approach involves calculating profit under each alternative and then comparing total profit.

- The incremental approach involves calculating only the change that would occur for items on the variable costing income statement.

CVP ANALYSIS: SALES-REVENUE APPROACH

- Instead of using units sold as the measure of sales activity, managers might prefer to use sales revenue.

Break-Even Point

- Break even in units can be converted to break even in sales revenue as follows:

Sales Revenue at Break Even = Selling Price Per Unit x Unit Sales at Break Even

- Also, break even in sales dollars can be calculated using the following equation:

$$\text{Sales Revenue at Break Even} = \frac{\text{Fixed Costs}}{\text{Contribution Margin Ratio}}$$

- The contribution margin ratio is the proportion of each sales dollar available to cover fixed costs and provide for profit.

- The contribution margin ratio can be calculated in three different ways:

  1. Contribution Margin Ratio = Total Contribution Margin/Total Revenues
  2. Contribution Margin Ratio = Contribution Margin per Unit/Selling Price per Unit
  3. Contribution Margin Ratio = 1 - Variable Cost Ratio

- The **variable cost ratio** is the proportion of each sales dollar that must be used to cover variable costs.

Variable Cost Ratio = Variable Costs/Sales Revenue

Profit Target

- Sales dollars necessary to earn a desired profit can be calculated as:

$$\text{Sales Revenue} = \frac{\text{Fixed Costs + Desired Profit}}{\text{Contribution Margin Ratio}}$$

GRAPHICAL REPRESENTATION OF CVP RELATIONSHIPS

The Profit-Volume Graph

- The **profit-volume graph** is a graphical portrayal of the relationship between profit and sales volume.

- The profit-volume graph is the graph of the linear equation:

$$I = PX - VX - F$$

where I = dependent variable (measured along the vertical axis)
X = independent variable (measured along the horizontal axis)

610

The Cost-Volume-Profit Graph

- The **cost-volume-profit graph** depicts the relationships among cost, volume, and profits. It contains a total revenue line and a total cost line.

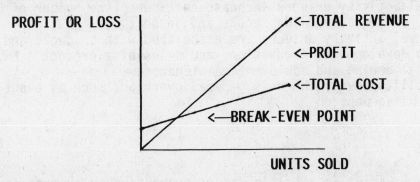

- The point where the total revenue line and the total cost line intersect is the break-even point.

LIMITATIONS OF CVP ANALYSIS

- Limitations of CVP analysis include:
  1. The analysis assumes a linear revenue function and a linear cost function.
  2. The analysis assumes that units produced are sold.
  3. The analysis assumes that fixed and variable costs can be accurately identified.
  4. The selling prices and costs are assumed to be known with certainty.

COST BEHAVIOR

- **Cost behavior** describes how a cost behaves or changes when the activity level changes. For example, a fixed cost remains the same, in total, as activity changes. A variable cost varies, in total, as activity changes.

- Three cost behavior patterns are:
  1. variable costs
  2. fixed costs
  3. mixed costs

- Determining whether a cost is fixed or variable depends on the time horizon. For example, in the long run, all costs are variable.

Activity-Level Measures

- Variable costs change, in total, with changes in <u>activity level</u>.

- Activity cost drivers are causal factors that explain the consumption of activities.

- Activity cost drivers fall into four categories.
  1. **Unit-level activity drivers** increase costs every time a unit is produced. Examples include direct materials and power to run the production equipment.
  2. **Batch-level activity drivers** increase costs when the number of batches increases. Examples include setups and inspections.
  3. **Product-level activity drivers** are associated with products and pertain to development, production, and sales of a product. Examples include engineering and equipment maintenance.
  4. At the **facility level**, there is general overhead, such as plant security and plant management.

Variable Costs

- A variable cost <u>varies in total</u> in direct proportion to changes in an activity cost driver. For example, if a unit-level activity cost driver is used and production increased 30 percent, total variable costs would increase 30 percent.

- The variable cost <u>per unit of activity remains constant</u>.

- Total variable cost is calculated as follows.

Total Variable Cost = Variable Cost Per Unit of Activity x Activity Level of Cost Driver

Fixed Costs

- Fixed costs remain <u>constant in total</u> during a specified period of time and within a relevant range of activity.

- The relevant range refers to the relatively wide span of output where fixed costs are expected to remain the same.

- To increase activity beyond a certain point (outside the relevant range), it may be necessary to incur additional fixed costs. For example, a company may incur $10,000 per year in rent for production levels up to 5,000 units. Beyond 5,000 units, the company would have to rent additional facilities.

- Fixed costs <u>in total remain constant</u>, but fixed costs <u>per unit of activity vary</u>.

Mixed Costs

- **Mixed costs** contain both fixed and variable components.

- A cost function can be used to estimate total mixed costs at different levels of activity.

- For example, if an equipment lease specified annual payments of $10,000 plus $2.00 per hour of machine usage, the cost function to estimate the total mixed cost at different activity levels would be:

$$\text{Total Mixed Cost} = \$10,000 + \$2.00X$$

where X = the number of hours the machine is used

- Because accounting records typically reveal only the total cost and the associated activity of a mixed cost item, it is necessary to decompose the total cost into its fixed and variable components.

METHODS FOR SEPARATING MIXED COSTS INTO FIXED AND VARIABLE COMPONENTS

- Three widely used methods for separating a mixed cost into fixed and variable components are:
  1. the high-low method
  2. the scatterplot method
  3. the method of least squares

- Each method assumes a linear cost relationship.

- Mixed costs can be estimated using the following equation for a straight line:

$$Y = F + VX$$

where:
Y = Total mixed cost (the dependent variable)
F = Fixed cost (the intercept parameter)
V = Variable cost per unit of activity (the slope parameter)
X = Activity level (the independent variable)

- Y (total cost) is called the dependent variable because it is dependent on the value of another variable, the activity level.

- The **intercept** of the line (where the line intersects the vertical or cost axis) is an estimate of the fixed cost component (F).

- The **slope** of the line is an estimate of the variable cost per unit of activity (V).

- A major goal of cost behavior analysis is to develop cost functions so costs can be estimated at various levels of activity.

The High-Low Method

- The high-low method uses two points (the high activity level and the low activity level) to determine the cost formula.

- The slope or variable cost per unit of activity is calculated as:

$$\text{Variable Cost Per Unit of Activity} = \frac{\text{Change in Cost Between High Point and Low Point}}{\text{Change in Activity Between High Point and Low Point}}$$

- Total variable costs can be calculated for different activity levels as follows:

$$\text{Total Variable Costs} = \text{Variable Cost Per Unit of Activity} \times \text{Activity Level}$$

- The fixed cost component is calculated as:

$$\text{Fixed Costs} = \text{Total Mixed Cost at High Point} - \text{Total Variable Costs at High Point}$$

or

$$\text{Fixed Costs} = \text{Total Mixed Cost at Low Point} - \text{Total Variable Costs at Low Point}$$

- The cost formula for total costs is:

$$\text{Total Cost} = \text{Total Fixed Cost} + (\text{Variable Cost Per Unit of Activity} \times \text{Activity Level})$$

- Weaknesses of the high-low method include:
  1. The method uses only two observations to develop the cost formula, and those two points could be outliers (points that do not represent typical cost-activity relationships). It is important that the high and low levels of activity used are representative of the general cost-activity pattern.
  2. The high-low method would not detect if the cost behavior is curvilinear rather than linear.

- The scatterplot method assists in determining if the high-low method produces acceptable results.

Scatterplot Method

- A **scattergraph** contains a vertical axis indicating the mixed cost being analyzed (the dependent variable) and a horizontal axis indicating the activity level (the independent variable). Past cost observations are plotted on the scattergraph.

- One purpose of the scattergraph is to see if there is a linear relationship. Also, the scattergraph may reveal points (observations) that do not seem to fit the general pattern of behavior (outliers) and perhaps should be eliminated.

- The scatterplot method involves visually fitting a line to the points on the scattergraph by selecting two points on the scattergraph that seem to best represent the relationship between cost and activity.

- The two points are used to determine:
1. the intercept
2. the slope of the line

- The slope or variable cost per unit of activity is calculated as:

$$\text{Variable Cost Per Unit of Activity} = \frac{\text{Change in Cost Between Point 1 and Point 2}}{\text{Change in Activity Between Point 1 and Point 2}}$$

- Total variable costs can be calculated for different activity levels as follows:

$$\text{Total Variable Costs} = \text{Variable Cost Per Unit of Activity} \times \text{Activity Level}$$

- The fixed cost component is calculated as:

$$\text{Fixed Costs} = \text{Total Mixed Cost at Point 1} - \text{Total Variable Costs at Point 1}$$

or

$$\text{Fixed Costs} = \text{Total Mixed Cost at Point 2} - \text{Total Variable Costs at Point 2}$$

- The cost formula for total costs is:

$$\text{Total Cost} = \text{Total Fixed Cost} + (\text{Variable Cost Per Unit of Activity} \times \text{Activity Level})$$

- The difference between the high-low method and the scatterplot method is the way the two points used in computing the cost formula are selected.

The Method of Least Squares

- The method of least squares is a statistical method for mathematically deriving a line that best fits a set of data.

- The **best fitting line** is one that minimizes the differences between the cost predicted by the cost formula (the line) and actual cost observations.

- **Deviation** is the difference between the cost predicted by a cost formula and the actual cost. It measures the distance of a data point (actual cost) from the cost line (predicted cost).

- The formula used to predict costs is the formula for a straight-line:

$$Y = F + VX$$

- The method of least squares arrives at values for F (fixed costs) and V (variable cost per unit of activity) that result in a line that fits the points (cost observations) better than any other line.

- The formulas to calculate V and F are:

$$V = [\Sigma XY - \Sigma X\Sigma Y/n]/[\Sigma X^2 - (\Sigma X)^2/n]$$

$$F = \Sigma Y/n - V(\Sigma X/n)$$

  where: n = number of cost observations
          X = actual activity associated with actual cost observations
          Y = actual cost observations

- To compute V and F, five inputs are needed:
  1. n   (the number of observations)
  2. ΣX (the sum of the actual activity levels associated with actual cost observations)
  3. ΣY (the sum of the actual cost observations)
  4. ΣXY (the sum of actual cost observations multiplied by actual activity levels)
  5. ΣX^2 (the sum of squared actual cost observations)

- Although the scatterplot method, the high-low method, and managerial judgment involve simpler calculations, the method of least squares produces a line that best fits the points (cost observations) on a scattergraph. (Calculators and software packages are available that perform the calculations for the method of least squares.)

KEY TERMS TEST

Test your recall of the key terms as follows: Read the following definitions of key terms and try to recall as many key terms as you can **without assistance**. Write your answers in the spaces provided. If you need assistance, refer to the list of key terms at the end of this section.

1. The _____ _____ _____ is calculated as variable costs divided by sales revenue.

2. The _____ _____ depends on the value of another variable.

3. The _____ _____ _____ is calculated as contribution margin divided by sales revenue.

616

4. The point where total sales revenue equals total costs is called the
_____ _____. It is the point of zero profits.

5. The _____ _____ is a method of fitting a line
to a set of data points using the high and low points in the data set.
For a cost formula, the high and low points represent the high and low
activity levels. This method is used to estimate the fixed and variable
components of a mixed cost.

6. The _____ _____ does not depend on the value of
another variable.

7. The _____ _____ is a method for fitting a line to a set of
data using two points that are selected by judgment. This method is used
to estimate the fixed and variable components of a mixed cost.

8. A(n) _____ _____ depicts the relationships among costs,
volume, and profits.

9. The line that minimizes the differences between the cost predicted by the
cost formula (the line) and actual cost observations is called the
_____ _____.

10. The _____ _____ is the point where the cost formula intercepts
the vertical axis.

11. The _____ _____ _____ _____ is a statistical
method for finding a line that best fits a set of data. It is used to
break out the fixed and variable components of a mixed cost.

12. A _____ is a plot of past cost observations at different
activity levels.

13. The _____ _____ is the variable cost per unit of activity,
represented by V in the cost formula $Y = F + VX$.

14. A(n) _____ _____ is a linear function, $Y = F + VX$.

15. _____ is the difference between the cost predicted by a cost
formula and the actual cost.

KEY TERMS:

best-fitting line
break-even point
contribution margin ratio
cost formula
cost-volume-profit graph
dependent variable
deviation
high-low method

independent variable
intercept parameter
method of least squares
scattergraph
scatterplot method
slope parameter
variable cost ratio

**Compare your answers to those at the end of the chapter and review any key
terms missed.**

Write your answers in the spaces provided.

1. Cost-volume-profit analysis enables a firm to determine _____ necessary to attain a desired level of _____.

2. Two approaches to CVP analysis are:
   1. the _____ approach, which measures sales in _____.
   2. the _____ approach, which measures sales in _____.

3. Variable costing income is calculated as follows:

   Sales

   - _____

   = _____

   - _____

   = Income

4. Break even in Units = _____ / _____

5. Sales Revenue at Break Even = _____ / _____

6. Before-Tax Profit = _____ / _____

Circle the single best answer.

7. Break even is the point where: (a) revenue equals variable manufacturing costs; (b) revenue equals variable manufacturing and variable selling and administrative costs; (c) revenue equals variable and fixed manufacturing costs; (d) revenue equals all variable and fixed costs

8. The contribution margin ratio equals: (a) revenue minus variable costs; (b) variable costs divided by revenue; (c) contribution margin divided by revenue; (d) variable costs divided by contribution margin

9. Limitations of CVP analysis include all of the following except: (a) a nonlinear revenue function and a nonlinear cost function; (b) what is produced is sold; (c) selling prices and costs are known with certainty; (d) costs can be separated into fixed and variable components

Use the following information to answer the next six questions.

Selling price per unit	$100
Variable manufacturing costs per unit	$20
Fixed manufacturing costs per unit	$30
Variable selling costs per unit	$25
Fixed selling costs per unit	$10
Expected production and sales	1,000 units

10. Contribution margin per unit is: (a) $15; (b) $50; (c) $55; (d) $80

11. The contribution margin ratio is: (a) 15%; (b) 45%; (c) 50%; (d) 55%

12. Break even for the product (rounded to the nearest whole unit) is:
(a) 727 units; (b) 888 units; (c) 1,000 units; (d) 1,500 units

13. If the firm wants to earn $70,000 in before-tax profit, sales revenue
must equal: (a) $60,500; (b) $110,000; (c) $200,000; (d) $244,444

14. If the firm wants to earn $70,000 in before-tax profit, contribution
margin must equal: (a) $98,000; (b) $110,000; (c) $125,000; (d) $155,000

15. If the tax rate is 40 percent, how many units must be sold to earn an
after-tax profit of $60,000? (a) 4,000; (b) 1,500; (c) 2,640; (d) 2,546

16. Cost behavior patterns include: (a) variable costs; (b) fixed costs;
(c) step costs; (d) mixed costs; (e) all of the above

17. Fixed costs: (a) remain the same in total; (b) vary per unit; (c) remain
constant per unit; (d) vary in total; (e) a and b; (f) c and d

18. Variable costs: (a) remain the same in total; (b) vary per unit;
(c) remain constant per unit; (d) vary in total; (e) a and b; (f) c and d

19. A car lease that specified a $100 fee per month plus $0.30 per mile would
be an example of a: (a) fixed cost; (b) variable cost; (c) mixed cost;
(d) step cost

20. Supervisors' salaries of $3,000 per month would be an example of a:
(a) fixed cost; (b) variable cost; (c) mixed cost; (d) step cost

21. Direct materials is an example of: (a) a fixed cost; (b) a variable cost;
(c) mixed costs; (d) step costs

22. The independent variable (activity) selected should have a high degree of
correlation with the dependent variable (cost) as indicated by a
coefficient of determination: (a) close to -1; (b) close to +1; (c) equal
to 0; (d) none of the above

Use the following information to answer the next three questions.

The following information was collected regarding maintenance costs at different activity levels measured in machine hours:

Number of Machine Hours	Total Maintenance Costs
8,000	$600,000
10,000	640,000
11,000	800,000
9,000	700,000
14,000	900,000
12,000	870,000

23. Using the high-low method, an estimate of the variable component for maintenance costs is: (a) $50.00; (b) $52.50; (c) $64.28; (d) $75.00
24. Using the high-low method, an estimate of the fixed component for maintenance costs is: (a) $165,000; (b) $200,000; (c) $224,000; (d) $300,000

25. Using the cost formula developed using the high-low method, the estimate of maintenance costs if 13,000 machine hours are scheduled for next month would be: (a) $650,000; (b) $950,000; (c) $850,000; (d) $882,000

Use the following information to answer the next three questions.

The method of least squares produced the following computer printout using direct labor hours as the activity.

Intercept	20,318.00
Slope	42.00

26. The estimate of the variable component for maintenance costs is: (a) $37.80; (b) $42.00; (c) $46.67; (d) $47.00

27. The estimate of the fixed component for maintenance costs is: (a) $18,286; (b) $20,276; (c) $20,318; (d) $20,360

28. If 5,000 machine hours are scheduled, an estimate of maintenance costs is: (a) $253,318; (b) $230,726; (c) $230,360; (d) $230,318

Compare your answers to those at the end of the chapter and review any questions missed.

EXERCISES

EXERCISE 1

AAH, Inc., manufactures a product that sells for $50. The variable costs per unit are:

Direct materials	$15
Direct labor	5
Variable manufacturing overhead	4

During 1995, the budgeted fixed manufacturing overhead is estimated to be $500,000, and budgeted fixed selling, general and administrative costs are expected to be $300,000. Variable selling costs are $6 per unit.

Required:

1. Determine the break-even point in units.

2. Determine the number of units that must be sold to earn $100,000 in profit before taxes.

3. What dollar amount of sales must be attained in order to earn $300,000 in profit before taxes?

4. If there is a 40 percent tax rate, determine the sales level in dollars that must be attained in order to generate an after-tax profit of $300,000.

EXERCISE 2

The Anton Company has developed the following income statement using a contribution margin format.

ANTON COMPANY
PROJECTED INCOME STATEMENT
FOR THE YEAR ENDING DECEMBER 31, 1995

Revenues		$200,000
Variable costs:		
Variable manufacturing costs	$60,000	
Variable selling costs	20,000	
Total variable costs		80,000
Contribution margin		$120,000
Fixed costs:		
Fixed manufacturing costs	$80,000	
Fixed selling, general and administrative costs	25,000	
Total fixed costs		105,000
Income		$ 15,000

The projected income statement was based upon sales of 10,000 units. Anton has the capacity to produce 15,000 units during the year.

Each of the following questions is independent of the others.

Required:

1. Determine the break-even point in units.

EXERCISE 2 (continued)

2. The sales manager believes the company could increase sales by 1,000
    units if advertising expenditures are increased by $16,000. Should the
    company increase advertising expenditures?

3. What is the maximum amount the company could pay for advertising if the
    advertising would increase sales by 1,000 units?

4. Management believes that by lowering the selling price to $17 per unit,
    the company can increase sales by 2,000 units. Based upon these
    estimates, would it be profitable for the company to lower its selling
    price?

AMK, Inc., believes their electricity costs are affected by the number of machine hours worked. Machine hours and electricity costs for 1995 were as follows:

Month	Machine Hours	Electricity Cost
January	1,500	$18,400
February	1,400	18,300
March	1,300	17,800
April	1,900	22,000
May	1,700	20,200
June	1,550	18,700
July	1,200	17,600
August	1,600	19,000
September	1,100	17,510
October	2,000	22,500
November	2,100	23,000
December	2,200	24,000

Required:

1. Using the high-low method, develop the cost function for monthly electricity cost.

2. Estimate total electricity cost for a month in which 1,800 machine hours are worked.

3. What are the weaknesses of the high-low method?

624

EXERCISE 4

The Koch Company incurred the following maintenance costs during the past six months:

Month	Machine Hours	Maintenance Cost
January	120,000	$456,000
February	100,000	420,000
March	140,000	492,000
April	160,000	528,000
May	130,000	474,000
June	90,000	402,000

Required:

1. Using the scatterplot method, the two points that seem to best represent the relationship between cost and activity are the activity levels of 100,000 and 140,000 machine hours. Using these two points, estimate the fixed and variable components of maintenance costs.

2. Develop a cost function that the Koch Company can use to estimate maintenance cost at different volume levels.

3. Estimate maintenance cost for July if the company expects to use 110,000 machine hours.

EXERCISE 5

Teddy Industries made the following observations of supply costs at different production volume levels:

Month	Supply Cost	Production (Units)
January	$ 960	420
February	1,060	580
March	1,180	760
April	980	480
May	840	380
June	900	400
July	1,120	620
August	1,260	840
September	1,200	800
October	1,360	900
November	1,160	720
December	1,040	540

Required:

1. Using the method of least squares, develop an estimate of total fixed costs and variable cost per unit. (Round your estimate of variable cost per unit to two decimal places.)

2. Develop a cost function to estimate supply cost at different volume levels, and then estimate supply cost if production is expected to be 700 units.

EXERCISE 6

Hentze Dental Center currently charges $20 per dental exam. A new company that recently located near the dental center asked if Hentze would be interested in providing dental services to their employees at a special rate of $15 per exam.

The dentists have agreed to offer the exams at the reduced fee if the $15 would cover the variable costs of the exam.

The dental center's accountant provided the following information about exams during the first six months of the year:

	Number of Exams	Total Cost of Exams
January	120	$1,850
February	150	2,020
March	110	1,600
April	140	1,960
May	100	1,450
June	80	1,200

Required:

1. Using the least squares method, determine the variable cost per dental exam.

EXERCISE 6 (continued)

2. Will the $15 reduced fee cover the dental center's variable cost of providing the dental exam?

3. Develop a cost function that can be used to estimate total exam costs at different activity levels.

4. If a total of 200 exams are expected to be performed in July, what would be the total expected cost of performing the 200 exams?

5. If 50 additional exams are performed each month at the special rate:

   a. What would be the incremental revenue resulting from the 50 exams?

   b. What would be the incremental cost of providing the 50 exams?

   c. What would be the incremental profit that would result from providing the 50 exams at the reduced rate?

EXERCISE 7

In order to better predict setup costs, the plant manager has asked the computer center to use the least squares method to generate a printout for use in estimating setup costs.

The following computer printout was generated and given to the plant manager.

Intercept	150.00
Slope	10.00
Correlation Coefficient	.98
Activity Variable	Number of setups

The plant manager brought the printout to you and said, "How am I supposed to use this to estimate setup costs? This printout is worthless!"

Required:

1. Explain how the printout information can be used to estimate setup costs.

2. Estimate setup costs if 30 setups are expected next month.

```
┌─────────────────────────────────────────────────────────────────┐
║  ANSWERS                                                          ║
└─────────────────────────────────────────────────────────────────┘
```

KEY TERMS TEST
1. variable cost ratio
2. dependent variable
3. contribution margin ratio
4. break-even point
5. high-low method
6. independent variable
7. scatterplot method
8. cost-volume-profit graph
9. best-fitting line
10. intercept parameter
11. method of least squares
12. scattergraph
13. slope parameter
14. cost formula
15. Deviation

CHAPTER QUIZ
1. sales, profit
2. units-sold, number of units, sales-revenue, dollars of sales revenue
3. Variable costs, Contribution margin, Fixed costs
4. Fixed Costs, Contribution Margin per Unit
5. Fixed Costs, Contribution Margin Ratio
6. After-tax Profit, (1 - Tax Rate)
7. d
8. c
9. a
10. c $100 - ($20 + $25) = $55
11. d $55/$100 = 55%
12. a ($30 + $10) x 1,000 = $40,000; $40,000/$55 = 727
13. c ($40,000 + $70,000)/55% = $200,000
14. b ($30 x 1,000) + ($10 x 1,000) + $70,000 = $110,000
15. d [$40,000 + ($60,000/(1 - .40))]/$55 = 2,546
16. e
17. e
18. f
19. c
20. a
21. b
22. b
23. a ($900,000 - $600,000)/(14,000 - 8,000) = $50
24. b $900,000 - ($50 x 14,000) = $200,000
25. c $200,000 + ($50 x 13,000) = $850,000
26. b
27. c
28. d $20,318 + ($42 x 5,000) = $230,318

630
```
```

EXERCISE 1

1.
$$\text{Break Even in Units} = \frac{\text{Fixed Costs}}{\text{Contribution Margin Per Unit}}$$

$$= \frac{\$800,000*}{\$20.00**}$$

$$= 40,000 \text{ units}$$

*Total fixed costs:

Budgeted fixed manufacturing overhead	$500,000
Budgeted fixed selling, general & administrative	300,000
Total fixed costs	$800,000

**Contribution margin per unit:

Selling price per unit		$50.00
Variable costs per unit:		
Direct materials	$15.00	
Direct labor	5.00	
Variable manufacturing overhead	4.00	
Variable selling costs	6.00	30.00
Contribution margin per unit		$20.00

2. Unit sales necessary to earn $100,000 in before-tax profit:

$$\text{Units} = \frac{\text{Fixed Costs} + \text{Desired Profit}}{\text{Contribution Margin Per Unit}}$$

$$= \frac{\$800,000 + \$100,000}{\$20.00}$$

$$= 45,000 \text{ units}$$

3. Sales dollars necessary to earn before-tax profit of $300,000:

$$\text{Sales Dollars} = \frac{\text{Fixed Costs} + \text{Desired Profit}}{\text{Contribution Margin Percentage}}$$

$$= \frac{\$800,000 + \$300,000}{40\%*}$$

$$= \$2,750,000$$

*Contribution margin percentage = $20.00/$50.00 = 40%

631

EXERCISE 1 (continued)

4. Sales dollars necessary to earn an after-tax profit of $300,000:

$$\text{Sales Dollars} = \frac{\text{Fixed Costs} + [\text{After-Tax Profit}/(1 - \text{Tax Rate})]}{\text{Contribution Margin Percentage}}$$

$$= \frac{\$800,000 + (\$300,000/.60)}{40\%}$$

$$= \frac{\$800,000 + \$500,000}{40\%}$$

$$= \$3,250,000$$

EXERCISE 2

1.

$$\text{Break Even in Units} = \frac{\text{Fixed Costs}}{\text{Contribution Margin Per Unit}}$$

$$= \frac{\$105,000}{\$12^*}$$

$$= 8,750 \text{ units}$$

*Contribution margin per unit:

Selling price per unit ($200,000/10,000)		$20
Variable cost per unit:		
Variable manufacturing costs ($60,000/10,000)	$6	
Variable selling costs ($20,000/10,000)	2	
Total variable cost per unit		8
Contribution margin per unit		$12

2. For this alternative to be profitable, the contribution margin from the additional sales of 1,000 units must at least cover the additional advertising expenditure.

Incremental contribution margin from 1,000 units ($12 x 1,000 units)	$12,000
Less: Incremental advertising expenditures	16,000
Decrease in income	($ 4,000)

632

EXERCISE 2 (continued)

To verify the effect on income, a new income statement that considers the effects on sales and costs could be prepared.

ANTON COMPANY
PROJECTED INCOME STATEMENT
FOR THE YEAR ENDING DECEMBER 31, 1995

Revenues (11,000 x $20)		$220,000
Variable costs:		
Variable manufacturing costs (11,000 x $6)	$66,000	
Variable selling costs (11,000 x $2)	22,000	
Total variable costs		88,000
Contribution margin		$132,000
Fixed costs:		
Fixed manufacturing costs	$80,000	
Fixed selling, general & administrative costs ($25,000 + $16,000)	41,000	
Total fixed costs		121,000
Income		$ 11,000

The Anton Company's income would decrease from $15,000 to $11,000 if the advertising expenditures were made.

3. The maximum amount the company could pay for additional advertising in order to sell 1,000 more units would be $12,000.

Additional contribution margin from 1,000 units	$12,000
Less: Additional advertising expenditures	12,000
Effect on income	$ -0-

The company also might want to consider the reliability of the estimates and the effect that advertising might have on sales in later periods.

EXERCISE 2 (continued)

4. A projected income statement based upon a $17 selling price and sales of 12,000 units follows:

ANTON COMPANY
PROJECTED INCOME STATEMENT
FOR THE YEAR ENDED DECEMBER 31, 1995

Revenues (12,000 units x $17)		$204,000
Variable costs:		
Variable manufacturing costs (12,000 x $6)	$72,000	
Variable selling costs (12,000 x $2)	24,000	96,000
Contribution margin		$108,000
Fixed costs:		
Fixed manufacturing costs	$80,000	
Fixed selling, general & administrative costs	25,000	105,000
Income		$ 3,000

If the company lowers its selling price to $17 and sells 2,000 more units, income will decrease from $15,000 to $3,000.

EXERCISE 3

1.

$$\text{Variable Cost Per Machine Hour} = \frac{\text{Difference in Total Cost}}{\text{Difference in High \& Low Levels of Activity}}$$

$$= \frac{\$24,000 - \$17,510}{2,200 - 1,100} = \frac{\$6,490}{1,100} = \$5.90$$

Total Cost at High Activity - Variable Cost at High Activity = Fixed Cost

$$\$24,000 - (\$5.90)(2,200) = \$11,020$$

Cost Function for Electricity Cost = $11,020 + $5.90X

where X = machine hours

EXERCISE 3 (continued)

2. Total Electricity Cost
   at 1,800 Machine Hours = $11,020 + ($5.90 x 1,800 machine hours)

   = $11,020 + $10,620

   = $21,640

3. Weaknesses of the high-low method include:
   1. The method uses only two points to develop the cost function, and the two points used must be representative of normal operations.
   2. The method does not detect if the cost behavior is curvilinear.

EXERCISE 4

1.

$$\text{Variable Cost Per Machine Hour} = \frac{\text{Difference in Total Cost}}{\text{Difference in Levels of Activity}}$$

$$= \frac{\$492,000 - \$420,000}{140,000 - 100,000}$$

$$= \frac{\$72,000}{40,000}$$

$$= \$1.80 \text{ per machine hour}$$

Total Cost at 140,000 Machine Hours	−	Variable Cost at 140,000 Machine Hours	= Fixed Cost
$492,000	−	($1.80 x 140,000)	= $240,000

2. Cost Function for Maintenance Cost = $240,000 + $1.80X

   where X = machine hours

3.

   Maintenance Cost at 110,000 Machine Hours = $240,000 + $1.80X
   = $240,000 + ($1.80 x 110,000)
   = $438,000

EXERCISE 5

1. Method of least squares:

Month	Units X	Cost Y	XY	X²
January	420	960	403200	176400
February	580	1060	614800	336400
March	760	1180	896800	577600
April	480	980	470400	230400
May	380	840	319200	144400
June	400	900	360000	160000
July	620	1120	694400	384400
August	840	1260	1058400	705600
September	800	1200	960000	640000
October	900	1360	1224000	810000
November	720	1160	835200	518400
December	540	1040	561600	291600
Totals	7440	13060	8398000	4975200

$$v = (\Sigma XY - \Sigma X \Sigma Y/n)/(\Sigma X^2 - (\Sigma X)^2/n)$$
$$= [8,398,000 - (7,440 \times 13,060/12)]/[4,975,200 - (7,440^2/12)]$$
$$= 300,800/362,400$$
$$= .83$$

The slope of the regression line and an estimate of the variable supply cost per unit is $0.83.

$$F = (\Sigma Y/n - v\Sigma X/n)$$
$$= [13,060/12 - (0.83 \times 7,440/12)]$$
$$= 573.73$$

The estimate of total fixed costs is $573.73.

The regression line equation is: Y = $573.73 + $0.83X

2. The cost function for supply cost would be:

$$\text{Total Monthly Supply Cost} = \$573.73 + \$0.83X$$

where X = the number of units

An estimate of supply cost at 700 units of production would be:

$$\text{Total Monthly Supply Cost} = \$573.73 + (\$0.83 \times 700 \text{ Units})$$
$$= \$573.73 + \$581$$
$$= \$1,154.73$$

EXERCISE 6

1.

Month	Units X	Cost Y	XY	X²
January	120	1850	222000	14400
February	150	2020	303000	22500
March	110	1600	176000	12100
April	140	1960	274400	19600
May	100	1450	145000	10000
June	80	1200	96000	6400
Totals	700	10080	1216400	85000

$$v = (\Sigma XY - \Sigma X \Sigma Y/n)/(\Sigma X^2 - (\Sigma X)^2/n)$$
$$= [1{,}216{,}400 - (700 \times 10{,}080/6)]/(85{,}000 - 700^2/6)$$
$$= 40{,}400/3{,}333.33$$
$$= 12.12$$

The slope of the regression line and an estimate of the variable cost per dental exam is $12.12.

2. Yes, the $15 reduced fee would cover the center's variable cost of $12.12 per exam.

3.
$$F = (\Sigma Y/n - v\Sigma X/n)$$
$$= [10{,}080/6 - (12.12 \times 700/6)]$$
$$= 266$$

The estimate of total fixed costs is $266.
The regression line equation is: Y = $266 + $12.12X

4. An estimate of costs for 200 dental exams would be:

$$Y = \$266 + (\$12.12 \times 200)$$
$$= \$2{,}690$$

5.a. Incremental Revenue = Special Rate x Additional Exams
$$= \$15 \times 50$$
$$= \$750$$

b. Incremental Cost = Variable Cost Per Exam x Additional Exams
$$= \$12.12 \times 50$$
$$= \$606$$

c. Incremental Profit = Incremental Revenue - Incremental Cost
$$= \$750 - \$606$$
$$= \$144$$

EXERCISE 7

1. If the intercept is within the relevant range, it is an estimate of total fixed costs.

   The slope is an estimate of variable costs.

   The printout information can be used to develop the following cost function to estimate setup costs at different activity levels.

$$\text{Total Setup Costs} = \$150 + \$10X$$

   where X = the number of setups

2.

$$\text{Total Setup Costs} = \$150 + (\$10 \times 30)$$
$$= \$450$$

CHAPTER 21

RELEVANT COSTS FOR SPECIAL DECISIONS INCLUDING SEGMENT ANALYSIS

CHAPTER REVIEW

RELEVANT COSTS

- Relevant costs:
  1. are future costs.
  2. differ among the alternatives.

- An irrelevant cost can be:
  1. a past cost or
  2. a future cost that does not differ among the alternatives being considered.

- Although past costs are never relevant, they are often used to predict what future costs will be.

- A **sunk cost** is a cost for which the outlay has already been made. Sunk costs are the result of past decisions and cannot be changed by current or future action. After sunk costs are incurred, they are unavoidable.

- Since sunk costs are past costs that do not differ among the alternatives, sunk costs are irrelevant costs.

- The acquisition cost of equipment purchased in the past is a sunk cost.

- <u>Depreciation</u> of equipment acquired in the past is an allocation of a past cost; therefore, depreciation of equipment already purchased is irrelevant.

- Allocations of common fixed costs are irrelevant if <u>total</u> common fixed costs do not differ among the alternatives.

DECISION-MAKING APPROACH

- The six steps in the decision-making process are as follows:
  1. Define the problem.
  2. Identify alternatives as possible solutions to the problem.
  3. Eliminate alternatives that are not feasible.
  4. Identify the relevant costs and benefits associated with each feasible alternative.
  5. Eliminate irrelevant costs and benefits from consideration.
  6. Express all relevant costs and benefits on a periodically recurring basis.
  7. Total the relevant costs and benefits for each alternative.
  8. Select the alternative with the greatest overall benefit.

639

RELEVANT COST APPLICATIONS

Make-or-Buy Decisions

- A **make-or-buy decision** involves deciding whether a product or component should be manufactured by the firm itself or acquired from another firm.

- The relevant costs of a make-or-buy analysis consist of the following avoidable costs:
  1. the variable costs associated with producing the product: direct materials, direct labor, and variable overhead
  2. avoidable fixed overhead

- The relevant (avoidable) costs of manufacturing the product are then compared to the outside supplier's price. The firm cannot afford to pay more to an outside supplier than it saves (avoids) by not manufacturing the component.

Other Uses of Capacity

- If the firm buys the component from an outside supplier, other uses of the manufacturing facilities may be possible, such as producing a different product.

- If the firm continues to produce the original component instead of buying it from an outside supplier, there is an opportunity cost associated with this choice: the firm foregoes the opportunity to produce a new product.

  The cost of foregoing this opportunity is the contribution margin lost by not producing the new product.

Short-Run Analysis

- If the firm can eliminate machinery and equipment as a result of buying a component from a supplier, there is an opportunity cost involved.

- If the firm continues to manufacture the component, the firm foregoes the opportunity to sell the machinery and equipment, invest the proceeds, and earn a return.

- If the alternative of making a component requires the acquisition of machinery and equipment, then it is a long-run investment decision rather than a short-run decision.

- Since long-run alternatives extend beyond one year, the time value of money must also be considered. The future cash flows must be discounted to determine their value in the present.

Qualitative Factors

• Qualitative factors are factors that cannot be quantified.

• Qualitative factors that should be considered are:
  1. How does the quality of the supplier's component compare to the quality of the component manufactured by the firm?
  2. Is the supplier reliable in terms of providing the needed quantities of the component on a timely basis?

Keep-or-Drop Decisions

• Keep-or-drop decisions concern whether to discontinue segments of an organization, such as the shoe department in a clothing store. Segments can be a product line or a territory.

• The analysis of dropping a segment relies upon the concept of relevant or avoidable costs.

• Based solely on quantitative factors, the segment should be kept if it contributes incremental profit.

• Incremental profit is determined by comparing the segment's revenues with avoidable costs associated with the segment.

• The loss in sales of other segments as a result of closing down a complementary segment should also be considered.

Keep-or-Drop Decisions with Alternative Use of Facilities

• If the space and resources used by the current segment could be used by another segment, an opportunity cost is involved.

• If the firm keeps the current segment, it foregoes the incremental profit generated by the other segment.

• If the incremental profit generated by the other segment exceeds the incremental profit generated by the current segment, then the current segment should be dropped (assuming all other factors are equal).

Special-Order Decisions

• A special order is a large order from a buyer usually seeking a quantity discount. Generally, the product is the same or similar to the firm's regular products.

- If there is excess capacity, the minimum acceptable price must cover the incremental costs associated with the special order:
  1. variable costs
     - direct materials
     - direct labor
     - variable overhead
  2. incremental fixed costs (out-of-pocket costs)

- If the firm is operating at full capacity, no additional production can occur without eliminating something that is currently being produced.

- Thus, if the firm accepts the special order, it foregoes the opportunity to produce and sell some of its regular products.

- When the firm is at full capacity, the minimum acceptable special order price must cover the following:
  1. variable costs
  2. incremental fixed costs
  3. contribution margin foregone on the regular units not produced

- A firm would want to accept special orders only when market segmentation is present. (Market segmentation is the separation or splitting of markets so that sales in one market have little or no effect on the other market.)

- A firm would not want to produce a special order that would be in direct competition with their regular products.

Decisions to Sell or Process Further

- Sell-or-process-further decisions involve situations where a market exists for a product prior to its completion in the normal production process.

- The alternatives are:
  1. sell the product at an intermediate stage.
  2. process further and then sell the product.

- In general, the product should be processed further if incremental revenues from further processing exceed the incremental costs of further processing.

- Joint product decisions concern whether the product should be sold at split-off or processed further.

- Any joint costs that have been allocated to a joint product are sunk and irrelevant for decision making.

- The relevant costs to be compared are:
  1. the market value of the product at split-off.
  2. the revenues resulting from further processing minus the incremental costs of further processing.

PRODUCT MIX DECISIONS

- In some cases, product resources, such as materials, labor, or equipment, may be limited. The firm must use the scarce resources in the most effective manner possible.

One Constrained Resource

- When there is one scarce resource, determine which product results in the most contribution margin per unit of the scarce resource.

- For example, if the scarce resource is machine hours, for each product calculate the contribution margin per machine hour as follows:

$$\text{Contribution Margin Per Machine Hour} = \frac{\text{Contribution Margin Per Unit of Product}}{\text{Machine Time Required Per Unit}}$$

- The quantity needed of the product with the highest contribution margin per machine hour should be produced before producing the other products.

Multiple Constrained Resources

- When more than one resource is limited, linear programming can be used to determine the optimal solution.

KEY TERMS TEST

Test your recall of the key terms as follows: Read the following definitions of key terms and try to recall as many key terms as you can without assistance. Write your answers in the spaces provided. If you need assistance, refer to the list of key terms at the end of this section.

1. Relevant costing analysis that focuses on whether a component should be made internally or purchased externally is a _____ _____.

2. Relevant costing analysis that focuses on whether a product should be processed beyond the split-off point is a decision to _____ _____ _____ _____.

3. The _____ _____ is the point where products become distinguishable after passing through a common process.

4. A relevant costing analysis that focuses on keeping or dropping a segment of a business is a _____ _____.

5. _____ _____ are future costs that differ between alternatives.

6. A _____ _____ is a cost for which the outlay has already been made and that cannot be affected by a future decision.

7. Relevant costing analysis that focuses on whether a specially priced order should be accepted or rejected is a _____ _____.

8. A _____ is a mathematical expression that identifies a resource limitation.

9. _____ _____ are products that are inseparable prior to a split-off point.

10. A _____ _____ is a specific set of procedures that, when followed, produces a decision.

KEY TERMS:

constraint
decision model
joint products
keep-or-drop decision
make-or-buy decision

relevant costs
sell or process further
special-order decision
split-off point
sunk cost

Compare your answers to those at the end of the chapter and review any key terms missed.

CHAPTER QUIZ

Write your answers in the spaces provided.

1. _____ _____ are the result of past decisions and cannot be changed by current or future actions.

2. _____ _____ is the sacrifice that results from pursuing one alternative and foregoing another alternative.

3. For a cost or revenue to be relevant to a particular decision, it must
   1. _____.
   2. _____.

4. Avoidable costs in a make-or-buy decision consist of two types of costs:
   1. _____
   2. _____

5. List two qualitative factors that should be considered when evaluating a make-or-buy decision.
   1. _____
   2. _____

6. When deciding whether to keep or drop a segment, if the decision is based solely on quantitative factors, the segment should be kept if it contributes _____ _____.

7. When there is a scarce resource, the product with the highest contribution margin per _____ should be produced first.

8. List two sunk costs.
   1. _____
   2. _____

9. If there is excess capacity, the minimum acceptable price for a special order must cover:
   1. _____
   2. _____

10. If the firm is at full capacity, the minimum acceptable price for a special order must cover:
    1. _____
    2. _____
    3. _____

11. In general, when considering a sell-or-process-further decision, the product should be processed further if _____.

Circle the single best answer.

Use the following information to answer the next three questions.

Liza Company produces a product with the following unit cost.

Direct materials	$ 2.75
Direct labor	1.25
Variable overhead	4.00
Fixed overhead	2.50
Unit cost	$10.50

Fixed selling costs are $600,000 per year, and variable selling costs are $1.50 per unit sold.

Production capacity is 500,000 units per year. However, the company expects to produce only 300,000 units next year. The product normally sells for $15 each. A customer has offered to buy 150,000 units for $10 each. The units would be sold in an area outside the market area currently served.

12. The incremental cost per unit associated with the special order is:
    (a) $8.00; (b) $9.25; (c) $9.50; (d) $10.00

13. Total incremental cost associated with the special order is:
    (a) $1,237,500; (b) $1,342,000; (c) $1,387,500; (d) $1,425,000

14. If the firm produces the special order, the effect on income would be:
(a) $75,000 increase; (b) $90,000 increase; (c) $2,500 decrease;
(d) $12,500 decrease

Compare your answers to those at the end of the chapter and review any questions missed.

EXERCISES

EXERCISE 1

The management of Garvin Industries is evaluating whether the company should continue manufacturing a component or buy it from an outside supplier. Based upon their accounting records, it appears that it costs the company $80 per unit to make the component. The $80 cost per component was determined as follows:

Direct materials	$16
Direct labor	30
Variable manufacturing overhead	12
Fixed manufacturing overhead	22
Total	$80

Garvin Industries uses 10,000 components per year. After Stinson, Inc., submitted a bid of $70 per component, some members of management felt they could reduce costs by buying from outside and discontinuing production of the component.

If the component is obtained from Stinson, Inc., $5 of fixed manufacturing overhead per unit would be avoided and Garvin's unused production facilities could be leased to another company for $30,000 per year.

Required:

1. Based upon relevant cost differences, should Garvin Industries make or buy the component? Include your supporting calculations.

Supporting calculations:

EXERCISE 1 (continued)

2. Prepare a memorandum to Garvin management with your recommendation. (See Appendix A: Guidelines for Memorandum Preparation.)

```
                        MEMORANDUM

    DATE:
      TO: Garvin Industries Management
    FROM:
 SUBJECT:
```

EXERCISE 2

The Critchfield Company has annual productive capacity of 60,000 units per year. Budgeted operating results for 1995 are as follows:

Revenues (50,000 units @ $10)		$500,000
Variable costs:		
Manufacturing (50,000 @ $3.20)	$160,000	
Selling (50,000 @ $0.80)	40,000	200,000
Contribution margin		$300,000
Fixed costs:		
Manufacturing	$100,000	
Selling and administrative	80,000	180,000
Operating income		$120,000

A wholesaler from another country wants to buy 5,000 units at a price of $8 per unit. All fixed costs would remain within the relevant range. Variable manufacturing costs would be the same per unit, but variable selling costs would increase by $2 per unit on the special order only.

Required:

1. Determine whether the company should produce the special order.

2. Assuming Critchfield's objective is to maximize profit, if the customer wants a special order of 20,000 units, should Critchfield accept or reject the special order?

EXERCISE 3

The Ahler Company manufactures three joint products: X, Y, and Z.

The cost of the joint process is $100,000.

Information about the three products follows:

	Anticipated Production	Selling Price Per lb. at Split-Off	Additional Processing Costs Per lb. After Split-Off (All Variable)	Selling Price Per lb. After Further Processing	Allocated Joint Costs
X	10,000 lbs.	$10	$2	$20	$24,000
Y	30,000 lbs.	5	6	10	36,000
Z	20,000 lbs.	8	4	16	40,000

Required:

Determine whether each product should be sold at split-off or processed further.

EXERCISE 4

The operations of the Schmollinger Corporation are divided into the Perry Division and the Nicholas Division.

Projections for the next year are as follows:

	PERRY DIVISION	NICHOLAS DIVISION	TOTAL
Sales	$250,000	$100,000	$350,000
Variable costs	80,000	40,000	120,000
Contribution margin	$170,000	$ 60,000	$230,000
Direct fixed costs	60,000	40,000	100,000
Segment margin	$110,000	$ 20,000	$130,000
Allocated common costs	70,000	30,000	100,000
Operating income (loss)	$ 40,000	$(10,000)	$ 30,000

Required:

1. Determine operating income for the Schmollinger Corporation as a whole if the Nicholas Division were dropped.

2. Should the Nicholas Division be eliminated?

EXERCISE 5

The Royer Company manufactures two products, 12-07 and 19-01. Contribution margin per unit is determined as follows:

	12-07	19-01
Revenue	$25	$20
Variable costs	15	12
Contribution margin	$10	$ 8

Total demand for 12-07 is 5,000 units, and for 19-01 it is 10,000 units.

Direct labor is a scarce resource. 40,000 direct labor hours are available during the year. Product 12-07 requires 5 direct labor hours per unit, while product 19-01 requires 2 labor hours per unit.

Required:

How many units of 12-07 and 19-01 should the Royer Company produce?

ANSWERS

KEY TERMS TEST
1. make-or-buy decision
2. sell or process further
3. split-off point
4. keep-or-drop decision
5. Relevant costs
6. sunk cost
7. special-order decision
8. constraint
9. Joint products
10. decision model

CHAPTER QUIZ
1. Sunk costs
2. Opportunity cost
3. 1. differ between the alternatives being considered.
   2. be a future cost.
4. 1. the variable costs associated with producing the product: direct materials, direct labor, and variable overhead
   2. avoidable fixed overhead
5. 1. How does the quality of the supplier's component compare to the quality of the component manufactured by the firm?
   2. Is the supplier reliable in terms of providing the needed quantities of the component on a timely basis?
6. incremental profit
7. unit of scarce resource
8. 1. acquisition cost of equipment purchased in the past
   2. depreciation of equipment purchased in the past
9. 1. variable costs
   2. incremental fixed costs
10. 1. variable costs
    2. incremental fixed costs
    3. contribution margin foregone on the regular units not produced
11. the incremental revenues from further processing exceed the incremental costs of further processing.
12. c ($2.75 + $1.25 + $4.00 + $1.50) = $9.50
13. d ($9.50 x 150,000) = $1,425,000
14. a ($10.00 - $9.50) x 150,000 = $75,000 increase

EXERCISE 1

1.

	BUY	MAKE
Outside supplier's price (10,000 x $70)	($700,000)	
Direct materials (10,000 x $16)		($160,000)
Direct labor (10,000 x $30)		(300,000)
Variable manufacturing overhead (10,000 x $12)		(120,000)
Fixed manufacturing overhead (10,000 x $22)		(220,000)
(10,000 x $17)	(170,000)	
Rental revenue	30,000	
Totals	($840,000)	($800,000)

There is a $40,000 difference in favor of manufacturing the component rather than buying it from the outside supplier.

The make-or-buy alternatives could also be analyzed as follows:

	BUY	MAKE
Outside supplier's price	($700,000)	
Direct materials		($160,000)
Direct labor		(300,000)
Variable manufacturing overhead		(120,000)
Avoidable fixed manufacturing overhead (10,000 x $5)		(50,000)
Rental revenue	30,000	
Totals	($670,000)	($630,000)

Notice that instead of including total fixed manufacturing overhead under each alternative, only the avoidable manufacturing overhead is included under the alternative of making the component. The difference in income is still $40,000 in favor of manufacturing the component.

EXERCISE 1 (continued)

2.

MEMORANDUM

TO: Garvin Industries Management

FROM: Management Consulting, Inc.

SUBJECT: Make-or-Buy Decision

This memo regards whether Garvin Industries should continue manufacturing one of its components or buy the component from an outside supplier.

Based on the attached calculations, I recommend that Garvin Industries continue manufacturing the component. There is a $40,000 difference in favor of manufacturing the component rather than buying it from an outside supplier. The net total cost of buying the component is $840,000. Fixed manufacturing overhead of $170,000 will be incurred even if the component is purchased. The net total cost of manufacturing the component is $800,000. Therefore, there is a cost difference of $40,000 in favor of manufacturing the component.

In addition, if we manufacture the component, we have control over the production scheduling and availability of the component. Another qualitative factor to consider is quality. Again, if the component is manufactured, we have control over the quality of the component produced.

If you have any questions concerning the analysis, please contact me at Extension 2531.

EXERCISE 2

1.

Incremental revenue (5,000 x $8)	$40,000
Incremental costs:	
Variable manufacturing (5,000 x $3.20)	(16,000)
Variable selling [5,000 x ($0.80 + $2.00)]	(14,000)
Incremental contribution margin	$10,000

Since the company would still be operating within the relevant range, fixed costs would remain the same.

If the company produces the special order, contribution margin and operating income would increase by $10,000.

2.

	Without Special Order	With Special Order
Revenues		
(50,000 x $10)	$500,000	
(40,000 x $10)		$400,000
(20,000 x $ 8)		160,000
Less: Variable costs:		
Manufacturing		
(50,000 x $3.20)	(160,000)	
(60,000 x $3.20)		(192,000)
Selling		
(50,000 x $0.80)	(40,000)	
(40,000 x $0.80)		(32,000)
(20,000 x $2.80)		(56,000)
Contribution margin	$300,000	$280,000
Less: Fixed costs:		
Manufacturing	(100,000)	(100,000)
Selling and administrative	(80,000)	(80,000)
Operating income	$120,000	$100,000

If Critchfield accepts the 20,000 unit special order, they would have to forego 10,000 units in regular sales because of capacity constraints. This would result in a $20,000 decrease in contribution margin and operating income.

EXERCISE 3

	Sell at Split-Off	Process Further Then Sell	Decision
X	$100,000	$200,000 (20,000)	Process further
		$180,000	
Y	$150,000	$300,000 (180,000)	Sell at split-off
		$120,000	
Z	$160,000	$320,000 (80,000)	Process further
		$240,000	

Notice that since the joint costs are incurred regardless of which action is taken, the joint costs are not relevant to the decision.

EXERCISE 4

1. If the Nicholas Division were dropped, the company's operating income would drop from $30,000 to $10,000.

Sales	$250,000
Variable costs	80,000
Contribution margin	$170,000
Direct fixed costs	60,000
Segment margin	$110,000
Allocated common costs ($70,000 + $30,000)	100,000
Operating income	$ 10,000

The $30,000 of common costs allocated to the Nicholas Division will be incurred even if the Nicholas Division is dropped.

2. The Nicholas Division should not be dropped, since it contributes $20,000 toward covering common corporate costs.

EXERCISE 5

Since direct labor hours are limited, the company should first produce the product that has the highest contribution margin per direct labor hour.

	12-07	19-01
Contribution margin per unit	$10	$8
Divided by: Direct labor hours required per unit	5	2
= Contribution margin per DLH	$ 2	$4

To maximize contribution margin, the Royer Company should produce 10,000 units of 19-01 and 4,000 units of 12-07.

Product	Units	DLH Per Unit	DLH
19-01	10,000	2	20,000
12-07	4,000	5	20,000
Totals	14,000		40,000

CHAPTER 22

CAPITAL BUDGETING

CHAPTER REVIEW

CAPITAL INVESTMENT DECISIONS

- **Capital investment decisions** involve planning, setting goals and priorities, arranging financing, and identifying criteria for making long-term investments.

- Capital budgeting is the process of determining which long-term capital assets to acquire.

- There are two types of capital investment projects:
  1. **independent projects** that do not affect the cash flows of other projects.
  2. **mutually exclusive projects** that, if accepted, preclude the acceptance of all other competing projects.

DECISION MODELS

- Capital budgeting decision models can be classified as:
  - nondiscounting models or
  - discounting models.

- **Nondiscounting models** do <u>not</u> consider the time value of money.

- Two nondiscounting cash flow models are:
  1. payback
  2. accounting rate of return (ARR)

- **Discounting models** consider the time value of money.

- Two discounting cash flow models are:
  1. net present value method (NPV)
  2. internal rate of return (IRR)

NONDISCOUNTING MODELS

Payback Period

- The **payback period** is the time required for a firm to recover its original investment.

- When the cash flows of a project are the same amount each period, payback is calculated as follows:

    Payback Period = Original Investment/Annual Cash Inflow

- If the cash flows are not the same amount each period, payback is calculated by adding the annual cash flows until the original investment is recovered.

- Firms may set a maximum payback period for all projects and reject projects that exceed the maximum payback period allowed.

- Reasons why the payback period may be used to screen projects are:
  1. The payback period may be used as a rough measure of risk. (The longer the payback period, the riskier the project may be.)
  2. Firms with liquidity problems may want to select projects with quick paybacks.
  3. Firms in industries where the risk of obsolescence is high may want to recover invested funds rapidly.
  4. If a division manager's performance is based on short-run measures, such as net income, the manager may select projects with short paybacks in order to affect net income as quickly as possible.

- Two weaknesses of the payback period method are:
  1. Payback ignores the time value of money.
  2. Payback ignores the profitability of investments beyond the payback period.

- Although payback should not be used as the sole evaluator for project selection, it may be used in conjunction with discounted cash flow methods that consider the time value of money.

Accounting Rate of Return

- The **accounting rate of return** measures a project's return in terms of accounting <u>income</u> instead of cash flows.

- The accounting rate of return is calculated as follows:

$$\text{Accounting Rate of Return} = \frac{\text{Average Income}}{\text{Investment*}}$$

or

$$\text{Accounting Rate of Return} = \frac{\text{Average Annual Net Cash Inflows} - \text{Average Annual Depreciation}}{\text{Investment*}}$$

*Either original investment or average investment can be used. Average investment is calculated as follows:

$$\text{Average Investment} = (\text{Original Investment} + \text{Salvage Value})/2$$

- The accounting rate of return may be used:
  1. as a screening measure to ensure that a new investment will not adversely affect accounting income.
  2. because bonuses of managers are often based on accounting income, and managers may want to ensure that a new investment has a favorable effect on net income (and the manager's bonus).

- The disadvantage of the accounting rate of return is that it does not consider the time value of money.

DISCOUNTING MODELS: THE NET PRESENT VALUE METHOD

- Discounting models consider the time value of money. (See the Present Value Module for a review of present value and future value concepts.)

- Two discounting models are:
  1. net present value (NPV)
  2. internal rate of return (IRR)

- When using the net present value method:
  1. the cash flows for each year are identified.
  2. all cash flows are stated in terms of their present value (discounted).
  3. the present values are added together to find the net present value.

- The present values are determined using the required rate of return as the discount rate.

- The **required rate of return**, or **hurdle rate**, is the minimum return that a project must earn in order to be acceptable.

- The **cost of capital** is often used as the minimum required rate of return. The cost of capital is the cost of investment funds, usually viewed as a weighted average of the costs of funds from all sources.
- Sources of funds for a firm are:
  1. debt
  2. common stock
  3. preferred stock

- The weighted average cost of capital is calculated by multiplying the proportion of long-term financing provided by each source by the cost of the source of capital and then summing the results.

Net Present Value: A Measure of Profitability

- Net present value is the profit of the investment expressed in current dollars.

- If the NPV > 0, this indicates:
  1. the initial investment is recovered.
  2. the cost of capital is recovered.
  3. a return in excess of the cost of capital is earned.
- If the NPV = 0, this indicates:
  1. the initial investment is recovered.
  2. the cost of capital is recovered.

- If NPV < 0, the investment should be rejected because the project earns less than the required rate of return.

- NPV analysis assumes that each cash inflow from a project is reinvested when received to earn the required rate of return during the rest of the project's life.

DISCOUNTING MODELS: INTERNAL RATE OF RETURN

- The **internal rate of return** is the interest rate (discount rate) that results in a NPV of 0.

- When NPV = 0, the present value of the project's cash inflows exactly equal the investment outlay. Therefore, the IRR is the interest rate that equates the present value of the <u>future</u> cash flows to the investment.

- If the cash flows are an annuity, the IRR can be determined as follows:

  1. Use the following equation to solve for the discount factor:

    Investment = Annual Cash Flow x Annuity Discount Factor

    Annuity Discount Factor = Investment/Annual Cash Flow

  2. Find the discount factor in Table 4, Appendix B, under the appropriate number of periods and determine the interest rate that corresponds with the discount factor. This is the IRR.

  3. If the discount factor computed falls between two discount factors listed in Table 4, the interest rate can be approximated using **interpolation**.

- If the cash flows are uneven, the IRR can be determined using trial and error to find the NPV that equals zero or by using a computer program.

- The IRR method assumes that the cash inflows from the project are reinvested to earn a return equal to the IRR for the remaining life of the project.

- The investment should be rejected if the IRR is less than the required rate of return.

MUTUALLY EXCLUSIVE PROJECTS: NPV VERSUS IRR

- When NPV and IRR produce different rankings for mutually exclusive projects, the NPV method correctly identifies the best investment alternative.
- Two major differences between NPV and IRR are:
  1. The NPV method assumes that cash flows from the project are reinvested at the discount rate.

     The IRR method assumes that cash flows are reinvested at the internal rate of return of the project.

  2. The NPV method measures the profitability of a project in absolute terms (in dollars), whereas the IRR method measures the profitability of a project in relative terms (as a percentage).

- Since the wealth of firm owners are maximized by total dollars of profit earned, not relative profits, NPV should be used when choosing among competing, mutually exclusive projects.

NET PRESENT VALUE AND MUTUALLY EXCLUSIVE PROJECTS

- When evaluating independent projects, a project is acceptable if the NPV is positive.

- When evaluating mutually exclusive projects, the project with the largest NPV is selected.

- The three steps in selecting the best project are:
  1. Determine cash flows for each project.
  2. Calculate the NPV of each project.
  3. Identify the project with the greatest NPV.

COMPUTATION OF CASH FLOWS

- Two steps in computing the cash flows for capital budgeting are:
  1. Forecast revenues, expenses, and capital investments.
  2. Convert the pre-tax cash flows to after-tax cash flows.

- The federal income tax rate is determined by a corporation's taxable income.

Taxable Income	Income Tax Rate
$0-$50,000	15%
$50,000-$75,000	25
$75,000-$100,000	34
$100,000-$335,000	39
Over $335,000	34

- In addition to federal income taxes, corporations often have to pay state income taxes.

After-Tax Cash Flows: Year 0

- The net cash outflow in Year 0 is the difference between the initial cost of the project and any cash inflows associated with the project in Year 0.

- The cost of the project includes:
  - the cost of land
  - the cost of equipment (including transportation and installation)
  - taxes on gains from the sale of old assets
  - increases in working capital

- Cash inflows occurring at the time of acquisition include:
  - tax savings from the sale of old assets
  - cash from the sale of old assets
  - tax credits, such as investment tax credits

- The net investment can be computed as follows:

  Total cost of new machine
  - Net proceeds from old machine (net of tax effects)
  = Net investment (cash outflow)

Cash Flows From Operations

- The incremental cash flow from operations can be calculated as follows:

  > Incremental cash inflow from sales
  > - Incremental cash operating expenses
  > = Cash flows from operations before taxes
  > - Income taxes
  > = Net cash flow from operations after taxes

- After-tax cash flows from operations also can be calculated as follows:

  After-Tax Cash Flows From Operations = (Pretax Cash Flows From Operations)(1 - Tax Rate)

Tax Savings From Depreciation

- Depreciation is NOT a cash outflow; however, since depreciation is deductible for tax purposes, it reduces the amount of income taxes a company must pay.

- For example, assume a company had cash inflows from operations of $100,000 and no deduction for depreciation. The company would pay $34,000 in taxes ($100,000 x 34%).

  If the company could deduct $10,000 of depreciation on their tax return, the company would pay only $30,600 in taxes.

	Without Depreciation Deduction	With Depreciation Deduction
Cash inflow from operations	$100,000	$100,000
Depreciation	-0-	10,000
Taxable income	$100,000	$ 90,000
Income taxes (34%)	$ 34,000	$ 30,600

$3,400
Tax savings

- Another way to calculate the tax savings from depreciation is to multiply the depreciation deduction by the tax rate.

  Tax Savings from Depreciation = Depreciation Deduction x Tax Rate
  = $10,000 x 34%
  = $3,400

- The amount of depreciation allowed for tax purposes is determined by the tax laws.

- The Tax Act classifies personal property (all depreciable business assets other than real estate) into different classes.

Class	Types of Assets
3 years	Most small tools
5 years	Cars, light trucks, and computer equipment
7 years	Most equipment, machinery, and office equipment

- Depreciation is calculated using
  1. straight-line or
  2. **MACRS (Modified Accelerated Cost Recovery System).**

- Both methods produce the same total amount of depreciation over the life of the asset; however, the amount of depreciation claimed each year will differ under the two methods.

- Both methods use a **half-year convention.** The asset is assumed to be in service for one-half of the taxable year in which it is acquired, regardless of when the asset is actually placed in service.

- This means 5-year property is depreciated over 6 years and 7-year property is depreciated over 8 years.

- MACRS depreciation is calculated as follows:

MACRS Depreciation = Asset Cost x MACRS Percentage

- The percentages are as follows:

Year	5-Year	7-Year
1	20.00%	14.28%
2	32.00	24.49
3	19.20	17.49
4	11.52	12.49
5	11.52	8.93
6	5.76	8.93
7		8.93
8		4.46
	100.00%	100.00%

- Tax savings from depreciation can be calculated as follows:

Tax Savings From Depreciation = (Depreciation Deduction x Tax Rate)

= (Asset Cost x MACRS% x Tax Rate)

- For example, if a company acquires an asset classified as 5-year property for $200,000, the tax savings from depreciation would be calculated as follows:

	Cost	x	Depreciation %	=	Depreciation Deduction	x	Tax Rate[a]	=	Tax Savings
Year 1	$200,000	x	20.00%	=	$ 40,000	x	34%	=	$13,600.00
Year 2	200,000	x	32.00%	=	64,000	x	34%	=	21,760.00
Year 3	200,000	x	19.20%	=	38,400	x	34%	=	13,056.00
Year 4	200,000	x	11.52%	=	23,040	x	34%	=	7,833.60
Year 5	200,000	x	11.52%	=	23,040	x	34%	=	7,833.60
Year 6	200,000	x	5.76%	=	11,520	x	34%	=	3,916.80
					$200,000				

[a]Assume a tax rate of 34 percent.

- Straight-line depreciation per year is calculated as:

Straight-Line Depreciation = Cost of Asset/Class Life

- Because the half-year convention is used, only half of the straight-line amount is deducted in the first and the last year.

- For example, if the company acquires 5-year property for $200,000, the tax savings from depreciation would be calculated as follows:

	Depreciation Deduction	x	Tax Rate	=	Tax Savings
Year 1	$ 20,000[a]	x	34%	=	$ 6,800
Year 2	40,000[b]	x	34%	=	13,600
Year 3	40,000	x	34%	=	13,600
Year 4	40,000	x	34%	=	13,600
Year 5	40,000	x	34%	=	13,600
Year 6	20,000	x	34%	=	6,800
	$200,000				

[a]($200,000/5)(1/2)
[b]($200,000/5)

- For the same investment, the present value of the tax savings from using MACRS is greater than the present value of the tax savings from using straight-line depreciation. Therefore, MACRS results in the higher NPV.

CAPITAL INVESTMENT: THE ADVANCED MANUFACTURING ENVIRONMENT

- Companies can realize benefits by:
  1. redesigning and simplifying the current manufacturing process.
  2. automating by adding robotics.
  3. automating by using flexible manufacturing systems.
  4. automating by using completely integrated manufacturing systems.
  5. automating by building **Greenfield factories** (new factories designed and built with a commitment to automation).

- Capital budgeting in the advanced manufacturing environment differs from the traditional approach in the following ways:

  1. Investment. For standard manufacturing equipment, the direct costs of acquisition represent virtually the entire investment. For automated manufacturing, the direct costs can be as low as 50 percent to 60 percent of the total investment. In addition, software, engineering, training and implementation costs must be considered as part of the total investment cost.

  2. Estimates of operating cash flows. Typically estimates of operating cash flows from investments in standard equipment were based on tangible benefits, such as direct savings from labor, power, and scrap. In the advanced manufacturing environment, it is important to consider intangible and indirect benefits, such as improved quality, greater reliability, improved customer satisfaction, and the ability to maintain or increase market share.

  3. Salvage value. Because of the uncertainty involved in estimating salvage value, it has often been ignored or heavily discounted. However, salvage value could make the difference between investing and not investing; therefore, a better approach is to use sensitivity analysis (calculate the NPV using different salvage values.) Being overly conservative with salvage values may result in the rejection of desirable projects.

  4. Discount rates. In practice, future cash flows are uncertain and managers often compensate for this uncertainty by using a discount rate that is greater than the cost of capital. If the rate selected is excessively high, it biases the selection process toward short-term investments. Because the cash returns of an automated manufacturing system are received over a longer period of time, it is more difficult for automated manufacturing systems to appear acceptable. Being overly conservative with discount rates may result in the rejection of automated manufacturing systems.

KEY TERMS TEST

Test your recall of the key terms as follows: Read the following definitions of key terms and try to recall as many key terms as you can <u>without</u> <u>assistance</u>. Write your answers in the spaces provided. If you need assistance, refer to the list of key terms at the end of this section.

1. The process of determining which long-term capital assets to acquire is referred to as making _____ _____ _____.

2. The time required for a project to return its investment is called the _____ _____.

3. Future cash flows expressed in present value terms are _____ _____ _____.

4. Projects that, if accepted, preclude the acceptance of competing projects are _____ _____ _____.

5. _____ _____ _____ _____ is the rate of return that equates the present value of a project's cash inflows with the present value of its cash outflows (the NPV equals zero).

6. Projects that, if accepted or rejected, will not affect the cash flows of another project are _____ _____.

7. _____ _____ _____ is the difference between the present value of a project's cash inflows and the present value of its cash outflows.

8. _____ _____ are capital expenditure models that identify criteria for accepting or rejecting projects without considering the time value of money.

9. _____ _____ _____ _____, or _____ _____, is the minimum rate of return that a project must earn in order to be acceptable.

10. The _____ _____ _____ _____ is calculated as income divided by the original or average investment.

11. A _____ _____ is any capital budgeting model that explicitly considers the time value of money in identifying criteria for accepting or rejecting proposed projects.

12. The _____ _____ _____ is the cost of investment funds, usually viewed as a weighted cost of funds from all sources.

KEY TERMS:

accounting rate of return
capital investment decisions
cost of capital
discounted cash flows
discounting model
hurdle rate
independent projects

internal rate of return
mutually exclusive projects
net present value
nondiscounting models
payback period
required rate of return

Compare your answers to those at the end of the chapter and review any key terms missed.

CHAPTER QUIZ

Write your answers in the spaces provided.

1. Capital expenditure decision models can be classified as nondiscounting models or discounting models. _____ models consider the time value of money. _____ models do not consider the time value of money.

2. Two nondiscounting cash flow models are:
   1. _____
   2. _____

3. Two discounting cash flow models are:
   1. _____
   2. _____

4. When the cash flows of a project are the same amount each period, payback is calculated as follows.

   Payback Period = _____ / _____

5. Accounting rate of return is calculated as follows.

   ARR = (_____ - _____)/ _____

6. Present values can be calculated using discount factors and the following formula.

   _____ = _____ x _____

7. The present value of an annuity can be calculated using an annuity discount factor and the following formula.

   _____ = _____ x _____

8. When NPV and IRR produce different rankings for mutually exclusive projects, the _____ method correctly identifies the best investment alternative.

9. The NPV method assumes that cash flows from a project are reinvested at the _____, while the IRR method assumes that cash flows are reinvested at the _____.

10. The tax savings from depreciation can be calculated as follows.

   Tax Savings From Depreciation = _____ x _____

11. Depreciation is calculated using the straight-line method or MACRS. The depreciation deduction using MACRS is calculated as follows:

   MACRS Depreciation = _____ x _____

   Straight-line depreciation per year is calculated as follows:

   Straight-Line Depreciation = _____ / _____

Circle the single best answer.

12. Which of the following methods is used as a screening measure to ensure that a new investment will not adversely affect income? (a) payback; (b) accounting rate of return; (c) internal rate of return; (d) net present value

13. Which of the following methods determines the interest rate which equates the present value of the future cash flows with the investment outlay? (a) payback; (b) accounting rate of return; (c) internal rate of return; (d) net present value

14. Which two of the following methods consider the time value of money? (a) payback; (b) accounting rate of return; (c) internal rate of return; (d) net present value

15. The discount rate is the rate used to compute: (a) payback; (b) accounting rate of return; (c) internal rate of return; (d) net present value

16. Discounting: (a) is the process of determining value at a future time; (b) is the process of converting future cash flows to their present value; (c) is a process that does not consider the time value of money; (d) is a process that can only be used for a single amount (not annuities); (e) all of the above

NOTE: For your convenience, present value factor tables are included in Appendix B of the study guide.

17. The present value of $10,000 to be received 5 years from now and earning an annual return of 8 percent is: (a) $6,210; (b) $6,806; (c) $4,000; (d) $4,693

18. The present value of a 5-year annuity of $10,000, earning an annual return of 8 percent is: (a) $31,700; (b) $34,700; (c) $37,910; (d) $39,927

<u>Use the following information to answer the next six questions</u>.

Duane Flowers is considering the purchase of a small business that costs $500,000. The business is expected to generate annual cash inflows of $80,000. Duane plans to operate the business for 15 years and then turn it over to his son. The cost of capital is 10%. Ignore income taxes, and round amounts to dollars.

19. Payback for the project is: (a) 6.11 years; (b) 6.25 years; (c) 7.96 years; (d) 8.33 years

20. If depreciation is $25,000 per year, the accounting rate of return based on the initial investment is: (a) 11%; (b) 12%; (c) 16%; (d) 17.2%

21. Using the cost of capital as the discount rate, the net present value of the project is: (a) $89,364; (b) $108,486; (c) $114,686; (d) $228,184

22. The approximate internal rate of return of the project is: (a) 8%; (b) 12%; (c) 12.5%; (d) 14%

23. Based on quantitative factors, should the project be accepted or rejected? (a) accepted; (b) rejected

24. Depreciation is a cash outflow that should be considered when evaluating capital investments: (a) true; (b) false

25. If an asset is sold for less than its tax basis, a loss results and the company will incur additional taxes: (a) true; (b) false

26. If a company purchases 7-year property for $210,000, the depreciation deduction using the straight-line method would be $30,000 in the first year: (a) true; (b) false

27. If a company had a depreciation deduction of $20,000 and a tax rate of 40%, the company would save $8,000 in taxes: (a) true; (b) false

28. If a company had pre-tax cash inflows from operations of $50,000 and a tax rate of 40%, after-tax cash inflows from operations would be $20,000: (a) true; (b) false

29. Under the Tax Act, cars and light-duty trucks are classified as 3-year property: (a) true; (b) false

30. Most manufacturing equipment is considered 7-year property under the Tax Act: (a) true; (b) false

31. For tax purposes, five-year property is fully depreciated after 5 years: (a) true; (b) false

Use the following information to answer the next three questions.

The Reelitz Company is considering the purchase of the following production equipment.

Acquisition cost	$400,000
Annual cash inflow from operations	90,000
Annual operating costs	30,000
Expected salvage value	0
Cost of capital	14%
Tax rate	34%
Depreciation method	MACRS

The company plans to keep the production equipment for 10 years. (Round amounts to dollars.)

32. The MACRS deduction in Year 1 would be: (a) $57,120; (b) $30,600; (c) $17,000; (d) $13,600

33. The tax savings from depreciation in Year 1 would be: (a) $13,600; (b) $19,421; (c) $30,600; (d) $57,120

34. The annual after-tax cash flows from operations would be: (a) $20,400; (b) $30,600; (c) $33,000; (d) $39,600

Compare your answers to those at the end of the chapter and review any questions missed.

EXERCISES

EXERCISE 1

A capital investment project requires an investment of $200,000. It has an expected life of 5 years with annual cash flows of $50,000 received at the end of each year. Ignore income taxes.

Required:

1. Compute payback for the project.

2. Determine the accounting rate of return for the project based on the initial capital investment.

3. Determine the approximate internal rate of return for the project.

4. Compute the net present value of the project using a 6% discount rate.

EXERCISE 2

A capital investment project requires an investment of $50,000 and has an expected life of four years. Annual cash flows at the end of each year are expected to be as follows (ignore income taxes):

YEAR	AMOUNT
1	$15,000
2	20,000
3	25,000
4	15,000

Required:

1. Compute payback assuming that the cash flows occur evenly throughout the year.

2. Determine the accounting rate of return for the project based on the initial investment.

3. Compute the net present value of the project using a 10% discount rate. (Round amounts to dollars.)

EXERCISE 3

The McEvers Company is considering a capital investment project that requires an investment of $37,910. The project is expected to have annual cash inflows of $10,000 occurring at the end of each of the next five years. Ignore income taxes, and round amounts to dollars.

Required:

1. Determine the internal rate of return for the project.

2. Determine the net present value of the project using discount rates of:
    a. 8%

    b. 10%

    c. 12%

3. What are your observations about the effect the discount rate has upon the project's net present value?

EXERCISE 4

The Martin Company is evaluating two mutually exclusive projects with three-year lives. Each project requires an investment of $10,000. The projects have the following cash inflows received at the end of each year. Ignore income taxes, and round amounts to dollars.

Year	Project 1	Project 2
1	$ 2,000	$ 6,000
2	4,000	4,000
3	6,000	2,000
Total	$12,000	$12,000

Required:

1. Determine the net present value of each project using an 8% discount rate.

2. What can you conclude about the effect the timing of the cash flows has upon a project's net present value?

EXERCISE 5

The Jensen Company is considering a project that requires an investment of $200,000. The project is expected to generate cash flows of $100,000 per year for 6 years. The cash flows would be received at the end of each year.

The asset is considered 5-year property for depreciation purposes and would be depreciated using MACRS. The asset has no salvage value and would be disposed of on the first day of the seventh year. Assume the weighted average cost of capital is 8 percent and the income tax rate is 34 percent.

Required:

Determine the net present value of the asset. (Round amounts to dollars.)

EXERCISE 6

W. A. Hartz & Co. is evaluating a project that requires an investment of $400,000. The property would be depreciated over 4 years using straight-line depreciation. (Ignore the half-year convention.) The company plans to dispose of the property at the end of the fourth year. Salvage value at that time is expected to be $0. Information about the cash flows associated with the project is as follows:

Revenues	$250,000 per year
Variable costs	$40,000 per year
Fixed out-of-pocket costs	$60,000 per year

Assume all the cash flows occur at the end of the year.

Assume the required rate of return is 12% and the tax rate is 34%.

Required:

1. Determine the net present value of the project. (Round amounts to dollars.)

2. Prepare a memorandum to management with your recommendation regarding
    whether Hartz should invest in the project. (See Appendix A: Guidelines
    for Memorandum Preparation.)

```
+---------------------------------------------------------------+
|                        MEMORANDUM                             |
|                                                               |
|           DATE:                                               |
|             TO:                                               |
|           FROM:                                               |
|        SUBJECT:                                               |
+---------------------------------------------------------------+
|                                                               |
|                                                               |
|                                                               |
|                                                               |
|                                                               |
|                                                               |
|                                                               |
|                                                               |
|                                                               |
|                                                               |
|                                                               |
|                                                               |
|                                                               |
|                                                               |
|                                                               |
|                                                               |
|                                                               |
|                                                               |
|                                                               |
|                                                               |
|                                                               |
|                                                               |
|                                                               |
|                                                               |
|                                                               |
+---------------------------------------------------------------+
```

EXERCISE 7

Magic, Inc., is evaluating whether they should use JIT techniques including the use of manufacturing cells. It is estimated that new equipment costing $2 million would be required. The new equipment would be considered 7-year property for tax purposes, and straight-line depreciation would be used. (Ignore the half-year convention.) The existing manufacturing equipment is fully depreciated for tax purposes and has no salvage value.

JIT manufacturing is estimated to save $400,000 per year resulting from reduced costs for maintenance, inspection, and materials handling. The cost savings would occur over the next 20 years. The tax rate is 40 percent and the cost of capital is 12 percent.

Required:

1. Using straight-line depreciation, calculate the net present value of the investment.

2. Prepare a memorandum to management with your recommendation regarding the new equipment. Include a discussion of any qualitative factors that influenced your recommendation.

MEMORANDUM
DATE: TO: FROM: SUBJECT:

KEY TERMS TEST
1. capital investment decisions
2. payback period
3. discounted cash flows
4. mutually exclusive projects
5. Internal rate of return
6. independent projects
7. Net present value
8. Nondiscounting models
9. Required rate of return, hurdle rate
10. accounting rate of return
11. discounting model
12. cost of capital

CHAPTER QUIZ
1. Discounting, Nondiscounting
2. 1. payback
   2. accounting rate of return
3. 1. net present value method
   2. internal rate of return
4. Original Investment/Annual Cash Inflow
5. (Average Annual Net Cash Inflows - Average Annual Depreciation)/Investment
6. Present Value = Future Value x Discount Factor
7. Present Value of an Annuity = Future Value Annuity x Annuity Discount Factor
8. NPV
9. discount rate, internal rate of return
10. Depreciation Deduction x Tax Rate
11. Asset Cost x MACRS%
    Cost of Asset/Class Life
12. b
13. c
14. c & d
15. d
16. b
17. b ($10,000 x .68058) = $6,806
18. d ($10,000 x 3.99271) = $39,927
19. b ($500,000/$80,000) = 6.25 years
20. a ($80,000 - $25,000)/$500,000 = 11%
21. b ($80,000 x 7.60608) - $500,000 = $108,486
22. d $500,000/$80,000 = 6.25; The present value annuity factor for 15 years and 12% is 6.81086. The present value annuity factor for 15 years and 14% is 6.14217. The internal rate of return is approximately 14%.
23. a
24. b False. Depreciation is NOT a cash flow. Depreciation can be deducted for tax purposes resulting in a tax savings and reducing the cash outflow for taxes.
25. b False. A loss produces a tax savings, which is viewed the same as a cash inflow.

26. b False. Because of the half-year convention, the depreciation deduction would be $15,000 for the first and the eighth year.

27. a True

28. b False. After-tax cash inflows from operations would be $30,000 [$50,000 x (1 - .40)].

29. b False. Cars and light trucks are classified as 5-year property.

30. a True

31. b False. Because of the half-year convention, 5-year property is depreciated over 6 years.

32. a ($400,000 x 14.28%) = $57,120

33. b ($400,000 x 14.28% x 34%) = $19,421

34. d ($90,000 - $30,000) x 66% = $39,600

EXERCISE 1

1.

$$\text{Payback} = \frac{\text{Capital Investment}}{\text{Annual Net Cash Inflows}}$$

$$= \frac{\$200,000}{\$50,000} = 4 \text{ years}$$

2.

$$\text{Accounting Rate of Return} = \frac{\text{Average Annual Incremental Income}}{\text{Initial Capital Investment}}$$

$$= \frac{\text{Average Annual Net Cash Inflows} - \text{Average Annual Depreciation}}{\text{Initial Capital Investment}}$$

$$= \frac{\$50,000 - \$40,000^*}{\$200,000} = 5\%$$

*Depreciation = $200,000/5 years = $40,000

3. Internal Rate of Return:

Use the following equation to solve for the present value factor.

Investment = Annual Cash Flows x Annuity Discount Factor

$200,000 = $50,000 x Annuity Discount Factor

Annuity Discount Factor = 4

Under 5 years in Table 4, Appendix B, the annuity discount factor of 4 falls between 7% (4.10020) and 8% (3.99271). The internal rate of return is approximately 8%.

EXERCISE 1 (continued)

4. NPV using a 6% discount rate:

Investment	($200,000)
Present value of cash inflows: (Cash Inflow x Annuity Discount Factor, 5 years, 6%) ($50,000 x 4.21236)	210,618
Net Present Value	$ 10,618

EXERCISE 2

1. If the cash flows occurred evenly throughout the year, payback would occur in 2.6 years:

Year	Projected Net Cash Inflows	
1	$15,000	
2	20,000	
3	15,000	(.6 x $25,000)
	$50,000	

2.

$$\text{Average Annual Net Cash Inflows} = \frac{\$15,000 + \$20,000 + \$25,000 + \$15,000}{4}$$

$$= \$18,750$$

$$\text{Average Annual Depreciation} = \$50,000/4 \text{ years}$$
$$= \$12,500$$

$$ARR = \frac{\$18,750 - \$12,500}{\$50,000} = 12.5\%$$

3. Net Present Value:

	0	1	2	3	4
Investment	($50,000)				
Cash flows		$15,000	$20,000	$25,000	$15,000
PV factors, 10%		x .90909	x .82645	x .75131	x .68301
Present values	59,193	$13,636	$16,529	$18,783	$10,245
NPV	$ 9,193				

EXERCISE 3

1. Use the following equation to solve for the annuity discount factor.

$$\text{Investment} = \text{Annual Cash Flows} \times \text{Annuity Discount Factor}$$
$$\$37,910 = \$10,000 \times \text{Annuity Discount Factor}$$
$$\text{Annuity Discount Factor} = 3.791$$

Under 5 years in Table 4, the annuity discount factor of 3.79079 corresponds to 10%.

2.a. NPV using an 8% discount rate:

Investment	($37,910)
PV of cash inflows:	
(Cash Inflow x Annuity Discount Factor, 5 years, 8%)	
($10,000 x 3.99271)	39,927
Net Present Value	$ 2,017

b. NPV using a 10% discount rate:

Investment	($37,910)
PV of cash inflows:	
(Cash Inflow x Annuity Discount Factor, 5 years, 10%)	
($10,000 x 3.79079)	37,908
Net Present Value	$ 2

c. NPV using a 12% discount rate:

Investment	($37,910)
PV of cash inflows:	
(Cash Inflow x Annuity Discount Factor, 5 years, 12%)	
($10,000 x 3.60478)	36,048
Net Present Value	($ 1,862)

3. There is an inverse relationship between the discount rate and the NPV. When the discount rate increased, the NPV decreased. Also, note that the discount rate of 10% that resulted in a NPV of almost zero was the IRR calculated in Requirement (1).

EXERCISE 4

1. NPV of Project 1:

	0	1	2	3
Investment	($10,000)			
Cash flows		$2,000	$4,000	$6,000
PV factors, 8%		x .92593	x .85734	x .79383
Present values	10,044	$1,852	$3,429	$4,763
NPV	$ 44			

NPV of Project 2:

	0	1	2	3
Investment	($10,000)			
Cash flows		$6,000	$4,000	$2,000
PV factors, 8%		x .92593	x .85734	x .79383
Present values	10,573	$5,556	$3,429	$1,588
NPV	$ 573			

2. Since money has a time value, the sooner the money will be received, the greater the present value will be.

EXERCISE 5

	0	1	2	3	4	5	6
Investment	($200,000)						
Cash inflows from operations before taxes		$100,000	$100,000	$100,000	$100,000	$100,000	$100,000
Income taxes on cash inflows from operations (34%)		(34,000)	(34,000)	(34,000)	(34,000)	(34,000)	(34,000)
Cash inflows from operations after taxes		$ 66,000	$ 66,000	$ 66,000	$ 66,000	$ 66,000	$ 66,000
Tax savings from depreciation[a]		13,600	21,760	13,056	7,834	7,834	3,917
Net cash flows after taxes		$ 79,600	$ 87,760	$ 79,056	$ 73,834	$ 73,834	$ 69,917
PV factors, 8%		x .92593	x .85734	x .79383	x .73503	x .68058	x .63017
Present values	360,281	$ 73,704	$ 75,240	$ 62,757	$ 54,270	$ 50,250	$ 44,060
NPV	$160,281						

[a]Tax savings from depreciation:

	Cost		Depreciation Percentage		Depreciation Deduction		Tax Rate		Tax Savings
Year 1	$200,000	x	20.00%	=	$40,000	x	34%	=	$13,600
Year 2	$200,000	x	32.00%	=	$64,000	x	34%	=	$21,760
Year 3	$200,000	x	19.20%	=	$38,400	x	34%	=	$13,056
Year 4	$200,000	x	11.52%	=	$23,040	x	34%	=	$ 7,834
Year 5	$200,000	x	11.52%	=	$23,040	x	34%	=	$ 7,834
Year 6	$200,000	x	5.76%	=	$11,520	x	34%	=	$ 3,917

EXERCISE 6

1.	0	1	2	3	4
Investment	($400,000)				
Revenues		$250,000	$250,000	$250,000	$250,000
Variable costs		(40,000)	(40,000)	(40,000)	(40,000)
Fixed out-of-pocket costs		(60,000)	(60,000)	(60,000)	(60,000)
Net cash inflows from operations before taxes		$150,000	$150,000	$150,000	$150,000
Income taxes on net cash flows from operations (34%)		(51,000)	(51,000)	(51,000)	(51,000)
Net cash flows from operations after taxes		$ 99,000	$ 99,000	$ 99,000	$ 99,000
Tax savings from depreciation[a]		40,000	40,000	40,000	40,000
Total cash flows		$139,000	$139,000	$139,000	$139,000
PV factors, 12%		x .89286	x .79719	x .71178	x .63552
Present values	422,191	$124,108	$110,809	$ 98,937	$ 88,337
NPV	$ 22,191				

[a]Tax savings from depreciation = $400,000/4 years = $100,000 x 40% = $40,000

689

EXERCISE 6 (continued)

2. A sample memo is shown below.

MEMORANDUM

> TO: W. A. Hartz & Co. Management
>
> FROM: Management Consulting, Inc.
>
> SUBJECT: Evaluation of Capital Budgeting Project

This memo regards your request for an evaluation of the capital budgeting project under consideration. Based on the information given, the project is acceptable because the project's return is greater than the required return of 12 percent. This is indicated by a positive net present value. (See attached calculations.)

Other factors to consider when evaluating this capital budgeting project include:
• the reliability of the estimates used
• the quality of the product produced
• environmental concerns
• customer satisfaction with the product
• competition and the market for the product

If you have any questions regarding the capital budgeting analysis, please contact me. We hope that we can serve your consulting needs in the future.

EXERCISE 7

1.

Investment	($2,000,000)
Tax savings: depreciation	
[($2,000,000/7) x 40% x 4.56376]	521,573
After-tax cost savings	
($400,000 x 60% x 7.46944)	1,792,666
Net present value	$ 314,239

2. Your memorandum should contain the following information:

The quantitative analysis indicates that the project has a return in excess of the cost of capital of 12 percent. Therefore, from a financial viewpoint, the project should be accepted. Qualitative factors to consider include the possibility of the new equipment producing an improved or higher quality product, greater production flexibility, and competitive advantages.

CHAPTER 23

DECISION MAKING IN
THE ADVANCED MANUFACTURING ENVIRONMENT

CHAPTER REVIEW

TRADITIONAL INVENTORY MANAGEMENT

Inventory Costs

- If inventory consists of goods purchased from an outside supplier, there
  are two inventory-related costs:
  1. ordering costs
  2. carrying costs

- If inventory consists of goods produced internally, the two inventory-
  related costs are:
  1. setup costs
  2. carrying costs

- If the goods are manufactured, the firm incurs setup costs instead of
  ordering costs.

- **Ordering costs** are the costs of placing and receiving an order. Examples
  include the clerical costs of processing an order and unloading costs.

- **Setup costs** are the costs of preparing equipment and facilities for
  production. Examples include wages of idled production workers, lost income
  from idled production facilities, and the costs of test runs (labor,
  materials, and overhead).

- **Carrying costs** are the costs of carrying inventory, such as:
  1. storage costs
  2. the opportunity cost of funds invested in inventory
  3. insurance on the inventory

- Since both ordering costs and setup costs are costs of acquiring inventory,
  they are treated in the same manner.

- **Stockout costs** are the costs associated with having insufficient amounts of
  inventory. Stockout costs include:
  1. lost sales
  2. costs of expediting (overtime or increased transportation costs)
  3. costs of interrupted production

- One reason companies hold inventory is to have a buffer to prevent
  stockouts.

- Ordering costs (or setup costs) are minimized by using fewer orders (or production runs) and <u>higher</u> inventory levels.

- Carrying costs are minimized by using <u>low</u> inventory levels.

- Since attempts to minimize ordering costs and carrying costs conflict, the objective becomes one of minimizing the combined ordering and carrying costs of inventory.

- Other reasons why firms carry inventory include:
  1. to take advantage of quantity discounts.
  2. to avoid anticipated price increases.

Inventory Policy

- An inventory policy addresses two questions:
  1. How much inventory should be ordered (or produced)?
  2. When should the order be placed (or the setup performed)?

Order Quantity

- The order quantity used should minimize the total cost of ordering and carrying inventory.

$$\text{Total Cost} = \text{Ordering Cost} + \text{Carrying Cost}$$

$$= PD/Q + CQ/2$$

where: P = the cost of placing and receiving an order
(or the setup cost for a production run)
D = annual demand
Q = quantity (number of units ordered each time an order is placed or the lot size for a production run)
C = the cost of carrying one unit for one year

EOQ

- The economic order quantity is the order quantity that minimizes the total cost.

- The economic order quantity is calculated as:

$$EOQ = \sqrt{(2DP/C)}$$

- The EOQ is the order size that results in ordering costs equaling carrying costs.

- The economic order quantity model can also be used to determine the most economical size of a production run. The only difference is that setup costs for starting a production run are substituted for ordering costs.

Reorder Point

- The **reorder point** is the point at which a new order should be placed (or a setup started).

- An order should be placed so it arrives just as the last item in inventory is used. This avoids stockout costs and minimizes carrying costs.

- The reorder point equals the amount of inventory that will be used from the time the order is placed until it arrives.

- **Lead time** is the time required to receive an order once an order is placed (or a setup initiated).

- The reorder point is calculated as follows:

Reorder Point = Rate of Usage x Lead Time

- **Safety stock** is extra inventory that serves as a cushion for preventing stockouts. Safety stock is calculated as follows:

Safety Stock = (Maximum Usage - Average Usage) x Lead Time

- With safety stock, the reorder point becomes:

Reorder Point = (Average Rate of Usage x Lead Time) + Safety Stock

EOQ and Inventory Management

- The traditional manufacturing environment has been characterized by mass production of a few standardized products that typically have a very high setup cost. The high setup cost encourages a large batch size and long production runs. Diversity is viewed as being costly and is avoided.

JIT AND INVENTORY MANAGEMENT: A DIFFERENT VIEW

- Competitive pressures have led many firms to abandon the EOQ model in favor of the JIT approach. JIT offers increased cost efficiency and simultaneously has the flexibility to respond to customer demands for better quality and more variety.

- JIT is a manufacturing philosophy that:
  1. focuses on increasing productivity by eliminating waste. (Inventories are viewed as waste because of the resources tied up in inventory.)
  2. maintains that goods should be purchased or produced only when there is a demand for the goods.
  3. reorganizes the manufacturing process into manufacturing cells.
  4. strives for zero defects (total quality control).
  5. emphasizes preventive maintenance, thereby reducing downtime for unexpected repairs.

- Two strategic objectives of JIT are:
  1. to increase profits.
  2. to improve a firm's competitive position.

- The objectives are achieved by:
  1. controlling costs (reducing waste, which enables better price competition).
  2. improving delivery performance.
  3. improving quality.

- JIT attempts to reduce inventories to zero.

- Traditional reasons for holding inventories are:
  1. to balance setup and carrying costs.
  2. to satisfy customer demand (meet delivery dates).
  3. to avoid shutting down manufacturing facilities.
  4. to take advantage of discounts.
  5. to hedge against future price increases.

- JIT challenges the traditional reasons for holding inventory and uses other solutions to the problems.

Setup and Carrying Costs: The JIT Approach

- The traditional approach takes setup costs as given and then tries to minimize total carrying costs and setup costs.

- JIT attempts to reduce setup costs (or ordering costs) by:
  1. reducing the time it takes to set up for production.
  2. reducing the number of orders through long-term contracting.

- If setup and ordering costs are insignificant, the only remaining cost to minimize is carrying cost.

- Carrying costs are minimized by reducing inventories to insignificant levels.

Due-Date Performance: The JIT Solution

- In the past, finished goods inventories have been used to ensure a firm's ability to meet a requested delivery date.

- JIT uses shorter lead times to meet requested delivery dates and to respond quickly to the demands of the market.

- JIT reduces lead time by:
1. reducing setup times.
2. using manufacturing cells to reduce travel distance between machines.

- Most companies experience at least a 90 percent reduction in lead times when they implement JIT.

Avoidance of Shutdown: The JIT Approach

- Most shutdowns occur because of one of three reasons:
1. machine failure
2. defective material or subassembly
3. unavailability of raw material or subassembly

- The traditional solution to the above problems is to hold inventory.

- JIT solves the problems by emphasizing:
1. total preventive maintenance to reduce machine failures.
2. total quality control to reduce defective materials or subassemblies.
3. the right kind of a relationship with suppliers to ensure the availability of raw material or subassemblies.

Total Preventive Maintenance

- The goal of **total preventive maintenance** is to have zero machine failures.

- Cell workers perform preventive maintenance during idle manufacturing time, thereby reducing downtime for unexpected repairs.

Total Quality Control

- The goal of total quality control is to have zero defects in internally produced and externally purchased materials.

The Kanban System

- The **Kanban system** is used to ensure that parts or materials are available when needed.

- The Kanban system is an information system that uses markers or cards to control production.

- The basic Kanban system uses three Kanban cards.
  1. A **withdrawal Kanban** specifies the quantity that a subsequent process should withdraw from a preceding process.
  2. A **production Kanban** specifies the quantity that the preceding process should produce.
  3. A **vendor Kanban** indicates to the supplier the quantity of materials to deliver and the time of delivery.

- The use of Kanbans ensures that the subsequent process withdraws the necessary quantity from the preceding process at the appropriate time. The Kanban system also controls the preceding process by allowing it to produce only the quantities withdrawn by the subsequent process. In this way, inventories are kept at a minimum, and the components arrive just in time to be used.

Discounts and Price Increases: JIT Purchasing Versus Holding Inventories

- Traditionally, inventories were held so that a firm could take advantage of quantity discounts and hedge against future price increases.

- JIT uses long-term contracts with a few suppliers.

- Suppliers are not selected based on price alone. Quality and reliability are important considerations.

- Benefits of long-term contracts include:
  1. stipulated prices.
  2. stipulated quality levels.
  3. reduction in the number of orders placed, thereby reducing ordering costs.

JIT: Some General Observations

- JIT stresses simplification and efficiency in plant layout by using:
  1. a cellular manufacturing layout with materials and components located adjacent to the work area.
  2. interdisciplinary labor where workers are trained to perform a variety of tasks.
  3. a quality standard of zero defects: "Do it right the first time."
  4. a commitment to continual improvement in efficiency.

STRATEGIC DECISION MAKING

- The three major objectives of the traditional management accounting system are:
  1. to assign a cost to services and products.
  2. to provide information for decision making.
  3. to provide information for planning and control purposes.

- The above three objectives are affected by JIT and automation.
  1. Product costing in the new manufacturing environment is discussed in Chapter 6.
  2. The effect of the new manufacturing environment on planning and control is discussed in Chapter 18.
  3. The new manufacturing environment affects decision making related to:
     - inventory management
     - capital budgeting
     - relevant costing
     - cost-volume-profit analysis
     - variable costing

Strategic Costing

- **Strategic decision making** is choosing among alternative strategies, with the goal of selecting a strategy or strategies that provides a company with a reasonable assurance of long-term growth and survival. Usually this goal is accomplished by obtaining a competitive advantage.

- **Strategic cost analysis** is the use of cost data to identify and develop superior strategies to produce a sustainable competitive advantage.

- The strategic role of management accounting must change, in part by switching from a short-term to a long-term focus.

- One aspect of strategic cost analysis is ensuring that the long run is considered—even for short-run decisions, such as special orders at reduced prices to use excess capacity. A long-term solution to excess capacity should be considered.

- Another aspect of strategic cost analysis is to identify and consider the strategic elements of a decision. For example, selling a product to discount department stores creates additional competition for the regularly priced product.

The Role of Activity-Based Costing

- Strategic product-related decisions include:
  - pricing decisions
  - product mix decisions
  - new product introductions
  - decisions on how to respond to competitors' products

- A unit-based system can result in distorted product costs and poor decisions. For example, a firm using unit-based costing with product diversity tends to overcost high-volume products and undercost low-volume products. This phenomenon has been blamed for the American giveaway of high-volume industries, such as VCRs, to foreign competitors.

- Activity-based costing (ABC) produces more accurate product costs for decision making.

- Strategic decision making is enhanced because activity-based costing can expand cost analysis to include post-plant, customer-level activities, such as marketing and distribution activities.

ACTIVITY-BASED COSTING, RESOURCE SPENDING, AND RESOURCE USAGE

- **Resource spending** is the cost of acquiring capacity to perform an activity.

- **Resource usage** is the amount of activity capacity used in producing output.

- Activity-based costing systems provide a key insight: Resource spending and resource usage can differ. For example, a firm's resource spending might provide the capacity for 100 setups but resource usage is the number of setups that actually occurred, which might be only 80 setups.

- In an activity-based costing system, only the amount of resource capacity used should be charged to products.

- Unused activity capacity is *not* assigned to products. Instead, it is shown as a common expense.

Resource Spending Versus Resource Usage

- The **activity rate** is the cost per unit of activity and is calculated as the resource expenditure for an activity divided by the practical activity capacity.

- The **cost of resource usage** is calculated as follows:

> Cost of Resource Usage = Activity Rate x Actual Activity Usage

- The **cost of unused activity** is calculated as:

> Cost of Unused Activity = Activity Rate x Unused Activity

- The relationship between resources supplied (resource spending) and resources used to perform activities can be expressed as follows:

> Resource Spending = Resource Usage + Unused Capacity

Units:

> Activity Availability = Activity Usage + Unused Capacity

Dollars:

Cost of Activity Supplied = Cost of Activity Used + Cost of Unused Activity

- The traditional accounting system provides information only about the cost of the resource supplied.

- An ABC system provides information about how much of an activity is used and the cost of its usage.

Activities, Resources, and Cost Behavior

- Resources are supplied in one of two ways:
  1. **Resources supplied as used (and needed)** are acquired from outside sources, and the organization is free to buy only the quantity of resource needed. Thus, the quantity of resources supplied equals the quantity demanded and thereby eliminates unused capacity.
  2. **Resources supplied in advance of usage** are acquired using either an explicit or implicit contract to obtain a given quantity of resource, regardless of whether the resource available is fully used or not. Resources supplied in advance may exceed the demand for their usage, resulting in unused capacity.

Resources Supplied As Needed and Cost Behavior

- The cost of resources supplied as needed generally can be treated as a variable cost. For example, in a JIT environment, raw materials are acquired and used as needed. Using units produced as the cost driver, as the units produced increase, the usage (and cost) of raw materials would increase proportionately.

Resources Supplied in Advance and Cost Behavior

- Two examples of resources that are acquired before actual demands for the resource are realized are:
  1. **multiperiod service capabilities**, where organizations pay cash up front or enter into an explicit contract that requires periodic cash payments, such as leasing buildings and equipment. The annual expense is independent of actual usage of the resource. These expenses correspond to **committed fixed expenses**--costs incurred to provide long-term activity capacity.
  2. **implicit contracts** (usually with salaried and hourly employees), resulting in the implicit understanding that the organization will maintain employment levels even though there may be temporary downturns in the quantity of the activity used. Resource spending for this category corresponds to **discretionary fixed expenses**--costs incurred for the acquisition of short-term activity capacity.

Activities and Cost Behavior

- Since it is possible that activities may have resources associated with them that are acquired in advance and resources that are acquired as needed, activity costs can display a mixed cost behavior.

- In a mixed cost setting, a need exists to compute both a *fixed activity rate* and a *variable activity rate*. These activity rates are computed using practical capacity.

  The *cost of unused activity* is the fixed activity rate x unused capacity.

- An activity-based resource usage model can improve managerial control and decision making. For example, eliminating excess activity capacity may decrease resource spending and increase profits.

- With respect to improved decision making, the activity-based resource usage model allows managers to calculate changes in resource supply and demand that result from implementing decisions, such as:
  - make-or-buy
  - special orders
  - keep-or-drop product lines

RELEVANT COSTING: ADVANCED MANUFACTURING ENVIRONMENT

- JIT and cell manufacturing result in many costs that formerly were common to several products that are now directly traceable to a particular product.

- Remaining common costs can often be traced directly to products using activity-based costing and multiple cost drivers.

- Many costs vary with activities associated with the individual products and activity-based drivers but may not vary directly with production activity or volume-based drivers.

SEGMENTED REPORTING BY COST BEHAVIOR

- **Segmented reporting** is reporting the profit contributions of activities or other units (e.g., divisions or products) within an organization.

- A **segment** is any profit-making entity within the organization.

- Segmented reporting is used to provide managers with information about:
  1. divisional profitability
  2. plant profitability
  3. product profitability

- Managers should not be held accountable for costs they cannot control. If noncontrollable costs are included in a segment report, they should be shown separately from controllable costs and labeled as noncontrollable.

- Absorption costing classifies expenses by function as:
  1. cost of goods sold or
  2. selling and administrative.

- Variable costing classifies expenses by behavior as either:
  1. variable or
  2. fixed.

- The different forms of segment reporting in <u>increasing</u> order of usefulness are as follows:
  1. absorption costing using functional classifications.
  2. variable-costing segment reporting using behavioral classifications.
  3. segment reporting using ABC classifications.
  4. segment reporting using JIT and ABC classifications.

- Segment reporting using variable costing provides more useful information than does absorption costing.

- Segment reporting using ABC classifications is more useful than variable-costing segment reporting.

- JIT provides even further improvement.

- JIT increases the number of traceable costs. Thus, responsibility for controlling these costs can be more readily assigned. In addition, the increased accuracy in segment reporting provides more useful information for such decisions as whether to keep or drop a segment.

Conventional Segmented Reporting

- Segmented income statements are usually prepared using a variable-costing approach.

- Fixed expenses are broken into two categories:
  1. **Direct fixed expenses**. Direct fixed expenses are fixed expenses that are directly traceable to a segment. They are sometimes referred to as avoidable fixed expenses because they are avoided if the segment is eliminated.
  2. **Common fixed expenses**. Common fixed expenses are caused by more than one segment and are not directly traceable to any one segment.

- **Segment margin** is the profit contribution a segment makes toward covering a firm's common fixed costs and is calculated as follows:

> **Sales**
> - **Variable costs**
> = **Contribution margin**
> - **Direct fixed costs**
> = **Segment margin**

- A conventional variable-costing segmented income statement calculates income in the following manner.

> **Sales**
> - **Variable costs (unit-based)**
> = **Contribution margin**
> - **Direct fixed costs**
> = **Segment margin**
> - **Common fixed costs**
> = **Income before taxes**

701

Segmented Reporting and ABC

• An activity-based segmented income statement calculates income in the following manner.

> Sales
> - Variable costs (unit-based)
> = Contribution margin
> - Traceable expenses:
>   Nonunit variable
>   Activity fixed expenses
>   Direct fixed expenses
> = Segment margin
> - Common expenses:
>   Unused activity
>   Facility-level costs
> = Income before taxes

• Resources acquired as needed vary with a cost driver and are labeled as:
1. unit-based variable expenses (such as direct materials).
2. nonunit variable expenses (driven by a cost driver other than units).

• Resources acquired in advance are labeled as *activity fixed expenses*. **Activity fixed expenses** are fixed expenses that are assigned to a segment by the use of a cost driver.

• Common expenses are not directly traceable to any one segment and consist of:
1. unused capacity.
2. facility-level costs (such as general administration costs).

Segmented Reporting and JIT

• JIT changes batch-level costs to unit-level costs. A segmented income statement using JIT and ABC classifications calculates income as follows.

• When JIT is used, direct labor often behaves as a fixed cost instead of a variable cost because cell workers perform preventive maintenance during idle time.

> Sales
> - Variable costs (unit-based)
> = Contribution margin
> - Traceable expenses:
>   Nonunit-based variable costs
>   Activity fixed costs
>   Direct fixed costs
> = Segment margin
> - Common expenses:
>   Unused capacity
>   Facility-level costs
> = Income before taxes

702

KEY TERMS TEST

Test your recall of the key terms as follows: Read the following definitions of key terms and try to recall as many key terms as you can <u>without assistance</u>. Write your answers in the spaces provided. If you need assistance, refer to the list of key terms at the end of this section.

1. _____ _____ is the time required to receive an order once placed or the time required to produce a product from start to finish.

2. _____ _____ are the costs of placing and receiving an order.

3. _____ _____ is extra inventory that serves as a cushion for preventing stockouts.

4. _____ _____ are costs of preparing equipment and facilities so that they can be used for production.

5. _____ _____ _____ is the process of choosing among alternative strategies, with the goal of selecting a strategy or strategies that provide a company with a reasonable assurance of long-term growth and survival.

6. _____ _____ _____ has a goal of zero machine failures.

7. A card or marker that specifies the quantity that the preceding process should produce is a _____ _____.

8. The point in time at which a new order (or setup) should be initiated is the _____ _____.

9. A card or marker that signals to a supplier the quantity of materials that need to be delivered and the time of delivery is a _____ _____.

10. A marker or card that specifies the quantity that a subsequent process should withdraw from a preceding process is a _____ _____.

11. _____ _____ are the costs of holding inventory.

12. _____ _____ _____, or _____, is the amount that should be ordered (or produced) to minimize the total ordering (or setup) and carrying costs.

13. An information system that controls production on a demand-pull basis through the use of cards or markers is a _____ _____.

14. _____ _____ are the costs of insufficient inventory.

15. _____ _____ _____ uses cost data to identify and develop superior strategies that will produce a sustainable competitive advantage.

16. _____ _____ _____ are fixed expenses that are assigned to a segment by the use of a cost driver.

17. The resource expenditure for an activity divided by the practical activity capacity equals the _____ _____.

18. _____ _____ _____ are costs incurred to provide long-term activity capacity.

19. _____ _____ is the cost of acquiring capacity to perform an activity.

20. The amount of activity used in producing an organization's output is called _____ _____.

21. The _____ _____ _____ _____ is calculated as: Activity rate (fixed) x Unused activity.

22. _____ _____ _____ _____ _____ are resources acquired by the use of either an explicit or implicit contract to obtain a given quantity of resource, regardless of whether the resource available is fully used or not.

23. The activity rate times the actual activity usage equals _____ _____ _____ _____.

24. _____ _____ _____ are costs incurred for the acquisition of short-term activity capacity.

25. _____ _____ _____ _____ are resources acquired from outside sources, where the terms of acquisition do not require any long-term commitment.

26. A _____ is any profit-making entity within an organization.

27. _____ _____ is the profit contribution each segment makes toward covering a firm's common fixed costs.

28. Reporting the profit contributions of activities or other units within an organization is called _____ _____.

29. _____ _____ _____ are fixed expenses that are directly traceable to a segment.

30. _____ _____ _____ are fixed costs that are caused by more than one segment and are not directly traceable to any one segment.

KEY TERMS:

activity fixed expenses
activity rate
carrying costs
committed fixed expenses
common fixed costs
cost of resource usage
cost of unused activity
direct fixed expenses
discretionary fixed expenses
economic order quantity, EOQ
Kanban system
lead time
ordering costs
production Kanban
reorder point

resource spending
resources supplied as used (needed)
resources supplied in advance of usage
resource usage
safety stock
segment
segment margin
segmented reporting
setup costs
stockout costs
strategic cost analysis
strategic decision making
total preventive maintenance
vendor Kanban
withdrawal Kanban

Compare your answers to those at the end of the chapter and review any key terms missed.

CHAPTER QUIZ

Write your answers in the spaces provided.

1. If inventory consists of goods purchased from an outside supplier, the two inventory-related costs are:
   1. _____
   2. _____

2. If inventory consists of goods produced internally, the two inventory-related costs are:
   1. _____
   2. _____

3. Three examples of carrying costs are:
   1. _____
   2. _____
   3. _____

4. The economic order quantity is the order size that results in _____ _____ equaling _____ _____. It is the order quantity that minimizes total inventory costs.

5. The reorder point is the point at which a new order should be placed. The reorder point is calculated as: _____ __ _____ X _____ _____.

6. Safety stock serves as a cushion for preventing _____.

7. If safety stock is carried, the reorder point is calculated as:
   [(_____ ___ _____ X _____ _____) + _____ _____].

705

8. List three reasons why companies have traditionally held inventory.

1. _____
2. _____
3. _____

9. The goals of JIT include:

1. _____
2. _____
3. _____

10. When JIT is used, during idle time cell workers perform _____ _____ .

11. When JIT manufacturing is used, suppliers are selected based upon:

1. _____
2. _____
3. _____

12. Benefits of using long-term contracts with suppliers include:

1. _____
2. _____
3. _____

13. Rank the following forms of segment reporting from 1 to 4 where 1 is the least useful and 4 is the most useful.

_____ Segment reporting using JIT and ABC classifications.

_____ Absorption costing using functional classifications.

_____ Segment reporting using ABC classifications.

_____ Variable-costing segment reporting using behavioral classifications.

14. A conventional variable-costing segmented income statement calculates income in the following manner.

        Sales

        - _____

        = Contribution margin

        - _____

        = Segment margin

        - _____

        = Income before taxes

15. An activity-based segmented income statement calculates income as follows.

        Sales

        - _____

        = Contribution margin

        - Traceable expenses:

            _____

            _____

            _____

        = Segment margin

        - Common expenses:

            _____

            _____

        = Income before taxes

16. Activity Rate = _____ / _____

17. Cost of Resource Usage = _____ x _____

18. Cost of Unused Activity = _____ x _____

19. Cost of Activity Supplied = _____ x _____

Compare your answers to those at the end of the chapter and review any questions missed.

Circle the single best answer.

20. Which of the following results in no unused capacity? (a) resources supplied as used; (b) resources supplied in advance of usage

21. Which of the following may result in unused capacity? (a) resources supplied as used; (b) resources supplied in advance of usage

22. Which of the following is usually labeled as a variable cost? (a) resources supplied as used; (b) resources supplied in advance of usage

23. Which of the following is usually labeled as an activity fixed expense? (a) resources supplied as used; (b) resources supplied in advance of usage

24. When ABC is used, which of the following is a fixed expense that is assigned to a segment using a cost driver? (a) nonunit variable expense; (b) activity fixed expense; (c) direct fixed expense; (d) facility-level costs

Use the following information to answer the next six questions.

The following unit cost information is provided for a product using three different cost systems: conventional, activity-based, and JIT. The conventional system assigns overhead using unit-based cost drivers. The activity-based system assigns overhead using both unit-based and nonunit-based cost drivers. The JIT system uses manufacturing cells, thus improving the traceability of costs, and activity-based costing is used for costs not directly associated with a manufacturing cell. If JIT is adopted, direct labor would behave as a fixed cost because the cell workers would perform preventive maintenance during idle time.

The company produces and sells 2,000 units of product each year. The finished product sells for $400 per unit.

	Cost System		
	Conventional	Activity-Based	JIT
Direct materials	$160	$160	$160
Direct labor	40	40	50[a]
Unit-based variable overhead	60	60	20
Nonunit-based variable overhead	-	30	20
Activity fixed overhead[b]	-	50	10
Direct fixed costs	20	20	20
Common fixed costs	90	20	20
Total	$370	$380	$300

[a] Cell labor, including maintenance, materials handling, and packing.
[b] Nonunit fixed costs assigned using a cost driver. In the short run, these costs do not vary with the level of the associated cost driver. Assume that all of the activity fixed overhead is avoidable and there are no unused activity capacity costs.

25. If a conventional cost system is used, variable expenses would be: (a) $320,000; (b) $440,000; (c) $490,000; (d) $520,000

26. If a conventional cost system is used, the product margin would be: (a) $224,000; (b) $240,000; (c) $280,000; (d) $320,000

27. If an activity-based cost system is used, variable expenses would be: (a) $520,000; (b) $490,000; (c) $440,000; (d) $320,000

28. If an activity-based cost system is used, the product margin would be: (a) $80,000; (b) $160,000; (c) $200,000; (d) $280,000

29. If JIT is used, variable expenses would be: (a) $440,000; (b) $280,000; (c) $360,000; (d) $520,000

30. If JIT is used, the product margin would be: (a) $240,000; (b) $260,000; (c) $280,000; (d) $310,000

Compare your answers to those at the end of the chapter and review any questions missed.

EXERCISES

EXERCISE 1

Below are listed 5 reasons why companies have traditionally held inventory. Indicate the JIT solution to each of the reasons for holding inventory.

Traditional Approach	JIT Approach
1. Hold inventories to minimize total carrying costs and setup costs.	
2. Use inventories to ensure the firm meets delivery dates and avoids stockouts.	
3. Hold inventory in case there is a shutdown due to machine failure.	
4. Hold inventory to avoid shutdowns due to defective parts.	
5. Hold inventory to take advantage of quantity discounts and hedge against future price increases.	

EXERCISE 2

The Georgia Company manufactures a special blend of tea. The company buys one of the spices used in the tea in 10-pound bags that cost $5.00 each. The company uses 50,000 of the bags per year, and usage occurs evenly throughout the year.

The average cost to carry a 10-pound bag in inventory per year is $1.00, and the cost to place an order is $12.00.

Required:

1. Determine the economic order quantity for the spice in terms of 10-pound bags.

2. If the company works 250 days per year, on the average how many bags of spice are used per working day?

3. If the lead time for an order is normally 5 working days, determine the reorder point.

4. If the company normally carries 50 bags as safety stock, determine the reorder point for the spice.

710

EXERCISE 3

Smith Manufacturing produces lawn mowers. In order to produce the frames for the mowers, special equipment must be set up. The setup cost per frame is $50. The cost of carrying frames in inventory is $4.00 per frame per year. The company produces 10,000 mowers per year.

Required:

1. Compute the number of frames that should be produced per setup in order to minimize total setup and carrying costs.

2. Compute the total setup and carrying costs associated with the economic order quantity.

EXERCISE 4

The following unit cost information is provided about a product using three different cost systems:
1. conventional
2. activity-based
3. JIT

The conventional system assigns overhead using unit-based cost drivers. The activity-based system assigns overhead using both unit-based and nonunit-based cost drivers.

The JIT system uses manufacturing cells, thus improving the traceability of costs, and activity-based costing is used for costs not directly associated with a manufacturing cell. If JIT is adopted, direct labor would behave as a fixed cost because the cell workers would perform preventive maintenance during idle time.

The company produces and sells 1,800 units of this product each year, and the product normally sells for $500 per unit.

	Cost System		
	Conventional	Activity-Based	JIT
Direct materials	$250	$250	$250
Direct labor	40	40	70[a]
Unit-based variable overhead	70	70	20
Nonunit-based variable overhead	-	30	25
Activity fixed overhead[b]	-	20	10
Direct fixed costs	30	40	40
Common fixed costs	60	20	20
Total	$450	$470	$435

[a] Cell labor, including maintenance, materials handling, and packing.
[b] Nonunit fixed costs assigned using a cost driver. In the short run, these costs do not vary with the level of the associated cost driver. Assume that all of the activity fixed overhead is avoidable and there are no unused activity capacity costs.

712

EXERCISE 4 (continued)

Required:

For each cost system prepare a product income statement that shows
contribution margin and segment margin.

	Conventional	Activity-Based	JIT

EXERCISE 5

Nance Manufacturing has idle capacity. A customer has offered to purchase
1,000 units of one of Nance's products for $5 each. The product normally
sells for $7.50.   The customer is located in a state not previously serviced
by Nance Manufacturing.   The activity-based accounting system provided the
following information:

	Cost Driver	Unused Capacity	Quantity Demanded*	Activity Rate Fixed	Variable
Direct materials	Units	-0-	1,000	--	$1.50
Direct labor	Direct labor hours	-0-	200	--	3.50
Setups	Setup hours	10	20	$25.00	4.00
Machining	Machining hours	3,000	2,000	2.00	0.50

*This only represents the amount of resources demanded by the special order
 being considered.

Any expansion of the setup resource must be acquired in "lumpy" amounts.
Each lumpy amount provides an additional 50 hours of setup servicing and is
priced at the fixed activity rate.

Required:

1. Compute the change in income for Nance Manufacturing if the order is
   accepted.

2. If the setup activity had 30 hours of unused capacity, how would this
   affect the analysis?

EXERCISE 5 (continued)

3. Prepare a memorandum to management stating your recommendation regarding whether the order should be accepted or rejected. Include a discussion of the strategic issues affecting the decision.

```
┌─────────────────────────────────────────────────────────────┐
│                        MEMORANDUM                             │
│                                                               │
│        DATE:                                                  │
│          TO:                                                  │
│        FROM:                                                  │
│     SUBJECT:                                                  │
├─────────────────────────────────────────────────────────────┤
│                                                               │
│                                                               │
│                                                               │
│                                                               │
│                                                               │
│                                                               │
│                                                               │
│                                                               │
│                                                               │
│                                                               │
│                                                               │
│                                                               │
│                                                               │
│                                                               │
│                                                               │
│                                                               │
│                                                               │
│                                                               │
│                                                               │
│                                                               │
│                                                               │
│                                                               │
└─────────────────────────────────────────────────────────────┘
```

ANSWERS

<u>KEY TERMS TEST</u>
1. Lead time
2. Ordering costs
3. Safety stock
4. Setup costs
5. Strategic decision making
6. Total preventive maintenance
7. production Kanban
8. reorder point
9. vendor Kanban
10. withdrawal Kanban
11. Carrying costs
12. Economic order quantity, EOQ
13. Kanban system
14. Stockout costs
15. Strategic cost analysis
16. Activity fixed expenses
17. activity rate
18. Committed fixed expenses
19. Resource spending
20. resource usage
21. cost of unused activity
22. Resources supplied in advance of usage
23. cost of resource usage
24. Discretionary fixed expenses
25. Resources supplied as used (needed)
26. segment
27. Segment margin
28. segmented reporting
29. Direct fixed costs
30. Common fixed costs

<u>CHAPTER QUIZ</u>
1. ordering costs, carrying costs
2. setup costs, carrying costs
3. storage costs, the opportunity cost of funds invested in inventory, insurance on inventory
4. ordering costs, carrying costs
5. Rate of Usage, Lead Time
6. stockouts
7. Rate of Usage, Lead Time, Safety Stock
8. 1. to avoid stockouts
   2. to avoid shutdowns
   3. to take advantage of quantity discounts and hedge against future price increases
9. 1. zero inventories
   2. zero defects (total quality control)
   3. total preventive maintenance
10. preventive maintenance
11. price, quality, reliability

CHAPTER 24

BUDGETING FOR PLANNING AND CONTROL

CHAPTER REVIEW

DESCRIPTION OF BUDGETING

Definition and Role of Budgeting

• Budgeting is a planning and control tool used by managers.

• A budget is a plan of action expressed in financial terms.

• A budget is a means of translating the goals and strategies of an organization into operational terms.

• Budgets are used as a control tool by comparing actual results with planned or budgeted amounts. Corrective action can be taken if needed.

• The steps involved in the planning and control process are:
  1. Develop a strategic plan. A **strategic plan** identifies strategies for future activities and operations, generally involving at least five years.
  2. Translate the strategic plan into long-term and short-term objectives.
  3. From the objectives, develop short-term plans.
  4. Develop budgets based upon the short-term plans.
  5. Compare actual results with planned (budgeted) amounts.
  6. Take corrective action if necessary.

Purposes of Budgeting

• The **master budget** is the collection of all budgets and is the comprehensive financial plan for the organization.

• Advantages of budgeting include:
  1. It forces managers to plan.
  2. It provides information that can be used to improve decision making.
  3. It assists in the control of resources and employees by setting a benchmark that can be used later to evaluate performance.
  4. It improves communication and coordination within the organization.

• **Control** is the process of setting standards, receiving feedback on actual performance, and taking corrective action whenever actual performance deviates significantly from planned performance.

Responsibility Accounting

• **Responsibility accounting** attempts to assign costs and revenues to the individuals who have the most control or influence over them.

• Responsibility centers are the areas of responsibility. Three types of responsibility centers are:
  1. **Cost center**: a responsibility center in which a manager is responsible for costs only.
  2. **Profit center**: a responsibility center in which a manager is responsible for both revenues and costs.
  3. **Investment center**: a responsibility center in which a manager is responsible for revenues, costs, and investments.

• The accounting system is used to set standards, measure actual outcomes, and report the performance of responsibility centers.

• The approach used in responsibility accounting is as follows:
  1. A responsibility center is identified.
  2. A standard or benchmark is set (usually through budgeting).
  3. A reward system is established to encourage good performance of managers.
  4. A manager's performance is measured by comparing actual performance with budgeted performance.
  5. A reward system is used to encourage managers to perform well.

The Master Budget

• The **master budget** is a comprehensive financial plan made up of the individual budgets.

• A master budget is divided into:
  1. **Operating budgets**: budgets concerned with income-generating activities. Operating budgets include the following:
     • sales budget
     • production budget
     • direct materials purchases budget
     • direct labor budget
     • overhead budget
     • selling and administrative budget
     • ending finished goods inventory budget
     • cost of goods sold budget
     • pro forma or budgeted income statement

  2. **Financial budgets**: budgets concerned with cash inflows, cash outflows, and expenditures for capital acquisitions. Financial budgets include the following:
     • cash budget
     • budgeted balance sheet
     • budget for fixed asset purchases (capital budget)

The Time Factor

• Most of the budgets in the master budget are for a one-year period.

• A **continuous budget** is a moving twelve-month budget. As a month expires in the budget, an additional month in the future is added so that the company always has a twelve-month plan on hand.

• A **capital budget** is a financial plan for the acquisition of long-term assets.

Directing and Coordinating

• The **budget director** is the individual responsible for coordinating and directing the budget process.

• The budget director is usually the controller or someone who reports to the controller.

• The **budget committee** is responsible for:
  1. Setting budgetary goals and policies.
  2. Reviewing the budget.
  3. Resolving any differences that arise as the budget is prepared.
  4. Approving the final budget.
  5. Monitoring actual performance and comparing it to the budget.

• Members of the budget committee usually include the president, vice presidents, and the controller.

Two Dimensions of Budgeting

• Two dimensions of budgeting are:
  1. How the budget is prepared (the mechanics of budget preparation).
  2. How the budget is used to implement the organization's plans (how individuals within an organization react to a budgetary system).

• The success or failure of budgeting depends upon how well management considers the second dimension—the behavioral implications.

Preparation of the Operating Budget

• The operating budget consists of a budgeted income statement accompanied by the following supporting schedules:
  1. sales budget
  2. production budget
  3. direct materials purchases budget
  4. direct labor budget
  5. overhead budget
  6. selling and administrative budget
  7. ending finished goods budget
  8. cost of goods sold budget

Sales Forecast

- Preparation of a sales forecast is the first step in the budget process.

- The sales forecast is usually the responsibility of the marketing department.

- Sales may be forecast using:
  1. time-series analysis
  2. correlation analysis
  3. econometric modeling
  4. the *bottom-up* approach based on feedback from salespeople

Sales Budget

- The sales forecast is the initial estimate of sales.

- The **sales budget** is the projection approved by the budget committee using expected sales in units and dollars.

Production Budget

- The **production budget** indicates the number of units of finished product to be manufactured in order to meet sales needs and inventory requirements.

- If production is related to sales of the next period, production needs for a manufacturer can be calculated as follows:

> **Budgeted sales in units**
> **+ Desired ending inventory in units**
> **= Total units needed**
> **- Beginning inventory (units on hand)**
> **= Units to be produced**

- For a retailer, the units to be purchased can be calculated as:

> **Budgeted sales**
> **+ Desired ending inventory in units**
> **= Total units needed**
> **- Beginning inventory (units on hand)**
> **= Units to be purchased**

Direct Materials Budget

- The **direct materials budget** is a budget of the expected usage of materials in production and the purchase of the materials required.

- The steps involved in preparing a direct materials purchases budget are:
  1. Determine the amount of direct materials necessary to manufacture the number of units to be produced based on the input-output relationship (the technological relationship between direct materials and output).
  2. Determine the quantity of direct materials to be <u>purchased</u> as follows:

    Quantity of direct materials needed for production
    + Desired ending inventory of direct materials
    = Total quantity of direct materials needed
    - Beginning inventory of direct materials
    = Quantity of direct materials to be purchased

  3. Determine the cost of the direct materials to be purchased by multiplying the quantity of direct materials to be purchased by the expected cost per unit of direct material.

Direct Labor Budget

- The **direct labor budget** is also based upon the production budget and is a budget of planned expenditures for direct labor. The direct labor budget indicates the rate per hour and the number of hours necessary to meet production requirements.

Overhead Budget

- The **overhead budget** shows the expected cost of all indirect manufacturing costs.

- Budgeted variable overhead costs are based on a budgeted variable overhead rate multiplied by budgeted activity.

- Budgeted fixed overhead costs remain unchanged as the activity level changes within the relevant range.

Selling and Administrative Expense Budget

- The **selling and administrative expense budget** is a budget of planned expenditures for nonmanufacturing activities, such as sales commissions and office salaries.

- Selling and administrative expenses have a variable component that varies with the level of production or sales and a fixed component that remains constant within the relevant range.

Ending Finished Goods Inventory Budget

- The **ending finished goods inventory budget** contains:
  1. calculations of the unit cost of the product.
  2. the cost of the planned ending inventory.

Budgeted Cost of Goods Sold

- Budgeted cost of goods sold is calculated as follows:

> **Direct materials used**
> **+ Direct labor used**
> **+ Overhead**
> **= Budgeted manufacturing costs**
> **+ Beginning finished goods**
> **= Goods available for sale**
> **- Ending finished goods**
> **= Budgeted cost of goods sold**

Budgeted Income Statement

- The budgeted income statement calculates net income as follows:

> **Sales**
> **- Cost of goods sold**
> **= Gross profit**
> **- Selling and administrative expenses**
> **= Operating income**
> **- Interest expense**
> **= Income before taxes**
> **- Income taxes**
> **= Net income**

Operating Budgets for Merchandising and Service Firms

- In a merchandising firm, the production budget is replaced with a **merchandise purchases budget** that identifies the quantity of each item that must be purchased for resale, the unit cost of the item, and the total purchase cost.

- In a for-profit service firm, the sales budget is also the production budget because the sales budget identifies the quantity of each service that will be sold.

- For a nonprofit service firm, the sales budget is replaced by a budget that identifies the levels of the various services that will be offered for the coming year and the associated funds that will be assigned to the services.

PREPARATION OF THE FINANCIAL BUDGET

- The financial budgets are:
1. The cash budget.
2. The budgeted balance sheet.
3. The budget for fixed asset purchases.

Cash Budget

- The cash budget is a summary of planned cash receipts and cash payments. A cash budget might include the following items:

>   Beginning cash balance
>   + **Cash receipts:**
>   Cash collections on accounts receivable
>   Cash sales
>   = **Cash available**
>   - **Cash payments:**
>   Cash payments on accounts payable (for material purchases)
>   Direct labor wages
>   Variable overhead
>   Fixed overhead[a]
>   Variable selling and administrative expenses[b]
>   Fixed selling and administrative expenses[a]
>   Income taxes
>   Dividends
>   Purchases of property or equipment requiring cash[c]
>   Total cash payments
>   - **Minimum cash balance**
>   = **Excess cash (or deficiency)**
>
>   **Investments:**
>   - Investment of excess cash
>   + Liquidation of investment of excess cash
>
>   **Financing:**
>   + Borrowings to cover deficiency
>   - Repayment of loan
>   - Interest payments
>   = **Ending cash balance**

[a]Depreciation is considered a fixed cost; however, it is not a cash outflow. Therefore, depreciation would not be included in the cash budget.

[b]Bad debt expense is included in the selling and administrative expenses budget; however, it is not included in the cash budget. Instead, bad debt expense is shown as a reduction in the amount the firm expects to collect on accounts receivable.

[c]Only purchases of property and equipment requiring cash would be shown on the cash budget. If the property or equipment purchase was financed by long-term debt, cash repayments of the debt would be shown as a cash payment in the cash budget.

727

- A firm may desire or be required to maintain a minimum cash balance.

- Excess cash should be invested to earn a return. A schedule of temporary investments may be used to account for the firm's temporary investments.

- If the firm has a cash deficiency, borrowing will be necessary to maintain the minimum cash balance.

Budgeted Balance Sheet

- The final statement to be prepared in the budgeting process is the pro forma balance sheet. Most of the amounts appearing in the pro forma balance sheet can be traced to one of the other budgets or schedules.

- See text Exhibit 24-3 for a diagram of the interrelationships of the budgets.

THE BEHAVIORAL DIMENSION OF BUDGETING

- Budgets are often used to judge the performance of managers.

- A manager's bonuses, salary increases, and promotions are affected by the manager's ability to achieve budgeted goals; therefore, budgets can have a significant effect on a manager's behavior.

- Whether the effect is positive or negative depends upon how the budgets are administered.

- An ideal budgetary system:
  1. promotes **goal congruence**: the manager's personal goals are congruent or consistent with the organization's goals.
  2. creates a drive in managers to achieve the goals.

- **Dysfunctional behavior** is behavior that is in conflict with the organization's goals. If the budget is improperly administered, dysfunctional behavior may result.

- A successful budgetary system emphasizes the behavioral considerations.

- Key features that encourage positive behavior are:
  1. Frequent feedback on performance.
  2. Flexible budgeting capabilities.
  3. Monetary and nonmonetary incentives.
  4. Participation.
  5. Realistic standards.
  6. Controllability of costs.
  7. Multiple measures of performance. The budget should NOT be the only means used to evaluate manager performance.

Frequent Feedback on Performance

- Frequent feedback on performance lets managers know how they are doing as the year unfolds. This gives managers the opportunity to take corrective action and adapt to changing conditions.

- **Management by exception** uses performance reports that show variances (deviations from planned results). This allows managers to focus only on the areas that need attention.

Static Budgets Versus Flexible Budgets

- A **static budget** is prepared for a particular level of activity. The problem with a static budget is that actual costs at one level of activity are compared with planned costs at <u>another</u> level of activity.

- A **flexible budget** computes expected costs for different activity levels. This permits comparison of actual costs and expected costs at the <u>same</u> level of activity.

- To compute the expected cost at different activity levels, the following cost formula is needed for each item in the budget.

$$Y = F + VX$$

  where:
  Y = the item's total cost
  F = the item's fixed cost
  V = the item's variable cost per unit of activity
  X = activity level

- The **flexible budget variance** is the sum of:
  - the price variance.
  - the efficiency variance.

- A *price variance* is caused by the difference between actual and budgeted costs of inputs (direct materials, direct labor, and overhead).

- An *efficiency variance* is caused by the difference between the quantity of planned inputs and the quantity of actual inputs needed to produce actual output.

- *Volume variances* are caused by differences in volume between the static budget and the flexible budget.

Monetary and Nonmonetary Incentives

- Incentives are used to induce a manager to work toward achieving the organization's goals.

- Negative incentives use fear of punishment to motivate.

- Positive incentives use the expectation of a reward to motivate.

- Monetary incentives are economic rewards, such as salary increases, bonuses, and promotions.

- Nonmonetary incentives are intrinsic factors that may motivate managers, such as the satisfaction of a job well done, recognition, and increased responsibility.

- Monetary awards alone are not sufficient to highly motivate managers.

Participative Budgeting

- **Participative budgeting** allows managers to participate in creating the budget used to evaluate their performance.

- Participative budgeting can:
  1. Increase goal congruence.
  2. Provide nonmonetary incentives. Individuals involved in setting their own standards work harder to achieve them.
  3. Use the knowledge of individuals who are aware of local conditions.

- Three potential problems of participative budgeting are:
  1. Standard-setting problems. If the goals are too low and too easily achieved, the manager's performance may drop because there is no challenge.

     If the goals are set too high, the manager may become frustrated and give up when he or she does not meet the goal.

     In participative budgeting, the goals should be high but achievable.

  2. Budgetary slack. Participative budgeting creates the opportunity for managers to build slack into the budget (pad the budget).

     Top management should conduct a careful review of budgets proposed by subordinate managers to decrease the effects of building slack into the budgets.

  3. Pseudoparticipation. Top management assumes total control, and subordinate manager participation is limited to endorsing the budget.

Realistic Standards

- Realistic standards should include allowances for seasonal variations and general economic conditions.

Controllability of Costs

- Managers should not be held accountable for costs they cannot control.

- Many firms still include noncontrollable costs in a manager's budget to make the manager aware of these costs. However, if noncontrollable costs are included in a manager's budget, they should be labeled as noncontrollable and separated from controllable costs.

Multiple Measures of Performance

- Budgets should not be the only measure used to evaluate manager performance.

- If budget performance is overemphasized, **myopic behavior** can occur, which is when the manager takes actions that improve budgetary performance in the short run but cause long-run harm to the firm.

- Since managers of responsibility centers usually spend only three to five years before being promoted or moving to another position, their successors are the ones who must deal with the effects of myopic behavior.

- The best way to prevent myopic behavior is to measure manager performance based on several measures of performance, such as market share, productivity, quality, and personnel development.

KEY TERMS TEST

Test your recall of the key terms as follows: Read the following definitions of key terms and try to recall as many key terms as you can <u>without assistance</u>. Write your answers in the spaces provided. If you need assistance, refer to the list of key terms at the end of this section.

1. A _____ is a plan of action expressed in financial terms.

2. The individual responsible for coordinating and directing the overall budgeting process is called the _____ _____.

3. The _____ _____ is responsible for setting budgetary policies and goals, reviewing and approving the budget, and resolving any differences that arise in the budgetary process.

4. A moving twelve-month budget where a future month is added as the current month expires is called a _____ _____.

5. The _____ _____ is the portion of the master budget that includes the cash budget, the budgeted balance sheet, the budgeted statement of cash flows, and the capital budget.

6. The collection of all area and activity budgets, representing a firm's comprehensive plan of action, is the _____ _____.

7. Budgets associated with the income-producing activities of an organization are called _____ _____.

8. The _____ _____ shows the planned expenditures for all indirect manufacturing items.

9. The _____ _____ shows how many units must be produced to meet sales needs and satisfy ending inventory requirements.

10. The _____ _____ describes expected sales in units and dollars for the coming period.

11. The _____ _____ _____ _____ _____ outlines planned expenditures for nonmanufacturing activities.

12. A _____ _____ is a financial plan outlining the acquisition of long-term assets.

13. The _____ _____ _____ shows total direct labor hours needed and the associated cost for the number of units in the production budget.

14. The _____ _____ _____ outlines the expected usage of materials production and purchases of indirect materials required.

15. The process of padding the budget by overstating costs and underestimating revenues is called _____ _____.

16. _____ is the process of setting standards, receiving feedback on actual performance, and taking corrective action whenever actual performance deviates significantly from planned performance.

17. Individual behavior that is in conflict with the goals of the organization is _____ _____.

18. A _____ _____ can specify costs for a range of activity.

19. A _____ _____ is a budget for a particular level of activity.

20. _____ _____ is the alignment of a manager's personal goals with those of the organization.

21. The _____ _____ _____ simultaneously achieves goal congruence and induces a manager to exert effort toward achieving the organization's goals.

22. Managerial actions that improve budgetary performance in the short run at the expense of the long-run welfare of the organization is called _____ _____.

23. _____ are positive or negative measures taken by an organization to induce a manager to exert effort toward achieving the organization's goals.

24. _____ _____ are economic rewards to motivate managers.

25. _____ _____ are psychological and social rewards to motivate managers.

26. _____ _____ allows managers who will be held accountable for budgetary performance to participate in the budget's development.

27. Claiming that a participative budgetary system exists when, in reality, budgets are dictated from above is called _____.

28. A _____ _____ is the long-term plan for future activities and operations, usually involving at least five years.

29. A _____ _____ is a detailed plan that outlines all sources and uses of cash.

30. _____ _____ are costs that managers have the power to influence.

31. A(n) _____ _____ is a responsibility center in which a manager has responsibility for incurrence of costs.

32. A responsibility center in which a manager is responsible for revenues, costs, and investments is a(n) _____ _____.

33. A(n) _____ _____ is an area or unit within an organization over which a manager is assigned responsibility for a specific activity or set of activities.

34. _____ _____ is the use of the accounting system to set standards, measure actual outcomes, and to report the performance of responsibility centers.

35. The _____ _____ _____ is the sum of price variances and efficiency variances in a performance report comparing actual costs to expected costs predicted by a flexible budget.

36. A(n) _____ _____ is a responsibility center in which a manager is responsible for revenues and costs.

KEY TERMS:

budget
budget committee
budget director
budgetary slack
capital budget
cash budget
continuous budget
control
controllable costs
cost center
direct labor budget
direct materials budget
dysfunctional behavior
financial budget
flexible budget
flexible budget variance
goal congruence
ideal budgetary system

incentives
investment center
master budget
monetary incentives
myopic behavior
nonmonetary incentives
operating budgets
overhead budget
participative budgeting
production budget
profit center
pseudoparticipation
responsibility accounting
responsibility center
sales budget
selling and administrative expense budget
static budget
strategic plan

Compare your answers to those at the end of the chapter. Review any key terms missed before proceeding.

CHAPTER QUIZ

Circle the single best answer.

1. Budgeting is a means of coordinating the activities of the organization and communicating the goals of the company: (a) true; (b) false

2. Budgeting is important only as a planning tool: (a) true; (b) false

3. The first step in the budgeting process is the preparation of the production budget: (a) true; (b) false

4. Bad debt expense is not included in the cash budget because it is shown as a reduction in the amount collected from accounts receivable: (a) true; (b) false

5. Depreciation is included in the cash budget because it is a cash outflow for equipment: (a) true; (b) false

6. On an income statement prepared using a contribution margin approach, costs would be classified by function (production costs versus selling and administrative costs): (a) true; (b) false

7. Responsibility accounting attempts to assign costs and revenues to the individuals who have the most influence over them: (a) true; (b) false

8. When participative budgeting is used, the flow of information for budgeting purposes is from the upper to the lower levels of the company: (a) true; (b) false

9. Capital budgeting refers to budgeting for expenditures for buildings and equipment: (a) true; (b) false

10. Equipment purchased using long-term debt would be shown in the cash budget as a cash outflow at the time the equipment is purchased: (a) true; (b) false

11. Budgets can affect managers' behavior because the managers' bonuses, salary increases, and promotions are often affected by the managers' ability to achieve budgeted goals: (a) true; (b) false

Write your answers in the spaces provided.

12. List the order in which the following budgets and schedules are prepared.

Cash budget   Purchases budget
Direct labor budget   Sales budget
Manufacturing overhead budget   Sales forecast
Production budget

    1. _____
    2. _____
    3. _____
    4. _____
    5. _____
    6. _____
    7. _____

13. The production needed for the period would be determined as follows:

Budgeted sales in units
+ _____
= Total units needed
- _____
= Units to be produced

14. The purchases budget for direct materials for a manufacturer is based upon the quantity of direct materials to be purchased. The quantity of direct materials to be purchased would be determined as follows.

_____
+ _____
= Total quantity of direct materials needed
- _____
= Quantity of direct materials to be purchased

15. List seven key features of a budgetary system that encourage positive behavior:

1. _____
2. _____
3. _____
4. _____
5. _____
6. _____
7. _____

Circle the single best answer.

Use the following information to answer the next six questions.

Projected sales for Silver, Inc., for next year and beginning and ending inventory data are as follows.

Sales	40,000 units
Unit price	$20
Beginning inventory	20,000 units
Targeted ending inventory	10,000 units

Each unit requires 5 pounds of material costing $3.00 per pound. The beginning inventory of raw materials is 5,000 pounds. The company wants to have 3,000 pounds of material in inventory at the end of the year. Each unit produced requires 2 hours of direct labor time, which is billed at $8 per hour.

16. Budgeted sales would be: (a) $580,000; (b) $600,000; (c) $800,000; (d) $840,000

17. According to the production budget, how many units should be produced? (a) 30,000; (b) 42,000; (c) 46,000; (d) 50,000

18. Pounds of material to be purchased would be: (a) 142,000; (b) 148,000; (c) 150,000; (d) 152,000

19. The budgeted total purchase cost of direct materials would be: (a) $456,000; (b) $450,000; (c) $444,000; (d) $426,000

20. The budgeted number of total direct labor hours needed would be: (a) 30,000; (b) 40,000; (c) 46,000; (d) 60,000

21. The budgeted total direct labor cost would be: (a) $320,000; (b) $442,000; (c) $480,000; (d) $496,000

Compare your answers to those at the end of the chapter. Review any questions missed before proceeding.

EXERCISES

NOTE: The following exercises are interrelated.

EXERCISE 1

The Baumberger Company manufactures oak bookcases that sell for $400 each. Budgeted sales for the first four months of the year are as follows:

Month	Budgeted Sales (Units)
January	1,000
February	1,500
March	2,500
April	2,000

Required:

Prepare a sales budget, in dollars, for each month and in total for the first quarter of the year.

January	February	March	Total

EXERCISE 2

Each bookcase requires 20 square feet of oak at a cost of $10 per square foot. The company wants to maintain an inventory of bookcases equal to 10% of the following month's sales. Inventory on January 1 consisted of 80 bookcases.

Required:

1. Prepare a production budget, in units, for each month and in total for the first quarter.

January	February	March	Total

EXERCISE 2 (continued)

2. Prepare a purchases budget, in dollars, for direct materials for each month and in total for the first quarter.

    The company wants to maintain an inventory of oak equal to 20% of the next month's requirements. Materials inventory on January 1 consisted of 11,000 square feet of oak. The company estimates an inventory of oak on hand at the end of March of approximately 8,000 square feet.

	January	February	March	Total

EXERCISE 3

Each bookcase requires 5 hours of direct labor at a cost of $8.00 per hour. Variable manufacturing overhead is budgeted at $2.00 per direct labor hour. Monthly fixed overhead consists of the following:

Supervisors' salaries	$ 6,000
Insurance	2,000
Depreciation on production equipment	500
Depreciation on production facility	10,000
Total	$18,500

Required:

1. Prepare a direct labor budget for each month and in total for the first quarter.

	January	February	March	Total

EXERCISE 3 (continued)

2. Prepare a manufacturing overhead budget for each month and in total for the first quarter.

	January	February	March	Total
	_____	_____	_____	_____

EXERCISE 4

The company expects 60% of the sales each month will be collected in that month, with 35% collected in the following month. Five percent of all sales are uncollectible and written off in the following month.

The accounts receivable balance at the beginning of the year is $200,000, (which is 40% of last year's December sales of $500,000).

Required:

Prepare a schedule of cash collections on accounts receivable for each month and in total for the first quarter.

	January	February	March	Total
	_____	_____	_____	_____

EXERCISE 5

The company normally pays for 70% of its purchases in the month of purchase. The remaining 30% is paid in the following month.

Accounts payable at the beginning of the year is $54,000 (which is 30% of December purchases of $180,000).

Required:

Prepare a schedule of cash payments on accounts payable for each month and in total for the first quarter.

January	February	March	Total

EXERCISE 6

Required:

Using the information from the previous exercises, prepare a pro forma income statement for each month and in total for the first quarter.

	January	February	March	Total
	_____	_____	_____	_____

EXERCISE 7

Use the information from the previous exercises and assume the company attempts to maintain a cash balance of $100,000 at all times. Any excess is invested in marketable securities of $10,000 denominations earning an 8% return.

Any deficiencies are covered by borrowing from a local bank at 10% interest. The cash balance at the beginning of the year is $105,000. Variable selling costs equal 5% of sales and are paid in the month following the sale.

Fixed selling, general, and administrative costs are $50,000 and, except for $10,000 of depreciation, are paid in the month incurred. Estimated tax payments, equal to 40 percent of estimated income for the quarter, are made at the end of each quarter.

Required:

Prepare a cash budget for each month and in total for the first quarter.

	January	February	March	Total
	_____	_____	_____	_____

ANSWERS

KEY TERMS TEST
1. budget
2. budget director
3. budget committee
4. continuous budget
5. financial budget
6. master budget
7. operating budgets
8. overhead budget
9. production budget
10. sales budget
11. selling and administrative expense budget
12. capital budget
13. direct labor budget
14. direct materials budget
15. budgetary slack
16. Control
17. dysfunctional behavior
18. flexible budget
19. static budget
20. Goal congruence
21. ideal budgetary system
22. myopic behavior
23. Incentives
24. Monetary incentives
25. Nonmonetary incentives
26. Participative budgeting
27. pseudoparticipation
28. strategic plan
29. cash budget
30. Controllable costs
31. cost center
32. investment center
33. responsibility center
34. Responsibility accounting
35. flexible budget variance
36. profit center

CHAPTER QUIZ

1. a True
2. b False. Budgeting is also an important means of controlling operations by comparing actual results with budgeted amounts.
3. b False. The first step in the budgeting process is preparation of the sales forecast.
4. a True
5. b False. Depreciation is not a cash outflow; therefore, it is not included in the cash budget.
6. b False. On an income statement prepared using a contribution margin approach, costs would be classified by behavior (fixed vs. variable costs).
7. a True
8. b False. When participative budgeting is used, the flow of information is from the lower to the upper levels of the company.
9. a True
10. b False. Equipment purchased using long-term debt would result in a cash outflow as the debt is repaid.
11. a True
12. 1. Sales forecast
    2. Sales budget
    3. Production budget
    4. Purchases budget
    5. Direct labor budget
    6. Manufacturing overhead budget
    7. Cash budget
13. Desired level of ending inventory
    Beginning inventory
14. Quantity of direct materials needed for production
    Ending inventory of direct materials
    Beginning inventory of direct materials
15. 1. frequent feedback
    2. flexible budgets
    3. monetary and nonmonetary incentives
    4. participative budgeting
    5. realistic standards
    6. controllability
    7. multiple measures of performance
16. c (40,000 x $20) = $800,000
17. a 40,000 + 10,000 - 20,000 = 30,000 units
18. b (30,000 x 5 pounds) + 3,000 pounds - 5,000 pounds = 148,000 pounds
19. c 148,000 pounds x $3.00/pound = $444,000
20. d 30,000 units x 2 hours = 60,000 hours
21. c 60,000 hours x $8 = $480,000

EXERCISE 1

SALES BUDGET IN DOLLARS

	January	February	March	Total
Budgeted sales in units	1,000	1,500	2,500	5,000
x Selling price	x $400	x $400	x $400	x $400
Budgeted sales	$400,000	$600,000	$1,000,000	$2,000,000

EXERCISE 2

1.

PRODUCTION BUDGET IN UNITS

	January	February	March	Total
Budgeted sales in units	1,000	1,500	2,500	5,000
Add: Desired ending inventory (10% of next month's sales)	150	250	200*	200
Total units needed	1,150	1,750	2,700	5,200
Less: Beginning inventory	80	150	250	80
Units to be produced	1,070	1,600	2,450	5,120

*2,000 units budgeted sales for April multiplied by 10 percent

2.

PURCHASES BUDGET IN DOLLARS

	January	February	March	Total
Units to be produced	1,070	1,600	2,450	5,120
Multiplied by: Sq. ft. of oak per unit	x 20	x 20	x 20	x 20
Sq. ft. of material needed for production	21,400	32,000	49,000	102,400
Add: Desired ending inventory (20% of next month's needs)	6,400	9,800	8,000	8,000
Total sq. ft. needed	27,800	41,800	57,000	110,400
Less: beginning inventory	11,000	6,400	9,800	11,000
Sq. ft. to be purchased	16,800	35,400	47,200	99,400
Multiplied by: Cost per sq. ft.	x $10	x $10	x $10	x $10
Cost of raw materials purchased	$168,000	$354,000	$472,000	$994,000

EXERCISE 3

1.   DIRECT LABOR BUDGET

	January	February	March	Total
Units to be produced	1,070	1,600	2,450	5,120
Multiplied by:				
Direct labor hours per unit	x 5	x 5	x 5	x 5
Direct labor hours needed	5,350	8,000	12,250	25,600
Multiplied by:				
Labor cost per hour	x $8	x $8	x $8	x $8
Total direct labor cost	$42,800	$64,000	$98,000	$204,800

2.   MANUFACTURING OVERHEAD BUDGET

	January	February	March	Total
Budgeted direct labor hours	5,350	8,000	12,250	25,600
Multiplied by:				
Variable overhead rate	x $2	x $2	x $2	x $2
Budgeted variable overhead	$10,700	$16,000	$24,500	$ 51,200
Budgeted fixed overhead:				
Supervisors' salaries	$ 6,000	$ 6,000	$ 6,000	$ 18,000
Insurance	2,000	2,000	2,000	6,000
Depreciation--equipment	500	500	500	1,500
Depreciation--facility	10,000	10,000	10,000	30,000
Total fixed overhead	$18,500	$18,500	$18,500	$ 55,500
Total budgeted overhead	$29,200	$34,500	$43,000	$106,700

EXERCISE 4   CASH COLLECTIONS ON ACCOUNTS RECEIVABLE

	January	February	March	Total
Accounts receivable, beginning of month	$200,000[a]	$160,000	$ 240,000	$ 200,000
Add: sales	400,000	600,000	1,000,000	2,000,000
Total amounts due from customers	$600,000	$760,000	$1,240,000	$2,200,000
Deduct: cash collections:				
60% of sales for current month	$240,000	$360,000	$ 600,000	$1,200,000
35% of sales for previous month	175,000[b]	140,000	210,000	525,000
Total cash collections	($415,000)	($500,000)	($810,000)	($1,725,000)
Deduct: write-offs:				
5% of previous month's sales	(25,000)	(20,000)	(30,000)	(75,000)
Accounts receivable, end of month	$160,000	$240,000	$ 400,000	$ 400,000

[a]40% of December sales of $500,000
[b]35% of December sales of $500,000

EXERCISE 5   CASH PAYMENTS ON ACCOUNTS PAYABLE

	January	February	March	Total
Accounts payable, beginning of month	$ 54,000[a]	$ 50,400	$106,200	$ 54,000
Add: purchases	168,000	354,000	472,000	994,000
Total amount owed	$222,000	$404,400	$578,200	$1,048,000
Deduct: cash payments:				
70% of purchases for the month	$117,600	$247,800	$330,400	$ 695,800
30% of purchases for previous month	54,000	50,400	106,200	210,600
Total cash payments	($171,600)	($298,200)	($436,600)	($ 906,400)
Accounts payable, end of month	$ 50,400	$106,200	$141,600	$ 141,600

[a]30% of December purchases of $180,000

EXERCISE 6

PRO FORMA INCOME STATEMENTS

	January	February	March	Total
	1,000 units	1,500 units	2,500 units	5,000 units
Sales revenue	$400,000	$600,000	$1,000,000	$2,000,000
Variable expenses:				
Production expenses[a]	$250,000	$375,000	$ 625,000	$1,250,000
S & A expenses (5% of sales)	20,000	30,000	50,000	100,000
Bad debts expense (5% of sales)	20,000	30,000	50,000	100,000
Total variable expenses	$290,000	$435,000	$ 725,000	$1,450,000
Contribution margin	$110,000	$165,000	$ 275,000	$ 550,000
Fixed expenses:				
Fixed mfg. overhead	$ 18,500	$ 18,500	$ 18,500	$ 55,500
Fixed S & A expenses	50,000	50,000	50,000	150,000
Total fixed expenses	$ 68,500	$ 68,500	$ 68,500	$ 205,500
Operating income	$ 41,500	$ 96,500	$ 206,500	$ 344,500
Interest income	-0-	1,000[b]	1,417[c]	2,417
Net income before tax	$ 41,500	$ 97,500	$ 207,917	$ 346,917
Income tax expense	16,600	39,000	83,167	138,767
Net income	$ 24,900	$ 58,500	$ 124,750	$ 208,150

[a]Consists of the following costs per unit:

Direct materials	(20 sq. ft. x $10 per sq. ft.)	$200
Direct labor	(5 hours per unit x $8 per hour)	40
Variable overhead	(5 hours per unit x $2 per hour)	10
Total variable production costs per unit		$250

[b]$120,000 invested at the end of January x 10% return x 1/12 = $1,000

[c]$120,000 + $50,000 invested at the end of February x 10% return x 1/12 = $1,417

EXERCISE 7

CASH BUDGET

	January	February	March	Total
Cash balance, beginning of month	$105,000	$101,900	$105,700	$ 105,000
Add: cash collected on accounts receivable	415,000	500,000	810,000	1,725,000
Cash available	$520,000	$601,900	$915,700	$1,830,000
Deduct: cash payments				
Accounts payable	$171,600	$298,200	$436,600	$ 906,400
Direct labor	42,800	64,000	98,000	204,800
Variable mfg. overhead	10,700	16,000	24,500	51,200
Fixed mfg. overhead[a]	8,000	8,000	8,000	24,000
Variable S & A[b]	25,000	20,000	30,000	75,000
Fixed S & A	40,000	40,000	40,000	120,000
Income taxes[c]	-0-	-0-	138,767	138,767
Total cash payments	$298,100	$446,200	$775,867	$1,520,167
Excess cash	$221,900	$155,700	$139,833	$ 309,833
Investing activities: Investment in marketable securities	(120,000)	(50,000)	(30,000)	(200,000)
Ending cash balance	$101,900	$105,700	$109,833	$ 109,833

[a]Excludes $10,500 of depreciation each month (noncash expense)

[b]5% of previous month's sales

[c]The amount of taxes to be paid in March is determined from the income statement for the quarter prepared in Exercise 6.

CHAPTER 25

STANDARD COSTING:
A MANAGERIAL CONTROL TOOL

```
╔═══════════════════════════════════════════════════════╗
║  CHAPTER REVIEW                                         ║
╚═══════════════════════════════════════════════════════╝
```

INTRODUCTION

- A **standard cost** is the expected or budgeted cost of materials, labor, and manufacturing overhead required to produce <u>one</u> unit of product.

- A standard cost card is a formal list of the standard cost for materials, labor, and manufacturing overhead to produce one unit of product. The costs are summed to arrive at the total standard cost for one unit of product.

- A **quantity standard** is the quantity of input allowed per unit of output.

- A **price standard** is the price that should be paid per unit of input.

PRODUCT COSTING METHODS

- Costs under the three product costing methods are summarized below:

PRODUCT COSTING SYSTEM	MANUFACTURING COSTS		
	Direct Materials	Direct Labor	Overhead
Actual Cost System	actual	actual	actual
Normal Cost System	actual	actual	budgeted
Standard Cost System	budgeted	budgeted	budgeted

UNIT STANDARDS

How Standards Are Developed

- Standards can be based on:
  1. historical experience
  2. engineering studies
  3. input from operating personnel

Types of Standards

- **Ideal standards** are standards that demand maximum efficiency and can only be achieved if everything operates perfectly.

  Such standards are virtually unattainable, and use of ideal standards can result in low employee morale and a decline in performance.

- **Currently attainable standards** are demanding but attainable under efficient operating conditions. Such standards allow for normal machine downtime and employee rest periods.

  Challenging but attainable standards tend to result in higher performance levels than ideal standards. If standards are too tight and never achievable, workers become frustrated and performance levels decline.

Why Standard Cost Systems Are Adopted

- Two reasons for adopting a standard cost system are:
  1. To improve planning and control. A standard cost system compares actual amounts with standard amounts to determine variances from the standard. The use of a standard cost system for operational control in an advanced manufacturing environment can produce dysfunctional behavior. However, standards in the advanced manufacturing environment are still useful for planning, such as developing bids.
  2. To facilitate product costing. Standard costing uses standard costs for direct materials, direct labor, and overhead. Standard cost systems provide readily available unit cost information that can be used for pricing decisions.

STANDARD PRODUCT COSTS

Standard Cost Sheet

- The standard cost sheet for one unit of product might appear as follows:

```
                    STANDARD COST SHEET
            Production Costs for One Unit of Product

   Direct materials
       (Standard quantity of material x Standard price for material)
   Direct labor
       (Standard direct labor hours x Standard direct labor rate)
   Variable manufacturing overhead
       (Standard direct labor hours x Standard variable overhead rate)
   Fixed manufacturing overhead
       (Standard direct labor hours x Standard fixed overhead rate)

       Total standard cost per unit of product
```

Standards for Direct Materials

• The standard cost for direct materials is calculated as follows:

Standard Cost for Direct Materials = Standard Quantity of Material x Standard Price for the Material

Standards for Direct Labor

• The standard direct labor cost for a unit of product would be calculated as follows:

Standard Direct Labor Cost = Standard Quantity of Direct Labor x Standard Rate Per Direct Labor Hour

VARIANCE ANALYSIS: DIRECT MATERIALS AND DIRECT LABOR

The Basic Variance Model

• **Variances** are differences between actual inputs and standard inputs allowed for units produced.

• There are two variances for variable production costs:
  1. price variances
  2. usage or efficiency variances

• **Price variances** focus on the difference between actual costs of inputs and what the inputs should have cost (standard prices).

• **Efficiency variances** (or usage variances) focus on the difference between the actual quantity used and the standard quantity allowed for units produced.

• The general model for calculating variable cost variances appears below:

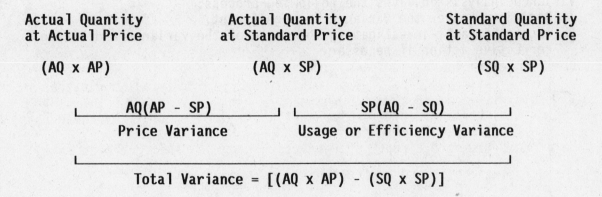

Actual Quantity at Actual Price	Actual Quantity at Standard Price	Standard Quantity at Standard Price
(AQ x AP)	(AQ x SP)	(SQ x SP)

AQ(AP - SP)	SP(AQ - SQ)
Price Variance	Usage or Efficiency Variance

Total Variance = [(AQ x AP) - (SQ x SP)]

- If the actual price or quantity is less than the standard, the variance is considered favorable.

- If the actual price or quantity exceeds the standard, the variance is considered unfavorable.

Direct Materials Price Variance

- The price variance for materials is calculated as follows:

Actual Quantity Purchased at Actual Price

(AQ x AP)

Actual Quantity Purchased at Standard Price

(AQ x SP)

AQ(AP - SP)

Direct Materials Price Variance

- The materials price variance can be computed at one of two points:
  1. when the raw materials are issued for use in production or
  2. when the raw materials are purchased.

- Variances should be calculated at the earliest point possible so management can take any necessary corrective action. Thus, the price variance for materials should be calculated at the time of purchase.

- Responsibility for the materials price variance is usually assigned to the purchasing agent.

- Using the materials price variance to evaluate performance can produce undesirable behavior. For example, if the purchasing agent feels pressured to produce favorable price variances:
  1. materials of lower quality might be purchased (perhaps resulting in unfavorable usage variances).
  2. in order to take advantage of quantity discounts, large amounts of inventory might be purchased (eliminating some of the benefits of JIT).

- Variance analysis involves the following process:
  1. Deciding whether the variance is significant.
  2. If significant, investigating the cause of the variance and taking corrective action if necessary.

Direct Materials Usage Variance

- The materials usage variance is calculated as follows:

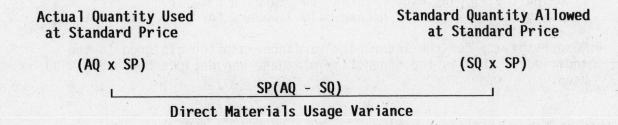

Actual Quantity Used at Standard Price	Standard Quantity Allowed at Standard Price
(AQ x SP)	(SQ x SP)

SP(AQ - SQ)

Direct Materials Usage Variance

- The production manager is usually responsible for materials usage because the production manager can minimize scrap, waste, and rework in order to meet the standard.

- Using the usage variance to evaluate performance can lead to undesirable behavior. For example, a production manager who is pressured to produce a favorable materials usage variance might allow defective units to be transferred to finished goods. Although this avoids the problem of wasted materials, it creates customer-relation problems.

- The materials usage variance is calculated at the time materials are issued or used in the manufacturing process.

- To facilitate the issuance of materials, many companies use three different forms.
  1. A **standard bill of materials** is presented to materials stores as a materials requisition form for the <u>standard</u> quantity allowed for the indicated output.
  2. **Excessive usage forms** are used to requisition material needed <u>in excess</u> of the standard quantity allowed. They provide immediate feedback that excess raw materials are being used.
  3. **Returned-materials forms** are used to return any <u>leftover</u> materials to materials stores.

Direct Labor Rate Variance

- The direct labor rate variance is calculated as follows:

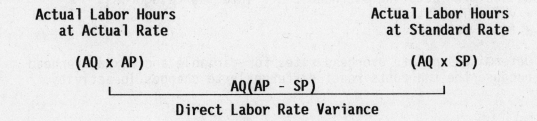

Actual Labor Hours at Actual Rate	Actual Labor Hours at Standard Rate
(AQ x AP)	(AQ x SP)

AQ(AP - SP)

Direct Labor Rate Variance

- Labor rates are largely determined by external factors, such as labor markets and union contracts.

- When labor rate variances occur, it is usually due to:
  1. using the <u>average</u> wage rate as the standard rate or
  2. using more skilled and higher paid laborers for less skilled tasks.

- Responsibility for the labor rate variance is often assigned to the individual, such as the production manager, who decides how labor will be used.

Direct Labor Efficiency Variance

- The efficiency variance for direct labor furnishes information about the efficiency of direct labor.

- The direct labor efficiency variance is calculated as follows:

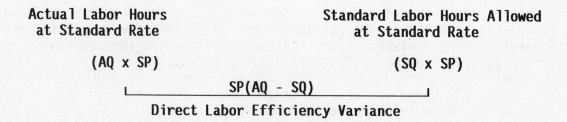

- Usually production managers are responsible for the direct labor efficiency variance; however, once the cause of the variance is discovered, responsibility may be assigned elsewhere.

- The total variance for direct labor would be the sum of the rate variance and the efficiency variance. The total variance can also be calculated as follows:

Total Direct Labor Variance = (Actual Quantity x Actual Price) - (Standard Quantity x Standard Price)

VARIANCE ANALYSIS: OVERHEAD COSTS

- One method of analyzing overhead variances is as follows.
  1. Divide manufacturing overhead costs into two categories:
     - variable costs
     - fixed costs

  2. Determine separate overhead rates for variable and fixed overhead because the two costs react differently to changes in activity.

The variable overhead rate is determined by analyzing how variable overhead costs react to changes in activity. For example, if a firm determines that $10.00 of variable manufacturing overhead is incurred for each direct labor hour worked, then the standard variable overhead rate (SVOR) would be $10.00 per direct labor hour.

The standard fixed overhead rate (SFOR) is calculated as follows.

$$\text{Standard Fixed Overhead Rate} = \frac{\text{Budgeted Fixed Overhead Costs}}{\text{Standard Hours Allowed for Denominator Volume}}$$

Denominator volume is the expected production volume selected at the beginning of the year when the standard fixed overhead rate is established. The standard fixed overhead rate is determined on an annual basis.

3. Apply manufacturing overhead using the standard variable overhead rate (SVOR) and the standard fixed overhead rate (SFOR).

   Manufacturing overhead in a standard costing system is applied based on the standard hours allowed for production achieved rather than on the actual hours worked.

   The Manufacturing Overhead Control account would include the following items.

MANUFACTURING OVERHEAD CONTROL

Actual overhead costs	Applied overhead costs (based on standard hours allowed for production)

4. Calculate the two variable overhead variances:
   • the variable overhead spending variance
   • the variable overhead efficiency variance

5. Calculate the two fixed overhead variances:
   • the fixed overhead spending variance
   • the fixed overhead volume variance

Variable Overhead Variances

• The two variable overhead variances are:
   1. the **variable overhead spending variance**
   2. the **variable overhead efficiency variance**

Variable Overhead Spending Variance

- The variable overhead spending variance indicates if a firm is paying the budgeted price for the variable manufacturing overhead used.

- The variable overhead spending variance is calculated as follows:

Actual	Standard Variable
Variable	Overhead Rate x
Overhead	Actual Hours
	(AQ x SVOR)

L_____J

Variable Overhead Spending Variance

- Price changes of variable overhead items are essentially beyond the control of supervisors; therefore, the variable overhead spending variance is usually assigned to the production departments.

- In order to determine how well costs of individual variable overhead items were controlled, a line-by-line analysis of each variable overhead item is essential.

Variable Overhead Efficiency Variance

- The variable overhead efficiency variance results from the efficient or inefficient use of the <u>base</u> used to apply variable manufacturing overhead.

- For example, if variable manufacturing overhead is applied using direct labor hours as the base and there is an unfavorable labor efficiency variance, there will also be an unfavorable variable overhead efficiency variance.

- The variable overhead efficiency variance is calculated as follows:

Standard Variable	Standard Variable
Overhead Rate x	Overhead Rate x
Actual Hours	Standard Hours
(AQ x SVOR)	(SQ x SVOR)

L_____ SVOR(AQ - SQ) _____J

Variable Overhead Efficiency Variance

- If variable overhead costs change in proportion to changes in the base, such as direct labor hours, then responsibility for the variable overhead efficiency variance should be assigned to the production manager because the production manager has responsibility for the use of direct labor.

Total Variable Overhead Variance

- The total variable overhead variance is calculated as follows:

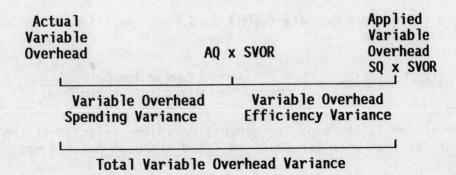

Actual Variable Overhead		AQ × SVOR		Applied Variable Overhead SQ × SVOR
	Variable Overhead Spending Variance		Variable Overhead Efficiency Variance	
		Total Variable Overhead Variance		

Fixed Overhead Variances

- Variance analysis for fixed manufacturing overhead differs from variance analysis for variable manufacturing costs because fixed costs react differently to changes in activity.

- Two variances calculated for fixed manufacturing overhead are:
  1. the **fixed overhead spending or budget variance**
  2. the **fixed overhead volume variance**

Fixed Overhead Spending Variance

- The fixed overhead spending variance compares <u>actual</u> fixed overhead to the fixed overhead <u>budgeted</u> for the production level achieved.

- The fixed overhead spending variance is calculated as follows:

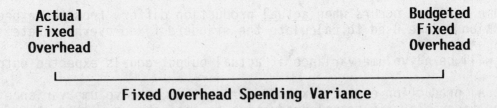

Actual Fixed Overhead		Budgeted Fixed Overhead
	Fixed Overhead Spending Variance	

- Because many fixed overhead items are not subject to change in the short run, fixed overhead costs are often beyond the immediate control of management.

- In addition, because fixed overhead consists of a number of items, such as salaries, depreciation, property taxes, and insurance, a line-by-line comparison of actual costs and budgeted costs provides more information about the causes of budget variances.

Fixed Overhead Volume Variance

- The fixed overhead volume variance is the difference between <u>budgeted</u> fixed overhead and <u>applied</u> fixed overhead. It is a measure of the utilization of plant facilities.

- The **standard fixed overhead rate (SFOR)** used to apply fixed overhead is calculated as follows:

$$\text{Standard Fixed Overhead Rate} = \frac{\text{Budgeted Fixed Overhead Costs}}{\text{Standard Hours Allowed for Denominator Volume}}$$

- Denominator volume is the expected production volume selected at the beginning of the year when the standard fixed overhead rate is established.

- The fixed overhead volume variance is calculated as follows:

Budgeted Fixed Overhead   **Applied Fixed Overhead**

                                                    (Standard Hours Allowed x SFOR)

Fixed Overhead Volume Variance

- The volume variance tells management if they operated at the expected production volume used to calculate the standard fixed overhead rate.

- The volume variance can also be calculated as follows:

$$\text{Fixed Overhead Volume Variance} = \text{SFOR} \times \left[\begin{matrix} \text{Expected Activity} \\ \text{Used in SFOR} \end{matrix} - \begin{matrix} \text{Standard Activity Allowed} \\ \text{For Actual Production} \end{matrix} \right]$$

- A volume variance occurs when <u>actual</u> production differs from the <u>expected</u> production volume used to calculate the standard fixed overhead rate.

- There will be no volume variance if actual output equals expected output.

- If actual production exceeds expected production, the volume variance is labeled favorable. If actual production is less than expected, the volume variance is labeled unfavorable.

- When a volume variance occurs, it might indicate that:
  1. management did not use the correct expected production level when calculating the standard fixed overhead rate or
  2. if the expected output is correct and the volume variance is unfavorable, production facilities were not fully utilized.

Total Fixed Overhead Variance

- The total fixed overhead variance is the sum of the fixed overhead spending and volume variances and is calculated as follows:

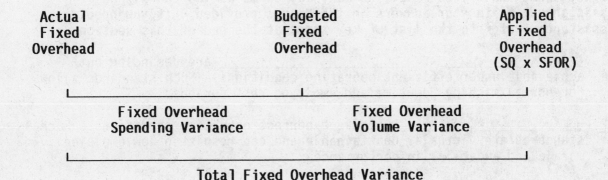

Actual Fixed Overhead	Budgeted Fixed Overhead	Applied Fixed Overhead (SQ x SFOR)

|———————— Fixed Overhead Spending Variance —————————|———————— Fixed Overhead Volume Variance ————————|

|————————————————— Total Fixed Overhead Variance —————————————————|

THE DECISION TO INVESTIGATE

- Variances indicate that actual performance is not going according to plan.

- Variances do not indicate the <u>cause</u> of the variance or responsibility.

- Usually the cause of a variance can be determined only by an investigation. For example, an unfavorable materials quantity variance may not be the fault of the production supervisor. Instead, it may be the result of the purchasing agent buying inferior quality material.

- As a general principle, variances should be investigated if the anticipated benefits of the investigation exceed the expected costs of investigating.

- Most firms adopt the general guideline of investigating variances only if they fall outside an acceptable range.

Lower Control Limit   Upper Control Limit

|————————————————————————————————————|

Acceptable Range

- The control limits of the acceptable range are calculated as follows:

Upper Control Limit = Standard + Allowable Deviation

Lower Control Limit = Standard - Allowable Deviation

- The control limits are often expressed as:
  - a specified amount and/or
  - a specified percentage of the variance.

- For example, management may investigate any variance that exceeds $1,000 or 5% of the standard amount to which the variance relates.

Test your recall of the key terms as follows: Read the following definitions of key terms and try to recall as many key terms as you can <u>without assistance</u>. Write your answers in the spaces provided. If you need assistance, refer to the list of key terms at the end of this section.

1. _____ _____ _____ are demanding but achievable under efficient operating conditions. Such standards allow for normal machine downtime and employee rest periods.

2. _____ _____ reflect perfect operating conditions. Such standards are virtually unattainable and can result in low employee morale and a decline in performance.

3. A _____ _____ _____ lists the standard costs and standard quantities of direct materials, direct labor, and overhead for a product.

4. _____ _____ establish the maximum allowable deviation from a standard.

5. A(n) _____ _____ is calculated as the difference between standard quantities and actual quantities, multiplied by the standard price.

6. A(n) _____ _____ results when the actual amounts are greater than the budgeted or standard allowances.

7. A(n) _____ _____ results whenever the actual amounts are less than the budgeted or standard allowances.

8. A _____ _____ ____ _____ is used as a requisition form from material stores for the standard quantity of materials allowed for a given output level.

9. _____ _____ _____ are the direct labor hours that should have been used to produce the actual output.

10. The _____ _____ _____ _____ is the difference between the actual direct labor hours used and the standard hours allowed, multiplied by the standard variable overhead rate.

11. The _____ _____ _____ _____ is the difference between the actual variable overhead and the budgeted variable overhead based on actual hours used to produce the actual output.

12. _____ _____ ___ _____ _____ is the quantity of materials that should have been used to produce the actual output.

13. The _____ _____ _____ is the difference between the actual price paid per unit of materials and the standard price allowed per unit, multiplied by the actual quantity of materials purchased.

14. The _____ _____ _____ is the difference between the direct materials actually used and the direct materials allowed for the actual output, multiplied by the standard price.

15. The _____ _____ _____ _____ is the difference between budgeted fixed overhead and applied fixed overhead and is a measure of capacity utilization.

16. The _____ _____ _____ is the difference between the actual hourly rate paid and the standard hourly rate, multiplied by the actual hours worked.

17. The _____ _____ _____ is the difference between the actual direct labor hours used and the standard direct labor hours allowed, multiplied by the standard hourly wage rate.

18. The _____ _____ _____ _____ is the difference between actual fixed overhead and budgeted fixed overhead.

KEY TERMS:

control limits
currently attainable standards
efficiency variance
favorable variance
fixed overhead spending variance
fixed overhead volume variance
ideal standards
labor efficiency variance
labor rate variance

materials price variance
materials usage variance
standard bill of materials
standard cost sheet
standard hours allowed
standard quantity of materials allowed
unfavorable variance
variable overhead efficiency variance
variable overhead spending variance

Compare your answers to those at the end of the chapter. Review any key terms missed before proceeding.

CHAPTER QUIZ

Circle the single best answer.

1. All of the following are true of currently attainable standards except: (a) they are based on an efficiently operating work force; (b) they are based on ideal conditions; (c) they allow for downtime and rest periods; (d) they are based on present production processes and technology.

2. There is a direct relationship between (circle two answers): (a) inputs of direct materials and output of finished product; (b) inputs of direct labor and output of finished product; (c) input of variable manufacturing overhead and output of finished product; (d) input of fixed manufacturing overhead and output of finished product

3. Standards can be based on: (a) historical experience; (b) engineering studies; (c) input from operating personnel; (d) all of the above

4. In order to facilitate control, actual overhead costs for the output level attained should be compared to budgeted costs at the expected activity level: (a) true; (b) false

5. Engineering relationships between inputs and outputs can be established for manufacturing overhead: (a) true; (b) false

6. Separate overhead rates should be calculated for variable and fixed manufacturing overhead because the two costs react differently to changes in activity: (a) true; (b) false

7. The standard fixed overhead rate is calculated as estimated fixed manufacturing overhead costs divided by estimated activity: (a) true; (b) false

8. The standard fixed overhead rate should be determined on a monthly basis: (a) true; (b) false

9. If the selected activity is direct labor hours, manufacturing overhead in a standard costing system would be applied based on the actual direct labor hours worked: (a) true; (b) false

10. The variable manufacturing overhead efficiency variance results from the efficient or inefficient use of the base upon which variable manufacturing overhead is budgeted: (a) true; (b) false

11. The fixed manufacturing overhead budget variance is a measure of the utilization of plant facilities: (a) true; (b) false

12. The fixed manufacturing overhead volume variance indicates to management whether they operated at the expected activity level used to calculate the standard fixed overhead rate. There will be no volume variance if the company operated at the expected activity level: (a) true; (b) false

13. As a general rule, variances should be investigated if the anticipated benefits of the investigation exceed the expected costs of investigating: (a) true; (b) false

Use the following information to answer the next eight questions.

The standard cost sheet for one of the Carver Company's products is presented below.

Direct materials (4 feet @ $6.00)	$24.00
Direct labor (1 hour @ $12.00)	12.00
Variable overhead (1 hour @ $5.00)	5.00
Fixed overhead (1 hour @ $3.00[a])	3.00
Standard unit cost	$44.00

[a] Rate based on expected activity of 12,000 hours

The following results for last year were recorded.

Production	10,000 units
Direct materials	
(39,000 feet purchased and used)	$241,800
Direct labor (10,500 hours)	$131,250
Variable overhead	$ 48,000
Fixed overhead	$ 40,000

14. The materials price variance is: (a) $7,800 unfavorable; (b) $7,800 favorable; (c) $8,400 unfavorable; (d) $8,400 favorable

15. The materials usage variance is: (a) $4,000 favorable; (b) $4,000 unfavorable; (c) $6,000 favorable; (d) $6,000 unfavorable

16. The labor rate variance is: (a) $5,250 favorable; (b) $5,250 unfavorable; (c) $5,000 favorable; (d) $5,000 unfavorable

17. The labor efficiency variance is: (a) $5,250 favorable; (b) $5,250 unfavorable; (c) $6,000 favorable; (d) $6,000 unfavorable

18. The variable overhead spending variance is: (a) $4,500 favorable; (b) $4,500 unfavorable; (c) $4,800 favorable; (d) $4,800 unfavorable

19. The variable overhead efficiency variance is: (a) $2,500 favorable; (b) $2,500 unfavorable; (c) $2,250 favorable; (d) $2,250 unfavorable

20. The fixed overhead spending variance is: (a) $4,000 unfavorable; (b) $4,000 favorable; (c) $8,000 unfavorable; (d) $8,000 favorable

21. The fixed overhead volume variance is: (a) $4,000 unfavorable; (b) $4,000 favorable; (c) $6,000 unfavorable; (d) $6,000 favorable

Compare your answers to those at the end of the chapter. Review any questions missed before proceeding.

EXERCISES

EXERCISE 1

The Luddeke Manufacturing Company has developed the following standards for one of their products, a walnut fern stand.

STANDARD VARIABLE COST CARD
One Walnut Fern Stand

Materials: 5 square feet x $8 per square foot	$40.00
Direct labor: 2 hours x $10/DLH	20.00
Variable manufacturing overhead: 2 hours x $5/DLH	10.00
Total standard variable cost per unit	$70.00

The company records materials price variances at the time of purchase. The following activity occurred during the month of April:

Materials purchased:	5,000 square feet costing $46,000
Materials used:	4,250 square feet
Units produced:	900 units
Direct labor:	2,200 hours costing $19,800
Actual variable manufacturing overhead:	$10,500

Required:

1. Calculate the direct materials price and usage variances.

EXERCISE 1 (continued)

2. Calculate the direct labor rate variance, the direct labor efficiency variance, and the total direct labor variance.

3. Compute the variable manufacturing overhead spending and efficiency variances.

767

EXERCISE 2

The Mills Company manufactures roofing shingles. The production process involves heating and compressing asphalt into sheets and then rolling coarse sand into the hot asphalt. The sheets are then cooled, cut into shingles, and packaged.

The following standard costs were developed:

STANDARD COST CARD
PER SHINGLE

Materials:		
Asphalt	2 lbs. x $0.08/lb.	$0.16
Sand	2 lbs. x $0.02/lb.	0.04
Direct labor	.01 hrs. x $7.00/hr.	0.07
Variable overhead	.01 hrs. x $3.00/hr.	0.03
Fixed overhead		?
Total standard cost per shingle		?

The following information is available regarding the company's operations for the period.

Shingles produced	500,000
Materials purchased:	
Asphalt	800,000 pounds @ $0.07 per pound
Sand	900,000 pounds @ $0.03 per pound
Materials used:	
Asphalt	775,000 pounds
Sand	850,000 pounds
Direct labor	5,100 hours costing $36,000
Manufacturing overhead incurred:	
Variable	$16,500
Fixed	$48,000

Budgeted fixed manufacturing overhead for the period is $60,000, and the standard fixed overhead rate is based on expected capacity of 6,000 direct labor hours.

Required:

1. Calculate the standard fixed manufacturing overhead rate.

EXERCISE 2 (continued)

2. Complete the standard cost card for roofing shingles.

3. Calculate the following variances:

   a. materials price and usage variances

   b. labor rate and efficiency variances

EXERCISE 2 (continued)

c. variable manufacturing overhead spending and efficiency variances

d. fixed manufacturing overhead budget and volume variances

EXERCISE 3

The Commodore Company uses standard costing for direct materials and direct labor. Management would like to use standard costing for variable and fixed overhead also.

The following monthly cost functions were developed for manufacturing overhead items:

OVERHEAD ITEM	COST FUNCTION
Indirect materials	$0.10 per DLH
Indirect labor	$0.40 per DLH
Repairs and maintenance	$0.20 per DLH
Utilities	$0.25 per DLH
Insurance	$2,000
Rent	$4,000
Depreciation	$20,000

The cost functions are considered reliable within a relevant range of 30,000 to 55,000 direct labor hours.

Commodore expects to operate at 40,000 direct labor hours per month.

Information for the month of September is as follows:

Actual overhead costs incurred:	
Indirect materials	$ 4,500
Indirect labor	17,000
Repairs and maintenance	8,000
Utilities	10,000
Insurance	2,100
Rent	4,000
Depreciation	20,000
Total	$65,600
Actual direct labor hours worked	42,000
Standard direct labor hours allowed for production achieved	44,000

Required:

1. Calculate the standard manufacturing overhead rate based upon expected capacity showing the breakdown between the fixed overhead rate and the variable overhead rate.

EXERCISE 3 (continued)

2. Calculate the variable manufacturing overhead spending variance.

3. Calculate the variable manufacturing overhead efficiency variance.

4. Calculate the fixed manufacturing overhead budget variance.

5. Calculate the fixed manufacturing overhead volume variance.

ANSWERS

KEY TERMS TEST
1. Currently attainable standards
2. Ideal standards
3. standard cost sheet
4. Control limits
5. efficiency variance
6. unfavorable variance
7. favorable variance
8. standard bill of materials
9. Standard hours allowed
10. variable overhead efficiency variance
11. variable overhead spending variance
12. Standard quantity of materials allowed
13. materials price variance
14. materials usage variance
15. fixed overhead volume variance
16. labor rate variance
17. labor efficiency variance
18. fixed overhead spending variance

CHAPTER QUIZ
1. b
2. a and b
3. d
4. b False To facilitate control, actual overhead costs should be compared to budgeted costs for the same level of output.
5. b False
6. a True
7. a True
8. b False The fixed manufacturing overhead rate should be determined on a yearly basis.
9. b False Manufacturing overhead would be applied based on the standard hours allowed for production achieved.
10. a True
11. b False The fixed manufacturing overhead volume variance is a measure of the utilization of plant facilities.
12. a True
13. a True
14. a 39,000($6.20 - $6.00) = $7,800 unfavorable
15. c $6.00[39,000 - (4 feet x 10,000)] = $6,000 favorable
16. b 10,500 hours($12.50 - $12.00) = $5,250 unfavorable
17. d $12(10,500 - 10,000) = $6,000 unfavorable
18. a $48,000 - (10,500 x $5) = $4,500 favorable
19. b $5(10,500 - 10,000) = $2,500 unfavorable
20. a $40,000 - ($3 x 12,000) = $4,000 unfavorable
21. c $36,000 budgeted - ($3 x 10,000) applied = $6,000 unfavorable

EXERCISE 1

1. Direct materials price variance:

Actual Quantity Purchased at Actual Price	Actual Quantity Purchased at Standard Price
5,000 sq. ft. x $9.20/sq. ft.	5,000 sq. ft. x $8/sq. ft.
$46,000	$40,000

$6,000 Unfavorable

Direct Materials Price Variance
5,000($9.20 - $8.00) = $6,000 Unfavorable

Direct materials usage variance:

Actual Quantity Used at Standard Price	Standard Quantity Allowed at Standard Price
4,250 sq. ft. x $8.00/sq. ft.	900 units x 5 sq. ft. x $8/sq. ft.
$34,000	$36,000

$2,000 Favorable

Direct Materials Usage Variance
$8.00(4,250 - 4,500) = $2,000 Favorable

2. Direct labor rate variance:

Actual Labor Hours at Actual Rate	Actual Labor Hours at Standard Rate
2,200 hours x $9/per hour	2,200 hours x $10/per hour
$19,800	$22,000

$2,200 Favorable

Direct Labor Rate Variance
2,200($9.00 - $10.00) = $2,200 Favorable

Direct labor efficiency variance:

Actual Labor Hours at Standard Rate	Standard Labor Hours Allowed at Standard Rate
2,200 hours x $10/per hour	(900 units x 2 hours) x $10 per hour
$22,000	$18,000

$4,000 Unfavorable

Direct Labor Efficiency Variance
$10(2,200 - 1,800) = $4,000 Unfavorable

EXERCISE 1 (continued)

Total direct labor variance:

Actual hours at actual price	$19,800
Standard hours allowed for production (900 x 2) x $10	18,000
Total direct labor variance	$ 1,800 U

The total direct labor variance can be broken down as follows:

Direct labor rate variance	$2,200 F
Direct labor efficiency variance	4,000 U
Total direct labor variance	$1,800 U

3. Variable manufacturing overhead spending variance:

Actual Variable Overhead	Standard Variable Overhead Rate x Actual Hours (AQ x SVOR) 2,200 hours x $5 per hour
$10,500	$11,000

$500 Favorable

Variable Overhead Spending Variance

Variable manufacturing overhead efficiency variance:

Standard Variable Overhead Rate x Actual Hours (AQ x SVOR)	Standard Variable Overhead Rate x Standard Hours (SQ x SVOR)
2,200 hours x $5 per hour	(900 x 2 hours) x $5 per hour
$11,000	$9,000

$2,000 Unfavorable

Variable Overhead Efficiency Variance

EXERCISE 2

1.

$$SFOR = \frac{Estimated\ Fixed\ Overhead}{Estimated\ Direct\ Labor\ Hours}$$

$$= \frac{\$60,000}{6,000\ DLH}$$

$$= \$10\ per\ DLH$$

2.

STANDARD COST CARD
PER SHINGLE

Direct materials:	
Asphalt	$0.16
Sand	0.04
Direct labor	0.07
Variable manufacturing overhead	0.03
Fixed manufacturing overhead	
.01 hr. x $10/hr.	0.10
Total standard cost per shingle	$0.40

3.a. Materials price variance--asphalt:

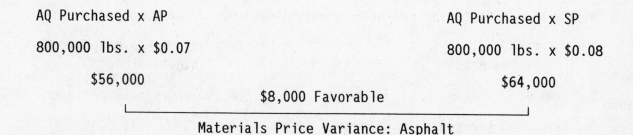

```
AQ Purchased x AP                              AQ Purchased x SP

800,000 lbs. x $0.07                           800,000 lbs. x $0.08

      $56,000                                         $64,000
                     $8,000 Favorable

               Materials Price Variance: Asphalt
```

Materials price variance--sand:

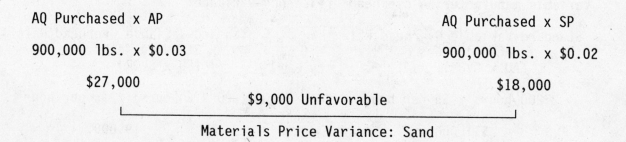

```
AQ Purchased x AP                              AQ Purchased x SP

900,000 lbs. x $0.03                           900,000 lbs. x $0.02

      $27,000                                         $18,000
                   $9,000 Unfavorable

                Materials Price Variance: Sand
```

Materials usage variance--asphalt:

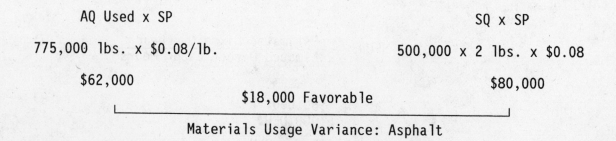

```
AQ Used x SP                                        SQ x SP

775,000 lbs. x $0.08/lb.                    500,000 x 2 lbs. x $0.08

      $62,000                                         $80,000
                     $18,000 Favorable

                Materials Usage Variance: Asphalt
```

EXERCISE 2 (continued)

Materials usage variance--sand:

AQ Used x SP		SQ x SP
850,000 lbs. x $0.02/lb.		500,000 x 2 lbs. x $0.02
$17,000		$20,000

$3,000 Favorable

Materials Usage Variance: Sand

b. Direct labor rate variance:

AQ x AP		AQ x SP
5,100 DLH x $7.06*/hr.		5,100 DLH x $7.00/hr.
$36,000		$35,700

$300 Unfavorable

Direct Labor Rate Variance

*rounded

Direct labor efficiency variance:

AQ x SP		SQ x SP
5,100 DLH x $7.00/hr.		500,000 x .01 DLH x $7.00/hr.
$35,700		$35,000

$700 Unfavorable

Direct Labor Efficiency Variance

c. Variable manufacturing overhead spending variance:

Actual Variable Overhead	Standard Variable Overhead Rate x Actual Hours (AQ x SVOR)
	5,100 DLH x $3.00/hr.
$16,500	$15,300

$1,200 Unfavorable

Variable Overhead Spending Variance

EXERCISE 2 (continued)

Variable manufacturing overhead efficiency variance:

Standard Variable Overhead Rate x Actual Hours	Standard Variable Overhead Rate x Standard Hours
(AQ x SVOR)	(SQ x SVOR)
5,100 DLH x $3.00/hr.	500,000 x .01 DLH x $3.00/hr.
$15,300	$15,000

$300 Unfavorable

Variable Overhead Efficiency Variance

d. Fixed manufacturing overhead budget variance:

Actual Fixed Overhead	Budgeted Fixed Overhead
$48,000	$60,000

$12,000 Favorable

Fixed Overhead Budget Variance

Fixed manufacturing overhead volume variance:

Budgeted Fixed Overhead	Applied Fixed Overhead
	(Standard Activity x SFOR)
	500,000 x .01 DLH x $10/hr.
$60,000	$50,000

$10,000 Unfavorable

Fixed Overhead Volume Variance

The volume variance could also be calculated as follows:

$$\begin{matrix} \text{FMO} \\ \text{Volume} \\ \text{Variance} \end{matrix} = \text{SFOR} \times \begin{bmatrix} \text{Expected Capacity} & & \text{Standard Hours} \\ \text{(Denominator} & - & \text{Allowed For Production} \\ \text{DLH Used)} & & \text{Level Achieved} \end{bmatrix}$$

```
= ($10)(6,000 DLH - 5,000 DLH Allowed)
= ($10)(1,000 DLH)
= $10,000
```

EXERCISE 2 (continued)

The Mills Company produced 500,000 shingles, a level for which 5,000 direct labor hours are allowed.

The Mills Company budgeted 6,000 direct labor hours. The volume variance resulted from the company operating at a level other than the budgeted level of 6,000 direct labor hours.

EXERCISE 3

1. Predetermined manufacturing overhead rate:

Manufacturing overhead items:		
Indirect materials		$0.10 per DLH
Indirect labor		0.40 per DLH
Repairs and maintenance		0.20 per DLH
Utilities		0.25 per DLH
Insurance	$ 2,000	
Rent	4,000	
Depreciation	20,000	
Variable manufacturing overhead		$0.95 per DLH
Fixed manufacturing overhead	$26,000	

SVOR = $0.95 per DLH

$$\text{SFOR} = \frac{\text{Estimated FMO}}{\text{Estimated DLH}} = \frac{\$26,000}{40,000 \text{ DLH}} = \$0.65 \text{ per DLH}$$

Total Manufacturing Overhead Rate = SFOR + SVOR
$$= \$0.65 + \$0.95$$
$$= \$1.60 \text{ per DLH}$$

2. **Variable overhead spending variance:**

Actual Variable Overhead	Standard Variable Overhead Rate x Actual Hours
	(AQ x SVOR)
($4,500 + $17,000 + $8,000 + $10,000)	42,000 DLH x $0.95/hr.
$39,500	$39,900

$400 Favorable

Variable Overhead Spending Variance

779

3. **Variable manufacturing overhead efficiency variance:**

Standard Variable Overhead Rate x Actual Hours	Standard Variable Overhead Rate x Standard Hours
(AQ x SVOR)	(SQ x SVOR)
42,000 DLH x $0.95/hr.	44,000 DLH x $0.95/hr.
$39,900	$41,800

$1,900 Favorable

Variable Overhead Efficiency Variance

4. **Fixed overhead budget variance:**

Actual Fixed Overhead	Budgeted Fixed Overhead
$26,100	$26,000

$100 Unfavorable

Fixed Overhead Budget Variance

5. **Fixed overhead volume variance:**

Budgeted Fixed Overhead	Applied Fixed Overhead
	(Standard Activity x SFOR)
	44,000 DLH x $0.65/hr.
$26,000	$28,600

$2,600 Favorable

Fixed Overhead Volume Variance

The volume variance could also be calculated as follows:

$$\text{FOH Volume Variance} = \text{SFOR} \times \left[\begin{array}{c} \text{Expected Capacity} \\ \text{(Denominator} \\ \text{DLH Used)} \end{array} - \begin{array}{c} \text{Standard Hours} \\ \text{Allowed For Production} \\ \text{Level Achieved} \end{array} \right]$$

= ($0.65)(40,000 DLH - 44,000 DLH Allowed)
= ($0.65)(4,000 DLH)
= $2,600 Favorable

CHAPTER 26

PLANNING AND CONTROL:
THE ADVANCED MANUFACTURING ENVIRONMENT

CHAPTER REVIEW

LIMITATIONS OF TRADITIONAL PERFORMANCE MEASURES

- Many of the traditional means used to evaluate and control conventional manufacturing are not suitable for JIT manufacturing.

- The traditional approach compares actual costs with budgeted or standard costs to determine variances.

- The variances are used as:
  1. an indication if the process is out of control.
  2. a means of evaluating performance.

- Standard costing encourages those being evaluated to produce favorable variances.

- Traditional variance analysis based upon currently attainable standards may encourage employees to take actions that are not consistent with the objectives of JIT manufacturing.

- The objectives of JIT are:
  1. total quality control (zero defects)
  2. continual improvement
  3. zero inventories

- Firms that adopt a philosophy of continual improvement usually alter the role of standard costing as a managerial control tool.

Materials Price Variance

- Purchasing agents may purchase large lots of low-quality material to produce a favorable price variance.

- The purchase of large lots would result in raw materials inventory, and low-quality materials would result in scrap, defective units, and rework costs.

- The results are the opposite of the JIT objectives of zero defects and zero inventories.

Materials Usage Variance

• To avoid unfavorable materials usage variances, workers may pass on poor-quality components.

• This results in increased defects and conflicts with the JIT objective of zero defects.

Labor Efficiency Variance

• Cell workers may produce more than needed in order to have a favorable efficiency variance. The increased inventory conflicts with the JIT objective of zero inventories.

• With JIT, idle cell workers use the time to perform other tasks, such as preventive maintenance.

Overhead Budget Variance

• To produce a favorable overhead budget variance, preventive maintenance may be postponed, resulting in downtime and conflicting with the JIT philosophy of total preventive maintenance.

Currently Attainable Standards

• Currently attainable standards allow for a certain level of inefficiency. JIT has an objective of continual improvement.

Summary of Limitations of Conventional Control Methods

Control Measure	Limitation	Advanced Manufacturing Objective Violated
Materials price variance	Encourages low quality and large lot purchases	Total quality control and zero inventories
Labor efficiency variance	Encourages overproduction	Zero inventories
Materials usage variance	Provides incentive for low quality	Total quality control
Budget variance: Maintenance	Provides incentive for downtime	Total preventive maintenance
Currently attainable standards	Encourages inefficiency	Continual improvement, zero inventories, total quality control, and total preventive maintenance

ACTIVITY-BASED MANAGEMENT

- Conventional responsibility accounting is characterized by four elements.
  1. A responsibility center is identified, responsibility is assigned to the individual in charge, and responsibility is defined in financial terms.
  2. Standards are set to serve as benchmarks for performance measurement.
  3. Performance is measured by comparing actual outcomes with budgeted outcomes. Individuals should be held accountable only for those items that they can control.
  4. Individuals are rewarded or penalized according to the policies and discretion of higher management. The reward system is designed to encourage individuals to manage costs—to achieve or beat budgetary standards.

- The emphasis of conventional responsibility accounting is on managing costs—not activities.

- The emerging consensus, however, is that managing activities—not costs— are the key to successful control in the advanced manufacturing environment.

- **Activity-based management (ABM)** is a systemwide, integrated approach that focuses management's attention on activities.

- The activity-based management model has two dimensions:
  1. a *cost view*
  2. a *process view*

- The *cost view* provides cost information about resources, activities, products, and customers. The cost of resources is traced to activities, and then the cost of activities is assigned to products and customers.

- The *process view* provides information about why work is done and how well it is done. The process view is concerned with cost driver analysis, activity analysis, and performance measurement.

- **Activity-based responsibility accounting** focuses on accountability for activities rather than costs.

- Costs are caused by activities; therefore, it makes sense to focus on managing the underlying causes of costs (the activities) rather than the costs themselves.

- Activity-based responsibility accounting emphasizes the maximization of systemwide performance instead of individual performance. Essentially, this form of control admits that maximizing the efficiency of individual subunits does not necessarily lead to maximum efficiency for the system as a whole.

- One key difference between the cost dimension and the control (process) dimension is the level of activity aggregation.

- For process costing, activities are grouped into homogeneous sets of activities.

- For control and activity improvement purposes, greater detail about individual activities is needed.

Activity Analysis

- **Activity analysis** is the process of identifying and describing the activities an organization performs.

- Activity analysis should reveal the following:
  1. what activities are done.
  2. how many people perform the activities.
  3. the time and resources required to perform the activities.
  4. an assessment of the value of the activities to the organization, including a recommendation to select and keep only those activities that add value.

- Activity management attempts to:
  1. identify and eliminate all unnecessary activities.
  2. increase the efficiency of necessary activities.
  3. add new activities that increase value.

- **Nonvalue-added activities** are either:
  1. unnecessary activities or
  2. necessary activities that are inefficient and improvable.

- Activity management attempts to eliminate nonvalue-added activities.

- **Nonvalue-added costs** are costs caused by nonvalue-added activities.

Examples of Nonvalue-Added Activities

- In a manufacturing operation, the following five major activities are often cited as wasteful and unnecessary:
  1. Scheduling: an activity that uses time and resources to determine when different products have access to processes (or when and how many setups must be done) and how much will be produced.
  2. Moving: an activity that uses time and resources to move raw materials, work in process, and finished goods from one department to another.
  3. Waiting: an activity where raw materials or work in process use time and resources by waiting on the next process.
  4. Inspecting: an activity where time and resources are spent on ensuring that the product meets specifications.
  5. Storing: an activity that uses time and resources while a good or raw material is held in inventory.

Target Costing

- A **target cost** is the difference between the sales price needed to capture a predetermined market share and the desired profit per unit.

 Sales price needed to capture a predetermined market share
    - Desired profit per unit

    = Target cost per unit

- Progress is measured by comparing actual costs and target costs.

- Both currently attainable standards and target costs generally share the same goal of cost reduction and continual improvement. However, target costs are <u>externally</u> driven, generated by an analysis of <u>markets and competitors</u>, while currently attainable standards are generated <u>internally</u> by <u>industrial engineers and production managers</u>.

Cost Driver Analysis: Behavioral Effects

- The cost driver selected can affect the behavior of employees. For example, if the cost driver for setup costs is setup time, the individual is motivated to reduce setup time.

LIFE-CYCLE COST MANAGEMENT

- **Product life cycle** is the time a product exists—from conception to abandonment.

- **Life-cycle costs** are all costs associated with the product for its entire life cycle.

- Life-cycle costs include:
  1. development (planning, design, and testing)
  2. production (conversion activities)
  3. logistics support (advertising, distribution, and warranty)

- **Whole-life cost** is the life cycle cost of a product plus post-purchase costs that consumers incur, including operation, support, maintenance, and disposal.

- Whole-life costing emphasizes management of the entire value chain.

- The **value chain** is the set of activities required to design, develop, produce, market, and service a product (or service).

- **Life-cycle cost management** focuses on managing value-chain activities so that a long-term competitive advantage is created.

  To achieve this goal, managers must balance the following:
  - a product's whole-life cost
  - method of delivery
  - innovativeness
  - product performance
  - features offered
  - reliability
  - conformance
  - durability
  - aesthetics
  - perceived quality

Cost Reduction

- Because 90 percent or more of a product's costs are <u>committed</u> (but not incurred) during the development stage, it is logical to focus on managing activities during this stage.

- Studies have shown that every dollar spent on premanufacturing activities saves $8-$10 on manufacturing and postmanufacturing activities.

- More opportunities for cost reduction exist during product planning than in production.

- The traditional emphasis has been on controlling costs during the production stage. In addition, development and logistics costs have been virtually ignored when computing product profitability for managerial purposes.

Whole-Life Product Cost

- A whole-life product cost consists of four elements:
  1. nonrecurring costs (planning, designing, and testing)
  2. manufacturing costs
  3. logistic costs
  4. the customer's postpurchase costs

Role of Target Costing

- Target costing is a useful tool for establishing cost reduction goals.

- If target profit exceeds estimated profit, the difference is the cost reduction goal.

Choosing the Quality Standard

The Traditional Approach

- The traditional approach uses an **acceptable quality level (AQL)** that permits a predetermined level of defective products to be sold.

The Zero-Defects Approach

- The **zero-defects** approach uses a quality performance standard that requires:
  1. all products to be produced according to specifications.
  2. all services to be provided according to requirements.

- Zero defects reflects a total quality control philosophy used in JIT manufacturing.

Quantifying the Quality Standard

- The goal for a company with a well-run quality management program is for quality costs not to exceed 2.5 percent of sales.

- If zero defects are achieved, quality costs are for prevention and appraisal activities.

Behavior of Quality Costs

- Quality costs are classified as:
  1. variable with respect to sales or
  2. fixed with respect to sales.

- Variable quality costs vary with changes in sales volume.

- Fixed quality costs do not vary with changes in sales volume.

- Actual variable quality costs are compared to budgeted variable quality costs using percentages of sales and/or actual dollars.

- Actual fixed quality costs are compared with budgeted fixed quality costs.

Interim Standards

- Because improving quality to the zero-defects level is a long-range goal, **interim quality standards** should be developed so that managers can evaluate progress made each year.

Types of Quality Performance Reports

- Two performance reports used to measure an organization's quality improvement are:
  1. **Interim standard performance report**, which measures the progress <u>achieved</u> within the period relative to the <u>planned</u> level of progress for the period. The interim standard report is a traditional approach to cost control.
  2. **One-year quality trend report**, which compares:
     - the current year's variable quality cost ratio with the previous year's variable quality cost ratio.
     - the current year's actual fixed quality costs with the previous year's actual fixed quality costs.

     The one-year trend report is more consistent with the new emphasis on tracking trends in actual costs.

PRODUCTIVITY: MEASUREMENT AND CONTROL

Productivity Measurement Defined

- Productivity is concerned with producing output efficiently.

- **Total productive efficiency** is the point at which technical efficiency and price efficiency are achieved.

- **Technical efficiency** is the point at which, for any mix of inputs that will produce a given output, no more of any one input is used than is absolutely necessary.

- **Price efficiency** is the least-cost, technically efficient mix of inputs.

- Productivity can be improved as follows:
  1. Improve technical efficiency by:
     - using less input to produce the same output or
     - using the same input to produce more output.
  2. Improve price efficiency by using a less costly mix of inputs.

- **Productivity measurement** involves measuring productivity changes so that efforts to improve productivity can be evaluated.

- Productivity can be measured using:
  1. a **partial productivity measure** that assesses productivity for each input separately or
  2. a **total productivity measure** that assesses productivity for all inputs at once.

- An **operational productivity measure** uses <u>physical quantities</u> to measure input and output.

- A **financial productivity measure** uses dollars to measure input and output.

4. _____ _____ _____ are incurred because products and services fail to conform to requirements where lack of conformity is discovered prior to external sale.

5. A(n) _____ _____ _____ _____ compares current-year quality costs with prior-year quality costs based on current-year sales.

6. _____ _____ _____ are expressed in physical terms.

7. _____ _____ is the least-cost, technically efficient mix of inputs.

8. The difference between the total profit change and the profit-linked productivity change is the _____ _____ .

9. _____ _____ _____ is a measure of how well a product meets its design specifications.

10. _____ _____ _____ refers to quality differences that arise for products with the same function but different specifications.

11. A(n) _____ _____ _____ , or _____ , is a predetermined level of defective products that a company permits to be sold.

12. _____ _____ are incurred to determine whether products and services are conforming to requirements.

13. _____ _____ _____ are costs incurred because poor quality may exist or because poor quality does exist.

14. A(n) _____ _____ _____ is a productivity measure that expresses inputs and outputs in dollars.

15. A(n) _____ _____ _____ _____ compares current actual quality costs with short-run budgeted quality targets.

16. _____ _____ are necessary and perfectly efficient activities.

17. A(n) _____ _____ is the quantity of a cost driver that should be used for an activity.

18. A(n) _____ _____ _____ is a ratio that measures productive efficiency for one input.

19. _____ _____ are incurred to prevent defects in products or services being produced.

20. _____ _____ concerns producing output efficiency, using the least quantity of inputs possible.

21. _____ _____ _____ is an assessment of the amount of profit change--from the base period to the current period—attributable to productivity changes.

22. _____ _____ _____ is an assessment of productive efficiency for all inputs combined.

23. _____ _____ is a quality performance standard that requires all products and services to be produced and delivered according to specifications.

24. _____ _____ is an assessment of productivity changes.

25. _____ _____ is the point at which for any mix of inputs that will produce a given output, no more of any one input is used than is absolutely necessary.

26. _____ _____ _____ is the point at which technical efficiency and price efficiency are achieved.

27. _____ _____ is the process of identifying and describing the activities an organization performs.

28. _____ _____ is the process of eliminating nonvalue-added activities.

29. _____ _____ decreases the time and resources required by an activity.

30. _____ _____ is the process of choosing among sets of activities caused by competing strategies.

31. _____ _____ increases the efficiency of necessary activities by using economies of scale.

32. _____ _____ is the difference between the sales price needed to achieve a projected market share and the desired per unit profit.

33. _____ _____ _____ is the time a product exists—from conception to abandonment.

34. _____ _____ is activity management during the development stage to ensure the lowest possible total life-cycle cost.

35. Costs associated with the product for its entire life cycle are called _____ _____.

36. _____ _____, or _____, is a systemwide, integrated approach that focuses management's attention on activities.

37. Costs caused by value-added activities are _____ _____.

38. _____ _____ is the set of activities required to design, develop, produce, market, and service a product (or service).

39. _____ _____ is the life-cycle cost of a product plus costs that consumers incur, including operation, support, maintenance, and disposal.

40. Costs caused by nonvalue-added activities are _____ _____.

KEY TERMS:

acceptable quality level, AQL
activity analysis
activity elimination
activity-based management, ABM
activity reduction
activity selection
activity sharing
appraisal costs
costs of quality
external failure costs
financial productivity measure
interim quality performance report
interim quality standard
internal failure costs
life-cycle costs
life-cycle cost management
nonvalue-added activities
nonvalue-added costs
one-year quality performance report
operational productivity measures

partial productivity measure
prevention costs
price efficiency
price-recovery component
product life cycle
productivity
productivity measurement
profit-linked productivity measurement
quality of conformance
quality of design
target cost
technical efficiency
total productive efficiency
total productivity measurement
value-added activities
value-added costs
value-added standard
value chain
whole-life cost
zero defects

Compare your answers to those at the end of the chapter and review any key terms missed.

CHAPTER QUIZ

Write your answers in the spaces provided.

1. The traditional approach compares actual costs with _____ _____ to determine variances.

2. Traditional variance analysis may encourage employees to take actions that are not consistent with the objectives of JIT manufacturing. The objectives of JIT are:

    1. _____
    2. _____
    3. _____

3. The emphasis of conventional responsibility accounting is on managing
   _____.

4. The key to successful control in the advanced manufacturing environment
   is to manage _____.

5. Activity-based costing is concerned with maximizing _____
   performance.

6. Nonvalue-added activities are either:
   1. _____ or
   2. _____

7. Value-added activities are _____ activities performed with
   _____ _____.

8. Value-added costs = _____ _____ x _____ _____

9. Nonvalue-added costs = (_____ _____ - _____ _____) x _____ _____

10. For nonvalue-added activities that are unnecessary, the standard quantity
    is _____.

11. Target cost = _____ - _____

12. Life-cycle costs include:
    1. _____
    2. _____
    3. _____

13. The traditional emphasis has been on controlling costs during the
    _____ stage; however, because 90 percent or more of a
    product's costs are committed during the _____ stage, it is
    logical to focus on managing activities during this stage.

Circle the single best answer.

14. Traditional variance analysis may encourage workers to pass on poor-
    quality components in order to avoid unfavorable materials usage
    variances: (a) true; (b) false

15. Currently attainable standards allow for a certain level of inefficiency:
    (a) true; (b) false

16. JIT uses a single volume-based cost driver: (a) true; (b) false

17. JIT uses an acceptable quality level approach: (a) true; (b) false

18. Many of the traditional means used to evaluate and control conventional
    manufacturing are also suitable for JIT manufacturing: (a) true;
    (b) false

19. The objectives of JIT are zero defects, zero inventories, and continual
    improvement: (a) true; (b) false

20. Standard costing encourages employees being evaluated to produce favorable variances and achieve the objectives of JIT: (a) true; (b) false

21. Value-added costs are standard costs based on currently attainable standards: (a) true; (b) false

Use the following information to answer the next seven questions.

King Manufacturing has developed optimal standards for labor usage, receiving, and packing. The optimal levels of the inputs for each of the activities, their actual levels achieved, and the standard prices are as follows:

	Cost Driver	SQ	AQ	SP
Labor usage	Labor hours	15,000	20,000	$ 10
Receiving	Purchase orders	600	750	120
Packing	Sales orders	700	1,000	90

The actual prices paid for the inputs equal the standard price.

22. Value-added costs for labor are: (a) $145,500; (b) $150,000; (c) $160,000; (d) $200,000

23. Nonvalue-added costs for labor are: (a) $50,000; (b) $60,200; (c) $68,400; (d) $105,000

24. Value-added costs for receiving are: (a) $68,000; (b) $72,000; (c) $84,600; (d) $90,000

25. Nonvalue-added costs for receiving are: (a) $15,600; (b) $16,200; (c) $16,800; (d) $18,000

26. Value-added costs for packing are: (a) $63,000; (b) $70,000; (c) $72,000; (d) $90,000

27. Nonvalue-added costs for packing are: (a) $18,900; (b) $25,200; (c) $27,000; (d) $28,400

28. If the company wants to reduce nonvalue-added costs for labor by 20 percent next year, the currently attainable standard for labor hours would be: (a) 17,000; (b) 18,600; (c) 19,000; (d) 20,000

Write your answers in the spaces provided.

29. List the four categories of quality costs.
    1. _____
    2. _____
    3. _____
    4. _____

30. In a quality cost report, quality costs are grouped into categories and then each category of quality costs is expressed as a percentage of _____ .

31. The goal is for quality costs not to exceed _____ .

32. There are two views concerning optimal quality costs:
    1. the traditional view, which uses an _____ quality level
    2. the world-class view, which uses _____ quality control

33. With a zero-defects approach, most of the quality costs should be for _____ and _____ activities.

34. Variable quality costs vary with changes in _____ .
    Fixed quality costs do not vary with changes in _____ .

35. Productivity is concerned with producing output _____ .

36. Productivity is measured as _____ divided by _____ .

37. List three ways productivity can be improved.
    1. _____
    2. _____
    3. _____

Use the following information to answer the next ten questions.

Classify the following costs as:
• Prevention Cost
• Appraisal Cost
• Internal Failure Cost
• External Failure Cost

_____	38. Warranty work
_____	39. Quality training programs
_____	40. In-process inspection
_____	41. Reinspection of reworked products
_____	42. Product recalls
_____	43. Inspection labor costs
_____	44. Downtime attributed to quality problems
_____	45. Product inspection
_____	46. Consumer complaint department
_____	47. Labor and overhead incurred for rework of defective products

Circle the single best answer.

48. Market shares of many U.S. firms have eroded because foreign firms have been able to sell higher quality products at lower prices: (a) true; (b) false

49. A quality product is a product that conforms to customer expectations: (a) true; (b) false

50. The two types of product quality are quality of design and quality of conformance: (a) true; (b) false

51. When quality experts refer to improving quality, they are referring to improving the quality of design: (a) true; (b) false

52. Quality refers to doing it right the first time: (a) true; (b) false

53. As prevention and appraisal costs increase, internal and external failure costs are expected to increase: (a) true; (b) false

54. JIT uses an acceptable quality level that permits a predetermined level of defective products to be sold: (a) true; (b) false

Use the following information to answer the next nine questions.

The following information pertains to the Sunshine Company.

	1994	1995
Output	8,000	10,000
Output prices	$12	$12
Materials (pounds)	5,000	5,500
Material unit price	$4	$5
Labor (hours)	3,000	2,500
Labor rate per hour	$10	$10
Power (kilowatt hours)	1,200	1,800
Price per kilowatt hour	$2.50	$3

55. The partial operational productivity measure for materials for 1994 is: (a) 0.625; (b) 1.60; (c) 1.67; (d) 1.10

56. The partial operational productivity measure for materials for 1995 is: (a) 1.82; (b) 1.87; (c) 2.0; (d) 1.55

57. From 1994 to 1995, productivity for materials: (a) increased; (b) decreased

58. The partial operational productivity measure for labor for 1994 is: (a) 2.67; (b) 4.00; (c) 0.375; (d) 1.20

803

59. The partial operational productivity measure for direct labor for 1995 is: (a) 2.5; (b) 2.8; (c) 4; (d) 4.2

60. From 1994 to 1995, productivity for labor: (a) increased; (b) decreased

61. The partial operational productivity measure for power for 1994 is: (a) 0.15; (b) 1.5; (c) 8.33; (d) 6.67

62. The partial operational productivity measure for power for 1995 is: (a) 5.52; (b) 5.56; (c) 7.24; (d) 16.67

63. From 1994 to 1995, power usage productivity: (a) increased; (b) decreased

Compare your answers to those at the end of the chapter and review any questions missed.

EXERCISES

EXERCISE 1

Traditional variance analysis may encourage employees to take actions that are not consistent with the objectives of JIT manufacturing. For each action listed below, indicate which JIT objective or objectives are not being met.

_____ 1. The purchasing agent received a reduced price on a purchase of raw materials because there were some seconds and irregulars in the order. This resulted in a favorable price variance and a favorable performance evaluation for the purchasing agent.

_____ 2. The production manager noticed employees were taking longer breaks when they were idle, so production volume was increased in order to reduce idle time.

_____ 3. To reduce setup costs, the number of setups was reduced.

_____ 4. To cut costs, one direct laborer per manufacturing cell was laid off resulting in less time for preventive maintenance.

_____ 5. To avoid being charged with an unfavorable materials usage variance, workers do not scrap defective material. Instead, it is passed on to the next production phase.

_____ 6. The purchasing agent produced a favorable price variance by buying large quantities of raw materials in order to take advantage of quantity discounts.

EXERCISE 2

For each activity listed below, determine the amount of value-added and nonvalue-added costs.

1. A company has 10 days of finished goods inventory on hand to avoid stockouts. The carrying costs of the inventory average $20,000 per day.

   Value-added costs $_____
   Nonvalue-added costs $_____

2. Setup time for a product is 5 hours. A firm that produces the same product and uses JIT has reduced setup time to 15 minutes. Setup labor is $10.00 per hour.

   Value-added costs $_____
   Nonvalue-added costs $_____

3. Warranty work costs the firm $1,000,000 per year. A competitor's warranty costs are $200,000 per year.

   Value-added costs $_____
   Nonvalue-added costs $_____

4. Downtime for bottleneck machinery averages 200 hours per year resulting in $600,000 in lost sales.

   Value-added costs $_____
   Nonvalue-added costs $_____

5. A time-and-motion study revealed it should take 12 minutes to produce a product that currently takes 30 minutes to produce. Labor is $15 per hour.

   Value-added costs $_____
   Nonvalue-added costs $_____

EXERCISE 2 (continued)

6. The company keeps 5 days of raw materials on hand to avoid shutdowns due to raw materials shortages. Carrying costs average $10,000 per day.

   Value-added costs $_____
   Nonvalue-added costs $_____

7. By redesigning the manufacturing layout, the time required to move materials can be reduced from 2 hours to 30 minutes. The labor cost is $12 per hour.

   Value-added costs $_____
   Nonvalue-added costs $_____

8. Each unit of product requires 10 pounds of raw material. Due to scrap and rework, each unit has been averaging 10.8 pounds of raw material. The raw material costs $5 per pound.

   Value-added costs $_____
   Nonvalue-added costs $_____

EXERCISE 3

Bass Company has developed ideal standards for four activities: labor, materials, inspection, and receiving. Information about each activity is provided below:

Activity	Cost Driver	Standard Quantity	Actual Quantity	Standard Price
Labor	Hours	5,000	6,000	$ 6.00
Materials	Pounds	20,000	24,000	$ 8.00
Inspection	Inspection hours	-0-	30,000	$ 7.00
Receiving	Orders	200	225	$500.00

The actual prices paid per unit of each cost driver were equal to the standard prices.

Required:

Prepare a cost report that lists the value-added costs, nonvalue-added costs, and actual costs for each activity using the following format.

Activity	Value-Added Costs	Nonvalue-Added Costs	Actual Costs
Labor	$_____	$_____	$_____
Materials	_____	_____	_____
Inspection	_____	_____	_____
Receiving	_____	_____	_____
Totals	_____	_____	_____

EXERCISE 4

Ashley, Inc., sells one of its products for $120 each. Sales volume averages 1,000 units per year. Recently, its main competitor reduced the price of its product to $100. Ashley expects its sales to plummet unless it matches the competitor's price. In addition, the current profit per unit must be maintained. Information about the product (for production of 1,000 units) is as follows:

	SQ	AQ	Actual Cost
Materials (pounds)	7,800	8,000	$40,000
Labor (hours)	1,800	2,000	20,000
Setups (hours)	0	1,000	10,000
Material handling (moves)	0	500	5,000
Warranties (number repaired)	0	300	15,000

Required:

1. Calculate the target cost for maintaining current market share and profitability.

2. Calculate the nonvalue-added cost per unit. If nonvalue-added costs can be reduced to zero, can the target cost be achieved?

EXERCISE 5

Michaels, Inc., developed the following budgeted life-cycle income statement for two proposed products. Each product's life cycle is expected to be two years.

	Product A	Product B	Total
Sales	$1,000,000	$1,400,000	$2,400,000
Cost of goods sold	(800,000)	(1,000,000)	(1,800,000)
Gross profit	$ 200,000	$ 400,000	$ 600,000
Period expenses:			
Research and development			(220,000)
Marketing			(180,000)
Life-cycle income			$ 200,000

An 11% return on sales is required for new products; therefore, because the proposed products did not have an 11% return on sales, the products were going to be dropped.

Relative to Product B, Product A requires more research and development costs but fewer resources to market the product. Seventy percent of the research and development costs are traceable to Product A, and 20 percent of the marketing costs are traceable to Product A.

Required:

1. Prepare a revised life-cycle income statement for each product.

	Product A	Product B

2. If an 11 percent return on sales is required, should Product A be produced?

3. If an 11 percent return on sales is required, should Product B be produced?

EXERCISE 6

The following information pertains to Magic, Inc., for 1995.

Sales	$30,000,000
External failure costs	900,000
Internal failure costs	1,800,000
Prevention costs	400,000
Appraisal costs	600,000

Required:

1. Calculate each category of quality costs as a percentage of sales.

2. Calculate total quality costs as a percentage of sales.

3. If quality costs were reduced to 2.5 percent of sales, determine the increase in profit that would result.

EXERCISE 7

At the beginning of the year, Westfall Company initiated a quality improvement program. The program was successful in reducing scrap and rework costs.

To help assess the impact of the quality improvement program, the following data was collected for the current and preceding year.

	Preceding Year	Current Year
Sales	$4,000,000	$4,000,000
Quality training	10,000	15,000
Materials Inspection	25,000	35,000
Scrap	200,000	180,000
Rework	250,000	200,000
Product inspection	40,000	60,000
Product warranty	300,000	250,000

Required:

1. Classify each of the costs as:

   • Prevention cost
   • Appraisal cost
   • Internal failure cost
   • External failure cost

   Quality training _____
   Materials inspection _____
   Scrap _____
   Rework _____
   Product inspection _____
   Product warranty _____

2. Compute each category of quality costs as a percentage of sales.

	Preceding Year	Current Year
Prevention costs	_____	_____
Appraisal costs	_____	_____
Internal failure costs	_____	_____
External failure costs	_____	_____

3.a. How much has profit increased as a result of quality improvement?

b. If quality costs can be reduced to 2.5 percent of sales, how much additional profit would result?

EXERCISE 8

The following pertains to the last two years of operation of the Lowell Company.

	1995	1996
Output	15,000	18,000
Selling price per unit	$20	$20
Input quantities:		
Materials (pounds)	5,000	5,000
Labor (hours)	4,000	4,500
Input prices:		
Materials (per pound)	$4	$4.50
Labor (per hour)	$8	$8.10

Required:

1.a. Calculate the partial operational productivity ratios for materials and labor for each year.

	1995	1996
Materials	_____	_____
Labor	_____	_____

b. Did labor and material productivity improve from 1995 to 1996?

2.a. Compute the profit-linked productivity measure.

b. By how much did profits increase due to changes in productivity?

EXERCISE 9

The following information pertains to the Starr Company.

	1995	1996
Output	4,000	4,500
Output prices	$8	$8
Materials (pounds)	2,500	3,000
Material unit price	$2	$3
Labor (hours)	2,000	1,800
Labor rate per hour	$7	$7
Power (kilowatt hours)	800	900
Price per kilowatt hour	$1.50	$2

Required:

1. Compute the partial operational measures for each input for 1995 and 1996. Discuss productivity improvement.

	1995	1996
Materials		
Labor		
Power		

2. Prepare an income statement for each year and calculate the total change in profits.

	1995	1996

3. Calculate the profit-linked productivity measure for 1996. Discuss the results.

4. Calculate the price-recovery component. Explain the results.

ANSWERS

KEY TERMS TEST
1. Nonvalue-added activities
2. External failure costs
3. Interim quality standard
4. Internal failure costs
5. One-year quality performance report
6. Operational productivity measures
7. Price efficiency
8. price-recovery component
9. Quality of conformance
10. Quality of design
11. acceptable quality level, AQL
12. Appraisal costs
13. Costs of quality
14. financial productivity measure
15. interim quality performance report
16. Value-added activities
17. value-added standard
18. partial productivity measure
19. Prevention costs
20. Productivity
21. Profit-linked productivity measurement
22. Total productivity measurement
23. Zero defects
24. Productivity measurement
25. Technical efficiency
26. Total productive efficiency
27. Activity analysis
28. Activity elimination
29. Activity reduction
30. Activity selection
31. Activity sharing
32. Target cost
33. Product life cycle
34. Life-cycle management
35. life-cycle costs
36. Activity-based management, ABM
37. value-added costs
38. Value chain
39. Whole-life cost
40. nonvalue-added costs

CHAPTER QUIZ

1. standard costs
2. 1. total quality control (zero defects)
   2. continual improvement
   3. zero inventories
3. costs
4. activities
5. systemwide
6. 1. unnecessary activities
   2. necessary activities that are inefficient and improvable
7. necessary, perfect efficiency
8. Standard Quantity x Standard Price
9. (Actual Quantity - Standard Quantity) x Standard rice
10. zero
11. Sales price needed to capture a predetermined market share - Desired profit per unit
12. 1. development
    2. production
    3. logistics support
13. production, development
14. a   True
15. a   True
16. b   False   JIT uses multiple activity-based cost drivers.
17. b   False   JIT uses a total quality control approach that strives for zero defects.
18. b   False   Many of the traditional means used to evaluate and control conventional manufacturing are NOT suitable for JIT and may even encourage employees to take actions that are not consistent with the objectives of JIT.
19. a   True
20. b   False   Standard costing encourage employees to produce favorable variances, but their actions may not be consistent with the objectives of JIT.
21. b   False. Value-added costs are standard costs based on ideal standards.
22. b   15,000 x $10 = $150,000
23. a   (20,000 - 15,000) x $10 = $50,000
24. b   600 x $120 = $72,000
25. d   (750 - 600) x $120 = $18,000
26. a   700 x $90 = $63,000
27. c   (1,000 - 700) x $90 = $27,000
28. c   5,000 hours x 20% = 1,000 hours; 20,000 - 1,000 = 19,000 hours
29. 1. Prevention costs
    2. Appraisal costs
    3. Internal failure costs
    4. External failure costs
30. sales
31. 2.5 percent of sales
32. acceptable, total
33. prevention, appraisal
34. sales, sales
35. efficiently
36. output, input

37. 1. use fewer inputs to produce the same output
    2. improve quality
    3. improve the manufacturing process
38. External failure cost
39. Prevention cost
40. Appraisal cost
41. Internal failure cost
42. External failure cost
43. Appraisal cost
44. Internal failure cost
45. Appraisal cost
46. External failure cost
47. Internal failure cost
48. a   True
49. a   True
50. a   True
51. b   False. They are referring to reducing the incidence of nonconformance.
52. a   True
53. b   False. As prevention and appraisal costs increase, internal and
            external failure costs are expected to decrease.
54. b   False. JIT uses total quality control and strives for zero defects.
55. b   8,000/5,000 = 1.60
56. a   10,000/5,500 = 1.82
57. a
58. a   8,000/3,000 = 2.67
59. c   10,000/2,500 = 4
60. a
61. d   8,000/1,200 = 6.67
62. b   10,000/1,800 - 5.56
63. b

EXERCISE 1

1. zero defects
2. zero inventory and total preventive maintenance
3. zero inventory
4. total preventive maintenance
5. zero defects
6. zero inventory

EXERCISE 2

1. Value-added costs: $ -0-
   Nonvalue-added costs: $200,000

2. Value-added costs: $10.00 x (15/60) = $2.50
   Nonvalue-added costs: $10.00 x 4.75 = $47.50

3. Value-added costs: $ -0-
   Nonvalue-added costs: $1,000,000

   Note that with zero defects there should be no warranty costs.

4. Value-added costs: $ -0-
   Nonvalue-added costs: $600,000

5. Value-added costs: $15.00 x (12/60) = $3.00 per product
   Nonvalue-added costs: $15.00 x [(30 - 12)/60] = $4.50 per product

6. Value-added costs: $ -0-
   Nonvalue-added costs: $50,000

7. Value-added costs: $12.00 x (30/60) = $6
   Nonvalue-added costs: $12.00 x 1.5 = $18

8. Value-added costs: $5 x 10 = $50
   Nonvalue-added costs: $5 x .8 = $4

EXERCISE 3

Activity	Value-Added Costs	Nonvalue-Added Costs	Actual Costs
Labor	$ 30,000	$ 6,000	$ 36,000
Materials	160,000	32,000	192,000
Inspection	-0-	210,000	210,000
Receiving	100,000	12,500	112,500
Totals	$290,000	$260,500	$550,500

The above amounts would be calculated as follows:

Activity	Value-Added Costs	Nonvalue-Added Costs	Actual Costs
	(SQ x SP)	(AQ - SQ)(SP)	(AQ x AP)
Labor	5,000 x $6	(6,000 - 5,000)($6)	6,000 x $6
Materials	20,000 x $8	(24,000 - 20,000)($8)	24,000 x $8
Inspection	0 x $7	(30,000 - 0)($7)	30,000 x $7
Receiving	200 x $500	(225 - 200)($500)	225 x $500

EXERCISE 4

1.

Current selling price	$120
Current cost ($90,000/1,000)	(90)
Current profit per unit	$ 30
Selling price to maintain market share	$100
Desired profit per unit	(30)
Target cost	$ 70

2.

	Nonvalue-Added Costs
Materials:	
$40,000/8,000 = $5/pound	
(8,000 - 7,800) x $5	$ 1,000
Labor:	
$20,000/2,000 = $10/hour	
(2,000 - 1,800) x $10	2,000
Setups	10,000
Material handling	5,000
Warranties	15,000
Nonvalue-added costs	$33,000
Nonvalue-added costs per unit	
($33,000/1,000 units)	$33.00/unit

If nonvalue-added costs can be reduced to zero, the cost per unit would be $57 ($90 - $33), which is below the target cost of $70.

EXERCISE 8

1.a. Partial operational productivity ratios:

	1995	1996
Materials	15,000/5,000 = 3.00	18,000/5,000 = 3.60
Labor	15,000/4,000 = 3.75	18,000/4,500 = 4.00

b. Yes. Both materials and labor productivity improved from 1995 to 1996.

2.a. Profit-linked productivity measure:

	(1)	(2)	(3)	(4)	(2) - (4)
	PQ^a	PQ x P	AQ	AQ x P	(PQ x P) - (AQ x P)
Materials	6,000	$27,000	5,000	$22,500	$4,500
Labor	4,800	38,880	4,500	36,450	2,430
		$65,880		$58,950	$6,930

^{a}Materials: 18,000/3.00 = 6,000
Labor: 18,000/3.75 = 4,800

b. Profits increased by $6,930 due to improvements in productivity.

EXERCISE 9

1. Partial operational measures:

	1995	1996
Materials	4,000/2,500 = 1.60	4,500/3,000 = 1.50
Labor	4,000/2,000 = 2.00	4,500/1,800 = 2.50
Power	4,000/800 = 5.00	4,500/900 = 5.00

Productive efficiency has decreased for materials, increased for labor, and remained the same for power. Overall productivity improvement can be evaluated by valuing the tradeoff.

EXERCISE 9 (continued)

2.

	1995	1996
Sales		
(4,000 x $8)	$32,000	
(4,500 x $8)		$36,000
Cost of Inputs:		
Materials		
(2,500 x $2)	(5,000)	
(3,000 x $3)		(9,000)
Labor		
(2,000 x $7)	(14,000)	
(1,800 x $7)		(12,600)
Power		
(800 x $1.50)	(1,200)	
(900 x $2.00)		(1,800)
Income	$11,800	$12,600

Total change in profit = $12,600 - $11,800 = $800 increase

3. Profit-linked productivity measure:

	(1)	(2)	(3)	(4)	(2) - (4)
	PQ[a]	PQ x P	AQ	AQ x P	(PQ x P) - (AQ x P)
Materials	2,813	$ 8,439	3,000	$ 9,000	$ (561)
Labor	2,250	15,750	1,800	12,600	3,150
Power	900	1,800	900	1,800	-0-
		$25,989		$23,400	$2,589

[a]Materials: 4,500/1.60 = 2,813
Labor: 4,500/2 = 2,250
Power: 4,500/5 = 900

The value of the increase in efficiency for labor more than offsets the decrease in efficiency for materials. There was no change in value of the productivity efficiency of power usage.

4. Price recovery:

Price Recovery Component = Total Profit Change - Profit-Linked Productivity Change
Price Recovery Component = $800 - $2,589 = $(1,789)

Without the productivity improvement, profits would have declined by $1,789. The $4,000 increase in revenues would not have offset the increase in the cost of inputs. It is only because of the productivity increase that the firm showed an increase in profitability.

824

APPENDIX A: GUIDELINES FOR MEMORANDUM PREPARATION

In general, a memorandum should contain the following sections. (See the sample memorandum on the following page.)

1 A brief introductory sentence to remind the reader of the memorandum topic.

2 A recommendation that is specific and concise.

3 A discussion of the reasons for your recommendations. Why should your recommendation be accepted? Any technical accounting terms should be explained in terms the reader would understand.

4 A closing. This may be as short as: If you have any questions, please contact me at Extension 303.

5 Supporting calculations shown on a separate sheet of paper and attached to the memorandum.

SAMPLE MEMORANDUM

DATE: January 2, 1995

TO: Claire, Inc. Management

FROM: Management Consulting, Inc.

SUBJECT: Selection of Manufacturing Process for the Plazer Gun

1 → This memo regards your request for an evaluation of two manufacturing processes under consideration for the production of the Plazer Gun.

2 → If sales are expected to exceed 2,000 units, I recommend that Claire, Inc. select the automated manufacturing process.

3 → Sensitivity analysis indicates that at 2,000 units the total costs of the two alternatives are equal. If sales exceed 2,000 units, the automated process will generate lower costs and more profits than the labor-intensive process. Below 2,000 units, the labor-intensive manufacturing process will generate lower costs and higher profits than the automated process.

In general, the cost structure of automated processes tends to result in lower variable costs and higher fixed costs. This often results in a higher breakeven for the automated manufacturing process. A higher breakeven might be viewed as riskier given the possibility that sales might not materialize as expected. However, in this situation, with expected sales of 3,000 units well above the breakeven for the automated process of 1,563 units, the automated process is recommended.

Other issues that should be considered include the quality of the product. Both manufacturing processes are believed to produce products of similar quality; however, this aspect should be investigated further.

An important consideration for any toy is product safety and the associated company liability. The safety of the Plazer Gun should be thoroughly evaluated before the project is undertaken.

4 → If you have any questions concerning the analysis, please contact me. Our firm looks forward to serving your consulting needs in the future.

5 → Supporting calculations would be shown on a separate page and attached to the memorandum.

Table 1

Future Value of a Single Amount

(n) Period	2.00%	2.50%	3.00%	4.00%	5.00%	6.00%	7.00%	8.00%
1	1.02000	1.02500	1.03000	1.04000	1.05000	1.06000	1.07000	1.08000
2	1.04040	1.05062	1.06090	1.08160	1.10250	1.12360	1.14490	1.16640
3	1.06121	1.07689	1.09273	1.12486	1.15763	1.19102	1.22504	1.25971
4	1.08243	1.10381	1.12551	1.16986	1.21551	1.26248	1.31080	1.36049
5	1.10408	1.13141	1.15927	1.21665	1.27628	1.33823	1.40255	1.46933
6	1.12616	1.15969	1.19405	1.26532	1.34010	1.41852	1.50073	1.58687
7	1.14869	1.18869	1.22987	1.31593	1.40710	1.50363	1.60578	1.71382
8	1.17166	1.21840	1.26677	1.36857	1.47746	1.59385	1.71819	1.85093
9	1.19509	1.24886	1.30477	1.42331	1.55133	1.68948	1.83846	1.99900
10	1.21899	1.28008	1.34392	1.48024	1.62889	1.79085	1.96715	2.15892
11	1.24337	1.31209	1.38423	1.53945	1.71034	1.89830	2.10485	2.33164
12	1.26824	1.34489	1.42576	1.60103	1.79586	2.01220	2.25219	2.51817
13	1.29361	1.37851	1.46853	1.66507	1.88565	2.13293	2.40985	2.71962
14	1.31948	1.41297	1.51259	1.73168	1.97993	2.26090	2.57853	2.93719
15	1.34587	1.44830	1.55797	1.80094	2.07893	2.39656	2.75903	3.17217
16	1.37279	1.48451	1.60471	1.87298	2.18287	2.54035	2.95216	3.42594
17	1.40024	1.52162	1.65285	1.94790	2.29202	2.69277	3.15882	3.70002
18	1.42825	1.55966	1.70243	2.02582	2.40662	2.85434	3.37993	3.99602
19	1.45681	1.59865	1.75351	2.10685	2.52695	3.02560	3.61653	4.31570
20	1.48595	1.63862	1.80611	2.19112	2.65330	3.20714	3.86968	4.66096
21	1.51567	1.67958	1.86029	2.27877	2.78596	3.39956	4.14056	5.03383
22	1.54598	1.72157	1.91610	2.36992	2.92526	3.60354	4.43040	5.43654
23	1.57690	1.76461	1.97359	2.46472	3.07152	3.81975	4.74053	5.87146
24	1.60844	1.80873	2.03279	2.56330	3.22510	4.04893	5.07237	6.34118
25	1.64061	1.85394	2.09378	2.66584	3.38635	4.29187	5.42743	6.84848
30	1.81136	2.09757	2.42726	3.24340	4.32194	5.74349	7.61226	10.06266
32	1.88454	2.20376	2.57508	3.50806	4.76494	6.45339	8.71527	11.73708
34	1.96068	2.31532	2.73191	3.79432	5.25335	7.25103	9.97811	13.69013
36	2.03989	2.43254	2.89828	4.10393	5.79182	8.14725	11.42394	15.96817
40	2.20804	2.68506	3.26204	4.80102	7.03999	10.28572	14.97446	21.72452

9.00%	10.00%	12.00%	14.00%	16.00%	18.00%	20.00%	22.00%	(n) Period
1.09000	1.10000	1.12000	1.14000	1.16000	1.18000	1.20000	1.22000	1
1.18810	1.21000	1.25440	1.29960	1.34560	1.39240	1.44000	1.48840	2
1.29503	1.33100	1.40493	1.48154	1.56090	1.64303	1.72800	1.81585	3
1.41158	1.46410	1.57352	1.68896	1.81064	1.93878	2.07360	2.21533	4
1.53862	1.61051	1.76234	1.92541	2.10034	2.28776	2.48832	2.70271	5
1.67710	1.77156	1.97382	2.19497	2.43640	2.69955	2.98598	3.29730	6
1.82804	1.94872	2.21068	2.50227	2.82622	3.18547	3.58318	4.02271	7
1.99256	2.14359	2.47596	2.85259	3.27841	3.75886	4.29982	4.90771	8
2.17189	2.35795	2.77308	3.25195	3.80296	4.43545	5.15978	5.98740	9
2.36736	2.59374	3.10585	3.70722	4.41144	5.23384	6.19174	7.30463	10
2.58043	2.85312	3.47855	4.22623	5.11726	6.17593	7.43008	8.91165	11
2.81266	3.13843	3.89598	4.81790	5.93603	7.28759	8.91610	10.87221	12
3.06580	3.45227	4.36349	5.49241	6.88579	8.59936	10.69932	13.26410	13
3.34173	3.79750	4.88711	6.26135	7.98752	10.14724	12.83918	16.18220	14
3.64248	4.17725	5.47357	7.13794	9.26552	11.97375	15.40702	19.74229	15
3.97031	4.59497	6.13039	8.13725	10.74800	14.12902	18.48843	24.08559	16
4.32763	5.05447	6.86604	9.27646	12.46768	16.67225	22.18611	29.38442	17
4.71712	5.55992	7.68997	10.57517	14.46251	19.67325	26.62333	35.84899	18
5.14166	6.11591	8.61276	12.05569	16.77652	23.21444	31.94800	43.73577	19
5.60441	6.72750	9.64629	13.74349	19.46076	27.39303	38.33760	53.35764	20
6.10881	7.40025	10.80385	15.66758	22.57448	32.32378	46.00512	65.09632	21
6.65860	8.14027	12.10031	17.86104	26.18640	38.14206	55.20614	79.41751	22
7.25787	8.95430	13.55235	20.36158	30.37622	45.00763	66.24737	96.88936	23
7.91108	9.84973	15.17863	23.21221	35.23642	53.10901	79.49685	118.20502	24
8.62308	10.83471	17.00006	26.46192	40.87424	62.66863	95.39622	144.21013	25
13.26768	17.44940	29.95992	50.95016	85.84988	143.37064	237.37631	389.75789	30
15.76333	21.11378	37.58173	66.21483	115.51959	199.62928	341.82189	580.11565	32
18.72841	25.54767	47.14252	86.05279	155.44317	277.96381	492.22352	863.44413	34
22.25123	30.91268	59.13557	111.83420	209.16432	387.03680	708.80187	1285.15025	36
31.40942	45.25926	93.05097	188.88351	378.72116	750.37834	1469.77157	2847.03776	40

Table 2
Future Value of an Annuity

(n) Period	2.00%	2.50%	3.00%	4.00%	5.00%	6.00%	7.00%	8.00%
1	1.00000	1.00000	1.00000	1.00000	1.00000	1.00000	1.00000	1.00000
2	2.02000	2.02500	2.03000	2.04000	2.05000	2.06000	2.07000	2.08000
3	3.06040	3.07562	3.09090	3.12160	3.15250	3.18360	3.21490	3.24640
4	4.12161	4.15252	4.18363	4.24646	4.31013	4.37462	4.43994	4.50611
5	5.20404	5.25633	5.30914	5.41632	5.52563	5.63709	5.75074	5.86660
6	6.30812	6.38774	6.46841	6.63298	6.80191	6.97532	7.15329	7.33593
7	7.43428	7.54743	7.66246	7.89829	8.14201	8.39384	8.65402	8.92280
8	8.58297	8.73612	8.89234	9.21423	9.54911	9.89747	10.25980	10.63663
9	9.75463	9.95452	10.15911	10.58280	11.02656	11.49132	11.97799	12.48756
10	10.94972	11.20338	11.46388	12.00611	12.57789	13.18079	13.81645	14.48656
11	12.16872	12.48347	12.80780	13.48635	14.20679	14.97164	15.78360	16.64549
12	13.41209	13.79555	14.19203	15.02581	15.91713	16.86994	17.88845	18.97713
13	14.68033	15.14044	15.61779	16.62684	17.71298	18.88214	20.14064	21.49530
14	15.97394	16.51895	17.08632	18.29191	19.59863	21.01507	22.55049	24.21492
15	17.29342	17.93193	18.59891	20.02359	21.57856	23.27597	25.12902	27.15211
16	18.63929	19.38022	20.15688	21.82453	23.65749	25.67253	27.88805	30.32428
17	20.01207	20.86473	21.76159	23.69751	25.84037	28.21288	30.84022	33.75023
18	21.41231	22.38635	23.41444	25.64541	28.13238	30.90565	33.99903	37.45024
19	22.84056	23.94601	25.11687	27.67123	30.53900	33.75999	37.37896	41.44626
20	24.29737	25.54466	26.87037	29.77808	33.06595	36.78559	40.99549	45.76196
21	25.78332	27.18327	28.67649	31.96920	35.71925	39.99273	44.86518	50.42292
22	27.29898	28.86286	30.53678	34.24797	38.50521	43.39229	49.00574	55.45676
23	28.84496	30.58443	32.45288	36.61789	41.43048	46.99583	53.43614	60.89330
24	30.42186	32.34904	34.42647	39.08260	44.50200	50.81558	58.17667	66.76476
25	32.03030	34.15776	36.45926	41.64591	47.72710	54.86451	63.24904	73.10594
30	40.56808	43.90270	47.57542	56.08494	66.43885	79.05819	94.46079	113.28321
32	44.22703	48.15028	52.50276	62.70147	75.29883	90.88978	110.21815	134.21354
34	48.03380	52.61289	57.73018	69.85791	85.06696	104.18375	128.25876	158.62667
36	51.99437	57.30141	63.27594	77.59831	95.83632	119.12087	148.91346	187.10215
40	60.40198	67.40255	75.40126	95.02552	120.79977	154.76197	199.63511	259.05652

9.00%	10.00%	12.00%	14.00%	16.00%	18.00%	20.00%	22.00%	(n) Period
1.00000	1.00000	1.00000	1.00000	1.00000	1.00000	1.00000	1.00000	1
2.09000	2.10000	2.12000	2.14000	2.16000	2.18000	2.20000	2.22000	2
3.27810	3.31000	3.37440	3.43960	3.50560	3.57240	3.64000	3.70840	3
4.57313	4.64100	4.77933	4.92114	5.06650	5.21543	5.36800	5.52425	4
5.98471	6.10510	6.35285	6.61010	6.87714	7.15421	7.44160	7.73958	5
7.52333	7.71561	8.11519	8.53552	8.97748	9.44197	9.92992	10.44229	6
9.20043	9.48717	10.08901	10.73049	11.41387	12.14152	12.91590	13.73959	7
11.02847	11.43589	12.29969	13.23276	14.24009	15.32700	16.49908	17.76231	8
13.02104	13.57948	14.77566	16.08535	17.51851	19.08585	20.79890	22.67001	9
15.19293	15.93742	17.54874	19.33730	21.32147	23.52131	25.95868	28.65742	10
17.56029	18.53117	20.65458	23.04452	25.73290	28.75514	32.15042	35.96205	11
20.14072	21.38428	24.13313	27.27075	30.85017	34.93107	39.58050	44.87370	12
22.95338	24.52271	28.02911	32.08865	36.78620	42.21866	48.49660	55.74591	13
26.01919	27.97498	32.39260	37.58107	43.67199	50.81802	59.19592	69.01001	14
29.36092	31.77248	37.27971	43.84241	51.65951	60.96527	72.03511	85.19221	15
33.00340	35.94973	42.75328	50.98035	60.92503	72.93901	87.44213	104.93450	16
36.97370	40.54470	48.88367	59.11760	71.67303	87.06804	105.93056	129.02009	17
41.30134	45.59917	55.74971	68.39407	84.14072	103.74028	128.11667	158.40451	18
46.01846	51.15909	63.43968	78.96923	98.60323	123.41353	154.74000	194.25350	19
51.16012	57.27500	72.05244	91.02493	115.37975	146.62797	186.68800	237.98927	20
56.76453	64.00250	81.69874	104.76842	134.84051	174.02100	225.02560	291.34691	21
62.87334	71.40275	92.50258	120.43600	157.41499	206.34479	271.03072	356.44323	22
69.53194	79.54302	104.60289	138.29704	183.60138	244.48685	326.23686	435.86075	23
76.78981	88.49733	118.15524	158.65862	213.97761	289.49448	392.48424	532.75011	24
84.70090	98.34706	133.33387	181.87083	249.21402	342.60349	471.98108	650.95513	25
136.30754	164.49402	241.33268	356.78685	530.31173	790.94799	1181.88157	1767.08134	30
164.03699	201.13777	304.84772	465.82019	715.74746	1103.49598	1704.10946	2632.34386	32
196.98234	245.47670	384.52098	607.51991	965.26979	1538.68781	2456.11762	3920.20061	34
236.12472	299.12681	484.46312	791.67288	1301.02703	2144.64890	3539.00937	5837.04658	36
337.88245	442.59256	767.09142	1342.02510	2360.75724	4163.21303	7343.85784	12936.53527	40

Table 3
Present Value of a Single Amount

(n) Period	2.00%	2.50%	3.00%	4.00%	5.00%	6.00%	7.00%	8.00%
1	0.98039	0.97561	0.97087	0.96154	0.95238	0.94340	0.93458	0.92593
2	0.96117	0.95181	0.94260	0.92456	0.90703	0.89000	0.87344	0.85734
3	0.94232	0.92860	0.91514	0.88900	0.86384	0.83962	0.81630	0.79383
4	0.92385	0.90595	0.88849	0.85480	0.82270	0.79209	0.76290	0.73503
5	0.90573	0.88385	0.86261	0.82193	0.78353	0.74726	0.71299	0.68058
6	0.88797	0.86230	0.83748	0.79031	0.74622	0.70496	0.66634	0.63017
7	0.87056	0.84127	0.81309	0.75992	0.71068	0.66506	0.62275	0.58349
8	0.85349	0.82075	0.78941	0.73069	0.67684	0.62741	0.58201	0.54027
9	0.83676	0.80073	0.76642	0.70259	0.64461	0.59190	0.54393	0.50025
10	0.82035	0.78120	0.74409	0.67556	0.61391	0.55839	0.50835	0.46319
11	0.80426	0.76214	0.72242	0.64958	0.58468	0.52679	0.47509	0.42888
12	0.78849	0.74356	0.70138	0.62460	0.55684	0.49697	0.44401	0.39711
13	0.77303	0.72542	0.68095	0.60057	0.53032	0.46884	0.41496	0.36770
14	0.75788	0.70773	0.66112	0.57748	0.50507	0.44230	0.38782	0.34046
15	0.74301	0.69047	0.64186	0.55526	0.48102	0.41727	0.36245	0.31524
16	0.72845	0.67362	0.62317	0.53391	0.45811	0.39365	0.33873	0.29189
17	0.71416	0.65720	0.60502	0.51337	0.43630	0.37136	0.31657	0.27027
18	0.70016	0.64117	0.58739	0.49363	0.41552	0.35034	0.29586	0.25025
19	0.68643	0.62553	0.57029	0.47464	0.39573	0.33051	0.27651	0.23171
20	0.67297	0.61027	0.55368	0.45639	0.37689	0.31180	0.25842	0.21455
21	0.65978	0.59539	0.53755	0.43883	0.35894	0.29416	0.24151	0.19866
22	0.64684	0.58086	0.52189	0.42196	0.34185	0.27751	0.22571	0.18394
23	0.63416	0.56670	0.50669	0.40573	0.32557	0.26180	0.21095	0.17032
24	0.62172	0.55288	0.49193	0.39012	0.31007	0.24698	0.19715	0.15770
25	0.60953	0.53939	0.47761	0.37512	0.29530	0.23300	0.18425	0.14602
26	0.59758	0.52623	0.46369	0.36069	0.28124	0.21981	0.17220	0.13520
27	0.58586	0.51340	0.45019	0.34682	0.26785	0.20737	0.16093	0.12519
28	0.57437	0.50088	0.43708	0.33348	0.25509	0.19563	0.15040	0.11591
29	0.56311	0.48866	0.42435	0.32065	0.24295	0.18456	0.14056	0.10733
30	0.55207	0.47674	0.41199	0.30832	0.23138	0.17411	0.13137	0.09938
32	0.53063	0.45377	0.38834	0.28506	0.20987	0.15496	0.11474	0.08520
34	0.51003	0.43191	0.36604	0.26355	0.19035	0.13791	0.10022	0.07305
36	0.49022	0.41109	0.34503	0.24367	0.17266	0.12274	0.08754	0.06262
40	0.45289	0.37243	0.30656	0.20829	0.14205	0.09722	0.06678	0.04603

9.00%	10.00%	12.00%	14.00%	16.00%	18.00%	20.00%	22.00%	(n) Period
0.91743	0.90909	0.89286	0.87719	0.86207	0.84746	0.83333	0.81967	1
0.84168	0.82645	0.79719	0.76947	0.74316	0.71818	0.69444	0.67186	2
0.77218	0.75131	0.71178	0.67497	0.64066	0.60863	0.57870	0.55071	3
0.70843	0.68301	0.63552	0.59208	0.55229	0.51579	0.48225	0.45140	4
0.64993	0.62092	0.56743	0.51937	0.47611	0.43711	0.40188	0.37000	5
0.59627	0.56447	0.50663	0.45559	0.41044	0.37043	0.33490	0.30328	6
0.54703	0.51316	0.45235	0.39964	0.35383	0.31393	0.27908	0.24859	7
0.50187	0.46651	0.40388	0.35056	0.30503	0.26604	0.23257	0.20376	8
0.46043	0.42410	0.36061	0.30751	0.26295	0.22546	0.19381	0.16702	9
0.42241	0.38554	0.32197	0.26974	0.22668	0.19106	0.16151	0.13690	10
0.38753	0.35049	0.28748	0.23662	0.19542	0.16192	0.13459	0.11221	11
0.35553	0.31863	0.25668	0.20756	0.16846	0.13722	0.11216	0.09198	12
0.32618	0.28966	0.22917	0.18207	0.14523	0.11629	0.09346	0.07539	13
0.29925	0.26333	0.20462	0.15971	0.12520	0.09855	0.07789	0.06180	14
0.27454	0.23939	0.18270	0.14010	0.10793	0.08352	0.06491	0.05065	15
0.25187	0.21763	0.16312	0.12289	0.09304	0.07078	0.05409	0.04152	16
0.23107	0.19784	0.14564	0.10780	0.08021	0.05998	0.04507	0.03403	17
0.21199	0.17986	0.13004	0.09456	0.06914	0.05083	0.03756	0.02789	18
0.19449	0.16351	0.11611	0.08295	0.05961	0.04308	0.03130	0.02286	19
0.17843	0.14864	0.10367	0.07276	0.05139	0.03651	0.02608	0.01874	20
0.16370	0.13513	0.09256	0.06383	0.04430	0.03094	0.02174	0.01536	21
0.15018	0.12285	0.08264	0.05599	0.03819	0.02622	0.01811	0.01259	22
0.13778	0.11168	0.07379	0.04911	0.03292	0.02222	0.01509	0.01032	23
0.12640	0.10153	0.06588	0.04308	0.02838	0.01883	0.01258	0.00846	24
0.11597	0.09230	0.05882	0.03779	0.02447	0.01596	0.01048	0.00693	25
0.10639	0.08391	0.05252	0.03315	0.02109	0.01352	0.00874	0.00568	26
0.09761	0.07628	0.04689	0.02908	0.01818	0.01146	0.00728	0.00466	27
0.08955	0.06934	0.04187	0.02551	0.01567	0.00971	0.00607	0.00382	28
0.08215	0.06304	0.03738	0.02237	0.01351	0.00823	0.00506	0.00313	29
0.07537	0.05731	0.03338	0.01963	0.01165	0.00697	0.00421	0.00257	30
0.06344	0.04736	0.02661	0.01510	0.00866	0.00501	0.00293	0.00172	32
0.05339	0.03914	0.02121	0.01162	0.00643	0.00360	0.00203	0.00116	34
0.04494	0.03235	0.01691	0.00894	0.00478	0.00258	0.00141	0.00078	36
0.03184	0.02209	0.01075	0.00529	0.00264	0.00133	0.00068	0.00035	40

Table 4
Present Value of an Annuity

(n) Period	2.00%	2.50%	3.00%	4.00%	5.00%	6.00%	7.00%	8.00%
1	0.98039	0.97561	0.97087	0.96154	0.95238	0.94340	0.93458	0.92593
2	1.94156	1.92742	1.91347	1.88609	1.85941	1.83339	1.80802	1.78326
3	2.88388	2.85602	2.82861	2.77509	2.72325	2.67301	2.62432	2.57710
4	3.80773	3.76197	3.71710	3.62990	3.54595	3.46511	3.38721	3.31213
5	4.71346	4.64583	4.57971	4.45182	4.32948	4.21236	4.10020	3.99271
6	5.60143	5.50813	5.41719	5.24214	5.07569	4.91732	4.76654	4.62288
7	6.47199	6.34939	6.23028	6.00205	5.78637	5.58238	5.38929	5.20637
8	7.32548	7.17014	7.01969	6.73274	6.46321	6.20979	5.97130	5.74664
9	8.16224	7.97087	7.78611	7.43533	7.10782	6.80169	6.51523	6.24689
10	8.98259	8.75206	8.53020	8.11090	7.72173	7.36009	7.02358	6.71008
11	9.78685	9.51421	9.25262	8.76048	8.30641	7.88687	7.49867	7.13896
12	10.57534	10.25776	9.95400	9.38507	8.86325	8.38384	7.94269	7.53608
13	11.34837	10.98318	10.63496	9.98565	9.39357	8.85268	8.35765	7.90378
14	12.10625	11.69091	11.29607	10.56312	9.89864	9.29498	8.74547	8.24424
15	12.84926	12.38138	11.93794	11.11839	10.37966	9.71225	9.10791	8.55948
16	13.57771	13.05500	12.56110	11.65230	10.83777	10.10590	9.44665	8.85137
17	14.29187	13.71220	13.16612	12.16567	11.27407	10.47726	9.76322	9.12164
18	14.99203	14.35336	13.75351	12.65930	11.68959	10.82760	10.05909	9.37189
19	15.67846	14.97889	14.32380	13.13394	12.08532	11.15812	10.33560	9.60360
20	16.35143	15.58916	14.87747	13.59033	12.46221	11.46992	10.59401	9.81815
21	17.01121	16.18455	15.41502	14.02916	12.82115	11.76408	10.83553	10.01680
22	17.65805	16.76541	15.93692	14.45112	13.16300	12.04158	11.06124	10.20074
23	18.29220	17.33211	16.44361	14.85684	13.48857	12.30338	11.27219	10.37106
24	18.91393	17.88499	16.93554	15.24696	13.79864	12.55036	11.46933	10.52876
25	19.52346	18.42438	17.41315	15.62208	14.09394	12.78336	11.65358	10.67478
26	20.12104	18.95061	17.87684	15.98277	14.37519	13.00317	11.82578	10.80998
27	20.70690	19.46401	18.32703	16.32959	14.64303	13.21053	11.98671	10.93516
28	21.28127	19.96489	18.76411	16.66306	14.89813	13.40616	12.13711	11.05108
29	21.84438	20.45355	19.18845	16.98371	15.14107	13.59072	12.27767	11.15841
30	22.39646	20.93029	19.60044	17.29203	15.37245	13.76483	12.40904	11.25778
32	23.46833	21.84918	20.38877	17.87355	15.80268	14.08404	12.64656	11.43500
34	24.49859	22.72379	21.13184	18.41120	16.19290	14.36814	12.85401	11.58693
36	25.48884	23.55625	21.83225	18.90828	16.54685	14.62099	13.03521	11.71719
40	27.35548	25.10278	23.11477	19.79277	17.15909	15.04630	13.33171	11.92461

9.00%	10.00%	12.00%	14.00%	16.00%	18.00%	20.00%	22.00%	(n) Period
0.91743	0.90909	0.89286	0.87719	0.86207	0.84746	0.83333	0.81967	1
1.75911	1.73554	1.69005	1.64666	1.60523	1.56564	1.52778	1.49153	2
2.53129	2.48685	2.40183	2.32163	2.24589	2.17427	2.10648	2.04224	3
3.23972	3.16987	3.03735	2.91371	2.79818	2.69006	2.58873	2.49364	4
3.88965	3.79079	3.60478	3.43308	3.27429	3.12717	2.99061	2.86364	5
4.48592	4.35526	4.11141	3.88867	3.68474	3.49760	3.32551	3.16692	6
5.03295	4.86842	4.56376	4.28830	4.03857	3.81153	3.60459	3.41551	7
5.53482	5.33493	4.96764	4.63886	4.34359	4.07757	3.83716	3.61927	8
5.99525	5.75902	5.32825	4.94637	4.60654	4.30302	4.03097	3.78628	9
6.41766	6.14457	5.65022	5.21612	4.83323	4.49409	4.19247	3.92318	10
6.80519	6.49506	5.93770	5.45273	5.02864	4.65601	4.32706	4.03540	11
7.16073	6.81369	6.19437	5.66029	5.19711	4.79322	4.43922	4.12737	12
7.48690	7.10336	6.42355	5.84236	5.34233	4.90951	4.53268	4.20277	13
7.78615	7.36669	6.62817	6.00207	5.46753	5.00806	4.61057	4.26456	14
8.06069	7.60608	6.81086	6.14217	5.57546	5.09158	4.67547	4.31522	15
8.31256	7.82371	6.97399	6.26506	5.66850	5.16235	4.72956	4.35673	16
8.54363	8.02155	7.11963	6.37286	5.74870	5.22233	4.77463	4.39077	17
8.75563	8.20141	7.24967	6.46742	5.81785	5.27316	4.81219	4.41866	18
8.95011	8.36492	7.36578	6.55037	5.87746	5.31624	4.84350	4.44152	19
9.12855	8.51356	7.46944	6.62313	5.92884	5.35275	4.86958	4.46027	20
9.29224	8.64869	7.56200	6.68696	5.97314	5.38368	4.89132	4.47563	21
9.44243	8.77154	7.64465	6.74294	6.01133	5.40990	4.90943	4.48822	22
9.58021	8.88322	7.71843	6.79206	6.04425	5.43212	4.92453	4.49854	23
9.70661	8.98474	7.78432	6.83514	6.07263	5.45095	4.93710	4.50700	24
9.82258	9.07704	7.84314	6.87293	6.09709	5.46691	4.94759	4.51393	25
9.92897	9.16095	7.89566	6.90608	6.11818	5.48043	4.95632	4.51962	26
10.02658	9.23722	7.94255	6.93515	6.13636	5.49189	4.96360	4.52428	27
10.11613	9.30657	7.98442	6.96066	6.15204	5.50160	4.96967	4.52810	28
10.19828	9.36961	8.02181	6.98304	6.16555	5.50983	4.97472	4.53123	29
10.27365	9.42691	8.05518	7.00266	6.17720	5.51681	4.97894	4.53379	30
10.40624	9.52638	8.11159	7.03498	6.19590	5.52773	4.98537	4.53762	32
10.51784	9.60857	8.15656	7.05985	6.20979	5.53557	4.98984	4.54019	34
10.61176	9.67651	8.19241	7.07899	6.22012	5.54120	4.99295	4.54192	36
10.75736	9.77905	8.24378	7.10504	6.23350	5.54815	4.99660	4.54386	40